Twiel Im Jahr 1641.

G. Fewr Mörser.   K. Schloß Stauffen.
H. Haupt Schantz.   L. Obe. Kellers Quartir.
I. Meyer'hofe.   M. Posten auf der Kelter.

The endpapers illustrate the siege of the fortress of
Hochen Twiel by an Imperialist army during the
Thirty Years' War.
C   Imperialist camp
D   Bavarian camp and communications trenches
E   Austrian camp
F   Artillery batteries
G   Mortar batteries
H   Main artillery trench

A History of Warfare

A History of Warfare

Field-Marshal Viscount Montgomery of Alamein

The World Publishing Company

Cleveland and New York

First published in the United States of America in 1968
by The World Publishing Company,
2231 West 110th Street, Cleveland, Ohio 44102

Library of Congress Catalog Card Number: 68–13718

This book was designed and produced by
George Rainbird Ltd,
Marble Arch House, 44 Edgware Road, London w.2
House Editors: John Hadfield, George Speaight
Picture Research:
Linda Knelman, Patricia Vaughan, Marianne Dumartheray
Designers: Ronald Clark, Anne Petrie
Index: Wing Commander Roger F. Pemberton
Maps, diagrams and battle plans:
John Flower, T. Stalker Miller MSIA
Weapon drawings: Ian Garrard

The text was phototypeset in Monophoto Plantin 110,
and the jacket and colour plates printed, by
Westerham Press Ltd, Westerham, Kent.
The origination of the jacket and colour plates was
carried out by Schwitter Ltd, Zurich, Switzerland.
The text was printed by Butler & Tanner Ltd,
Frome, Somerset.
The book was bound by
Butler & Tanner Ltd, Frome, Somerset.

PRINTED IN GREAT BRITAIN

PREFACE

I have not written this book to glorify war. I have sought to highlight the human endeavour of men and women which is brought out in wartime – on the home front as well as in battle. The need to understand this human factor and to avoid all unnecessary suffering and loss of life, makes it vital that national leaders should be decisive regarding the political object of a war and should then give clear instructions to Service Chiefs on this and all other relevant matters. Two verses from the New Testament, Corinthians I 14, might well be their guide:

8. If the trumpet give an uncertain sound, who shall prepare himself to the battle?
9. Except ye utter by the tongue words easy to be understood, how shall it be known what is spoken?

The aim of the general must be not only to win wars but also to play his part in preventing them. Some years ago Sir Winston Churchill said: 'Peace is the last prize I seek to win.' Nobody knows better than a soldier the overwhelming value of that prize, because nobody knows better than a soldier the monster called War.

In a full life I have seen much fighting in major conflicts, which have ended without the secure and lasting peace for which we fought. But I am not weighed down under the bitter burden of despair in the world of politics and so-called peace in which we live in 1968; indeed, my gaze is hopefully and steadfastly directed forward and outward. It is in that sense that I offer this book to the public, dedicating it to my comrades-in-arms on the battlefields of Africa and Europe – many of whom gave their lives that we who remain might have that freedom in the West for which we all fought, and which we now enjoy.

Thucydides, writing of the Peloponnesian War, is reputed to have said: 'If anybody shall pronounce what I have written to be useful, then I shall be satisfied.' And that is exactly what I and my research team would like to say.

Isington Mill,   Montgomery of Alamein
Alton, Hampshire.   F.M.

CONTENTS

Author's Acknowledgments   11

1   The Nature of War   13
2   Generalship   19

PART ONE   ANCIENT WARFARE

3   War in Earliest Times   28
4   The Ancient Greeks   58
5   The Expansion of Rome   84
6   The Roman Defensive and the
Barbarian Migrations   108

PART TWO   MEDIEVAL WARFARE

7   Early Medieval Warfare   134
8   The Norman Conquests and the Crusades   156
9   The High Middle Ages   182

PART THREE   EUROPEAN WARFARE

10   The Greatness of Spain   210
11   The Ottoman Turks   242
12   European War in the Seventeenth Century   262
13   Marlborough and his Times   290

14 European War in the Eighteenth Century 314
15 The Era of Nelson, Napoleon and Wellington 334

PART FOUR EASTERN WARFARE
16 The Mongols, the Chinese and the Japanese 368
17 India 392

PART FIVE WARFARE 1815–1945
18 The Beginnings of Modern War 410
19 Learning the Hard Way 442
20 The 1914/18 War 460
21 Twenty Years After: 1939/45 496

PART SIX INSCRUTABLE DESTINY
22 The Ethics of War 546
23 The Iron Curtain and the Cold War 553
24 The Nuclear Age 558
25 Epilogue – The Ideal of Peace 565

Selected Bibliography 568
Acknowledgments for Illustrations 570
Index 573

MAPS AND BATTLE PLANS

The Fertile Crescent   32

The battle of Kadesh   46

The ancient Greek world   65

The battle of Salamis   66

The route of Alexander's conquests   72

The battle of Gaugamela   79

The campaigns of Hannibal and Scipio   90

The battle of Cannae   92

The battle of Zama   95

The extent of Roman domination in the
time of Julius Caesar   98

The frontiers of the Roman empire and
the barbarian migrations   116–7

Arab conquests in the seventh and eighth
centuries   136–7

The Carolingian empire and Viking and
Magyar incursions   148

Norman conquests in Europe   158

The battle of Hastings   164

The crusader kingdoms   176

The battle of Crécy   203

Western Europe in the sixteenth century   213

The battle of the Garigliano   218

The Ottoman empire   245

The battle of Lepanto   259

Germany at the time of the Thirty Years' War   268

The battle of Breitenfeld   272

England at the end of the Civil War   284

The area of Marlborough's campaigns   299

The battle of Blenheim   306
North America in the eighteenth century   318
Central Europe at the accession of Frederick the Great   324
The battle of Leuthen   326
The battle of Aboukir Bay   337
The Austerlitz campaign   350
The battle of Austerlitz   352
Napoleon's empire   356
The Peninsular War   359
Asia   374–5
India   394
Central Europe in the nineteenth century   431
The battle of Gravelotte-Saint-Privat   433
The American Civil War   439
The Balkans, 1876–8   454
The Russo-Japanese War   457
The Schlieffen Plan and the Western Front   465
The battle of Tannenberg   466
The fronts in eastern and south-eastern Europe   484
The war in the Middle East   488
The German campaign in north-western Europe, 1940   501
The war in the Mediterranean   507
The war in eastern Europe, 1942–4   509
The battle of Normandy   519
The defeat of Germany, 1944–5   528
The Japanese war, 1941–5   531
The Allied recovery of Burma   538
The battle of Meiktila   541

COLOUR PLATES

The Egyptian chariot	49
Egyptian soldiers	50
Single combat in ancient Greece	75
An Asiatic nomad archer	76
The Norman conquest of England	173
A crusader castle	174
Medieval warfare: French	199
Medieval warfare: German	200
The battle of Pavia	225
The Spanish Armada	226
The battle of Lepanto	251
The relief of the last Turkish siege of Vienna	252
The battle of Montjuic	277
An Anglo-Dutch naval engagement	278
The battle of Malplaquet	303
The battle of Ramillies	304
An Anglo-French naval engagement	341
The battle of the Pyramids	342–3
The battle of Borodino	344
A Japanese warrior	381
The last stand of the Kusunoki	382
The capture of Bakadur Khan	407
Akbar's forces besiege Rauthaubhor Fort	408
The defence of Chateaudun	421
The battle of the Alma	422–3
The battle of Gettysburg	424
Battleships in action	521
Rocket-firing Typhoons at the Falaise Pocket	522–3
American troops landing on Iwo Jima	524

AUTHOR'S ACKNOWLEDGMENTS

The leader of my research team, Alan Howarth, was selected personally by me from a number of possible candidates for the post. He was a scholar at Rugby, then a major scholar at King's College, Cambridge, where he studied history. I could not have made a better choice. This very gifted, brilliant young graduate, only twenty-one when he joined me, brought to bear on our work the full power of his abilities and organized the research with remarkable success. He chose as his team-mate Anthony Wainwright who was at Rugby with him; he was at Loughborough College but agreed to leave before his time and join the team; he also was only twenty-one and he proved a splendid second to Alan Howarth.

That was the research team – I the soldier and they the young historians. Some might wonder how it worked, the soldier being nearly eighty, and the historians only twenty-one! My answer is that it worked well; what they thought of me I have yet to learn; I thought the world of them and they helped to keep me young in my old age. There is no doubt about one thing – they were made to work hard. There were no set office hours or trade union rules, it was solid work day in, day out, with no holidays; but we had a great deal of fun, and many happy days were spent together at my home in Hampshire.

Then I needed somebody who would be apart from the research team, but who would help me by reading the chapters as they were produced, and comment freely. I looked for an experienced military historian; his further task would then be to draw sketch plans as references for the diagrammatic battle plans we needed. I found exactly what I needed in Antony Brett-James, Lecturer in Military History at the R.M.A. Sandhurst, and himself an author of military works. His knowledge and help were invaluable.

We had behind us the experience and willing help of the editorial staff of George Rainbird Ltd. And finally I must mention our typist, Miss Bunney, who typed the chapters – and some of them more than once.

And the final result – this book.

An immense number of works were read by the research team, too many to enumerate; the bibliography gives those we have found the most useful. We were confronted from the outset with the problem of deciding which writer was correct in his presentation of historical facts, since they often differed. In this matter we have done our best, and we can quote an authority for all statements of fact which we have made. The team also needed advice as to the best books to study for any particular era. Certain people were consulted and gave valuable advice – university dons, historical experts and the like. Libraries were most cooperative – the London Library, British Museum and others. In particular we received valuable help and guidance from the Chief Librarian at the

Ministry of Defence, Mr D. W. King, O.B.E., F.L.A., and his staff.

Personally, I read with great interest certain books which are sent me from time to time by authors and publishers – not for comment, but as a gesture of friendship. Two were most instructive:

Men in Arms, written by two Canadians, Professors Preston and Wise of the Royal Military College of Canada, and one American, Mr Werner of the U.S. Naval Academy. It is published by F. A. Praeger, Inc., New York and Thames and Hudson of London. I had some correspondence with Professor Preston, and the authors and the publishers gave permission for me to make any use desired of the book. It is a standard work for cadets at the Royal Military College of Canada, and I was most interested to find it in use at Saldanha Bay, the Military Academy of South Africa, when I was there a few years ago.

Design for Survival, written by General Power of the U.S. Air Force, who was Commander-in-Chief, Strategic Air Command of the United States. General Power, now retired, is a friend of mine; he is a very great airman and the copy of his book which I received was inscribed personally to me with the words 'Keep the Free World Strong.' How right he is! I found his book helpful. It is published by Coward-McCann, Inc., New York.

Then there were certain friends of mine, all authors, whose books I studied carefully – – notably Sir Basil Liddell Hart, Cyril Falls, Alan Clark, Corelli Barnett and the late Major-General Fuller. I also read with interest *Links of Leadership* by John Laffin, sent me by his publisher Walter Harrap. I do not suggest for a moment that any of my friends will agree with what I have written; the military comment is based on my own practical experience in war, and I accept full responsibility.

Finally, I have enjoyed the time spent on this book and I extend my grateful thanks to all who have helped me.

Montgomery of Alamein
F.M.

1 The Nature of War

War is not the concern of soldiers only. Throughout history civilian life has always been affected by warfare, and in modern times the higher direction of war has become the responsibility of politicians, who are themselves civilians, and not professional soldiers, sailors or airmen. Furthermore, in total war, industry and civilian energies are absorbed into the war effort. For these reasons military history is inseparable from the general historical background, and the history of warfare is worth studying by everybody – both civilians and members of the fighting services.

In this book my emphasis will be upon methods and techniques (which include weapons), strategy and tactics, and leadership. Where more general historical factors are discussed they will be those scientific, technological, social, economic or political factors which have had a particular and definite influence on the course of the history of warfare. This is not meant to be a book of reference; my hope is that the reader will feel he is absorbed in a momentous and engrossing story. Therefore my main task will be to indicate and discuss what is significant in wars, campaigns and battles, and the technological developments which characterized them and the generals and men who fought them – and to comment, where it seems appropriate, on the basis of my own military experience.

In this first chapter I shall try to indicate the fundamentals of a subject about which the reader may know little, particularly if he is a civilian and has made no great study of military history or techniques. As man became more and more civilized so wars became more and more frequent, and the fundamental matters emerged more clearly.

Man's progress in all fields has been basically affected for good and for ill by the impact of armed conflict – the *verdict of war* being, time and again, a deciding factor in the process of historical change – though of course not the only one. It is impossible to study the history of warfare as if war has always existed in a vacuum. For example, William the Conqueror, as his name indicates, exercised his influence upon the history of England because of a successful war. As another example I quote the suggestion made by some historians that the beginning of large-scale metal industries was due to a certain extent to the demand for cannon (though I must admit that others claim it was due to the need for church bells!).

Why do wars happen? Some will say that war is the child of civilization, others that war stems from raw human nature. But one thing is clear: war has always been the arbiter when other methods of reaching agreement have failed. The judgment which it has given has been based on might rather than on right – although at times right has prevailed.

Causes and types of war have varied in different parts of the world. With nomadic peoples, such as the Magyars, movements of population were mainly determined by the locations of good grazing lands and the prospects of easy plunder. The Persian wars, on the other hand, were fought to save Greece, and therefore Europe, from Asiatic tyranny. The Roman empire was established by warfare, and warfare contributed to its destruction; the same is true of the German empire created by Bismarck.

There was a time when religion was one of the great causes of international strife. Later, the possession of colonies brought wealth to the colonial powers of western Europe, wealth which was gained by armed strength; it was commercial rivalry that then pushed nations into conflict.

At this stage some definitions may be useful:

WAR is any prolonged conflict between rival political groups by force of arms. It includes insurrection and civil war. It excludes riots and acts of individual violence.

GRAND STRATEGY is the co-ordination and direction of all the resources of a nation, or group of nations, towards the attainment of the political object of the war – the goal defined by the fundamental policy. The true objective of Grand Strategy must be a secure and lasting peace.

STRATEGY is the art of distributing and applying military means, such as armed forces and supplies, to fulfil the ends of policy. TACTICS means the dispositions for, and control of, military forces and techniques in actual fighting. Put more shortly: strategy is the art of the conduct of war, tactics are the art of fighting.

Throughout history certain factors have been constant in warfare. For example, since the earliest days there have been the problems of movement and of firepower: how to be able to move one's own forces freely and to prevent the enemy from moving. The requirements of mobility, firepower and security have always to a certain extent conflicted. The development of the armoured fighting vehicle, dominating the land battle as it ranges over ever wider fronts, and the parallel development of wireless communications to maintain control over distances previously considered unthinkable – these are only the latest forms of one of the fundamental exercises of war.

The strategical background to a campaign or battle is of great significance. What was the aim? What was the commander trying to achieve? An objective may be very desirable strategically; but that which is strategically desirable must be tactically possible with the forces and means available. The precise facts are important; but the general picture must be drawn and the feel of the campaign shown.

SEAPOWER has had a decisive influence on warfare since very ancient times. In their wars against the Persians the Athenians realized that the enemy could not be beaten so long as the Persian fleet could transport men and supplies across the Aegean and land them at will along the Greek seaboard. Athens, by a supreme effort, built up her naval power and defeated the Persians in the sea battle of Salamis in 480 B.C. The Persian campaign ended a year later. Greece then dominated the eastern Mediterranean, enjoying an age of commercial prosperity and producing a great civilization.

Similarly, Rome collided with the mercantile state of Carthage in North Africa, whose navy controlled the western Mediterranean. She declared war on Carthage but soon found that it was necessary first to defeat her on the sea. Rome then became a naval power and defeated Carthage – the most formidable enemy the Romans were ever called upon to face.

It was because Britain had defeated the French and Spanish fleets at Trafalgar that the invasion of England was rendered impossible and in 1808 a British army was able to land in Portugal. Some years later Britain beat Napoleon, who wielded far greater military power but was confined to a land strategy.

Seapower has been just as important in more modern times. It is interesting to note that the dates of Trafalgar (21st October) and Alamein (23rd October) are so close; but the two battles have more in common than that: both marked the turning point in a long war against a powerful continental enemy. Because the Allies were masters of the sea, Alamein was fought and won. If they had not been able to build up their forces and supplies faster than Rommel the issue would have been lost, and with it Egypt, the Suez Canal, and possibly the whole of the Middle East.

The lesson is this: in all history the nation which has had control of the seas has, in the end, prevailed.

AIR POWER, when developed to its full potential, made a profound impact on war at sea, as well as on land. In 1941 and 1942 the Japanese showed in south-east Asia and the Pacific what could be attempted with superior sea and air power. At Pearl Harbour on 7th December 1941 they revealed the tremendous offensive power of a carrier task force, launching over 300 aircraft which sank most of the battleships of the U.S. Pacific Fleet – in water considered by the Americans to be too shallow for the use of aerial torpedoes. Shortly afterwards Japanese land-based aircraft sank the British battleship *Prince of Wales* and the battle-cruiser *Repulse* off the coast of Malaya.

In 1942 two naval battles were fought between American and Japanese naval forces which clearly demonstrated the dominant role of air power in modern naval warfare. The first was in the Coral Sea between 4th and 8th May, when the U.S. fleet foiled a Japanese amphibious attack on Port Moresby and removed the threat to Australia. The second was off Midway Island between 3rd and 6th June; the U.S. navy had broken the Japanese code and was fully prepared to meet a powerful enemy concentration both north and south-west of Midway. These two naval battles, both resulting in crippling Japanese losses, marked the real turning point of the war against Japan. The action in the Coral Sea was remarkable as being the first naval battle in which the opposing war-ships never once sighted each other – not one direct shot was exchanged.

In war on land the advent of the aeroplane enabled commanders to see 'the other side of the hill'. As air power grew and developed it was able to prevent movement in daylight to any appreciable degree, so much so that it became necessary to gain mastery in the air before beginning a land battle. The mighty weapon of air power enabled armies to win victories more quickly than before and to win them with fewer casualties than would otherwise have been the case. And to add to it all, air bombing could carry war deep into the heart of the opponent's homelands, causing heavy civilian casualties and tremendous damage to property on the home front, with a cumulative adverse effect on the war effort of the nation so attacked.

GENERALSHIP is a theme which will run like a golden thread throughout this book. I will only touch on it here but will deal with it more fully in Chapter 2. 'Captaincy', or leadership in the higher sense, is of supreme importance in warfare. Many qualities go to make a leader, but two are vital – the ability to make the right decisions, and the courage to act on the decisions. These are, of course, the qualities most prized in other fields, such as industry and politics.

A commander must know what he himself wants. He must see his objective clearly and then strive to attain it; he must let his subordinates know what he wants and what are the fundamentals of his policy. He must, in fact, give firm guidance and a clear lead. It is necessary for him to create what I would call 'atmosphere', and in that atmosphere his staff and subordinate commanders will live and work.

He must have the 'drive' to get things done; he must have the character and ability which will inspire confidence in his subordinates. Above all, he must have that moral courage, that resolution, and that determination which will enable him to stand firm when the issue hangs in the balance. Only one thing is certain in battle, and that is that everything will be uncertain. Therefore one of the greatest assets a commander can have is the ability to radiate confidence in the plan and operations even (perhaps especially) when he is not too sure in his own mind about the outcome.

To make this philosophy work with all those under his command, a commander-in-chief must watch carefully his own morale. A battle is, in effect, a contest between two wills – his own and that of the enemy commander. If his heart begins to fail him when the issue hangs in the balance, his opponent will probably win.

I believe that generals can be divided broadly into two classes. To make the distinction I will use two very expressive French definitions. *Le bon général ordinaire* is the general who is good so long as his superior will tell him in detail what to do, will stand by him and help him, and will see that he does what he is told. *Le grand chef* requires only a general directive covering the operations which are envisaged; he requires no detailed instructions, he knows what to do and can safely be left alone to do it; he is a very rare bird.

As we study history from the earliest beginnings of warfare up to present times, many remarkable and well-known figures pass across the military stage. We shall have the opportunity to decide in our own minds to which class each belongs.

But generals can be judged fairly only in the exercise of their own profession and on military grounds. Some campaigns have been undertaken, and some battles have been fought, for political reasons only; those have been the graveyard of the reputation of many soldiers.

INTELLIGENCE AND SECRET SERVICE must never be underrated by a commander. Polybius, a Greek historian (201–120 B.C.), wrote that a general must 'apply himself to learn the inclinations and character of his adversary'. About two thousand years later, von Moltke, chief of the general staff of Prussia for thirty years from 1857, said to his officers: 'You will usually find that the enemy has three courses open to him; of these, he will adopt the fourth.'

A good military leader must dominate the events which encompass him; once events get the better of him he will lose the confidence of his men, and when that happens he ceases to be of value as a leader. He has therefore got to anticipate enemy reactions to his own moves, and to take quick steps to prevent enemy interference with his own plans.

For these reasons a first class Intelligence organization is essential and the head of it must be an officer of brilliant intellectual qualities, who need not necessarily be a professional fighting man. He must be a very clear thinker, able to sort out the essentials from the mass of incidental factors which bear on every problem concerning the enemy. Service Intelligence organizations must be in the closest touch with the Secret Service.

A general must understand the mind of his opponent, or at least try to do so. For this reason I always had in my caravans during Hitler's war a picture or photograph of my opponent. In the desert, and again in Normandy, my opponent was Rommel; I would study his face and see if I could fathom his likely reaction to any action I might set in motion; in some curious way this helped me. I must admit that I do not know of any other commander-in-chief – except Slim – who adopted the same practice! Yet the study of opposing commanders has always been a prime necessity. Any battle can very quickly go off the rails. If this should happen the initiative may well pass to the enemy. If there is one lesson which I have learnt in my long military career it is that without holding the initiative it is not possible to win. Hence the value of Intelligence.

In all Secret Service activities, which are handled by the central government, the operations of spies, saboteurs and secret agents generally are regarded as outside the scope of national and international law. They are therefore anathema to all accepted standards of conduct. Nevertheless history shows that no nation will shrink from such activities if they further its vital interests.

While the factors of command and control play a large part in the winning of battles, the greatest single factor making for success is the spirit of the warrior. The best way to achieve a high morale in wartime is by success in battle.

The raw material with which the general has to deal is men. It is essential to understand that battles are won primarily in the hearts of men. An army is not merely a collection of individuals with so many tanks and guns, and its strength is not just the total of all these added together. The real strength of an army is, and must be, far greater than the sum of its parts; that extra strength is provided by morale, by fighting spirit, by mutual confidence between the leaders and the led (and especially between field leaders and the high command), and by many other intangible spiritual qualities.

Discipline and comradeship play a large part. Why does the soldier leave the protection of his trench or hole in the ground and go forward in the face of shot and shell? It is because of the leader who is in front of him and his comrades who are around him. Comradeship makes a man feel warm and courageous when all his instincts tend to make him cold and afraid.

A commander must understand that bottled up in men are great emotional forces which have to be given an outlet in a way which is positive and constructive, and which warms the heart and excites the imagination. In modern times if the approach to the human problem is cold and impersonal, a commander will achieve little; but if he can gain the trust and confidence of his men, and they feel their best interests are safe in his hands, then he has in his possession a priceless asset and the greatest achievements become possible. This is vital because in the end a battle is won by the fighting spirit of junior officers and men – whatever the quality of the higher commanders.

I say 'in modern times' because it was not always so. Generals are meant to win battles, and the good general of today will do so with the least possible loss of life. Throughout the Middle Ages in the Western world the manpower of a nation was considered of small account; the serf was expendable in battle. Then came the series of epidemics in Europe in the fourteenth century known as the Black Death; manpower was scarce, the economic value of the serf increased, and his life had to be safeguarded: he was less expendable.

In modern times when a nation goes to war the ranks of its armed forces are filled with men from civil life who are not soldiers, sailors or airmen by profession – and who never wanted to be. Such men are very different from the serf or the mercenary of by-gone days; they are educated, they can think, they can appreciate, and they are prepared to criticize. They want to know what is going on, and what the general wants them to do, and why, and when; they also want to know that in the doing of it their best interests will be absolutely secure in the general's hands. And, of course, they want to see him and decide in their own minds what sort of person he is. If all these things are understood, morale will be high.

It will be clear from what I have written that there is a human side to warfare which, unfortunately, has often been neglected by historians. It will be referred to frequently throughout this book and for that I make no apology, because it is the crux of the whole matter. Tiredness, fear, appalling conditions, great privations, the virtual certainty of wounds and the probability of death – all will be faced by the fighting man if he has a stout heart, knows what he is fighting for, has confidence in his officers and his comrades, and if he knows he will never be required to do anything which is not possible. These matters must be understood by all those who study warfare and, of course, especially by those who follow the profession of arms.

Modern war is *total war* and over the centuries has become very complicated, embracing the life and activities of a nation to an ever increasing extent – so that the morale of the whole nation is involved. This is vital. In the days of levies and mercenaries comparatively few men did the fighting or were engaged in the national war effort. But today the whole manpower of a nation, and womanpower too, together with its industrial strength, is mobilized in order to provide the necessary sinews of war. Furthermore today, whether a man is drafted to the fighting services or employed in industry, he is subject to dangers almost wherever he may be; this has necessitated the introduction of an organization for what has come to be called Civil Defence – but a more inspiring title would be Home Defence.

These facts have made modern war a complex affair; a great power must be prepared not only for a conventional type of warfare but also for a nuclear one. Scientific and technical resources now must be harnessed to the limit, if nations are to have any hope of survival in total war.

In the last part of this book we shall look into the future and examine the pattern which future wars may be expected to take.

2   Generalship

Talleyrand is reported to have said: 'War is much too serious a thing to be left to military men.' This was quoted by Briand to Lloyd George during the 1914/18 war, and is of course very true. Equally it could be said that war is too serious a thing to be left to politicians. The truth is that in modern war the closest cooperation between the two is vital, and where it is lacking the desired outcome of a war will always be in doubt. But more of that later; let me first give my views on the responsibilities of Talleyrand's 'military men'.

I interpret the word 'general' in its widest sense, to include all those of high rank in any fighting service. In the Concise Oxford Dictionary the word 'generalship' is defined as: 'Office of a general; strategy, military skill; skilful management, tact, diplomacy.' My own definition would be that generalship is the science and art of command. It is a science in that it must be studied theoretically by officers, and an art because the theory must then be put to practical use. Above all, it involves an intimate knowledge of human nature.

Mao Tse-tung, no mean commander, has written (*Selected Military Writings*):

> All military laws and military theories which are in the nature of principles are the experience of past wars summed up by people in former days or in our own times. We should seriously study these lessons, paid for in blood, which are a heritage of past wars. That is one point. But there is another. We should put these conclusions to the test of our own experience, assimilating what is useful, rejecting what is useless, and adding what is specifically our own. The latter is very important, for otherwise we cannot direct a war. Reading is learning, but applying it is also learning and the more important kind of learning at that.

Mao Tse-tung is right. I remember during the 1914/18 war suggesting to an officer that he ought to go to one of the junior staff college courses which were held in France. He ridiculed my suggestion, saying that the thing which really counted in war was practical experience in the trenches. I then told him of Frederick the Great's remark about officers who relied only on their practical experience and who neglected to study – that he had in his army two mules which had been through forty campaigns, but they were still mules!

Both study and practice are necessary: first, a study of the science of war, and, secondly, learning to apply the study practically in battle. The first is always possible and there is no excuse for its neglect; the opportunity for the second may not often come – although it did come my way in no small measure.

A vast amount of experience lies buried in the story of past warfare, and commanders could not do without the military historians who uncover it for them. (Nor could they do without us; if there were no generals or admirals to criticize a lot of them would go out of business!) Their value is in establishing the facts and in drawing lessons from them (rather than in embarking on discussions of what should have been done). The facts which are stated must, of course, be true and above dispute; comment is free and an expression of individual opinion.

It may be of interest, and not inappropriate to this book, if I give some details of my own habits of study, beginning as an inexperienced and ignorant young officer serving with my regiment in India in 1909, and continuing until high command came my way. My object was, and always has been, to study the past intelligently, in order to seek guidance for the present and the future.

My reading and study of military history has been extensive, but it has been confined mostly to books written by British historians during my own lifetime. I did make attempts to read the writings of Clausewitz, a Prussian, and of Jomini, a Swiss. Both were well-known military writers, but I couldn't take them in, and I turned to historians of my own nation and language. The first book I then tackled was *The Science of War* by G. F. R. Henderson; this was a series of his lectures, published after his death. I gathered from the lectures that the War between the States would well repay study, so I read *Stonewall Jackson and the American Civil War*, also by Henderson; this interested me enormously.

I then decided that I would learn more if I turned to more recent historians, and particularly if I studied the lives of the great captains of the past to learn how they thought and acted, and how they used the military means at their disposal. A knowledge of the detailed dispositions of an army at any time was not what mattered to me; I wanted to know the essential problem which confronted the general at a certain moment in the battle, what were the factors which influenced his decision, what was his decision – and why. I wanted to discover what was in the great man's mind when he made a major decision. This, surely, was the way to study generalship.

Of the military historians of my own nation, language and times, I found Sir Basil Liddell Hart far and away the best. To my mind he is the military historian *non pareil* – very readable, absolutely clear, and an expert in analysis and comment. For over forty years I have known him personally and read his works; his military thinking has always appealed to me and it had a definite influence on my own conduct of war as I rose in military rank. Some historians are wise after the event; one has only to read the volumes of Liddell Hart's *Memoirs* to realize that he was wise before the event – a prophet at last honoured in his own country. Where Liddell Hart stands high above all other military writers is that not only is he an historian, able to analyse and comment, but he is also a theorist, and has produced from his vast knowledge a philosophy or doctrine of war, as did Clausewitz and Jomini. But whereas they were often wrong, Liddell Hart has proved to be generally right.

Other historians from whose works I have in the past learned much are Sir Arthur Bryant, the late J. F. C. Fuller, Cyril Falls and A. J. P. Taylor. The last named's book *The Origins of the Second World War* is the best I have read on the German problem – a classic. A new and younger generation of military historians is now arising – men who themselves have never seen war. Of these I consider Correlli Barnett outstanding;

his book *The Sword-Bearers*, studies of certain commanders in the 1914/18 war, is on a high level, showing great powers of analysis and comment. Another I would commend is Alan Clark; his book *Barbarossa*, the story of the Russian-German conflict 1941–5, is quite first-class. These two authors have a good future and anything they write is worth reading.

By the very nature of things, skill in the profession of arms has to be learnt mostly in theory by studying the science of war – since the opportunity of practice in the art does not come often to the general. For this reason the great captains have always been serious students of military history. Bismarck wrote that wise men profit from the experience of others. And T. E. Lawrence rightly said that we of the twentieth century have two thousand years of experience behind us, and, if we still must fight, we have no excuse for not fighting well. My reading over the years has convinced me that nobody in this twentieth century can become a great commander, a supreme practitioner of the art of war, unless he has first studied and pondered its science.

In the light of my own experience of high command in war I have come to certain conclusions about generalship.

One of the first responsibilities of a commander-in-chief is to create what I have called 'atmosphere' as a state of mind in which his staff, his subordinate commanders, and his troops will live and work and fight. His armies must know what he wants; they must know the very fundamentals of his policy; and they must be given firm guidance and a clear lead. Inspiration and guidance must come from above and permeate the whole force. If this happens all concerned will go ahead on the lines laid down, the force will acquire balance and cohesion, and the results will be evident in battle. Nelson exemplified this principle ideally.

In addition to 'atmosphere', there are two basic requirements of generalship. The first is to create the fighting machine and forge the weapon to his own liking. This involves a profound knowledge of the conduct of war, and of training. The second is to create an organization at headquarters which will enable the weapon to be wielded properly. The fighting machine must be so set in motion, at the appropriate time, that it can develop its maximum power rapidly. The troops must be launched into battle in a way which promises the best prospect of success – and the troops must know this. The 'stage-management' of the battle must be first-class.

The essence of tactical methods in battle lies in the following factors:

> Surprise
> Concentration of effort
> Cooperation of all arms
> Control
> Simplicity
> Speed of action
> The initiative.

A commander has got to be a very clear thinker: able to sort out the essentials from the mass of lesser factors which bear on every problem. Once he has grasped the essentials of the problem which faces him, he must never lose sight of them – he must never allow a mass of detail to submerge what is essential to success. Military problems are in essence simple; but the ability to simplify, and to select from the mass of detail those things and only those things which are important, is not always so easy. The general must have this capacity for essential detail, without loss of vision. He is likely to fail unless he has an ice-clear brain at all times and a disciplined mind; this implies being abstemious, particularly in such things as drinking and smoking. The plan of operations must be made by the commander; it must not be forced on him by his staff, or by circumstances, and never by the enemy.

Most opponents are at their best if they are allowed to dictate the battle; they are not so good when they are thrown off balance by manoeuvre and are forced to react to your own movements and thrusts. Surprise is essential. Strategical surprise may often be difficult, if not impossible, to obtain; but tactical surprise is always possible and must be given an essential place in planning. The enemy must be forced to dance to your tune all the time. This means that the commander must foresee his battle. He must decide in his own mind, and before the battle begins, how he wants operations to develop; he must then use the military effort at his disposal to force the battle to swing the way he wants.

As the battle develops, the enemy will try to throw you off your balance by counter-thrusts. This must never be allowed. Throughout the battle area the whole force must be so well balanced and poised, and the general layout of dispositions so good, that one will never be dictated to by enemy thrusts. Skill in grouping forces before the battle begins, and in regrouping to meet developing tactical situations, is one of the hall-marks of generalship. By grouping, I mean seeing that each corps in the planning and conduct of the tactical battle is suitably composed for its task. I mentioned in Chapter 1 that an essential quality of a general is the ability to understand the mind of his opponent, in order to be able to anticipate enemy reactions to his own moves and to take quick action to prevent enemy interference with his own plans.

Of course, all generals are different; each will develop his own methods and techniques in accordance with his study, experience and make-up. My own military doctrine was based on unbalancing the enemy by manoeuvre while keeping well balanced myself – as I have been indicating. A short title for this tactic would be 'off-balancing manoeuvre'. I planned always to make the enemy commit his reserves on a wide front in order to plug holes in his defences. Having forced him to do this, I then committed my own reserves in a hard blow on a narrow front. Once I had committed my reserves, I always sought to create fresh reserves.

The initiative, once gained, must never be lost; only in this way will the enemy be made to dance to your tune. If you lose the initiative against a good enemy you will very soon be made to react to his thrusts; and once this happens you may well lose the battle. In large-scale operations it is very easy to lose the initiative. A firm grip on the battle is necessary to prevent this from happening, combined with a willingness to adjust plans to meet the developing tactical situation. In a campaign a commander should think two battles ahead – the one he is planning to fight and the next one. He can then use success in the first as a springboard for the second.

While operational problems will tend to be the main preoccupation of a general, he must never forget that the raw material of his trade is men, and that generalship is, basically, a human problem. The soldier can feel intense loneliness during moments in battle. In the early stages of the 1914/18 war, as a young platoon commander on a patrol at night in no-man's-land, I was several times cut off from my men. I was alone in the neighbourhood of the enemy, and I was frightened; it was my first experience of

war. I got used to it, of course. But in those days I came to realize the importance of the
soldier knowing that behind him were commanders, in their several grades, who cared
for him. The general who looks after his men and cares for their lives, and wins battles
with the minimum loss of life, will have their confidence. All soldiers will follow a
successful general.

A general, therefore, has got to 'get himself over' to his troops. My own technique in
the 1939/45 war was to speak to them whenever possible. Sometimes I spoke to large
numbers from the bonnet of a jeep, sometimes I spoke to just a few men by the roadside
or in a gun pit. I would also address them less directly by means of written messages at
important phases in the campaign or before a battle. These talks and messages fostered
the will to win and helped to weld the whole force into a fighting team which was
certain of victory.

In the 1914/18 war Sir Douglas Haig never seemed to me to get himself over to the
soldiers. He would inspect troops in complete silence. There is a story told that one of
his staff suggested it would create a good impression if he would occasionally stop and
speak to one or two men. He took the advice and asked one man: 'Where did you start
this war?' The astonished soldier replied: 'I didn't start this war, sir; I think the Kaiser
did.' I understand that Haig gave it up after this encounter! Nevertheless, it is the
spoken word above all which counts in the leadership of men.

A main responsibility of a general is to organize training, not only for the campaign
which is to be opened up but also for any particular battle during the campaign. The
fighting man must have confidence in his weapons and in his ability to use them effectively in all types of situation, of ground, and of climate. This confidence can be achieved
only by intensive training – which, if successful, will raise morale.

A general must never be chary in allotting praise where it is due. People like to be
praised when they have done well. In this connection Sir Winston Churchill once told
me of the reply made by the Duke of Wellington, in his last years, when a friend asked
him: 'If you had your life over again, is there any way in which you could have done
better?' The old duke replied: 'Yes, I should have given more praise.'

By studying the actions and methods of some of the great captains of the past we can
learn how the practical side of war was handled in their day. Such a study will illustrate
the evolution of the art of war but also the uniformity of its basic conceptions. It will
show the student that the same principles of war which were employed in the past
appear again and again throughout history, only in different circumstances. Although
weapons have become more powerful and the problems of the battlefield have grown
more intricate and more complex, nonetheless the art of war is fundamentally the same
today as it was in the days of ancient Greece, or when Rome and Carthage joined in
battle.

As the centuries passed, commanders in their several grades were forced to grapple
with the problem of administration: often called logistics. In my own case, I very soon
learnt by hard experience that the administrative situation in rear must be commensurate
with what I wanted to achieve in battle in the forward area. Another lesson I learnt was
the need for robustness, or the ability to stand up to the shocks of war – which will come
as surely as the dawn follows the night. Perhaps *toughness* is a better word for this
quality.

I have mentioned my sense of loneliness as a young platoon commander. There is also a loneliness about high command. A C-in-C has immense responsibilities which he cannot pass on to his staff or to his subordinates; his are the decisions, and his the responsibility for success or failure and for the lives of his men. This aspect of generalship applies particularly in adversity, but it is of permanent relevance and is a severe test for a commander. Wellington was faced with this problem, so was Napoleon – and to a lesser extent myself in Normandy in the summer of 1944. When things are not going exactly as planned, all eyes look to the commander-in-chief for confidence, fortitude, or even 'what do we do now?' In such conditions of adversity, when things may not be going too well, a commander, besides commanding his armies, has got to learn to command *himself* – which is not always too easy, as I know well.

In the Civil War in America, Lee retained the devotion of his army even although he lost. Wavell wrote of Lee: 'He was possibly too much of a gentleman for the ungentle business of war.'

Let us now return to the subject mentioned by me in the opening paragraphs of this chapter. I have always held that 'captaincy', or leadership in the higher sense, is of supreme importance in war – in the political as well as in the military sphere.

Until political leaders can find some sensible way of settling international disputes, war will remain with us. When a nation decides to resort to armed force to achieve its political ends, or is itself attacked, all must understand that the responsibility for the higher direction of the war lies in political hands. But service chiefs will find it difficult, indeed impossible, to give success to a government which vacillates, lacks courage and clear-sightedness, and has no clear conception of what is important and what is not in the campaigns which will follow. It is vital that the political aims and the strategy be clearly defined in simple language which cannot be misunderstood. Commanders-in-chief having been selected wisely, directives must be given to them in such terms. The issue then passes to the generals – who must be backed to the utmost. These matters need to be emphasized often: and very clearly.

In a major war, resources may be relatively equal between the nations involved; in such a case victory will go to that side which is best trained, best led, and of higher morale. However skilful the general may be, there comes a stage in every battle against a determined enemy when victory hangs in the balance; the power then is out of the hands of the general and goes finally to the soldiers; victory will depend on their courage, their training, their discipline, their refusal to admit defeat, their steadiness and tenacity in battle. During the long march from Alamein to Berlin in the 1939/45 war, I had pinned in my caravan the following quotation from Shakespeare's *Henry V*:

O God of battles! steel my soldiers hearts.

As our study of war unfolds, I hope the reader will recognize the truth of what I have written. Many of the battles we shall examine were won, in the end, by the soldiers or sailors. When planning the battle, a general is faced with the fog of war; but provided he has a sound plan, the soldiers will disperse the fog.

It is my belief that good generals are made, rather than born; no officer will reach the highest rank without prolonged study. The conduct of war is a life study and if the study has been neglected a general can expect no success. I once said to an A.D.C. of mine who was ambitious, but inclined to be idle: 'Remember that without great toil those who triumph are very few in any profession.' Of course, certain natural gifts are essential: the power of rapid decision, sound judgment, boldness at the right moment, toughness. We shall see how the training and experience of veteran troops have led to some surprising victories over numbers and circumstances. We shall see how the good general is one who has shown his quality in adversity as well as in success. And finally, our study will show that, given all this, there is no more important factor leading to military success than the energy, driving power, and will force of the commander; and he who has these in the highest degree has established his claim to be enrolled among the great captains. When all is said and done, the crucible of war will determine the fine metal of which a general is made.

I will finish these few thoughts about generalship on a note which will be clear as the historical chapters are read. The late Field-Marshal Wavell once told me that when the Spartans were at the height of their military fame they sent a deputation to the oracle at Delphi and demanded, somewhat arrogantly: 'Can anything harm Sparta?' The answer came quickly: 'Yes, luxury.'

I have visited Delphi, and spent some hours at the scene of this somewhat disturbing interview. But how true was the answer! Throughout our study it will be seen that national history is no story with a happy ending, but a fight which goes on from age to age: each advance has to be won, each position gained has to be held. In war, the enemy is plain and clear. In peace, a nation is confronted with a more insidious foe: the weakness within, from which alone great nations fall. If an example from modern times is needed, it is France – a great nation by any standards. But in the years before the 1939/45 war the weakness within attacked her soul; and the crash came in 1940. She was given back her soul in 1958 by General de Gaulle, and has risen again phoenix-like from the ashes – under a very great leader.

Among all the nations whose soldiers have served under my command in war, and those I got to know well during my ten years' service in the Western defence organization, naturally I know best my own race, the British. We have always been a sturdy and independent people and for many years have not known final defeat. Freedom is in our blood and has given us a sturdy and unique strength. The Industrial Revolution disturbed this spirit, but the desperate struggle for existence in the slums of Britain toughened at the same time as it physically hurt the people. Economic oppression has not broken the spirit of the British. It has produced the Glasgow Scot, the lad from Lancashire, the man from the Midlands, the London cockney. With such men all things are possible, and once set in motion in battle they are unbeatable – given good generalship, adequate equipment and sinews of war, and leaders they trust. But the danger from within is always present and must be kept in subjection. All in all, the oracle was right: if undue luxury gets a hold on the manhood of a nation, and martial qualities are neglected, that nation is likely to fall.

Morale is the most important factor on which war potential is built up. Francis Bacon, a very wise man, wrote the following:

Walled towns, stored arsenals and armories, goodly races of horse, chariots of war, elephants, ordnance, artillery and the like; all this is but sheep in a lion's skin, except the breed and disposition of the people be stout and warlike.

A study of the history of warfare proves the absolute truth of this statement. The main

Alexander the Great   Hannibal   Scipio   Julius Caesar   Jenghiz Khan

Gonzalo de Córdoba   Drake   Gustavus Adolphus   Wallenstein   Cromwell

Marlborough   Turenne   Anson   Maurice de Saxe   Frederick the Great

Napoleon   Nelson   Wellington   Von Moltke   Skobelev

Some famous commanders

responsibility for ensuring it belongs to political leaders, but generals have their part
to play.

High morale is allied with physical fitness; the soldier cannot be mentally fit for
battle unless he is physically fit, and the same applies to sailors and airmen. Kipling in
his preface to *Land and Sea Tales* wrote:

> Nations have passed away and left no traces,
> And history gives the naked cause of it –
> One single, simple reason in all cases;
> They fell because their peoples were not fit.

Generals must see to it that their troops are imbued with that infectious optimism
and that offensive eagerness which comes from physical well-being. Given this, and in
the sure knowledge that they have a great and righteous cause, then must follow the will
to persevere in battle in the face of all difficulties – and finally to conquer.

War has existed in almost all primitive societies. An archer engaged in combat with a rival tribe is depicted in the rock paintings of Tassili, *c.* 3000 B.C.

PART ONE

ANCIENT WARFARE

3   War in Earliest Times

War has been constant in human affairs since the earliest societies of which there is record. If we go back to about 7000 B.C. and consider Jericho, we find that it was strongly fortified by a wall 21 feet high encompassing an area of 10 acres, and by an outer moat 15 feet wide and 9 feet deep hewn through solid rock. Of possibly 2,500 citizens, 500 to 600 would have been fighting men. Surviving flint arrowheads indicate that as well as being experienced and skilled in engineering and fortification, these people had developed the bow and arrow. I know the area well, and in 1931 spent many hours exploring the excavations and the walls of the ancient cities in the Dead Sea valley. To have made such large-scale military preparations they must have had powerful enemies to fear.

But the art of warfare had clearly been evolving for long before those days. How then did war first arise?

War is a basic part of history because it is concerned with the essentials of life. Food, and a secure place in which to live, were the two absolute necessities for primeval man – just as they are for us. But these things which man needs, as well as many other things which he desires, such as mates, wealth, power and prestige, are often available only in short supply. The basic reason why individual men and societies have almost incessantly fought each other lies in this economic fact – they have always had to compete for the minimum conditions of existence. Animals and insects fight each other for the same reason. Indeed, ants have highly complex wars, involving espionage, ambushes and surprise attacks, battles and sieges conducted by masses of disciplined creatures, subordinated to an officer hierarchy and working to a long-term strategy.

It was Sir Winston Churchill who first instructed me in ant warfare, and a prized possession is Maeterlinck's *The Life of the Ant* which he gave me on one of his visits to my headquarters in Germany in the autumn of 1944. Since ants possess organized armies and undertake offensive wars, maybe he thought the book would give me some ideas in offensive operations against the Germans!

Anyhow, it is clear that war is in the very nature of things. Yet there is no reason to suppose that if they had not been compelled to make war the mass of mankind would have chosen to do so. The record of human achievement shows that cooperation is at least as normal as struggle. The urges of rage, aggression and fear are natural only because in a competitive social situation each creature represents a frustration or a danger to his neighbour. Societies of animals, such as the street dogs of Istanbul, birds and monkeys, stake out territories. Within societies individuals do the same. The frontiers are generally respected, and force is normally used only to drive out intruders if threats are seen to be of no avail or there is no room for flight. Domestic hens and cattle have hierarchies, in which junior defers to senior when there is a clash of interests – for example over food. In this way, outright crude fighting has practically been eliminated among certain animal species. Humans also have many such rituals to avoid physical violence, of which the whole process of formal diplomacy is the most obvious. Humans, of course, have been much less successful than animals in avoiding the resort to violence. One of the reasons is that the strains under which they have had to live, such as over-crowding, have been much greater, and their problems are more complicated.

Aggressiveness and bellicosity in individual men are not the inevitable result of any instinct or inbuilt psychological urge; yet in societies they are natural. What traces we can discover of the primitive peoples of ancient times show that, from the first, men have had to organize themselves for defence. It was because their dwelling-places had to be refuges as well as shelters that they so frequently lived in cliff-side caves which were difficult to get at, on hill-tops such as Windmill Hill in Wiltshire and Homolka in Bohemia, or, like the first inhabitants of Northern Italy and the present-day people of Brunei, in houses built on piles in lakes and marshes so as to be moated. The same sticks and stones as were used for domestic purposes and hunting were also used for fighting. Among the palaeolithic instruments which could be used as weapons of war were stone cleavers and knives, and blades and lance-heads of bone, flint and reindeer horn. How-ever, since it is virtually impossible for archaeologists to work out what would have been the causes and modes of warfare among the earliest peoples of Europe and western Asia, the most instructive approach for us is to look at the primitive peoples of other continents, some of whom in our twentieth century are passing through their stone ages. In particular we may learn why they go to war, and what their attitude is to violence.

It is immediately clear that no generalization can be made about the bellicosity of primitive peoples. Motives for war vary, and the degree of ferocity depends on circum-stances – such as bitterness of feeling, fear of the consequences, and so on. Some tribes slaughter all their prisoners, while others treat them leniently. The pygmies are ex-tremely peaceable, but for that very reason, and because they are weak, they have been driven into the least habitable area of Africa by other more aggressive peoples. The Australian aborigines dislike war. But in many parts of the world there are tribes which, at any rate until very recently, obviously regarded war as normal and acceptable. Examples are the Masai of East Africa, the Guaranis of Brazil, the Apaches of North America, and the Dyaks and Kenyahs of Oceania. Tribes ruled by kings are usually more prone to war than those with more democratic forms of government. A hundred years ago Sir Richard Burton noticed that tribal wars were much less frequent and ferocious in the Gaboon and Lower Niger, where the consent of the elders was needed before a tribe could go to war, than in East Africa where the kings were absolute.

The most common and infallible cause of war among primitive peoples is over-crowding, which can be caused both by a sudden rise in the population of an area and by the failure of food or water supplies. Malthus was correct in observing that the birthrate usually tends to rise faster than the physical environment can accommodate. Population has to be kept down, and this has generally been brought about by war or by nature, i.e. disease. The history of the Red Indian tribes of North America illustrates well how territorial possessiveness can lead to war. From about A.D. 1600, when enough Europeans were established on the east coast with superior weapons, the Indians were driven back westwards. There was more than a century of continuous war among the tribes as each was forced back to intrude into the territory of its westerly neighbour. A succession of great battles was fought between the Chippewa and the Sioux, at Mille Lacs in the seventeenth century, at Elk River in the eighteenth century, and at Cross Lake in 1800. These were no mere raids for amusement and glory, but serious wars fought by men who had to defend their homes against invaders who had equally to escape from their own overrun homes to the east. In the nineteenth century the situation was aggravated by the disappearance of the buffalo, the main food of the Indians, and by the need to compete for horses and firearms. The chain of enforced migration continued, the defeated Sioux in their turn pushing other tribes such as the Cheyenne farther west. The Cheyenne eventually drove the Comanche back towards Mexico.

Another fundamental explanation of the frequent occurrence of war may be the deep-rooted desire of men to belong to groups. If loyalties and a sense of group identity and patriotism are to develop in a society, it must be exclusive and positively antagonistic to its neighbours; it is significant that the Latin word *hostis* meant both 'stranger' and 'enemy'. Different peoples hold most strongly to their different cultures and there is an intimate connection between culture and military institutions. This is especially apparent in religion, as for example in initiation ceremonies. It was actually a religious belief among the Mbaya of South America that they should live by assaulting and plundering all other tribes. When the Polynesians were prevented from warring by Europeans, they underwent a profound social and cultural crisis; their values had been related to conditions of constant war; when that had to stop they lost their energy, dignity and religion.

War can appeal because it is exciting, and can be amusing; many Red Indian tribes had organized mock wars, often resulting in numerous casualties. War can also satisfy demands for easy profits, colour and romance, discipline and ritual, self-sacrifice and comradeship, status, and the admiration of women. Women especially are a strong inducement. The warrior such as Achilles is the type of the attractive male. Among the Tahitians a sufficient reason for going to war was the custom that a youth might not marry unless he had the tattoo which signified that he had killed a man in battle. The Bible several times mentions raids by one tribe to plunder the women of another – one of the many kinds of war for loot. There are the classic legends of Helen of Troy and the Sabine women. In the late eighteenth century Barbary corsairs raided a French coastal village for women to sell to Arab harems. Some weak tribes disfigure their women to make them unattractive to raiders.

It is probably reasonable to suppose that the causes and methods of warfare, and the significance of military institutions in shaping the culture and structure of primitive societies, were much the same in very ancient times as they are in the twentieth century. We cannot be sure, because there is a gap of over three thousand years in our direct archaeological knowledge of the ancient world, between the fortifications of Jericho in 7000 B.C. and the history of Mesopotamia and Egypt in the fourth millenium B.C. When we do pick up the story, it is immediately clear that the factor which underlay all military and political developments in the history of the Near East during the four thousand years before Christ was overcrowding of population. The first civilizations arose in

great river valleys, Babylonia and Sumeria on the lower reaches of the Euphrates and
the Tigris, and Egypt astride the Nile. Warfare was inevitably continuous because of
the competition to possess the small quantity of very fertile land which there was in a
densely populated and otherwise very arid area. The inhabitants of the valleys fought
each other for every inch of precious, well-watered land they could get.

As well as competing with each other, the fortunate dwellers of the river valleys had
to defend themselves against the jealous peoples of the desert. Neither Egypt nor
Babylonia was protected by any natural barriers. Egypt had continually to thrust back

The Fertile Crescent in ancient times, showing the area of the Egyptian and Assyrian empires

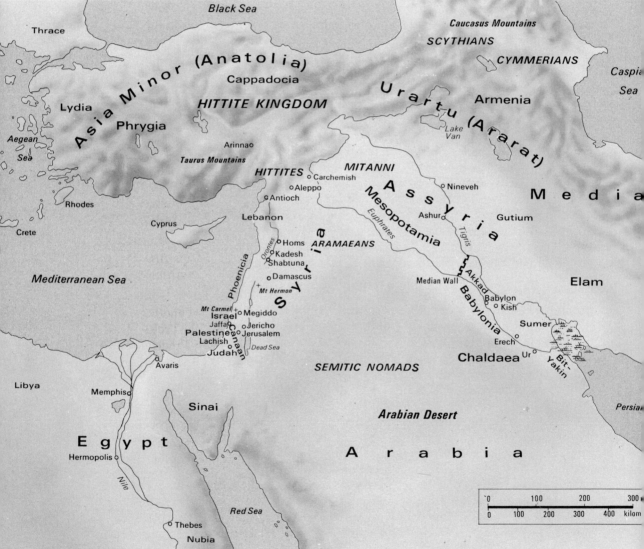

from its frontiers aggressive and less civilized neighbours – the Nubians in the south, and Semitic nomads in Sinai to the east. Semerkhet, about 3370 B.C., was the first king of Egypt actually to invade Sinai. He left carved upon the rocks there a record of his campaign, in which he is shown striking down the king of the Bedouin. There is a picture on the tomb walls of Sahure, 2950 B.C., of a naval expedition sailing across the Red Sea to Sinai, and then returning with Semitic prisoners on board. Similarly, Babylonian kings undertook continuous border police operations against the Arabian Semites and the upland peoples of Assyria and of Elam (a hill country, east of Babylonia and across the Tigris).

But occasionally these raids from the wilds developed into much bigger onslaughts, when great masses of migratory peoples – Semitic at first, but later Indo-European – were attracted to the river valleys. The Semitic population of the Middle East and North Africa originates from the Arabian desert. Yet although the area is such a breeding-ground, much of it is frequently uninhabitable. When the hollows of moist ground dry up, as often happens, nomadic people are forced by drought to seek new territories. Since the land slopes gently downwards to the east, the tribes are most naturally drawn to the Persian Gulf, the Euphrates and Mesopotamia. At the risk of oversimplifying the story of a complicated ethnic process, it may be said that in ancient times there were three great eruptions of the Semites of Arabia.

Legends suggest that as early as 4500 B.C. there was a Semitic dynasty in northern Mesopotamia. Further semi-legendary accounts point to a Sumerian dynasty established shortly afterwards in the south. A later southern kingdom at Ur was eclipsed by a Semitic kingdom at Akshak on the Tigris in 3200. This struggle for Mesopotamia, between the Sumerians and the Semites, was the first great clash of cultures in history. Some time in the fourth millenium the southerners built the Median Wall from the Euphrates to the Tigris to keep out the nomadic invaders – an identical strategical conception to that of the Great Wall of China, but of no avail. The struggle between north and south for dominance over Mesopotamia continued unceasingly for thousands of years.

The first dynasty really to hold sway over both north and south was founded about 2872 by Sargon, a low-born priest of Ishtar, goddess of battle. By then the Semites had been reinforced by the first great migration from Arabia into Syria and northern Mesopotamia, some time before 3000. Sargon chose Akkad as his capital probably for military reasons, since at that point the Tigris and the Euphrates flowed only fifteen miles apart. In the second year of his reign he conquered Elam, and thereafter he subdued the west as far as the Mediterranean and Cyprus. Frequent revolts were firmly dealt with; for example, as the chronicle puts it, 'he turned Kazalla into dust and heaps of ruins; he destroyed even the resting-places of the birds'. Hittites advancing out of Asia Minor in the north-west were decisively driven back.

The next successful soldier-king of the Akkadians was Naram-Sin. His success must be attributed to his own generalship, and an efficient and obedient army. When he died he was the ruler of the largest empire the world had yet seen, stretching from Armenia to the Persian Gulf and the Red Sea, and from Elam to the Mediterranean shore. Later the empire was shattered by internal revolts, and invasions by barbarians from Gutium in the north. Within forty years of Naram-Sin's death Akkad itself had lost its independence.

Chariots were the basic instruments of Mesopotamian warfare. Babylonian four-wheeled chariots drawn by four asses. The soldiers are wearing mail coats

The second half of the fourth millenium, and the third millenium, the period of the clash between the Semites and the Sumerians, of the Akkadian empire and the Egyptian Old Kingdom (3500–2400 B.C.), was thus an age of great military activity. Except for cavalry it saw the first real development of the principles of warfare and the types of weapons and fortifications which were to prevail for three thousand years – until the use of gunpowder in the fourteenth century A.D. The Mesopotamians were a great deal more advanced in military technique than the Egyptians, whose warfare was on a smaller scale altogether until the invasion of the Hyksos in 1800 B.C. The Egyptians, for example, did not use a chariot until twelve hundred years later than the Mesopotamians.

I have found Yigael Yadin's book on *The Art of Warfare in Biblical Lands* instructive on the subject of weapons and the technique of warfare in ancient times. He was Chief of Staff of the Israeli Army in 1948 when Israel was conducting its war for independence against the British Army – of which I was the Chief of Staff. I cannot recall that we have ever met.

The basic instrument of war in Mesopotamia after 3500 B.C. was the chariot. From the start there were two types, two-wheeled and four-wheeled. Drawn by four asses, the early models were heavy and clumsy. The chariots found in the royal tombs at Kish have a high and upright protective panel at the front, which suggests that they were normally used for direct frontal assault. The crew consisted of two – the driver, and a soldier armed with a javelin and a spear. The chief function of the Mesopotamian chariot was to charge and panic the enemy, the crew joining battle first at medium range with javelins, and then at short range with the spear. It was already a formidable and decisive instrument of war. Later, between 2000 and 1500, revolutionary developments made the chariot a far more effective mobile firing platform. Improved mobility

A clay model of a two-wheeled Sumerian chariot with solid wheels and protective front panel *left*. A relief of two two-wheeled Assyrian chariots with spoked wheels *right*

was achieved with the discovery of the spoked wheel and the means of making a lighter car. The axle could then be shifted to the rear, and the vehicle was far more manoeuvrable. Asses were replaced by horses, which first appeared in Mesopotamia from the northern steppes about 2000. Improved firepower came with the introduction of the composite bow.

The mace was always a weapon in constant use, and was particularly valued by the Egyptians; but when strong helmets were introduced its blunt head was less effective, and the axe became more important. In the third millenium axes with copper blades were developed for both piercing and cutting; they were used by infantry spearmen and charioteers. The sword was slow in appearing in Mesopotamia, where the technical ability to produce and fashion a long blade of hard metal was acquired late. The first swords were like daggers: short, straight and double-edged. Later came curved, sickle swords for striking. Already Anatolian armourers were experimenting with iron-work to make longer blades. But the knowledge spread slowly, and elsewhere iron swords were used regularly only from the fourteenth century B.C. Before that the standard weapon of the Mesopotamian phalanx was the spear, a long wooden staff with a leaf-shaped metal blade, shoulder-sloped on the march, and carried horizontally in assault.

The bow is depicted on many monuments from the end of the fourth millenium. In Egypt it was double-convex in shape, but in Mesopotamia single-arc. It is strange that it was not used by charioteers till after 2000 B.C. Arrowheads were made of flint. The victory monument of Naram-Sin (2800) portrays for the first time the composite bow. It was then that the bow emerged as a battle weapon of first importance; the success of the Akkadian empire builders was due above all to its possession. Hitherto the bow had always been made out of one material, but there was no single material of sufficient strength and elasticity to give it much range. The new composite bow was made of four materials – wood, animal horn, sinews and glue – so stuck or bound together that, before the string was attached, the arms of the body bent the other way. When it was strung it was thus very tense. It was now possible to make a light bow with an effective range of 300 to 400 yards. The impact of the composite bow was revolutionary: for the first time, enemies could be surprised and attacked from beyond their range of hearing, vision and retaliation. The composite bow was perfected when the Egyptians gave it a double-convex form. It was their chief weapon. In reaction to this bow, shields were made larger, and armour was introduced. The first mail coat was a cape worn by the Sumerians, studded with small circular pieces of metal.

Egyptian weapons

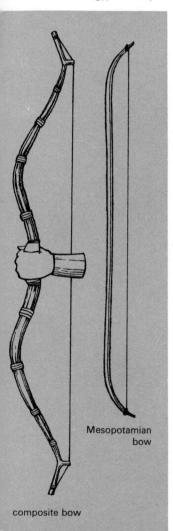

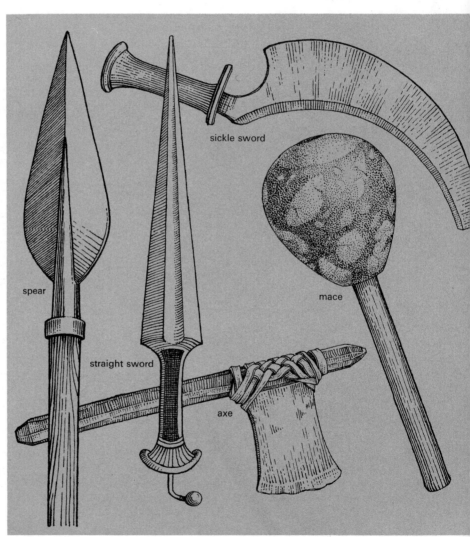

composite bow

Mesopotamian bow

spear

straight sword

sickle sword

mace

axe

Illustrations of open battles in this very early period are few. But it is clear that in open country the functions of infantry and chariots were closely integrated. The phalanx probably went into action in the immediate wake of the chariot charge. The chariots would first confuse, scatter and trample the enemy by storming through their ranks. The phalanx would follow up the charge from the flanks or centre (the men protecting themselves with large rectangular shields) and finish off the enemy with piercing axes and spears.

The organization of the phalanx was methodical and disciplined. The unit would move forward as a column of six files, with eleven men in each file – perhaps ten men and an N.C.O. – then present itself for battle by a right or left wheel, which would offer a

A Babylonian phalanx, armed with spears and large rectangular shields, followed behind the charge of the chariots

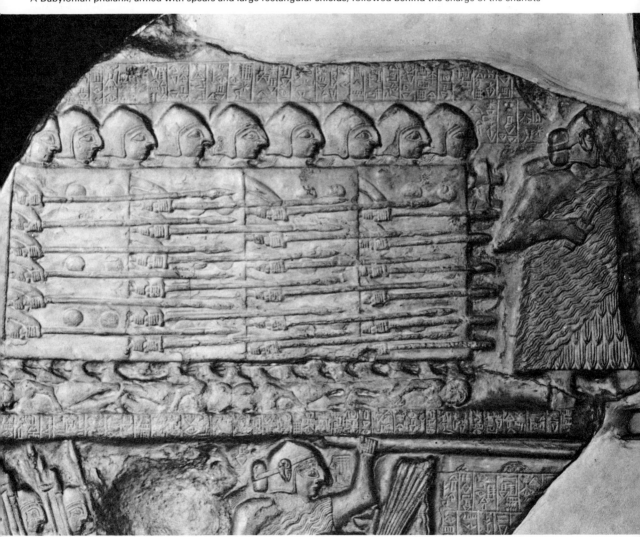

line six ranks deep. Archers were added to this battle formation by the Akkadians; but long-range archery units were possibly only fully integrated with chariots, and with infantry armed with spears and swords, by the Egyptians – when they fought the Hittites a thousand years later.

Advanced techniques of siege warfare did not appear until the time of the Assyrians. But in the third millenium cities were fortified. They were effectively defended by bowmen firing from square or semi-circular bastions. Fortifications were generally built of a mixture of brick and stone, extremely thick, not so much to prevent them being breached, but so that the walls could be built too high for the enemy's scaling-ladders. The monument of the siege of Deshashe in Egypt indicates clearly how a fortified city was attacked in this period. The assailants are climbing a scaling-ladder, which has wheels. They are covered by archery fire. Meanwhile a battering-ram is being used to breach the wall, probably at the gate – which would be the weakest point.

Having examined the weapons and techniques of warfare between 4000 and 2000 B.C., let us now resume the brief account of the political history of war in the ancient Near East. The second great wave of Semitic migration began about 2500 and penetrated from Arabia first of all into Canaan on the Mediterranean coast. It was then that those Semitic tribes with sinister names, the Ammonites, the Edomites and the Moabites, first appeared in the history of Israel. The Canaanites swept on, along the path of the first migration, into Mesopotamia, where they introduced their gods Rimmon and Dagan. It was they who first made Babylon an important city; they refounded Ur, and united all southern Mesopotamia in the Chaldean kingdom.

In Egypt the Middle Kingdom had begun about 2375 when the Theban rulers of the south conquered the Nile delta. Kings of Egypt had still to fight continuously against internal troubles and frontier raids. Nubia was conquered and kept in tyrannical subjection. On the pharaoh's fortress at Semneh was an inscription: 'This is my fortress here. No negro shall pass north of it. I am King and what I say I do.' But under the great Amenemhet III (2061–13), Egypt entered a prolonged phase of peace and high civilization. The result was that the Egyptians became totally unwarlike. Although they had plenty of asses and wheeled carts it never occurred to them to make a chariot; their military technology was centuries behind that of the other peoples of the Near East. This was the situation when in about 1800 the north was invaded and enslaved by Saltis, the first of the Hyksos or 'Shepherd Kings'. The Hyksos were an offshoot of the second wave of Semitic migration, and had come south-west from Syria to the other great river valley. The Egyptians could put up no resistance to their horses and chariots and bronze scimitars; after a period of savage destruction a Hyksos, Semken, became king of Egypt.

Thebes was the last city to bow before the Hyksos, and it was from Thebes in about 1630 B.C. that the Egyptian struggle for liberation was begun. Eventually the Theban king Ahmose carried the war up into the Nile delta, took Avaris, and around 1580 finally defeated the Hyksos who fled from the southern tip of Palestine up to the valley of the Orontes river, which flows northwards from Homs into the sea near Antioch. Ahmose was the founder of the New Kingdom (1580 onwards).

The occupation of Egypt by the Hyksos did not last more than 250 years, but it had a profound effect. By the time the conqueror was thrown off Egypt had become a powerful military state. What was the nature of the Egyptian army in the liberation struggle at the end of the Middle Kingdom ? Its warriors continued to use piercing axes and spears, but the chief weapon was the bow. However, although it was so important, the bow was slow in developing; the Nubians had no armour, and before the coming of the Hyksos there had been no stimulus to develop a long-range piercing weapon. The Hyksos in fact introduced into Egypt the powerful double-convex composite bow as well as the horse and chariot. As regards defence, there does not seem to have been a standardized shield. Shields tended to be smaller and lighter for assault, to give mobility. Fortifications for some time had been highly organized. Yigael Yadin has made a reconstruction of the XIIth dynasty fortress of Buhen, working from the wall-paintings of Beni-Hasan and excavations. The fortress, surrounded by a dry moat, has all the elements of solid defence. The battlements would facilitate defensive fire, and the balconies on the walls would make it possible to fire vertically downwards on assaulting troops. The ingeniously designed gate would also be a formidable obstacle to attackers.

By this time it had become quite common for tribes to settle small disputes, over wells and so on, by single combat, which was considered an honourable and binding way – a practice which looks forward to the duel between David and Goliath. Major campaigns were not, however, settled like this, and the Egyptians had developed a complex military organization. The king had his body of professional guards – perhaps captive Libyans or Sudanese – and every local ruler had to supply a contingent. Until the Hyksos invasion the whole male population of Egypt had been subject to this feudal levy. Then it became necessary to have a more professional army (and the levée en masse did not return to Egypt until Mehmet Ali's reforms in the early nineteenth century A.D.). In the Middle Kingdom the militia was divided into units, the size of which depended on their function. The 300-man unit, made up of three companies of 100, was for assault; a guards unit consisted of ten soldiers only.

The systems of communications, intelligence and administration were efficient. There was a code of torch signals; runners relayed messages and orders on the battlefield; sometimes semaphore and trumpet calls were used. With large bodies of troops campaigning in unfamiliar and difficult terrain it was necessary to have good intelligence services. The Egyptians used to send out reconnaissance units to spy and to capture prisoners for interrogation. Rapid and frequent reports from officers in the front line were relayed to their superiors at headquarters to provide battle intelligence. It was a rule that the source of their information must always be stated, and the form of report was probably very like that used in a modern army. Receipts of detailed lists of equipment and supplies which have been discovered indicate that the army had a well-organized administrative machine. It had a medical service; there were companies of engineers to construct siege equipment, and a transport service of ships and wagons to carry it long distances.

After Ahmose had completed the expulsion of the Hyksos he became master of Egypt. Since very few of the nobles had supported him he confiscated their estates, and made all Egypt the pharaoh's domain and the basis of a military state. The taste of successful war gave the Egyptians in the New Kingdom an appetite for further conquest. Amenhotep I (1554–30) consolidated control of Nubia and Libya, and then invaded Asia, penetrating through Syria as far as the Euphrates. His son Thutmose I maintained this advance, and conquered the people of Mitanni, away to the west of Nineveh

Ramses II extended the Egyptian empire with campaigns against the Hittites and the Nubians. A relief showing the pharoah with Libyan and Negro prisoners

(on the Tigris opposite modern Mosul). He then turned his attention to the restoration of the temples and the regeneration of Egyptian civilization.

During this peaceful period Egyptian control of Mitanni, Syria and northern Palestine was dangerously relaxed, and on his succession Thutmose III had to face a revolt led by the king of Kadesh. If the Egyptian empire was to survive it was vital to control Kadesh, a city near Lake Homs in Syria, commanding the upper valley of the Orontes river, because the city was the key to the great trade link with Asia, stretching up between the Lebanon land-ridges towards the Euphrates and Assyria. This it was decided to do. With an army of about 30,000 men Thutmose marched from the Nile delta on 19th April 1468. He reached the southern slopes of Mt Carmel by 10th May, having covered sixteen miles a day. Meanwhile the Asiatic army under the command of the king of Kadesh had occupied the strong fortress of Megiddo on the north slope of Mt Carmel. The battleground was well chosen, for this ridge is the first real natural barrier to confront an army marching north out of Egypt. Megiddo commands the trade route to Anatolia, Syria and the Euphrates. It is the site of several battles and has always been important in the history of the Near East. The Egyptians attacked and won an easy victory. But Thutmose foolishly allowed his troops to waste time in looting instead of ordering an immediate pursuit. However, in due course he reached Kadesh; the city was sacked, but the king escaped.

In later ages both Napoleon and Allenby were to advance over the same country as Thutmose III. In 1931 when on garrison duty in Palestine I paid several visits to Mt Carmel and surveyed the battlefield of Megiddo.

Thutmose established a strong hold on the rich Phoenician coast, attacking it by land and sea. Later he returned to attack once again his long-standing enemy, Kadesh. Kadesh itself was the most impregnable fortress of Syria by reason of its water defences. It lay between the Orontes and a tributary stream, and to complete the moat a canal had been cut above the town between the two streams. The siege was long and difficult, but eventually Thutmose captured the city. Thus the last vestige of Hyksos power disappeared. Finally, Thutmose III reconquered Mitanni, and received tributes and gifts from many cities of Mesopotamia. When he died in 1447 the Egyptian empire had entered the height of its extent and wealth.

The third great migration of Semites out of Arabia began about 1350. It is known as the Aramaean migration, after the area between the Lebanon and the Euphrates, where the confederate Semitic tribes eventually established a great power – with its capital at Damascus, dominating the westerly desert trade routes for two hundred years. These were the 'Syrians' who constantly threatened Israel from the time of David to the time of Ahab. After the death of Thutmose III the military strength of the Egyptian empire was undermined by attacks from the Aramaeans and Hittites, and by internal religious troubles. However, the Egyptian army was revived after about 1350, and in 1292 Ramses II, a young man of great ability and energy, became pharaoh. He was determined to recover the former extent of the Egyptian empire. The previous period of peace had given the Hittites time to become very strong in Syria, making Kadesh the bulwark of their southern frontier. It was at this point that Ramses decided to attack. But before examining the battle of Kadesh, let us first consider the weapons and organization of the Egyptian armies of the New Kingdom, from the time of Amenhotep I to that of Ramses II.

A great deal of evidence in documents and monuments has survived from the New Kingdom to tell us about this. The axe remained in use, but in this period, after 1500 B.C., it was less prominent than the sword which, like other important weapons, was introduced to Egypt from Asia. The sword replaced the mace as the symbol of the pharaoh's power. The sword of Ramses III was long and wide; the short dagger-like sword of earlier times was also still in use, and these were the most effective weapons for the phalanx in hand-to-hand fighting. The spear was also a basic infantry weapon, and at last the stronger socket-type, leaf-shaped head, known for centuries in Mesopotamia, was adopted in Egypt. A phalanx would have consisted of spear, axe, and sword units. The spear was also used for defending ramparts, but not by charioteers – in contrast to Asiatic practice.

Egyptian charioteers used javelins. This difference arises from their different chariot tactics. The Asiatic chariot would charge into the enemy, with a crew consisting of a driver and two spearmen. If the fighting became too congested for the chariot to be able to manoeuvre, the driver would join in as a spearman. Egyptian chariots, on the other hand, operated more as a unit; the chariots would charge in a solid mass, driving the enemy before them, and never allowing themselves to be surrounded individually in the battle. Chariots, which constituted a large proportion of the Egyptian army, were divided into units of fifty, each unit under an officer. Cavalry was still not used. But as weapons had developed in power, and conversely armour had been developed to give better protection, the outcome of a battle was increasingly likely to be decided by troops of the maximum mobility, and it is for this reason that the chariot now became of prime importance. At the beginning of the New Kingdom it was a light vehicle with a wooden frame, drawn by two horses; everything was designed to make it strong, yet fast and manoeuvrable; the wheels had four spokes, and the parts were bound together with strips of birch. From the reign of Thutmose IV the Egyptians developed a special heavier chariot. Chariot maintenance was provided along regular campaign routes by repair workshops, which kept stores and spares and also saw to repairs of transport vehicles. There is a picture which shows Ramses II charging through the ranks of the Hittites, in a chariot equipped with quivers for both javelins and arrows.

In all large armies of this period the bow was the decisive weapon. It was difficult and expensive to make, and it was largely because they had the money and specialized factories to produce good bows that the Egyptians could deal so easily with the smaller states of Palestine and Syria. The bow was supplied to both chariot and infantry troops. A composite bow was used, which in shape could be either triangular or recurved; to prevent warping it was kept in a case. The arrows had reed shafts and bronze heads, and at a reasonably short distance could penetrate the armour of the time. The infantry archer would carry on a shoulder-strap a quiver of up to thirty arrows. Archery training was a popular pastime, and practice ranges were available under the supervision of experienced instructors. The training system laid particular stress on firing from a chariot with the horses at full gallop.

In the Middle Kingdom (2375–1580) Egyptian soldiers had worn no armour but carried large shields. In the New Kingdom (1580 onwards) charioteers and bowmen, who needed to have both hands free, took to wearing coats of mail and helmets, and used only a small shield or none at all. As weapons developed more penetrating power, armour was correspondingly strengthened. The armour was made of metal scales, but

Heavy infantry of the period of the Middle Kingdom carried shields as their only protection. The spear, with a leaf-shaped head, was the basic infantry weapon

Egyptian soldiers assaulted a fortified city by scaling the walls with ladders, protecting themselves with their shields

was flexible and fairly light. Expense was a problem, and generally mail armour was worn only by those who had to have both hands free; others, such as spearmen and swordsmen, used shields. All troops wore helmets, which were often highly decorated. A chariot relief of Thutmose IV illustrates the armour of a Canaanite charioteer; the coat of mail made of rectangular scales covers his body and upper arms; his neck is protected by a leather collar covered with metal scales. The artist has indicated the weak spot by showing an arrow protruding from the armpit.

Military administration became more highly organized in the New Kingdom than it had been before. One central authority was no longer sufficient to deal with all the aspects of recruitment, supply and organization. Detailed records of military establishments, equipment and pay were kept by a quartermaster and adjutant services. These were also responsible for the distribution of supplies to be ready at the various depots *en route*, and they made lists of captured booty. They arranged the transport of supplies in wagons drawn by asses and oxen, and on occasion provided boats to ferry troops across rivers.

A new kind of defence in this period was the *migdol*, a square fort with rectangular bastions built to guard important military points such as wells and roads. Great ingenuity and engineering ability is apparent in fortifications of the second millenium. For example water supply in time of siege was always a problem. At Megiddo the well lay outside the city walls; the inhabitants therefore sank a vertical shaft 60 feet down inside the fort as near to the well as possible, and connected it to the water supply 140 feet away by a horizontal tunnel through the rock. Egyptian armies did not now use battering-rams in sieges, since walls were usually too thick. The usual method of assaulting a fortified city was by beating down the gates with axes and scaling the walls. The soldier would grip the ladder with both hands, and protect himself as he climbed with a shield slung over his back. The defenders countered the attack with archers, and spearmen would pick off the enemy one by one as they reached the top. Assaulting a strongly fortified place in this way obviously involved heavy casualties; generals, therefore, often besieged a city, attempting to starve it into surrender. Stratagems and ruses were also used. For example, Thot, a general of Thutmose III, captured Jaffa by pretending to surrender and then, when the inhabitants of the city opened the gates, storming it. The legend of the Trojan horse relates to this period.

The Egyptians were skilled at ambushing, but with their superior resources they preferred to fight with large formations in the open. Megiddo is the first battle in history which can be reconstructed in any detail. But since we know so much more about the battle of Kadesh between Ramses II and the Hittites in 1288, it will be better to take that as an illustration of battle in open terrain.

In the respite given them by Seti, the Hittites under Mutallu had built up a more formidable army than the Egyptians had ever before had to face. But by 1288 Ramses had an equally large army, which included mercenaries. Late that spring he reached the valley of the upper Orontes, overlooking the plain in which lay Kadesh, a day's march away. He divided his army into four, and with himself at the head of the division of Amon set off to ford the river, leaving the others to follow. He crossed the river in the vicinity of Shabtuna, six miles or so south of Kadesh, and advanced northwards. He was anxious to begin the siege, and was completely confident about pushing on ahead of his main army because two Hittite deserters had told him that the bulk of the Hittite

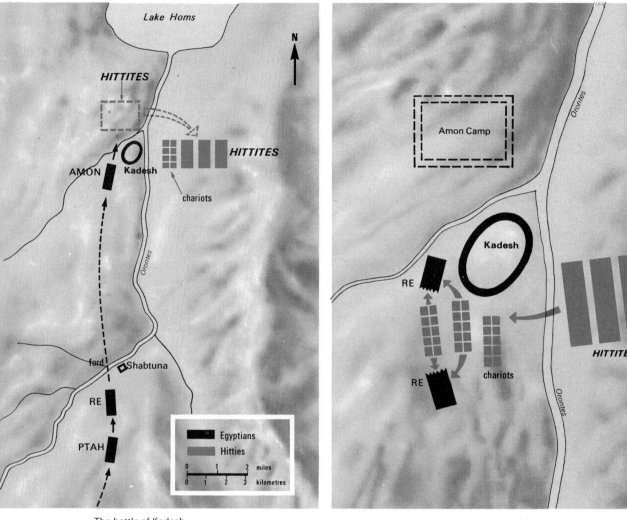

The battle of Kadesh

army was far to the north, near Aleppo. But he had been deceived. The two 'deserters' had been sent by Mutallu to lure him northwards, and make him fall unsuspectingly into the trap laid by the Hittite army concealed north of Kadesh.

As Ramses approached and passed northwards to the west of Kadesh, the Hittite army first moved across to the east of the river, and then south, always keeping the city between themselves and the enemy – to avoid being seen. Finally they completed a brilliant manoeuvre by closing in on Ramses from the south-east. The Egyptian army was now completely cut in two. Ramses was isolated and faced by overwhelming numbers. His other divisions were straggled out so far to the south that it was doubtful if they would be able to join in the battle at all. Mutallu had his whole army based on Kadesh, which could give him concealment and shelter. The Egyptian king perceived

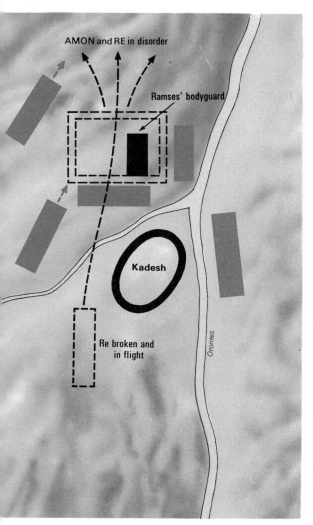

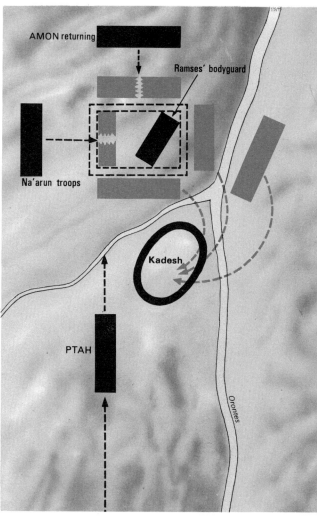

his desperate plight only when he captured two Hittite spies – genuine, this time – who admitted that the Hittite army was behind Kadesh.

The Hittites first attacked the second division of the Egyptian army, called Re. Taken completely by surprise, Re was broken in two and cut to pieces. Part of the remnants fled towards the pharaoh's camp, followed closely by the chariot units and phalanxes of the Hittites, in all about 17,000 men. Ramses' division of Amon was at first bewildered and driven back in chaos. The rout seemed to be complete. But then Ramses launched a desperate counter-attack. He could not halt the Hittites in the centre, but he observed that their eastern flank by the river was thin, and it was here that he flung his chariots. The Hittites should still have won. They were victorious in the centre, and they needed only to concentrate their forces against the Egyptian king on the eastern flank to secure a complete victory. But instead their discipline broke, and they began looting the Egyptian camp. This was the crucial moment of the battle. While the Hittites in the centre were looting and off their guard, they were attacked and overwhelmed by the Na'arun troops. These were a crack Canaanite unit of phalanxes ten ranks deep, serving with the Egyptian forces; they only now arrived from the western flank where they had originally been deployed. At the same time that the situation in the centre was thus being salvaged, the Egyptians were pressing their attack relentlessly on the eastern flank. At this point the technical superiority of the Egyptian chariot, armed with the long-range composite bow, was decisive. The Hittite chariots were less mobile, and were armed only with a short-range spear.

Mutallu was driven back across the Orontes, and halted on the far side of the river with 6,000 men. He was now crippled, since he had already committed all his chariots in the first attack in the centre, and his infantry was powerless against the Egyptian chariots. By this time it was evening, and the third division (Ptah) of the Egyptian army was arriving. The Hittites then retired into Kadesh, and there prepared for a siege. But the Egyptians also retired without attempting to take the city. The battle thus ended indecisively. Ramses had been outmanoeuvred strategically, but in the actual course of the battle he led his men so well that disaster was averted, although the Egyptian losses were severe. Mutallu, after a brilliant start, had lost his advantage because of faulty command and control; he also suffered from technical inferiority.

Both the Hittite and the Egyptian empires began to decay rapidly after this time. The Egyptians had exhausted their imperialistic drive, and the Hittites were already feeling the rising power of Assyria. Furthermore, ever since about 1400 migratory Indo-European tribes had been sweeping down into the south-east Mediterranean from the direction of the Aegean, in raids which were becoming increasingly frequent and serious. The whole movement of the Aegean peoples was irresistible, and by 1200 they had overrun the country of the Hittites, had advanced into Syria, and were threatening Egypt. The Egyptian army was reorganized by Setnakht and Ramses III, and its archers were still powerful enough in the 1190's to beat the invaders by land and sea on the Phoenician coast. That this invasion was an armed migration is quite clear from the fact that the land force was accompanied by the families of the soldiers and their property in large wagons. When Ramses had defeated them, he settled the non-combatants of the Philistines, as they were called, on the coast. No invader actually penetrated Egypt until the Assyrians in the seventh century B.C., but the pharaohs were very weak.

One of the chief beneficiaries of the decline of the Egyptian empire was Israel. The children of Israel were led out of Egypt by Moses about 1290. Whether it was because of the will of Jehovah, or because their path through Sinai and around the Dead Sea area was blocked by other tribes, or, as is most likely, because Moses needed time to train his people as a fighting force – they did not reach their 'promised land' of Palestine for forty years. But under Joshua they captured Jericho and the land as far north as the Lebanon and Mt Hermon. The Israelite kingdom reached its height under Saul, David and Solomon around 1000, when it stretched from the Euphrates to the border of Egypt. But after that it split into two kingdoms, Israel and Judah; and the northern kingdom of Israel was soon completely obliterated after its conquest by Assyria, which had risen to be the most powerful military state of the Middle East.

The Egyptian chariot. A cast of a temple relief depicting Ramses II's conquest of Nubia

Company of negro archers marching in fours from the tomb of an officer Mesehti. The coffin on one side and the boat on the other, are from the same tomb.

... ne compagnie d'infanterie légère, formée de quarante hommes.

Company of light in forty strong.

I first became interested in the Assyrians as a small boy in Tasmania. An officer going off to the South African War quoted to me some lines of Byron's 'Destruction of Sennacherib':

> The Assyrian came down like a wolf on the fold,
> And his cohorts were gleaming in purple and gold.

I then read about them in the Bible, in the Second Book of Kings, and learnt about Sennacherib, king of Assyria, who was murdered by his two sons.

The first people of Assyria (as the hilly country of the Tigris north of Babylonia came to be called) were probably an offshoot of the second Semitic migration (2500 B.C.). The cooler climate and an infusion of non-Semitic mountain blood made them rugged and vigorous. They were the greatest military people, with the most advanced technique of war, before the Romans. Nineveh was the capital of their empire which eventually incorporated all the peoples of the Near East.

In the second millenium B.C. Assyria had been cut off from the mainstream of events, and her power grew only slowly until the thirteenth century B.C. Then the exhaustion of the Egyptians and the Hittites left a power-vacuum. Between 1276 and 1233 the Assyrians advanced rapidly in the north and north-west. By the reign of Tiglathpileser I (1115–02) they were strong enough to annex extensive areas of the Hittite empire, march down the Mediterranean coast, and capture Babylon. But then civil war and attacks from Aramaean tribesmen caused the power of Assyria to collapse for two hundred years. Recovery began only under Adad-Nirari II (911–889) who penetrated into Babylonia, and in the north-west drove a wedge between the peoples of the plain and the hills. For the next hundred years Assyrian kings followed a consistent and ruthless policy of thorough conquest.

The Assyrians never bothered to justify their empire, or even to wait for any excuse for an invasion. These ferocious people worshipped the stern god Ashur. The winged disc, within which Ashur was shown leading his people, was always carried on the king's chariot in battle and set up in every conquered place. Senior army officers were also priests, and the word 'rebel' meant the same as 'sinner': a man to be punished with the utmost severity. It was enough that the city of Arinna had 'despised the god Ashur' for it to be destroyed. After a victory prisoners were slaughtered while religious rites were performed. The Assyrians brought no benefit to their subject peoples. On the contrary, they pillaged every land, and cruelty and mass deportations to swell the population of Assyria were regular policies. The feelings of all their subjects were expressed in the cry of the Jewish prophet Nahum: 'Woe to the bloody city!' Tiglath-pileser I boasted of his victims that 'their blood in the valleys and on the high places of the mountains I caused to flow. Their heads I cut off, and outside their cities, like heaps of grain, I piled them up. Their spoil and their possessions in countless number I brought out. Six thousand men . . . I took away and as inhabitants of my country I counted them.' The royal annals consist of little more than such frank and revolting accounts of devastating conquests.

Yet this policy was realistic. Assyria was situated in an infertile area of the upper Tigris and had the alternative of remaining small and poor, or becoming rich by conquest. If she was to expand she had to be secure on her eastern and southern frontiers, and

Egyptian soldiers. A company of Negro archers of the period of the Middle Kingdom completely dominant to the north and west. There was little trouble in the east until the seventh century, when a threat arose from the Medes and masses of migratory Iranians. Nor was there too much difficulty in the south, although every king had to give his attention to that area. At first the Assyrian policy there was to strengthen the authority of the king of Babylon over the tribes. But after a long period of revolt Sennacherib (705–681) sacked Babylon in 689, and in 639 Ashurbanipal (668–26) destroyed the kingdom of Elam (thus, in fact, leaving a vacuum for the rise of Persia). The major problems lay in the north and west. The hill peoples of the north, particularly the Urartians and, later, the migratory Scythians and Cymmerians, had to be held back and disciplined by periodic punitive expeditions. In the west experience had shown that the tribes could be kept in proper submission, and commercial possibilities fully exploited, only if the whole area at least as far as Carchemish was systematically conquered and integrated with Assyria herself. This was achieved by the greatest of Assyrian conquerors, Tiglathpileser III (745–27). He first eliminated the smaller powers; then he dealt knock-out blows to his two major enemies, Urartu and Damascus. In a series of campaigns he advanced northwards up the Tigris, striking alternately east and west, against the Medes and into Syria. Urartu was thoroughly crushed. Likewise Damascus was captured, after the rulers of Phoenicia, Palestine and many lesser states had submitted. He then dealt with the south.

When he died, after eighteen years of systematic and ruthless campaigns, Assyria, as the king himself said, 'ruled the lands . . . from the salt waters of Bit-Yakin to Mount Bikni in the east, from the Western sea as far as Egypt, from the horizon of heaven to its zenith.' For the next century the Assyrians maintained this supremacy in the Near East. The advancing Cymmerians were checked by Sargon II in a great battle in 705. In 671 the army of King Esarhaddon of Assyria captured all upper Egypt.

How were the military successes of the Assyrians achieved? They appear to have been interested in few things but warfare, which was their constant occupation. The character of their history is clearly revealed to us in the paintings and sculpture in the royal palaces, which depict military subjects and little else. We therefore have a full knowledge of the development of Assyrian weapons and military techniques. The Assyrians were the first great military power of the iron age, and their weapons were stronger and sharper than any before.

They were also the first people to use cavalry, shortly before 1000 B.C. There were two branches of cavalry – bowmen and spearmen – both of which were used in short- and long-range combat, but never in assaulting fortified places. In a battle the mounted spearmen would open the charge, followed by infantry spearmen. Mounted archers attacked mostly from the rear or the flanks, operating in pairs, one horseman with a bow and the other holding both sets of reins and a large shield big enough to protect two men. The horses were sometimes protected with leather armour. Chariots were the main strength of an army. In the time of Ashurbanipal the crew of a chariot was increased from two to four – driver, archer and two shield-bearers. The chariot itself became much heavier and was pulled by four horses.

The infantry consisted of spearmen, archers and slingmen. The spearmen wore heavy coats of mail and helmets. Various experiments were made with the size, shape and weight of shields, to achieve the right balance between security and mobility, but no fixed pattern was settled. Spearmen were generally shock troops who led the assault in hand-to-hand fighting, but they were also very important in assaults on fortified cities. The main power of the Assyrian infantry rested with its archers, who with their highly advanced composite bow were used in all types of attack. In the earlier period they wore long coats of mail; then, under Tiglathpileser III (745–27), who made radical changes

The Assyrians were the first nation to use cavalry *above*. Their archers at first wore long coats of mail *below left* and later sheltered behind large hooded shields *below right*

The Assyrian army included units of slingmen, whose high-angled fire was particularly effective in assaults on cities or up steep slopes

in all arms, they used a huge shield with a hood, taller than a man and carried by a special bearer. Light archery units also existed. The bow was improved in the eighth century, when the tips of the arc were curled back, making it easier to string. Tiglath-pileser III was the first Assyrian king to use slingmen. One of Sennacherib's reliefs shows them operating in pairs behind archers. Their high-angled fire was particularly effective in assaults up steep slopes on cities. All infantrymen were armed, in addition to their special weapon, with a long straight sword carried in a sheath over the left thigh.

    In four hundred years of almost incessant warfare, in two empires, the Assyrians were rarely beaten. Their armies were often outnumbered, and, of their enemies, the Urartians, Syrians, Babylonians and Elamites were certainly as well armed as they were. Their success was partly due to the fact that most of the kings of Assyria were first-rate field commanders. But it was also to a great extent the result of sound organization. As the original oriental despots, the Assyrian kings had absolute power to direct all the resources of the state to military ends, and an application to detail made them very efficient administrators. There was a regular army, and all adult males had to do a period of military service – although in practice the rich could, if they wished, commute service for a payment, or send a slave in their place. Conquered peoples had to supply contingents. The military formations, or *kisri*, varied in size, and were divided into 'fifties' and 'tens'. The troops and officers were probably well provided for by the central government and from exactions in the areas they occupied. At the close of a campaign a share of the spoil was divided among the troops. The army was backed by an efficient intelligence system, and civil officials in the provinces regularly sent in information which could be of military use.

The formidable power of the Assyrian army meant that practically all other peoples stood little chance in open battle, and relied on defending fortified places. There are no detailed records of open battles, and it is impossible to be sure of what the strategy and tactics of the Assyrians would have been in such operations. The key part was probably played by chariots charging from all directions and engaging in battle at all ranges; the other formations would mop up what was left by the chariots. The best evidence is a series of reliefs of Ashurbanipal, depicting the battle against the Elamites and Arabs on the river Ulai. The Elamite army of light archers, infantry and a few cavalry appears in a desperate plight. The Assyrian army, using units appropriate to the terrain, consists mainly of cavalry armed with bows and spears, and of infantry spearmen. Most of them are heavily armoured, but in addition lightly-clad auxiliary archers are moving through the field doing considerable damage. The scenes, from left to right, begin with the initial onslaught, and end with the retreat of the Elamites into the river and the decapitation of prisoners. It is clear that the cavalry and infantry are launched after the chariots have caused confusion among the enemy. The cavalry operates mainly on the flanks, to prevent any of the enemy escaping; they are all to be forced back into the river and slaughtered.

The Assyrians were good fighters in all kinds of country, from the mountains of Urartu to the marshes of Bit-Yakin and the desert. A relief of Sennacherib shows infantry advancing through wooded country. The unit of foot spearmen proceeds line abreast in separate ranks, while small scattered forces follow to secure the rear and flanks. In combat in partly wooded and hilly regions mounted archers and spearmen play the chief part, closely co-ordinated with infantry. They move forward in column, their flanks in the wooded areas protected by the infantry. The best example of the ability of Assyrian troops to deal with difficult terrain is the amphibious operations of Sennacherib in the marshland of the Tigris delta. The infantry appear as marines, charging into the swamps in light boats, manoeuvring among the reeds, seeking out the enemy and burning their refuges. The Assyrian army, capable of moving large formations over long distances in hilly country, reached a new level of ingenuity and technical skill in surmounting natural obstacles, particularly rivers. Another relief shows a chariot corps crossing a wide river with all its heavy gear. The vehicles are ferried across in large boats which are rowed and assisted on the far bank by an advance party hauling or. ropes. Whereas the horses swim behind, tied to a rope held in the boat, the troops swim across with the aid of inflated goatskins, and take great care to prevent their weapons getting wet. Assyrian sappers could build pontoon bridges across smaller streams.

To oppose the Assyrians, smaller nations, particularly Syria and Palestine, developed the technique of fortification. The Assyrians correspondingly developed the art of siege warfare. Their great success here was due to the maximum co-ordination and exploitation of all military possibilities open to them. They used, both separately and together, various techniques of siege: storming of ramparts, breaching of walls and gates, scaling, tunnelling, and even psychological warfare. In the early period battering-rams were somewhat clumsy and large, on six wheels, and perhaps 15 feet long; at the front was a round turret about 18 feet high, from the inside of which the ram was suspended on a rope, so that it could be swung. The head of the ram, shaped like an axe, would be forcibly inserted into the gate or the wall, and then levered left and right to make the walls collapse. Long sharp-headed levers were also used by individuals. Tiglath-pileser III owed much of his success to the introduction of a new and lighter four-wheeled ram. The operators of battering-rams were obviously in great danger from defending archers, and so were given continuous covering fire from their own archers in mobile towers.

Simultaneously the walls would be assaulted by spearmen carrying scaling ladders, and these could either divert the defenders from dealing with the rams or else take advantage of weak points in the defence – the defenders having concentrated elsewhere to repel the battering assault. Later, when walls became stronger, scaling ladders were increasingly used in preference to rams, some being up to 30 feet long. All methods of assault were used at the same time, together with sustained archery fire, and assaults

The Assyrians developed siege warfare to a high degree, inventing several types of battering rams mounted on wheels. The ram was in the form of an axe-head, which could be levered sideways

became even more devastating after the reign of Sennacherib, when slingers were added. When manpower posed a definite problem, or the fortifications were exceptionally strong, siege or stratagem would be employed. In the Second Book of Kings, 18: 19–23, it is described how Rabshakeh called to the defenders of Jerusalem, in their own tongue, to surrender despite Hezekiah's orders – an early example of psychological warfare.

The survival of Jerusalem in 710 against the Assyrian siege by Sennacherib was probably due above all to Hezekiah's foresight in ensuring a good water supply. Chapter 32 of the Second Book of Chronicles tells how he 'stopped the upper watercourse of Gihon, and brought it straight down to the west side of the city of David'. By a remarkable feat of engineering, he built a conduit leading through some 650 yards of solid rock to a reservoir inside the city. He had also built up reserve stores of oil, wine and flour.

An example of improved fortifications is the massive new wall of Megiddo, built at the beginning of the nineteenth century B.C.: 7 feet thick at the base, it is constructed with 18-foot-wide salients and recesses, and crowned by a balcony with a crenellated parapet; a lower outer wall gives additional strength. The reliefs of Sennacherib's assault on Lachish show that the defenders along the ramparts built special wooden frames, on which their shields were hung so as to form a screen behind which the archers could stand upright and operate freely.

Some sieges were heroically and brilliantly sustained against the Assyrians, perhaps most notably by the kings of Judah and Israel – Rehoboam, Ahab, Uzziah, and, as we have seen, Hezekiah.

By 639 Ashurbanipal had established good order in his empire. There was peace in the south-west, Lydia had been secured as an ally, Elam had been finally crushed, and the king was on good terms with the Scythians in the north and with the puppet king of Babylon. Then disaster struck. We do not know exactly what happened, but it is certain that the king's death was followed by a long and weakening dispute for the succession in Assyria. Nabopolassar, king of Babylon, and Cyaxares of Media allied to destroy the Assyrians, whose manpower had been seriously depleted in the civil wars of the 620's. The enemy generals were very able, and the Assyrians found themselves slowly hemmed in to the fortified quadrilateral of their homeland, until in 616 Nabopolassar inflicted a severe defeat on them at Kablinu. Two years later Cyaxares marched almost up to Nineveh, then turned south and joined the Babylonians to sack Ashur. Even now, the Assyrian empire did not finally disintegrate. But in 612 the Scythians joined the Medes and Babylonians in the assault on Nineveh. Between May and July the city held out, but at length it fell before a coalition of powers which had been trained in warfare by the Assyrians themselves. Sin-Shar-Ishkun, the last king of Nineveh, threw himself into the flames of his city. So complete was the defeat and enslavement, and so extensive the slaughter and deportation of the victims, that the separate Assyrian nation ceased altogether to exist.

So ended the history of a people who had made war all over the Near East for over six hundred years, unceasingly and relentlessly – being generally victorious in battle.

A young Greek warrior receives the armour of the 'heroic' age : helmet, breast-plate, greaves, shield and spear

4 The Ancient Greeks

Chapter 3 covered nearly seven thousand years of the history of warfare and it ended with the collapse of the Assyrian nation in 612 B.C. While those events were taking place in the Near East, the war clouds were gathering further to the west.

It can be said that the 'heroic' age of Greek warfare began in 1400 B.C. when the Achaeans wrested supremacy in the Aegean from Crete. From about 1200 the piratical and migratory raids of these and other Aegean peoples exhausted the Egyptian and Hittite empires. The story of one such raid, against Troy, was told by Homer. Battles in those days were trials of valour between mighty warriors: Ajax, Diomedes, Hector – and he who was the greatest of them all:

> High o'er the scene of death Achilles stood,
> All grim with dust, all horrible in blood.

The warriors would ride on to the field in chariots, dismount, and engage in single combat, cheered on by their retainers. Lightly equipped for agility, each carried a round shield, two throwing spears, and a straight sword. The bow was despised as a cowardly weapon. If the spears did not settle the matter, a sword duel would follow. Whatever else was to change, the spear always remained the first weapon of the Greeks.

Two generations after the Trojan War Greece was invaded from the north by the Dorian migration. Four dark centuries of racial struggle and fusion followed, during which Greece entered the Iron Age. Until the eighth century B.C. Argos, a Dorian city, ruled all the eastern Peloponnese. Then began the age of Sparta, a city in the southern Peloponnese. Between 740 and 710 King Theopompus of Sparta annexed Messenia and Laconia, thereby securing iron supplies, and a labour force of slaves or 'helots'. But in 669 the defeat by the king of Argos, Pheidon, in the valley of Hysiae, and a 19-years' revolt of the helots, temporarily exhausted Sparta. However, by the beginning of the sixth century she revived, and entered upon 250 years of military pre-eminence in Greece.

Between 620 and 600 Lycurgus, the reputed founder of the Spartan constitution, introduced a new social and political system. Sparta became a military state, and education was designed solely to produce efficient soldiers. Weakling babies were exposed to die on Mt Taygetus, and Spartan boys from seven to thirty were trained to discipline and hardship in barracks. The whole male population constituted an intensely professional standing army, every man dedicated to the law that he must 'conquer or die'. The two kings of Sparta commanded the army. Economic needs were supplied by the helots.

This system gave Sparta unique political stability, and the strength, despite her small population, to dominate the helots and the Peloponnese. In 560 King Anaxandridas allied with Tegea, an Arcadian city in the central Peloponnese, in the first stage towards building up a Peloponnesian League under Spartan political leadership. In 546 Sparta defeated Argos in the Battle of the Champions, and under Cleomenes finally shattered her at Sepeia in 495.

But by now the first of the great wars between Greece and Persia was looming ahead.

In 552 Cyrus the Great, founder of the Persian empire, had grasped the opportunity left by the disappearance of Assyria, and within thirty years he and his son Cambyses had conquered Media, Babylonia, Lydia and Egypt. In 512 King Darius I extended the Persian empire westwards to the Danube. In 500 the Greek cities of the Ionian islands revolted, and appealed to mainland Greece for help. Darius then decided that all Greece must be conquered. In the face of this peril for the first time the Greek cities united, under Spartan leadership. The first massive invasion by the Persians in 490 was repelled at Marathon, and the second in 480–79 at Salamis and Plataea. The Greeks won these great victories against the vast and supposedly invincible Persian forces because they had perfected two superb instruments of war, the hoplite phalanx and the trireme (described later).

Shortly after 700, battles at long range and in loose formations gave way to conflicts between close-order phalanxes of heavy infantry, or 'hoplites'. It was natural that the men of a city-state community should fight shoulder to shoulder, and as smelting techniques improved and prosperity grew, more people could afford the panoply of the hoplite. This consisted of an 8-foot thrusting spear, a sword, helmet, breast-plate, greaves, and a round shield about 3 feet in diameter held on the left arm. The helmet was crested, and the shield often emblazoned with birds or wild beasts. The first true hoplite army was the Argive force at Hysiae in 669. Within twenty years this mode of fighting had become standardized among the city-states.

The tactics of the hoplite phalanx consisted essentially in confronting the enemy with a firm and solid line of alternate shields and spears. At the clash each man struck with his spear at his opponent's throat. The continuity of the line was vital, for every man depended on his neighbour. Personal distinction was to be sought not on the battlefield but in athletics. At Plataea there were eight ranks in the Spartan phalanx. The function of the rear ranks was to fill the gaps as they appeared in front, to carry spare weapons, and to deal with the wounded – killing those of the enemy and tending their own. Discipline and tenacity were needed to maintain cohesion and to prevent dangerous gaps in the front rank, discipline being based on morale. The battle was decided by steadiness and weight of numbers, and was usually short. Since it was important to be as powerful as possible in the initial charge, the whole strength of an army was committed straightaway. Once a line was broken the defeated hoplites turned and fled; there being no reserves, a second assault was impossible. There was little pursuit, since the strenuous nature of the fighting was exhausting for heavy troops. The verdict of battle was quickly accepted; it was the custom for the vanquished to admit defeat by sending heralds to ask permission to collect the dead for burial.

Tactics were thus extremely limited. There was no possibility of manoeuvre other than the charge. But with their superior training and discipline the Spartans were

The hoplite phalanx advanced into battle to the music of flutes

supreme in this kind of war. They developed a simple refinement of the hoplite charge, which for almost three centuries invariably gave them victory. Advancing troops had a natural tendency to edge towards their right, as each man sought the protection of his neighbour's shield. The right wing of the phalanx was therefore likely to some extent to outflank the enemy's left, and the Spartans exploited this tendency. After outflanking the enemy they would wheel and roll up his line. Their slow, steady charge to the music of flutes allowed them sufficient flexibility for the manoeuvre.

These narrow limits of tactics set limitations on strategy and originality. Flat ground was always chosen for battle since neither side would concede the advantage of fighting downhill, and on broken ground the all-important solidity of the line was liable to be lost. One short battle was generally enough to decide a campaign. In any case bad roads, mountainous country, and rigid formations limited the scope for strategical or tactical conceptions, such as surprise. Wars were restricted to the summer months, since the only way to force the enemy to emerge from his walled city and fight was by ravaging his crops and herds. Sieges were rare; the Spartans failed to take Argos in 495, and there is no record of a city ever being stormed before 424. Hoplites hardly ever fought other arms. Cavalry would have been effective if the Greeks had had more and stronger horses; but Greece was not a suitable country for horse breeding on account of poor pasture land. Athens had an aristocratic corps of knights, but only the Thessalians regularly relied on cavalry, and their defeat of a force of Spartan hoplites in 511 was unique. Archers and chariots could not check the phalanx; indeed the chariot was used by the Greeks only as a ceremonial and sporting vehicle. The Persians, who had conquered Asia with their archers and cavalry, confronted the Greeks with new methods of war. But they met their match in the Greek phalanx. After they had endured the rain of arrows at Plataea (479), Pausanias timed the charge of the Spartan hoplites perfectly, to hit the enemy while they were massed together.

Guards of Darius I, under whom the Persian threat to Greece reached its climax

I know Greece well and reconnoitred it thoroughly during my years of service in NATO. My comment on the Greek military organization of those days must begin with the observation that in a land three-quarters of which is mountainous, and maybe more, the Greeks based their tactical conceptions on formations which could be effective only on level ground. Battles became slogging matches; there was no manoeuvre, no fire and movement, no opportunity for skilful generalship. Indeed, the most a general could do was to draw up his line of battle, put his best soldiers in the right place, encourage them to fight well, and then fight with them himself just as another hoplite. There was no command structure, no intermediate officer hierarchy.

The point to note here is that the Greeks had no urge to develop further their organization for warfare. All except the Spartans resented discipline and disliked fighting. They could fight well enough when they had to, but they were interested in better things. Their philosophy in this matter was that 'the bravest spirits are those who, having the clearest sense both of the pains and of the pleasures of life, do not on that account shrink from danger'. When Pericles heard of the young men of Athens who were killed in Samos he felt 'it was as if the spring had been taken from the year'.

The Persian approach to warfare was different; so was their organization. In their army infantry was not the most important arm. Persian society was organized around the aristocracy of great landowners, with their retainers, and this group provided the formidable cavalry so feared by the Greeks. Serfs and hill tribesmen formed the bulk of the infantry, which could not compete with the highly disciplined, middle-class infantry of Greece. For instance, at Marathon in 490 B.C. the Athenian phalanx had no difficulty in dealing with the Persian infantry, and the Persian cavalry had little scope for manoeuvre and attack since the battle took place in a confined beach head. Again, at Thermopylae in 480 the Persian infantry refused to close with the hoplites; the Spartans were eventually worn down by archery fire from the front and rear. It will be noted that Greek victories against the Persians were based on an initial defensive, fought on ground of their own choosing where the Persian cavalry would be unable to develop its full potential – tactics which, in the circumstances, were very sound.

In the heroic age of Greece there had been no naval warfare; ships were used only as transports. But by the seventh century B.C. there were proper warships, with bows specially strengthened for ramming, and decks to carry marines who would bombard or board the enemy ship. From about 650 the emphasis in naval tactics was on ramming, and ships became longer, faster and lower in the water. The standard warship was the 'penteconter', rowed by twenty-five men on each side. Then, between 550 and 500, rivalry with the Phoenician fleet of the Persians caused the Greeks to develop a far more powerful ship. This was the trireme, which for two hundred years was to rule the waves in the eastern Mediterranean, and became the prototype of the galley which dominated naval warfare until the battle of Lepanto in A.D. 1571. A trireme might be rowed by as many as 170 men, each pulling one oar; the oars were probably arranged in three superimposed tiers, with outriggers to support them and even-out the leverage; fast and manoeuvrable, the trireme offered great scope to skilled navigators. The first battle involving fleets of triremes was fought at Lade in 494 when the Persians with greatly superior forces crushed the Ionian revolt.

By the 490's it was obvious that Persia was going to invade Greece by land and sea. In 493 Miltiades, an Athenian general, began to fortify the Piraeus as a naval base for Athens. The Persian landing at Marathon (about twenty miles to the north-east of Athens) in 490 was part of an amphibious strategy designed to lure the army away from Athens, so that it could be taken by a fifth column inside the city and by another Persian landing at Phalerum. The Athenian hoplites had to march south at all speed from Marathon immediately after the battle, and only just prevented the landing at Phalerum. Themistocles, the leading Athenian statesman of the 480's, realized that there would be a second invasion, and that if Athens did not become the greatest naval power in the Aegean she and all Greece would be doomed. During the respite given to the Greeks by a revolt of Egypt against Persia and by the death of King Darius I in 486, he persuaded the Assembly to build 100 triremes. In 484 Xerxes, the successor of Darius, began large-scale preparations to invade Greece by land, supported by a fleet. Harpalus, a Greek engineer employed by the Persians, bridged the Hellespont between Abydus and Sestus. He constructed wooden roadways over two bridges of boats, each of over 300 triremes and penteconters linked by six cables. Then in the spring of 480 the Persian forces under Xerxes, some 160,000 troops and, according to Herodotus, 1,207 warships and 3,000 transports, advanced into northern Greece.

At a pan-Hellenic congress under the presidency of Sparta the Greeks concerted their plan of defence. To minimise the effect of Persian numerical superiority it was decided to meet them in the narrow pass of Thermopylae, some eighty miles to the north of Athens, and in the Euboean Channel to the east. Thermopylae was to be a holding operation to induce Xerxes to try to outflank the Greeks in a sea battle, on which everything was staked. A fleet of 324 triremes and 9 penteconters, under the command of the Spartan Eurybiades, was sent to the north of the Euboean Channel. Its main force was the Athenian contingent under Themistocles. The Persians aimed to force the Thermopylae Pass and bottle up the Greek fleet in the Euboean Channel. But as the Persian fleet was sailing down the east coast of Magnesia it was caught in a gale and severely damaged. Themistocles then persuaded the reluctant Greek admiral to attack immediately while the enemy fleet was in disorder. Two days of hard but indecisive fighting followed off Cape Artemisium. The Persians came off rather the better, and the Greeks were considering a retreat at the end of the second day. Then news reached them that Thermopylae had fallen. Leonidas, the Spartan king, and 7,000 hoplites (of whom only 300 were Spartans) had held out for three days against the whole Persian army. But in the end a traitor revealed to the Persians how the pass could be turned. The Spartans died to a man, and the Persian army having won the pass moved southwards towards Athens. During the night the Greek fleet sailed south down the channel and round Attica.

In 1933 I visited Thermopylae and saw the Memorial commemorating the Spartans who died defending the pass – the English version reading:

> Go, tell the Spartans, thou that passest by,
> That here, obedient to their laws, we lie.

The Spartan law is recorded earlier in this chapter – 'conquer or die'.

Now, only the fleet could save Greece. The problem was to induce the Persian fleet to give battle in water that suited the Greeks. Themistocles decided that the place to fight was off the island of Salamis, which lies in the mouth of the bay of Eleusis. The bay can be approached from two directions, from the west between Megara and Salamis, and from the east between the Piraeus and the promontory of Cynosura on Salamis. The eastern approach to the bay is divided by the island of Psyttaleia into two very narrow channels, neither more than three-quarters of a mile wide. In these narrow waters the large Persian fleet would be cramped, and with their superior seamanship the Greeks should have a good fighting chance. The Persians, however, did not now need a sea battle. Would they choose to ignore the Greek fleet? The morale of the Greeks was low since Xerxes had now ravaged Attica and slaughtered the defenders of the Athenian Acropolis. Eurybiades was in a state of indecision. But Themistocles adopted a very bold, probably risky, scheme to induce the Persians to attempt to capture the Greek fleet. He left the channel between Salamis and Megara unguarded, and on 22nd September 480 sent a message to Xerxes telling him that 'fear has seized the Greeks and they are meditating a hasty flight'.

Xerxes fell into the trap. That night his fleet blocked the two straits of Salamis, and Persian troops landed on Psyttaleia. By dawn the bulk of the Persian fleet was deployed in a triple line from Cynosura across to the Piraeus. The Greeks rapidly deployed their fleet of 366 triremes and 7 penteconters. The Corinthian squadron was sent to oppose the Egyptian ships in the western channel, and the rest were drawn in a line from the town of Salamis across to the Heracleion on the mainland. Eurybiades was on the right

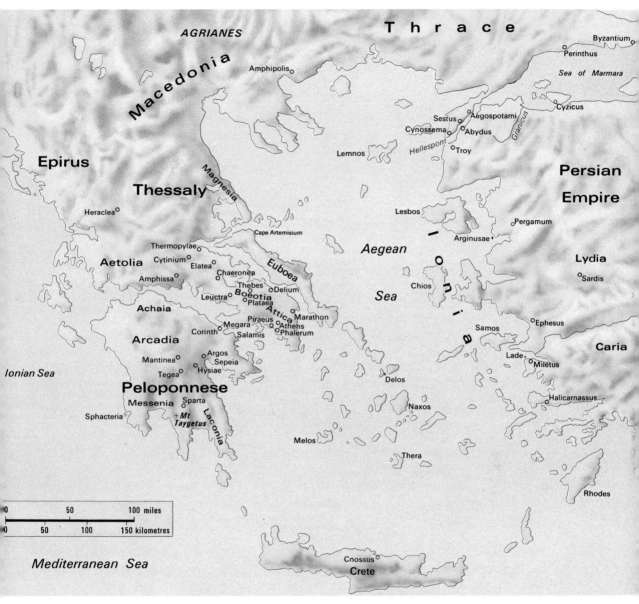

The ancient Greek world

with his sixteen Spartan ships; Themistocles with more than half the Greek triremes was on the left; the remainder were in the centre. The two fleets were as yet out of sight of each other.

The Persians opened the battle. Because the channel was narrow their three lines had to break up into two columns, the Phoenicians on the right and the Ionians on the left. Almost immediately they fell into disorder, either because they were too congested

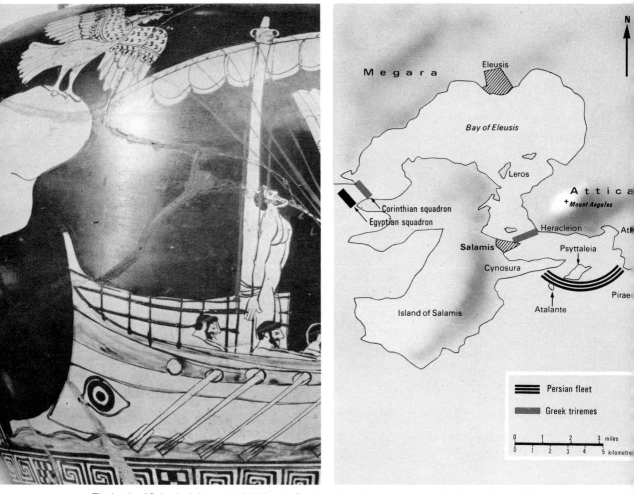

The battle of Salamis *right* was decided by the Greek tactics of ramming the enemy ships with specially strengthened bows *left*

or the sea was rough. The Greek ships charged at them, and a *mêlée* began. The tactic of the Greek triremes was to shear away the oars of the enemy ships, rendering them uncontrollable, and then ram them amidships, and sometimes board them. The decisive action was fought by the Athenians and Aeginetans on the left. Rowing close inshore, they turned the Persian right, and drove it in towards the centre. The Persians became more and more jammed up and confused. In the centre at first the fighting was evenly matched, and on the right the Greeks looked to be in trouble. But after seven or eight hours of hard fighting the wave of Greek victory spread across the battle area and the Athenians threatened to take the Persian left in the rear. The Ionians thereupon gave up and withdrew. Psyttaleia was cleared, and the Persians retired to Phalerum. Casualty figures are uncertain, but in any case the Greeks were not in a position to pursue and their fleet put in to Salamis.

Tactically the battle of Salamis was unremarkable, but its strategic importance was enormous. Without a fleet to provide transport and secure his communications, Xerxes dared leave only a small army in Greece, and this the Greeks were able to defeat at Plataea in 479. Greece was not again invaded from Asia until the fifteenth century A.D.

In the fifth century B.C. Athens was a great naval power. In 478 the Delian League was formed by the Aegean and Ionian Greeks, to drive the Persians right out of the Aegean. The League was so called because its treasury was established on the sacred island of Delos, members of the League being required to contribute either ships or money. Athens gradually emerged as leader. In 467 Cimon, the Athenian general and son of Miltiades, heavily defeated the Persians at the river Eurymedon in Pamphylia. When, ten years later, a fleet was sent to aid a revolt in Egypt, the expedition was a disaster; but by this time the fortifications of the Piraeus were complete and in 454 the treasury of the Delian League was transferred to Athens. As a result the League became an Athenian empire, with over a hundred and fifty states paying tribute, from which Athens built up a great fleet.

From now on, however, in the words of Thucydides, 'the growth of the power of Athens, and the alarm which this inspired in Sparta, made war inevitable'. In 431 the Peloponnesian War broke out. Almost every state in Greece was to be involved in it at some time during the next twenty-seven years. The first decade saw a deadlock between the power of Athens at sea under Pericles and Phormio, and the supremacy of Sparta and her allies, commanded by Brasidas and Pagondas, on land. From 421 to 418 the war languished. Then the Spartans won the biggest land battle of the war at Mantinea, and Athens replied in 415 with an invasion of Sicily, to cut off the enemy's food and trade. But the indifferent Greek command of Nikias allowed the Syracusans, led by Gylippus, the Spartan C-in-C in Sicily, to blockade and finally destroy the Athenian fleet in the Great Harbour at Syracuse, and then to annihilate the army. Sparta, subsidized by Persia, now built a hundred warships and moved the theatre of war into the eastern Aegean, to cut the Athenian supply routes. Athens still managed to win the naval battles of Cynossema, Cyzicus and Arginusae between 412 and 406. But then in 405 the Spartan admiral Lysander surprised the Athenian fleet at Aegospotami, when 170 ships were beached, and captured it almost without a blow. Defenceless at sea, and therefore hamstrung everywhere, in 404 Athens was captured and subjected to humiliating peace terms.

The fall of Athens, with the division of political and cultural leadership, ended the greatest period of Greek civilization. The most interesting feature of the Peloponnesian War is its history written by Thucydides. He was the first real historian. The Assyrian and Egyptian annals are no more than incomplete and biased diaries of events. Herodotus is a *raconteur*. But Thucydides sets out to describe and explain events objectively, clearly and profoundly. His analysis of the Athenian ideal, in the 'funeral speech' attributed to Pericles, and his description of the Athenian disaster in Sicily, are historical and literary masterpieces.

The period of the Peloponnesian War (431–04) marked the zenith of the Athenian navy. Yet it can be said that Pericles laid too much emphasis on a purely naval strategy. He failed to realise that Athens could not win the war without a proper army, with sea and land power nicely balanced, and this negligence led to the final defeat of Athens.

The Peloponnesian War could not be decided by the conventional phalanx duel, and in its duration and scale of operations it was greater than any previous war in Greece. During this period, and in the first half of the fourth century while the struggle between Sparta, Thebes and Athens was going on for supremacy in Greece, land warfare developed beyond the old Spartan methods. Thebes, one of the earliest Greek fortified cities, lay some fifty miles to the north of Athens. Its military security tended to give it a leading position, and this enabled it to establish a supremacy over neighbouring towns and, in due course, to become a military power.

There were several sieges during the Peloponnesian War. Plataea successfully defended her walls with hides against the flaming missiles of the Athenians. The Syracusans destroyed the Athenian battering-rams with an incendiary mixture made of pitch, sulphur, tow and pounded gum of frankincense and pine sawdust. Delium, in 424, was the first Greek town to be taken by assault; its hastily built palisades were burnt by fire propelled through a gigantic blowpipe. The first Greek master of siegecraft was Dionysius I of Syracuse (405–367). In his defence against the Carthaginians he made the island of Ortygia impregnable, and built a magnificent fortress on the heights of Epipolae. In 398 he took the island city of Motya by advancing siege-towers containing battering-rams and catapults along a mole; after an initial bombardment his men scaled the walls by night. The introduction of siege-towers and torsion catapults (invented by the Phoenicians) was revolutionary. There were two types of catapult. The small *katapeltes* could project arrows, javelins, and an eight pound stone accurately up to 250 yards; the bigger *petrobolos* and *onager* could hurl stones of about 55 pounds weight. In each case the motive power came from twisted skeins of sinew or women's hair. Towns were still, however, more often taken by the old methods of starvation, fifth column and treachery.

During this period arms began to be diversified, and more value became attached to cavalry and lightly armed troops. In 415 Nikias took only thirty horses to Sicily; but he soon found that he had to protect his foragers, and so he raised 400 cavalry locally and sent home for more. Agesilaus of Sparta raised a force of cavalry which in 394 defeated the Thessalians. The best cavalry commander of this period was the Theban, Pelopidas. The old limitations on the use of cavalry still existed. Fodder and water were scarce during the summer campaigning months, and the Greeks had no horseshoes or stirrups – horseshoes were invented by the Celts in the fourth century B.C., and the stirrup appeared in central Asia at about the same time. The Greek horses were not strong enough to support armour; hence they were vulnerable to spears, particularly at the moment when cavalry wheeled away after a charge. But the obvious value of cavalry in the broken countryside of Greece was increasingly recognized.

It was realized, similarly, that lightly armed troops were far more suited to Greek terrain than hoplites; but in the past they had been despised as barbarian. The Athenians learnt a sharp lesson in 426 when 120 hoplites under Demosthenes were annihilated by Aetolian javelin-men who refused to close with them. Demosthenes immediately raised a force of light troops and in 425, to the astonishment of Greece, he used them to capture the Spartans on Sphacteria. Light foot soldiers were cheap, and their development was furthered by the growth of the mercenary system. Many Greeks who had fought in the Peloponnesian War had no other skill when it ended in 404, so they became professional soldiers. There had been Greek mercenaries before; some of them had

Cavalry began to play a greater part in Greek warfare in the fifth century

carved their names on the column at Abu Simbel, and others had been bodyguards to
Persian satraps. But now their numbers increased. In 401 Cyrus hired 10,000 Greeks to
fight for him in revolt against his brother Artaxerxes, king of Persia. At the battle of
Cunaxa, near Babylon, they were irresistible, although Cyrus deployed them so badly
that he lost. The Ten Thousand then had to extricate themselves. Xenophon, one of
their generals, wrote a description of the 'Anabasis', their five-month retreat to the
Black Sea, and how they learnt much about light-armed warfare, particularly archery,
from the mountain tribes through which they fought their way. Between 399 and 375,
25,000 Greeks took service as mercenaries abroad, and many of them brought back the
techniques they learned, such as those of the Rhodian slingers and the Cretan archers.
In Athens, shortly after 400, Iphicrates raised a body of mercenary javelin-men,
modelled on the Thracians and called 'peltasts'. They wore leather jerkins, carried a
sword and a small shield, and were trained to rapid manoeuvre. In all but big set battles
they were the most effective infantry of the time; for example, in 390 near Corinth, they
annihilated 600 Spartan hoplites.

As these new arms became organized, so tactics began to alter. Brasidas, the victor
of Amphipolis in 422, was the last of the great Spartan hoplite generals in the old
tradition. In 424 the Theban general Pagondas used novel tactics to defeat the Athenian
army at Delium, deepening the right flank of his phalanx and using cavalry as a mobile
reserve. At long last there was some forward military thinking in Greece. In *Laches*
Plato portrayed the man skilled in war; Thucydides analysed the war going on around
him; and Xenophon observed that 'wise generalship consists in attacking where the
enemy is weakest'. It was a maxim of Iphicrates that 'the light-armed troops are like the
hands, the cavalry like feet, the line of men-at-arms itself like chest and breast-plate,
and the general like the head'. The army of Dionysius I of Syracuse consisted of integrated bodies of hoplites, light infantry and cavalry – a great advance in organization.

Phalanx warfare was revolutionized at the battle of Leuctra in 371 by Epaminondas,
the Theban general. His tactics were simple, though requiring skill to execute. They consisted essentially of concentrating his strength at the crucial point of the battle, instead
of applying it, as in the past, in such a way that he was weak everywhere and strong
nowhere – like butter is spread on bread. Facing a Spartan army, he knew that the
enemy would concentrate strength on their right, and aim to turn his left. Epaminondas
therefore confronted the Spartan phalanx with an oblique line. He held back his right,
and placed his striking force on his left in a column fifty ranks deep, guarded by a force
of cavalry. He thus met the Spartan shock with counter shock, won the battle on the left,
and had enough reserve force not to lose it in the centre and on his right. As Adcock
observes, Leuctra, like Rocroi in A.D. 1643, destroyed a legend of invincibility. The
way in which Epaminondas followed up his victory the following year also showed new
strategical vision. He marched from Thebes to Laconia, freed Messenia (the basis of
Sparta's economic strength), and unified Arcadia – thus balancing what was left of the
power of Sparta in the south.

The death of Epaminondas in 362 B.C. removed the strongest force from Greek politics.
In 359 Philip II became king in Macedonia. Ambitious and always ready to seize opportunities, but also clear-sighted and a first class organizer, he reckoned that the city-
states of Greece, having been perpetually at each other's throats for seventy years,

would not unite to expel an intruder backed by a powerful army. 'Fraud before force, but force at the last' was Philip's political method. In the 350's he conquered Illyria (modern Yugoslavia), Thrace and Thessaly, and began to play off the Greek states against each other. In 338 he won a battle against Thebes and Athens at Chaeronea, in Boeotia, which finally brought him the mastery of Greece. After his victory, Philip called the Greek states to a congress at Corinth, and proposed to them that they should unite under his leadership, for two purposes: the prevention of further strife within Greece, and the invasion of the Persian empire as revenge for the desecration of Greece by Persia in the fifth century. Such an idea had for some time been in the air, and Sparta alone refused to fall in with Philip's plan. But before he could carry it out he was assassinated, in 336, and the project was left to his successor – Alexander.

An idea was not all that Alexander inherited from his father. Philip's army, and his military conceptions, were the basis for Alexander's future achievement. Philip's strategy against Athens was a trial run in the Macedonian art of war, which Alexander was to develop. Considerable geographical vision, mobility, and the coordination of arms were its principal features. Philip was anxious to control both the north-east and the south; to this end he decided to kill two birds with one stone and deal with Athens by cutting off her supplies from the Dardanelles. He failed in this plan because the Persians took alarm and helped the Greeks to break the sieges of Perinthus and Byzantium. But the indirect strategy worked in reverse. His defeat of the Athenians at Chaeronea gave him control of their policy, and thus of the Hellespont and of the path into Asia Minor.

The campaign before Chaeronea was a model of mobility. Long forced marches had been very rare in Greek warfare. Philip's path into Boeotia was barred both at the western route from Cytinium to Amphissa, and farther east from Elatea to Chaeronea. Concealing his intentions, he first placed himself at Elatea, and put the defenders of the western route off their guard. Then he marched rapidly by night to Amphissa, delivered a crushing attack on the 10,000 mercenaries there, and thus eliminated the extreme left of the extended defensive line which for a long time had thwarted him. He could now bring about the pitched battle with the Thebans and Athenians which he desired. But he did not at once advance due eastwards against the main enemy force, using a route which would have been more direct but which, by its terrain, favoured defence. Instead, he switched his army back to Elatea, and then descended rapidly through the pass of Parapotamii to come upon the enemy at Chaeronea.

There his conduct of the battle showed for the first time that a Greek army had learnt how to co-ordinate all arms successfully on the battlefield. The enemy presented a solid line, with the flanks protected by high ground and a river. Philip created a gap in their line by causing his highly trained phalanx on the right to conduct the difficult manoeuvre of a fighting withdrawal. The enemy left was then drawn into an advance, while their right clung to the protection it had on that flank. The moment a gap thus appeared, Philip launched the decisive charge of the cavalry from his left, led by his 18-year-old son, Alexander. At the same instant, with great speed and force, the phalanx went over to the attack.

The Macedonian army which Alexander commanded after the death of his father, Philip, was the most superbly organized, equipped and trained that Greece ever produced. Philip had welded the old local levies of Macedonia together with his own royal

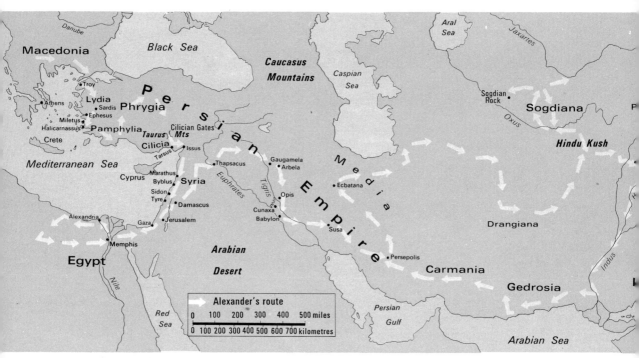

The route of Alexander's conquests *above*. Persian chariots were defeated by Greek cavalry at Issus *below*

retainers into an integrated force of all arms, in which the function of the 'Territorial Army' was to provide a tactical base for decisive action by the 'Royal Army'. The latter consisted of two *corps d'élite*, the Companion Cavalry and the 'hypaspists'. The Macedonian horsemen had always been good, and their role in battle was now to deliver the decisive shock, on the flanks or in a gap, when the enemy had been checked by the phalanx. There were eight squadrons or *ilai* of the Companions, each of two to three hundred horsemen under an officer. They were armed with a cuirass, and a short thrusting spear or *xyston*. The hypaspists were foot soldiers, probably armed in the same way as the hoplites, but distinguished as a professional *élite*. Their primary function was to form the tactical junction in battle between the cavalry and the remainder of the phalanx; but at different times they were also used for following up the cavalry, for rapid night marches, and for storming fortifications. They were divided into three battalions, each of 1,000 men. One squadron each of the hypaspists and the Companions formed the king's guard. Alexander himself usually led the Companions, but occasionally he led the hypaspists and the phalanx, and once even the archers.

The Territorial Army consisted of the main body of infantry, the phalanx. It was formed of six, later seven, battalions, each of 1,536 men, subdivided into units of 512 and ranged in files of 16 men. Each battalion had its commander, and Philip introduced the first officer hierarchies into Greek armies. He also armed his hoplites in a new way, making the shield smaller, and replacing the 8-foot spear with a 13-foot pike, called *sarissa*. The phalanx fulfilled the subordinate but vital function of holding the enemy while the cavalry dealt the decisive blow. Because they had this firm support, Alexander's Companions could beat the Persian cavalry, who were little inferior to them. Philip and Alexander also raised contingents from their subject and allied peoples, the most important of which were the Thessalian heavy cavalry, the Thracian lancers, the Cretan archers and the Agrianian javelin-men. Alexander was the first general to integrate fully his light troops with other arms; they proved devastating against the Persian chariots, and in mountain campaigns against tribesmen. He also relied increasingly on mercenaries to guard his communications, and in the last years of his wars raised a force of horsemen from the nomads of eastern Iran.

Alexander's siege equipment was probably modelled on that of Dionysius I; it consisted of towers, rams, pent-houses and catapults, and it never failed him. He was the first general to use field artillery, which was organized in sections and carried on pack animals in all his campaigns. Unfortunately little is known about his system of supply. He had a personal staff of thirteen, and an informal council of about eight. With the army travelled sappers, water and mining engineers, naval experts, architects such as Deinocrates who designed Alexandria in Egypt, surveyors and geographers, botanists, physicians, a secretarial department and an official historian.

The net result was the best balanced and most powerful army of ancient times – an army equipped to fight in any type of country and against any enemy. The essence of the Macedonian technique of warfare under Alexander was the combination of the rock-like phalanx with light and heavy cavalry. The union of a dependable infantry base with the mobile shock supplied by cavalry was too much for the Persian masses, whose chief advantage lay in numbers. But numbers alone were of no avail against steadiness, missile fire, shock action and first class generalship.

Alexander spent the years 336 and 335 securing his home base. The barbarians were pushed back beyond the Danube, after his troops had crossed the river at night on rafts made of tent covers stuffed with straw. He then astonished the Greeks by marching from the Illyrian border to Thebes in fourteen days, and the Delphic oracle hailed him as invincible. In the spring of 334 he invaded Asia Minor with 30,000 infantry, 5,000 cavalry, 160 ships, and almost no money. Among his senior officers were four future kings, Ptolemy, Lysimachus, Seleucus and Antigonus. Within nine years he was to conquer the Persian empire from the Dardanelles to the Punjab. The feebleness of Darius III and the chaotic condition of his empire favoured an invader, yet the numbers and wealth of the Persians were prodigious. The ingredients of Alexander's success were his bold and imaginative leadership, the courage and technical quality of the army, the systematic development of his strategy over two million square miles, four great battles and a famous siege.

Darius was not expecting an invasion, and Alexander was met by only a scratch force raised by the Persian officials, and some Greek mercenaries. He defeated them overwhelmingly in a battle at the river Granicus, and thereby gained control of western Asia Minor. This, the first of his great victories, was fought along his usual lines, with himself leading the decisive charge of the Companions on the right. After this he proceeded round Asia Minor, by way of Sardis, the coastal cities of Ephesus, Miletus and Halicarnassus, then through Phrygia in winter when the tribes were forced into the accessible valleys by snow, and finally down with great speed to take the defenders of the Cilician Gates unawares. His purpose was to secure his communications before striking farther east, and to eliminate the strong Persian fleet by depriving it of its bases. He won over most of the country by the mildness of his conquests. Furthermore, by supporting democratic movements in the cities, he induced many crews in the Persian navy to desert. In the winter of 334–3 he sent a large number of married soldiers home to Greece on leave – characteristic of the human touch which won the devotion of his soldiers.

Alexander's rapid advance ahead of his main troops through Cilicia to Tarsus was for once miscalculated. Darius, who was looking for battle, marched round him and severed his communications. But in November 333 at Issus (Turkey, near Adana), thanks partly to the Persian failure to follow up their advantage, Alexander won another great victory. The treasury at Damascus fell into his hands and his financial worries were over. At this point he did not immediately pursue Darius, but concentrated on destroying the other bases of the enemy's fleet in Phoenicia. Marathon, Byblos and Sidon quickly submitted. But Tyre proved difficult.

Alexander's siege of Tyre is the classic example of his determination and skill, and was one of his most brilliant feats of arms. It was the greatest siege of antiquity; Demetrius' operations against Rhodes in 305 were on a more massive scale, but less skilful. Tyre had held out against a siege by Nebuchadnezzar for thirteen years. But, as Alexander told his generals, it had to be taken, for then the Phoenician fleet would be without any base, and would have to come over to the Greeks or wither away into nothing. Cyprus and the Aegean would thus be completely secured and the way into Egypt opened. However, to capture the city posed formidable problems. Built on a rock half a mile off from the shore, it was surrounded by a wall two and three quarter miles long and at points 150 feet high. There were two harbours on the eastern side: the northern called the Sidonian harbour and the southern called the Egyptian.

The siege was opened in January 332. Alexander, and Diades, his chief engineer,

Single combat in Ancient Greece. An Attic black-figured neck amphora, c. 550 B.C.

started by building a mole out from the shore towards the rock, and progress at first was easy. But farther out the water was deep, and the workers began to be in trouble from gales as well as from missiles fired from the walls and from Tyrian warships. With some difficulty Alexander's men got two siege-towers out to the end of the mole. They were 150 feet high, and were covered with hides to protect them against blazing arrows. Catapults on the different storeys bombarded the defenders on the walls and the enemy galleys. The Tyrians dealt with this assault by sending against the mole two fire-ships filled with pitch, sulphur and shavings. When the towers had been burnt down, they sallied out in small boats and dismantled what was left of the mole. It was now clear to Alexander that he had to deal with tough opponents, so he ordered that a bigger mole should be built, and himself sailed northwards to Sidon to gather a fleet.

The cities of Phoenicia had always been deadly rivals, and it did not take long to raise a fleet of 220 ships to fight the Tyrians. But when Alexander returned, King Azemilk of Tyre refused to give battle. Alexander therefore blockaded both the harbours – although without a proper anchorage this was difficult. By this time the new mole had been constructed, and another battery of siege-towers with rams and catapults was set up. Since only about 200 yards of the city wall could be bombarded from the mole, Alexander also mounted some battering-rams on ships, which could sail all round the rock. But once again the Tyrians were ready. By dropping rocks into the sea they made it impossible to approach the island closely, and their volleys of fire-arrows harried the assailants. When Alexander brought up ships to sweep the underwater obstacles, and warships to protect the sweeps, Tyrian divers cut their cables. So he moored them with chains – to which the defenders had no reply. Next, thirteen Tyrian warships sailed out from the Sidonian harbour and surprised Alexander's fleet while the crews were having a meal on shore. Several of his ships were destroyed. But Alexander reacted quickly; he ordered a blockade of the Egyptian harbour, himself rowed round Tyre with a few ships, took the enemy in rear and beat them back.

By now the battering-ships had found a weak point in the wall, just south of the Egyptian harbour. A general assault was vigorously pressed, from the mole by the Cypriot and Phoenician fleets blockading the harbours, and by a squadron of galleys circling round the island. When a good breach had been made Alexander brought up two transports, carrying bridges and storming parties. He himself and Admetus led the royal guard of the hypaspists, and Coenus followed with a battalion of the phalanx. The assault pressed through successfully to Azemilk's palace, and the city was occupied. Tyre thus fell after a siege of seven months. The Greeks, bitterly angered by the way the defenders had ostentatiously murdered their captives, retaliated by killing 8,000 Tyrians and selling 30,000 more into slavery.

After the battle at Issus in 333 Darius had offered peace and an alliance; but Alexander had scorned the suggestion, telling his enemy that he must 'send to me as lord of Asia'. During the siege of Tyre, Darius offered better terms: 10,000 talents, the hand of his daughter, and overall rule west of the Euphrates. Parmenion, his second-in-command, urged Alexander to accept, for the Greeks imagined that with the conquest of Asia Minor the object of the war had been gained. But Alexander's vision was now wider. First he marched through Syria and Egypt. These submitted easily enough, although Alexander was severely wounded at Gaza. Then he turned towards Persia, to challenge Darius for his throne.

An Asiatic nomad archer, *c.* 500 B.C.

In the summer of 331 he sent Parmenion ahead to bridge the Euphrates at Thapsacus. Alexander was the first commander to apply the principle of 'march divided, fight united'. He himself crossed the river in July, and pushed forward north-eastwards to the Tigris, the Persian advance guard falling back before him. His army crossed the river on 19th September, and four days later scouts told him that the enemy army was encamped on the plain near Gaugamela. The best policy for the Persians would have been to harry and exhaust the invading army rather than to give battle. However, Darius had decided that he would fight. Alexander was delighted, telling his men that this battle would decide the fate of Asia.

In the twenty months since Issus the Persians had made an effort to build up a respectable army. But they had long before abandoned the methods of warfare by which the empire had been won in the sixth century. The famous archers and the 10,000 'Immortals', who had been the *élite* of their heavy infantry, no longer existed. Apart from the small royal guard, their infantry now comprised only untrained levies and undisciplined tribesmen. The best part of the Persian army was the cavalry, notably the royal horse guards and the Cappadocians; these were now equipped with link armour, a thrusting spear instead of a javelin, and a longer sword. To supplement his cavalry, Darius had brought back into service the long disused scythed chariots, but there had not been time to train the drivers properly. The trouble with the Persian army was, to quote Fuller, that it had 'plenty of mobility, but little stability'. Besides that, it was saddled with Darius as commander-in-chief. It included twenty-four nationalities, and decidedly outnumbered its opponents.

The Persian strategy was dictated by the composition of their army. The plain of Gaugamela was carefully levelled to make the terrain as suitable as possible for chariots. Darius took advantage of his numerical superiority and presented a long front with two powerful cavalry wings. He himself commanded in the centre, behind the 1,000 horse guards and the Indian and Carian cavalry. With him waited the only trained foot soldiers in the army, the guard of spearmen, and 2,000 Greek mercenary hoplites. On the left, under Bessus, were the cavalry detachments from the eastern provinces of the empire, including 1,000 heavily armoured cavalry from the Jaxartes known as the Saca 'cataphracts'. On the right, commanded by Mazaeus, were the western cavalry, including the Cappadocians. The infantry units were in rear of the cavalry. In the front were drawn up about two hundred chariots. In the centre of the Persian position were fifteen elephants. Horses dislike facing up to elephants, and if Darius had known what to do with his elephants they could have been very effective against Alexander's cavalry; but there is no record of their use in the battle.

Alexander had the largest army he ever commanded. He had recruited a number of Greek mercenaries and been reinforced by three cavalry units, bringing the whole total up to 40,000 foot and 7,000 horse. It was certain that he would be outflanked and that the front line of Persian chariots and cavalry would attack all out, early in the battle. He therefore assumed a defensive order of approach, his front consisting of a rock-like phalanx only about half the length of the enemy's line, supported by deep columns on the flanks. In the centre he put the six battalions of the phalanx and the hypaspists. On the left of the centre Parmenion commanded the Thessalian cavalry, half the allied horse, and some archers and mercenary infantry. On the right was the main strength, the Companion cavalry under Philotas, some other cavalry, and in front of them javelin-

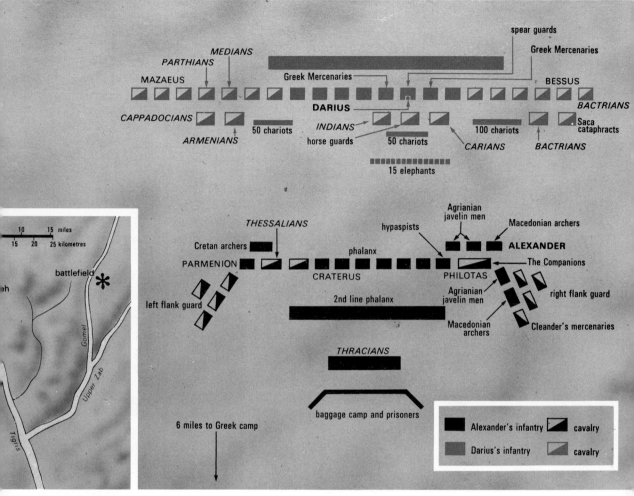

The battle of Gaugamela

men and half the Macedonian archers. The left wing column was made up of more allied cavalry. The far right consisted of cavalry, including Cleander's veteran mercenaries, and the remaining archers and Agrianian javelin-men. A second line of mercenary hoplites would resist enveloping tactics by the Persian wings. Behind them were the baggage and prisoners guarded by the Thracian foot, and, about six miles to the rear, the Greek camp.

Alexander's dispositions were perfectly planned to accord with Napoleon's battle principle of 'a well reasoned and extremely circumspect defensive followed by rapid and audacious attack'. It was a question of whether the instability of the Persians or the weakness of the Greek left would count first. The night before the battle Darius stood his men to arms all night – a foolish and unnecessary tactic, since it merely tired them before the battle began.

Alexander *right* forged 'the Companions' cavalry and the hypaspists infantry *left* into an irresistible army

Alexander, having made his dispositions in the early evening, slept well into the morning of 1st October 331. When he led his army out, he saw that the Companions were opposite the scythed chariots, so he inclined his advance to the right to bring the infantry opposite the chariots. This move brought the Companions almost to the edge of the levelled ground. Darius saw that he must stop the enemy moving to their right, or his chariots would be no use. So he launched the Saca cataphracts, followed by the Bactrian cavalry, against Alexander's extreme right. A hard fight took place, during which Alexander skilfully fed in new units one by one to produce the best results with fresh troops. But the Persians were only checked after some time by the Companions, and were then driven back by the lancers.

Meanwhile the charge of the Persian chariots had been launched. It proved a complete failure. Volleys of javelins threw the chariots into confusion, the horses panicked, and many of the drivers were killed; when what was left of them reached the phalanx, the hypaspists opened their ranks and let them run through – to be dealt with by the second line of infantry.

When Darius saw that Alexander had engaged his last mobile reserve on the Greek right, he thought that Bessus must be doing better than was in fact the case. Consequently he decided that the moment had come to launch the two decisive enveloping attacks. The whole Persian line of cavalry moved forward. Now came the crucial point of the battle. Instead of the Persian left concentrating their attack against the Companions, they headed towards the far right of the Greek army. This mistake may have been due to orders being misunderstood, or, as Fuller suggested, to the tendency of cavalry to follow the path of a previous charge – as happened to some of the French at Waterloo. It may also have been that the horses could not face the missiles in the centre. Anyway, the result was that a gap appeared in the Persian front.

Arrian describes how Alexander instantly seized the opportunity:

> When the Persians had made a break in the front line of their army, in consequence of the cavalry sallying forth to assist those who were surrounding the [Greek] right wing, Alexander wheeled round towards the gap, and forming a wedge as it were of the Companion cavalry and of part of the phalanx which was posted here [four battalions and the hypaspists], he led them with a quick charge and a loud battle-cry straight towards Darius himself. For a short time there ensued a hand-to-hand fight; but when the Macedonian cavalry, commanded by Alexander himself, pressed on vigorously, thrusting themselves against the Persians and striking their faces with their spears, and when the Macedonian phalanx in dense array and bristling with long pikes had also made an attack upon them, all things together appeared full of terror to Darius . . . so that he was the first to turn and flee.

In fact Darius got well away, while most of his foot guards were killed.

However, the battle was not yet won, since the advance of four battalions of the phalanx in the wake of the Companions had left a gap in the Greek line, and the Persian cavalry of the guard had flung themselves into it – cutting the phalanx in two. Most of them foolishly threw away the chance of helping Mazaeus destroy the Greek left, by riding on and looting the transport lines in the rear. But Parmenion's troops on the Greek left were surrounded and very hard pressed. Parmenion sent a desperate call for help to Alexander, which reached him as he was following up his victorious charge with an attack on the Persian left. It is an indication of Alexander's extraordinary control that he succeeded in turning the Companions immediately, and led them across to the other side of the battle area. There they encountered some of the Persian guard returning with the Parthian and Indian cavalry, and, according to Arrian, 'the fiercest cavalry engagement of the whole action' then took place. But the Persian soldiery were now becoming aware that Darius had deserted them, and they lost heart. The Thessalians on the Greek left, who had been beaten back, made a second charge, this time successfully. The Persian right collapsed, while their left under Bessus made an orderly retreat.

Alexander ordered an immediate general pursuit. As Tarn says, 'he was determined that the enemy should never reform as an army'. His men chased the Persians for thirty-five miles as far as Arbela, pausing only to rest for a short time at midnight.

Gaugamela is one of the world's great battles, not only as the classic instance of

Alexander's military genius, but in its historical consequences. It uncovered the heart of the Persian empire and made Alexander master of Asia, with all that this was to imply.

Darius fled north-eastwards into the hills of Media. But again Alexander refused to be lured from his principal objective. Instead he marched on to take the great Persian centres of Babylon, Susa and Persepolis, all of which surrendered easily. On his way to Persepolis Alexander led a flying campaign against the hill tribes. He wintered at Persepolis, where he burnt the palace of Xerxes to signify that Greece was fully revenged on Persia. In the summer of 330 Alexander marched to Ecbatana in Media, in pursuit of Darius. His mission for the Greeks was now completed, and he paid off those of the Greek troops who wished to return home.

From Ecbatana, Alexander set out to conquer the East. In the early summer of 326 he reached the Indus, after four years of fighting. On the way, he and his army performed a number of remarkable military feats. In his pursuit of Darius towards the Caspian he covered 400 miles in eleven days, and then mounted 500 phalangists on horseback to ride another 50 miles at night. He defeated the nomads at the Oxus in 329 by bombarding them with catapults from boats, and then attacking with a force of heavy cavalry interspersed with javelin-men and archers. In the winter of 328 Alexander's men captured the stronghold of the Sogdian Rock, by climbing 300 feet in the snow with the aid of ropes. In 327 he crossed the Hindu Kush with 27,000 men and, after very hard fighting against the Bajaur tribesmen, reached the Hydaspes river in the following year. There he won the fourth of his great victories. He had first to cross the river while the enemy were massed on the other bank, and then fight against elephants which put his cavalry out of action. He crossed after a series of feints, and won a hard battle with his infantry.

But shortly after, at the river Beas, his army mutinied and would go no further. It was eight years since they had left Greece, and they had marched 17,000 miles. Now, exhausted by the rains, and dismayed at the prospect of fighting their way through the apparently innumerable warriors and elephants of India, their morale failed. Alexander led them back down the Indus, through Gedrosia and Carmania to Susa, which they reached in spring 324. That last phase of the war was the toughest of all. Alexander was wounded, and he died in June 323 at the early age of thirty-three, after a reign of twelve years and eight months.

It has never been disputed that Alexander belongs to the top flight of military captains. He is known to history as Alexander the Great, and versions of 'The Romance of Alexander' are found in the languages of practically all peoples from China to Iceland. Yet in another respect Alexander has been more generally underrated than most other great men. For his was a great civilizing imagination. Everywhere that he carried his wars he introduced new standards of humanity and tolerance. At Ephesus he installed the democrats, and refused to allow them to murder the oligarchs. In Caria he respected the matriarchal system, and appointed a female satrap. He was always careful not to violate the religion of his subjects; for example, at Babylon he rebuilt the temple of Marduk which had been destroyed by Xerxes. He is said to have founded seventy new cities in his empire. He was responsible for the hellenization of the Near East. But Alexander's greatness lies above all in his departure from the traditional idea, expressed by Aristotle, that civilized Greece must be apart from the barbarians of the rest of the world. He told the priest of Ammon in Egypt that God was 'father of all men'. This, as Sir William Tarn believes, was the first assertion in the western world of the principle of the brotherhood of mankind. All Alexander's subject peoples were respected and treated equally, and it was his intention to fuse them into one race. He and eighty of his officers married Persian women, and at a great feast at Opis in 324 some nine thousand guests of every people in his empire sat down together.

Alexander's dream of the brotherhood of man, *homonoia*, was not fulfilled because no stable political structure was ever established in the lands which he conquered. Once the personality and stature of Alexander had been removed, the empire disintegrated. But his vision was one of the great milestones in the development of civilization; it looked forward to the ideas of Stoicism, of the Roman empire, and of Christianity.

Alexander's death was followed by a massive and many-sided struggle between his successors to appropriate portions of the empire, and four kingdoms emerged after the battle of Ipsus in 301. The Hellenistic art of war did not develop beyond the high level attained by Alexander. His successors, particularly Lysimachus and Seleucus, were good generals, but their armies became too unwieldly and complex, and the battles produced no lessons. During Alexander's Indian campaign, elephants had made a strong impression on his generals. They were useful against cavalry because horses would not face them, and they could be effective against troops who had not seen them before – for instance in the battle of Heraclea in 280, when Pyrrhus, king of Epirus, defeated the Romans. But it must be said that on the whole elephants were not a success in battle. Pyrrhus was defeated by the Romans at Beneventum in 275 B.C. mainly because one elephant, maddened by its wounds, rushed into his own ranks and trampled a great many to death. Nor did the attempts of Pyrrhus to solve the problems of the growing inflexibility of the Greek phalanx work. The heavy casualties he suffered in his victorious battles, for example the 4,000 at the 'Pyrrhic victory' of Heraclea, have given him a notorious reputation. Nonetheless, the Albanians today claim Pyrrhus as a national hero.

The Roman soldier of the Republic

5 The Expansion of Rome

We now move forward to the age of Rome. As the story unfolds it will become clear that the Romans possessed the political and administrative capacity to consolidate, for the benefit of the republic and later of the empire, the conquests of their generals – a capacity which was lacking in ancient Greece. We shall see how social development and military organization influenced each other profoundly as Rome expanded from city-state to empire. In the wars waged by Rome against the successors of Alexander the Great it will be interesting to note that the Romans, who at first used the phalanx formation in battle, decided that advantages lay in a more open order – and the legion emerged.

Rome was founded, according to the legend, in 753 B.C. At that time she was just one among many modest city-states, but five hundred years later she dominated the Italian peninsula and seven hundred and fifty years later she ruled western Europe and the Mediterranean world. Rome emerged as supreme in Italy by a process that was natural yet almost accidental: the survival of the fittest. The constant demands of self-defence made her people increasingly militaristic and aggressive.

Over the centuries the Etruscans, the Volsci and the Samnites were conquered, and invasions of the Gauls beaten back. A humiliating defeat at the Caudine Forks in 321 was revenged by the victory won over the combined Gauls and Samnites at Sentinum in 295. This gave Rome the mastery of central Italy, and the defeat of Pyrrhus at Beneventum in 275 gave her control of the south.

Little is known about the Roman army before the fourth century B.C. In the sixth century an Etruscan king, Servius Tullius, is supposed to have built the first fortifications of Rome and organized the state on a military basis. The Romans became a nation in arms, with all male citizens between seventeen and forty-six liable for military service, and those between forty-six and sixty available as a reserve. The Assembly was summoned by a trumpet call, and met on the Field of Mars outside the walls. The citizens were divided into classes – knights, seniors and juniors – according to their liability for service and war-tax. The juniors furnished the main military striking force. The richer among them were armed with the full panoply of the hoplite – bronze helmet, shield, cuirass and greaves, spear and sword; the poorer, called *velites*, had no defensive armour, and were equipped only with slings and stones. The Assembly also contained professional armourers and trumpeters. The tactics of the Romans at this time were almost certainly the conventional hoplite tactics of the period, and the knights were merely mounted infantry.

A severe defeat at the hands of the Gauls at the Allia in 391 necessitated a new start.

In the following two generations, at the inspiration of Marcus Furius Camillus, Rome was refortified and her army reorganized. The army remained a citizen levy, paid when on active service, but the phalanx was replaced by the legion. The main troops of the legion were heavy infantry; it also contained *velites* and cavalry. The infantry was organized in three lines – the *hastati* in front, behind them the *principes*, and in the rear the *triarii*. Each of these lines was broken up into ten companies called 'maniples' (handfuls), the light infantry being interspersed among the maniples of the heavy infantry. The whole infantry force of the legion was drawn up in a chequered formation, the maniples of the second rank covering the intervals between those of the first, and the third those of the second. Each line was probably four files deep; the front two contained 1,200 men each, or 120 to a maniple, and the *triarii* 600. The cavalry was disposed on the wings, and numbered altogether 300 in ten squadrons. Later the numbers in the legion rose towards 6,000 and troops were increasingly recruited from the Italian allies.

The *hastati* and the *principes* were protected by a bronze helmet and a breast-plate, and a semi-cylindrical rectangular shield. The shield was made of two layers of wood glued together and covered with canvas and leather; its upper and lower edges were rimmed with iron to resist the long Gallic sword. Their weapons consisted of two javelins, a dagger, and a pointed double-edged sword 2 feet long, of a type which originally came from Spain. The *triarii* were similarly armed, except that instead of javelins they had a thrusting-spear. The *velites* were armed with a sword, two javelins, a round shield 3 feet across, and wore a head-dress of wolf's skin. The Romans probably copied their javelin from the Gauls. It was 6 feet long, with a barbed iron head. The head bent on impact, so that the enemy would not be able to make use of the weapon themselves. If it lodged in a shield it was heavy and difficult to extricate. It could be thrown with the aid of a thong attached to the shaft behind the centre of gravity; when pulled this worked like rifling, causing the javelin to rotate in flight, thus increasing its range and accuracy. The device went out in the second century, when tactics required only a short throw of about 25 yards. The legionary cavalry units were poorly armed, with a leather shield, a lance and a sword.

The virtue of the manipular formation was that it made possible both an elastic defence and a flexible attack, whether against the stiff hellenistic phalanx or the loose mass of the Gauls. The legion's attack was begun by the *velites*, who as light skirmishers covered the advance of the heavy infantry. When the *hastati* got within range they hurled their javelins, and immediately advanced to engage the enemy with their swords. During the struggle the rear ranks supplied support to those in front who fell or tired. The legionaries were thoroughly drilled to execute relay manoeuvres, by which one whole line replaced another and launched a new drive forward. If things went badly the *hastati* and the *principes* could form into one line, and retire through the intervals of the *triarii* – who would then fight as a phalanx. Cavalry was used for scouting and pursuit, but it had no part in the classical tactics of the legion, and the troopers in fact often fought on foot. The Romans applied this system with a high degree of discipline and training.

The youngest trained men were put in the front line where sheer force counted for most, while the older men were in the *triarii* – where they would be spared the fighting in the event of a quick victory, yet as a reserve could be fed in to give additional support in front. A third and final assault with fresh troops could well clinch a victory. The

Roman infantry of the fourth century B.C.: a light foot soldier of the *velites* (far left); heavy foot soldiers of the *hastati* or *principes* (centre left and right)

system of three lines was good for morale in that it kept two-thirds of the soldiers out of the danger area for as long as possible, and gave a defeated front line a good chance to retire safely.

Fuller considered that the Romans were 'the greatest entrenching army in history'. The legion was always backed by a fortified camp. If necessary a new camp was built at

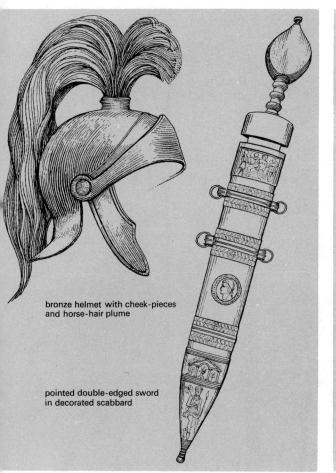

bronze helmet with cheek-pieces
and horse-hair plume

pointed double-edged sword
in decorated scabbard

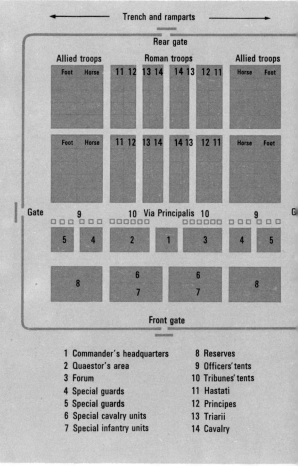

Trench and ramparts

Rear gate

Allied troops		Roman troops				Allied troops	
Foot	Horse	11 12	13 14	14 13	12 11	Horse	Foot
Foot	Horse	11 12	13 14	14 13	12 11	Horse	Foot

Gate   9   10   Via Principalis   10   9   G

5	4	2	1	3	4	5
8	6 7			6 7	8	

Front gate

1 Commander's headquarters	8	Reserves
2 Quaestor's area	9	Officers' tents
3 Forum	10	Tribunes' tents
4 Special guards	11	Hastati
5 Special guards	12	Principes
6 Special cavalry units	13	Triarii
7 Special infantry units	14	Cavalry

Weapons of the Roman soldier *left*. The lay-out of a Roman camp *right*

the end of every day, even at the cost of reducing marching time to three or four hours in the morning so that the afternoon could be spent digging. The size and shape of the camp varied according to the terrain, but where possible it was built square and large enough to accommodate two legions. It was fortified by ramparts, palisades and ditches.

The Romans took trouble to build these camps for two reasons. First, they recognized the value of security and comfort. They used much of the time spent in the camp in drill and physical training, in order to instil the qualities of steadiness, regularity and order which were necessary for the tactics of the legion, and which in any case seem to have been natural to the Roman soldiers. Secondly, the legions generally did not offer battle unless they had a fortified area near at hand to retire into if the fighting should go against them. As a result, the reverses they suffered were rarely disastrous.

Apart from their weapons, the Roman soldiers on the march had to carry a considerable load – including entrenching tools and cooking equipment. The men were not

particularly well fed. They seldom ate meat, and the staple food in camp was un-
leavened bread made of wheat baked on hot stones or embers.

The army was commanded by two consuls, elected annually; these were generally
politicians who had received no training in generalship. This peculiar dual command
was designed to lessen the possibility of military tyranny, but it was a military nonsense.
For one thing the annual change made continuity of policy difficult; for another, the
day-to-day rotation of command resulted in deadlock when the consuls disagreed – a
situation which could be broken only by the election of a dictator for an emergency
period. In the *Lays of Ancient Rome* Macaulay relates in 'The battle of Lake Regillus'
how an elder consul said to the Conscript Fathers when things didn't look too good:

> In seasons of great peril
> 'Tis good that one bear sway;
> Then choose we a dictator,
> Whom all men shall obey . . .
> Then let him be Dictator
> For six months and no more.

Excellent advice. Maybe it would be easier in the world today if dictators were elected
for the same period!

The ancient Romans did not have an aristocratic officer class. The maniples, the
essential tactical units, were each led by two centurions, who were experienced soldiers
of the same social background as the privates. The tactical functioning of the legion
was thus in the control of tried professionals who understood their men. Polybius
describes the centurions as

> not so much bold and adventurous as men with a faculty for command, steady and rather of a
> deep-rooted spirit . . . who, in the face of superior numbers or overwhelming pressure, would
> endure and die in the defence of their post.

They were steady and brave; they understood war and they treated it as a job which
had to be done. It was largely because she could always produce first class N.C.O.'s and
privates that Rome proved so successful in her campaigns.

Such was the legion – a force consisting of three lines of heavy infantry armed with
javelins and swords, hardly supported at all by light infantry or cavalry, and much
addicted to spadework. For over seven hundred years after the middle of the fourth
century B.C. this remained the standard Roman military system. Individual commanders
varied it sometimes, but the legion did not fundamentally change. Its strengths and
weaknesses will become apparent as the wars fought by the Romans are studied.

By the middle of the third century Rome, with her widening political and commercial
interests, came up against the challenge of Carthage, the richest city of the west. The
First Punic War (265–41) went in Rome's favour. But by 220 Carthaginian power was
reviving in Spain. In 218, after certain provocations, Hannibal, a 29-year-old Carthaginian general, crossed the Pyrenees to invade Italy. Both for its influence on world
history, and for the outstanding generalship on both sides, the Second Punic War

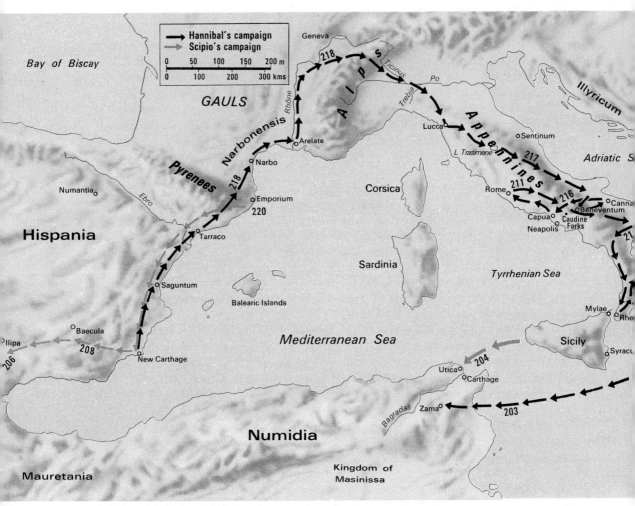

The campaigns of Hannibal and Scipio

(218–01) is worth studying. Rome and Carthage were evenly matched, and each knew that she must win or be for ever ruined. The Carthaginian territory is well-known to me, being in Tunisia, and I visited the site of the ancient city after the end of the war in North Africa in the spring of 1943.

Hannibal had been schooled in arms since early boyhood, and had made a wide study of Hellenistic and Roman warfare. Already he had commanded armies for three years, and he was completely confident that he knew how to beat the Romans. He crossed the Pyrenees with a motley army of about 40,000 men and 37 elephants; the troops were recruited from different parts of Africa and Spain and supplemented on his way to Italy with Gauls. The army consisted mostly of mercenaries held together only by Hannibal's leadership and the prospect of plunder. The main constituent was light infantry, armed with a short sword, spear, shield, and little body armour. The best troops were the

Numidian mounted javelin-men under a brilliant cavalry commander, Maharbal. Polybius says 'the army was not so much numerous as highly efficient, and in an extraordinary state of physical training'. All through the war the Carthaginians were to be heavily outnumbered by the Romans, who by 217 had raised their legions from five to eleven, and in the last stages of the war to over twenty – or 100,000 men. Hannibal's strategy in the war was not to destroy Rome, but by his victorious presence in Italy to break her hold over the Italian confederacy, and force her to agree to coexist with Carthage. He posed as a liberator, and proclaimed that 'I am not come to fight against Italians, but on behalf of Italians against Rome.'

Hannibal advanced rapidly round the Mediterranean. During his crossing of the Alps he was so beset by tribesmen and early snows that his army debouched into northern Italy reduced to 20,000 foot and 6,000 cavalry. After a successful engagement at the River Ticinus he crossed the Po, and at the Trebia stream in December 218 won the first of three great victories. His elephants and cavalry drove the Roman wings into the stream; although 10,000 legionaries burst through in the centre and got away, more than two-thirds of the Roman army was destroyed. In 217 the Romans decided not to meet the Carthaginians with their superior cavalry in the plain, but further south in the Apennines. However, in April Hannibal caught the army of Flaminius between the hills and the northern shore of Lake Trasimene. The Romans had neglected their intelligence and reconnaissance. Screened by a mist, the Carthaginian forces launched a sudden attack from the foothills and in three hours destroyed or captured all the enemy. After this victory Hannibal declared Italy free from Roman overlordship; he marched down the Adriatic coast and in the spring of 216 he captured the Roman supply base at Cannae (north of Bari). There, in August, he brought the Romans to battle again.

Hannibal drew up his army in a convex crescent formation, with the Spanish and Gallic infantry in the centre, the Africans on either side of them, and on the wings powerful detachments of cavalry. The Roman infantry army was drawn up in conventional parallel formation. Hannibal began the battle by routing the Roman cavalry. Then he let the Roman infantry advance and press the Carthaginian crescent back till it was concave. At that point he suddenly advanced his African infantry from left and right and turned them inwards on to the Roman flanks. The battle was completed when his cavalry returned from the pursuit and fell on the Roman rear. Assailed on all four sides, as Fuller put it, 'the Roman army was swallowed up as if by an earthquake'. At the battle of Cannae in 216 B.C. a large Roman army (70,000 men) was destroyed because of the sound generalship of Hannibal and the stupidity of its commander – who that day was the consul Tarentius Varro, a business man whose turn it was to be general! Cannae was a crowning disaster for Roman arms.

After Cannae most of southern Italy went over to the Carthaginians, including the important city of Capua (modern Caserta). But a large nucleus of Roman territory stood firm, and the Roman fleet was definitely in command of the seas. Maharbal urged Hannibal to march on Rome straightaway. He refused. As we have said, his strategy was not to prosecute a war to the death, but simply to bring Rome to terms; and in any case he lacked the resources to undertake a massive siege. A war of attrition followed, in which the Romans, chiefly led by Quintus Fabius Maximus, known as *Cunctator* or the Delayer, sought to avoid pitched battles; they took advantage of their fortresses and their greater numbers to wear Hannibal down, and contained him in the south of Italy.

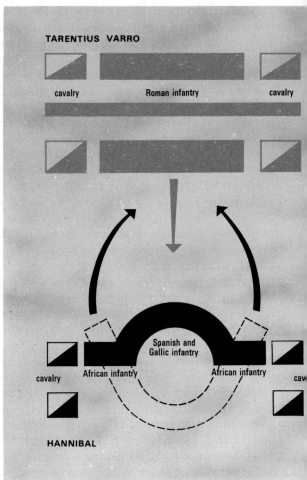

Hannibal's army included elephants *left*. The battle of Cannae *right*

But they did not dare attack him. A naval victory in 208 gave Rome absolute supremacy at sea, making possible a future invasion of Africa.

This turn of fortune in Rome's favour in Italy in the ten years after Cannae coincided with success in the Spanish theatre. An army had been sent to Spain in 218 and at first had done well. But in 211 some of the Spanish allies deserted and the Romans were severely beaten, the remnants of the army falling back north of the Ebro. In 210 the Spanish command was given to Publius Cornelius Scipio, aged twenty-five, known later as Africanus. Scipio Africanus was to become the greatest of all Roman generals. He had been present as a young lad at the disasters of the Ticinus and Cannae, where he had distinguished himself by his courage and become popular. He had studied war carefully and with an open mind.

Late in 210 Scipio landed in Spain at Emporium. He had with him 10,000 foot and 1,000 cavalry, with which to bring the shattered Roman army up to a strength of four legions. Scipio immediately set about organizing his army and raising the morale of his men, and then, by a most daring and dramatic move, stamped his imprint on the Second Punic War. Instead of engaging any of the three enemy armies in Spain he decided to make straight for New Carthage, their main base 300 miles down the coast to the south. The enemy armies were all a good ten days' march from New Carthage, and Scipio reckoned there was time. He covered the 300 miles with his army and navy in about a week. The fortress, built on a rocky promontary, was supposed to be strong, but Scipio took the defenders by surprise. Wading with his men through the lagoon, he had scaling-ladders placed at the weakest part of the wall, and New Carthage was quickly taken. Scipio thus captured the enemy's base, and established himself on their eastern flank and rear.

In 208 Scipio caught Hasdrubal's army at Baecula in Andalusia, and defeated it. The Carthaginians were reinforced and in 206 Scipio met the combined armies of Mago and Hasdrubal Gisgo at Ilipa. Although outnumbered, he won a decisive victory. The Romans attacked with their thin centre held back, and the strongest legions on the wings thrown forward. The legions destroyed the Spanish levies on the Carthaginian wings before the armies had even met in the centre, and then turned inwards to decide the battle. Scipio pursued the enemy to the sea, where they surrendered. In 205, when the Carthaginians had been completely cleared out of Spain, he returned to Rome.

Carthage had now lost Spain, Sicily and Sardinia, Macedonia had made peace, and Hannibal was contained in lower Italy. The Roman Senate intended to strangle his army where it was. But Scipio proposed a different strategy. He was in favour of keeping Hannibal contained in southern Italy while striking at Carthage in North Africa. The Senate was dubious, but it allowed him to go to Sicily with two legions. There Scipio set about recruiting, organizing and training his army. He also secured the alliance of Masinissa, king of Numidia, who could supply him with first-class cavalry. In the spring of 204 Scipio landed in Africa. He had 25,000 men and the support of Masinissa. He was opposed by a Carthaginian army of 20,000 foot, 6,000 cavalry and 140 elephants under another Hasdrubal and Syphax, king of Masaesylli. After successfully besieging Utica he wintered on the promontary of Castra Cornelia. There he was almost cornered by Syphax, but extricated himself by pretending to seek an armistice and then ordering his army to burn the enemy's camp.

It was essential for Scipio to deal with Hasdrubal's army before Hannibal returned to Africa. Accordingly in the spring of 203, after a four day march, Scipio with one legion and some cavalry caught the enemy on the Bagradas plain, and defeated it by the very un-Roman tactics of launching two decisive cavalry charges from the wings. The victory was complete and Syphax was captured. Carthage now sued for peace and recalled Hannibal; but when in the summer of 203 he landed in Africa with 15,000 men, the Carthaginians decided after all to go on fighting. In the following year Scipio ravaged the rich Bagradas valley, and in the autumn he was met by Hannibal's army at Zama, five days' march to the south-west of Carthage.

At Zama in 202 B.C. was fought the final battle of the Second Punic War. Each army was about 40,000 strong. Hannibal's forces may have been slightly more numerous, but most of Scipio's infantry had received a longer training, and he had the advantage in cavalry, with more than 4,000 to Hannibal's 2,000. For the first time in his career Hannibal was inferior in cavalry, and this meant that he could not use the enveloping tactics which had been so successful – for example, at Cannae. It may therefore have been partly out of apprehension, as well as out of personal curiosity, that on the eve of the battle Hannibal did a most extraordinary thing. According to Livy, he proposed to Scipio that the two of them should meet between the armies and talk things over. I find it hard to imagine such a thing happening in the twentieth century; if Rommel had asked me to meet him between our lines before Alamein for a discussion on the situation, I would have declined – although I would have been intensely interested to meet my famous opponent, which I never did. The meeting between Hannibal and Scipio took place with interpreters, and very probably Hannibal offered peace terms which Scipio refused. Each then returned to his own camp.

On the following day at dawn both sides drew up their forces. Hannibal's dispositions indicate that he was well aware of the inferior nature of his army, and that he did his best to make up for it. In front of his forces he placed 80 elephants. His infantry stood in three lines. The first consisted of Ligurian and Gallic heavy infantry interspersed with Moorish light infantry and Balearic slingers. In the second line he placed the troops in whom he had least trust – the newly-levied Carthaginians and Africans. The third line, consisting of his own veteran infantry from Italy, was held about 200 yards behind the second, so that it should not get involved before it could deliver the decisive blow. Hannibal posted 1,000 Carthaginian cavalry on the right wing and 1,000 Numidians on the left. His aim was simply to break the Roman front. Much would depend on the elephants.

Scipio adapted the normal dispositions of the legion to deal with the enemy's elephants and to exploit his own cavalry superiority. Instead of drawing up the maniples of the three lines chequer-wise he disposed them in columns, leaving gaps so that the elephants could pass through and be dealt with on the way by the *velites* in the lanes. The lines were also spaced farther apart than usual, with the *triarii* particularly far back, to give the *velites* room to retire between them if necessary. He put his main force of cavalry, Masinissa's Numidians, on the right wing, and the Italian cavalry under Laelius on the left.

The battle opened with a skirmish between the opposing forces of Numidian cavalry. Hannibal then launched the charge of his elephants. As they pounded towards the Roman army Scipio ordered a blast of trumpets and horns along the whole of his line. The sudden blare caused the elephants to panic. Those on the left turned and crashed back into Hannibal's Numidians. When Masinissa saw that the enemy's prize cavalry was in confusion he seized the opportunity to charge, and drove the Numidians from the field. In the centre Scipio's disposition of his maniples in lanes paid off, for although the elephants punished the *velites* severely, most of them passed straight through the Romans without touching the heavy infantry. Some were driven back from the lanes towards the Carthaginian right, pursued by javelins from the Roman cavalry. Laelius exploited the confusion thus caused among the enemy's cavalry in the same way as Masinissa had on the other wing, and hurled his cavalry at the Carthaginian right. Thus Hannibal's cavalry on both sides of the battle area were routed at the start, and his flanks exposed. Once again elephants had proved to be a disastrous liability.

The Roman cavalry pursued the Carthaginians into the distance, and the second phase of the battle, the infantry engagement, now began. Hannibal's Gauls and Ligurians at first got the better of the struggle because of their mobility; but they could

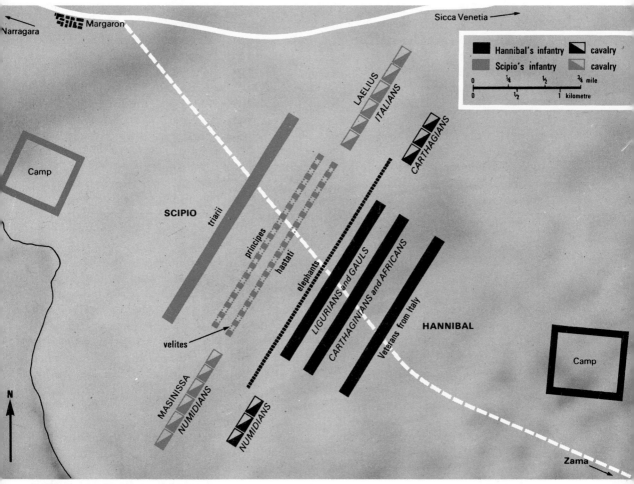

The battle of Zama

not actually break the Roman line which, with its superior weight, gradually began to press them back. When the Roman *principes* came into action the Carthaginian second line failed to support their front; and when it seemed to the Gauls that they had been let down they gave up the fight and melted away, leaving the second line to face the Romans. The ground was now encumbered with corpses and slippery with blood, which made fighting difficult. For a while the Roman *hastati* were driven back by the new Carthaginian front. But then the Roman officers rallied the *principes*, and with their longer line the Romans forced back the Carthaginian second line and cut it to pieces. The survivors, as before, fled back towards the next line for refuge, and, as before, Hannibal refused to allow fresh and disciplined troops to get involved with defeated ones; his veteran *triarii* levelled their spears, and the remnants of the Carthaginian second line disappeared towards the flanks.

The third and toughest phase of the battle now opened. The Romans had routed two lines of the enemy already, and no doubt were elated at their success. On the other hand, except for the *triarii*, they had exerted themselves heavily and now had to face Hannibal's veteran infantry in perfect order and completely fresh. With extraordinary coolness, Scipio at this point checked his highly disciplined troops. He had the wounded carried to the rear, ordered the exhausted *hastati* to the flanks, and reformed the *principes* and *triarii* together, in close order and on a more extended front so as to concentrate the shock of the charge while at the same time overlapping the enemy. Polybius relates that, when this had been done, 'the two lines charged each other with the greatest fire and fury. Being nearly equal in numbers, spirit, courage and arms, the battle was for a long time undecided, the men in their obstinate valour falling dead without giving way a step.' The infantry struggle was for some time very evenly matched.

Then, finally, the Roman cavalry of Masinissa and Laelius returned from their pursuit of the Carthaginian cavalry and struck Hannibal's infantry in the rear. 'The greater part of his men were cut down in their ranks; while of those who attempted to fly very few escaped with their life.' The battle was over. Scipio's cavalry made thoroughly sure of the victory, and the outcome of the war, by scouring the whole countryside. Hannibal himself escaped. Scipio did not march on Carthage because he had not the means to conduct a siege, and he wished to impose moderate rather than vindictive peace terms.

We should now discuss the relative merits of the two generals – Scipio and Hannibal. Liddell Hart's comment on the battle of Zama is that 'a master of war had met a greater master', and the fact is that on this, the only occasion when Scipio and Hannibal faced each other in battle, Scipio won. Nonetheless the comparative merits of the generalship of the two cannot be so simply evaluated. It is clear that Hannibal was the better tactician; indeed his tactical genius at Cannae can compare with the conduct of any battle in the history of warfare. It must be borne in mind that Hannibal's army at Zama was inferior in quality to Scipio's. A considerable proportion of his infantry was semi-trained, and he was at a grave numerical disadvantage in cavalry, with the result that he could not use the tactics of envelopment which had brought him his previous victories. He had to take a chance with the elephants, and everything depended on their behaviour. In the event they let him down disastrously. And yet even after that, by holding his best infantry back till the end, and by letting the Roman infantry blunt its attack on his secondary troops, he almost pulled it off. Scipio made no mistakes at Zama, and his cool reorganization of his troops in mid-battle was masterly. Even so, it was the providential return of his cavalry in the nick of time, together with the fighting quality of the Roman infantry, which really won the battle. Hannibal did everything he could have done; but by 202, after sixteen years of continuous high command, he may well have been past his best, whereas at that time Scipio was undoubtedly at the top of his form.

Scipio was definitely the most original of Roman tacticians. He perceived that the great weakness of Roman armies was lack of cavalry. The legionary infantry was superior to any that the world had yet seen, but without a good cavalry arm Roman armies were gravely handicapped. For this reason the Romans could never have been a match for the Macedonian armies of the fourth century. Scipio temporarily repaired this deficiency and won the battles of the Bagradas and Zama. But here, both in his recognition of the need for cavalry and in his method of using it, Scipio acknowledged Hannibal's mastery. His use of cavalry was in the classic pattern set by Alexander and Hannibal, and his crescent formation at Ilipa was closely similar to Hannibal's at Cannae. Unfortunately Scipio relied for cavalry on allied or mercenary contingents, instead of training Romans. In the wars of the second century, when the Romans found themselves opposed by enemies who fought in an infantry phalanx, Scipio's tactical lessons were entirely forgotten.

Both Hannibal and Scipio were outstandingly good at handling men. Hannibal invaded Italy with a motley army recruited from all parts of the western Mediterranean. He trained it and led it to win great victories. Altogether, as Polybius says, 'for sixteen continuous years' Hannibal maintained the war with Rome in Italy, without once releasing his army from service in the field, but keeping the vast numbers under control . . . without any sign of disaffection towards himself or towards each other'. He was a master of psychology, not only as regards the maintenance of morale in his own army, but also in his ability to mislead and mystify his opponents – for example, before Trasimene. Both generals were personally courageous and popular with their men. Scipio possibly showed a deeper appreciation of the human factor in war when before the battle of Zama he rode up and down the ranks of his men personally inspiring them, whereas Hannibal merely ordered his subordinate commanders to encourage the troops. However, Hannibal's failure here may well have been due to the language problem in his multi-national army.

Where Scipio was undoubtedly superior to Hannibal was in strategy. It was this which in the end mattered most, and which marks out Scipio as one of the great captains of history. Hannibal's strategy in Italy was a complete failure. His three quick victories between 218 and 216 did not cause the Roman people to crack up as he had hoped. Maharbal was right when he told Hannibal after Cannae that he did not know how to use a victory. It is extraordinary that he never raised a proper siege-train, if not to attack Rome at least to reduce the fortresses upon which the Fabian strategy of the Romans depended. After Cannae, Hannibal apparently ran out of ideas. He lost the initiative, allowed Fabius to turn the tide of war against him, and eventually found himself trapped in southern Italy. Clearly he never understood fully the importance of seapower.

By contrast, Scipio showed his military greatness in the originality and vision of his strategy. Whenever possible he struck direct at the enemy's base, each time with the most successful results. His lightning capture of New Carthage reversed the course of the war in Spain. His plan of leaving Hannibal contained in lower Italy and striking straight at Africa, thus devastating the enemy at home and forcing them to abandon activities in Italy, was the strategy of a genius. The way in which Scipio brought Hannibal to the final battle at Zama was also brilliant. By marching up the rich valley of the Bagradas, ravaging it as he went, he threatened Carthage with the destruction of one of her chief sources of supply, drew Hannibal away from Carthage itself, and at the same time shortened the distance which Masinissa had to cover in order to reinforce him and thereby produce the superiority in cavalry which would be decisive. The ultimate victory of Rome over Carthage in the Second Punic War was due to the endurance of her people after the disaster at Cannae in 216, to her superiority at sea, and to the strategy of Scipio.

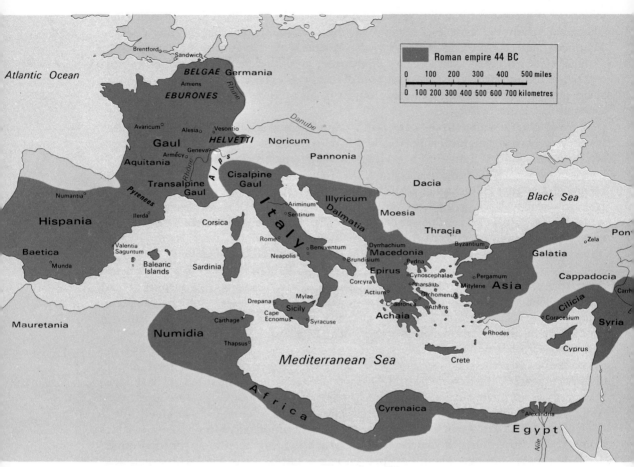

The extent of Roman domination in the time of Julius Caesar

Both sides at Zama were fully aware of the importance of the battle. As Livy writes, 'before nightfall, they would know whether Rome or Carthage should give laws to the nations . . . For not Africa . . . or Italy, but the whole world would be the reward of victory.' Certainly the battle decided the fate of the western Mediterranean. By the terms of the peace Carthage was disarmed and had to pay an indemnity. Numidia became a Roman protectorate and Spain was made into two Roman provinces, with an army permanently stationed there and its inhabitants subject to taxation and military service. Thus out of the Second Punic War emerged the beginning of the Roman empire.

During the second century Rome was continually at war to preserve and extend her power in the Mediterranean. In 146 Carthage was finally destroyed. Three wars were fought in Macedonia. At the battles of Cynoscephalae (197) and Pydna (168) the greater flexibility of the legions brought them victory over the rigid Hellenistic phalanx. But some of these campaigns were notable only for incompetent generalship and the indiscipline of the legions. Furthermore the character of Roman imperialism was becoming sinister; for example, many of the victims after Pydna were slaughtered or enslaved. In 167 all direct taxation in Italy was abolished and from that time Rome lived off imperial tribute and slave labour. Such an economy necessitated the constant subjugation of further territories. Africa, Macedonia, Greece and Asia Minor became provinces. The extortionate rule of the Romans made them hated. In 154 the unpopularity of Roman rule in Spain led to a revolt; four years later some of the rebels surrendered to the Roman general Galba, and were massacred in cold blood. Nonetheless the Spaniards continued to fight, led by the guerrilla chieftain Viriathus, until eventually in 133, after an 8-year siege, their stronghold of Numantia was captured by the Romans and, like Carthage and Corinth, totally annihilated.

In 135 a revolt of the Sicilian slaves, known as the First Servile War, opened a dismal and confused century of revolt and civil war. War in Numidia from 112 to 106 was terminated by Gaius Marius and Lucius Sulla, and an invasion of northern Italy by Germanic tribes in 102–1 was thrown back by Marius.

Between 104 and 101 Marius made important reforms in the army, particularly as regards the organization and recruitment of the legions. His changes were mostly a matter of regularizing tendencies which had been growing for some time. For example, Aemilius Paulus, at Pydna, had formed his maniples together into larger groups. Now, Marius, in order to give the legion more cohesion while retaining flexibility, enlarged its basic tactical unit from the 120-man maniple to the 600-man 'cohort'. At the same time he fixed the total number in the legion at 6,000. There were thus ten cohorts in a legion. Each of these was divided into six 'centuries', under centurions. The thrusting-spear so far used by the *triarii* was abolished, and all three lines were armed with an improved javelin. The *velites* and the legionary cavalry disappeared, and from now on all cavalry and light troops were supplied by the allies. A more unified and formidable legion of heavy infantry emerged, which was to be the instrument of Julius Caesar's conquests. Marius also gave every legion an eagle standard. Originally standards had been poles with twists of hay tied to them, which could be used to give signals and served as a rallying point. The new eagles really became symbols of the legions, and their loss in battle came to be regarded as the worst of disgraces; they were what the Colours are today in infantry units in many armies, or the eagles given by Napoleon to his regiments.

The most important change in the army made by Marius was to widen the basis of recruitment. A low-born man himself, who owed his political success to popular support, he did not require that his army should be drawn from the men of property; instead he threw it open to all who would volunteer to join. This change led to a rapid professionalization of the legions, and its effect on politics was revolutionary. The rich and parasitic imperial capital contained huge numbers of idle citizens, who volunteered for the army and made it their life. Because the state did not undertake to provide pay, and pensions on demobilisation, the loyalty of the soldiers was given not to the state, but to the general who recruited them. He equipped them, and they followed him for as long as he was successful and there were prospects of loot. It was this innovation which made possible the careers of a succession of soldier-politicians in the first century B.C. – Marius, Sulla, Pompey and Caesar. It was more than anything the cause of the struggle which, Sallust wrote, 'threw everything, human and divine, into confusion, and rose to such a pitch of frenzy that civil disorder ended in war and the devastation of Italy'. If the development of mercenary armies meant that the Romans more often defeated their enemies abroad, it also meant that their internal politics became more and more a matter of naked force. The field of recruitment to the legions was further widened when the Italian allies were granted citizenship.

The relations between Sulla and Marius had been unfriendly ever since 106, and now their political ambitions clashed. In 88 Mithridates IV of Pontus (in eastern Anatolia) invaded the province of Asia and the liberated subjects of Rome rose up in Greece and Asia Minor, and murdered their governors. Sulla was elected to the consulship and given the eastern command. But Marius was jealous, and while Sulla was still crushing a revolt in Campania he got the appointment transferred to himself. Sulla in fury marched on Rome, and violating the tradition that no army should enter the capital he marched his men through the streets. The Marians were scattered in street fighting; Marius himself was outlawed and fled.

Early in 87 Sulla set out for the east with five legions. He first captured and sacked Athens, and then defeated Archelaus, the Pontic general, at Chaeronea and Orchomenus. In these battles Sulla made full use of the new legionary formation, and introduced into Roman infantry tactics a new flexibility and thrust. Meanwhile at Rome the Sullans had again been supplanted, but Sulla did not resign his command. In 83 he returned with his army to southern Italy. Marius was now dead, and in 82 Sulla entered Rome. In November of that year he defeated the last of his opponents in a battle outside the Colline Gate. The prisoners were slaughtered in the circus, and Sulla set himself up as dictator. He secured his power by arranging for the murder of some 3,500 of his enemies, and then ruled till 79, when he retired.

Sulla's government proved to be quite beneficial. But the sinister fact remained that this was dictatorship backed by military force. The Roman legions, now recruited predominantly from the poor and idle proletariat of Italy, would apparently sell their support to any leader, however unscrupulous. Already another such *condottiere* was appearing, Gnaeus Pompeius, an officer of Sulla, and better known as Pompey.

During the 70's three serious revolts broke out against Rome. In 76 Pompey was sent to Spain to deal with the rebellion of an ex-Roman general, Quintus Sertorius. Sertorius, a pupil of Marius, had trained his army to be proficient in both legionary and guerrilla tactics. He had gained control of all Spain, and at first outgeneralled Pompey. Gradually, however, numerical superiority told, and in 72 the revolt petered out. In that year Marcus Licinius Crassus stamped out a slave revolt led by the gladiator Spartacus. The slaves were hemmed in to the toe of Italy by an earthwork thirty-seven miles long, and 6,000 prisoners were crucified along the Appian Way from Rome to Capua. At the same time Lucius Lucullus was engaged in dealing with further trouble caused by Mithridates. Between 73 and 69 he cleared Asia Minor, but when he advanced into Armenia his men mutinied and he had to return leaving the job half finished. A brilliantly efficient and daring commander, Lucullus was too humane a conqueror and too rigorous a disciplinarian to keep the personal loyalty of the mercenary-minded Roman soldiers. He gave up military life and became a gourmet.

The most powerful individual in Rome in the 60's was Pompey. During the Mithridatic Wars piracy had become a serious nuisance. The pirates operated all over the Mediterranean in close cooperation, based on strongholds in Crete and Cilicia, and were supposed to have a thousand ships painted in gold, silver and purple. They had given support to Sertorius and Mithridates, and their raids were becoming bolder. Cities and islands in the Aegean were captured, the coasts of Italy were raided, and rich people, for example the young Julius Caesar, were kidnapped. Most serious of all, the Roman corn imports were being cut off. So in 67 Pompey was commissioned to liquidate the pirates. For this purpose he raised 270 ships, 20 legions and 6,000 talents. The Mediterranean and the Black Sea were divided into thirteen commands, each under a *legatus*, who was to round up pirate squadrons and reduce any strongholds in his area. The *legati* were to cooperate to keep the pirate forces from coming to each other's help.

In the spring of 67, with a roving squadron of sixty ships, Pompey began to sweep the whole Mediterranean from west to east, forcing the pirates into the arms of his waiting flotillas. In forty days the whole area west of Italy was cleared. He paid a rapid visit to Rome to check over political affairs, and then resumed his operations from Brundisium (modern Brindisi). As the Romans moved east, the blockade of the Cilician ports which had been maintained while the west was secured was stepped up into a full-scale attack. Many of the pirates were induced to surrender quickly by the example of the lenient treatment given to the first prisoners. The most determined and desperate of them fled into various fortresses. Pompey had ready a powerful force of siege-engines, and after the last of the pirates still at sea had been defeated off Coracesium, he laid siege to the

The catapult, or *onager*, was one of the most effective Roman siege-engines

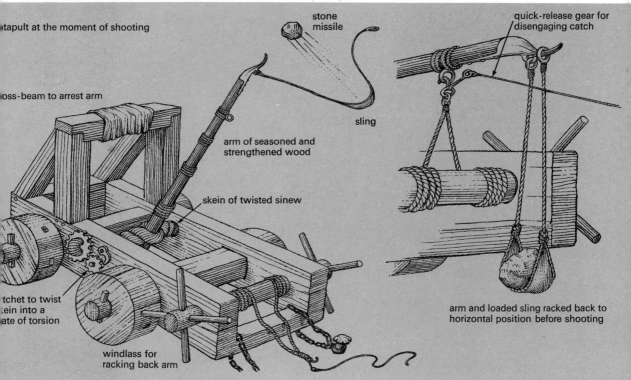

catapult at the moment of shooting

cross-beam to arrest arm

ratchet to twist skein into a state of torsion

windlass for racking back arm

stone missile

sling

arm of seasoned and strengthened wood

skein of twisted sinew

quick-release gear for disengaging catch

arm and loaded sling racked back to horizontal position before shooting

stronghold there, an eyrie perched on a steep rock high above the sea and connected to the land only by a narrow isthmus. When the defenders capitulated, the other strongholds of Cilicia followed suit. The whole operation from start to finish was thus completed within three months.

Pompey's ability as an admiral is remarkable, not only because he himself had always fought on land, but also because the Romans were, by inclination, landlubbers. When the occasion demanded in the past they had been capable of taking to the seas with great success, but when the necessity passed they returned to dry land with relief, and framed all foreign policy and strategy to achieve their aims as far as possible by staying there. Only when they went to war against the great naval and mercantile power of Carthage had the Romans built a proper fleet. In 260, within sixty days, a fleet of 20 triremes and 100 quinqueremes was constructed. The tactic adopted was to lay the Roman ship alongside the enemy; marines would then cross over a gangway to board. In 260 Duillius won a spectacular victory with the new fleet off Mylae in Sicily, sinking or capturing forty-four of the enemy's ships. The effects of a second victory off Cape Ecnomus in 256 were offset during the next year when most of the fleet was lost in a storm. Throughout her naval history Rome lost more ships to the elements than to the enemy.

The First Punic War was concluded in 241 by the naval victory of Drepana, and in the Second Punic War (218–01 B.C.) Rome's superiority at sea contributed largely to her ultimate victory, since Hannibal could not be reinforced in southern Italy, while Rome could invade Africa. During the second century Rome allowed her own navy to rot, and relied on the fleets of her allies, Rhodes and Pergamum – to her disadvantage in the Macedonian wars. As Rome became the dominant power in the whole Mediterranean world she neglected her responsibility of policing the seas, with the result that piracy became rife.

At the end of 59 B.C. news reached Rome that the Helvetii were on the point of migrating from Switzerland across to the south-west of Gaul. As soon as he was free of his duties as consul for that year, Julius Caesar, governor of Illyricum, Cisalpine Gaul and the unbounded region of Transalpine Gaul, set off for Geneva at top speed. At this time Caesar was forty-one years old. His previous military experience had been very limited.

In 81 B.C. he had served in Asia Minor, and at the storming of Mitylene he had won a civic crown for saving the life of a fellow soldier. But after that he had concentrated on a political career. He had secured the consulship in 59 by coming to an arrangement with Pompey and Crassus. A nephew of Marius, he got his way as consul by a combination of rabble-rousing oratory and the threat of military force.

It is probable that when he hastened to Geneva in 58, with Labienus his second-in-command, Caesar had no definite idea of conquering Gaul, let alone anything more. But he was ambitious, and if he was to maintain himself at the top of Roman politics he had to have fame – and also an army. In the early summer of 58 he checked the Helvetii by building a 19-mile chain of fortifications along the valley of the Rhône, and then defeating them at Armécy. Posing to the Gauls as a saviour and not a conqueror, he then advanced north of the old Roman frontier to clear Alsace of the Germanic invaders who had recently settled there. Near Vesontio (Besançon) Caesar's six legions in triple line overwhelmed seven German tribes. In the winter of 58–7 Caesar left his legions quartered in that area.

The penetration of Roman arms into their country now aroused the hostility of the Belgae, the part-Germanic confederacy of tribes which inhabited northern Gaul. In the spring of 57 Caesar hurried northwards to meet the Belgic army of 300,000 men led by Galba, on the Aisne. The fighting methods of the Belgae were those of primitive barbarians; they fought as an undisciplined horde of infantry. Most of them were armed only with a long cutting-sword and a wooden or wattle shield, and fought half-naked, though their chiefs wore breast-plates of bronze and highly decorated helmets. Occasionally the shock of their savage onslaught prevailed, but generally when they fought the Romans, as Fuller put it, 'courage shattered itself on the rocks of discipline'. Dissensions among the Belgae allowed Caesar to deal with the different tribes separately. By the end of 56 all Gaul except for the Massif Central had been conquered.

In the autumn of 55 Caesar made his first expedition to Britain, on what was really nothing more than a reconnaissance trip. In July 54 possibly the biggest fleet ever seen in the Channel before the 1939/45 war sailed for Sandwich, carrying five legions and 2,000 Gallic cavalry.

The Britons were too terrified to oppose the landing, and Caesar hurriedly pursued them inland. But within twenty-four hours he heard that his transports had been damaged by the weather. The Britons were encouraged, and under the leadership of Cassivellaunus conducted a vigorous guerrilla war. However, Caesar defeated them at a battle near Brentford, and captured the stronghold of Cassivellaunus on the other side of the Thames. It was now time for him to return to Gaul, so he imposed moderate terms and withdrew. The Romans did not again come to Britain for a hundred years, and the tribute was probably never paid. Caesar's own accounts of the two invasions of Britain should be read with some suspicion; they give the impression of trying to cover up failure.

It was more than time for Caesar to turn his attention to Gaul, for revolt was breaking out in many places. In 53 a rebel leader emerged in Ambiorix, chief of the Eburones. He annihilated a legion near Amiens, and then laid siege by Roman methods to a Roman camp. After a forced march Caesar relieved it, but he had to spend the rest of that year crushing the Eburones. Ambiorix was driven into the Ardennes, another chieftain was flogged to death, and the Eburones were systematically harried. Their crops and cattle were destroyed, and as Caesar tells us, 'every hamlet, every homestead that anyone could see was set on fire'.

So far dissensions between rebel chieftains had enabled Caesar to get the better of them. But in 52 a new leader arose who was capable, principally by means of extra-ordinarily cruel discipline, of uniting the rebel Gauls. This was Vercingetorix, chief of the Arverni (from Auvergne). At the beginning of the year Caesar threw the enemy into some confusion by a succession of lightning marches through the snowy hills. Then he laid siege to the stronghold of Avaricum (Bourges). Vercingetorix intended to fight a war of attrition, avoiding battle between his guerrillas and the legions. He attempted to relieve Avaricum by reducing the whole country around to a smoking wilderness, to deprive the Romans of food. But Caesar took the town, massacred its inhabitants and appropriated its corn stores. Caesar eventually caught Vercingetorix at his citadel of Alesia (near Dijon) and there besieged him. Attacked by a powerful relieving army, so that he was both besieged and besieger at the same time, he held twenty-five miles of entrenchments and defeated two enemy armies. This remarkable victory broke the back

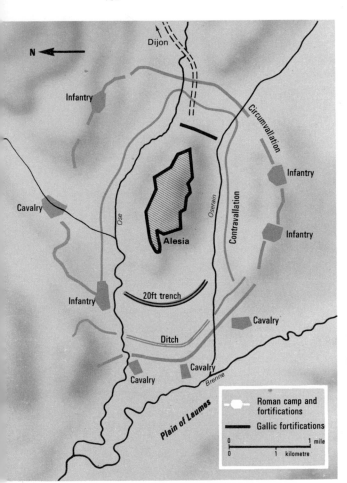

The siege of Alesia *left* concluded many years of fighting between Romans and Gauls *right*

of the Gallic revolt. A liberal peace was made, and thereafter Gaul caused no trouble to Rome.

Meanwhile the political situation in Italy had altered completely, since in 53 Crassus had been removed from the scene. With grandiose ideas of an eastern conquest to rival that of Pompey or even Alexander, he had gone off with 28,000 infantry, 4,000 light troops and 4,000 cavalry to invade Parthia. In the previous century the Parthians had established a powerful empire to the west of the Euphrates, and so far the Romans had been careful not to provoke them. Their army was composed entirely of cavalry, of two sorts. The nobles, mounted on large and strong armour-clad Nesaean horses, fought much like medieval knights, covered with armour and charging with a lance. The mass of their retainers were light horsemen, armed with a bow which was specially shortened below the grip for use in the saddle. From boyhood they were trained to execute the famous Parthian shot, galloping away from the enemy in simulated flight and turning to fire low over the crupper.

In the spring of 53 Crassus crossed the Euphrates and met the enemy at Carrhae. He was opposed by an army of 1,000 heavy lancers and 10,000 horse-archers, backed by a corps of 1,000 camels carrying spare arrows, and commanded by Surenas. In typical tactics the Parthians drew on his advance guard, and then turned to encircle and annihilate it. The main body of the Romans formed a square and held out under showers of arrows till nightfall. During the night Crassus started to withdraw towards some hills, but he was misled by his guide and trapped. He and his senior officers were murdered while parleying with Surenas, and out of the original total of 36,000 only about 10,000 of his men eventually escaped. Carrhae was ranked by the Romans as a disaster to compare with the Caudine Forks and Cannae.

When in the autumn of 50 Caesar returned to Italy, he and Pompey were thus left face to face. Caesar's ruthlessness in Gaul was known at Rome, and many feared that he would be another Sulla. Some of the senators said publicly that they would prosecute him for treason on his return. In the circumstances, civil war was inevitable. Caesar had a successful and devoted army of nine legions. Pompey had ten, seven of which were in Spain, and he also had command of the seas. Caesar was more likely to have popular support than Pompey. Labienus went over to Pompey's side. In January 49 Caesar committed himself to war by crossing the river Rubicon (near Ariminum) and pressing south. Pompey had not seen active service since 62 and with his poorly trained troops he had no wish to fight a battle against the conqueror of Gaul and his veterans, so at the end of March he shipped his army to Macedonia from Brundisium, with Caesar hard on his heels. Within ten weeks of crossing the Rubicon Caesar had mastered Italy, and he entered Rome without a blow.

In April 49 Caesar departed for Spain, and there in seven months secured the submission of Pompey's seven legions without any bloodshed. Fording the Sicoris near Ilerda, by speed of marching he trapped the enemy in a defile, and they surrendered. In January 48 he was ready to cross with his army to Macedonia, and one calm day he slipped past Pompey's patrolling vessels to land seven legions just north of Corcyra. After being besieged for some time in Dyrrhachium, Pompey's army burst out. Eventually the crucial battle of the civil war was fought at Pharsalus in Thessaly on 9th August. Pompey had still wished to avoid battle, but his officers were impatient. He was defeated primarily because Labienus bungled the cavalry engagement on the left. On the following day the remnants of his army surrendered, and he himself fled to Egypt, where he was murdered.

Caesar still had to mop up the Pompeians in various provinces. He first followed his enemy to Egypt; there he fell in love with Queen Cleopatra, and lingered for nine months. Then in July 47 he set out for Pontus, where at Zela he defeated the rebel Pharnaces and sent a dispatch to Rome telling the senators, '*Veni, vidi, vici.*' By now over a year had passed since Pharsalus and the Pompeians had rallied under Labienus in Africa. In December 47 Caesar landed in Africa with one legion and 600 cavalry. He was at first very hard pressed, but after receiving reinforcements the following spring he successfully concluded the African campaign with a victory at Thapsus. In 45 Caesar defeated the last of the Pompeians in Spain at Munda (near Cordoba), and thus became master of the world. He became life-dictator at Rome. Although his rule was not unpopular he was assassinated on the ides of March 44 B.C. by the republicans Brutus and Cassius.

Roman naval tactics consisted in oarsmen rowing their ship alongside the enemy, while marines stood ready to board. Ships of this type took part in the battle of Actium

For a general who achieved such total overall success Caesar is extraordinarily open to criticism. He failed to make those changes in the organization of his army which were obviously necessary. Without proper light infantry it took him much longer to defeat the Gauls than it need have done. He did not train any proper cavalry, but relied on barbarian auxiliaries; again and again this deficiency handicapped him. His reconnaissance was often bad. He neglected his communications; through carelessness his fleet was twice almost lost off the British coast, and when this happened he had no proper repair equipment. His supply system broke down so completely at Ilerda and Dyrrhachium that his troops were almost starving.

As a strategist Caesar was, to say the least, erratic. He systematically overran Gaul, but then spent a summer in an island which was remote and unimportant economically, politically and strategically, while massive revolt was brewing behind him. The swift, bloodless conquests of Italy and Spain contrast completely with his conduct of the later phases of the civil war. He threw away the advantage of his surprise crossing into Macedonia by informing Pompey of his presence, and by wasting time in Egypt and Pontus he allowed the Pompeians to rally and reorganize in Africa. He landed for the first time in Africa with absurdly few troops – one legion and 600 cavalry.

As a tactician Caesar showed no originality. He neglected cavalry, and fought all his various enemies with a three-line legion which was basically extremely traditional. He was, however, by far the greatest Roman infantry commander, and he raised the legion to its highest point. As in politics, so in tactics: when he saw his way he was swift in decision, rapid in action and bold to a degree. Before crossing into Macedonia he encouraged his men to face the difficulties ahead by saying: 'I consider rapidity of movement the best compensation for all these things . . . Let us oppose our good fortune to the winter weather, our courage to the smallness of our numbers, and to our want of supplies the abundance of the enemy, which will be ours to take as soon as we touch the land.' He was often too rash and hasty, but overall his reliance on mobility paid off – as against the Helvetii and Vercingetorix, in the descent to Brundisium, and before Ilerda and Thapsus.

As great a factor as any in bringing Caesar success was his own personality and character. His mere presence with his troops seems to have filled them with the same overwhelming certainty of victory that he had. His cheerfulness and wit, as well as his success, made his men devoted to him. Women could not resist him. He was a brilliant and popular politician with remarkable oratorical gifts, and it was above all because he was so popular with the masses that Italy fell to him immediately in the civil war. His only concern was power, and to secure it he was completely ruthless and amoral. No man ever made war so horrible as Caesar did in Gaul, yet when it suited him better, in the civil war and after, he was lenient and tolerant to his enemies. It is open to question whether towards the end of his life he was altogether sane. Caesar is certainly the most disappointing of great conquerors.

After his death Caesar's empire was fought for by various politicians. Eventually his great-nephew Octavian defeated Antony and Cleopatra at the sea battle of Actium in 31 B.C., and became the first Roman emperor.

The Praetorian Guard constituted an *élite* corps as the emperor's personal bodyguard

6

The Roman Defensive and the Barbarian Migrations

Octavian, who assumed the title *Augustus* in 27 B.C., had few of Caesar's military qualities; but he possessed the qualities of a statesman which Caesar lacked. We shall now see how the Roman empire of the Mediterranean, after it had been extended by Caesar, was, for over four hundred years, garrisoned by soldiers posted along the frontiers. The defensive was the order of the age, and this tended to react unfavourably on the fighting qualities of the Roman army – which will always happen in any army when the offensive spirit is allowed to die and gives way to a 'Maginot' complex. As the years passed barbarians were enlisted more and more into the army: mainly because of a manpower problem due to a falling population and to a dislike of military service by the Italians. This barbarizing of the Roman army gradually resulted in the disintegration of the old Roman military traditions, because it destroyed the discipline and efficiency of the legions and fundamentally changed their character. The empire slowly decayed from within. This decay, coupled with a series of migratory invasions from barbarian peoples, finally brought to an end the Roman empire in the west.

Augustus soon became aware that the condition of the Roman army which he had inherited was far from satisfactory: consisting in the main of short-service private retinues. In order to garrison the long frontier, to police the conquered areas, and to keep out raids and invasions, a disciplined long-service army was necessary – loyal to the state rather than to its various commanders. In 31 B.C. altogether sixty legions were under arms – far more than the state could afford. They were also more than it would need, although the frontier enclosed all the countries on the Mediterranean shore and eventually ran along the Danube, the Rhine and through Scotland. Natural barriers – the Atlantic and Sahara respectively – gave a degree of protection in the west and south; Augustus considered that the east could be better secured by diplomacy than by force; only in the north would a powerful garrison be needed. Accordingly he reduced the number of legions to twenty-eight, keeping some of those which Antony had raised in the east.

Besides this standing force of 168,000 legionaries, he kept about 150,000 *auxilia*; these provided most of the cavalry and light infantry, and were organized in cohorts of infantry and squadrons of cavalry between 500 and 1,000 men strong. Augustus also founded the Praetorian Guard, organized in nine cohorts of 1,000 strong and recruited in Italy, to form the garrison of the city of Rome and to be the emperor's personal bodyguard. The Guard was better paid than the rest of the army and went on active service only with the emperor – for which reason it was not popular. The Praetorians soon became conscious of their potential political power – and used it, becoming a

In the imperial era the Roman navy was enlarged

menace to the well-being of the state. Sejanus, the captain of the Guard, was a favourite of Tiberius, and in A.D. 68 Nero committed suicide to avoid being put to death by his guards.

Seapower was no longer underestimated at Rome, even if it was now likely that the functions of a fleet would be limited to police and convoy duties in friendly waters. Augustus founded two new naval bases in Italy, at Misenum and Ravenna; all provincial governors had ships at their disposal; and squadrons were maintained on the river frontiers. A naval career carried far less prestige than a military one, and the rowers of the ships were usually slaves.

The equipment, strategy and tactics of the imperial army remained for three and a half centuries much as they had been under Scipio, Marius and Caesar. The army normally moved in a long column. When Vespasian entered Judaea in A.D.67 the van-guard was composed of light troops and archers of the *auxilia*; then came detachments of legionary infantry and cavalry, followed by a unit of engineers. The baggage of the senior officers moved next, guarded by cavalry, and then the commander-in-chief himself with a picked bodyguard of infantry and cavalry. The main body of the troops followed with the cavalry leading; next came a unit carrying siege apparatus on mules, and then the legionary commander and his staff, the standard, the trumpeters, and the legion itself drawn up six deep. Lastly came the legionary baggage and the rearguard of

Cavalry took an important place in the line of battle

The infantry cohorts often adopted a two-line formation

mercenary troops. Through difficult country, or when attacks were expected, the army changed its formation to four parallel columns, so that a line of battle could more readily be formed.

The fighting formation of the Roman army in the first century A.D. remained normally a triple line of infantry cohorts, but a two-line formation was not uncommon, and during the second century the army reverted to phalanx tactics. The *auxilia*, by this time very efficient, carried out the initial reconnaissance and probing, and the solid phalanx then bore the brunt of the heavy fighting. Another formation was the *testudo*, or 'tortoise', used when under heavy missile fire, both in advance and retreat. The soldiers of the front rank held their shields up in front of them, and those in the ranks behind raised their shields above their heads. A shell of shields thus protected them all. The only new weapon to be introduced before the third century A.D. was the *lancea*, a lighter spear than the old *pilum* of the legionaries.

At the beginning of the empire the northern frontier was not fixed. Augustus aimed to push forward to the Danube and the Elbe, and between 17 and 11 B.C. Tiberius, one of his stepsons, secured the line of the Danube. Meanwhile Drusus, brother of Tiberius, built fortified camps on the Rhine and undertook the advance towards the Elbe. Moving through wild, forested country, by 9 B.C. he reached the Elbe, but then he died. The German command was then given to Tiberius; but between A.D. 6 and 9 he was called away to Pannonia to deal with a serious revolt, and during that time the Roman grip on Germany was fatally loosened.

The Germans were not a people to be cowed by a display of Roman military power. Though their military organization was crude they made up for it in fierce energy and restless independence. Warfare between the Romans and the Germans was described by Tacitus, in his *Germania* and *Annals*, tersely, vividly and acutely. The German philosophy was, he says, that it is 'limp and slack to get with the sweating of your brow what you can gain with the shedding of your blood'. He described the characteristics of their warfare as follows:

> Few have swords or the longer kind of lance: they carry short spears, in their language *frameae*, with a narrow and small iron head, so sharp, and so handy in use that they fight with the same weapon both at close quarters and at a distance. The mounted man is content with a shield and *framea*; the infantry launch showers of missiles in addition, each man a volley, and hurl these to great distances, for they wear no outer clothing, or at most a light cloak. There is no bravery of apparel among them: their shields only are picked out with choice colours. Few have breastplates: scarcely one or two at most have metal or hide helmets. The horses are conspicuous neither for beauty nor speed . . . On a broad view there is more strength in their infantry, and accordingly cavalry and infantry fight in one body . . . The battle-line itself is arranged in wedges: to retire, provided you press on again, they treat as a question of tactics, not of cowardice . . .
>
> To have abandoned one's shield is the height of disgrace . . . many survivors of war have ended their infamy with a noose . . . Certain totems . . . and emblems are . . . carried into battle. The strongest incentive to courage lies in . . . family and kinship . . . Some lost or losing battles have been restored by the women, by the incessance of their prayers and by the baring of their breasts.

Germany was deceptively quiet for some time after the departure of Tiberius; but

Arminius, a chieftain of the Cherusci, was preparing trouble, and in A.D. 9 he ambushed three Roman legions in the Teutoburger Forest (north-west Germany). The Romans were marching through the thickets and swamps of the forest during a thunderstorm when the Germans hurled their volleys of javelins at them. The storm lasted all the next day and the attacks continued until the soldiers could beat them off no longer. The commanding officer, Publius Quintilius Varus, and the senior officers committed suicide; the soldiers who were not killed in the fighting were crucified, buried alive or sacrificed to the German gods.

Between A.D. 14 and 17 Germanicus made one more attempt to subdue the territory between the Rhine and the Elbe. But operations were rendered difficult by the wooded and marshy nature of the country, and the enemy general, Arminius, took full advantage of these conditions.

However, eventually at Idistaviso on the Weser (west of Hanover) Germanicus defeated Arminius. Like Henry V at Agincourt, on the eve of the battle Germanicus disguised himself and wandered about the camp incognito. He discovered that although the morale of his men was very low at least they were devoted to him. During the night an enemy soldier rode up to the Roman stockade and promised any deserter a wife, land and money. The Romans indignantly shouted back that they would help themselves to German women and land after the morrow's battle. When next morning Germanicus addressed his troops before battle was joined, he instructed them in the best tactics to adopt against the German foe, and raised their morale by promising victory.

Idistaviso was a plain curving between the Weser and the hills, with a forest in rear. Tacitus describes the battle thus:

> The Germans occupied the plain and the outskirts of the forest. The Cherusci alone occupied the heights waiting to charge down when the battle started. The Roman army moved forward in the following order: first, Gallic and German auxiliaries followed by unmounted bowmen; next, four Roman brigades [legions] and Germanicus with two battalions [cohorts] of the Guard and picked cavalry; then four more brigades, each brought by light infantry and mounted bowmen to divisional strength, and the remaining auxiliary battalions. The troops were alert and ready to deploy from column of march into battle order.
>
> Units of the Cherusci charged impetuously. Seeing this, Germanicus ordered his best cavalry to attack their flank, while the rest of the cavalry . . . was to ride round and attack them in the rear; and he himself would be there at the right moment. He saw a splendid omen – eight eagles flying into the forest. 'Forward,' he cried, 'follow the birds of Rome . . .!' The infantry attacked, and the cavalry, which had been sent ahead, charged the enemy's flanks and rear . . .
>
> The Cherusci . . . began to be dislodged from the slopes: among them Arminius, striking, shouting, wounded, trying to keep the battle going. His full force was thrown against the bowmen . . . by sheer physical strength . . . he got through. To avoid recognition he had smeared his face with his own blood . . . The rest were massacred. Many tried to swim the Weser. They were battered by javelins, or carried away by the current, or finally overwhelmed by the mass of fugitives and collapse of the river banks. Some ignominiously tried to escape by climbing trees. As they cowered among the branches, bowmen amused themselves by shooting them down . . . The slaughter of the enemy continued from midday until dusk.

The Romans might slog and hack their way through to the Elbe, but it was clear that

Despite stern measures, such as the execution of prisoners, the Romans never subjugated the Germanic tribes

Germany would never submit passively to their rule, and after the semi-victorious campaigns of Germanicus they retired to the Rhine, where the frontier could more easily be held. This failure of Roman arms, and the fact that Roman civilization did not penetrate to Germany, was of profound significance for the whole development of German, and hence European, history.

After the death of Augustus in A.D. 14 only two new additions of territory were made to the empire: Britain, and Dacia (modern Rumania). In A.D. 43 Aulus Plautius landed in Britain at Richborough with four legions and auxiliaries. After two days of battle the Britons were driven back across the Thames, and the city of Camulodunum (modern Colchester) was captured. Later the emperor Claudius (41–54) came over with more troops and some elephants, and gradually southern Britain as far as the Fosse Way from Lincoln to Exeter was subdued.

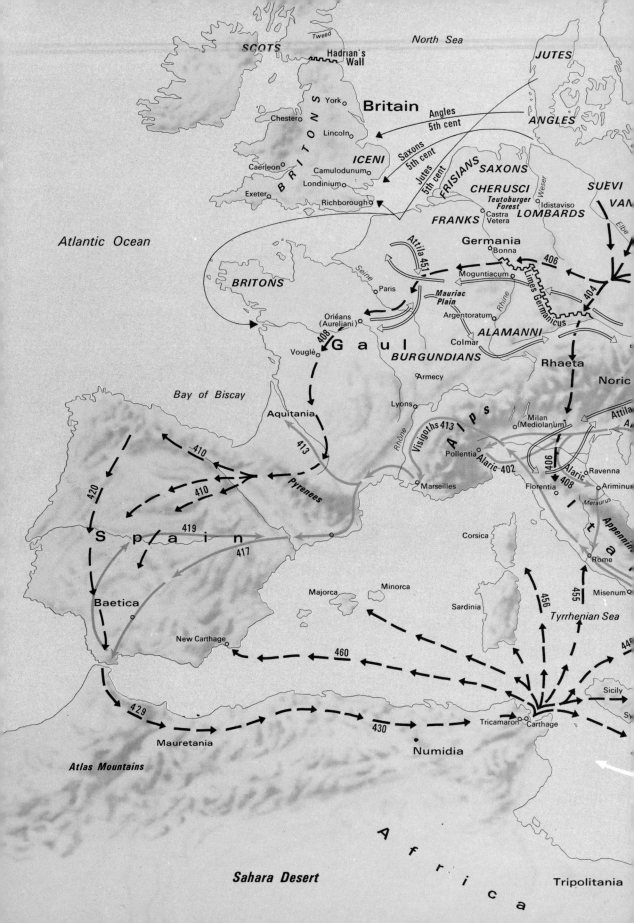

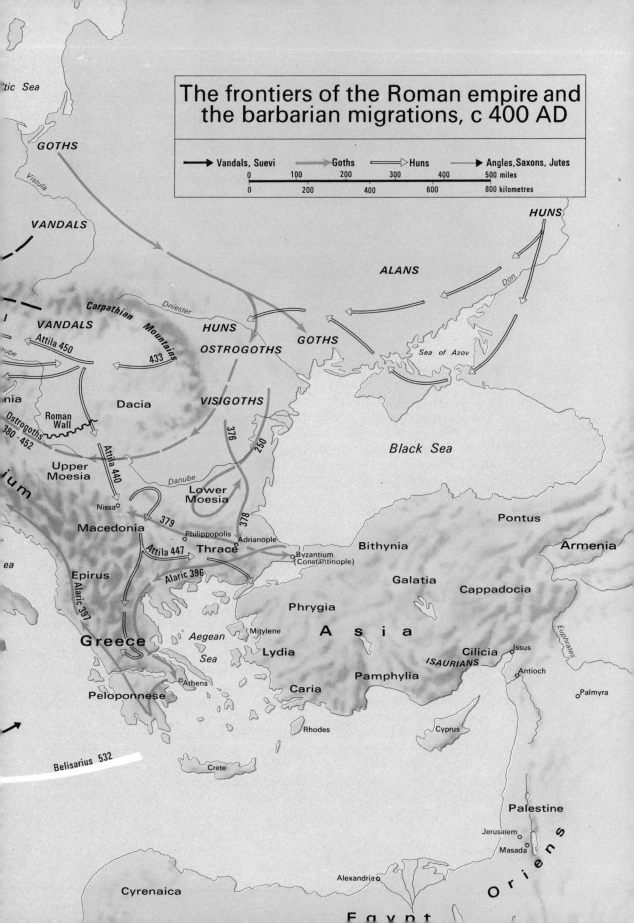

The frontiers of the Roman empire and the barbarian migrations, c 400 AD

Vandals, Suevi →   Goths →   Huns ⇨   Angles, Saxons, Jutes →

0   100   200   300   400   500 miles

0   200   400   600   800 kilometres

ltic Sea

GOTHS

Vistula

VANDALS

HUNS

VANDALS

ALANS

Carpathian Mountains

Dniester

Don

HUNS

Attila 450

433

OSTROGOTHS

GOTHS

Sea of Azov

nia

Dacia

VISIGOTHS

be

Ostrogoths
380 - 452

Roman
Wall

376

250

Black Sea

Upper
Moesia

Attila 440

Danube

ium

Nissa

379

Lower
Moesia

378

Pontus

Macedonia

Philippopolis

Adrianople

Bithynia

Armenia

Attila 447

Thrace

Byzantium
(Constantinople)

Epirus

Alaric 396

Galatia

Cappadocia

Alaric 397

Phrygia

Euphrates

Greece

Aegean
Sea

Mitylene

A s i a

Cilicia

Issus

ea

Lydia

ISAURIANS

Antioch

Peloponnese

Athens

Caria

Pamphylia

Palmyra

Rhodes

Cyprus

Belisarius 532

Crete

Palestine

Jerusalem

Masada

Oriens

Cyrenaica

Alexandria

Egypt

Under Domitian, the Dacians, led by Decebalus, became dangerously powerful on the Danube frontier, and in 87 annihilated a Roman force. The emperor Trajan (98–117), a Spaniard, decided that the only way to deal with Decebalus was by conquest, which he carried out in two campaigns: in 101 and 105–6. Dacia was always a most difficult province to hold since it lay on the other side of the Danube in the natural path of a series of barbarian movements, and in about 273 the emperor Aurelian abandoned it.

Between 66 and 73 there was a revolt in Palestine. Since the Jews were ferocious guerrilla fighters, and since some of their fortifications were, in the opinion of Sidney Toy, 'the finest works of military architecture at . . . the beginning of our era', it taxed all the available skill and resource of Rome to deal with them. Jerusalem was fortified with a triple belt of walls: the outer one 15 feet thick, 30 feet high, battlemented and strengthened at frequent intervals with large square towers. The siege equipment of the Romans, however, was on a corresponding scale. Titus used engines which could hurl stones of 1 cwt to a distance of a quarter of a mile, and he had three siege-towers 60 feet high and covered with iron plates. The walls were taken one after the other, and in August 70 the Temple was burned and the inhabitants of Jerusalem were massacred – a disastrous moment for Jewish religion and nationhood. But the Jewish revolt was not yet crushed; the last of the guerrillas held out till 73 in the stronghold of Masada. This fortress was strikingly like a medieval castle, with its rectangular keep near the curtain wall of an extensive bailey. When the Romans entered Masada they found that all the defenders and their families had killed each other rather than be taken alive.

As the frontiers became secure in the first century A.D. and as the armies became defensive garrisons rather than field forces, so the military camps of the Romans became more elaborate and permanent. In the reign of Augustus the walls of the camps on the Rhine were earthworks; by the time of the Flavians (70–96) they were built of stone. The layout of a military town was interesting. The walls formed a rectangular enclosure; they were surrounded by one or more ditches, and strengthened with towers. There was a gate in each wall. In the centre of the camp, facing the main gate, stood the administrative buildings and residence of the commanding officer, and the chief store houses. The camp was crossed by two streets at right angles to each other, and a road ran right round it immediately inside the walls. The main area was filled with blocks of barracks, and generally a market-place.

Between 70 and 130, during the reigns of Vespasian, Domitian and Hadrian, the main work of consolidating the fortifications of the frontier was undertaken, although the Roman 'iron curtain' was not completed until the early years of the third century. On the German frontier a line of fortifications stretched for 300 miles between the Rhine and Danube. The western part of this *Limes Germanicus* consisted of an earthen mound and a ditch; the eastern part, known as the Devil's Wall, was a stone wall 4 feet thick; both parts were reinforced by numerous signal towers and camps built of stone. Similar *limites* were constructed along the eastern and southern borders of the empire, and in the north of Britain.

The occupation and fortification of Britain may be regarded as typical of Roman military policy in a frontier province. South-eastern Britain offered little resistance to conquest; but the Fosse Way was only a road and therefore not a satisfactory frontier, and the Roman advance beyond this line proved difficult. Under the leadership of Caractacus the Welsh resisted the Romans for thirty years. In 61 Boadicea, the widow of

An incident from a Danubian campaign: Roman infantry adopt a *testudo* formation

a chieftain of the Iceni, led a savage uprising in East Anglia; this was brutally put down, and Boadicea, defeated, took poison. Between 80 and 84 Agricola, the Roman governor, pushed forward into the far north of England and into Scotland. He won a decisive victory at the Mons Graupius (somewhere in Perthshire) over the combined Caledonian tribes, who foolishly took on the Romans in open battle rather than relying on guerrilla fighting. After Agricola's recall the Romans retired south of the Tweed. No tenable frontier had yet been established, and between 115 and 120 a great revolt in northern Britain shook the Romans badly.

Hadrian himself came to Britain to deal with this revolt, and at last he established a frontier. Hadrian's Wall, built between 122 and 125, stretches for seventy-three miles from Tyne to Solway. Built of stone with a concrete core, at most parts it is $7\frac{1}{2}$ feet thick, though at some points it is more. In Roman times the height to the wall-walk was probably about 15 feet. As well as being sited at the shortest distance across the country, the wall follows a naturally defensible line: for long distances running along the top of high ridges, with precipitous slopes on the northern side. On lower ground, to give added strength, a ditch was dug. It was further strengthened by sixteen forts at intervals of approximately four miles. At every Roman mile (a thousand paces) there was a mile-castle between the forts, and between the mile-castles the wall was again divided into three sections by turrets which served as signal stations.

Hadrian's Wall was more a deterrent than a defence. It could not have checked a large-scale invasion, but it was a difficult obstacle to petty raids and provided a good sentry walk. Considerable disorder still remained in northern Britain during the second century; in particular there were two great revolts, in 158–60 and again in 183. But between 208 and 211 the emperor Septimius Severus was in Britain, and he restored the security of the northern frontier lands, with the result that the third century was a peaceful period in Britain.

Forts were constructed along the frontiers of the empire

Britain had been conquered by four legions; after 85 she was garrisoned by three legions and 35–40,000 auxiliaries. The legions were each based on a fortress: Caerleon-on-Usk, Chester and York. When required, detachments were sent out from these centres: for example, as expeditionary forces or to build fortifications. To regulate and police the province there was also a whole network of small forts, in size between two and seven acres, each garrisoned by 500 to 1,000 auxiliaries. Most of these were in the north of England and Wales, sited along important roads or at strategic points about fifteen or twenty miles apart.

The province had a network of roads, most of which had been built by the army for military purposes. For example, in the north there were three main routes. One ran north from York to the lower Tyne, Carbridge, Newcastle and Shields; a second diverged from this at Catterick Bridge and ran to Carlisle; a third passed from Chester northwards into the Lake District and then branched through Cumberland, Westmor-

Hadrian's Wall marked the limits of Roman power in Britain

land and west Northumberland. The building of the famous Roman roads was one of the most important and enduring achievements of the Roman army, and throughout the period of the empire this activity continued unabated in all the provinces. In this way, above all, the army contributed to unification in the areas under Roman rule, and to the spread of civilization.

In the first two centuries of the empire the total size of the imperial army fluctuated only slightly. The distribution of the army depended upon the military and political situation throughout the Roman world: the legions being moved from point to point and concentrated where they were needed. Hadrian (117–35) made important changes in the workings of the Augustan system. From his reign onwards locally raised *auxilia* were used for the first line of frontier defence, and the legions were located further back, in garrisons linked with the front by good roads.

In theory, in the first century the legions were recruited from Roman citizens only, and served in a different part of the empire from that in which they were raised. But in practice the convenience of recruiting the legions in areas where they were stationed proved irresistible. The citizenship was granted to all who would enlist and, after Hadrian's changes, a legion would consist almost entirely of soldiers recruited in its area of service. During the second century the distinction between *auxilia* and legions died out.

It was in some way an advantage to defend vulnerable areas on the frontiers with troops familiar with the district, because it meant that they were defending their own homes. But there were two dangers in such a policy. First, the idea of imperial unity could be lost, as the troops on one frontier had no contact with those on another. The worst instance of this occurred in 69, when different armies rose up and struck down three candidates for the emperorship before a fourth, Vespasian, secured the position, backed by the armies of the east and the Danube. Secondly, it could happen that the garrison forces would degenerate into a local militia of rather idle and inefficient peasants, confident in the imperial peace and reckoning on an easy life. Quite often troops who were willing to serve in their own country were unwilling to be posted elsewhere. The legions of the eastern frontier were notoriously inefficient and indisciplined.

Corbulo, a Roman commander in the east, restored discipline by severe measures. Stealing and physical unfitness were punished by flogging administered by a centurion, desertion was punished by death, and the army was toughened in a winter campaign in the Armenian highlands. The most severe punishment which could be inflicted was decimation of a unit; this was very rare, but in the year 20 Apronius, the governor of Africa, had every tenth man of a battalion which had run away in battle flogged to death. Units which had disgraced themselves might be disbanded altogether. Vespasian cashiered four legions which had lost their eagles or had joined in the revolt on the Rhine led by the Batavian chieftain Civilis in 69, and he raised two new legions in their place. At the other end of the disciplinary scale a centurion might lose his rank, or a soldier be required to parade all day outside the orderly room. Hadrian in particular fought against luxury and the lowering of standards in the army; but at the same time he reorganized the leisure of the soldiers to make life more pleasant, and improved their legal position and economic status.

The army offered a secure but dull life. The normal term of service was twenty years, during the last four of which a man served as a veteran in the reserve, being excused the more arduous camp duties. Good pay and pensions were provided from the *aerarium militare*, the military budget instituted by Augustus. A soldier could possibly live off five-sevenths of his pay; he had to buy his own food, weapons and uniform, and contribute to the funds of the annual camp dinner and the soldiers' burial fund; but there was little opportunity to spend the remainder unless he dabbled illicitly in trade. He was encouraged to use the camp bank, where his savings were likely to be supplemented by occasional imperial bonuses. Soldiers of the rank of centurion and below were not supposed to marry, but many of them formed unions with women and these were tolerated.

There were various military awards and decorations. A victorious commander would be permitted to hold a triumphal procession in Rome. The Civic Crown was the coveted award for valour in the Roman army; Tiberius awarded it, for example, in 20 to Rufus

Helvius, a private soldier who had saved a comrade's life during a battle in Africa. A *corona vallaris* might be awarded to the first man over the enemy's wall, and a *corona aurea* to a centurion for bravery on the field of battle. Other decorations included a silver spearhead or a miniature silver standard for officers, and bracelets, necklaces and embossed discs for the privates.

Vegetius, a military writer, describes the peace routine of a legion. Three times a month the infantry did a ten-mile route march, varying the rate of marching so as to give practice in rapid advances and retirements. During field training, open order fighting was given great prominence, and tactics suitable for repelling sudden attacks and ambushes were practised. Considerable emphasis was laid on arms drill and barrack-square drill generally, as being an aid to discipline.

Although military activities at no time ceased, the second century saw the fulfilment of the ideal of Augustus. It was the period of the *Pax Romana*. Gibbon indeed considered that 'if a man were called to fix the period in the history of the world during which the condition of the human race was most happy and prosperous, he would, without hesitation, name that which elapsed from the death of Domitian to the accession of Commodus' (96–180). But by the end of the century things were altering. The death of Commodus in 192 was followed by a struggle for the throne. Pertinax was murdered by the Praetorians, who elevated in his place Didius Julianus. There was yet another candidate in the person of Septimus Severus, governor of Pannonia, and eventually he secured the throne for himself because he was the best soldier among the aspirants, whom he defeated in battles at Issus and Lyons.

From the time of Severus the army was the chief and, indeed, the disastrous force in Roman politics. To maintain his power every emperor in the third century had to bribe and pamper the soldiers. Severus increased their pay by one third, allowed the soldiers to marry and to farm their own plots of land around the camps, and accorded the centurions certain new social privileges. His dying advice to his son Caracalla was to enrich the soldiers and disregard the rest, and that was exactly what Caracalla did. In the sixty years following the death of Commodus no less than twenty-one emperors rose and fell. It was a period of anarchy and misery, during which the army terrorized the civil life of the empire while becoming demoralized and inefficient, and the security of the frontiers was lost for ever. A disastrous inflation was largely caused by the continual increases in pay which the emperors had to give the army if they were to keep their thrones.

Hadrian's army reforms had been of doubtful benefit. The troops who were now stationed permanently in the same frontier areas were enlisted mainly from the local farmers, who paid as little attention as possible to their military duties. Furthermore, the defensive strategy of armed forces strung out along the frontiers was unsuccessful; they were weak everywhere and strong nowhere; there was no defence in depth, and no reserves were kept for counter-attack. By 250 the fighting qualities of the legions was deteriorating; imaginative tactics were needed to deal with new enemies who fought in ways strange to the Roman soldiery: and these were lacking. However, three emperors in the second half of the third century, Gallienus, Aurelian and Diocletian, reformed the army and pulled the empire together again. It was an Augean task but carried out in no uncertain way, and when completed it enabled the empire to hold out against final ruin for almost another two centuries.

Stern measures were taken to restore order and discipline both in civil and military affairs, and under Diocletian civil government took on a stronger military character. Furthermore the Roman army began to assume a barbarian character; senators were excluded from it, and, since plagues had caused a serious manpower problem, Aurelian took the momentous step of forming *auxilia* from among the Vandals and Alamanni, the Germanic tribes which were pressing most heavily on the northern frontier. The barbarians were to conquer the empire as much by infiltration as by force. The emperors had a bodyguard of German soldiers, and German troops were allowed to keep their native fighting dress and traditions. The eagle standards of Rome were replaced by barbarian dragons. As another method of maintaining the numbers of the army, sons were compelled to follow their fathers as soldiers – the army, in fact, became a hereditary caste – and the conscription laws were revived. Diocletian enormously increased the nominal size of the army – to sixty legions, although most of them soon fell below their nominal strength of 6,000 men. Road buildings and fortifications were energetically kept up.

Gallienus realized the strategical mistake of the garrison policy of the previous 250 years. At the cost of permanently weakening the frontier forces, he created reserve armies based on northern Italy which provided defence in depth and could be used for counter-attack in an emergency. The long-established tactical traditions were discarded and reforms ordered which were more suited for dealing with new enemies, whose tactics were generally sudden cavalry attacks or long-range missile fire. Gallienus took the decisive step of relegating the legions to a subordinate position, and making cavalry the 'queen of the battlefield'. In 258 he formed corps of Dalmatian horsemen and Moorish mounted javelin-men who rode bareback. Further variety was added to Roman arms by an increasing reliance on oriental archers, particularly the Osrhoënians with their powerful nomadic composite bow. There were also corps which used the long Iranian thrusting spear, barbarian infantry who fought in wedge formation, a camel corps, and heavy cavalry of the Parthian and Persian type. The throwing spear and short thrusting sword of the legionaries were replaced by the lance and long slashing swords of the barbarians.

This military overhaul came none too soon, for pressure on the frontiers was building up to an unprecedented intensity. The rise of the Sassanid Persian empire threatened to deprive Rome of all her eastern provinces. The low point of Roman imperial prestige came in 260 when Valerian was captured by the Persian ruler Shapur. Fortunately Odenathus, governor of Palmyra, succeeded in repelling the Persian forces. But the situation was even worse on the northern frontier. The period of the barbarian migrations had begun.

After Caesar's conquest of Gaul the old Celtic power in central and western Europe had crumbled, leaving a power vacuum both north and east of the Roman frontier. Into this area new peoples began to move, at first from Scandinavia, driven probably by climatic changes and over-population. But these people themselves were, by the third century, being driven further south and west by a new influx of migratory peoples from Asia. The Franks and the Alamanni burst across the Rhine, and the Goths pressed south over the Danube. The Ostrogoths (east Goths) overran the Balkans, sacked Philippopolis, and defeated and killed the Emperor Decius in battle in 251. Dacia was lost for ever to Rome, but in 268 Claudius won a great victory over the Goths at Nissa (modern Nish) and checked their advance. Farther west the Alamanni, after crossing the Rhine, pushed south into Italy itself, until Gallienus defeated them at Milan in 258. They again attacked in the reign of Aurelian, but after an initial defeat the emperor raised a new army and destroyed the Alamannic army at the Metaurus. By the almost superhuman efforts of these emperors the barbarians were thus checked, and with the newly strengthened army the empire remained relatively secure for almost another century.

During the fourth century, in the reign of Constantine (306–37), two important developments took place. Proclaimed emperor at York, Constantine had to defeat various political rivals before he could install himself at Rome. One afternoon in 312, on his march to Italy, somewhere between Colmar and Saxa Rubra, it is said that he saw in the sky a bright cross, and above it the words *Hoc vince*: 'Herein conquer'. In a dream that night Christ told him to take the sign for his standard. Thus inspired, by a skilful flank march Constantine forced his enemy Maxentius to fight with the Tiber behind him at the Milvian Bridge. He won an overwhelming victory, and thereafter took the Christian sign as his own helmet badge and put it on the shields of his soldiers. Constantine then proclaimed toleration for Christianity, and later in the century Theodosius (379–95) made it the official religion of the empire. The issue of religion was to be a further cause of antagonism between the barbarians and the empire, for they were almost all heretical Arian Christians (disciples of Arius, a deacon from Antioch, who died in 336).

The other important development at this time was the foundation by Constantine of a second imperial capital, better placed strategically to resist the barbarian invaders, called Constantinople, or Byzantium. From that time until 476 there were usually two emperors, one in each capital; after that Constantinople became the sole capital of the Roman empire.

It is arguable that, fundamentally, the fall of the Roman empire was not a military phenomenon. Economic weakness and the withering of the cities, the fall in population, the assimilation of provincial and barbarian culture, the adoption of Christianity, and the establishment of a new imperial capital at Constantinople: all these were deeper causes and more significant symptoms of the passing of ancient Rome. But all the same, some of the most unmistakable landmarks in the process were military.

The key events in the military collapse of Rome were the defeat of the emperor Valens by the Goths at Adrianople in 378, the first sack of Rome by Alaric the Visigoth in 410, the second sack by the Vandals under Geiseric in 455, and the deposition of the last western Roman emperor, Romulus Augustulus, in 476 by the Herul chieftain Odovacar. The Goths were a people of Teutonic race – barbarians, who came originally from Sweden, settled first in the area of the Vistula, and later moved southwards towards Pannonia (modern Hungary) and the valley of the Danube. As the different barbarian peoples (primarily Goths and Vandals) overran the provinces of the empire, lured by the civilization and wealth of Rome and driven from behind by the Huns, it became clear that the military power of Rome, upon which all else depended, was at an end – at any rate in the west.

The fate of Britain was characteristic of what happened to the outlying Roman provinces in this age. After its pacification by Severus between 208 and 211 the country remained pretty well unmolested by invaders for 150 years. But it was one of the most rebellious provinces during the imperial anarchy of the third century, and in the next century Britain produced her own soldier candidates for the emperorship. Just before 350, Picts from the north and Scots (Irish) from the north-west began to be a serious nuisance, but in 368 Theodosius (the father of the emperor) cleared the country as far north as Hadrian's Wall. But now the Saxons were raiding heavily from across the North Sea and, from being raids with the object of pillage, these expeditions soon grew into invasions with the object of settlement. The native 'Roman' troops were hard pressed. Forts were built along the coasts of Sussex and Yorkshire, but to no avail; even the Orkneys, according to one contemporary, were 'moist from the slain Saxon'. In 406–7 a great horde of barbarians crossed the Rhine into Gaul, and Britain was thus cut off from contact with the Mediterranean. At about the same time Rome abandoned Britain, ceasing to send out officials or to organize military activities.

The Franks were probably a confederation of the north German tribes which Tacitus had described. They travelled the shortest distance of any of the migratory peoples and settled in Gaul or France, finally establishing their occupation by a victory over the Visigoths at Vouglé (near Poitiers) in 507. These people, and several others, the Burgundians, the Alamanni, the Saxons, the Langobardi (eventually Lombards) were all much alike. The same Celtic armourers on the Rhine and the Danube may indeed have made iron weapons for them all. Many of their swords were beautifully decorated with similar motifs: birds of prey, or elongated interlacing snake-like animals which seemed to devour themselves. The long slashing sword was their most valued weapon, but metal was rare, and maybe only chieftains had swords. Good weapons were passed on from generation to generation, and the most famous of them, such as Arthur's sword Excalibur, feature prominently in the sagas of the peoples. Mail armour was also highly prized, but very costly. The great weapon of the Langobards was the broadsword, but they also used lances, some so strong that when the victim had been run through he could be held aloft, wriggling on the end. Another very popular weapon was the 'sax', a short, broad, slightly curved single-edged weapon, the ancestor of the sabre. The northern peoples also fought with spears up to 11 feet long. The shields of the chiefs were often highly decorated, and some of them were quartered in a way which anticipated medieval heraldry. The helmets were more or less skull caps made of bands of metal; some had neck and cheek guards, others a visor, and others again were adorned with beasts' heads. The Franks used another weapon too: a short light throwing-axe.

Such weapons could not be afforded by every man of the tribe. The mass fought, almost as in the time of Tacitus, protected by leather caps and by round shields of wood or wicker covered with hide, and armed with a lance or club. Most of the migratory peoples preferred to fight on horseback, but the Franks fought as a horde of undisciplined and ill-armed infantry, the only mounted men being the king's guard. Their army was divided roughly into units: hundreds, thousands and clans. The most common battle formation was the V-shaped wedge. They fortified themselves with circular ramparts on the hills, and in the plains with leaguers of locked wagons. Physically they appeared formidable to the Mediterranean peoples; Sidonius wrote that the Burgundians were 7 feet high, greased their hair with rancid butter, ate vast quantities, and spoke in stentorian voices.

Some of these peoples were good seafarers; the pirate ships of the Saxons, with their leather sails, were the terror of the British coasts. Among the maritime tribes, boats evolved from dugouts holding thirty men to plank-built galleys of the Viking type which held over a hundred. The Vandals, having travelled farther than any other people, from the Baltic in the first century, through Gaul and Spain (they gave their name to Andalusia), and to North Africa by 429, dominated the western Mediterranean with their piratical fleets – as the Barbary corsairs were to do from the same seaboard in a later period. In 455, led by Geiseric, they sailed up the Tiber with their galleys and fire-ships and sacked Rome. The Romans had long since lost their naval supremacy in the Mediterranean, and it was far too late when a law was passed at Constantinople forbidding the teaching of ship-building to the barbarians on pain of death. Between 253 and 267 the Goths had carried their raids by sea into Greece and Asia Minor, and already by then Rome could find ships only by borrowing them from the commercial ports of the eastern Mediterranean.

The Goths were the first of the migratory peoples to smite the empire; it was they who penetrated to its heart and who are of most significance in the history of the art of war. In 376 the Visigoths (west Goths) under a new pitch of pressure from the Huns, besought the emperor Valens to allow them to settle within the empire; he allowed them to cross the Danube from Dacia and settle in lower Moesia (Bulgaria), on condition that they disarmed. But then the Ostrogoths (east Goths) made the same request, and this time the emperor, fearful of the numbers of the barbarians, refused. They crossed the Danube nonetheless, armed to the teeth, and the Visigoths rose up to join them. Valens met the Goths at Adrianople in 378.

It was a terrible battle. The imperial army came upon the Goths encamped in a vast wagon leaguer. Despite the changed character of the Roman army and all that should have been learnt from experience of fighting the barbarians, Valens drew up his forces in the historic Roman fashion, with the legions massed in the centre and the squadrons of auxiliary horse on the wings. It being reported that all the enemy were in the leaguer, Valens attacked. But he did not know that the bulk of the Gothic horsemen were away foraging; they were quickly recalled and formed together, and, as the battle raged, they charged down on the Roman left, 'like a thunderbolt which strikes upon a mountain top and dashes away all that stands in its path'. The Roman cavalry on the left disintegrated instantly, and the Goths crashed on to roll up the infantry. The right fled, and the legions were crushed together in the centre by the cavalry of the Goths from the left and their infantry in front. The Roman infantry, thus left on the field to their fate, were cut down as they stood, so packed together that they could not move.

A total disaster for the Roman empire, the battle of Adrianople is also of great significance as the first victory of heavy cavalry over infantry. The success of the Parthians and the reforms of Gallienus had hinted at the future, but it was the Gothic horsemen who first crossed the threshold of medieval warfare. From then on, until the English archers and the Swiss pikemen challenged them in the fourteenth century, heavy cavalry were to be supreme in Europe. The advent of medieval warfare was due more to the barbarians than to the Romans. The heavily armoured knight with his lance, his retainers, and the characteristic features of his warfare (chivalry and heraldry), derived from the barbarians and was in opposition to the whole Roman infantry tradition.

The Gothic cavalry had developed into this formidable power for two reasons. First, in the long period of their migration through the plains of southern Russia and central Europe they had become splendid horsemen. Secondly, they possessed a vital piece of

Heavy cavalry, riding with the aid of a stirrup, were introduced from the East

equestrian equipment, the stirrup. Only with this support could the heavy cavalryman keep his seat in the saddle, bearing the weight of his armour and the shock of the lance's impact. The stirrup probably originated in the east as early as the fourth century B.C., and horsemen riding with stirrup loops are depicted in Buddhist sculptures of the second century B.C. It was brought to the west, together with a stronger type of horse, by the Scythians and Sarmatians from Asia in the first century A.D. The Goths displaced the Sarmatians during the next century, and combined Sarmatian military techniques with their own energy, ferocity and efficiency as they launched their attack on the Roman empire. After Adrianople the Byzantines began to model their fighting methods on those of the Goths, and the emperors finally discarded the infantry legions. The emperor Maurice emphasized the value of the stirrup for cavalry in his treatise on 'The Art of War' in 590.

The Goths, it seemed, could not be resisted by force; therefore the Romans fell back on the doubtful policy of assimilating them on suitable terms, and playing them off against other barbarian peoples. The western Roman armies, commanded by a very able Vandal general, Stilicho, succeeded in 397 in driving the Visigoths, led by Alaric,

out of Greece. But Alaric merely turned into Italy. Stilicho even managed to get the
better of Alaric with an infantry army in an encounter at Pollentia in northern Italy in
402, and four years later he surrounded 20,000 Langobards at Florence and forced them
to surrender. But again hordes of tribesmen – Suevi, Vandals, Heruls and the like –
were being forced over the Alps by the Huns, and there was a general movement
southwards. The emperor Honorius foolishly murdered Stilicho, and a massacre
provoked the 30,000 Gothic mercenaries in the imperial army to mutiny. In 410, 800
years after the first sack of Rome by the Celtic barbarians in 390 B.C., Alaric captured
the city. Although, according to Gibbon, 'the want of youth, or beauty, or chastity, protected the greatest part of the Roman women from the danger of a rape', and although
the Goths being Christians respected some of the religious treasures, the damage and
shock of the sack was tremendous.

For some years after 410 there was a lull in warfare. The Vandals established themselves in Africa, the Burgundians in Burgundy, the Franks in northern France, and the
Visigoths having pillaged Italy came to terms with the emperor and moved on to found
kingdoms in Spain and south-west Gaul. It seemed that the peoples of Europe could
draw breath. But then, in the middle of the fifth century, the most terrible invasion of all
fell on the Mediterranean world. Under a great khan, Attila, 'the scourge of God', the
Huns were organized into a vast army and given an objective.

For centuries this Mongol people of horsemen had been on the move. The Chinese
had known them as the Hiung-nu, and, under the Han dynasty between 207 B.C. and
A.D. 39, had repelled their attempts at invasion and sent them westwards. They were
feared with loathing and revulsion by all the peoples of the west who knew them,
barbarian and Roman alike. The Scandinavian and German barbarians at least invaded
the Roman empire with the object of enjoying it; the sole object of the Huns in their
random raids on the west, as with their lineal descendants the Mongols, appeared to be
to destroy. In the past the disorganized Huns had fought sometimes for the barbarians –
there were Huns with the Gothic army at Adrianople – and sometimes even as Roman
auxilia, and only the pressure of their numbers had actually caused wars. But now,
deliberately, unitedly and systematically, the Asiatics made war against the Europeans.

Ammianus Marcellinus, a contemporary soldier, described his impressions of the
Huns:

The nation of the Huns . . . surpasses all other barbarians in wildness of life . . . They all . . .
have strong and well-knit limbs and fine necks. Yet they are of portentous ugliness and so crook-
backed that you would take them for some sort of two-footed beasts.

Wandering at large . . . they are trained to bear from their infancy all the extremes of cold, of
hunger, and of thirst . . . They are almost welded to their horses, which are hardy, though of
ugly shape, and on which they sometimes ride women's fashion. On horseback every man of that
nation lives night and day . . . on horseback he takes his meat and drink, and when night comes
he leans forward upon the narrow neck of his horse and there falls into a deep sleep . . .

When attacked, they will sometimes engage in regular battle. Then, going into the fight in order
of columns, they fill the air with varied and disordered cries. More often, however, they fight in
no regular order of battle, but being extremely swift and sudden in their movements, they disperse, and then rapidly come together again in loose array . . . It must be owned that they are
the nimblest of warriors . . .

The Huns were probably not, in fact, as numerous as they seemed. Their ferocity and ugliness, which made them seem diabolical or subhuman, were a valuable psychological weapon of war. Above all, their incredible mobility, both as a migrant nation on a continual war footing and as a tactical force, made them devastating. They had horses which could gallop twenty miles at a stretch and a hundred miles in a day. Superb horsemanship in rapid charges and retreats, and clouds of arrows, proved too much even for the Gothic cavalry. Their principal weapon was the bow. According to Lattimore, the composite bow of the steppe horseman 'is notably short for its great power and is made of horn – a steppe material – and short pieces of wood spliced double'. The Huns were amazingly accurate marksmen. They also used iron swords; these were probably looted or bartered from the European peoples, since they themselves had no opportunity to do metal work. A notable tactic in close fighting was for one man to entangle the enemy soldier with a lasso or a net while he was intent on parrying the sword blows of another. They hardly bothered with armour, though a few did carry shields.

Attila became ruler of the Hunnic empire in 433, and he soon exercized a loose sway over the Ostrogoths and Slavs between the Don and the Danube, and over the German tribes on the Danube and further west. For some years he was content to ravage his empire, receive tribute and bribes from the peoples on the edge of it, and hire out the Huns as mercenaries. But between 440 and 447 he invaded the Balkans. When resistance stiffened there, Attila began to look farther west. At Easter 451 the Huns crossed the Lower Rhine on rafts and advanced on Orléans. The Visigoths of Aquitaine joined with the Romans under Aëtius, and at a battle on the Mauriac Plain (Champagne) they repelled the Huns and their subject-allies, the Langobards, the Heruls and the Ostrogoths. Nothing certain is known of the battle except, as was written, that it was *atrox multiplex immane pertinax* ('savage and tenacious, complex and vast'). Aëtius did not follow up his victory, for fear that if the Huns were destroyed the Visigoths would become too powerful. As a result, the following year, Attila invaded northern Italy. But he was checked by famine, disease, imperial reinforcements from the east, and the diplomacy of Pope Leo I. In 453 Attila took a new wife, and died as a result of a blood-vessel burst during his wedding night. As Chaucer later commented:

> Loke, Attila, the grete conquerour,
> Deyde in his sleep, with shame and dishonour,
> Bledinge ay at the nose in dronkenesse;
> A capitayn shoulde live in sobrenesse.

It would seem that the episode of the Hunnic invasions, although undoubtedly sensational, was made into a melodrama. Had the forces of Europe combined sooner to fight the Huns, they would have shaken them off easily by force of numbers. The armies that opposed them in the Balkans, and the army that eventually did beat them, were hurriedly assembled forces of motley and indifferent troops. Attila fought at the Mauriac Plain on ground of his own choosing which should have suited the style of warfare of the Huns. He must have had a very remarkable personality to have united such a people and to have led them for so long. He was clearly a good military leader of an Asiatic people, but when opposed by a disciplined force his generalship failed; he cannot be counted among the great captains like Jenghiz Khan.

The Hun horsemen overran the Roman empire and established the predominance of cavalry

The defeat of the Huns did not save Rome, for in 476 Odovacar, the Herul commander of a 'Roman' army composed entirely of barbarians, finally threw off all pretences and deposed Romulus Augustulus, thus ending the Roman empire of the west. He in turn was driven out by Theodoric the Ostrogoth, who established a highly civilized kingdom at Ravenna. When Theodoric died, Justinian (527–65), the emperor at Constantinople, made a bid to restore the Roman empire in the west. In the pursuit of this chimerical objective the Danube and eastern frontiers were neglected, the eastern provinces were exhausted by taxation to finance the armies of the west, and Africa, Spain and Italy were subjected to twenty years of warfare. But the wars produced one outstanding general: Belisarius.

The Byzantine army had for some time been adapting itself to be able to compete in the new era of Gothic warfare. It was formed almost entirely out of mercenaries from the various barbarian tribes, and consisted mostly of cavalry, with a few units of heavy infantry. Belisarius had passed through the imperial cadet school with distinction, and received a commission in the Guards. In the 520's he set about training an *élite* corps of heavy cavalry armed with both bow and lance, trained to be skirmishers as well as shock troops. He also armed them with feathered darts which were thrown by hand at close quarters. Finally, in case the lance should fail they carried a heavy broadsword. It required a lot of drill to become proficient with all four weapons and to be able to control the horse at the same time. Since two hands were needed to use the bow, Belisarius trained his men to support themselves in the saddle by the stirrups and to control the movements of the horse with their knees. The saddles were wide and comfortable. The men had a small shield strapped to the left arm, and wore sleeveless mail shirts of thigh length and tall boots of raw hide. When not in use, the bow was slung over the shoulder; the arrows were kept in a quiver next to the broadsword on the left thigh, and the twelve darts carried in a receptacle attached to the shield; the lance was carried in a leather bucket on the right side. The archery methods were copied from the Huns, and tilting with the lance from the Goths. The training exercise to improve the skill of the knight was to gallop towards a stuffed dummy hanging from a gallows. The rider had to string his bow as he approached, fire three arrows at the swaying figure, and finish the charge with the lance or darts. Pay, rations and rank were awarded according to proficiency in this and other exercises.

Before the great wars of Justinian's reign, Belisarius had learnt his profession in operations on the Danube and in the east. For example, against the Hunnic mounted archers of Bulgaria he devised an original and successful tactic. The problem was to come to close quarters with them; his solution was to tempt them with live bait: a few men on swift horses, who would draw the eager Huns into a position where their retreat could be cut off. To deal with their wagon barricades, Belisarius ordered his men to ride to windward of them and set them alight with fire arrows. For four years he had also been director of military training, and had spent that time touring the garrisons of the eastern frontier and organizing their training. In the operations against the Persians he had been notably successful. His only failure so far had been in an attempt to kill the great whale called Porphyry which was the terror of the Bosphorus, and this had only been because his sailors lost their nerve and failed to aim the catapult correctly.

In 532 Belisarius was given the command in the war against the Vandals. He set out from Byzantium with a multi-national mercenary army of 10,000 infantry and 5,000 cavalry. Most of these were mercenaries, but many were the general's own retainers and in a sense this was the first feudal army. The infantry soldiers were, on the whole, of good quality: Isaurian mountaineers trained by Belisarius himself. Among the cavalry were 600 Huns and 400 Heruls, as well as Belisarius' own Household Regiment of 1,500 cuirassiers. His chief of staff was an Armenian eunuch called Solomon, and with his headquarters went the historian of Justinian's reign, Procopius. As usual on his campaigns, Belisarius was accompanied by his wife, Antonina – a woman of sure courage and doubtful morals. The army sailed by way of Italy and Sicily in a fleet of 500 transports of different sizes, and escorted by a flotilla of 92 fast single-banked galleys, called 'dromons', decked in, and each rowed by twenty oarsmen. Belisarius impressed himself on his men as a disciplinarian by executing two Huns who had murdered a man during a drunken party.

The landing in Africa met with no resistance, and the army marched towards Carthage along well-shaded roads and through luxuriant orchards. Every night they entrenched themselves in a camp, in the ancient Roman manner. At the tenth milestone (Ad

Decimum) outside Carthage the Romans met the Vandal forces. The Vandals were good horsemen, but their cavalry fought only with lance and broadsword and their only bowmen were infantry; they could muster altogether perhaps 80,000 fighting men, but their army was far less experienced than that of Belisarius, and not so well trained.

In the first skirmish some of the Roman cavalry met a detachment of Vandal horsemen in a defile. Charging immediately they routed the Vandals, whose leader, the brother of their king Gelimer, was killed by a dart which hit him in the forehead. Meanwhile, in a nearby plain, Gelimer with a large force ran into the Huns; their showers of arrows and outlandish appearance caused the Vandals to panic. But soon the whole Vandal army assembled and occupied the defile, a strong defensive position. Belisarius, greatly outnumbered, was in a difficult situation. But then events took an improbable turn. The temperamental Gelimer, learning of the death of his brother, gave way to fits of grief and refused to take any further interest in the battle. Belisarius, quick to seize the opportunity, divided his forces into two, and sent them up the hills on either side of the defile. By repeated simultaneous volleys of arrows, followed by charges, they practically annihilated the Vandals, and on the following day Carthage surrendered. To avoid a sack, Belisarius refused to allow his troops to enter the city. Later, in December 535, Belisarius' victory of Tricamaron ensured the conquest of the Vandals in Africa.

The war was next carried into Italy. Between 535 and 540, with a force of only about 7,500 and hampered by the schemings of his enemies at the Byzantine court and by the indecision and jealousy of his emperor Justinian, Belisarius conquered the Ostrogoths. The most spectacular episode of this war was his defence of Rome. Twelve miles of walls were held by 5,000 men for a year. In 540 Ravenna surrendered; but revolt broke out almost immediately. Belisarius, and a new commander, the 80-year-old eunuch Narses, fought the Goths for another fourteen years. When peace came, it was a peace of exhaustion, and an empty victory: for Italy was too devastated to be able to defend itself against the Lombards, when they swept over the north in 565. Belisarius had done all that he could. He is the classic example of a loyal and capable soldier compelled by a second rate political chief to pursue an unrealistic strategical objective.

Justinian's reach had far exceeded his grasp. In 540 Antioch was sacked by the Persians. The drain of troops from the east hopelessly weakened that frontier, despite the massive building programme which he undertook in order to fortify the whole of the east and north-east. However, the 700 or more fortifications built by Justinian marked an enormous stride forward in military architecture. Already in the fifth century the Byzantines had built the great defences of Constantinople: a triple belt of walls and two moats, which were to resist repeated attacks until they fell for the first time in 1204. The curtain walls, baileys, dungeons, battlements and keeps of Justinian's castles were a direct inspiration to the engineers and architects of the middle ages.

The failure of Justinian's scheme of reconquest in the west finally rang down the curtain on the western Roman empire. Militarily, ethnically and culturally it had long since disappeared; now the last political illusions were dispelled. The Lombardic invasion of Italy was the last of the 'barbarian migrations'. North Africa and Visigothic Spain now awaited the invasion of the Arabs, the Franks consolidated themselves in France, and the Anglo-Saxons were firmly settled in England. The new era of medieval warfare, characterized by the heavy-armed knight and his retainers, was already two centuries old.

ETSYRIAM SOBAL · ET CONYERTIT

Under the feudal system the mounted knight developed as the chief figure on the battlefields of western Europe. A detachment of Carolingian cavalry preceded by a standard bearer.

PART TWO
MEDIEVAL WARFARE

7   Early Medieval Warfare

When the western Roman empire disintegrated, its eastern counterpart at Byzantium lived on, and its struggle for survival, first with the Arabs and later with the Turks and Bulgars, is a fascinating story. After Byzantium had got the better of the Arabs, the latter made their way across northern Africa, conquered Spain by 713, and seven years later penetrated into southern France. Then the Franks come back into prominence – the Germanic group of tribes which had moved into Roman Gaul from their original homelands in north-west Europe. Finally, in the eighth century, the Vikings began raiding down from Scandinavia into Britain and western Europe, and it was not until the tenth century that the Franks and the English finally found themselves able to deal satisfactorily with their attacks.

During these troublesome times old Europe produced many able generals to defend herself, and we shall come across some of them as we examine the period. The interesting feature to observe in the history of western European warfare between the seventh and eleventh centuries is the continued rise of cavalry: the feudal system was emerging, with the mounted knight as the main figure. There were areas, however, where infantry did not cease to be a power.

In 622 Mohammed, founder of Islam, moved with his followers from Mecca to Medina, and began the expansion of both Arabianism and Islam. The Prophet himself led 300 of his adherents in an attack on a Meccan caravan, and won the first military victory. In 628, with 1,400 followers, he imposed terms on Mecca, and added as recruits to his cause two men who were to be the great leaders of Islam on the march: Khalid ibn-al-Walid and Amr ibn-al-As. Within twelve years of Mohammed's death in 632 his disciples wrested Syria and Egypt from the Byzantine empire and an exhausted Persia was quickly overthrown. Within a hundred years the Islamic empire extended from the Aral Sea to the upper Nile, and from the confines of China to the Bay of Biscay. Before their drive was exhausted only one power was able to resist the Arabs, Byzantium – and even she lost the south-eastern part of her empire. In 636 Heraclius, the eastern emperor, sent an army of 50,000 men to meet the Arabs. At the valley of the Yarmuk, a tributary of the Jordan, Khalid confronted them with half their numbers. In one of the hottest and dustiest places in the world the Byzantines were routed and slaughtered by the people of the desert, and their frontier contracted to the Taurus mountains. Alexandria, protected by powerful walls, a garrison of 50,000 and the Byzantine fleet, fell to Amr even though he had no proper equipment or experience in siegecraft. The Berbers of Libya and Tunisia resisted the Arabs for twenty-five years, but then they were converted to Islam,

Arab conquests in the seventh and eighth centuries.

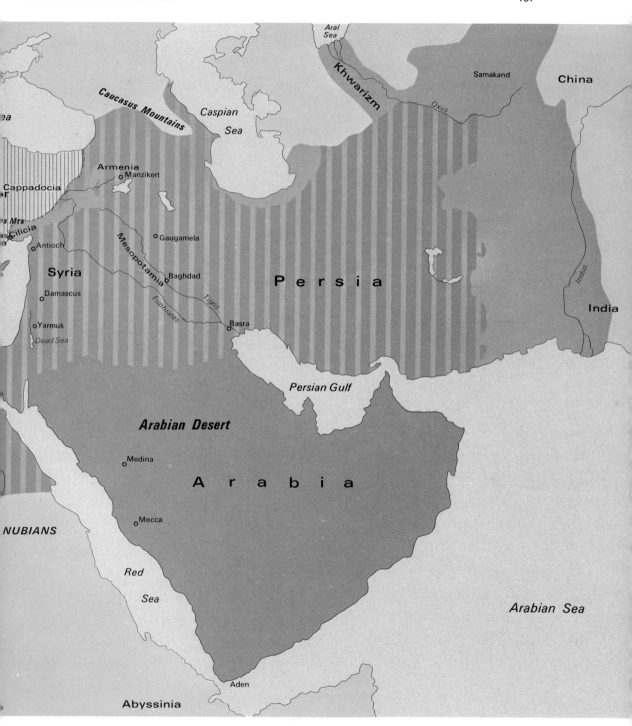

and they themselves provided the main forces of the armies which conquered Spain between 710 and 713.

The Arabs made their conquests by applying intelligently the techniques of camelry and cavalry in areas which were suitable for them, the open lands of North Africa and western Asia. But their organization and battle tactics were primitive, and their armour was poor. They usually fought in one, but sometimes two or three, closely packed lines, different tribes forming separate units. At the beginning of a battle individual champions might challenge and fight one another; this would be followed by a mass charge. It was the numbers and appearance of the Arabs which made them so formidable. As the Byzantine commander Nicephorus Phocas noted, 'they are very bold when they expect to win: they keep firm in their ranks, and stand up gallantly against the most impetuous attacks. When they think that the enemy's vigour is relaxing, they all charge together in a desperate effort.' The infantry, except for the Abyssinian archers, were inefficient and ill-armed plunderers; their strength lay in their cavalry, which in the early part of the seventh century was very lightly equipped, hence its great mobility. But in succeeding centuries the Arabs learnt many lessons from their most stubborn enemies, the Byzantines, and relied increasingly on mounted archers and lancers, protected by chain-mail shirts, helmets, shields and greaves. But the Arabian cavalry was never as heavily armoured as the Byzantine.

All in all, the best qualities of the armies of Islam lay not in equipment or organization but in morale, which was the product of religion, mobility due to camel transport, and endurance bred of hard living in the desert.

Other factors also contributed to their extraordinary drive. Success breeds success, and such an impulse did not quickly run down. But the Arabs were driven by the strongest impulses to make war. Many of them, particularly in the early stages of the conquests, were motivated by religious ardour; the crusading idea of the *jihad*, the holy war, was very real to the close followers of Mohammed. Moslems make much less distinction between Church and State than do Christians. If ever the religious impulse weakened there was still a profound cultural antagonism between the Arabs and the peoples of the Mediterranean world. A perhaps deeper cause of Arab aggression in the seventh century was economic: the old story of overcrowding in the Arabian peninsula. For some centuries southern Arabia had been becoming more arid, and the inhabitants had been drifting northwards. The Arab explosion of the seventh century was the fourth, last, and greatest of the Semitic migrations. In the traditional and natural pattern, the migrants went first for the Fertile Crescent, before overspilling towards and beyond the valleys of the Euphrates and the Nile. They conquered much farther afield than they had in ancient times, not only because they were now more numerous, but also because practically everywhere they went they were welcomed as the deliverers of subject peoples. Their tolerance, humanity and impressive civilization, as well as their inevitability, converted almost as many people as it defeated. Except for Spain, the areas which they conquered in the seventh century have remained Islamic in religion and culture to this day.

The first check to the Arabs came from the Byzantines. After the battle of the Yarmuk the Arabs realized that the capture of Constantinople would give them valuable security and be a striking symbol of success. Their early triumph in the Near East had been due partly to the fact that the Persian and Byzantine empires were exhausted from fighting each other. In six campaigns after 623 the emperor Heraclius had driven back hordes of barbarians from his north and north-eastern frontiers. During that time the Persian emperor Chosroes had taken advantage of his rival's critical condition, and attacked him from the east. Heraclius had defeated him too, but when the Arabs attacked they caught the military power of Byzantium at an abnormally low ebb of exhaustion. However, after the Yarmuk the Byzantines held the line of the Taurus, and rebuilt their strength. The Byzantine army and navy between the eighth and the eleventh centuries were, in fact, the most efficiently organized of any in Europe and the Mediterranean world; this the Arabs discovered when they began seriously to attempt to conquer that empire. In 668, and again every year from 672 to 677, the Arabs attacked the Byzantine empire at various points, only to be frustrated each time by the Byzantine fleet.

The galleys of the Arabs and the Byzantines were more or less identical. There were two types: the small reconnaissance craft, and the large fighting dromon. The characteristic Pamphylian dromon was about 110 feet long, 14 feet wide, had a draught of 3 feet, and was rowed by 100 men in two banks. The upper bank of oarsmen were armed, and there was a complement of marines. A larger dromon could be 140 feet long, and rowed by as many as 230 men. There were two reasons for the success of the Byzantines at sea. First, their ships and equipment were better made; secondly, they had the weapon of 'Greek fire'. This was an incendiary mixture; its formula is uncertain, but it probably contained naphtha, bitumen, pitch, sulphur, resin, oil and quicklime. It could be shot out of a tube in the bows of a ship, or thrown in pots by *ballistae*. If water was thrown on it, Greek fire merely burnt the more fiercely. The Greeks had possessed something like it for a long time, possibly as early as the siege of Delium in 424 B.C., but apparently a Syrian called Callinicus had recently improved the mixture.

The turn of fortune in the struggle between the Arabs and the Byzantines did not come till the siege of Constantinople in 717–18. Under the caliph Walid (705–15) the Arab empire reached its greatest strength, and it was determined that Byzantium should at last be reduced. When the Arabs invaded Asia Minor, the emperor Theodosius III retired to a monastery, leaving the throne to a professional soldier – Leo the Isaurian, who quickly repaired and stocked the massive fortifications of Constantinople. Before the age of gunpowder such walls were impregnable to assault and the only way the city could be taken was by blockade. Since it was built on a promontary, and surrounded on three sides by water, all would depend on the relative strength of the opposing fleets. The exact numbers involved are doubtful, but it is certain that the Arabs, drawing ships from all the ports of the eastern Mediterranean, had a vast superiority.

In August 717 the Arab general Maslama assaulted the landward wall of Constantinople. Having been decisively repulsed by catapult fire he duly set about a blockade. He ordered Suleiman, the admiral, to divide his fleet into two squadrons. One of these was to be based at Anthemius and Eutropius on the coast of Asia Minor, to cut off supplies and communication from the Mediterranean; the other was to pass through the Bosphorus and block the passage between Constantinople and the Black Sea. Meanwhile Leo built two towers, one on either side of the entrance to the harbour of the Golden Horn, and he suspended a great chain between them as a boom. At the beginning of September the Arab squadron set out to sail up the Bosphorus. As it passed Seraglio Point the strong current threw it into confusion, and at that moment Leo lowered the chain, launched his galleys, and attacked the enemy fleet with Greek fire. Having lost

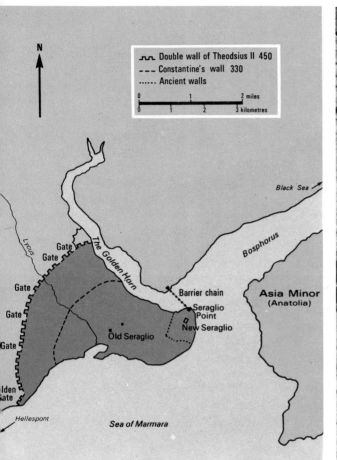

Constantinople 717 *left*. The line of fortifications was substantially the same in 1453 when the city fell to the Turks. Cavalrymen *right* were the main strength of the Byzantine armies.

over twenty ships the Arabs retired, and Leo returned to the Golden Horn. The Arabs made no further attempt for the time being to force the strait and, as a result, their blockade during the winter was only partial. Supplies poured into the beleaguered city from the Black Sea, while the Arabs suffered greatly from the unusual cold.

In the spring the Arabs received heavy reinforcements from North Africa, and again they attempted to move up the Bosphorus and complete the encirclement of the city. But it so happened that many of the crews of the new ships were impressed Christians, and they revealed the plan. Just as in the previous autumn, Leo's fleet sallied out from behind the boom at the crucial moment, and when numerous Arab ships went over to the Byzantines he gained a complete victory. This success was crowned by a land victory won by his Bulgarian allies between Constantinople and Adrianople. Eventually the Byzantines spread rumours among their enemies that the Franks were marching to fight for Christendom; the caliph then gave up, and in August 718 the twelve-month siege of

Constantinople was raised. Leo's fleet pursued the enemy down the Hellespont; there it ran into a storm and only a small proportion of the Arab forces survived. It was a great disaster for the Arabs, which they did not forget. By his further victory at Acroinon in Phrygia in 739, which forced the Arabs to evacuate western Asia Minor, Leo ensured that Islam should not penetrate into Greek Europe for centuries.

The major credit for the victory of Constantinople must be accorded to Leo the Isaurian; he grasped the leadership of Byzantium at a moment of crisis, and then in the face of an enemy with a great reputation and enormous numerical superiority he conducted a long defence with courage and brilliance. But he could not have succeeded if he had not inherited an army and navy built up over a long period in a tradition of military efficiency. The army founded by Belisarius, by Maurice (emperor from 582 to 602), and by Heraclius, the victor of the Slavic and Persian wars of 622 and 628, was in the future to prove itself again and again more than a match for the energetic Arabs.

For the rest of Byzantine history the heavy cavalry of Belisarius provided the main strength of the armies. The trooper was protected by a long shirt of mail reaching down from the neck to the thighs, a round shield of medium size, a tufted steel cap, gauntlets and steel shoes. The horses of the officers and front line troopers were also protected by a steel poitrel. All the horses were equipped with large comfortable saddles with iron stirrups. In hot weather the trooper wore a light linen surcoat over his armour, and a woollen cloak when it was cold. His offensive armour consisted of a broadsword, a dagger, a short bow and quiver, and a long ornamented lance fitted with a thong near the butt. Sometimes an axe was also carried, strapped to the saddle. Like its Roman predecessors, and unlike any other western army before the sixteenth century, the Byzantine army can be said to have worn uniform; the surcoat, the lance-pennon, and the tuft of the helmet were of a particular colour for each unit. The cavalryman had to be well off to afford this equipment. All the officers, and every four or five troopers, had soldier servants; this also was expensive, but it was considered worthwhile if the soldiers could concentrate on their purely military tasks and keep in good physical condition by being well fed. The history of the rich Byzantine empire illustrates that a little comfort does not necessarily have a harmful effect on military standards – provided it is regulated carefully.

The infantry of the Byzantine army was not the 'queen of the battlefield'. Its functions were limited to the defence of defiles and mountainous country, and the garrisoning of fortresses and important cities. Most of the light infantry were archers, though some were javelin-men. The bowman sometimes wore a mail-shirt, but more often only a tunic and stout boots. Besides his bow, he carried a quiver containing forty arrows, an axe at his belt should he have to engage the enemy at close quarters, and a small round buckler which could be slung over his back. The heavy infantryman, called the *scutatus*, was protected by a mail-shirt, a large round shield, gauntlets, greaves and a pointed steel helmet with a tuft. His offensive weapons were a lance, a sword, and an axe with a cutting blade on one side and a spike on the other. Like the cavalry, the infantry had a considerable body of camp-followers. For every unit of sixteen men, two carts carried ammunition and food, cooking utensils including a hand mill, and entrenching tools: spades, mallets, axes and saws. There were also pack-horses to carry supplies on forced marches.

A variety of tools were needed because the Byzantines maintained the classical Roman practice of regularly building fortified camps. A corps of engineers always marched with the vanguard of the army, and there was a regular routine for encampment. First the engineers would plan the camp and mark out its lines with ropes. Then, when the main part of the army arrived, the horses and carts would move into the centre, where the carts would be arranged in a leaguer to form an inner line of defence. An outer line of pickets kept watch as the troops dug the camp defences.

Besides the engineers and the military train, the army was accompanied by an ambulance corps. Every unit of 400 men had its medical officer and six or eight stretcher bearers. Besides stretchers, the bearers had horses equipped with a flask of water and a side-saddle with two stirrups on the same side, so as to be able to carry a wounded man comfortably. The bearers were paid a bonus for every casualty brought in from the battlefield – not for humanitarian reasons but because the state was interested in restoring the wounded to battle fitness as early as possible.

The keynote of the Byzantine military system was impressive tactical organization; they fought cunningly and efficiently. The Byzantines rightly considered that the methods to be employed in battle must be varied according to the tactics of their opponents. So they studied carefully everything of importance which could be ascertained about the methods of probable opponents, and evolved scientifically the tactics best suited to defeat each enemy. Their most important military writings are the *Strategicon* of Maurice, written in about 580, the *Tactica* of Leo the Wise (emperor 886–912), and a very interesting manual on frontier warfare by Nicephorus Phocas (conqueror of Crete and Cilicia from the Arabs, and emperor 963–9).

The basic structure and recruitment of the army was reorganized by Maurice. Under Justinian there had been no permanent unit larger than the *numerus*. Maurice regarded this unit of about 400 men, which he called a *tagma*, as the basic unit, but he organized a whole hierarchy of larger units, culminating in the *meros* – a division of 6,000 to 8,000 men. As in Napoleon's army the sizes of units were deliberately not standardized. There was an officer hierarchy which descended from the 'moirarch' in charge of 2,000 men to the 'decurion' in charge of a file of 16. The appointment of all officers above the rank of centurion rested in the hands of the central government. The terminology used in the army was a mixture of Roman, Greek and Teutonic words, correctly indicating a mixed heritage though misleading if it suggested that the organization was anything but coherent.

The number of Teutonic mercenaries in the Byzantine army greatly decreased after Justinian's wars. There remained three important barbarian corps, the *Foederati*, the *Optimati* and the *Buccellarii*, the last of whom were the sworn personal bodyguard of the emperor and who by the tenth century were composed of Vikings called Varangians. Despite the efforts of several emperors there was no universal male conscription in the empire, but a system called on every estate to send a certain number of men for training and active service when required. The burden of service naturally fell most heavily on the inhabitants of the frontier areas. The tenth-century poem, *Digenes Acritas*, describes life on the Cappadocian frontier, with warlike barons dominating the country from their castles, and making endless forays into the Arab territories of Cilicia and Mesopotamia. The best professional soldiers came from Cappadocia, Isauria and Thrace. Under Constans II, about 650, when the desperate Arab pressure on the Taurus frontier was beginning to slacken, the Byzantine empire was divided into territorial provinces of civil and military administration called 'themes' – each providing up to about 10,000 men for the army, based on the principle that quality must be the yardstick in recruitment. The frontier areas were further divided into districts called 'clissuras', one of which might consist, for example, of a mountain pass and a fortress; the command of a clissura was frequently the road to a successful military career.

Byzantine tactical theory was built up from the basic principle of delivering a series of heavy cavalry charges. Often the battle line was composed entirely of cavalry, as in the formation adopted by Nicephorus Phocas in his victory over the Arabs before the walls of Tarsus in 965. According to Leo the Wise, in principle a cavalry force should be divided into a front fighting line, a second supporting line, a small reserve behind the second line, and a detachment thrown well forward on each wing with the role of turning the enemy flank or, alternatively, of protecting its own. Up to about one-half of the available strength was in the front line, with the balance distributed in depth as the tactical situation demanded, and on the flanks. The commander-in-chief would normally position himself with the second line. There were no intervals in the front line, but three in the second through which the front might pass in case of retreat – each line having a depth of up to ten files.

There were, naturally, many variations in tactical dispositions. Infantry and cavalry would often act together against Slavs or Franks, whose armies were mostly foot-soldiers, or against large-scale Arab invasions. On such occasions the infantry would be placed in the centre, and the cavalry on the wings and in reserve. The *scutati* fought in the centre of the infantry and the archers and javelin-men on the wings. If the enemy was expected to open the battle with a cavalry charge, the light troops would retire behind the *scutati*, 'just as', Oman remarks, 'a thousand years later the musketeers of the sixteenth and seventeenth centuries used to take cover behind their pikemen'. For offensive operations the infantry fought in two lines, whereas in a defensive battle they usually fought in one thick line near their camp. But in no circumstances did a Byzantine army ever fight all together in one line, with no reserves. In hilly country and in passes, when cavalry could not be used, the infantry were disposed in a crescent formation, the heavy *scutati* blocking the enemy in the centre, and the light troops showering missiles down from above on the enemy flanks.

The Byzantines were the best soldiers of early medieval Europe, but the least spectacular; this was because their strategy was mostly defensive, and they preferred to rely on brain rather than brawn. They had constantly to operate defensively, either in keeping the Arabs out of Asia Minor or in holding back the Lombards and the Franks from the Italian provinces, and the Slavs, Bulgars, Avars, Magyars and Patzinaks from Greece and the Balkans. By their constant efficiency and vigilance they were highly successful in defending the frontiers; that was their main task, and only very rarely did Byzantium become an aggressive power – as, for example, in the middle of the ninth century and at the end of the tenth.

The Byzantines were quite unimpressed by the contemporary western European attitude to war. Chivalry and impetuous valour did not seem to them the way to secure victory at the minimum cost to themselves. They had professional pride and probably a good deal of religious enthusiasm, but always skill was rated higher than force and they went in a good deal for ambushes and night attacks. Indeed, that was the only possible attitude for them, since they were continually beset by fierce and numerous enemies. They never fought a battle until as many circumstances as possible had been turned to their advantage. They often used ruses and stratagems, such as spreading false intelligence or fomenting treason among the enemy. But they were not cruel to prisoners or in the habit of going back on their word; with them, treachery was strictly a strategical device.

The Byzantine theorists worked out different methods of conducting war against their many enemies. For example, Leo the Wise laid down special instructions about how to deal with the Bulgars, the Magyars, and the Patzinaks or 'Turks', as he calls them. These peoples were the familiar light horsemen of the eastern European and western Asiatic plains; they fought in innumerable small bands, armed principally with the bow, but also with the javelin and scimitar. They were wary fighters, efficient at scouting and fond of ambushes. In attack they would dash up and down the enemy front, showering it with volleys of arrows and delivering short stinging charges. Leo recommended that if the heavy Byzantine cavalry could close with them, they should do so – charging at the first opportunity. Foot-archers could also be very effective against the Turks, since their larger bows outranged the enemy, and if the steppe fighter lost his horse he was helpless. But while always attempting to close with the Turks, the commander had to watch his flanks, and beware of every defile or marsh where he might be ambushed. Careless pursuit by cavalry was likely to be fatal, since in Parthian style the Turks liked to rally from simulated flight and turn on disorderly pursuers. These battle instructions by Leo contained valuable lessons for the Byzantine officers and soldiers.

A different style of fighting was suitable against the Slavonic tribes of the northwestern Balkans. In the second half of the ninth century these were converted to Christianity, became vassals of the empire, and for a long time gave little trouble. Having practically no cavalry they were formidable only in the mountains, and a vigilant advance was the best way to forestall the danger of ambush by their archers and javelinmen. In the plains the Slavs were easily ridden down by the Byzantine cavalry, since they were poorly armed and indisciplined. By the second half of the tenth century the Russians, learning from the Vikings, had become better fighters. They armed themselves with mail-shirts, kite-shaped shields and battle-axes, and organized themselves in disciplined columns.

The Arabs were the most formidable enemy Byzantium had to face, particularly since after their first century of disorderly conquest they systematically modelled their army on the Byzantine system. Their mailed lancers became a powerful force, although man for man they were always lighter than the Byzantine cavalry and no match for them. They also copied some of the Byzantine methods of fortification and siegecraft, which had changed very little since the sixth century. On the other hand, the Arabs never appreciated the real merits of organization, and of drill as an aid to discipline, and they never maintained professional troops other than the royal bodyguards. Although to be feared because of their numbers and mobility, the Arab forces remained basically just masses of aggressive and energetic tribesmen. According to Leo, 'they are no regular host, but a mixed multitude of volunteers; the rich man serves from pride of race, the poor man from hope of plunder. They say that God, "who scattereth the armies of those that delight in war" is pleased by their expeditions, and has promised victory to them.'

The Arabs were profoundly impressed by their failure at Constantinople in 718, and after that time they made only two serious attempts at conquest beyond the Taurus, in 806 and 838: both of them unsuccessful. The impulse of Arab aggression rapidly weakened after 750, when in an 11-day battle on the Greater Zab (near Gaugamela) the Abbasid family wrested the caliphate from the Ommayads. The Abbasids raised Islamic civilization to a new height in their capital at Baghdad and were the heroes of the Arabian Nights, but they were not interested in military affairs. The Islamic world now slowly broke into several different caliphates, and Arab attacks on Asia Minor became raids rather than attempts at conquest. This was fortunate for Byzantium, since in the eighth and ninth centuries religious and political controversy began to weaken the empire internally, and at the beginning of the tenth century the Bulgarian empire reached its height under Simeon, who in 923 actually laid siege to Constantinople – but without success. In 941 the city was again besieged by Igor, prince of Kiev.

Leo the Wise also worked out the best strategy against the Arab raiders. Usually an Arab army would cross the Taurus and advance at high speed, hoping to reach its objective before the people of the countryside were even fully aware of what was happening. The Byzantine commanders of the provinces had a good system of frontier vigilance, and Leo ordered that they must assemble their forces the moment it was reported that the Arabs were on the move. The infantry were then to block the passes while the cavalry, having collected at a central point, must maintain contact with the raiders and attack them. If a commander found himself outnumbered he was to avoid open battle, but must obstruct the enemy in every way possible – tapping in on the raiders at every opportunity, defending fords and defiles, blocking up wells and barricading roads. More troops would then be raised from distant provinces, and the aim would be to oppose the Arabs in due course with a trained army of some 30,000 cavalry. In 863 this method of operating was tested and found to work, with the result that the Arab army of Omar, emir of Malatia, was surrounded and exterminated by the converging contingents of ten provinces.

In most of their encounters the successive shocks of the Byzantine lines proved too much for the loose mass of the Arabs, who were particularly vulnerable if attacked while foraging or just as they were retiring from Byzantine territory loaded with booty. In such instances Nicephorus Phocas recommended a night attack: 'Send three infantry bands . . . to charge into each flank of their camp, assail the front a little later with the main body of your foot, and leave the rear, where lies the road to their own land, unattacked. In all probability the enemy will instinctively get to horse, and fly the only way that seems to lead to safety.' Victory was surest of all if the Arabs were attacked in mountainous country, when they could be assaulted in rear by the infantry guarding the passes.

In the second half of the tenth century Byzantium took the offensive against the Arabs and the Bulgars. Nicephorus Phocas captured Crete in 961, Tarsus and Cyprus in 965, and in 969 Antioch. Perhaps the greatest soldier of the late Byzantine empire was Basil II (976–1025). By 995 he had suppressed the rebellious barons of Asia Minor and fortified a strong defensive frontier in Armenia. Then he turned to deal with the Bulgars. In 1014, at Bêlasitza, Basil annihilated the Bulgarian army, earning his title of 'Bulgar-Slayer'. He blinded 15,000 prisoners, leaving every hundred with a one-eyed man to lead them back to their tsar. For a hundred and fifty years the Balkan Slavs remained subject to Byzantium. The eastward advance continued for some time, and in 1045 with the annexation of Armenia the emperor could boast that his territories extended farther than in the reigns of any of his predecessors since Trajan.

But in the middle of the eleventh century a new enemy, the Seljuk Turks, began to press on the eastern frontier. In their methods the Turks did not differ from the Patzinaks described by Leo the Wise; the Byzantines held them off for some time, but they were eventually heavily outnumbered. Unfortunately, too, in 1068 a new emperor came to the throne, Romanus Diogenes, who rashly threw aside all the traditional Byzantine principles of circumspection and efficiency. In the spring of 1071 Romanus marched to Armenia with 60,000 men to meet 100,000 of the Turks under Alp Arslan. By careless movements he had already lost considerable numbers when he met the main force at Manzikert. Battle was joined and the Turks were driven back. But in the early evening they rallied, just when the Byzantines began to retire and lose their cohesion, thinking themselves victorious. The treacherous commander of the Byzantine reserve refused to support Romanus, and in the twilight the army was encircled and cut to pieces. The emperor himself was taken prisoner. With the flower of the Byzantine army thus annihilated, and no leadership at the capital, the Turks flooded into Asia Minor and within ten years had reduced it to a waste.

Meanwhile in western Europe, since the seventh century, the history of the Franks had followed a rather similar pattern to that of Byzantium. With an army in which cavalry played an increasingly important part, they had succeeded in checking the Arab advance; and then, after a period of military and cultural supremacy, they had weakened before the attacks of a different barbaric people: the Vikings.

For two centuries after the victory of Clovis at Vouglé in 507 the Franks, now dominant in Gaul, did not change their military organization. Agathias, the Greek poet and historian of the mid-sixth century, describes the warfare of the Franks in the Merovingian period (the name given to the first dynasty which ruled over the Franks):

> The arms of the Franks are very rude; they wear neither mail-shirt nor greaves, and their legs are only protected by strips of linen or leather. They have hardly any horsemen, but their foot-soldiery are bold and well practised in war. They bear swords and shields, but never use . . . the bow. Their missiles are axes and barbed javelins. These last are not very long, they can be used either to cast or to stab.

The *francisca* or throwing-axe was the most characteristic Frankish weapon. Its heavy head consisted of a single long blade, curved on the outer face and deeply hollowed in the interior. Like the Red Indian tomahawk it was carefully weighted, so that it could be thrown with great accuracy, as well as being used in close combat. The shield was broad and oval, with an iron rim and boss; the sword was about three feet long, double-edged and pointed, so that it could be used for both thrusting and slashing; a broad-bladed dagger was also used. The Frankish helmet was crested and round-topped with a peak at the front, and came down low over the nape of the neck. Right up till the second half of the eighth century Frankish armies fought thus armed, in massive disorderly columns of infantry. The rule of the Merovingian house (*c.* 450–750) was weak and barbaric; the warfare of the Franks was mostly among themselves and not against outside enemies.

The Franks were, however, aware that other peoples fought on horseback and with

The Frankish army was originally limited to lightly armed foot soldiers.

more body armour, and as they began to clash more frequently with these different types of armies so they were forced to change their methods. In the late sixth century wealthy men began to use protective armour of metal. In 574 Bishop Gregory of Tours commented that Bishop Sagittarius had ridden to battle 'armed not with the sign of the heavenly cross, but with the secular cuirass and helm'. In the seventh century the Roman breast-plate disappeared and the *brunia* or 'byrnie', the Teutonic chain-mail shirt, was increasingly used. The use of the horse developed at the same time as armour. The earliest known instance of a Frankish cavalry charge was in the battle fought by Clothar II against the Saxons in 626. But at least for another century after that time only the rich men went to war with horses, and normally they used them solely for transport, dismounting for battle and fighting on foot.

In 718 the Arabs burst over the Pyrenees. The Franks were not sorry to see the Visigothic kingdom of Aquitaine ravaged for a while, but the situation became more alarming when in 732 Abd-al-Rahman led an Arab army as far north as Tours. Charles Martel (or Charles the Hammer), mayor of the Merovingian palace, collected the Frankish forces, and advanced against the Arabs, who were retiring with their plunder towards Poitiers. For seven days the Arab army of light cavalry and the Frankish infantry army faced each

The Carolingian empire and Viking and Magyar incursions.

other. When Abd-al-Rahman at last attacked, according to the chronicler Isidorus Pacensis,

the men of the North stood as motionless as a wall; they were like a belt of ice frozen together, and not to be dissolved, as they slew the Arabs with the sword. The Austrasians, vast of limb, and iron of hand, hewed on bravely in the thick of the fight; it was they who found and cut down the Saracen king.

It was a defensive victory won by infantry, and there was no pursuit. It cannot be said that the Franks had checked the Arabs in the same way as the Byzantines had done; the Arabs had merely travelled as far as their resources allowed. In 743 they advanced again up the Rhône to capture Lyons, and they did not relinquish their military base at Narbonne till 759. The importance of the battle of Tours was that it confirmed Charles Martel as the most powerful individual in France. In 751 Martel's son Pepin deposed the Merovingian Childeric III, and in 768 Pepin's son Charles, known as Charlemagne, succeeded to the throne as king of the Franks.

When considering Charlemagne's military activities, it is difficult to understand some of his motives. One factor was no doubt the thrill of success, which encouraged him to go further. Certainly there was much disorder and danger to his kingdom, and if aggressive neighbours such as the Saxons would not respond to mild treatment the only policy was thorough conquest. It is also a fact that Charlemagne regarded himself as a universal ruler, the partner of the Pope, and God's regent to command on earth in temporal matters. His missionaries advanced with his armies, often in a real sense as psychological shock-troops, and he regarded it as an essential completion of the conquest of a heathen people to convert them to Christianity. As he wrote to Leo III:

Our task is, with the aid of divine piety, to defend the Holy Church of Christ with arms against the attack of pagans and devastation by infidels . . . Your task, most holy father, is to lift up your hands to God, like Moses, so as to aid our troops; so that through your intercession the Christian people may, with God as its leader and giver [of victory], always and everywhere be victorious over the enemies of His Holy Name.

On Christmas Day, 800, Charlemagne was crowned at Rome as emperor by the Pope. Many of his methods were crude, such as the massacre in 782 at Verden of 4,500 insubordinate pagan Saxons in a single day; another was the law which made it a capital offence to evade baptism or to break the Lenten fast. But eventually he learned better, and throughout the Middle Ages he was regarded as the model of a Christian emperor. Certainly his government was one more truly claiming divine authority, and his wars were more genuinely crusades, than those of many more cynical and hypocritical medieval rulers of a later date.

Between 768 and 814, in almost annual campaigns, Charlemagne fought against the Lombards, the Saxons, the Spanish Moslems, the Serbs, the Avars, the Byzantine provinces of southern Italy, the Bretons, the Frisians and the Duchy of Benevento. His empire eventually included the areas which are now France, Belgium, Holland, Switzerland, West Germany, most of Italy, northern Spain and Corsica. The war for which he was later most famed took place in Spain – a crusade of Christian against Moslem; it was famous because of the massacre by the Basques of his rearguard during the march home through the Pyrenean pass of Roncesvalles in 778, which became the subject of a poem, the *Song of Roland*. The Saxon wars were less romantic. The constant raids by these barbaric and pagan people, the inhabitants of the north German plain between the Rhine and the Elbe, at first led Charlemagne only to strengthen his frontier. By about 776 he had organized a march along the River Lippe, with strong points at Paderborn, Eresburg and Sigeburg. From these bases he made constant demonstrations of his military power, but the Saxons would not desist from their raids; whenever he appeared they pretended to submit, but whenever he was absent, as in 778, they burst into the Rhineland. Between 782 and 785 Charlemagne therefore carried out a thorough conquest. The Saxons led by Widukind slowly collapsed under the brutal and brilliant generalship of Charlemagne as he co-ordinated the swift and devastating marches of three armies.

The army of Charlemagne was very different in character from that of his grandfather, Charles Martel – the essential difference being in its striking force of heavy cavalry. Cavalry was essential for his far-flung campaigns against such enemies as the mounted bowmen of the Avars and the heavy Lombard lancers. The value of cavalry had long been recognized, but the expense of raising it had hitherto been an insuperable problem for the Franks. Apart from the cost of the armour, it was not easy for the knight to afford a suitable horse, strong enough to carry him when fully armed, sufficiently trained not to bolt or panic in a battle, and fast enough to take part in a charge at full gallop. Such a horse had to be specially bred and trained. Even the expense of stabling and providing winter fodder was considerable, and a knight had to have at least two attendants, one to deal with his armour and the other as groom for the horse; furthermore, he himself had to be able to give much time to training and active service. In the Merovingian period no ruler of the Franks was rich enough to pay an army of heavy cavalry.

This problem and various others were solved by the development of feudalism. The essence of the system was that the 'lord', the king or a great man, granted some land and his protection to the 'vassal', in exchange for a sworn undertaking to furnish specific services, sometimes civil but generally military in character. The power of Charles Martel had largely been built up by binding important individuals to him in this way. Charlemagne feudalized his kingdom to a very great extent. The system appealed both to those who were rich and to those who desired protection in troubled times. In the disorder of the ninth century following the death of Charlemagne in 814, when his empire was divided and Europe was beset by the attacks of the Magyars and the Vikings, society became honeycombed with this pattern of mutual obligation: protection and service. The effect of feudalism on warfare was twofold. On the one hand, vassals with considerable lands could afford, and were required, to furnish knightly service; on the other hand, the bonds of loyalty and mutual interest improved the discipline of armies. After his conquests of Italy, Charlemagne had recruited another force of cavalry in Lombardy, and it is a measure of his commanding force that he induced these traditional enemies of the Franks to undertake distant campaigns against the Avars in eastern Europe.

The heavy cavalry were the core of the Frankish army. Although not particularly numerous, they were of high quality. The knights were all equipped with a mail-shirt, helmet, shield, lance and axe. The old Frankish *levée en masse* of infantry did not entirely disappear. The infantry was reduced, and the quality improved by better armament; no man was allowed to appear at the 'March Field', the annual assembly of the Frankish army, armed only with a club – he must also have a bow. An interesting document survives, in which Charlemagne summons an important vassal, Fulrad, Abbot of Altaich, to the royal army in 806:

> You shall come to Stasfurt on the Boda, by May 20th, with your 'men' prepared to go on warlike service to any part of our realm that we may point out; that is, you shall come with arms and gear and all warlike equipment of clothing and victuals. Every horseman shall have shield, lance sword, dagger, a bow and a quiver. On your carts you shall have ready spades, axes, picks and iron-pointed stakes, and all other things needed for the host. The rations shall be for three months . . . On your way you shall do no damage to our subjects, and touch nothing but water, wood, and grass . . . See that there be no neglect, as you prize our good grace.

There is no clear evidence as to the tactical dispositions of the Franks in battle; probably the infantry archers did some preliminary probing and skirmishing, and then the cavalry delivered the decisive charge *en masse*. Superior organization, the quality of the highly trained and well armed soldiery, and the strategical vision of Charlemagne were perhaps more responsible for his success than any tactical brilliance. The thoroughness of his conquests was due above all to his policy of building a system of fortified posts along the frontiers and in disturbed areas, usually on hills near rivers. Charlemagne's forts, copied from the remains of Roman camps and *limites*, were not built particularly strongly; but it was rare for any of them to fall to an enemy, and many of them were the sites of later towns.

In the ninth century, without any able kings, the quality of the Frankish army declined. In composition it remained the same, basically a feudal host of cavalry, but some of the old weaknesses of Merovingian times reappeared and the Byzantines of southern Italy were never defeated by the Franks. Leo the Wise noted some of their characteristics and failings:

> The Franks and Lombards are bold and daring to excess . . . they regard the smallest movement to the rear as a disgrace, and they will fight whenever you offer them battle. When their knights are hard put to it in a cavalry fight, they will . . . dismount, and stand back to back against very superior numbers rather than fly. So formidable is the charge of the Frankish cavalry with their broadsword, lance and shield, that it is best to decline a pitched battle with them till you have put all the chances on your own side. You should take advantage of their indiscipline and disorder; whether fighting on foot or on horseback, they charge in dense, unwieldy masses, which cannot manoeuvre, because they have neither organization nor drill . . . There is nothing to compare to our own orderly division into battalions and brigades . . . They readily fall into confusion if suddenly attacked in flank and rear – a thing easy to accomplish, as they are utterly careless and neglect the use of pickets and vedettes and the proper surveying of the countryside. They encamp, too, confusedly and without fortifying themselves, so that they can be easily cut up by a night attack . . . They are impatient of hunger and thirst, and after a few days of privation desert their standards . . . They are destitute of . . . respect for their commanders . . . Nor are their chiefs above the temptation of taking bribes . . . On the whole, therefore, it is easier and less costly to wear out a Frankish army by skirmishes, protracted operations in desolate districts, and the cutting off of its supplies, than to attempt to destroy it at a single blow.

Charlemagne's empire began to fall apart very soon after his death. This was partly because of civil war in the reign of his successor, Louis the Pious, but above all it was due to the combined effect of simultaneous raids from three directions during the ninth and tenth centuries – by the Arabs, the Magyars and the Vikings. It is an indication of the general insecurity of western Europe in this period that the unlucky abbey of Luxeuil in Burgundy suffered at the hands of all three in turn. The Arabs, or Saracens as they were called by the Franks, contented themselves with occupying Sicily and southern Italy, and with relatively minor piratical raids on the Mediterranean coast of France. The Magyar horsemen caused much terror farther east, repeatedly raiding right through Germany and into Provence and Burgundy in the years after 900; these raids continued until the Magyars were checked by the Saxon ruler Henry the Fowler at the battle of the River Unstrut in 933, and then finally shattered by the victory of Otto the Great at the Lechfeld in 955. By far the most serious danger to Europe came from the Vikings of Scandinavia, and it is with them we must now deal.

There is no satisfactory explanation for the dramatic outburst of the Vikings, or Norsemen, at the end of the eighth century. The purpose of the raids which they conducted all over Europe seems at first to have been chiefly plunder rather than colonization, though later many of them settled in parts of the lands which they overran. The first recorded expedition of the Vikings is the appearance of three ships at Wareham in Dorset in 789. In the following decade the abbeys of Lindisfarne and Wearmouth on the Northumbrian coast were sacked, and Ireland and France were attacked. From then on the raids built up. In 832 a large force of Vikings under Thorgils invaded the interior of Ireland; two years later the cathedral city of Utrecht was sacked; and in 851 London and Canterbury suffered the same fate. During the next fifty years the raids became incessant. North and eastern England was definitely conquered by the Vikings, and in 911 the area that was to be called Normandy was ceded to them by the Frankish king Charles the Simple. Eventually the whole of England became part of the Scandinavian empire of the Danish king Canute (995–1035). Meanwhile the Vikings also penetrated to Iceland, Greenland and America, Spain, Morocco and Italy, Novgorod, Kiev and Byzantium.

The strength of the Vikings lay in their seamanship. Their ships were their supreme technical achievement and their great pride, and they themselves were sailors of outstanding skill and hardiness. Various Viking ships have been excavated, and one of the most interesting to have been found is the Gokstad ship, still almost completely intact, which I have seen in Oslo. It is about 70 feet long, 16 feet in beam, nearly 6 feet deep from rail to keel and built of oak – weighing over 20 tons. In its construction it is highly advanced. Instead of a flat bottom plank, a strong keel made of one piece of timber makes a backbone; the bow and stern are also made of one piece of wood. There are sixteen rows of planking, nine of which are below the water-line; these are riveted together, caulked with tarred rope, and lashed to the ribs. Amidships is a block in which the 40-foot pine mast was stepped. The sail was probably square; the Sagas tell of red sails, and some with blue and red stripes. For voyages sail was used, but when fighting the ship was rowed. It had sixteen pairs of oars, some 16 feet long and some longer, each oar being pulled by two men. The shields were hung along the rail, painted alternately yellow and black. The rudder was a single piece of oak, shaped like the blade of a huge oar, and attached to the starboard side of the ship by a riveted cleat. There were no

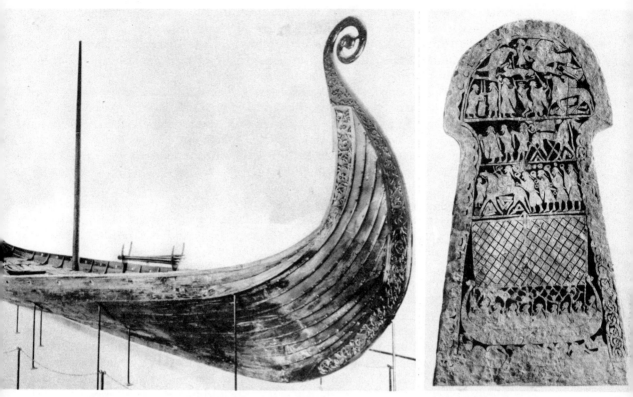

A Viking ship *left* and a gravestone *right* depicting a Viking raid. The ships sailed under square sails, sometimes in striped colours; oars were used for sea battles; horses might be captured ashore.

thwarts for the rowers to sit on, and probably they used their sea-chests. By the tenth century the ships were much larger, some of them holding as many as 200 men, and these could sail 150 miles in a day. Food on board was preserved with ice and salt.

The sea battles of the Vikings were always fought close inshore, and usually developed in three stages. First the commander reconnoitred the enemy and selected the best position from which to attack, then he would begin to close, manoeuvring for a favourable approach. The captain of the ship always steered it in battle. As the fleets closed together, a missile bombardment would begin, usually volleys of arrows but sometimes just lumps of iron and stone. Finally the Vikings would grapple, and decide the issue by hand-to-hand fighting.

The fleet then remained the base of operations for inland raids. Generally, Viking strategy was to work their way up an important waterway, living off the country and plundering the abbeys and towns on either bank. When they got so far up the stream that it was no longer navigable, or if they found further progress blocked by fortifications, they would moor their ships or run them ashore – leaving them protected by a stockade and a garrison, while they raided the surrounding country. In the early days they would return to their ships on the appearance of a hostile force, and drop back downstream. Later they grew bolder. But since they were not numerous and their main object was plunder, they avoided heavy fighting. Eventually they took to building fortresses, or strongholds, to which they would often return – for example, the island of Oiselle in the Seine above Rouen, Noirmoutier near the mouth of the Loire, Walcheren for their attacks on Flanders and Austrasia (the eastern part of the Frankish kingdom), and Thanet (England).

These water-girt camps, strengthened by stakes and a ditch, and defended by the Viking axemen, were immensely difficult to take. The Frankish king, Arnulf, captured the important camp in the marshes at Louvain in 891 : a remarkable feat. The Vikings had been ravaging Austrasia and had slaughtered a large number of Franks. Arnulf had been fighting the Slavs on the Bavarian frontier but he immediately returned, bitterly enraged. Regino of Prüm describes his victory:

> The Northmen, elated by the previous battle, set out in full strength on a plundering raid, and the king advanced against them with his army. The Northmen seeing him approach in battle array over the river which is known as the Dyle, constructed a fortification of wood and piled up earth in their usual manner, [and] assailed the [Frankish] line of march with jeers and insults.

The Franks defeated the Vikings – although the battle of the Dyle was somewhat uncharacteristic since it was fought in marshland and the Frankish cavalry thus could not be used.

The battle is of interest to me personally, since my first encounter with the German army in the 1939/45 war was in this very same area. The 3rd British Division which I commanded had moved up into Belgium from the Lille area on 10th May 1940, passed through Louvain that night, and occupied defensive positions on the general line of the Dyle before dawn on 11th May – shortly before the leading German troops reached the area. I can confirm that the river valley was still marshy in 1940.

When the Vikings began their offensives they were probably poorly armed; one of their chief aims in plundering was to secure weapons and armour, and by the middle of the ninth century they had captured plenty and had themselves learnt the techniques of manufacture. Practically all Viking warriors had a long shirt of chain-mail, and in other respects their body armour resembled that of the Franks, except that the helmet was pointed, with a nose-guard. At first the wooden shield was round, but later it was kite-shaped, and was often painted in bright colours. Their great offensive weapon was the axe. This was not the light tomahawk of the Franks, but a massive weapon with a single broad iron blade welded on to a handle five feet long. Sometimes the blade was marked with runes. They also fought with short and long swords, spears, and long bows and arrows. Unlike other peoples they regarded the bow as a highly honourable and useful weapon.

The Vikings were, basically, infantry – preferring to wield their great axes on foot. Since they could not transport horses on their ship-borne raids, they achieved mobility when on land by rounding up horses from the neighbourhood for use as transport animals. The fighting formation they liked best was a shield-wall, and of necessity their tactics were defensive since they were infantry opposed to cavalry. They usually chose to fight at their camp, or behind a stream as at Edington (Wiltshire) in 878, or on a steep hillside as at Ashdown (Berkshire) in 871. Being professional soldiers, man for man they could almost always get the better of the hurriedly raised levies of farmers which opposed them; and they had the advantage of being exceptionally large and strong in physique. They had two particularly formidable classes of warrior. The first of these was the 'berserks' who, astonishingly enough, were probably a specially organized corps of madmen, selected for their exceptional strength and ferocity. The other, equally astonishingly, was the 'shield-maidens', women who accompanied the Viking champions, and who might themselves be formidable female warriors, like Vebjorg, who

> attacked the champion Soknarsoti; she had accustomed herself . . . to the use of helmet, mail-shirt and sword . . . she dealt the champion heavy blows . . . and with a blow at his cheek cut through his jaw . . . he put his beard into his mouth and bit it, thus holding up his chin. She performed many great feats . . . [but] finally . . . she fell, covered with wounds.

Towards the end of the ninth century the Franks and the English began to get the measure of the Vikings. In the preceding years of chaos feudalism had grown apace, and the Franks could now raise a large force of efficient cavalry. Only cavalry had a hope of catching the swift-moving Vikings, and a cavalry charge had the impetus to break the Viking shield-wall. The Vikings themselves did not learn the art of equestrian warfare until too late, although their Norman descendants in the eleventh and twelfth century were the finest cavalry in Europe. In 866 Charles the Bald issued an edict that every Frank who owned a horse must hold himself ready for military service, and it can be said that from that date infantry was of negligible importance in France. Charles's most successful method against the Vikings was to build castles along the Seine, the Loire and the Oise. The most important of these was at Paris, where the Ile de la Cité was fortified with two strong bridges. Paris successfully resisted the great Viking siege of 885–6. The Vikings used much the same methods of siegecraft as had been used in Justinian's wars at the other end of Europe three centuries before – the same kinds of towers, catapults, rams, bores and mines. But all their assaults failed, and they neglected to surround the city so as to ensure a complete blockade – in contrast to the Germans in the Franco-Prussian War of 1870.

In England at the same time, Alfred the Great (died 899) was using a similar system of strong fortifications to check the Viking Danes. Instead of cavalry, however, he relied on an *élite* force of heavy infantry, which proved its worth by the victories of Ashdown and Edington. He also took the bold step, which the Franks ever since the time of Charlemagne had neglected to do, of building up a strong fleet modelled on the ships of his Viking enemies. Alfred's fleet won considerable successes, and for a thousand and fifty years after his death England always had a strong navy in which to put her trust.

The annexation of England by Canute in 1016 was a political and not a military affair. Already by this time Europe was breathing more easily, freed at last from the incessant barbarian raids which had lasted for seven hundred and fifty years without respite. In the east, Byzantium was to remain for a short while at the height of its military power achieved by Basil. In the west, the Viking energy was inherited by the Normans, about to become the new military leaders of Europe.

Norman heavy cavalry carried all before them as they imparted a new energy to Europe

8

The Norman Conquests and the Crusades

Our study has now reached a highly important period in military history – the central Middle Ages, between 1000 and 1200. In this period the outstanding military people were the Normans, the descendants of those Northmen to whom the French monarchy had granted the Duchy of Normandy as a feudal holding in 911 – being convinced that the best defenders against Vikings were other Vikings. The Northmen were basically infantry soldiers; but the Normans became famous as horsemen, and when Duke William invaded England the main element of his army was cavalry.

The Normans adopted and improved the methods of warfare which they found in France, as well as much else, and they became Europe's greatest exponents of heavy cavalry and strategic fortification. The great period of their expansion was the eleventh century, followed by consolidation in the twelfth. Two separate areas of Norman rule were established by conquest – southern Italy and Sicily, and the British Isles and western France. They imparted energy to Europe and, as might be expected, they also played a leading part in the movement which endeavoured to express Europe's revived vitality – the crusades. As it seemed to William of Malmesbury, 'they are a race inured to war, and can hardly live without it'.

To me, this part of our story is exciting and full of interest since my family has its origins in Normandy. Falaise, of which city I am a Freeman, has many Montgomery memorials; Roger Montgoméry, a cousin of the Conqueror, fought on the right wing of the army at Hastings; and, curiously enough, my old enemy Rommel received the wound which removed him from the battle of Normandy (1944) in the village of Ste Foy de Montgomery near Lisieux – when I myself was commanding an army operating in the opposite direction to the one which Duke William had commanded.

Balanced armies like those of the eastern Roman empire, composed of all arms, were not compatible with feudal society. During the years from about 400 to 1000 most armies of Europe and Asia had consisted primarily of mounted warriors, with weak elements of badly equipped infantry, and several centuries were still to pass before infantry again became the queen of the battlefield. From the time of the defeat of the Anglo-Saxon axemen at Hastings in the eleventh century to the rise of the Swiss and English infantry in the fourteenth, the cavalry soldier was the dominant figure in warfare. Under feudalism the mounted knight was regarded as the ideal soldier and the real backbone of an army.

We shall find that the armies of the crusades differed from a feudal array in that they contained more volunteers; they were also more incoherent because of the mixture of races, and the jealousy and friction between the leaders. Although I know those areas

The Normans conquered extensive areas of Europe *left*. Norman soldiers before a battle *right*

well, from Turkey through Syria and Palestine to Egypt, and have examined the country over which some of the battles were fought, I have found it difficult to raise any great enthusiasm over the operations of the crusaders. Indeed, it can be said that warfare learned little from the experiences of their battles.

The exploits of the Norman adventurers in the Mediterranean were short-lived, but daring and brilliant. The first Normans to penetrate into southern Europe were pilgrims, but many of these were little more than adventurers. In 1016 a band of forty, on their way home from the Holy Sepulchre at Jerusalem, came across a Saracen force besieging Salerno; they collected arms and horses and attacked the infidels – scattering them. During this period the activities of the Normans were little more than the haphazard exploits of freebooting mercenary individuals and their followers; but from about 1040 the family of Hauteville gave direction to their energies. Tancred, baron of Hauteville near Coutances, had twelve sons; he could not provide for them all, and some – William of the Iron Arm, Drogo, Robert and Roger – journeyed southwards to make their fortunes. By 1046 Robert, known as Guiscard or 'the Wary', was making a good living as a part time mercenary, part time brigand and cattle thief, in the mountains of Calabria in southern Italy.

In 1053 a papal army marched against the Normans at Civitate (south-east of Termoli) and was decisively defeated. But such a victory was embarrassing to follow up, and in 1059 Guiscard, now recognized as their leader by the Normans in Italy, swore fealty to the Pope in return for investiture of his lands – which he continued to expand. In 1084, during the 'Investiture' struggle, the emperor Henry IV took possession of Rome, and imprisoned Pope Gregory VII in the castle of St Angelo. Guiscard was called in to the rescue. The Germans retreated northwards and the Pope was released; but at the hands of the Normans and their Saracen troops Rome suffered a slaughter and pillage far worse than anything perpetrated by the Vandals.

By this time the conquest of Sicily was almost complete. Begun in 1061 by Roger, assisted by Guiscard, the turning-point came in 1072 with the siege and capture of Palermo, although the last Saracen stronghold did not fall until 1091. By that time Roger I was ruling over a consolidated principality, tolerantly embracing Greeks, Moslems and Normans, and strengthened by a Norman fortress in every important town. For defence, Norman feudal and Saracen subject contingents provided some power; but the armed strength of Sicily lay with her fleet of galleys, and in George of Antioch she produced one of the most brilliant admirals of the Middle Ages. In 1130 the Pope recognized Roger II as king of Sicily, Malta and southern Italy. From such rough beginnings the Norman kingdom of Sicily developed into one of the best governed and most universally cultured areas of Europe, uniting the energy of the north with the experience of the Mediterranean.

The other great conquest by the Normans in the eleventh century was England. In 1066, the year of his invasion and victory at Hastings, Duke William of Normandy had already ruled for thirty-one years. He had acquired a reputation as an able general, as a good tactician but even more resourceful in strategy and ruses, and as a far-sighted, patient and masterful ruler of men. He was ruthless in the execution of his policy. As was later written in the Anglo-Saxon Chronicle:

> He caused castles to be built, and oppressed the poor. The king was also of great sternness . . . The rich complained and the poor murmered, but he was so sturdy that he recked nought of them . . .

On the other hand,

> . . . the good order that William established is not to be forgotten; it was such that any man . . . might travel over the kingdom with a bosum-full of gold unmolested; and no man durst kill another.

Such a peaceful state was attained only after many years of war, rebellion and struggle. In 1047 William had defeated a baronial revolt at Val-des-Dunes near Caen. He had also grappled with Geoffrey the Hammer, Count of Anjou, for the possession of Maine, and in 1064 had finally decided the issue in favour of Normandy by the capture of Le Mans.

In 1066 William was thus an experienced and successful ruler and soldier, familiar with every feature of war in his time. His expedition against England was not a raid on the spur of the moment, but a drive of expansion – long prepared and well practised. Indeed, when Edward the Confessor died on 5th January 1066, William, as the result of an obscure history of marriage connections and secret oaths, had a better theoretical claim to the throne of England than had Harold – earl of Wessex, and the most powerful man in England. On 6th January Harold was chosen as king by the *witan*, or national council, and crowned, but he was in no real sense a national leader. When William crossed the Channel in September, after eight months of careful propaganda and preparation, he had the great moral asset of the blessing of Pope Alexander II, as well as the encouragement of the German emperor and the king of the Danes.

The Norman threat was not the only one which Harold had to face that year; there was also danger in the north. Harold's brother Tostig had allied himself with the aggressive king of Norway, Harold Hardrada, and a Norse invasion was possible. In May, Tostig had raided the Humber. Harold reckoned that William's threat was by far the more serious of the two, so he called out the limited naval strength of his realm, and all through June, July and August he maintained patrols in the channel between Dover and the Isle of Wight. At the same time the earls and sheriffs were ordered to keep the militia of the realm, the *fyrd*, ready for instant mobilization. The *fyrd* was the main strength of the English army and was recruited on the basis of one man for every 600 acres, but it could be called out only for two months at a time. There was another class known as 'thegns'; these were above ordinary freemen in status but below the aristocracy, each owing military service directly to the king.

The English army fought on foot, the soldiers being armed with spear, javelin, two-edged sword, and the massive Danish axe. Archery was a popular sport but was little used in fighting. The shields were round or kite-shaped. All who were rich enough wore a metal helmet and coat of mail. The king had a personal force of professionals, the 'housecarls', and these waited with him in Sussex during the summer of 1066.

It is unlikely that William and Hardrada had an agreed strategy, but it turned out for Harold as if they had – the crisis in the north coming at an awkward time for him. On 8th September the English fleet ran out of supplies and was forced by damage suffered in the rough August weather to return to London for revictualling and repairs. A week after he had thus been forced to abandon his watch in the Channel, Harold heard that 300 Norse ships had appeared off the Yorkshire coast, and that Cleveland and Scarborough had fallen to the invaders. He decided to leave the south coast undefended and march his troops north at all speed. On his way he heard that the northern earls Edwin and Morkar had been defeated in a pitched battle at Fulford, outside York, and that the city was on the point of surrendering. He reached York in time to prevent that disaster, and on the afternoon of 25th September he brought the Norsemen to battle at Stamford Bridge on the Derwent, seven miles from the city. Here the English thegns won their greatest victory, Hardrada and Tostig being killed, and their forces decisively defeated – only a small number escaping by sea.

On 28th September William of Normandy and his army landed on the south coast, unopposed. On that day Harold and his army were resting at York, 250 miles away, celebrating the victory over the Norsemen.

William had been hard at work since January preparing for the invasion of England. First he had to raise an army and, secondly, acquire a fleet of at least 450 transport vessels. In the strong Norman state the obligations of feudalism were clearly laid down. Every baron and bishop held his land from the duke on condition that he maintained for the duke's service a given number of knights, or heavily armoured cavalrymen. The knight was the characteristic medieval soldier. He was protected by a long mail-shirt, a peaked or conical helmet with a nose-guard, and a shield which was usually kite-shaped – round at the top and pointed at the bottom – and 3 to 4 feet high. The shields were decorated, but the patterns did not yet have any heraldic significance. The principal weapon of the knight was a lance with an untapered wooden shaft between 8 and 9 feet long, and tipped with a broad iron head. When not in use the butt of the lance would be rested on the stirrup. By the mid-eleventh century the medieval sword had reached its full development, and was to remain essentially unchanged for 400 years – two-edged, tapering to a point, some 44 inches from pommel to tip. Besides the lance and sword, the knight carried on his saddle a broad-bladed battle-axe or an iron-headed mace, which-ever he preferred.

By 1066 the Norman knights were well used to serving under William. But feudal custom had decreed that knightly service should be limited to forty days within the bounds of the duchy, and it was clear that William's feudal resources would not be sufficient for the conquest of a foreign country. Fortunately, however, most of the barons were willing to go with him. Condoned by the Pope, the conquest of the large and reputedly wealthy country of England was tempting, especially to an energetic people already feeling the economic pressure of a rising population. And so William secured volunteers and mercenaries not only from Normandy but also from all parts of France, and even from among the Norman adventurers in southern Italy. By these means he raised altogether between 2,000 and 3,000 knights, of whom at least 1,200 were Normans – these latter being the hard core of his army.

To supplement his knights William enlisted between 3,000 and 4,000 infantry, con-sisting of bowmen and possibly crossbowmen, with foot soldiers armed with pike and sword. The Norman infantry soldiers, unlike most of the English *fyrd*, were protected by mail-shirts. The Norman bow was some 5 feet long, and to fire it the arrow was drawn back to the chest. The crossbow may have come into use shortly after the beginning of the eleventh century; it is supposed to have been used by some of William's forces in 1066, but it is not shown in the Bayeux tapestry, the chief historical source for our knowledge of the conquest. (In 1804 Napoleon had the Bayeux tapestry exhibited at Paris to arouse enthusiasm among Frenchmen for his projected invasion of England.) The crossbow was a great deal more powerful than any previous bow; it did not involve any new principle, but derived from both the *ballista* and the ordinary bow.

At the end of August 1066 William had assembled his army at the mouth of the River Dives, with the intention of crossing the Channel at the first opportunity. Strong nor-therly winds prevented the sailing for six weeks, and the duke had to exercise all his qualities as a disciplinarian to keep his mixed army in order during that time. At last a westerly wind allowed the fleet to move to the mouth of the Somme; then on the evening of 27th September, when the wind had changed to the south, the army embarked and the fleet crossed the Channel that night. Early the next morning William landed on an empty beach in Pevensey Bay, a few miles west of Hastings. A prefabricated fort was erected during the day within the old Roman harbour in order to protect the ships and, in the evening, according to the poet Wace, 'all ate and drank enough and were right glad

Norman ships carried William's army across the Channel to England

they were ashore'. On the 29th the Normans marched to Hastings, and the fleet was brought into the harbour. The countryside was then systematically ravaged.

Harold meanwhile was still at York, allowing his men to recover from their recent battle at Stamford Bridge. He heard the news of the Norman landing on 1st October and the next day started for the south with his housecarls, reaching London about one week after the Norman landing. There he had to wait while his army assembled after the long march, and it was not until the evening of 13th October that Harold reached the appointed rallying place of his forces, the landmark of the 'hoary apple tree', on a spur of the South Downs about six miles north of Hastings – near the present town of Battle.

We must now examine Harold's strategy, and plans. His intention would appear to have been to act as he had done at Stamford Bridge – to move with all speed and attack William with the best of his troops, hoping to gain surprise. William's information from spies was that Harold and his army were 250 miles away, resting after a hard battle, and it is doubtful if such a move by Harold would gain surprise. Careful consideration of the problem would have revealed to Harold that the Normans must fight a decisive battle as early as possible – and, what is more, must win it. William was indeed on English soil with his army; but behind him was the English Channel, now again being patrolled by the English fleet. The longer the battle was put off, the more the Norman forces were likely to be depleted and their morale to sink, and the more troops would Harold be able to raise. William had gambled heavily; some might say that he had taken a 'calculated risk' – to use an expression which was in frequent use by American generals in the 1939/45 war when things went wrong! The gamble had so far paid a dividend in that the Norse invasion and the unpredictable English weather had, together, enabled him to gain an easy footing on the south coast of England. But now he was to prove his generalship by cool and skilful calculation.

William had known Harold personally for some time, and estimated that he would be most likely to adopt an impetuous course. The devastation of Sussex was one of the duke's most characteristically intelligent and unscrupulous acts – that country being part of Harold's own earldom of Wessex, it was unlikely that he would quietly watch it suffering. Harold's best strategy was to wait in some suitable area to the south of London, to collect a strong army, and to order his fleet to attack the Norman ships in Hastings harbour. Then, if he could bring the Normans to battle in the Weald, the forest between Hastings and London, he might gain a major victory. This, it is interesting to note, is exactly what the English planned to do three centuries later, when in 1386 the French were threatening an invasion which, like that of 1803–5, never came. William had to fight Harold quickly, or risk a major disaster, and this Harold should have realized.

In the event Harold did none of these things, but acted impetuously as William reckoned he would. He left London and marched direct on Hastings 'before a third of his army was in fighting order' – according to Florence of Worcester. And he did not achieve the surprise which he desired, since William's scouts reported his approach. The Normans spent the night of 13th October in prayer and preparation for battle. Then, striking camp before sunrise the next morning, they marched the six miles to Telham Hill, opposite the hoary apple tree ridge. It was the English who were surprised; many of those who had arrived during the night were still asleep, and many more of the *fyrd* were still only just coming in. To maintain his fiction of legality, William sent an embassy to Harold to seek an eleventh-hour peaceful settlement, and he took advantage of the opportunity to unnerve at any rate some of his enemy by telling them, plausibly if untruly, that they had been excommunicated.

William had the advantage of surprise; but Harold's position, on ground of his own choosing which he had probably reconnoitred earlier in the summer, had great natural strength and was well suited to defensive tactics. The English army occupied a ridge some 700 yards long, with the ground sloping away gently to the west and east, and rising steeply to the north. To the south and south-east the ground sloped down at a gradient of about 1 in 13 to a boggy valley, and then rose up to the Norman positions on Telham Hill – about a mile and a half from the hoary apple tree. Harold extended his line of battle, the shieldwall, the whole length of the ridge, making it difficult for the Normans to take him in rear or flank. He set his two standards, his own Fighting Man and the Dragon of Wessex, in the centre, and drew up the housecarls on either side of them. Each man in the front rank probably occupied about two feet of the line, the depth being altogether ten or twelve ranks. The English force totalled 6,000 to 7,000 men, about the same as the Normans.

Many of Harold's men were tired after the forced march from London the day before, and some had not been properly re-equipped since Stamford Bridge. Also, he lacked the archers who had served him well at Stamford Bridge, and who might have caused havoc among the Norman horse. Some of the hurriedly raised troops of the southern *fyrd* had little to fight with except clubs, picks and staffs; but all wanted to expel the harsh invader. In particular, the housecarls had the reputation of being the finest infantry in Europe, and if depleted in numbers they still had confidence in their fighting ability. When the line of battle had been drawn up, Harold rode along it, reminding his men that nothing could go wrong so long as the solidity of the shield-wall was maintained. In this he was right; but let us see what happened.

The Normans, who had marched from Hastings early on 14th October, were drawn up in three divisions: on the left the Bretons commanded by Count Alan of Brittany; on the right the French and other mercenaries under Eustace of Boulogne; and in the centre the Normans, under William's personal command. There were three lines in each

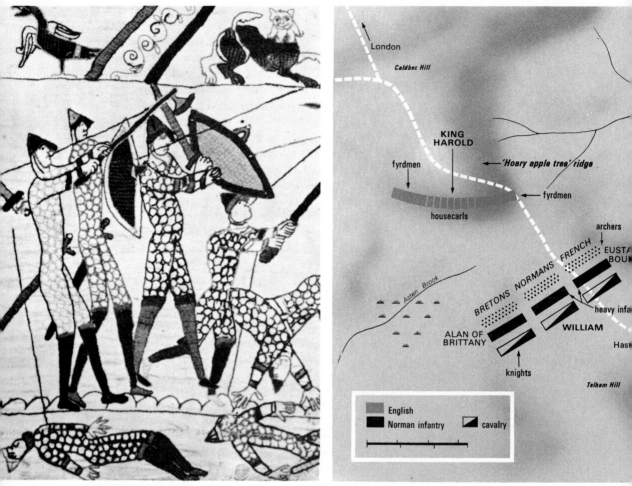

At the battle of Hastings *right* the English army was composed solely of foot soldiers *left*

division: in front, the bowmen; next, the heavy infantry; and lastly, the knights. The papal banner was carried in front of the army. Before battle was joined the knights put on their heavy armour, having preserved their strength to the last moment. Finally, William hung round his neck the bones which were the holy relics of Bayeux. He was accompanied into battle by his half-brothers, Robert, Count of Mortain, and Odo, Bishop of Bayeux, and by his friends William Giffard and William Malet. When the Norman advance began from Telham Hill their ranks deployed outwards so as to cover the full line of the English; they were led by the minstrel Taillefer, riding ahead of the army, twirling his lance and singing the *Song of Roland* – until he was cut down.

The first serious attack began at about nine o'clock. As the Normans closed, their archers began to fire; but since they had to shoot uphill most of their arrows passed over the heads of the English or were caught on their shields. The heavy infantry immediately took up the attack. According to William of Poitiers the English put up a very tough and successful resistance. 'The shouts both of the Normans and of the barbarians were drowned in the clash of arms and by the cries of the dying, and . . . the battle raged with the utmost fury.' The English took advantage of their strong position, maintaining their front intact. 'They bravely withstood and successfully repulsed those who were engaging them at close quarters.' In fact the attack of the Norman archers and heavy infantry against the shield-wall was a failure, and at last 'the foot soldiers and the Breton knights, panic-stricken . . . broke in flight'. Soon, apparently, 'the whole army of the duke was in danger of retreat'.

So long as the shield-wall was unbroken and stood firm in its strong positions, the English army had nothing to fear. But some of the raw levies of Harold's army moved out in pursuit of the Breton knights retreating down the slope; for infantry to pursue mounted men was to court disaster, and it is unlikely that Harold would have ordered such a counter-attack so early in the battle. Actually, at that time William had been unhorsed and a shout went up that he had been killed. But he quickly mounted another horse, showed himself to his troops, and took a firm grip on the battle. Although some of the English right wing had broken out in pursuit, the rest of the line stood firm; on the soft ground of the valley the pursuing infantry soon wavered, and the Normans rallied under William's leadership.

William himself now led a renewed attack of the knights, and for several hours con-fused mass assaults continued. In the eleventh century, knights did not charge in one cohesive mass, but rode up to the line in groups or individually, hurling their lances rather than thrusting with them, and then hacking at close quarters with their swords, maces and axes. William himself took an outstanding part in this fighting, and had several horses killed under him, although he himself was not wounded. According to William of Poitiers, 'he dominated this battle, checking his own men in flight, strengthen-ing their spirit, and sharing their dangers'. On the other hand,

> the English fought confidently with all their strength, striving in particular to prevent the attackers from penetrating within their ranks, which indeed were so closely massed together that even the dead had not space in which to fall.

On balance, as Wace says, 'both sides stood so firm and fought so well that no one could guess which would prevail'.

In the early afternoon William tried a ruse. Remembering how the retreat of his left in the morning had led the English right to break forward and lose cohesion, he decided to carry out a feigned retreat on the other flank. The device, an old Byzantine one, worked admirably. Most of the English left, certainly without orders from Harold and possibly against them, chased down the slope to the valley. When they were at the bottom the Norman horsemen turned and savagely attacked them with great effect.

But the housecarls in the centre and part of the left stood rock-like, and as the sun began to set in the later afternoon the Norman knights became tired, discouraged, and more than ever apprehensive of the English axes. Once again William showed himself a resourceful general. His archers, who had been unsuccessful in the morning, were at any rate now fresh. Let them try a different attack! Drawing up the archers in a long, loose line, with gaps through which the knights could ride, he sent them up the hill at a run, with the horsemen trotting behind. A hundred yards short of the English line the archers halted, and loosed their arrows almost vertically into the sky. The arrows rained down on to the English, and, Wace says, 'all feared to open their eyes or leave their faces unguarded'. At the same moment the knights charged together, hitting the English a few seconds after the arrows had caused sudden confusion and terror. Even then, for a while the fighting was hard. But the English left cracked before Eustace of Boulogne's men and finally the whole shield-wall began to disintegrate, many fleeing headlong. The house-carls retreated in good order, until William rode in pursuit and scattered them. He returned to the field of battle after dark, to find Harold's body stripped and hacked almost beyond recognition.

We should now discuss briefly the generalship of the two commanders. I hold the view that Harold might well have defeated William, and pushed him and his army into the sea. It was strategically desirable to do this as quickly as possible; but it was not tactically possible to implement this strategy with the resources immediately available without a sound plan. Harold pursued an unsound strategy and his plans are open to criticism. To leave the south coast entirely undefended, indeed even unwatched, while he moved his forces northwards to York was most unwise; furthermore he did not make the best use of the weapon of seapower when the English fleet had been revictualled and repaired after the August storms. A threat from the sea against their ships would have been disturbing to the Normans and lowered their morale, particularly if delivered at the right moment – for example, when Harold's army was approaching Hastings from the north. In all he did Harold pursued the strategy which best suited William, and played into his hands. William was the better and more experienced general of the two; he was undoubtedly lucky; but he was bold, and boldness deserves luck. William conquered England when he won the battle of Hastings, and that one battle altered the course of English history. And maybe it was for the best; the Normans had much to give England.

The Conqueror had still much work to do even after he was crowned in Westminster Abbey on Christmas Day, and some of it cruel work – for example, the humbling of Exeter and the harrying of the north. Norman warriors, administrators, churchmen and merchants completed the conquest enthusiastically. The Scandinavian element in English life was submerged, and the history and civilization of England became intimately connected with that of France – England being thoroughly feudalized, to the benefit first of the king and then of the Norman lords. In the twelfth century the Norman empire became the greatest power in Europe, reaching its highest point under Henry II, when it stretched from Scotland and Ireland through England and western France to the Pyrenees. But in 1214 the foolishness of Henry's sons, Richard and John, allowed Philip Augustus, the greatest statesman of the kings of France, to bring it to final ruin at the battle of Bouvines – King John of England being vanquished and humiliated, his own knights finally rebelling against him.

Norman society in the central Middle Ages was divided clearly into three classes, as was all European society: those who fought, those who prayed, and those who laboured. The foundation of the strength of the military class and of all defence policy was the castle; it was also the most visible symbol of feudal government. Between 1000 and 1300 military architecture developed strongly; on the other hand there was no comparable advance in the offensive weapons and techniques of siegecraft. It thus came about that during this period the defensive was reckoned to be more profitable than the offensive in the conduct of war. Because of this reasoning large-scale pitched battles became rare; men preferred to be secure inside strong fortifications rather than accept risks in operations in the open country. Rulers who could control a network of castles, such as most of the kings of England, were thus in a strong position; those who could not prevent the barons from holding castles independently were liable to be in bad trouble – for example, most of the German emperors.

In the twelfth century tactical conceptions made little progress, and there was a disappointing failure to apply under western conditions the lessons learnt during the great wars in the east. At intervals battles of considerable political importance were fought – for example, the victories of Henry I of England at Tenchebrai (1106) and at Bremûle (1119). But, in fact, these could hardly be called battles, being no more than brief clashes of a few hundred knights. The so-called battles of this period are much less interesting to the military historian than the fortifications.

The building of wooden fortifications and earthworks had been revived in France and England as the best strategy against the Vikings – being mostly modelled on the remains of ancient fortifications. But by the middle of the eleventh century the Normans had developed, and introduced to most of Europe, a new type of fortification – the motte and bailey castle. The motte was a mound surrounded by a ditch. Surmounting it was a wooden stockade, and a keep or *donjon* which was the residence and stronghold of the baron, his family and retainers. The bailey was a forecourt protected by another ditch and stockade, its original purpose being to protect the domestic animals. The outer entrance to the castle was by way of a drawbridge, consisting of some planks across the ditch which could be drawn back by the defenders. The keeps of the eleventh century were nearly all made of wood, with certain exceptions – for example at Brionne in Normandy, where stone was on the site. In due course stone was increasingly used as the building material since timber was not durable and was vulnerable to fire, and further-more it was the ambition of feudal lords to have strong castles.

From the end of the eleventh century stone castles became larger and more elaborate. Tamworth is an example of the type of early stone keep known as a 'shell-keep'. It is built on a mound, surrounded with a circular curtain wall averaging 100 feet in internal diameter, and with a square tower on the eastern point. In the twelfth century a more compact form of citadel, the rectangular keep, gradually supplanted the shell type – built on the firm ground of the bailey, and not on a mound. Examples are the Tower of London, still standing, and Corfe Castle – which was defended by Lady Bankes and her household over some three years against the artillery of Cromwell's army in the 1640's. The rectangular keeps were very massively built. An example is Dover Castle, built in the 1180's, with walls 83 feet high, square corner turrets rising another 12 feet, buttresses about 20 feet thick, and three towers strengthening the forebuilding. The principal rooms are two large halls on the third storey. It also contains two chapels. There is a well 350 feet deep, water being conveyed through lead pipes within the walls to different parts of the building.

Rectangular keeps presented vulnerable corners to assault by battering or mining, which was a disadvantage, because the enemy could be attacked only from one side – being protected by the corner itself against attacks from the other. A circular or mul-tiangular wall could offset this danger to some extent, as the crusaders had learned by experience when besieging Levantine castles. By the middle of the twelfth century the form of the keep was changing. The keep of Houdan in France, built about 1130, is square on the inside; but on the outside it is circular with four projecting round turrets, from which the whole length of the outside walls could be swept by missile fire. Arrow-loops were pierced in the walls and towers; these were more effective than battlements, since the defenders could shoot at the enemy outside while themselves remaining unseen and protected. The early ones were merely long slits, but later they were cut in the form of a cross – to allow the archer a wide lateral sweep.

Towards the end of the twelfth century, bows and stone-throwing engines became more powerful. The reply of military architects was to build greater curtain walls and multiple baileys. The motte and keep shrank in size and importance. The powerful fortress of Château Gaillard, completed by Richard I of England in 1198, included the features most characteristic of the best fortification of that time. The site selected was a precipitous cliff 300 feet above the Seine. The castle consisted of three baileys in line downhill, as advance fortifications astride the only possible direction of approach. The

The Normans were Europe's greatest castle builders. Dover Castle still preserves its fine rectangular keep

inner bailey and the keep were on the edge of the cliff. The side of the keep which faced into the courtyard – the only side which could be attacked – was thickened and V-shaped like the prow of a ship, so that missiles would be deflected by the oblique alignment of the walls. It was protected against sapping by a deep plinth, and against battering attacks by 'machicolations', or openings beneath the battlements through which pitch and missiles could be dropped on to the heads of assailants below. It had two tiers of battlements. The baileys were each separated from the next by a moat and a curtain wall. While the curtains of the middle and outer baileys were strengthened by circular projecting towers, the inner curtain was given a continuous series of corrugations – which served even better the purpose of wall towers to enable the defenders to cover the outside of the wall at all points.

Only a small proportion of the numerous sieges of the Middle Ages were successful; the siege and capture of Château Gaillard by Philip Augustus in 1203–4 was therefore exceptional. But that example will serve to illustrate the contemporary methods of

Château Gaillard, plan *left* aerial view *right*, occupied an apparently impregnable position.

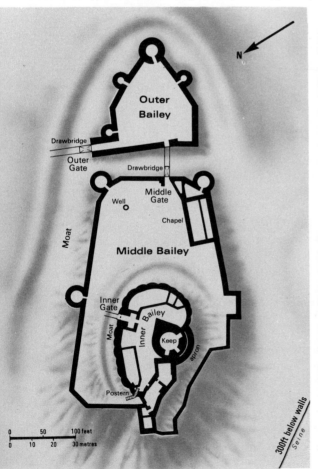

The crusades canalised the warlike energies of western Europe against an external foe. The capture of Antioch during the first Crusade

siegecraft, and make clear what ingenuity was needed in such a formidable operation. The weapons, tools and techniques of siegecraft had still not significantly changed since the time of the fall of the Roman empire; at best, some of them had been made more powerful. They consisted for the most part of battering-rams, siege-towers or *beffrois*, scaling-ladders, pent-houses and mantlets, and projectile-throwing engines. The projectiles might be stones, darts, poles, fire, or even carrion. The engines ranged in size from the *trébuchet*, with its beam made of a whole tree trunk, to the crossbow; but it is doubtful whether these medieval engines were as effective as the Roman versions had been. The best means of taking a castle were still mining, starvation and treachery. Throughout history starvation has proved to be one of the most powerful weapons of a besieger.

In the late summer of 1203 Philip Augustus began the siege of Chateau Gaillard, the chief defence of King John of England's Duchy of Normandy. His plan was first to weaken the garrison by starvation. For this purpose his army dug two lines of trenches to cut off the garrison from the river, built wooden towers at intervals between them, and then acted passively for three months. When supplies in the castle began to run short, the commander, Roger de Lacy, sent out 400 women, children and infirm men, but the French refused to let them pass. Since the garrison would not have them back, these unfortunate people were compelled to pass a hard winter between the lines, so short of food that they ate first their dogs and then their infants. The problem for the besieged of *les bouches inutiles* remained unsolved; the opposing general would never assist the defenders by allowing them to send out their women and children after the siege had begun.

In the spring of 1204 Philip began his active assault, using large missile-engines and a siege-tower. His initial bombardment was met with a hot return of similar missile fire from the walls. The next tactic of the French was to mine the salient tower of the outer bailey, which was successful; the besiegers then advanced to the middle bailey. Against the curtain on the south side was a building containing latrines on the lower storey, and a chapel above it. Searching along the moat a Frenchman found the outlet of the drain from the latrines, and crawled up through the pipe to emerge just below one of the windows of the chapel. With the aid of a rope he hauled up some of his comrades, and they burst into the chapel with loud shouts. The startled and emaciated garrison put up little resistance before retiring to the inner bailey. The French now began to undermine the last curtain wall. The garrison counter-mined from the other side, broke into the French tunnel, and drove the attackers out. But the foundations of the wall were by now greatly weakened, and after a battering by powerful catapults the wall fractured. The French poured through the breach, and at the end of a long and stiff fight the garrison surrendered. With the fall of Château Gaillard Normandy was, in effect, lost to King John.

We must now examine the crusades. In 1071, following the disastrous defeat of the Byzantines at Manzikert, the emperor Alexius Comnenus had appealed to the Pope for help from the West. But it was not until 1095 that the papacy could divert its attention sufficiently from its quarrel with the German emperor to respond to the Byzantine appeal. In that year Urban II called a council at Clermont and preached his call to Europe:

> All Christendom is disgraced by the triumphs and supremacy of the Moslems in the East . . . The Holy Land, which is dear to all Christian hearts and rightfully a Christian possession, is profaned . . . Christian kings should therefore turn their weapons against these enemies of God, in place of warring with one another as they do. They ought to rescue the Holy Land and the Holy City, they ought to roll away the reproach of Christendom and destroy for ever the power of Moslem attack. The war to which they are called is a Holy War and *Deus vult* is the fitting battle-cry. Those who lose their lives in such an enterprise will gain Paradise and the remission of their sins.

The Christian army was to set forth on the Day of the Assumption in the next year, commanded by Adhemar, Bishop of Le Puy. There were no detailed plans; God would provide.

The response to the Pope's appeal was tremendous. In 1096 contingents set off from most parts of western Europe, except from Germany which was plunged in civil war. Adhemar and Raymond, Count of Toulouse, led the largest force from the south of France. Hugh of Vermandois, brother of the king of France, Robert, Count of Flanders, and Robert, Duke of Normandy, the son of William the Conqueror – these led the contingent from northern France. Godfrey de Bouillon, Duke of Lower Lorraine, and his brother Baldwin, led a third contingent from the Rhineland area. And a fourth contingent, from southern Italy, set out under the Norman Bohemund, son of Robert Guiscard, and his nephew Tancred. By the late spring of 1097 between 25,000 and 30,000 crusaders had crossed the Bosphorus.

There were many reasons for the appeal of the crusading movement. For a hundred years or more the population of western Europe had been increasing, and agricultural output had not kept pace. The restlessness which this caused was particularly intense after the famine of 1094. Furthermore, there was a limit to the number of subdivisions which could be made in feudal holdings; also, many of the younger sons of the nobility contributed to the general restlessness – wanting to find new lands for themselves, with adventure and excitement. Peasants enrolled in the hope of thereby gaining freedom from serfdom. Many other people, particularly the merchants of Venice and Genoa, saw an opportunity for commercial profit, either from the disintegration of the Byzantine empire or in supplying the crusading armies. But the prime motive of the first generations of crusaders was undoubtedly religious. The eleventh century had witnessed the revival of monasticism, the papacy and pilgrimage; in the twelfth century this religious enthusiasm coursed through the laity of Europe. Christ's enemies were profaning the scene of His earthly life, and the Crusade was a new and urgently necessary pilgrimage. The feeling was caught in a song of the second Crusade:

> God has fixed a day for you to be at Edessa: there the sinners will be saved who hit hard and who serve Him in His need.

St Bernard's method of recruiting in 1146 was to preach thunderously: 'I tell you, the Lord is testing you.'

Ever since the time of Charlemagne, European warfare had become increasingly involved with religion and infected with scruple. More than one battle of the Carolingian era (751–987) had been fought in a strange atmosphere of religious exaltation. Duke William had taken great pains to secure the Pope's approval for his invasion of England. Before Hastings, Harold made a pilgrimage to the Holy Rood of Waltham; and during the battle itself William wore the relics of Bayeux around his neck, while Odo, Bishop of Bayeux, fought with a mace rather than with a sword – since as a priest he ought not to shed blood.

The 'Truce of God' was a long-sustained attempt by the Church to regulate and restrict the depredations of private war, and to protect women, peasants, clerics and pilgrims, as well as agriculture and buildings. It is first heard of in southern France in 990, supported by the influential monastic order of Cluny. A Synod at Elne in 1027 prohibited all warfare at weekends. In 1042 the Truce was introduced by William to Normandy, and the Normans thereafter carried it to many parts of Europe. The papacy took up the idea, and in successive councils reaffirmed increasingly elaborate regulations. For example, the Lateran Council of 1139 forbade the use of the crossbow – except against infidels – as being a weapon too murderous for 'Christian warfare'. In the twelfth century those who accepted the Truce undertook to abstain from fighting for three-quarters of the year, on pain of excommunication. Except where the temporal authority intervened to enforce the Church's pronouncements, the Truce of God was not on the whole effective. But until kings became strong enough to impose their own peace, the efforts of the Church were worthwhile.

The Norman conquest of England. A detail from the Bayeux tapestry

The first Crusade was successful. Although the crusaders were not on good terms with the Byzantines, they were not thereby discouraged. They marched across Asia Minor, suffering with immense fortitude the discomforts of hunger and thirst – the result of the inefficiency of their commissariat. After defeating the Turks at Dorylaeum they captured Antioch in June 1098, where they were smitten by dysentery and were themselves besieged by the Turks. In this critical position the crusading leaders abandoned their rivalries and appointed Bohemund commander-in-chief. Having discovered a holy lance they then sallied out, and, aided by St George, so it is said, and other saints mounted on white horses, they defeated the Turks. At the beginning of January 1099 the crusaders continued on their way to Jerusalem and in July, after a five weeks' siege, captured the city – massacring its inhabitants. The crusaders had met practically no Moslem resistance, since, luckily for them, their enemies were divided; at that time, the Fatimid caliph of Egypt, to whom Jerusalem belonged, was in fear of attack from the Seljuk Turks of Asia Minor.

Having accomplished their mission the crusaders then had to undertake the defence of the Holy Land. Several of the leaders had already broken off with their followers from the main army – Bohemund declared himself Prince of Antioch, others set themselves up as Counts of Edessa and Tripoli, and in 1100 Baldwin became king of Jerusalem. These Latin States, as they were called, were, in fact, held very precariously. The bulk of the crusading contingents returned home after having completed their pilgrimage to Jerusalem, and Baldwin found that he had only 300 knights with whom to defend the city. Not until after the second Crusade were the armies to be supplemented by mercenaries. At an early stage the support of the Genoese and Venetian fleets was purchased to hold the coastal towns and keep the crusaders supplied. Numbers also increased to some extent after the foundation of the orders of warrior monks – the Knights Hospitaller (1113) and the Knights Templar (1119).

The Templars, or Poor Knights of Christ and of the Temple of Solomon, were founded by a Burgundian knight called Hugues de Payns, and undertook to protect the pilgrims who now flocked to Jerusalem. They vowed to live in chastity, obedience and poverty according to the rule of St Benedict, and 'to fight with a pure mind'. Supported by St Bernard, they rapidly gained recruits, and found official favour in all parts of Europe. They provided Christian heroes in almost all the crusading battles of the twelfth century, but in the thirteenth they became too powerful to be popular, and in 1312 Pope Clement V abolished the order. The Teutonic Knights, a similar order founded in 1191 and chiefly active in eastern Germany, survived till the nineteenth century.

It was necessary for the crusaders to formulate a strategy appropriate to their shortage of manpower. Their doctrine was to avoid open battles as far as possible, and to rely, even more than in the West, on castles. First, good relations had to be cultivated with the local inhabitants; these were well used to frequent changes of overlord and appeared willing to be docile subjects, despite the religious difference. The government of the Latin States was similar to that established by the Norman conquerors in England – feudal rule by a military aristocracy based on castles. Many of the castles of the crusaders, such as those on the coastal plain, were built on sites chosen for administrative, economic and social purposes rather than for strategical reasons. There was no attempt to hold strongly the frontier of the Lebanon mountains and the river Jordan, it being recognized

A crusader castle. Krak des Chevaliers

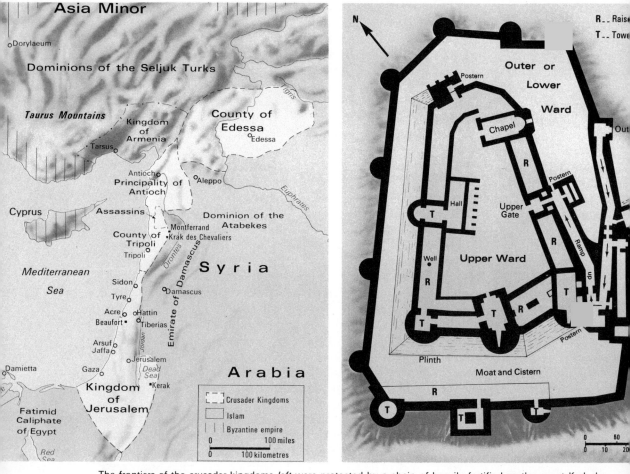

The frontiers of the crusader kingdoms *left* were protected by a chain of heavily fortified castles, as at Krak des Chevaliers *right*

that castles could be only bases or retreats, and not barriers. Indeed, the mountain route from Damascus and the crossing of the Jordan at Al-Sann Abra south of Lake Tiberias were left virtually undefended. But the crusaders eventually did build a large number of castles at points along the frontier, such as Kerak of Moab, Beaufort, Krak des Chevaliers and Montferrand.

During my service in Palestine in 1931, and again in 1938, I visited the sites of many crusader castles. It was interesting to note that they were visible one from the next in a chain across the country, visual signals being used for intercommunication; this inter-visibility was clearly considered important. I have read that when Kerak of Moab was besieged by Saladin in 1183, the garrison communicated nightly by fire signals across the Dead Sea with King David's Tower at Jerusalem – fifty miles away. In some cases pigeons were used to carry messages.

Krak des Chevaliers, which belonged after 1142 to the Hospitallers, is perhaps the finest of these powerful fortifications, being outstanding in size and strength. Sidney Toy wrote:

> The castle stands on a hill, with precipitous falls on the east, west and north sides and a more gradual descent on the south, where it is defended by a moat. It is surrounded by two lines of powerful walls with wall-towers, enclosing two wards of which the innermost, following the steep rise of the hill, is on a much higher level than the other, its towers and battlements dominating the whole fortifications. On the south and west sides, where the rise from the outer to the upper ward is greatest, the curtains of the latter are strengthened by massive battered plinths, which soar up to a great height, engulfing the lower parts of the towers.

The early success of the crusaders was due at least as much to the disunity of the Saracens as to their own courage and faith. The beginning of failure came in 1127 when Imad ed-Din Zangi set out to extend his power in Syria, capturing Edessa in 1144. The gravity of this disaster was recognized in the West, and in 1147 Louis VII of France and the emperor Conrad III responded to St Bernard's call for a second Crusade – which was a total failure, the newly arrived crusaders being shocked at the tolerant regime of the Latin States, and disagreeing about the strategy of the campaign. The resident crusaders urged an attack on Nur ed-Din, Zangi's successor, whose rising power thay saw as a serious danger. But the second crusaders proposed to attack Damascus, even though its emir was an enemy of Nur ed-Din and well disposed to the Latin States. Eventually the attack on Damascus was made, with depleted forces – and failed. Most of the second crusaders then returned home, and Nur ed-Din renewed his aggression. In 1154 he captured Damascus, and in 1169 gained control of Egypt. The crusaders had failed to appreciate the strategical importance of holding the centre of the north-south desert communications east of the Jordan, in order to prevent the unification of the forces of Syria and Egypt. In 1174, on the death of Nur ed-Din, Saladin became king of both Egypt and Syria.

Saladin was a most able ruler, a devout Moslem, and a sound strategist. He systematically built up military strength, and by able preaching prepared his subjects for the *jihad* – the holy war against the Christians. The crusaders now became more seriously threatened than ever before: their enemies in the north and south were working on a common plan, and their supply lines were put in danger by Saladin's Egyptian fleet. But instead of uniting in this crisis the leaders, particularly Raymond, Count of Tripoli, and Reynald of Chatillon, Master of the Temple, wrangled ever more bitterly. There were a few minor hostilities, but Saladin did not open the attack until 1187, when Reynald gave him provocation by plundering a caravan. Then Saladin marched across the Jordan, annihilated a force of 130 knights which included most of the strength of the Templars, and laid siege to Tiberias. Reynald and Guy de Lusignan urged that the crusaders should march to relieve the fortress. Raymond argued that such an advance would be to fall into Saladin's trap; the crusaders would be greatly outnumbered, and, it being the hottest time of year, they would suffer greatly from lack of water; he considered it would be best to remain on the defensive until the situation was more favourable for an offensive. But his wise counsel was disregarded. On 3rd July 1187 Guy de Lusignan led out the crusading forces to meet their greatest disaster – at the battle of Hattin, in the hills west of the Sea of Galilee.

As has already been observed, the strategy of the crusaders was dictated by shortage of numbers. The backbone of their armies was the knights: either feudal tenants or members of the religious orders. These were increasingly supplemented by mercenaries and 'Turcopoles' or renegade Moslems. The efficiency of the knights of the twelfth century had developed somewhat since 1066, their defensive armour becoming more elaborate. The mail-shirt now came down to the knees, and the extremities of the body, the hands and legs, were protected by pieces of chain armour. A mail coif was worn to protect the neck. The conical helmet had been replaced by the pot-helm, which was a flat-topped iron cylinder, covering the whole head, with slits to enable the wearer to see and breathe. The horse was a specially bred animal called a *destrier* – also protected by mail armour or quilting. The lance had become slightly longer. The chief striking power of the crusader forces lay in the impact of the heavy cavalry charge, although this was still a combination of individual assaults rather than a mass charge. Foot soldiers carried out camp and siege duties. The most important infantry were the bowmen, in particular mercenary crossbowmen from northern Italy.

The main strength of the Saracen armies lay with their horse archers; these were more lightly equipped than the cavalry of the crusaders, the horses being faster and handier. Besides his bow, the mounted archer carried a small round shield, a short lance, a sword

The Saracen mounted archers sometimes made feigned retreats, firing Parthian shots as they went

and a club. A major problem for the Saracens was disunity of command. For example, the emirs commanding the Saracen forces at the battle of Aarran in 1104 failed to follow up their victory because they were quarrelling over the spoils. Saladin was the first undisputed leader of the forces of Islam.

The Saracens usually took the tactical offensive – exploiting the superior mobility of their light cavalry, harassing the crusaders on the march, and in battle encircling them. The offensive strength of the crusaders lay in their heavy cavalry. To avoid having to withstand this shock and also to break the cohesion of their enemy, the Saracens used tactics of evasion, adopting loose formations and keeping at a distance from the enemy until they could launch a sudden attack at the right moment. They made feigned retreats, and sometimes actual retreats, firing Parthian shots as they went and then returning to harass their enemy – like flies which could be beaten off only momentarily. Sometimes they retreated for days on end, in order to draw the crusaders into difficult country and wear them out. Frequently, for example with great effect against Louis VII's forces in Asia Minor, they ambushed or sniped at the enemy on the march. Their bows were not powerful enough for the arrows to penetrate mail armour, so they often directed their fire on the enemy's horses.

The tactics of the crusaders, which were largely worked out by Bohemund during the

The backbone of the crusader armies was the mounted cavalry

first Crusade, were on the whole defensive – being designed to counter the Saracen tactics. Byzantine military ideas and local experience led to certain changes in the relatively crude tactics current in the West. For example, care was taken in the order of march and in deployment for battle to guard against encirclement or surprise – the crusading force moving with strong advanced flank and rear guards of archers, which would cover the ranks of the knights until the moment was right for their charge. The harassing tactics of the Saracens were unpleasant, and it was not easy to restrain the knights from taking individual and reckless action. But it had to be done. The Templars laid down severe penalties for any knight who left the ranks without authority; nonetheless, in 1191 at the battle of Arsuf in the third Crusade, Richard Coeur-de-Lion could not restrain the Hospitallers from charging too soon. When strictly disciplined, with co-ordination between infantry and cavalry action, the crusaders were often successful. But generally they avoided open battle, in which they were always outnumbered. In any case, since it was usual for the Saracens to abandon their campaigns at the beginning of winter, there was little point in fighting to drive them away. Nevertheless, it was bad for morale to allow the enemy to overrun the country around the crusader castles.

With a century's experience behind them the crusaders had eventually developed a sound doctrine of warfare against the Saracens. But at the battle of Hattin, Guy de Lusignan threw experience and good sense overboard. In order to raise an army of 1,200 knights, 2,000 native light cavalry, and 10,000 infantry, Guy deprived the castles of the region of all but the most meagre garrisons. Abandoning the proven strategy of avoiding the risk of open battle and keeping close to protective castles, he led his men into the barren and dry hills of Galilee – where Saladin lay with 20,000 men.

When it was reported to Saladin that Guy's army was advancing, he sent forward units of skirmishers to begin harassing the enemy. The first attacks were delivered in the heat of the day. The thirsty crusaders soon had no water left and, becoming tired, they lost cohesion. The van crawled on, but the important compact order of march was lost, and finally the rearguard and most of the centre became encircled by swarms of bowmen. The main body of the crusading army, the Templars, Hospitallers and Turcopoles, by now exhausted, bivouacked on the slopes of a hill with two hummocks on its crest called the Horns of Hattin – which I know well. There they spent a sleepless night, without water for themselves or their horses. The Saracens continued to subject them to volleys of arrows and unnerving taunts – even setting fire to the scrub, thus adding to their discomfort with suffocating smoke.

In the morning Saladin still refused to close with the crusaders; seventy camels laden with arrows supplied his archers, who continued to rain missiles unceasingly on the enemy. In desperation, Guy decided to try and put an end to the torture suffered by his infantry, and loosed his knights in a charge; but no good resulted. Realizing the situation, some of the infantry began to panic, but Guy stopped the rot by holding aloft the True Cross. The knights charged again, and for a while the Saracens seemed to be in difficulties; but their horsemen closed in and eventually the crusaders, now completely encircled, concentrated round the Cross. This time the Saracens moved in for the kill. Raymond, and some of the knights whose horses were not wounded, made a desperate charge to cut their way through the enemy and escape. Most of the crusaders were annihilated; but some of the leaders, as well as the True Cross, were captured by the Moslems.

Saladin marked his victory over the crusaders by the capture of the True Cross at Hattin

Saladin had now all but destroyed the forces of the crusaders. By the end of 1187 almost the whole kingdom of Jerusalem was in his hands, the city itself falling in October – its inhabitants being mercifully treated. In the West a third Crusade was at once preached, with some success. The emperor Frederick Barbarossa set out from Germany in 1189, but his army was decimated by the Saracens in Asia Minor. The kings of France and England, Philip Augustus and Richard Coeur-de-Lion, reached the Holy Land and recaptured Acre and Jaffa – but had to turn back before Jerusalem. The degeneration of the crusading ideal was apparent in their continual quarrels, as well as in the conduct of the emperor Henry VI – who kidnapped Richard on his way home and held him to ransom – and of Philip who took advantage of Richard's absence to raid Normandy. The fourth Crusade (1202–4) represented a further decline. The strategical plan of conquering Egypt to secure a base for the invasion of the Holy Land was sound. But in the end the hard bargaining of their Venetian suppliers prevented the crusaders from getting any further than Constantinople, where, in April 1204, Baldwin of Flanders so far forgot his original purpose as to enter the city with his army and set himself up as emperor.

There were further Crusades in the thirteenth century, and for short periods the Christians recovered Jerusalem. St Louis, king of France (1226–70), indeed revived the highest ideals of the movement, even if others such as the emperor Frederick II and Simon de Montfort (the father of the parliamentarian) debased them further than ever before. But the story is complicated, and its military history presents little further interest. The really important developments were by this time again taking place in the West.

The knight in armour remained the symbol of military glory, though his effectiveness declined during the later Middle Ages. South German armour for man and horse, *c.* 1475—85

9   The High Middle Ages

During the High Middle Ages, between the battles of Bouvines (1214) and Morat (1476), warfare was the rule in Europe almost everywhere – and for our purpose it was a period of particular importance and interest. The disintegration of the Holy Roman Empire was furthered by the struggle in the thirteenth century between the Papacy and the Hohenstaufen imperial family, by the Swiss wars of independence fought after 1291 by the League of the Forest Cantons, and by the wars of the Bohemian Hussites between 1419 and 1436. The power of the English state was consolidated by Edward I's conquest of Wales (1277–95), although the English attempt to conquer Scotland (1296–1328) was a failure. Then came the great clash between England and France – the series of English invasions between 1337 and 1453, together known as the Hundred Years' War. The overall political effect of these wars was that Germany became still further fragmented and Rome lost much of her moral authority, while England and France passed beyond the feudal stage that had characterised medieval society to emerge as the leading nation-states of Europe.

From the military point of view these wars are immensely important. The hundred years between 1250 and 1350 was a most revolutionary period in the history of the art of war. The knight, the castle and feudalism gave way to the infantryman, to firearms, and to professionalism. Strategically, it became clear that the defensive with the weapons available could win battles provided the enemy could be induced to attack; but to win campaigns offensive action was necessary. Tactically, superiority passed to new missile weapons, and these, rather than shock action, became the decisive factor in battle. Eventually the gun was to prove the most powerful instrument of war during the next six hundred years. But although artillery was effective by the beginning of the fifteenth century, the full impact of firearms was not felt for a long time after their first appearance. Interest in this period focuses rather on one outstanding development: the revolutionary achievement of infantry, both spearmen and archers, who wrested from heavy cavalry its thousand-year mastery of the battlefield.

The battle of Hastings had confirmed the exclusive supremacy of heavy cavalry inaugurated by the battle of Adrianople in 378. Infantry became despised, and no commander in western Europe before the mid-thirteenth century grasped the lesson of the crusades: that the tactical sum of infantry and cavalry when carefully co-ordinated was far greater than the sum of the two parts when acting separately. Yet some proficient infantry did exist in the Netherlands and in northern Italy. Flemish pikemen had been employed by William at Hastings, and were used by Philip Augustus at Bouvines in 1214; they continued to win battles in the thirteenth century. By this time, however,

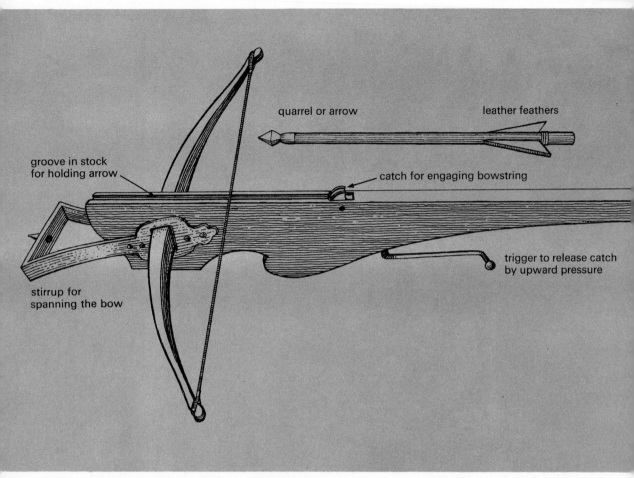

quarrel or arrow

leather feathers

groove in stock
for holding arrow

catch for engaging bowstring

trigger to release catch
by upward pressure

stirrup for
spanning the bow

The crossbow proved an effective weapon, though the firing rate was slow. The bow was at first made of wood, then of a composition of horn and wood, and finally of steel

they were supplanted as the chief mercenary infantry of Europe by the crossbowmen of the north Italian cities, principally Genoa.

The Genoese were well protected by a steel cap and mail-shirt. Their weapon, the crossbow, continued to evolve right up till the end of the fifteenth century. It remained basically a miniature *ballista*, a small stiff bow being set crosswise at the end of a stock. Eventually the bow was made of steel, being drawn either by a cord-and-pulley or by a rack-and-pinion, and discharging a short square bolt, with an iron head, wooden shaft, and leather 'feathers'. The weapon was heavy, slow to operate, and did not work in wet weather. But it had advantages: it was accurate up to a range of about 100 yards, could be handled by relatively untrained men who were not strong enough to draw a longbow, and was a particularly good weapon for defensive loop-hole shooting.

Good infantry units existed, but often were not properly used. In some of the most important battles of the thirteenth century, such as the Marchfeld in 1278 (the victory

Mail-shirts gave way to plate armour by the end of the fourteenth century. A vizored bascinet, Italian, *c.* 1380 *left;* a kettle hat, south German, *c.* 1460 *right*

by which Rudolph of Habsburg founded the power of his family on the Danube, which was to last till 1918), neither side used infantry. There were other cases where only one side had infantry – for example, Legnano in 1176. Generally, only a raw peasant levy was raised, for use in menial duties, or at best for skirmishing – as at Benevento in 1266. Infantry obviously lacked mobility compared to knights, but it is odd that commanders were so little aware at any rate of its defensive capacity. The pike was longer than the lance, and horses feared arrows. In 1237, at the battle of Cortenuova, the infantry units of the North Italian League massed together and stubbornly held off a surprise attack by Frederick II's cavalry, until they could melt away under cover of darkness. Occasionally considerable tactical perception was shown; a good example, again, is Legnano in 1176, when the steady Milanese foot gave the Lombard cavalry time to rally and then defeat the purely cavalry army of Barbarossa.

Heavy cavalrymen were divided into two grades, knights and sergeants. In the thirteenth century the sergeants, who were the retainers of the barons, bishops and abbots, rode lighter horses and wore less armour. But in the fourteenth century equipment was standardized, and the distinction of terminology became purely social. All men equipped with the full panoply of the heavy cavalryman were bracketed together for military purposes as 'men-at-arms'.

Armour was in a continual process of development. In 1200 the conical helmet was giving way to the pot-helm, a visor being added by 1300. The long mail tunic was supplemented by the surcoat and quilted protections called *gambesons*. Poorer men might wear the *gambeson* alone, without metal armour. Chain-mail was made finer, more supple and close fitting. Plate armour was a development of the fourteenth century, but by 1250 men began to improve their mail armour by the addition of metal plate caps for the knees, elbows and shins. Then the cuirass appeared; this provided a tougher protection against sword blows, but was heavy and left gaps. At Benevento there were 1,200 German cavalry armed with breast-plates, whose advance was irresistible until the French noticed that they could stab them in the armpits with rapiers.

Light cavalry, such as the German *panzerati* and the English 'hobilars', was used only for skirmishing and reconnoitring, and never had an integral part in the tactical systems of the Middle Ages. In the thirteenth century an army of men-at-arms still often relied for victory on weight and main force alone. Groups of horsemen would hurl themselves against the enemy, hacking with sword or battle-axe. Some commanders adopted a different tactic, dividing their men-at-arms into three 'battles' or divisions – success depending on the timing of each successive mass charge. Simon de Montfort is an example of an efficient commander of this time. Decisive, swift and cool, it was because he chose his ground well, surprised the enemy, and used his reserve line at the right time and place, that he won the battle of Lewes against Henry III in 1264 (making possible the institution of Parliament). To take another example, at Benevento in 1266 both sides drew up their cavalry in three corps, each a thousand strong. First came a preliminary infantry skirmish, which did not affect the main battle and which some chronicles do not even mention. Then each side launched its men-at-arms – Charles of Anjou defeated Manfred because he timed his charges better. Such was the normal tactical system of Europe in the 1300's, although towards the end of the century new conceptions appeared in Switzerland and England. But in France, commanders stuck rigidly to the old ways – until they met repeated disaster.

By the thirteenth century the feudal recruiting system was generally breaking down, although in principle the armies of the king of France continued to be raised in this way even in the Hundred Years' War. Obligations had become confused, and the feudal system was irregular and unreliable. The contingents tended to obey only their particular lord, and would serve no longer than forty days. A great disadvantage was that feudal levies consisted of amateurs, most of whom were probably not fully proficient in the use of their weapons. It is true that many knights had little to occupy themselves with except fighting; but their followers were farmers, who had other occupations and little time to spare for training.

Everywhere an increasing dependence was placed on mercenaries. In England the king was glad to allow his tenants to commute their feudal service for payment of a tax called 'scutage'. With these funds he could hire mercenary adventurers and their troops – landless younger sons, adventurers, refugees from serfdom – who were to be found all

By the fifteenth century heavy cavalrymen were completely encased in suits of plate armour

over Europe. These were trained and experienced professionals, used to working together. They would serve their paymaster for as long as required. Sometimes, however, they could be a great nuisance. Many mercenary recruits had been criminals, and when peace came these private armies might turn into gangs of bandits, living off the countryside. One of the causes of John's unpopularity was that he brought over to England the mercenary crossbowmen of Fawkes de Bréauté; these ruffians were still around in the next reign. Roger de Flor's 'Great Company', more than a thousand strong, was formed from discharged mercenary bands at the end of the Sicilian wars.

The best training in arms was to be had in tournaments. In the thirteenth century these were more like war than sport, for knights armed themselves and fought exactly as they would in actual battle. There were various types of tournament. The 'joust' was a combat of individual knights, who charged each other full tilt with their lances – three times. Then, if neither had been unhorsed, they dismounted and each dealt the other three blows with sword, mace or axe. The 'tourney' was much the same exercise, but performed by a group of knights. William the Marshal – pilgrim to Jerusalem, and regent of England for Henry III – as a young man was passionately keen on tournaments. He spent several years going from one to the next, fighting about once a fortnight, winning renown all over northern France, and making considerable profit – in one tournament he captured ten horses, and twelve knights whom he held to ransom. Commoners also had their war-games; these might be bouts with the quarter-staff or sword and buckler, and tilting at a dummy with a bucket of water on it. The crusades were sometimes described as a 'tournament between heaven and hell'.

With time, as life became more comfortable and tournaments produced too many serious injuries, elaborate rules were made. By the fifteenth century they were more popular than ever and far less dangerous. The knights charged each on his own side of a wooden fence; they used brittle lances which broke easily; and saddles were designed so that a man could slide down the tail of his horse. Even so, in a tournament in 1559 King Henry II of France was accidently killed by a Norman ancestor of mine, who had to flee the country quickly. That was unlucky, for by then the tournament was more of a pageant than a combat.

The last tournament ever held was arranged by the Earl of Eglinton in 1839 (Lord Montgomerie, the Scottish branch of my family). The participants travelled up to the earl's estate by train, and there was a full press coverage. 'Within the gothic hall be-

Tournaments provided valuable training for war, but they developed into little more than pageants

jewelled beauties occasionally flitted among the mailed knights.' Unfortunately a large part of the programme was cut short by rain.

By the beginning of the thirteenth century the status of knighthood had become associated with the concept of chivalry. Hitherto the knight had merely been the man who did military service on horseback in exchange for a grant of land. But in the twelfth century the crusades, and the institution of orders such as the Templars, had made knighthood first respectable and then even sacred. The theory came to be accepted that a knight was a man of particular virtue and valour who had been formally initiated into his caste. The old method of bestowing the status of knighthood, the accolade, still survived for the battlefield. The candidate knelt before another knight, who touched him with the flat of his sword on either shoulder, and pronounced a short formula of creation and exhortation. But a more elaborate initiation, later described by Selden, was now normal:

> The ceremonies and circumstances at the giving this dignity . . . were of two kinds . . . which we may call courtly and sacred. The courtly were the feasts held at the creation, giving of robes,

arms, spurs and the like. The sacred were the holy devotions . . . in the church . . . before the receiving of the dignity.

These included the vigil, the taking of arms from the altar, and the vow to protect all things weak, good or holy. John of Salisbury wrote:

> For what purpose is knighthood ordained? To protect the Church, to attack infidelity . . . to protect the poor, to keep the peace, to shed one's blood . . . for one's brethren.

John's description would have seemed sentimental to many knights. The *Song of Roland* expressed more realistically the qualities that were idealized. It is a good story of heroism and treachery, and it emphasizes the virtues of personal valour, loyalty to one's comrades, and confidence in the aid of the saints. This was the best expression of the chivalrous spirit, and reflected a just pride in the achievement of knightly arms in Europe by the thirteenth century: the stabilization of the borders, the recovery of political order, and the possibility of economic progress which resulted from a measure of security. Otherwise, it can be said that chivalry was a force for good in reminding the upper classes of a standard of decency worthy of their privileges. But it would be an illusion to regard the later literature of chivalry, the romances of Chrétien de Troyes and Thomas Malory, however beautiful, as an expression of anything that ever really happened. The knight is portrayed as engaged in a mysterious quest for virtue. But in fact, compared to our own day, the manners of the medieval gentleman were lacking in discipline and refinement. He relied on serf labour, and, if he had reverence for the Virgin Mary, there is not much evidence that he often had it for any other women. The wardship system became a racket, courtesy was shown only to captives who were worth a ransom, and the rest of the victims were usually slaughtered.

Another development of the thirteenth century was heraldry. This developed with the pot-helm, which by concealing the wearer's face made it necessary for him to carry some identifying mark. Individuals assumed more or less elaborate emblems, which were painted on the shield and embroidered on the surcoat. Crests were worn on top of helmets. Richard Coeur-de-Lion was the first king to display the arms of England, the three golden lions on a red ground. The heraldic system was also convenient for marshalling, each knight carrying a banner to rally his retinue.

Possibly the most momentous invention in the history of warfare has been gunpowder. But when the formula was originally published it passed unnoticed by soldiers. It is not known for certain who first discovered gunpowder, who thought of using it to force a projectile out of a tube, nor when and where the earliest gun was used in anger. The first man in the western world to record the formula for gunpowder was Roger Bacon, an English monk, in his *De Secretis Operibus Artis et Naturae et de Nullitate Magiae*, in 1260. His formula is seven parts of saltpetre, five of charcoal, and five of sulphur. 'With such a mixture you will produce a bright flash and a thundering noise, if you know the trick . . .' But, for fear of the Church, Bacon concealed his formula in a cipher and an anagram.

Fifty years at least then passed before the first gun appeared. In a treatise by an Englishman, Walter de Milemete, in 1326, there is an illustration of the earliest type of

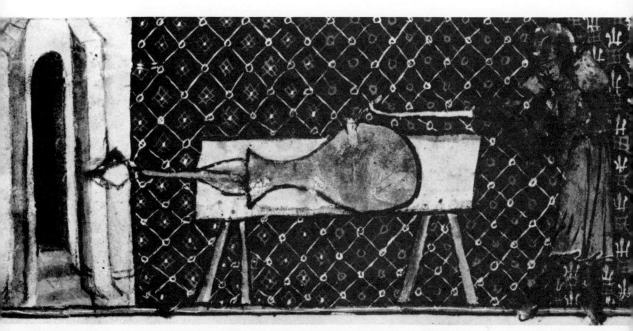

The earliest known gun in Europe is illustrated in a manuscript of 1326

cannon. This was known as a *pot-de-fer* or *vaso*, because it was shaped like a vase, with a fat body and a thin neck. In the picture it is mounted on a bench, and loaded with a large crossbow-type arrow with metal 'feathers'. The gunner has just fired it by thrusting a red-hot rod into the touch-hole. From the same year a Florentine document survives, ordering the Council to see to the production of cannon and iron bullets.

The first definite instance when a gun was fired in anger was in 1324 at Metz in France. In the next fifteen years they are heard of increasingly. Edward III probably used cannon against the Scots at Berwick in 1327. Certainly the French used *canons et bombardes* to fire arrows at the English at Quesnoi in 1340, and Edward used artillery in his siege of Calais in 1346. There was also another firearm, the *ribauldequin*. It was built of several metal tubes mounted on a sort of chariot and capable of being fired simultaneously. This would appear to have been a sort of primitive rocket battery, similar to those used by the Canadian Army on the Meuse, and by the Second British Army at the Rhine crossing in 1945. Edward ordered a hundred of these to be made in 1345. Thus by the mid-fourteenth century firearms were coming into regular use; but for some years they were not to make any real impact on the conduct of war.

Eventually guns were to break the impregnability of castles, the second great element of Norman warfare. But the castle long outlived the knight as a force to be reckoned with, and between 1260 and 1320 some of the most efficient fortifications of any age were built. The main principle of fortification now was to build a series of concentric powerful curtain walls, great attention being given to the outworks. The moat was often a lake. The gatehouses were strong and square, of three or four storeys and surmounted by twin towers. Approaches could be defended by one or more drawbridges, and then the gate by

Caerphilly, plan *right* aerial view *left*, was one of the finest concentric castles

machicolations, portcullises, two-leaved doors and loop-holes. The central bailey
enclosed by the walls frequently included a town, as at Flint, Conway and Caernarvon.
These castles, built in Edward I's Welsh wars (1277–95), served a strategic purpose
comparable to the chain of forts built by the Teutonic Knights to hold down the
barbarians of Prussia.

Sidney Toy described Caerphilly, built 1267–77, one of the earliest but also the best
of concentric castles:

> Caerphilly Castle stands on . . . an island in a lake, the lake being fed by a stream and held in by a
> great screen wall, or dam, forming the barbican. The main portion of the castle is rectangular,
> and is surrounded by two lines of walls, the inner wall having a tower at each corner and a large
> gatehouse [on the east and west sides], and the outer wall a gateway east and west in line with
> those of the inner wall. The towers of the inner wall have such bold projection beyond the corners
> that the outer faces of the . . . wall between them . . . could be swept from end to end by missiles

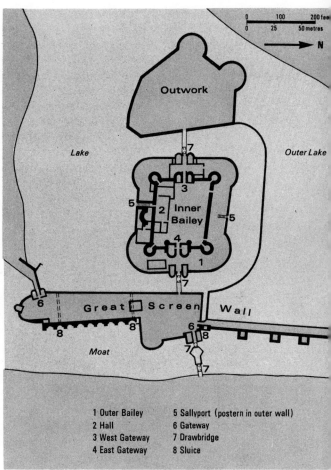

1 Outer Bailey   5 Sallyport (postern in outer wall)
2 Hall   6 Gateway
3 West Gateway   7 Drawbridge
4 East Gateway   8 Sluice

from the arrow-loops and battlements. The outer wall is lower and thinner than the inner, and in place of towers the curtain takes a circular sweep round the corners. The east gateways look towards the barbican, from which they were approached by a drawbridge. The west gateways look towards an outwork, which stood in the same lake . . .

In addition to the main gateways, there are three posterns in the inner bailey. The . . . doorways are each protected by a portcullis. From the posterns in the outer wall supplies could be brought in, sorties made, or escapes effected by boat.

The massive screen wall, sustained on one wing by a series of huge buttresses and on the other by three strong towers, is a most powerful and impressive work of military engineering. Through it run three sluices, by which the level of the water in the lake was regulated.

Caerphilly was never assailed, not surprisingly: for it would have been necessary to pass two moats and three walls built to include every defensive refinement.

In the fourteenth century powerful fortifications of this type were still being built. An example is the Bastille at Paris (1370–83). Rectangular in plan it had eight wall towers, and thick walls rising as high as the towers and crowned by a continuous machicolated parapet. There was a wide moat. With a little spirit in the defence, the Bastille could easily have held out on 14th July 1789. Many churches of the thirteenth and fourteenth centuries were fortified – for example, Les Saintes Maries near Arles, and the cathedral at Albi. Domestic architecture in the new towns of Italy also had a defensive aspect. In San Gimignano there were at least twenty houses which had their own fortified towers, and even during the Renaissance many town houses were built with severe plain walls and windows with strong grills. All the same, by the fourteenth century the demands of comfort increasingly overbore the requirements of security.

It is true to say that before the second half of the thirteenth century, no commander in western Europe perceived the tactical potentiality of infantry acting in co-ordination with cavalry, let alone of infantry used as the decisive striking force – despite the lessons of Legnano and the crusades. However this situation now altered dramatically, primarily because of the tactical conceptions of Edward I of England and of the Swiss leader, Rudolph of Erlach. Between 1282 and 1346 infantry won an outstanding but logical series of victories, which constituted a revolution in tactical history. At Courtrai (1302), Morgarten (1315) and Laupen (1339) spearmen defeated mounted men-at-arms. At Orewin Bridge (1282), Falkirk (1298) and Halidon Hill (1333) longbowmen defeated spearmen. Finally the battle of Crécy (1346) announced to Europe the downfall of the heavy cavalry arm after its thousand-year supremacy. That battle showed beyond doubt that cavalry could not win against archers supported by men-at-arms and drawn up in a strong position. At Poitiers (1356) and Agincourt (1415) the English longbowmen confirmed the power of their tactical system. Meanwhile in central Europe the Swiss pikemen, using a different method, continued to win victories. A little later in eastern Europe the Bohemian Hussites, using guns, demonstrated at Sudomer (1419) a third method by which foot soldiers could get the better of cavalry.

The first serious shock which heavy cavalry received on the Continent was at the battle of Courtrai in 1302, when a Flemish army consisting almost entirely of infantry pikemen destroyed a French army of knights. The Flemings were strongly assembled in a phalanx behind a stream; but the French commander, repeating the medieval cliché that 'a hundred horse are worth a thousand foot', ordered his men-at-arms to attack. As they reached the stream they got bogged down, and were helpless when the Flemish mass attacked them with their heavy pikes. This battle caused considerable discussion, but in the end the bog was blamed rather than the Flemings, and the moral was shirked: that courageous infantry, in a strong defensive position and intelligently led, could defeat cavalry. When the French later defeated the Flemings it seemed to confirm that Courtrai had been a departure from the normal.

A second shock for cavalry, comparable to Courtrai, was the victory of the Swiss Confederate spearmen over their Austrian overlords at Morgarten in 1315. Duke Leopold neglected to make a reconnaissance before sending his army up a narrow, steep and slippery Alpine pass in November. The Swiss barricaded the road and ambushed the Austrians. The Austrian men-at-arms were more numerous, but they were taken by surprise and jammed together. 'The mountain folk slew them like sheep in the shambles.' Still, again, it was possible to lay the blame on unfavourable terrain and poor command.

The Swiss victory over their feudal lords at Laupen in 1339, however, put the matter beyond doubt, for here the battle between infantry and cavalry was fought out on an open slope. Rudolph of Erlach, the Swiss commander, being outnumbered, adopted a defensive plan. He stationed his few cavalry on the right where the slope was steeper, and the bulk of his infantry on the left where the severest attack was expected. His tactical plan was to wait for the enemy to begin the ascent towards him, and then charge down in a dense mass. The Bernese, on the right, were immediately successful. But on the left the men of the Forest Cantons, clashing with the baronial cavalry far down the slope, soon found themselves in trouble. Their charge downhill was halted, they were surrounded and forced to make a stand back to back with their halberds bristling – in the 'hedgehog' formation which was to become famous. The fighting was close and ferocious, but the mountaineers held firm until the Bernese came to their relief, charging the enemy cavalry in flank and rear to win the battle. It had been a fair fight. The Swiss peasants captured 27 feudal banners and 70 crested helms.

At Laupen the Swiss were still using the halberd, a heavy spear, the head of which had both a spike and a blade. But the halberd was only 8 feet long, and already they were changing over to the weapon which they were to keep, the 18-foot pike: an ash shaft with a 10-inch steel head, held level at shoulder height, and totally effective against cavalry. In battle the Swiss presented an impenetrable bristling hedge, with the pikes of the first four ranks projecting together in front. The hedge was equally effective in a defensive wall or in a mass advance. The tactical system of the Swiss was so efficient and simple, like that of the Spartans and the Romans, that it was hardly ever varied. Their light armour (due originally to poverty, but then found to be an advantage) gave them great mobility, and they usually took the offensive. Machiavelli considered that 'no troops were ever more expeditious on the march, or in forming themselves for battle'. They marched brigaded in fighting order, and were the first modern troops to march in step to music. Their usual method of attack was to advance in an *échelon* of three parallel columns, one slightly behind the next. This gave flank protection and a reserve to the attacking column in the lead.

During the two centuries after Morgarten (1315) the Swiss pikemen suffered no serious reverses. But rivalry between the cantons, and their system of command by a council, always prevented the Swiss from following up their victories strategically, and they never established themselves as a first-class political power. Instead they became the leading mercenary soldiers of Europe. At Sempach in 1386 they won another important victory, this time over dismounted men-at-arms. The Austrian commander, not understanding that the past successes of the Swiss had been due to their particular weapons and formation, reckoned that if his men fought on foot they ought, with their heavier equipment, to be able to cut down the peasants. But the weight of their armour exhausted the Austrians before they ever closed, and the experiment was a disaster. In 1476 the Swiss pikemen won the two most famous of all their victories, over Charles the Rash of Burgundy, at Granson and Morat.

It was in England that the infantry revolution first manifested itself. The man responsible was Edward I (1274–1307), conqueror of Wales, victor at Falkirk in 1298, a great military organizer and a fine commander. In his Evesham campaign in 1265 Edward evinced remarkable strategical imagination, timing a series of rapid manoeuvres to prevent two enemy armies joining, and all the while maintaining a river front of fifty

Swiss pikemen *left* and English longbowmen *right* outfought the medieval cavalry

miles – until he could dispose of one enemy and then turn swiftly to trap Simon de Montfort in a loop of the Avon. In his Welsh wars (1277–95) Edward again showed his strategic vision, in building a systematic network of roads and castles. He also saw that the Welsh mountaineers could not be conquered by the conventional army of the time, a cavalry host limited to a short period of service in the summer. So he made two innovations of major and enduring importance: he relied on a hired, professional army contracted to serve all the year round, and he exploited the potentialities of the longbow.

The professionalization of armies had started with the increasing dependence on mercenaries. The unsuitability of normal feudal forces in the Welsh situation forced Edward I to abandon that method of recruitment, but in any case the feudal system was breaking down for various economic and constitutional reasons. Specialization and professional armies would be further necessitated by economic factors in the next century, when the new types of armour became very expensive, and plague carried off much of the population of Europe.

Edward I's solution to the problem of recruitment was to encourage many of his feudal tenants to commute their service for 'scutage', referred to earlier in the chapter. He asked his other tenants to bring fewer but better troops, and contracted to pay them after the expiry of their feudal period of service – the first such military contract, known as an 'indenture', being made in 1277. The system was developed by Edward III in his Scottish and French wars. The 'indentures' were precise written agreements between a professional officer and the king. They laid down the exact size and composition of the force provided, the place, duration and type of service, the rates of pay, bonuses and so on. Most commonly the force provided was of all arms, and included such personnel as artificers, surgeons, miners, chaplains and interpreters, as well as archers and men-at-arms. The term of service ranged from the old forty days to 'the king's pleasure'. The Earl of Kent, for example, in 1360 contracted to serve the king 'at the accustomed wages of war' for three months; he was to provide 60 men-at-arms and 120 archers, all with horses. From 1340 onwards Edward III's armies had no feudal element. They consisted mostly of his own subjects, but also a few bands of foreign mercenaries, all serving on 'indentures', under highly capable professional officers. The population of France during the Hundred Years' War was roughly five times that of England, but because the French stuck to the feudal system of recruitment they had no proper infantry, and their men-at-arms, although more numerous, were less highly trained and disciplined than the English.

Edward I's other revolutionary innovation was to make the longbow the chief English weapon. The archers at Evesham (1265) were still armed with the crossbow, but in the Welsh wars (1277–95) the longbow came to the fore, and the English victory at Orewin Bridge in 1282 was won by means of it. It was in fact originally a Welsh weapon. The English longbows were 6 feet 4 inches in height, and required a muscular pull of about 100 pounds to draw them. They were usually made of yew or elm. In the middle they were $1\frac{1}{2}$ inches wide, $1\frac{1}{4}$ inches thick, flat on the outside, and rounded in the belly. The ends tapered, and were tipped with horn in which a notch was cut to hold the bowstring. The string might be of hemp whipped with light linen cord. The arrow, or 'cloth-yard shaft', was some 37 inches long, made with a small, not particularly sharp, lozenge-shaped head, and was 'fletched' with the halves of three goose feathers. The 6-foot bow was a weapon that could be used only by a very tall and strong man. In an almost continual motion it was drawn back to the angle of the jawbone, aimed and loosed. The accurate range was 250 yards, and the extreme range 350 yards.

The only armour worn by longbowmen was a metal cap and a quilted tunic or, exceptionally, a cuirass. They carried, besides the bow, a sword and sometimes an iron-headed cudgel. They had leather protections on their hands. To stop the bowstring being entangled they kept their hair cut short, thus founding an important British military tradition. From 1252 onwards all forty-shilling freeholders were required to possess a bow, and the yeomen thus became a standing archery militia. Archery practice was at various times compulsory, and took such forms as shooting at a popinjay on top of the church tower after mass on Sundays, and the game of 'rovers' – medieval golf – in which archers progressed from field to field shooting at one target after another.

The tactical potentialities of missile fire received their first full recognition in Edward I's Welsh wars. A rain of arrows might, as a preliminary, unnerve the enemy and destroy their cohesion, and it could cover the advance of one's own men-at-arms. In December 1282, at Orewin Bridge, the English, led by Edward Mortimer and John

Giffard, defeated the Welsh. The Welsh spearmen were in a strong position, massed on a slope. But the English surprised them, their longbowmen bombarding them with arrows from the flank; then, and only when this attack had taken effect, they launched the charge of their men-at-arms. Much the same pattern unfolded in a battle near Conway in 1295, and in 1298 Edward I himself tried out the new tactics against the Scots at Falkirk. William Wallace was determined to face the English only from the strongest possible defensive position, and the Scots were drawn up in four great masses of spearmen, on a steep slope backed by a forest and fronted by a morass. Edward was short of supplies, was far from his base, and he himself had two broken ribs. Nonetheless, he decided to attack. The battle opened when the English men-at-arms on the left and right rode round the morass and charged the Scots in each flank. The spearmen checked them easily. Instead of ordering a second charge Edward now brought up his longbowmen, and from very close range a concentrated archery fire was loosed against particular points in the enemy masses. Many of the Scots soon fell, and the rest became unsteady. A second charge of men-at-arms at the weakened parts of the enemy front decided the battle, which ended in a great slaughter.

The English defeat by the Scots under Bruce at Bannockburn in 1314 happened because Edward II reverted to outdated methods, failing to co-ordinate his archers with his men-at-arms. But this was a temporary lapse. At Dupplin Moor in 1332 Edward Baliol developed the new English system further, by combining archers with dismounted men-at-arms in a defensive formation. The men-at-arms waited in the centre for the advance of the enemy. The archers on either wing were thrown out in a half-moon, scattered thinly in the heather so that they presented no solid body for the enemy to attack. When the struggle became locked in the centre, the archers poured simultaneous volleys into the flanks of the Scots columns. The Scots became unnerved and jammed together, and the second drive of the English men-at-arms was again decisive. The following year Edward III, with several of the senior officers who had fought at Dupplin, repeated this tactical plan with equal success at Halidon Hill.

In 1337 the Hundred Years' War between England and France began. A variety of antagonisms made this long struggle a matter of national interest on both sides. The issues included the feudal status of the English Duchy of Guienne (in south-west France), Edward III's alleged claim to the throne of France, the recent French support of the Scots, rivalry over the Flemish wool trade, and a long-standing border warfare between English and French sailors in the Channel. From a few disjointed invasions by the English, it developed into a war of devastation and attrition, with a few big clashes and no decisive battles. It really amounted to the repeated devastation of the farms and monasteries of Artois, Normandy, Brittany and Aquitaine by ruffianly bands of professional soldiers. But from the moment, in 1337 when the Earl of Derby fought his way ashore at Cadzand in Flanders, the most powerful weapon was the longbow.

The first considerable battle of the war was at sea, off Sluys in 1340. For a hundred and fifty years after Hastings, ships had not altered from the Viking pattern, and there had been no large naval operations in northern waters. In the thirteenth century there had been a continuous and more or less ferocious war in the Channel. The style of ships had developed, and the flagship of Edward III, the *Thomas*, was about 275 tons, with a crew of 137. Ships now had high sides and raised poops and forecastles. They were

Medieval warfare. A miniature from a fifteenth-century French manuscript

generally driven by one large square sail. Tactics at sea corresponded to those on land, as did differences in armament. The French at Sluys fought with swords and pikes and a few crossbows, while the English relied on men-at-arms and above all on longbowmen (firing special arrows tipped with broad heads to slash through rigging and sails). Edward III himself was in command, and he had 147 ships to the 190 of the French. Both sides drew up their ships in three divisions. While the French chained their ships together to make three massive floating platforms for their men-at-arms, the English adopted a more flexible formation – alternate ships containing archers and men-at-arms. The English tactics were to launch a preliminary missile bombardment from long range to weaken the enemy, and then to close – so that the men-at-arms with swords and lances could board the enemy ships. After eight hours of fighting the French broke, and finally they lost seven-eighths of their ships and three-quarters of their men.

Although no great land battle was fought until the war had been going for almost ten years, there were several campaigns during which each side had time to get the feel of the other. The weapons and equipment of the men-at-arms on both sides were very similar. Armour was in the process of transition from mail to plate. The helm was tough, the shield was becoming smaller and the spurs more prominent. The main weapons were the sword, a 14-foot long lance, and the dagger or 'misericord'. The units of organization were the retinues of the knights, which were broken down into groups or 'lances' of three to four fighting men. Both sides had some firearms, the *pots de fer*, but these were as yet tactically insignificant. Where they differed, and where the English held the advantage, was in training, recruitment and the quality of the infantry. The English professionals were fresh from their successes in Scotland; on the other hand the French feudal levies had experienced no battle fighting during the past twenty-five years beyond occasional expeditions into Guienne. And whereas the few infantry units the French possessed consisted of crossbowmen, the English had a large force of archers, using a weapon which gave twice the range and six times the firing rate of the crossbow.

Before the first great encounter at Crécy in 1346 the French were given two sharp foretastes of the English longbow. At Morlaix in 1342 the Earl of Northampton entrenched his men on a ridge behind a marsh, with the men-at-arms dismounted and the archers on the wings. The French cavalry were so bombarded as they attacked that they were in dismayed confusion when the English men-at-arms charged down on them. The second time, a flying column of English was caught by the French at St Pol de Léon in Brittany and surrounded. The English stood their ground, and poured such a stream of arrows into the enemy that 'a veritable massacre' ensued.

In 1345–6 Edward III conceived the ambitious strategy of attacking King Philip VI of France on exterior lines, from Brittany, Gascony and Flanders. The Earl of Northampton and Sir Thomas Dagworth conducted successful campaigns in Brittany, and the Earl of Derby in the south-west. In 1346 Philip bestirred himself to march against Derby, only to be forced to return north by the news, in July, that Edward had landed near Cherbourg with more than 10,000 men. Derby immediately launched a diversionary campaign in Poitou.

Edward presumably hoped that these simultaneous attacks would induce Philip to offer terms or meet him in battle, but his precise strategical purpose is not clear. The English army marched on a broad front through much of the same country over which the Allied armies fought after the invasion of Normandy in June 1944. Enemy ships and

Medieval warfare. A detail from 'Die Alexanderschlacht' by Albrecht Altdorfer

Ships had raised poops and forecastles, and were driven by one large square sail

installations along the coast were destroyed, Caen was captured on 26th July, and the advance continued up to the Seine. Edward was then faced with a problem. Many of his ships had returned to England, and he had no secure communications behind him; a large French army was coming up from the south. Would it not be safer to move away north-eastwards towards Flanders, where he could at least hope to effect a junction with an Anglo-Flemish force which was advancing south from Ypres? But he was unable to cross the Seine at Rouen, as he had hoped: the bridge had been destroyed.

Nothing daunted, he quickly decided to march his army up the Seine until he could find a crossing place – which he did at Poissy, near Paris. Fortunately for him Philip failed to attack and he was able to cross the Seine and head for the Somme at top speed. He reached Abbeville on 22nd August. But Philip was already at Amiens. On the 23rd the English rearguard left Airaines only two hours before the first of the French came up. Edward's situation was now unpleasant; the Somme, an awkward obstacle, had to be

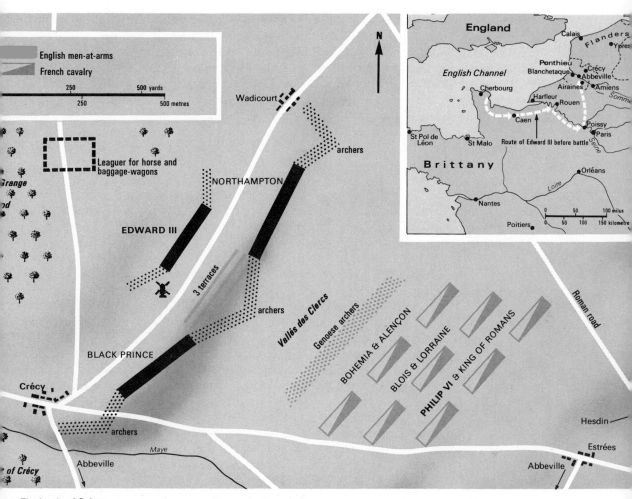

The battle of Crécy

crossed. I know all that area very well, having fought over it in two world wars; I can well imagine Edward's feelings.

But in the moment of adversity his decision and courage saved him. On the night of the 23rd he offered a large reward to anyone who would tell him of a practicable ford. A local man betrayed the French and guided the English during the night to Blanchetaque, on the Somme ten miles below Abbeville. The river here was very wide, and the enemy had a force of 500 men-at-arms and 3,000 infantry on the opposite bank. At ten o'clock next morning the English archers advanced. Despite damp bowstrings and the waist-deep water they cleared the edge of the far bank, and the men-at-arms forced their way on. The rearguard then began to cross, fighting off the French coming up behind – who, curiously enough, did not pursue any further. The English extrication at Blanchetaque was a fine feat of arms.

On 25th August the English army rested at the edge of the forest of Crécy-en-

Ponthieu, nine miles north of Abbeville where Philip's army lay. Edward had made up his mind to fight a battle, and apparently he knew that Philip had decided likewise. Edward felt himself bound to defend his grandmother's territory of Ponthieu, and since Blanchetaque the morale of his army was high. The Anglo-Flemish advance had stopped fifty-five miles away to the north, so he could expect no help. But friendly Flanders was only three days' march to the north, and there was no natural obstacle to block retreat.

On the morning of 26th August 1346 Edward III prepared his army for battle. He had the choice of position, and plenty of time to array his forces. Knowing that he would be heavily outnumbered, and since it suited his tactics, he chose a strong defensive position. This was the ridge which runs north-eastwards for about 2,000 yards from the village of Crécy to the cluster of houses at Wadicourt. A stream called the Maye ran from east to west, passing by Crécy. The ridge, therefore, at its southerly end, the English right, sloped down steeply, for about 100 feet, to the stream. But to the north-east the slope became more gradual until, on the English left, there was very little gradient. A few hundred yards behind the ridge was a wood. The natural strength of the ridge was increased by three terraces near the centre, built for cultivation, each about 350 yards long and very difficult for cavalry to negotiate. The English right was well protected in flank by the village and the stream. Though the left was much weaker, this did not matter since the French must advance along the Abbeville-Hesdin road on the right. Edward had no more than 12,000 or 13,000 men to fill a line almost 2,000 yards long. But, if it was safe to leave the terraces thinly manned, this was enough.

Intending, on the lines of Halidon Hill and Morlaix, to use his men-at-arms on foot, Edward left the horses, together with the baggage, in a leaguer by the wood. The main force of the men-at-arms was placed on the right, well down the slope, only about 300 yards from the valley bottom; the nominal commander was the 17-year-old Black Prince, assisted by Godfrey Harcourt and the Earl of Warwick. The left was held by the division of the experienced Earl of Northampton, placed rather higher up the slope. The third division of men-at-arms, the king's, was in reserve, slightly behind the centre of the line. The main force of the archers was drawn up in 'herce' or wedge formation on the flanks of the divisions of men-at-arms. There were three wedges: the outer two each linking one of the front divisions with a village, and the central wedge connecting the two divisions. Edward's own division was also flanked by archers. The overall proportion of archers to men-at-arms was about two to one. Pitfalls, or *trous de loup*, were dug in front of the Black Prince's division. Edward's command post was a windmill, on the highest point of the ridge about 700 yards from Crécy. From here he could command the whole English line, as well as the presumed approach route of the French along the road from Abbeville.

When the soldiers had been assigned to their positions by the marshals, the king rode along the lines inspecting his forces and giving them words of encouragement. On their performance his crown depended. Towards midday there was no sign of the enemy, and the men were given permission to fall out and have a meal. Each archer laid his bow and quiver at his position on the ground, and each man-at-arms his helmet. At the hour of vespers, about half past four o'clock, there was a sudden flurry of rain, and the archers rushed to cover their bowstrings. There was still no sign of the French.

Philip, misled by his intelligence service, had supposed that the English were nearer the Somme. He had given orders for an advance from Abbeville at dawn, but his scouts began looking for the English in the wrong direction. It was only just after the rain ended that the French came down from the Abbeville direction towards the Maye stream. When Edward saw them from the windmill the trumpet was sounded, and the English soldiers went quickly to their places.

Philip's feudal army was led by a motley galaxy of princes and nobles. With him were the almost blind King John of Bohemia and his son Charles, king of the Romans; James III of Majorca; and many of the leading chivalry of France and the Rhineland. The best troops in the army were the royal household knights and 6,000 mercenary crossbowmen from Genoa. The total strength of the French army is very uncertain; estimates range from the 100,000 boastfully alleged by contemporary English chroniclers to the face-saving 12,000 suggested by Professor Lot. I have always assumed that 40,000 was about right.

Even at a distance the French were seen already to be in some disorder, possibly as a result of changing the direction of their march. The situation was made worse when Philip, seeing the English array, decided that he would rather postpone the battle until the next day and gave the order to halt. The order was obeyed by the van of the army, but not by the rear. The men in front were forced on from behind, with no clear orders. Furthermore, the French were approaching the English front from the road at an oblique angle, and had to wheel half left at the last moment to face it directly. Inevitably over the last mile disorder increased to chaos. Descriptions of the French formation as they met the English are most obscure. But it is likely that, at any rate in theory, the French men-at-arms were in three divisions: the first under the king of Bohemia and the Count of Alençon; the second under the Count of Blois and the Duke of Lorraine; and the third commanded by King Philip and the king of the Romans. The Genoese were in front. The French had the low evening sun in their eyes, a tremendous disadvantage in battle – whether in attack or defence. I adopted this tactic at the battle of Mareth in March 1943, when I launched my left hook against the German 'last ditch' positions at the north end of the Matmata Hills – attacking in a north-easterly direction in the late afternoon, with the bright African sun low in the sky and directly in the eyes of the Germans.

As the French advanced with loud battle cries, confident at least in their numbers, the English waited silently. When the Genoese came within range of the longbow, which was before they could touch their enemy, the first English volley was loosed. In a few minutes the Genoese were in confusion. Terror reigned when the English let off their cannon – the first ever to be used in an important battle. It is recorded that the guns 'made a sound like thunder', and if that was the only impact they made it was nonetheless momentous. The French cavalry, however, was surging forward and many of the mercenaries were ridden down by their own employers.

The longbow continued to work execution among the French men-at-arms.

> The bowmen let fly among them at large, and did not lose a single shaft, for every arrow told on horse or man . . . So the knights . . . fell, slain or sore stricken, almost without seeing the men who slew them.

Probably not a single man in the first French division even got within hand-striking distance of the English. But already the next wave of French cavalry was charging through the carnage of those in front.

The continuation of the battle was no more than a succession of suicidal charges by masses of French men-at-arms, and the English reckoned afterwards that from first to last they had fought off fifteen successive attacks. With desperate *élan* the French hurled themselves up the slope, each time heading for the English men-at-arms, partly through outmoded tradition, but actually because neither they nor their horses could face the arrows. The English archers held their position and formation throughout. As each charge began they first loosed volleys to break the enemy into disorder and slow their impetus, and then they raked their flanks. Handfuls of the bravest knights in the French army, such as a group of followers of the king of Bohemia, reached the line of the English men-at-arms, only to be cut down by more numerous and fresher men. Each successive wave was muddled and hampered by the retreating remnants of its predecessors. The attacks went on until long after dark, but they grew ever more haphazard and ineffectual, and the English shield-wall, this time, did not waver.

Completely confident in his tactical arrangements, Edward observed the whole course of the action from his mill. In the evening he advanced the left division a little downhill, wheeling it round to face the French right flank and ease the pressure on the Black Prince's division. But he never needed to use his central reserve. He kept his men under arms on the field all night, and in the morning they disposed of a few French reserves unaware of the true situation. There was no pursuit. August 27th was foggy, and the English spent the day clearing the battlefield.

At Crécy a trained, well-armed, confident English army, under a commander who was a tried expert in the most efficient new tactics of the age, defeated a larger army which was hastily raised, diverse, untrained, out of date, and indecisively led. The only sane course for Philip to adopt was to halt for the night of 26th August, which, in fact, he ordered. But some of his subordinates had other ideas. All in all, it is clear that he lacked that tight grip on his army, so necessary in war and particularly in the encounter battle – with the result that the French army was committed to battle when out of control and undeployed. Tactically, Crécy was the logical culmination of the series of victories won by longbowmen since Orewin Bridge sixty-four years earlier. Edward followed up his victory by the capture of Calais, which as a military and commercial bridgehead abroad was to be as useful to England for two hundred years as Gibraltar in a later age. But the strategic result of Crécy in the Hundred Years' War was, above all, moral. The English emerged as the leading military people of Europe, and there would be no question of them abandoning their adventure in France until the French could find means to force them out.

Edward III remained the English commander-in-chief until 1360, when the Treaty of Calais brought a pause in the war. Another great victory was won, by the Black Prince at Poitiers in 1356, and the morale of the army remained as good as ever. For twenty-two years altogether – a period as long as the Napoleonic War – Edward III had consistently pursued one strategy, and his soldiers were always confident in his leadership. He was successful, and soldiers will always follow a successful general. Furthermore, the continuity and loyalty within the ranks of his high command – Derby, Warwick, Northampton, Hawkwood, Chandos – was outstanding.

War was resumed in 1369. Desultory and unprofitable fighting went on, much of it mere brigandage, until Henry V's invasion in 1415 altered its character. The dominant figure was the Constable of France, Bertrand du Guesclin. His Fabian strategy, of avoiding large pitched battles and pouncing on isolated English columns, worked so well that by 1377 the French had reduced the English possessions in southern France to an area of twenty miles radius around Bordeaux. The French, however, did not overhaul their army, and the English, unbeaten in actual battle, refused to give up. Every so often an English commander set out on a *chevauchée*, taking a column of men through enemy country and achieving no more than a passage of destruction. The most famous *chevauchée* was John of Gaunt's in 1373. With 15,000 men he set out from Calais to relieve Guienne. He was caught by winter in the Massif Central, but proceeded down the valley of the Dordogne to reach Bordeaux, having marched a thousand miles in five months and losing half his army without fighting a single battle.

The armour and tactics of the French men-at-arms were somewhat developed after Crécy in an attempt to deal with the problem of the arrow. The transition from mail to plate armour was completed by 1400, by which time a man-at-arms was encased from head to foot in metal. But the quest for security meant a loss of mobility, which more than countered any benefit in the change – the mounted man being so burdened with protective armour that he became virtually immobilized. At Poitiers in 1356, as the Austrians were to do thirty years later at Sempach, King John II of France dismounted his men-at-arms, and suffered the same fate. Trying to beat infantry at its own game without understanding how it had been won, he merely sacrificed his assets of superior mobility and impact. Nonetheless men-at-arms remained dismounted for the next hundred years, and the lance was abandoned. At Agincourt in 1415 the English archers, although handicapped by diarrhoea, had no difficulty in mowing down the French men-at-arms herded together, exhausted and stumbling in the mud.

In the second half of the Hundred Years' War, from 1415, artillery began to affect the shape of warfare. Cannon by now had evolved from the vase to the cylindrical shape, and improved methods of casting had made it possible to manufacture guns sufficiently strong and large to hurl projectiles of 200 pounds weight. At the outset of his campaign in 1415 Henry V laid siege to Harfleur. When mining failed he resorted to artillery. He had ten cannon, three of which were exceptionally large, with names such as 'London' and 'The King's Daughter'. The chief engineer, Master Giles, organized a steady bombardment, night and day, particularly concentrated against the walls flanking one gate. After twenty-seven days the gate and barbican were in ruins. Master Giles then set alight the woodwork with an incendiary shell, and as the breach was stormed the town surrendered. When Henry V's artillery battered down the walls of Harfleur in 1415 the era of impregnable fortifications passed. There was no reaction in military architecture till the end of the fifteenth century.

By 1419 Henry V had recovered all Normandy. But in 1422 he died, and between then and 1453 the French gradually drove the English off their soil. One of the leading spirits in the French recovery was Joan of Arc, a peasant girl who presented herself at the court of the lethargic French king, Charles VII, telling him that she knew how to win the war. Her presence at the raising of the siege of Orléans in 1429 seems to have inspired the French, and they went on to clear the English out of central France. The Duke of Alençon reported that Joan was an expert at 'the preparation of the artillery'. Eventually she was captured, and burned to death by the English in 1431. I have never been able to decide whether Joan had any God-given military ability herself or whether she was merely a tool in the hands of the French generals. One thing is clear: she certainly restored the morale of the French soldiery, sapped by a long succession of disasters – showing that she possessed psychological genius.

The superiority of the French in artillery was the chief cause of their success at the end of the war. The first great artilleryman was Jean Bureau. He is first heard of in 1439 at the successful French siege of Meaux. In 1449–50, within one year, Bureau and his brother conducted, it is said, sixty successful siege operations in the reconquest of Normandy. At the battle of Castillon in 1453 the French army under Bureau's command had 250 cannon. The cross-fire and enfilade by the French field artillery caused the English heavy casualties.

Already, some years earlier, field artillery had been used in eastern Europe as a third formula for the defeat of heavy cavalry by infantry. John Zizka was the military leader of the Hussite movement in Bohemia, a religious, nationalistic and popular uprising which began in 1419. After some street fighting in Prague, Zizka retired to the Hussite stronghold of Tabor in the south, with 400 followers and 12 wagons carrying guns. At the village of Sudomer they met 200 royalist cavalry. Zizka deployed his men where the ground gave the maximum flank protection, and arranged his gun-wagons in a leaguer. Victory went to the Hussites. By 1420 Tabor was organized as a theocratic community on a war footing. The Pope declared a crusade to root out the Hussites, and large Catholic forces mustered.

In the following wars Zizka was to show himself a highly original military thinker. Ignoring the medieval axiom that mounted men-at-arms were invincible, he adapted the resources that he had at his disposal. Having seen knights powerless before fortifications, he hit on the idea of making a wagon fortress. He used ordinary peasant wagons of a suitable size, mounted guns on them, and arranged them in a circle – just as the American pioneers were to do four hundred years later. For defence, the system of wagon leaguers defended by firearms gave him the advantages of a fortress combined with mobility. Zizka had an excellent eye for terrain; the wagons were usually on a small hilltop. The gaps between them were stopped up with mantlets. Each wagon carried two or three small guns, and heavier guns were mounted on special carriages. Zizka was the first commander to use field artillery systematically since the experiment of Alexander at the Hydaspes. The rest of the Hussite army consisted of a few cavalry for scouting, and infantry crossbowmen. The organization of the army was efficient.

When Zizka was satisfied with the training of his army in 1420 he set out for Prague. Using his new system he defeated the royalists at Vitkov, and by the end of the campaign of 1421 the Hussites were in control of most of Bohemia. Zizka himself was blinded by an arrow, but he continued to command, planning his battles on the basis of exact information about the enemy's forces and dispositions given to him in answer to his questions. He defeated the crusaders at Mount Vladar in 1421, and the king at Kutna Hora in 1422. In 1423–4 there were dissensions among the Hussites, and the Taborite sect led by Zizka defeated the Utraquist sect. The wars went on till 1436, when reasonable terms were agreed with Rome.

Zizka himself died of plague in 1424, aged only forty-eight. 'The whole army was overcome by immense sadness', and his soldiers were thereafter called 'orphans'. Undoubtedly they had lost a great leader. Zizka was a man of enormous personal courage and force of character. Unfettered by tradition, he ingeniously exploited limited assets to produce an original and successful tactical formula. He was to exercise a powerful influence on tactics and strategy in eastern Europe for the next two hundred years.

As the fifteenth century wore on gunpowder began to turn all other existing tactical traditions and methods upside down. Of the three weapons which had ruined the heavy cavalryman, the longbow, the pike and field artillery, the last named was to survive longest in its original form. The longbow was to be dropped as the authorised weapon of England by an edict of Elizabeth I's Privy Council in 1595. The Swiss pikeman survived for a time to be accepted in the earliest continental regular armies of the seventeenth century. However the bowman as well as the pikeman are equally the ancestors of the post-medieval European infantryman: the marriage of the missile principle with the pike produced the rifle with bayonet; and the alliance of gunpowder with the other resources of the national state produced the beginnings of modern warfare.

Cannons were normally fired from fixed positions for battering castle walls *left*, but in the Hussite wars they were given mobility for use against cavalry by being mounted on wagons *right*

The Spanish became the dominant military power in Europe and founded a great empire overseas. A detail from a mural depicting the capture of Oran from the Moors

PART THREE

EUROPEAN WARFARE

10

The Greatness of Spain

In the history of European warfare in the sixteenth century the leading nation was Spain. Obscure and backward in the Middle Ages, she acquired unity and bold purpose at the beginning of the century under Ferdinand and Isabella, reached the height of her power by 1550 under Charles I, and retained that importance under Philip II – although by 1600 the sun was beginning to set on her vast empire. Spain took a major part in all the great nationalistic-dynastic wars in Europe in the sixteenth century: the Valois-Habsburg struggle between 1494 and 1559, the French wars of religion from 1562 to 1598, and the Dutch war of independence from 1568 to 1609. Furthermore, in the great new commercial offensive of European imperialism the ships of Spain, with those of England snapping at their heels, were responsible for the tremendous development and expansion of the strategic and diplomatic horizon of Europe to include the Atlantic and the newly colonized continent of America.

In the development of military and naval technology and tactics Spain was again a leader. The overriding question was clearly what was to be the future of guns. At the battle of Cerignola in 1503 Gonzalo de Córdoba, known with justice by the Spaniards as their *gran capitán*, demonstrated that the handgun or arquebus would for many years be the dominant weapon in battle. The irresistible forays of Europeans over the seas of the world in this period were made possible by the development of the sailing ship armed with cannon – described by Professor Cipolla as 'essentially a compact device which allowed a relatively small crew to master unparalleled masses of inanimate energy for movement and destruction'. Here the most creative individual, both in the navigation and tactics of these revolutionary ships, was an Englishman – Francis Drake. But Spanish seamen, though outclassed at the defeat of the Armada in 1588, had been as ready to experiment as any. Land warfare after about 1525 became almost entirely a matter of manoeuvre and siegecraft, open battles on any large scale being avoided. But of the three outstanding military commanders in the European wars of the later part of the sixteenth century – Alexander of Parma, Ambrogio Spinola, and Maurice of Nassau – the first two were in the service of Spain.

The explanation of the rise of any people to military greatness must ultimately be obscure, but one or two preconditions to the greatness of Spain stand out. Castile was a barren country and bred a tough people. The Spaniards had just completed the work of three centuries in reconquering their country from the heathen Arabs. The rich port of Seville, the gateway to the Atlantic, had been taken in 1248. In 1492 Granada fell, the last centre of Moorish resistance. The Spaniards were thus left with an impetus of military success. Economic demands were not likely to distract their energies from war, since most commerce was still in Moorish hands and the pastoral economy of the countryside needed little labour. Besides, war was expected to be profitable.

During the Italian wars, which we are about to consider, for the first time a distinctly modern European attitude to war can be discerned. It was an age of political realism, the age of Machiavelli and the doctrine of *raison d'état*. In place of the moral and arbitrating authority of the Church, there developed systems of international law, diplomacy and secret service. Old clichés died hard, and for a long time firearms were denounced as a cowardly and unchivalrous threat to Christian morality and the social order. The point was, however, that they worked, and they were used. In the military theory of the *Nef des Princes et des Batailles* (1502) Robert de Balzac epitomized the new attitude. Behind a smoke-screen of conventional moralizing he stresses the efficient use of firearms and modern formations, and the necessity of ruthlessness in such matters as the maintenance of discipline and scorched earth policies. He encourages the keeping of treaties, but warns his readers never to rely on the honour of other powers. With the same freedom from sentimentality he observes that 'success in war depends on having enough money'.

In 1494 Charles VIII of France invaded Italy. He occupied Florence against little resistance since the people had been discouraged by Savonarola's explanation that the French were like the Assyrians of old – the sword of the Lord. Then he marched on Rome. The next year, having captured Naples as well, he decided to extricate himself from Italy, and on their way northwards the French shattered an Italian army at Fornovo. Whatever the pretext, the motives of Charles in 1494–5, as of his successors Louis XII and Francis I, were vainglory together with the attractive possibilities of plunder in a rich, accessible and disunited country. The details of the wars of the next sixty years make a tedious story of hit-and-run invasions and a kaleidoscopic complex of alliances and fratricidal counter-alliances. French aggression aroused not only all the little Italian states to war, but also the king of Spain who claimed Naples as his, and the emperor who had commercial interests in the security of north Italy and the Alpine communications. The Swiss leaped at the opportunity to make money as mercenaries, and fought indiscriminately on either side. After 1519 the Italian wars developed into a wider conflict between the Valois and Habsburgs, when King Charles I of Spain became also the emperor Charles V – as well as being ruler of the Netherlands, and having pretentions to rule in Burgundy and northern Italy. But from the military point of view the interest in these wars is concentrated in certain campaigns and battles of the earlier Italian phase.

In 1495 the victory of the French under Charles VIII at Fornovo against the combined armies of Venice and Milan under Gonzaga ended the somewhat absurd era of *condottiere* warfare. For the past two hundred years the wars of the Italian cities had been conducted by bands of medieval cavalry under professional soldiers known as *condottieri*. Many campaigns had by this time become so 'scientific' that battles were no more than man-oeuvres, in which armies would surrender as soon as they were technically outflanked or cut off from their base. They were, as Sir Charles Oman called them, 'games of chess in which checkmate was accepted with little acrimony, and still less bloodshed'. The Italians therefore got a rude shock when the French with their Swiss mercenaries crossed the Alps, with the intention of taking towns by storm and slaughtering prisoners. The Italians had laid a neat trap at Fornovo, but when they were hit by the charge of the French men-at-arms – now mounted again after their century of disastrous floundering on foot – the Italians were scattered like chaff. But they learned their lesson. Although their commanders, such as Prosper Colonna, retained their preference for intricate manoeuvre, they now took a more down-to-earth attitude to war and adapted themselves to the more up-to-date arms and techniques of the pikeman and arquebusier.

Charles VIII's irresistible progress up and down the length of Italy in 1494–5 showed what a siege-train could do. In recent years Jacques de Genouillac had made certain technical improvements to artillery weapons, and the Italians were amazed to see the

Western Europe in the sixteenth century

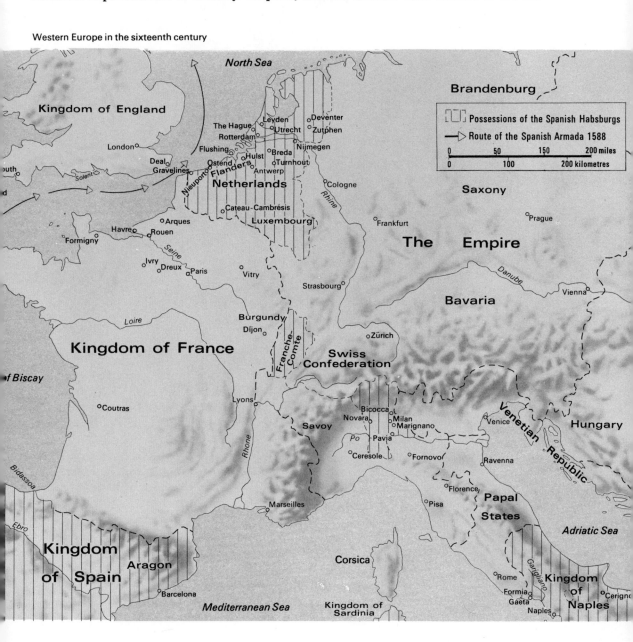

Field guns played a decisive part in the battle of Marignano

new cannon, 'lighter and all cast in bronze . . . drawn by horses . . . They could keep up with the marching speed of the army . . . [and] shot at very short intervals'. Particularly important developments included the introduction of gun carriages, of trunnions to elevate guns, and the use of metal instead of stone cannon balls. City walls were still of the medieval type, high and defended primarily by crossbowmen, and the Italian cities could make no effective defence against Charles's siegecraft.

The French were also ahead of the rest of Europe in the use of field artillery. At the battle of Formigny (1450) the unendurable pounding of two culverins had forced the English longbowmen to break their formation. The French victory at Ravenna (1512) was won in a similar way; the Spanish-Papal army was entrenched in a defensive position, but was forced by the battering of field artillery to take the offensive – with disastrous results. At Marignano (1515), the first great defeat of the Swiss by the French under Francis I, field guns again played a crucial part.

The Swiss at this time had a tremendous reputation in Europe. The prestige of the victories of Granson and Morat against the Burgundians had recently been reinforced by their victory over the French at Novara (1513). After a brilliant feint to mask their real intention, the three columns of pikemen in *échelon* had made havoc of the French

German *landsknechte* were formed to fight the Swiss pikemen with their own weapons

cavalry. They had pressed home their victory as far as Dijon, before they were bought off for an enormous sum. The Florentine historian Guicciardini wrote:

> Never did the Swiss nation make a finer . . . resolve, a few against many, without horsemen or field-pieces to attack an army so admirably provided with both . . . Many have ventured, considering the courage . . . to reckon this deed of arms more highly than most of the memorable actions recorded of . . . the Romans.

The emperor Maximilian had already decided that the only way to beat the Swiss was to play them at their own game, and he had introduced corps of pikemen into his armies, called *landsknechte*. The only difference between the Germans and the Swiss was in the way they operated their pikes. The *landsknechte* held the pike low down and pointed it upwards; the Swiss grasped it nearer the middle, thrusting it slightly downwards. The Germans soon showed the same mercenary tendencies as the Swiss.

Novara was, however, the last major victory of massed pikemen, and Francis I's campaign in 1515 introduced them to a different future. Advised by the great Spanish engineer, Pedro Navarro, he took his army over the Alps by traversing the high Col d'Argentière, and surprised his enemies by appearing in rear of them with 30,000 men and 72 guns. At Marignano he brought overwhelming force to bear against the Swiss mercenaries of Milan. The Swiss probably had no more than 15,000 men, and, as usual, they were virtually without cavalry. Their organization, in any case, was in some confusion, since they had spent the last day or two discussing Francis' proposition that they should sell the Duke of Milan to him. Several of their commissioners were in favour; some proportion of the forces had been withdrawn and the rest rallied only just in time. The two-day battle which ensued was a disorderly affair, but the main principle by which the French defeated the Swiss is clear – the columns of Swiss pikemen attacked, but were first halted and then repelled by alternate salvos of field artillery and cavalry charges.

Marignano was a severe jolt for the Swiss. But it was not taken as a very significant portent, since they had been outnumbered by two to one; furthermore they made a skilful withdrawal from the field.

High hopes were now raised for field artillery, but they did not mature. Machiavelli was right in arguing that the immobility of field artillery was such that an intelligent tactician should be able to deal with it. In order to be more formidable, guns were being made ever larger. For the purpose of battering down walls this was sound, but there was as yet no differentiation between cannon for use on the field and cannon for siegecraft. Mobile and rapid-firing field artillery was not developed until the seventeenth century.

By the beginning of the Italian wars the handgun had at last been developed into a weapon of very great potentiality. In the Hundred Years' War it had been so unwieldy and inefficient as to be virtually unserviceable, two men being required to operate it; but recently there had been improvements. The weight was reduced to 30 pounds, and its butt so shortened that one man could support the gun against his shoulder. The barrel was lengthened to over 3 feet and the calibre reduced, thus giving great range and accuracy. But the most important development was the invention of the match-lock. Previously the method of firing the gun had been to apply a smouldering piece of impregnated fibre called 'match' to the touch-powder. To do that, while at the same time holding the gun in the position of correct aim, required at least three hands and three eyes. The match-lock now gave the gunner the chance to be efficient, by making the firing automatic. The match was clipped to a cock, which swung over to ignite the touch-powder when the trigger was pulled. The handgun fitted with the match-lock was known as an 'arquebus'.

The man who first recognized the tactical potentialities of the arquebusier, the infantryman armed with a handgun, and who first integrated him in a successful tactical system, was Gonzalo de Córdoba of Spain. In 1495 Gonzalo was sent to defend Spanish interests in southern Italy. His army consisted of crossbowmen, men-at-arms, and light cavalry called 'genitors' – armed with javelins and originally developed to fight the Moors in southern Spain. At Seminara he was defeated by a French combination of men-at-arms and pikemen, and this defeat caused Gonzalo to ponder. Within a few years he had radically altered the nature of his army.

He came to the conclusion that the key to success lay with the arquebusiers; accordingly he greatly increased their numbers. He equipped them with the latest handguns, each man also having a bullet pouch, a match, cleaning materials, a ramrod, and powder in small tubes hung on a bandolier. In addition they were armed with a sword and pro-

The arquebus now developed into the most effective weapon in battle

tected by a helmet, but had little other body armour. Gonzalo considered that sufficient arquebusiers strongly entrenched would be able to check the assault of any number of crossbowmen, pikemen or cavalry – just as the English longbowmen had done. The arquebusiers would need to be backed by pikemen, who were the best hand-to-hand fighters of the time; these would reinforce them should the enemy succeed in closing, and would be necessary in counter-attacks. The most important cavalry were the genitors, who would be useful for scouting, skirmishing and harassing the enemy. Only a very few crossbowmen and men-at-arms were retained.

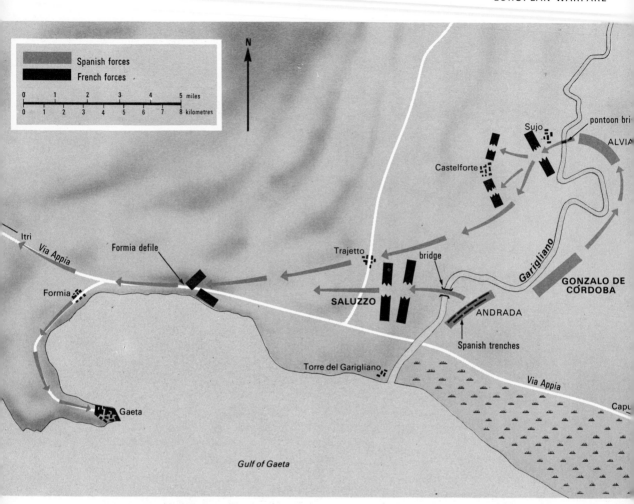

The battle of the Garigliano

Gonzalo's system was tested against the French at Cerignola in April 1503. The Spanish infantry units – a few ranks of arquebusiers in front and the pikemen behind them – were entrenched on the lower slopes of a hill. Just below ran a ditch, the bank of which was raised into a sort of rampart with earth and vine-props. Gonzalo induced the enemy to attack him by sending out clouds of genitors who harassed the French and drew them forward. The French men-at-arms and pikemen in *échelon* made a head-long attack, thinking that the force of their rush would break the meagre-looking station-ary Spanish line. As they came within range the Spanish arquebusiers opened heavy fire. The leaders of the advancing columns were shot down or fell into the ditch. The French assaults were repeated but with the same result, and their commander, Nemours, was killed by a bullet. Only when it was clear that victory was in sight did Gonzalo order his men forward from the line of their entrenchment – to complete the destruction of the enemy.

Cerignola was a battle of small political significance, and relatively small armies were engaged; but in the history of warfare it was a major turning-point. Gonzalo de Córdoba had raised the infantry soldier armed with a handgun to the status of the most important fighting man on the battlefield – a status which he was to retain for over four hundred years. In the 1914/18 war the combination of machine-guns and barbed wire was to cause his lustre to shine less brightly. But he came into his own again in the 1939/45 war when the armoured fighting vehicle roamed the battlefield helping him to gain ground in the face of small-arms fire. The lesson was then learned that battles are won by the skilful combination of all arms, although any one might be more important than others at certain periods. But more of that in due course.

Gonzalo de Córdoba's outstanding military ability was again evinced at the end of 1503 in the campaign and battle of the Garigliano. The French remnants of Cerignola had been heavily reinforced, and in October Gonzalo tailed a French army twice the size of his own down the valley of the Garigliano. The enemy were heading for Naples, but because of torrential autumn rains they decided, rather than attempt the mountain route, to make for the coast and then proceed along it. When Gonzalo realised this, he moved his army through the mountains at top speed to get across the river before the enemy, and early in November he confronted them across the swollen lower reaches of the Garigliano. The French threw a pontoon bridge across, but were driven back by the artillery and arquebus fire of the Spaniards. The weather was worsening, and after one more attempt to cross the river the French gave up trying.

The River Garigliano will be well known to soldiers of the Allied armies who fought in Italy in the winter of 1943–4. It flows into the sea to the south of Cassino and formed part of the southern end of the German 'Winter Line' – which ran from Ortona on the Adriatic southwards across the mountains to the mouth of the Garigliano, the upper reaches of which today are called the River Liri. In the autumn and winter the Italian rivers become seas of mud, as I know very well – the Eighth Army which I commanded having to cross the Sangro before it could capture Ortona. We used to say that *la boue* was a more formidable enemy than *les Boches*!

To return to Gonzalo's battle. A deadlock of six weeks followed, during which both sides sat fast, guarding the muddy banks of the Garigliano – the weather continuing exceptionally wet and cold. Gonzalo knew that it would be fatal to retreat even as far as the drier foot-hills, since once the superior forces of the French crossed the river Naples was doomed. Morale then played a decisive part. Gonzalo himself lived in a hut about a mile back, and visited the forward positions daily – exhorting and keeping his drenched and inactive army in good heart. On the other hand, the French officers rapidly lost interest, many of them retiring to live in comfortable quarters in the nearest towns, while the commander-in-chief, the Marquis of Mantua, developed a diplomatic 'fever' and handed over his command to the Marquis of Saluzzo. The soldiers soon became thoroughly demoralized; many deserted, and their lines straggled farther and farther back from the mud of the river bank. In such weather it seemed highly improbable that the Spaniards, who were outnumbered and had hitherto adopted the defensive, would attack; consequently French vigilance was neglected.

The deterioration of the French was perceived by Gonzalo, and he planned a surprise attack. Well behind the lines the parts of a pontoon bridge had been prepared, under the supervision of the outstanding specialist in gunnery and engineering for siege-craft

– Pedro Navarro. The parts of the bridge were made small and light enough to be carried on mules, and they could be fitted together quickly. At Christmas there was a two-day truce, and some fraternization took place between the armies – the French soldiery continuing their celebrations for several days. On 27th December the mass of the Spanish army and the components of the bridge were moved up to the north end of the Spanish position, opposite the extreme left of the French at the village of Sujo, where the river was a little narrower, the ground less wet, and preparations could be concealed. The assault was planned for dawn on the 29th. In command of the bridge-builders and the van was Alviano; Gonzalo commanded the 'main battle'; the rear units occupied the trenches along the river opposite the main force of the French, with orders to cross at that point if the battle went well.

The scheme worked as planned. The bridge was laid by dawn, and the few French infantry at Sujo were not even under arms to resist the light horse of the Spanish van when they fell upon them. Alviano dashed on downstream through several villages occupied by Swiss infantry, who were not given time to form up for battle. The French men-at-arms were mostly well back from the river, and Saluzzo was able to collect only a small party, which made one charge – but in vain. The genitors pursued the enemy for ten miles before a considerable body of French succeeded in holding them in the defile of Formia. Gonzalo's infantry of the 'main battle' were already at hand, and behind them the rearguard had crossed the river. The only real battle of the Garigliano took place in the defile. After an hour's hard fighting the French broke, and the chase and captures of men and guns continued as far as Gaeta.

The Garigliano was his last campaign, and a fitting crown to the career of the 'Great Captain'. In 1515 Gonzalo de Córdoba died, full of honours. His tactical system received general acceptance. Spain continued to increase the proportion of arquebusiers in her forces, and their effectiveness was repeatedly demonstrated in striking fashion. In 1513 at the battle of La Motta against the Venetians the Spanish cavalry was actually driven off the field, but the arquebusiers and pikemen won the day on their own. By the time the enemy got as far as the Spanish infantry line they were so broken and disordered by volleys of arquebus fire that they could not stand up against the final assault of the pikemen.

The victory of the Spaniards under an Italian commander, Prosper Colonna, over the Swiss at Bicocca in 1522 was won by following Gonzalo's pattern. Colonna prepared a very strong defensive position, where a sunken lane ran between the edge of a garden and some fields. He built up the bank on the garden side into a rampart, mounted some artillery on it, disposed his arquebusiers four deep to man the rampart, and in rear of them placed continuous units of pikemen. As the Swiss pikemen advanced across the fields they were mown down first by artillery and then by arquebus fire. Those who succeeded in pressing forward to jump down into the lane found themselves trapped in an abattoir, and were slaughtered by the arquebusiers who were so high above them that the Swiss pikes could not even touch them. Immense numbers of the Swiss were shot down while making this hopeless assault. Eventually the Spanish pikemen descended to finish them off.

Bicocca was a day of total disaster for the Swiss; thereafter they never recovered their former confidence and pugnacity. Guicciardini wrote: 'They went back to their mountains diminished in numbers, but much more diminished in audacity'. At Zürich the reformer Zwingli, who had been an army chaplain at the first defeat of Marignano, found sympathetic audiences in his denunciation of the demoralizing mercenary trade. Lack of alternative employment in their own country, however, compelled the Swiss to continue providing recruits for all the armies of Europe in the sixteenth century. They maintained a reputation as good steady troops. But the future tactical role of pikemen was to serve in small units together with more or less equal numbers of arquebusiers, and the Swiss adapted themselves only slowly and reluctantly to this new subordinate function. They had no proper command structure. In misjudged deference to democratic tradition, over-all command was vested not in one individual but in a committee of old soldiers. There were very few officers and soldiers of N.C.O. rank. The result was that the Swiss remained good at a few old and well-practised manoeuvres, but lacked flexibility and the capacity for improvisation; consequently, in battle they were unable to vary plans to fit developing tactical situations.

For the Spaniards, by contrast, Bicocca was a total vindication of their new system. Having defeated the most renowned infantry in Europe, the Spanish arquebusiers gave further notable evidence of their prowess by the victory under the Marquis of Pescara over the French cavalry outside Pavia in 1525. Here they did not win by waiting behind good cover for an attack; they defeated the French by surprising them on open ground, turning their flank, and then pouring unremitting volleys into the massed ranks of cavalry. The enemy infantry was also all but destroyed, and Francis I himself was taken prisoner.

At the battle of Pavia the Spanish infantry routed a French army

Sleeping soldiers. Armour was now becoming largely decorative and would soon fall into disuse

Gonzalo de Córdoba's system had now been proved repeatedly against cavalry and all types of infantry. Crossbowmen and mounted men-at-arms began to disappear rapidly from almost all European armies, to be replaced by the arquebusier and the pikeman. Since most soldiers naturally preferred to do the shooting rather than be shot at, arquebusiers were easy to recruit. Pikemen everywhere adapted themselves perforce to a new tactical function: of backing arquebusiers rather than themselves leading the attack in *échelon*. Body armour offered no effective protection against the new bullets, and, since it conduced to immobility, after passing through an ornamental phase it was largely abandoned.

The defensive power of arquebusiers, above all, was now the most prominent tactical consideration in the minds of commanders, and once again the defensive in warfare became dominant, with the result that after Pavia large-scale open battles on land became extremely rare – Ceresole (1544) and Nieuport (1600) being the only examples in the rest of this period. Arquebusiers, in the system developed by Gonzalo de Córdoba, remained the most powerful type of troops, and those of Spain were the best of all. But after 1525 they got little opportunity to prove themselves again in the field in any except petty clashes.

The warfare of the last three-quarters of the sixteenth century in Europe produced some able soldiers, but there were no campaigns to compare in interest with those of the Italian wars. In the second phase of the Habsburg-Valois struggle, between 1525 and 1559, there were, in fact, fourteen years in which no fighting took place at all.

By the Treaty of Cateau-Cambrésis in 1559 Burgundy and certain frontier fortresses including Calais were conceded to France, and she gave up her claims to Savoy and Italy. From the political point of view the whole long episode had been singularly negative; all parties had been prevented from giving attention to more important matters. The passage of thousands of men back and forward across the Alps may have contributed to the communication of the Italian Renaissance to northern Europe. The wars left the prestige of the French crown at a very low ebb and the country bankrupt, divided in religion, and full of unemployed soldiers.

The stage was thus set for renewed fighting, and in 1562 the French wars of religion began – nine phases of civil war. They were fought ostensibly over the right to worship according to the dictates of conscience, but their most important outcome was Henry IV's success in maintaining the absolute authority of the crown. They have been described by V. H. H. Green in terms that would be appropriate to most of the wars of this period:

> Inextricably confused, tedious if considered in detail, on some occasions dramatic, occasionally revealing intense devotion to principle but more often complete lack of it, frequently throwing into grim relief the depths of human treachery and greed.

At the same time, after 1568, the Dutch were fighting to gain independence from Spain. Had Spain's maritime commitments not prevented her from concentrating her force to crush the revolt, the Dutch would certainly have lost; but, as it was, they threw off their yoke in a struggle of epic endurance. By 1584 all seemed lost: the Catholic provinces in the south (Belgium) had capitulated; the first Dutch patriot leader, William the Silent, was dead; and the great Spanish commander, Alexander, Duke of Parma, was advancing relentlessly to capture Ghent and Antwerp. But the struggle was carried on at sea, and in the desperate resistance of the townspeople against Spanish sieges. By 1590 the tide was turning. Parma was diverted to take part in the French wars, and the Dutch found a fine military leader in Maurice of Nassau. Two brilliant siege campaigns, and the victories of Turnhout (1597) and Nieuport (1600) carried them forward. Even the outstanding generalship of Ambrogio Spinola after 1600 could not prevent the Dutch gaining *de facto* independence at the armistice of 1609.

These wars saw the definition of the innovations which had appeared in the Italian wars. They were fought very largely by mercenary troops, and all armies were of mixed nationality. The Swiss were still much in demand in France, and Italy was regarded as a source of good officers and arquebusiers. There was internal peace in Germany between 1555 and 1618, for one reason because division in the face of the Turkish menace would have been fatal. But large numbers of mercenary *landsknechte* and cavalry fought outside Germany, particularly for the Protestant armies in France and the Low Countries.

England's part in the history of land warfare in the sixteenth century was practically nil. She was a relatively underdeveloped country, with a population of only 4 million, as against the 7 million of Spain and the 10 million of France. After the trivial fighting of the Wars of the Roses (1455–85) the new Tudor dynasty was concerned with domestic matters: the replacement of feudalism by parliamentary government, and the introduction of Protestantism. Apart from occasional small and mostly unsuccessful ventures, England avoided involvement with continental politics. Because they maintained no national forces the English for a long time fell badly behind in military techniques; it was not until Elizabeth I's reign (1558–1603) that the longbow gave way to the arquebus. English mercenary troops, and soldiers of fortune such as Francis Vere, were, however, prominent in the Dutch war.

The legacy of Gonzalo de Córdoba made defensive tactics normal; commanders preferred manoeuvre, feinting and seeking to attack the enemy on the march, to cut his communications or starve him out – rather than frontal attacks. The technical developments which were made in firearms did not alter this situation. The Dutch war was fought, in any case, over a terrain of bogs, dykes and canals, appropriate mainly for defensive campaigning. Much poor leadership and unsound military theory was a reason for the poor conduct of the fighting in France. The French soldier, La Noue, complained about his countrymen:

> The young have been reading too many romances of reckless adventure, full of *amours déshonnêtes* and objectless fighting. The old have been reading and rereading Machiavelli.

The generalship in the early years of the French wars was indeed remarkable for sustained incapacity: at the battle of Dreux (1562) each side captured the other's commander. Simultaneous petty campaigns were too often not integrated in any overall strategy. No state, except Spain, could recruit or afford to pay more than a very small regular national army, and the high proportion of mercenary troops in all armies largely accounts for the general lack of initiative, offensive spirit, and strategic unity of purpose. Even the national troops of Spain were inclined to go on strike when their pay was not forthcoming; the mutiny of 1576 caused terrible damage to Antwerp. Lack of funds was a cause of numerous campaigns petering out, and the stinginess and caprice of both Philip II and Elizabeth I repeatedly irritated and frustrated their generals. The ablest soldier of the time was Parma. But he seldom had enough funds, and at times orders from the king of Spain, with typical disregard of strategic continuity, prevented him from carrying out his main task of defeating the Dutch rebels: in 1588 he was told to stand by for an invasion of England, and between 1590 and 1592 he was sent to France.

During the fifteenth century siegecraft had got the better of fortification, at any rate up to the 1494–5 campaign of Charles VIII of France. The situation changed in the sixteenth century, as military architects at last reacted constructively to the existence of artillery, and scientific fortification developed rapidly along new lines. Once again fortifications became well-nigh impregnable. Together with the defensive pattern in tactics and the shortage of funds common to all the governments of Europe, this factor led to the prevalence, after the Italian wars, of defensive strategy – or at any rate of long-term strategy and political manoeuvre in preference to quick results by force of arms. People naturally retired into their safe fortresses, and opposing commanders did not dare leave them unreduced. After Pavia (1525) the annals of warfare are increasingly a record of sieges, culminating in the three years' beleaguerment of Ostend (1601–4) by Spinola.

The chief principle in the new fortifications from the 1520's was to build them compact and low, indeed partly below ground level, so as to be a difficult mark for artillery, and thick enough to withstand bombardment and also the recoil of their own guns. The outworks were strengthened with covered ways and glacis, and by making larger ditches. Cannon were to be used for defence, and walls were built with bastions, redans and horn-

The battle of Pavia demonstrated that the handgun had established a mastery over the armoured horseman. A detail from a sixteenth-century Flemish tapestry.

works in order to command as wide a range as possible. In the majority of cases, for example Rhodes, medieval fortifications were merely adapted to something like this very different pattern. Deal is an example of a new fortress of the period, one of a chain built by Henry VIII in the 1530's to guard against the eventuality of a wind blowing an enemy fleet towards England's south coast while confining the home fleet to harbour. Deal consists of two sexfoil clovers one within the other, and a low round central tower. Some 145 guns were mounted round the flat roofs of each perimeter, thus commanding in tiers all approaches. One part of the outer wall was lapped by the sea; the whole fortress was moated, entrance being by a drawbridge. In France, Havre and Vitry are examples of the many new fortresses built in the sixteenth century. Dutch fortifications in most cases were particularly strong, being surrounded by water. In 1574, the siege of Leyden was relieved by cutting the dykes and flooding the besiegers out of their camp.

There was no development in artillery to compete with the increased strength of fortifications. Bronze cannon had already attained vast dimensions in the fifteenth century. A gun called 'Mad Margaret' made in Flanders was 18 feet long, had a 33-inch bore, and weighed 15 tons. In the 1520's the efficiency of artillery was somewhat improved by the introduction of a coarser gunpowder which burned rapidly and projected the missile with greater punch, and by more accurate techniques of casting and boring which increased accuracy. The design of muzzle-loading cannon thereafter remained basically unchanged for three hundred years.

There was little standardization. In 1550, English artillery ranged through sixteen sizes, from the 'cannon-royal' weighing 4 tons and firing a 75-lb shot, to the 'rabinet' which weighed 300 lbs and fired a 5-oz shot. The cannon used in ships were from the smaller range, such as 'culverins' and 'sakers'. In the early sixteenth century, when Henry VIII decided that he wanted to acquire 'cannon enough to conquer hell', he had to order them from the Flemish manufacturer, Hans Poppenruyter – an indication of English military backwardness at that time. But in 1541 there was an important development: the Rev. William Levett began to make iron cannon in Ashdown Forest. Though iron guns were brittle, very heavy, and generally less efficient than bronze, they were much cheaper and very popular. Indeed, by 1574 so many iron guns were being exported that politicians became alarmed, and the trade was forbidden. The best cannon at this time were German, made in the factories of Beck at Augsburg and Sattler at Nürnberg. The Germans also invented the mortar, a short gun designed to lob a shot on to the enemy. Spain had no efficient manufacture of artillery, and thereby suffered a grave disadvantage.

In siegecraft, treachery or guile or starvation were generally more successful after the Italian wars than bombardment. The firing rate of artillery had not yet surpassed that of the *ballista,* and *trébuchets* were still occasionally used. In 1546 Niccolo Tartaglia, a Venetian, published an important treatise on ballistics, teaching the artilleryman to estimate range and elevation with the use of a quadrant. Although siegecraft was such a laborious business, with the odds piled against the besieger, the wars of this period did produce two masters – Alexander of Parma (Spain) and Maurice of Nassau (Holland). In 1586 Parma took Antwerp after fourteen months by constructing a fortified bridge of boats across the mouth of the Scheldt, thus cutting the city off from communication with the sea. Four years later, when Parma was away in France, his opponent Maurice of Nassau began a series of brilliant campaigns. He started with Breda, which he captured

The Spanish Armada. A detail from a sixteenth-century oil painting design for a tapestry

Castles were now built compact and low, to withstand bombardment. The double sexfoil design at Deal enabled guns mounted on the roofs to bear upon attackers from all directions

Muzzle-loading cannon now assumed a design that was to continue unchanged for three hundred years. Mortars,
capable of lobbing a shot over a short distance, were also developed

Handguns consisted of the arquebus *left* or the heavier musket with its rest *middle*. Light cavalry and special infantry were provided with pistols *right*

by a stratagem, bringing his men right up to the quayside hidden in turf-boats. In June and July 1591 he took Zutphen and Deventer, both north of Nijmegen. Maurice next moved his troops at top speed by barge to Hulst (west of Antwerp) at the other end of the Spanish line of fortresses. Hulst fell in five days, and he dashed back to Nijmegen, which was taken in another six days. Maurice's usual method was to concentrate an intense artillery fire on a small section of the *enceinte*, thus creating a breach. He would persuade his victims to surrender by allowing them the full honours of war and by forbidding pillage. The next year, when Parma was back in France engaged in the campaign in which he received a fatal wound, Maurice took two more major fortresses in the Low Countries. These campaigns permitted the Dutch in the following years to drive the Spaniards entirely out of the country north of the lower Rhine and the Waal. Despite Spinola's skill in siegecraft, Spain was never able to recover that ground.

In such open fighting as took place, until at least 1600, the Spanish infantry – arquebusiers, musketeers and pikemen – were the best in Europe; their self-confidence and skill in the conventional tactics of the time were outstanding. Despite difficult circumstances, in the small clashes of the early part of the Dutch war they swept all before them. One notable feat – of the same type, but more remarkable than Wellington's crossing of the Bidassoa in 1813 – was the march of 3,000 men under Mondragon to relieve Tergoes in 1572. They waded for six miles through water up to the waist and over, knowing that if the tide came in before they were across they would all be drowned. The introduction of

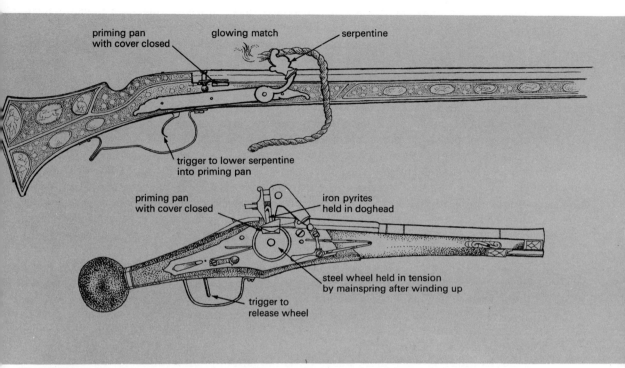

The charge in an arquebus or musket was detonated by a smouldering match; that in a pistol, however, was fired by a milled wheel striking a piece of pyrites – known as a wheel-lock

the musket made no difference to tactics. It was a handgun of greater range and accuracy than the arquebus, but it had the disadvantages of being so heavy that it had to be rested on a fork, and of having a firing rate appreciably slower even than the forty rounds an hour of the arquebus. The Spaniards had only fifteen musketeers to a hundred arque-busiers in the 1570's, but by 1600 the proportions in most armies were about level. It is an interesting reflection on the age that in 1534 the number of chaplains in a brigade (3,096 men) of the Spanish army was 13, while the number of medical staff was 3. France produced no good infantry in this period; but after 1590 Maurice of Nassau trained some excellent Dutch foot, and at the battle of Nieuport (1600), together with Vere's English, they were a good match for the Spaniards. There was a tendency during these years to reduce the size of units, in both infantry and cavalry. In place of the enormous units of Gonzalo's day, smaller 'regiments' commanded by 'colonels' appeared in the Spanish army.

The medieval heavy cavalry armed with the lance was now rapidly disappearing; the publication of *Don Quixote* in 1605 finally ridiculed into extinction the armoured knight of the age of chivalry. The javelin was replaced as the weapon of light cavalry by the pistol – a German invention, first conspicuous in the campaign of Mühlberg in 1547. The pistol of course differed from the arquebus in size, and also in that it was detonated by a 'wheel-lock' – which was an improvement. Rather than obtaining fire from an inflam-mable material, it worked like a cigarette lighter. When the trigger was pulled a milled wheel struck a spark off a piece of pyrites (later flint). Since this mechanism was delicate and expensive it was not usually used for arquebuses and muskets.

All armies rapidly adopted the pistol as the main cavalry weapon. The best pistoleers were the Germans, known as *reiter* – each of whom carried three pistols, in holsters, and wore black armour. Their characteristic tactical manoeuvre was the 'caracole'. Each line in succession rode up to the enemy, fired, and then swerved off – to reload and form up again in the rear. It was a hazardous system, since the complicated manoeuvre could lead to confusion, and it took a brave man to ride up close enough to the enemy to be within effective pistol range. This deep formation contradicted the principle of shock tactics, since the impetus of the back ranks was wasted, and if the enemy had cannon or even arquebuses the casualties among the *reiter* were bound to be heavy. However Henry of Navarre, the French Protestant leader in the wars of religion, won the battle of Coutras in 1587 using his pistoleers in three squadrons each of six ranks. His enemy's cavalry was disposed in a long line of two ranks. Although outnumbered, the pistoleers broke the thin enemy line at their three points, and then turned sideways to roll up the fragments by flank charges.

Most of the battles in the French wars were in fact decided by cavalry, since the quality of the infantry was generally bad. However, even the standard of cavalry fighting was not high, because too many noble officers were truculent, careless and imprecise. In general, the terrain of Holland was particularly unsuitable for cavalry operations, but a most memorable incident in the Dutch war was the occasion on which Sir Philip Sidney was killed, the heroic but tragic charge of 1,000 English horse at Warnsfeld, near Flushing, in 1586. In the early years there was nothing to match the Spanish horse. But Maurice of Nassau studied this problem and did not neglect cavalry in his general improvement of the Dutch forces. At the battle of Turnhout (1597) the Dutch cavalry drove the Spanish cavalry off the field, and then turned in conjunction with their infantry to break the enemy's foot. At Nieuport in 1600 it was the clear superiority of the Dutch horseman which decided the greatest battle since Pavia. While the infantry struggle was locked on the sand dunes, the Dutch cavalry repeatedly charged the Spaniards on the coastal road, and eventually drove them off altogether. The fortune of the infantry contest swung against them, but a last cavalry charge by the Dutch, this time across the dunes and into the disordered third line of the Spanish infantry, achieved victory on all parts of the field.

Henry of Navarre was a daring, rash, but on the whole successful cavalry leader, who believed in winning victories by dashing charges in the style of Pappenheim and Murat. His defence of the defile of Arques in 1589 is also a classic of its type. But as a strategist he was second-rate. Instead of following up the victory of Ivry in 1590 by a quick march on Paris, he took a fortnight off to lay twenty-two standards at the feet of his mistress in Béarn. Later in 1590 Parma outmanoeuvred him by drawing his forces away from Paris, and in 1592 Rouen was relieved in the same pattern. Whenever they clashed Henry was outclassed by Parma, a master of economic strategical manoeuvre, as well as of siegecraft and engineering.

We now move on to the history of naval warfare which is more rewarding than the study of military developments between 1525 and 1609. In the fifteenth and sixteenth centuries Europe at last broke out of its beleaguerment by alien peoples – Goths, Arabs, Vikings,

Mongols, Turks – which had gone on throughout the Middle Ages. There is no simple explanation for the new advance of Europeans across the seas of the world. The navigators and *conquistadores* were generally conscious of the motives of wanting to bring Christianity to the heathen world, and to perform great deeds for themselves and their countries. Curiosity drew them further, but the strongest urge of all was the desire to become rich. European imperialism was a commercial affair, backed by speculators and carried forward by adventurers. Francis I of France only meant to be rude when he called Manoel of Portugal *le roi épicier*, but historically his analysis was correct. If commerce supplied the energy, and religion the pretext, the means lay in the new developments in technology, in sailing ships and in guns.

The first offensive drive came from Spain and Portugal. In 1493, the very next year after the fall of Granada, the report of Columbus' voyage to the Bahamas suggested an adventurous, just, and profitable outlet for Castilian energy in a new world. By 1509 the first Spanish colony had been set up in America. The whole American continent contained only two significant native states: the Aztec empire in Mexico which was overpowered by Hernando Cortés between 1519 and 1522, and the Inca empire of Peru annexed by Francisco Pizarro during 1532 and 1533. The empire finally acquired by the Spaniards in less than fifty years was thereafter maintained intact for three hundred years. The European empires founded in the sixteenth century – Spanish, Portuguese, English and Dutch – remained essentially maritime trading empires, certainly until the eighteenth century. The Europeans were not numerous enough to occupy in a real sense the vast interiors of the new continents, nor did they have the same overwhelming technical superiority in land warfare over the non-European peoples as they had at sea.

The square-rigged sailing ship, armed with cannon and manned by sailors with advanced navigational knowledge and skill, was the key to these adventures. The Portuguese made the first crucial navigational discoveries. Prince Henry the Navigator patronised seamen and collated knowledge at his court at Sagres in the 1430's and 1440's. In 1497–8 Vasco da Gama made his great voyage round the Cape to India. The seamen of the Middle Ages, hugging the shore and taking compass bearings from familiar landmarks, had been pilots. New instruments and experience in the fourteenth and fifteenth centuries turned them into navigators. Improvements in the cut of sails made it possible to tack against the wind, and the 'traverse board' kept track of the ship's course while doing so. By 1456 the Portuguese were using astrolabe, quadrant and cross-staff to measure the altitude of the Pole Star and Southern Cross above the horizon in order to determine latitude. Schools of navigation were set up at Lisbon and Seville. However, there was still no way to measure longitude, and charts remained rudimentary. Seamen in the sixteenth century had to depend above all on calculated guesses based on measurement of latitude, and on accumulated knowledge of winds and currents. The 'caravels' used in the early age of exploration constituted some advance from the medieval merchant ships; they were tubby, with three masts, square-rigged, and with guns mounted in castles fore and aft. Gradually their lines were made finer, and the sail area was increased to give speed. The cannon were small or medium-sized, of the same type which were used on land.

Much development had to take place, but already no other ships in the world could rival this powerful combination of mobility and destructive power. In 1509 the Portuguese under Francisco de Almeida shattered the combined Egyptian and Gujerati fleets off Diu (a port about 300 miles south of Karachi), and thus replaced the Arabs as the dominant seafaring people in the Indian Ocean.

The Spanish conquests of Mexico and Peru were not strictly military episodes, for both were gigantic bluffs. Cortés and Pizarro, each with bands of adventurers under 1,000 strong, only a few horses, and firearms which were not particularly up-to-date, took over the empires they coveted by playing on the superstitious fears of their enemies. The picture of the 'active iron of Spain against the passive feathers of Peru' (Peter Shaffer) is dramatic but unhistorical. It was fear of strange white gods mounted on horses and wielding instruments of thunder and lightning which really caused the Indian rulers to capitulate with hardly a blow, while their terrorised subject peoples welcomed the release. The introduction of smallpox by the Europeans to the American continent, where the natives had little or no immunity, also played some part in destroying their enemies' resistance. But the story at any rate merits a prominent place in the annals of courage, leadership and psychological warfare.

On the occasions when Spanish arms did clash with Indian in South America, their technical superiority was strikingly demonstrated. The Indians had only slings, bows, obsidian-headed spears, and axes, whereas the Europeans had guns, steel swords, and horses. The Aztec capital of Tenochtitlan (site of Mexico City) was built on an island in the lake of Texcoco. For the final siege in 1521 Cortés had thirteen brigantines constructed to support the assault of his men along three causeways. These craft were 42 feet long, had a beam of 9 feet, with 4 to 7 feet of freeboard. Some had one mast and others two. Each had a crew of twenty-five men, armed with arquebuses and crossbows, and a small cannon mounted in the bows. Cortés regarded his brigantines as 'the key to the whole war', and committed to them a third of his total force and almost 80 per cent of his artillery. They did indeed play a vital part in the combination of blockade, bombardment and assault by which Tenochtitlan was reduced. The brigantines annihilated a vast Indian fleet of canoes by ramming and gunfire. They performed the tactical function of cavalry in supporting the flank and rear of assault forces on the causeways, and at night they guarded the men at rest. They carried out supply and liaison duties, severed the enemy's communications, and formed pontoon bridges. Eventually their bombardment destroyed the native fortifications, and they penetrated along the canals which led into the heart of the city. Cortés' siege of Tenochtitlan was an efficient sustained amphibious operation, original in conception and brilliantly executed. Even such an improvisation demonstrated the overwhelming power of guns and sail combined.

Warlike competition between the European imperial powers themselves was bound to arise sooner or later. For one thing the extension of European interests into new areas was seen as an expansion of the diplomatic and strategic horizon of Europe. During the Habsburg-Valois wars, after about 1520, the Spaniards and French preyed on each other's colonies and shipping, and the terms of the treaty of Cateau-Cambrésis specifically excluded the non-European theatre. But in any case when the initial period of exploration was past, and interest in 'the great southern continent', in the 'north-west passage', and in other explorations was flagging, the concerns of the European governments became definitely commercial. Certain rich areas, notably the Caribbean, became areas of competition between aggressively monopolistic powers. The Portuguese succeeded on the whole in avoiding war; they had no political pretentions in Europe, and they had an agreement with the Spaniards to operate in separate areas. In 1580 the thrones of Portugal and Spain were united, thus producing a single very powerful navy. The Dutch seaborne empire began to develop only at the end of the sixteenth century, as independence was gained from Spain. Spain's chief rival in this period was England.

Sir Walter Raleigh summed up the strategical attitude of all sides in the maritime competition:

> Whosoever commands the sea commands the trade; whosoever commands the trade of the world commands the riches of the world, and consequently the world itself.

In the 1540's and 1550's the Spaniards developed the silver mines of South America, and in a short time the volume of bullion crossing the Atlantic doubled. The whole lucrative Spanish trade was tempting, both to peaceful 'interloping' traders and to more adventuresome piratical 'privateers'. In the 1560's the volume of Spanish commercial shipping in the Pacific also increased rapidly. Although England was economically backward in the first part of the century, and had played only a minor part in the first explorations and in the expansion of trade, a slump in the north European market in the late 1540's stimulated the English to investigate the New World. At first they concerned themselves with the North Atlantic – but by the 1560's English interest was firmly fixed on the Caribbean.

The development of British seapower in the sixteenth century was a haphazard process. The most important factor at the outset was that, being on the edge of the Atlantic, the English nautical tradition was of sail rather than oars. Sailing ships were used both for fighting and for cargo, since they had greater sea endurance. Henry VII (1485–1509) increased the size of sailing vessels to about 100 tons, and added more sail area. It was he who made Portsmouth the home of the British navy and built there the first dry dock. He encouraged navigators, and as a matter of policy supported a new class of rich man – whose enterprise was to build British maritime power in the years to come. But the large English armed merchant ship, called the 'carrack', remained, in his reign, as a fighting vessel not much more than a mobile strongpoint – and not too mobile at that.

The great step forward in the rise of British seapower was made by Henry VIII (1509–47). Having acquired some new cannon he found that they were too heavy to go in the flimsy gun castles of his carracks; he therefore installed them along the cargo deck, cutting holes in the freeboard. Henry's ships were thus the first to be armed with a broadside. The muzzle-loading cannon were swung inboard for reloading on two-wheeled carriages, which recoiled between chocks in the deck. The problem of the sailing ship's lack of striking power was now overcome. Henry VIII also made his ships more manoeuvrable by removing the gun castles altogether and streamlining the hulls – so that they could sail closer to the wind. The new type of sailing ship, with vastly developed offensive power and manoeuvrability, was called the 'galleon'. By 1550 there were galleons of 600 tons, and by the 1580's there were some, such as the *Triumph*, of over 1,000 tons. These were the ships of Hawkins and Drake. Smaller armed sailing vessels, called 'pinnaces', were also used. To supplement the Lord Admiral, Henry VIII also set up a bureaucratic system: the Navy Board and Comptroller. In the 1550's the Spanish admiral, Alvaro de Bazan, adopted the galleon to protect his country's Atlantic shipping, and in the 1560's a regular routine of armed convoys was established.

Until 1569 Anglo-Spanish relations remained more or less friendly. The chief figure of this period was Admiral Sir John Hawkins. He improved the design of the galleon, and in 1562 and 1564 he raised fleets by subscription, which poached very successfully in the Caribbean. Hawkins then arranged a third voyage, subscribed by Elizabeth herself, and in which Francis Drake was introduced to the Caribbean. The English were making repairs to their ships in the harbour of San Juan de Ulúa (Gulf of Mexico) in 1568 when they were set upon by a large Spanish force. Only a very small part of the expedition got back to England. This was a turning-point. From 1569 to 1580 there was definite semi-official hostility between England and Spain in the Caribbean. Queen Elizabeth made it clear that she supported the activities of privateers so long as they did not provoke open war. The antagonism of commercial rivalry was sharpened by religious differences and by a mounting record of maltreatment of prisoners by the Spaniards.

Francis Drake now emerged as the leading seaman of the galleon age. In twenty years of successful enterprise his name became a terror to the Spaniards and a by-word at home – although he incurred the jealousy of some of his less brilliant compatriots. His contribution to the development of British seamanship, strategy and tactics was immensely important. In 1572–3 he avenged the disaster of San Juan de Ulúa, when with two ships and seventy-five men he made a successful raid on Nombre de Dios, a key point in Spain's maritime communications. Several months were then spent in pillaging the Spanish Main and destroying shipping. At one point he took to the land and in alliance with the natives captured a valuable Spanish silver caravan. Between 1577 and 1580 Drake made his famous 'circumnavigation' of the world. After losing two ships in the Magellan Straits he sailed on with the *Golden Hind*. Raiding the Pacific coast of South America he found the harbours there unequipped to deal with his ship's cannon. The capture of a great silver-ship, the *Cacafuego*, ensured the financial success of the voyage, and there was a good deal more wealth to be grabbed on the way through the Spice Islands of the Moluccas. When the *Golden Hind* arrived back in the Thames Drake anchored off Deptford. Elizabeth then announced her intention to knight the circumnavigator on board his ship: which was done on 4th April 1581. The queen made Drake kneel before her and then handed the sword to a French diplomat to perform the actual dubbing – possibly to give a direct affront to the king of Spain and to embroil the French with him.

But the end of the easy period had come. English ships and seamen were better than ever before, but the Spaniards had also taken measures to deal with the marauders. Their cargo ships had been made larger and were equipped with guns. They adhered strictly to the convoy system; two great fleets left America for Spain at fixed times of the year, accompanied by a powerful protecting squadron of galleons. For a long time the Spaniards, being a Mediterranean people, had been reluctant to abandon the oared ship for the sailing ship. If endurance was the key to strategy, mobility was essential for tactics. At the time of the great Mediterranean sea battle of Lepanto (which we shall deal with in Chapter 11) against the Turks, in 1571, the Spanish fleet consisted wholly of galleys. In the 1570's, however, the qualities of sailing ships were admitted. Experiments were made with the 'galleass', a compromise ship which was driven by oars and sails, and fired a broadside over the heads of the rowers. At the union with Portugal in 1580 Spain acquired a large number of galleons. Finally, in 1587, when the galleass had proved a failure, the Spaniards went over altogether from the galley to the galleon.

In 1580 Elizabeth was still unwilling to precipitate open war, and in refusing to join

The oar-propelled galley remained the principal vessel in the Mediterranean, but it was gradually being replaced by the galleon, fitted with sails

with the French in a raid on the Azores she missed an opportunity to strike a great blow at the seapower of Spain. Nevertheless relations deteriorated rapidly, and in 1585 when Philip seized some English traders in Spain and it was reported, correctly, that he was planning an invasion of England, war was officially declared.

Unlike the previous periods of war in English history, when fleets had been used merely to transport and assist troops to fight on land, there was now a genuine naval strategy. British ships were used systematically to cut the vital maritime links of the enemy – a strategy of indirect approach comparable to that used by Sparta to defeat Athens in the last ten years of the Peloponnesian War. The communications between the Spanish armies in the Netherlands and their home base were attacked; the military expedition sent to aid the Dutch in 1585 was a complementary part of the strategy. At the same time England continued Drake's policy of cutting off Spain's American resources. In 1585 Drake sailed for the Caribbean with 20 ships and 2,300 men, his object being to capture the major Spanish emporium of Havana. He succeeded in causing much damage to Spanish shipping and installations, but he did not have enough men to achieve complete success. It was characteristic of the queen's indecision that she kept him short of men. Too many troops were sent to the Low Countries, when it would have been better to make sure merely that the Dutch held the Spaniards, while England made her main effort in the Caribbean. Nevertheless Elizabeth proved to be an inspiring national leader. Since Henry VIII's time the British navy had dwindled considerably; Elizabeth was short of money and preferred to conduct her maritime policy by subscribing to private joint-stock enterprises. All Drake's expeditions had been backed in this way. But now the British fleet was also built up again.

The Spanish strategy in the war was to destroy the saboteurs of the empire in their nest, and strike a blow against heresy, by invading England with the great Armada in conjunction with Parma's army from the Netherlands. The preparations were long drawn, and two plans were rejected before 1588.

Rumours of these preparations spread through Europe, and in 1587 the English made an attempt to nip the invasion in the bud. Leaving a flotilla to watch the Flemish coast, Drake sailed to Spain with 23 ships, on his most brilliant mission of all – 'the singeing of the king of Spain's beard'. His instructions were

> . . . to impeach the joining together of the King of Spain's fleet out of their several parts, to keep victuals from them, to follow them in case they should come towards England . . .

In the harbour of Cadiz he found about 80 ships of various kinds being fitted out, but only 12 galleys were in fighting condition. Seizing the advantage of surprise, he sailed his ships into the harbour. The galleys were fighting in ideal conditions, but they were defeated by the gunfire of the galleons. Drake then destroyed all that he could find in the harbour; altogether the Spaniards lost 30 ships. The British fleet spent some time longer on the Spanish coast, but eventually illness and shortage of provisions forced it to return to England. Drake's Cadiz expedition is the first example of a future essential of British naval strategy: the interception of the enemy on his own coast. The most important direct consequence was the Spanish decision to abandon galleys for galleons. All the preparations for the Armada had to begin again. In 1588 Drake urged that his offensive-defensive strategy should be repeated. But the queen's hesitation, followed by unfavourable winds, confined the English fleet to home waters.

The Armada which finally set out for the English Channel in May 1588 was a seemingly imposing force. Philip II's administrative ability had raised 65 galleons since the Cadiz disaster. There were only 4 galleys and 4 galleasses; but a host of smaller pinnaces and transports brought the total size of the fleet to 130 vessels, raised from all parts of Spain and the New World. The total of the English fleet at Plymouth was 197, of which 34 were the queen's and 163 were privately owned; they included about 25 first-rate galleons and another 40 very good fighting ships; the remainder did not fight. The largest ships on either side were of about 1,000 tons. The fighting strength of each side was thus equally strong: 60 to 70 galleons, with a core of about 20 very powerful ships. The Spanish vessels, however, were higher out of the water, with large forecastles, which rendered them considerably less manoeuvrable than the lower English galleons. And, very important, the English had more seamen experienced in sail.

The quality of command on the English side was also superior. The titular commanders-in-chief, the Duke of Medina Sidonia and Lord Howard of Effingham, were grandees who both had tact and charm but lacked naval experience. The real Spanish commander was Diego de Valdez, a sailor of great experience, but unable to control his subordinates. The English had Drake, then in his prime.

There were considerable differences between the armament of the fleets, which corresponded to differences in tactical approach. The tactical intent of the Spaniards was to bombard the enemy from short range so as to damage his rigging and the fighting capacity of his men, and then to close, grapple and board. They therefore armed each galleon with about 40 heavy, short-range guns: full 'cannons', 'demi-cannons' and 'cannon-perriers'. The purpose of the English was to bombard the hulls of the enemy ships when on the 'downward roll' and from as long a range as possible, in order to sink them. They therefore armed their ships principally with lighter-shotted, long-range 'culverins'. In armament, the Spaniards thus had the advantage in weight, the English in range.

On 19th July 1588 the Armada appeared off the Lizard. For some time a southwesterly wind had confined the English fleet to Plymouth Harbour, and its officers to playing bowls. But on the 20th the English ships beat out of harbour towards the Armada. Drake was determined to steal the initiative by getting to windward of the Spaniards. The first instance of the superiority of the English as seamen came when their fleet beat acros the enemy's front on short tacks to put themselves to windward. The Armada, in its westward-trailing crescent, could now be compelled to fight a rearguard action at the English convenience all the way up the Channel.

This was, in fact, what happened during the next five days. The English decided to exploit their superior mobility and firing range, tailing the enemy, and day after day picking on the weathermost ships in their rear. At first they pounced in small groups; later the fleet was organised in four squadrons – the beginning of coherent fleet tactics. (The principle of a squadron advancing in line ahead, so that each ship could deliver its broadside in turn, had not yet developed.) Time and again the English ships outsailed the enemy. But their chosen tactics worked no more than did those of their enemy. The English guns proved to be too light to inflict any serious damage from the distance which was regarded as safe; only when the Armada ran out of ammunition on 29th July did the English dare approach close enough, and by the end they had only sunk 11 of the defeated fleet. The Spanish tactics, which were hardly adapted from the medieval galley system, were a failure; not one of their ships ever closed with the English on its own terms.

The English got the better of the struggle; their objectives were achieved each time by superior seamanship, aided by the distinct incompetence of the enemy. Having gained the first initiative, Drake kept the windward position, thanks to the consistent blowing of a 'Protestant' wind. By anticipating minor variations in wind and water, on the 25th he forced the Spaniards to go past the Solent and head on up the Channel, with no further possibility of finding the safe anchorage which they needed – since Parma had not synchronised the assembly of his troops on the Flemish coast. The decisive moment came when the English dispersed the Armada with fireships off Gravelines before dawn on 29th July. The Spaniards panicked, and at last the English were able to get in among them – thanks to the Spanish inefficiency in running out of ammunition. The greatest losses that the Armada finally suffered were from storms as the broken fleet fled round the north of Scotland.

The defeat of the Spanish Armada saved English Protestantism and national sovereignty. But in other respects, during the fifteen years of the war which remained, the full

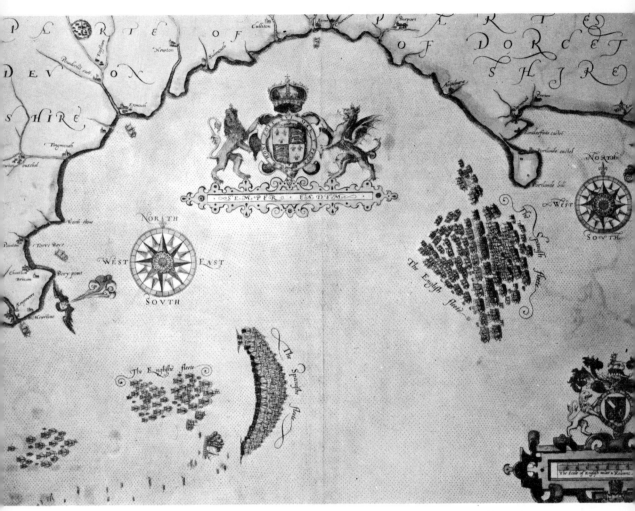

Four stages in the engagement between the English fleet and the Armada in the English Channel

results of the victory were thrown away. The trouble was again Elizabeth's refusal to follow a resolute strategy. As Raleigh wrote:

> Her Majesty did all by halves, and by her petty invasions taught the Spaniard how to defend himself and to see his own weaknesses.

Only 53 heavily battered ships had returned out of the 130 of the Armada which originally sailed, but in an amazingly short time the wealth of Spain raised up a great new fleet of galleons. At the very same time, as so often happens after a major victory, English naval expenditure was being cut down, and disgracefully inadequate expeditions were sent out. Grenville's immortal action off Flores in the Azores in 1591 should never have happened. An English squadron of only 16 ships faced 140 Spanish. Many got away; but

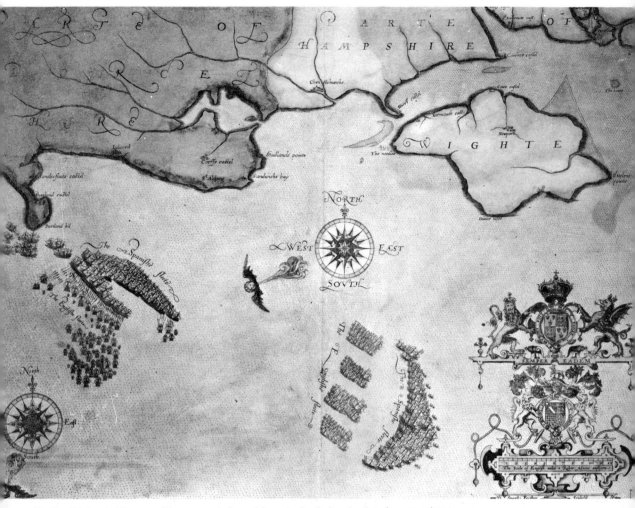

The English harried the rear of the crescent-shaped Armada, finally forming into four squadrons

the *Revenge* was caught, and after she had fought all day and had sunk one of the enemy, the Spaniards grappled and captured the battered hulk. When peace came in 1603 England had lost the dominance of the seas gained for her by Drake. Never once did the privateers achieve their dream of capturing a great Spanish treasure fleet. In the trade war against Spain, England had lost.

It did not matter over much, for by this time many other factors were causing Spain to decline. The chief cause was the inflation produced by the unregulated influx of bullion from the New World. In any case, the task of ruling such an immense empire, and defending it against predators of all nations, was exhausting. Political inefficiency soon led to chaos and indecision. The defeat by the Dutch was a stinging blow. Nonetheless, for some considerable time to come, even after the Armada and Nieuport, the efficiency of Spanish arms, both on land and sea, continued to command general respect.

The Turks carried their empire deep into Europe. They besieged Rhodes unsuccessfully in 1480, as shown here, but were successful nearly fifty years later

11   The Ottoman Turks

The beleaguerment of medieval Europe by barbarians was raised in the west and north sooner than in the south-east. By A.D. 1000 the aggressors from the north had been assimilated, and by 1500 technological progress had enabled western Europe to adopt an offensive world strategy. But the Turkish assault on the south-east was more formidable and prolonged. The crusades may be regarded as a series of defensive sorties; the first of them took the enemy by surprise and was a success, but subsequently each one was increasingly hesitant. The failure of medieval Europe's most vigorous counter-attack emphasizes the strength of this particular enemy.

The Turks had, first of all, an overwhelming advantage in numbers. They were a vast group of semi-nomadic peoples, distinguishable by their language; they had advanced towards the eastern Mediterranean from central Asia, driven by Mongol expansion and lured by the failure of Arab power. Their western spearhead had infinite resources of manpower. By contrast Europe's population, previously stagnant, was greatly reduced between 1347 and 1351 by the Black Death. Moreover Turkish morale was good, and possibly superior to that of their European opponents. The Turks were no primitive people, but heirs to the fusion of two mature cultures: of Islam, and of the steppe. There could be no hope that the Turkish warrior, a fiercely dynamic Moslem, would be disarmed and converted by the insipid *élan* of chivalry, or by the passivity of Orthodoxy and the dying civilization of Byzantium.

But the major reason for Europe's long failure to make headway against her Asian assailants was technological. The native Asiatic technology of war had throughout history been superior to that of Europeans – except in one phase, when Alexander produced a cavalry with mobility as well as stamina and tactical purpose. Otherwise, at every great clash in the Levant, Asiatic mobility had triumphed. Carrhae and Hattin tell the same story, and in the High Middle Ages as the European men-at-arms became heavier and heavier the perennial nomad light horse found it still easier to run circles round them. The continuing success of the Turks in the age when Europe was expanding on other fronts is also to be explained by a technological factor: that the Turks grasped as quickly as any Europeans the revolutionary implications of firearms.

Although they were Asiatic in origin, the Turks must be associated in military history with the European peoples. In the period of their military greatness, between 1300 and 1550, the direction of their drive was westwards against Europe on two fronts: the Danube and the Mediterranean. They regarded their eastern front as their rear, and governed their strategy in that direction largely by European considerations. The Ottoman empire was in fact the leading military and political power of south-east Europe.

The victory of the Seljuk Turks over the Byzantines at Manzikert in 1071 opened the way for the Turkish advance into Asia Minor, which was at first a matter of chance rather than policy. The interest of the Seljuk rulers was fixed on Arabia rather than on Byzantium, but many Turkish warriors preferred the attractive and defenceless land of Anatolia. Turkish chieftains and their followers drifted westward. They were looking for homes, but they were also inspired by their faith as *ghazis*: warriors for the Moslem faith. They obeyed the *futuwwa*, a military and moral code as formal as chivalry, and more dynamic. They acknowledged only in a loose sense the authority of the Seljuk sultan. It therefore made little difference to the western *ghazis*, and did not help Europe at all, when in 1243 the Seljuks were overthrown by the Mongols. The Mongols quickly departed, but their pressure had reinforced the westward impulse of the Turks. Thus both pressure and faith lured the *ghazis* to attack the tumbledown Byzantine empire.

The Ottoman state originated as one among many small *ghazi* powers. It was founded by the semi-legendary Ertughrul, and set on the way to greatness by his successors Osman (1281–1326) and Orkhan (1326–62). Soon after the fall of the Seljuks, the Ottomans emerged as leaders of the Turks. This was due initially to their westerly position which allowed them to survive the Mongol onslaught and made them a rallying point for other *ghazis*. But it was due also to the genius of their early leaders, who knew how to organize and where to lead the energy of the westward-flooding Turks.

Europe was in no condition, then or later, to repel the Turkish threat. The end of the political and military power of Byzantium had been signalled by the crusaders' sack of Constantinople in 1204, and this ruin was completed when western Anatolia, the empire's chief source of manpower and food, was finally lost to the Turks. Furthermore, the expansion of the Ottoman Turks was always facilitated by the divisions of their enemies. The religious difference between Byzantium and the West was the first problem. As long as Byzantium embraced the schismatic Orthodox faith, Europe had an excuse not to help her; yet the consequent movement in Byzantium for unity with Rome demoralized the people. The former subject peoples of Byzantium, the Bulgars and the Serbs, had no love for her. The peoples of western Europe at first failed to understand that Byzantium was doomed without their help, and when they did realize it they hardened their hearts, and pursued their own differences. As Pope Pius II wrote:

> Who will unite the Genoese and the Aragonese? Who will reconcile the Germans with the Hungarians and Bohemians? If you lead a small army against the Turks you will easily be overcome; if a large one it will soon fall into confusion.

The Europeans knew in any case that they were faced by a superior military power. When they did oppose the Ottoman advance, the depressing experience of the crusades was confirmed by a succession of resounding defeats.

In 1301 Osman started to clear the Byzantines out of Asia Minor. His cavalry met no effective opposition as they swept over the countryside, and although some cities held out for a few years like islands, all the interior was quickly submerged. By 1356 the Turks were ready to cross into Europe. For the time being they were content to skirt round the great city of Constantinople. Adrianople was taken, and masses of Turks began to migrate into the Balkans. Orkhan at the same time expanded his power in Asia, completing the welding together of the Turks of Asia Minor into one force. The advance towards the Danube was then pressed forward, the stages being marked by the victories over the Serbs at the River Maritza (1371) and Kossovo (1389), and by the destruction by Bayezit I of a crusader army composed mostly of Hungarians at Nicopolis (1396). Constantinople was surrounded and doomed. Three times the Turks prepared the final siege but were distracted. Europe had one great chance of ruining the military power of the Ottomans when in 1402 Timur, half Turkish by birth but the khan of the Mongols, invaded Asia Minor and defeated Bayezit at Ankara. But no move was made, Timur departed, and the Ottoman power quickly revived. Two more crushing victories in the Balkans, at Varna in 1444 and at Kossovo in 1448, ensured that when Mehmed II finally undertook to capture Constantinople Europe would not attempt to prevent the operation.

The Turkish military system was essentially the creation of Orkhan and Murad I. There was no distinction in the Ottoman state between civil and military functions – it owed its origin to a conquering drive, and developed as an organization for further conquest. The sultan was commander-in-chief as much as emperor, and the heads of governmental departments constituted his military staff. The soldiers in the Turkish army owed their duty to the sultan as an individual rather than to the state. The system was comparable to the European feudal system, but it worked a great deal better. The bulk of the army was a regular militia, settled on land in return for military service as

The Ottoman empire

Ottoman empire 1568
100 200 300 miles
200 400 kilometres

The Spahis were the *élite* Turkish cavalry

required. Feoffees were graded from holders of smaller provinces – *timars, sanjaks,* and so on – up to the ten *beylerbeys,* who ruled great provinces and commanded their contingents in war. The feudal troops, which were cavalry, constituted the main reliable mass of the army. There were also hordes of irregular troops, infantry called *bashi-bazouks* and cavalry called *akibi,* who were unpaid and fought for plunder. The *élite* troops of the Turkish army were the sultan's own corps of guards, the 'Janissary' infantry and the 'Spahi' cavalry.

The Janissaries were rightly the most celebrated troops in the Turkish army. They were professional infantry, a remarkable fact considering the circumstances of their institution – organized by a people whose only tradition was of cavalry and at a time, in the fourteenth century, when infantry was despised in most of the West. It is possible that the last-ditch stand of the long-decadent Byzantine legions had taught Orkhan to appreciate the potentiality of a good infantry force. The method of recruitment to the Janissaries was extraordinary, but, as it turned out, sound. They were taken as children from Christian families, mostly in the Balkan countries, and trained in special communities. They were then affiliated to a religious order of dervishes, and thus received in their monastery-barracks an education which made them fanatical Moslems. They were also given the best physical education possible, and were highly trained in the handling of their weapons. As the sultan's own guard, they occupied a privileged position in the state, not subject to other departments of government, and with responsibility for the maintenance of order in the capital. In other respects they were not pampered – receiving little pay, being strictly subject to the Moslem rules of temperance, and being expected to maintain absolute devotion to their profession of arms and their allegiance to the sultan. Veteran Janissaries, however, received great honour and adequate pensions.

At the height of their greatness, in the first half of the sixteenth century, the Janissaries numbered between 12,000 and 15,000 – of which in time of peace about half were stationed in the provinces and half in the capital. The basic tactical unit was the *orta*, which ranged in size at different periods from 100 to 3,000 men. The titles of the officers, of whom there were many, were taken from the titles of household departments – for example, 'chief soup-maker' and 'chief of the bloodhound keepers'. The commander of the Janissaries was the *agha*; he was not necessarily himself a Janissary, but otherwise promotion was always by merit or seniority within the corps.

The armour of the Janissaries varied as time went on. Their original weapon was the bow, a short composite weapon which far outranged any other type. To qualify for admission to the archers' guild founded by Mehmed II it was necessary to have shot an arrow 630 yards. These ranges were achieved only by using light arrows with a tail wind; the effective range of the bow for fighting was much less, and as soon as the arquebus appeared as a practicable weapon it was adopted by the Janissaries. Sabres and daggers were also standard equipment. Other weapons at various times used by them as well as by the *bashi-bazouks* included slings, crossbows, javelins, lances, straight swords, pikes, axes, maces, scythes, flails and whips. The essential weapons continued to be firearms. The men were not heavily laden with protective armour. In the fifteenth and sixteenth centuries they had a small round shield, a metal helmet shaped like a *fez* with a sharp point on top, and possibly some light mail. There was a colourful uniform for each section, and the soldier wore the emblem of the corps, which for the Janissaries was a wooden spoon; they also went in a great deal for tattooing.

The mass of Turkish forces were horsemen, and of these the Spahis – the word has the same derivation as sepoy – were the *élite* cavalry, which acted as a nucleus for the rest. In the 1520's the Spahis numbered between 10,000 and 12,000. Each man was responsible for recruiting and training between two and six additional horsemen; these he brought to battle rather as a western knight was accompanied by his 'lance'. The Spahis were the original sultan's bodyguards. They were highly paid, and did not have the Janissaries' peculiar system of recruitment and training. The chief weapons of the Turkish cavalry were bow, lance and short sword. They had no defensive armour. Besides the cavalry there were also specialist corps of marines, gunners, armourers, smiths, commissariat officials, and bandsmen. At certain periods the Tartars of the Crimea furnished contingents.

The theoretical total of men of all arms and functions in the Turkish army in its heyday, under Mehmed II (1451–81), Selim I (1512–20) and Suleiman the Magnificent (1520–66), was in the region of 300,000 men, and such was the organization of the

Ottoman state that mobilization was remarkably rapid and complete. The professional nucleus of infantry and cavalry numbered at least 25,000. These were savagely cruel to their enemies, but they were highly trained and well-disciplined, being imbued with religious zeal and owing strict allegiance to the sultan. European observers were profoundly impressed; Giovio wrote:

> The Turks surpass our soldiers for three reasons: they obey their commanders promptly; they never show the least concern for their lives in battle; they can live a long time without bread and wine, content with barley and water.

In 1451 Mehmed II became sultan. He was nineteen years of age, taciturn and cruel, a homosexual, inclined to drink, but resolutely ambitious and a capable soldier. His chief aim at his succession was to complete the conquest of the Byzantine empire by capturing Constantinople. That he succeeded in doing this in 1453 is not remarkable; the city had long been encircled, and the Turks brought an army of 100,000 to besiege its fourteen miles of walls garrisoned by 7,000 men. The fall of Constantinople to the Turks is principally significant in that it meant the final extinction of the civilization of Greece. It is also interesting in that it showed very clearly that the age of chivalry had passed; no Christian force attempted to raise the siege. From the military point of view the chief point to note in the siege is that it was a landmark in the history of artillery.

The main reason for Europe's inability to repel the Turks was that the Ottoman invaders were just as advanced as any other people in the use of firearms. The technique of artillery spread from the Christians to the Moslems in Spain, and thence along North Africa. By 1364 the Ottomans were manufacturing cannon in Asia Minor, and in 1389 they used field artillery at Kossovo. Fifteenth-century cannon were, however, suitable only for battering walls, and the Turks soon recognized this. In the field they continued to rely on mobility, horsemanship and numbers. But for siegecraft they quickly learned to apply the new weapon to good effect. The triple land walls of Constantinople were among the strongest of all medieval fortifications, and during a siege in 1422 it had very soon become obvious that *ballistae* would be ineffective. Before the advent of artillery the strength of their medieval fortifications had been the one comfort for the Byzantines. But when Mehmed II prepared a massive siege train the citizens of Constantinople knew their end was near.

In 1452 a Hungarian engineer called Urban came to the emperor Constantine, offering his services as the best manufacturer of cannon in the world. But Constantine could not pay him what he asked nor provide the necessary raw materials. Urban therefore, the first of many renegade westerners who were to sell their services as technical advisers to the Turks, crossed the Bosphorus and approached the sultan. Mehmed offered him four times the salary he had asked and gave him all the technical assistance he needed. By the beginning of 1453 Urban had produced at Adrianople the largest cannon ever seen, with a barrel nearly 27 feet long, and capable of throwing stone balls of over 1,000 pounds weight. When it was tested the projectile travelled a mile, and the bang is said to have caused pregnant women twelve miles away to have miscarriages. Mehmed was delighted, and Urban's monster-cannon set out for Constantinople drawn by sixty oxen. At the siege it broke down, but that did not matter overmuch because of the efficiency of the other Turkish artillery.

The massive fortifications of Constantinople were unable to resist the Turkish cannon fire. The walls of the city before its capture *above* and as they are today *below*

The Turks kept up a ceaseless bombardment for six weeks, concentrating fire on the most vulnerable points in the walls. Some of their cannon were exceptionally large, and these were difficult to get into position as well as to maintain on their platforms – particularly when rain made the ground soft. Since the barrels cracked if they were not left to cool between shots, the larger cannon could not be fired more than seven times a day. But every shot did tremendous damage. Within a week the outer wall of Constantinople was completely destroyed at several points. Thereafter the gallant defence worked night and day to repair a stockade and earthwork behind the outer wall. But the bombardment, unhurried and relentless, gradually destroyed the fortifications. The Turks demonstrated their technical ingenuity by floating cannon on platforms attached to a pontoon bridge across the Golden Horn, thus reinforcing their bombardment from a new angle. Twice when Mehmed thought that his bombardment had already done enough he was mistaken, for the first two Turkish assaults were beaten off. But the third time he succeeded.

The capture of Constantinople was the prelude to a period of dramatic advance by the Turks and the height of their military greatness. Greece and Serbia were for the first time effectively conquered during the next fifteen years. The resistance of the Albanians, led by George Scanderbeg, at last collapsed in 1468. The limit of Turkish expansion in the west was set for the time being by Mehmed's failure to capture Belgrade. In the east, Trebizond, the last significant Christian area in Asia Minor, was mopped up in 1461. Only isolated and remote strongpoints in the Peloponnese and Anatolia fought on, such as the castle of Kordyle which was defended for several weeks by a peasant girl; gradually even these were extinguished. Mehmed, though cruel to individuals and rigorous in the exaction of Christian tribute children for the Janissaries, was however in many ways a liberal conqueror. The Orthodox religion was tolerated, and apart from the conversion of some Greek temples into mosques the major monuments of Greek and Byzantine architecture were not molested structurally. (It was not until the Venetian siege of the Acropolis in 1687 that the Parthenon, used by the Turks as a powder magazine, was ruined by an explosion).

During this time the advance of Turkish power on land had been balanced by the development of naval strength in the eastern Mediterranean. From the first, as a natural extension of the original *ghazi* drive, some Turks had taken to the sea as corsairs. When the expansion into Europe began it became necessary for the Ottomans to have a navy, if only to protect the crossing of the Bosphorus, and in 1352 a bridgehead was established with a naval base at Gallipoli. Thereafter Turkish seapower grew, and a definite policy was formulated for controlling the trade between the Black Sea and the West, and for the blockade of Constantinople. The chief European naval power in the Mediterranean at this time was Venice. Pietro Loredano destroyed a large part of the Turkish fleet off Gallipoli, and the Turks were temporarily confined to the east of Tenedos. But trade was the great concern of Venice, and she did her best to maintain peace in the Levant. From 1430 Venice was preoccupied with struggles with rival Italian states, and again owing to the disunity of their enemies the Turks were able to make progress westwards. Indeed, by 1453 Turkish ships were plying even the Adriatic with impunity, and one of Mehmed II's soundest reasons for confidence in besieging Constantinople was that he had a strong fleet to cut the sea communications of the city.

The Turks of course had no native seagoing tradition of their own, and when they

The battle of Lepanto. A detail from a painting of the Venetian school

die Belägerüng Wien von Türgau
16   83

reached the Mediterranean they adopted without criticism or modification the ancient Mediterranean naval tradition of the galley – not only in ship design but also in tactics. Fundamentally, little ever changed in galley warfare between the battles of Lade in 494 B.C. and Lepanto in A.D. 1571.

The Greek and Roman trireme had been taken over as the basic ship of war by the Byzantines, who called it the dromon, and increased it in size till it ranged in displacement from 78 to 175 tons, with from 100 to 200 rowers. When Byzantium went into decline Venice and Genoa became the leading Mediterranean sea powers; they called their ships 'galleys' and used only a single tier of oars. Sail was used only for cruising; in action the mast was usually lowered. Some grudging attention was paid in Venice to western developments in sail, and the hybrid 'galleass' appeared in the fourteenth century. But conservatism and inexperience with sail ensured that the oared ship continued to hold sway in the Mediterranean. Galley tactics were simple and had been stereotyped by their most efficient practitioner, Ruggiero de Lauria, in the Sicilian wars of the last twenty years of the thirteenth century. The principle was to advance in line or crescent formation, to ram the enemy in the hope of damaging his oars, and then after a bombardment to board and capture the ship. The majority of the fighting men were slingers and crossbowmen. Refinements in assault included the use of liquid soap to make the enemy's decks slippery, and of broad-tipped and incendiary arrows to damage his rigging. The only subsequent changes were that the size of galleys increased slightly and *ballistae* were replaced by small cannon as bow artillery. Tactics did not change, and the outcome of fighting continued to depend on the 'grapple and board' method.

When the Turks at last captured Constantinople they gained a great ship-building centre, and the reign of Mehmed II then saw an important growth in Turkish seapower. The systematic advance of Turkish dominion on land was paralleled further south by control of the Aegean, and by the occupation of numerous islands and coasts in the eastern Mediterranean. The Black Sea trade was taken over from the Italians, and the export to the West of military and naval supplies was forbidden. There was war with Venice between 1463 and 1479, which the Venetians lost, because they had not realized how rapidly the Turkish fleet had grown, and they were outnumbered as well as being unsupported by the other Italian states – which were jealous of their wealth. The most significant Turkish gains in this war were the capture of the Venetian Dardanelles base of Negroponte in 1470, and the occupation of the Albanian coast eight years later. In 1480 Mehmed failed to take Rhodes from the Knights Hospitaller of St John of Jerusalem, but when he died in 1481 he was preparing a full-scale invasion of southern Italy. It was fortunate for the European peoples that the next Ottoman sultan, Bayezit II (1481–1512), was a man of peace, because during the next thirty years they were cutting each other's throats for the spoils of Italy and disregarding the eastern question. Nevertheless, during his reign Turkish power on land and sea still continued to develop.

As a seafaring people the Turks were unoriginal and conservative, and they had no ambition to participate in the oceanic expansion of Europe which took place from about 1500. But they did aspire to dominate the peoples and trade of the eastern Mediterranean, and they could not afford to ignore the rise of Spain and Portugal. Spanish power was extending threateningly along the North African coast: Pedro Navarro captured Oran in 1509, and Tripoli was occupied in the following year. Furthermore, when the Portuguese entered the Indian Ocean there seemed a real danger that the westerners

The relief of the last Turkish siege of Vienna. A detail from a seventeenth-century painting

In the east the Turks extended their conquests into Persia

might outflank the Turks, gain control of the economy in their rear, and even join forces with their Persian enemies – who in any case were becoming too strong for comfort. In fact, such a purpose hardly crossed the minds of the European politicians. But it was too great a risk to tolerate. Selim I the Cruel during his short reign (1512–20) gave his whole attention to the southern and eastern fronts of the empire. At a time when Europe was most vulnerable to a stab in the back, this allowed a further respite on the Danube and in the Adriatic. But it was definitely in accord with the wider European purpose of the Ottomans.

To clear the way behind him Selim had first to deal with the Persians, whom he defeated on the plain of Chaldiran lying to the west of their capital at Tabriz. But he did not press his victory far into the Persian territories in the east. Instead he set out to realize his chief purpose: the conquest of the Mameluke state in Syria and Egypt. The Mameluke numbers were small and they had no infantry and virtually no firearms, despite attempts by Venice to sell them guns. In 1516 Selim gained his first victory over

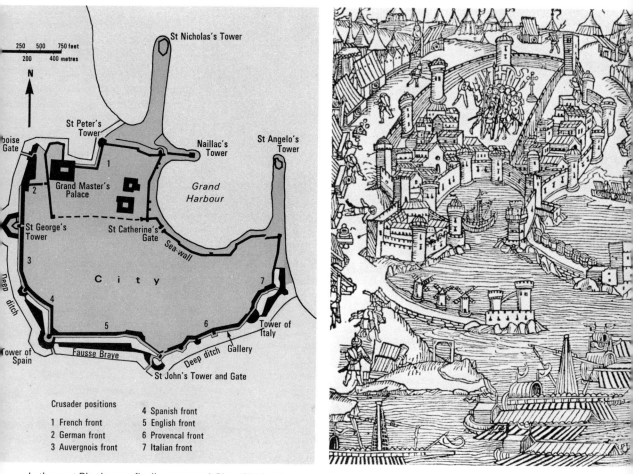

In the map (left):

250 500 750 feet
200 400 metres

N

St Nicholas's Tower

St Peter's Tower

boise Gate

Naillac's Tower

St Angelo's Tower

1

Grand Master's Palace

Grand Harbour

2

St George's Tower

St Catherine's Gate

Sea-wall

3

Deep ditch

C i t y

7

4

5

6

Tower of Italy

Tower of Spain

Fausse Braye

Deep ditch Gallery

St John's Tower and Gate

Crusader positions

1 French front
2 German front
3 Auvergnois front

4 Spanish front
5 English front
6 Provencal front
7 Italian front

In the west Rhodes was finally conquered. Plan of its fortifications *left*, woodcut view *right*

the Mamelukes at Dabik in Syria. He was assisted by treachery in the enemy's ranks, but as at Chaldiran the steadiness of his infantry and the effect of his guns gave him victory. In 1517 a second victory at Ridanieh allowed the Turks to enter Cairo.

Selim's conquest of Egypt was part of an overall strategy to gain control of the eastern Mediterranean and the Near East, in which seapower also had a vital part to play. He decided it was essential to meet the challenge of Spanish power along the north coast of Africa; the occupation of Egypt was the first stage in this strategy. It was followed up in 1519 when Khairredin Barbarossa, the foremost pirate of the Barbary coast, was induced to give his allegiance to the sultan, and was appointed *beylerbey* of Algiers. The Turks also gained control of the Red Sea to enable them to ward off any Portuguese threat from the south-east. There still remained in the Mediterranean one glaring weakness in the Turkish lines of communication: the continued possession by the Knights of St John of the island of Rhodes.

The first great siege of the citadel of Rhodes, by Mehmed II in 1480, had been a failure. Since that time the defences had been much improved, and the fortifications strengthened to withstand artillery bombardment. In place of the original high curtain there was now a wall some 30 feet high and 40 feet thick, bastioned and mounted with guns. The ditch had been widened and deepened, and at points outside it, including the western and southern sides, there was an outer rampart protected by further ditches and steep slopes. There were altogether about 700 knights, and various auxiliaries raised the total of fighting men in the citadel to some 6,000. There was a large stock of ammunition; but in the event of a siege by a power with naval superiority the defenders had no chance of receiving supplies or reinforcements from outside sources.

Selim I had died in 1520 and it must have been clear to Suleiman the Magnificent, his successor, that the assault and capture of Rhodes would be a formidable task; but Turkish strategy in the eastern Mediterranean demanded the possession of the fortress and in June 1522 he decided to go ahead. The siege was begun by landing a force of some 10,000 men on the island in advance of the main army, to make preparations and reconnoitre battery sites. A total of five divisions eventually formed the besieging army; the fortress was surrounded on the landward side, trenches were dug as close to the walls as the fire of the defenders would permit, and a strong force of heavy artillery was deployed. Turkish galleys cruised outside the harbour to complete the investment.

The leaders of the defence were the Grand Master, Villiers de L'Isle Adam, and a Brescian engineer called Gabriel Martinengo. A determined resistance was maintained, but by the end of August the outer ditch had been filled in by the Turks and covered approaches pushed forward to the ramparts. Then the Turks began to mine; the defenders counter-mined; mines were exploded by both sides; desperate hand-to-hand encounters took place; positions were lost, retaken, and lost again. In all, four Turkish assaults were beaten off during September. Three more assaults were launched in October, and a massive general assault in November; all were unsuccessful. There would seem to be no end to it. But although the resistance was unbroken, the strength of the garrison had been reduced by half; furthermore, ammunition and food were running short.

On the Turkish side Suleiman was becoming discouraged and his army fed up. Winter was closing in so he decided to offer generous terms if the fortress would surrender. His offer was accepted and a truce arranged to discuss details; the garrison could depart with all their possessions; those inhabitants who wanted to remain were promised good treatment. On 21st December, six months after the siege had begun, the capitulation was ratified. But only 180 knights and 1,500 other ranks of the garrison survived.

Suleiman kept his word. The knights departed to Malta, and the inhabitants who stayed on were well treated. It had been a great and noble defence; the acceptance by the Grand Master of the generous terms offered by Suleiman saved the inhabitants from Turkish cruelty and looting. Suleiman himself was well satisfied; Turkish supremacy in the eastern Mediterranean was ensured, which was in accord with his strategy.

Having dealt with Rhodes, the sultan's chief concern was the improvement of the internal ordering of the empire, but his reign was also a period of military and naval expansion. In 1525–6 he led a major Turkish campaign on the Danube front, the first for more than fifty years. There was no united opposition from the barons of the frontier nor from the states of eastern Europe. Despite ample warning the Hungarians had not prepared a strong army by the time the Turks reached Belgrade in July 1526. Some of the forts along the Danube made a spirited defence, but Turkish numbers were too great. The armies of Suleiman and King Louis of Hungary met on the plain of Mohacs on 29th August. Suleiman's army of 70,000 was drawn up in a deeper formation than the Turks normally had used on their eastern front. Two lines of cavalry were backed by the Janissaries and Spahis. Such artillery as there was had been deployed at the back. The Christian army of only 35,000 was in two long lines, each of mixed horse and foot. The first cavalry attack of the Hungarians appeared to throw the Turks into disarray, and Louis ordered a general advance. But he had misjudged the depth of the Turkish army, and the elements of the best Hungarians which penetrated through to the rear of their enemy were destroyed without difficulty by the Janissaries. The victory was complete, many leading Hungarians and Bohemians were killed; no obstacle now stood between the Turks and Vienna.

In 1529 the Turks advanced with fire and sword and laid siege to the city. But a desperate defence and the onset of winter determined Suleiman to abandon the siege, since he was now so far from home. The effective limit of the empire in the west was thereafter not extended beyond a line drawn north-east from Zengg on the Adriatic to Gran on the Danube.

On his south-eastern front Suleiman extended the empire as far as Basra. Mesopotamia was in itself a valuable gain, and the acquisition of a port in the Persian Gulf assisted the maritime strategy against the Portuguese which he had inherited from Selim I. In 1526 Suleiman allied with Bahadur, prince of the Indian state of Gujarat, and in 1538 a large fleet was sent to besiege the Portuguese in Diu. The expedition was not a success, and the Turks thereafter abandoned their policy of obstructing the Portuguese in the Indian Ocean; in any case they found they had overestimated the danger in this direction, since Portugal was interested not in the acquisition of an empire on land but rather in peaceful profits from trade by sea. But in the Mediterranean, where Spain had definitely replaced Venice as the leading European maritime power, the competition was fierce. The expansion of Turkish power westwards was vigorously prosecuted in Suleiman's reign. The chief agents were the Barbary corsairs, and in particular Khairredin Barbarossa.

Barbarossa rapidly built up his fleet, and expanded his activities. The leading admiral in the service of Spain, Andrea Doria (a Genoese by birth), commanding a combined Christian fleet, was defeated at Prevesa off the Albanian coast in 1538. Venice then acknowledged Turkish supremacy at sea east of Italy. Thus between 1541 and his death in 1546 Barbarossa was virtually unopposed. By 1551 the Turks had a new corsair leader, Dragut, who captured Tripoli and inflicted another major defeat on Andrea Doria. France and Spain finally made peace between themselves in 1559, but the war between Spain and the Turkish corsairs continued.

Philip II of Spain was also striving to build up the strength of his navies, both in the Atlantic and the Mediterranean, and at last in 1565 the tide began to turn. In that year there was a massive attempt by the Turks to capture Malta, the key point in the communications between the eastern and the western Mediterranean, and still held by the Knights of St John. The knights managed to survive until a Spanish fleet arrived to relieve the island. During the fighting Dragut was killed. The rejoicing in the West was cautious, however, for it seemed certain that there would be a great Turkish reprisal in the next year. But in 1566 Suleiman died. He was succeeded by Selim II, the Drunkard.

In 1570 Selim turned his attention to Cyprus, the last important Venetian possession.

Venice appealed for help to Rome and Spain, and in May 1571 the three powers formed a 'perpetual' league and agreed to prepare a united fleet under the command of the king of Spain's half-brother, Don John of Austria, aged twenty-six. By the end of August 1571 Don John's Christian fleet was concentrated at Messina, and on 16th September it set out for Corfu. Meanwhile a Turkish fleet was assembling at Lepanto in the Gulf of Corinth; its admiral was Ali Pasha, who had once been a *muezzin* – until his beautiful voice had charmed one of the sultan's wives and by her favour he had risen from his lowly position.

The Christian fleet consisted of over 200 galleys, 6 galleasses, 24 large transports, and 50 light rowing craft. In all there were about 50,000 seamen; these worked in appalling conditions, most of them being fettered to their rowing benches. The total number of fighting men was some 30,000, of whom the greatest number and the best in quality were Spaniards. The Turkish fleet was slightly larger, having 250 galleys, 40 galliots, and 20 smaller craft – with some 25,000 fighting men.

The only change in galleys since the thirteenth century had been an increase in size and armament. A large war-galley now displaced about 170 tons as compared to 140, was 131 feet long on the waterline where it had been 128 feet, and was driven by 75 instead of 60 oars. The ships on both sides were basically identical in type. But a few small technical differences were of considerable importance. The Christian galleys had 5 guns mounted in the bows which fired directly ahead; the Turks had only 3 guns. Only the Christian fleet had galleasses; these each carried about 30 guns, mounted on a deck above the rowers, 2 in the bow, 6 in the stern, and 11 lighter cannon on each broadside. The individual soldiers in the Christian fleet were better armed, and most of them had arquebuses. The Turkish bow was, however, a powerful weapon, with a faster rate of fire. The Turks thus had more ships and a high prestige, but certain technical advantages favoured the Christians.

On the morning of 7th October 1571 the fleets sighted each other off Point Skropha, some twenty-five miles west of Lepanto at the mouth of the Gulf of Corinth. Both sides prepared for action. The Christian fleet was in three squadrons in line abreast, spread across about four miles. In the centre Don John commanded 63 galleys; on the left Augustino Barbarigo also commanded 63; on the right Giovanni Andrea Doria had 64 (he was a nephew of the Andrea Doria mentioned earlier); in reserve were 35 under the Marquis of Santa Cruz; and half a mile ahead, spread out in front of the whole line, were the 6 galleasses. The Turks were also in three main squadrons: 90 galleys in the centre under Ali Pasha; 55 on the right under Mahomet Sirocco; 60 on the left commanded by Uluch Ali; with a reserve of 10 galleys, and 20 *fustae* (light rowing vessels). The Turkish line was more extended than that of the Christians.

The admirals on both sides inspected their fleets and exhorted the men to religious fervour and cupidity. Don John on his flagship called for his pipers, and danced a galliard in full armour in sight of all. The battle was joined soon after 10 o'clock.

The first encounter took place on the north, nearest the shore, where the Christian left and the Turkish right were both thrown forward. At the third discharge from two Christian galleasses a Turkish galley was sunk. The galleasses were too heavily armed and too high out of the water for the Turks to risk boarding, and they hoped to pass quickly by. But as they moved forward the galleasses backed water, spun slowly round, and poured gunfire into the massed Turkish galleys, with the result that when they met

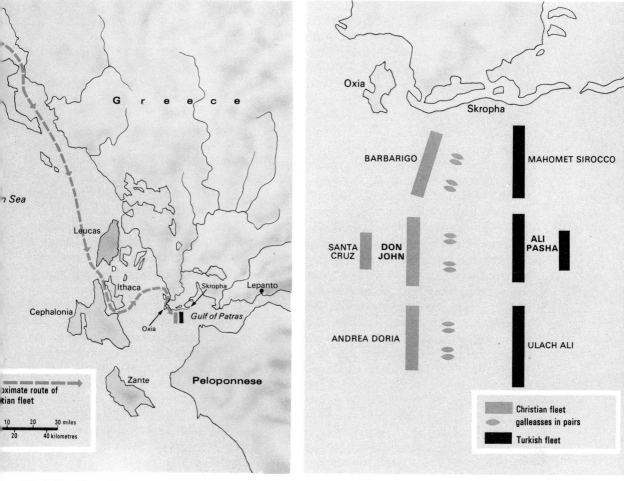

The battle of Lepanto

the main Christian squadron many of them were damaged and the line was disordered. When the two lines met, a desperate hour-long *mêlée* ensued. Barbarigo was killed, but undismayed the Christians fought on. The Turks began to yield, and some of their Christian galley-slaves seized weapons, knocked off their fetters, and joined in the fighting against them. Tempted by the proximity of land many Turks fled to the shore, where they were pursued by the Christians. The victory on the left was complete, and every Turkish vessel was sunk or captured.

Meanwhile the battle had been joined in the centre. The fighting raged principally around the two flagships, which made for each other straightaway and grappled, to the noise of shouting, the rattle of arquebuses and the hail of arrows, and the explosion of artillery. There was a general sword fight as the men of each side struggled to board the ships of their enemy. The fighting spread until 25 or 30 vessels were engaged in an area of some 250 by 150 yards. More than once Ali's men reached and occupied the forecastle of the enemy flagship, but Santa Cruz, his eye on the battle, put 200 Christian reinforcements aboard her. The fury of the fighting lasted for over an hour and a half. The Christians then slowly gained the upper hand, but they were three times driven off the decks of Ali Pasha's galley before it was successfully rammed and most of the Turks were shot down. Don John took the Turkish standard and towed away the flagship. Ali Pasha himself was decapitated in the last of the fighting. By 1 o'clock the battle in the centre had been clearly won by the Christians.

Realizing at the start that there was a danger of being outflanked by the more extended Turkish line, Giovanni Andrea Doria on the right had at first edged some way southwards, and both squadrons here were still manoeuvring for position after the fighting had begun elsewhere. But Doria's delay in joining battle had led some of his captains to doubt his courage, and the 15 vessels on the left of the squadron turned back towards the battle in the centre. Uluch Ali thereupon abandoned the attempt to outflank the Christians, and chased after the splinter group. With an advantage in numbers of five to one the Turks quickly overwhelmed 11 of the 15. Their gain was rather offset, however, when one Christian captain, Benedetto Soranzo, fired his ship's magazine, thus destroying several of the enemy as well as himself. Uluch now moved on towards the centre. But there he found that the battle was already lost; so with Doria's ships attacking him from behind and Santa Cruz's reserves from another angle, he gave up the unequal contest and extricated himself with all speed.

By 4 o'clock the battle was over. Dirty weather was threatening and the Christians concentrated on securing the prizes and searching for a safe anchorage. Altogether 117 captive Turkish galleys were found worth keeping as well as 274 guns.

Lepanto is an interesting battle for several reasons. In *Great Sea Battles*, Oliver Warner wrote:

> At Lepanto, as in most earlier naval battles, the fleets were like armies. Their formation was rigid; the commanders were military; and tactics were based on experience by land. The sailors got the ships where they were wanted: the generals and their soldiers fought it out.

Don John had received his early training as a soldier. Indeed, Lepanto was his first, and last, major naval battle; but he had gained experience in fighting Algerian pirates, and also the Moors at Granada. He died seven years after Lepanto in the Netherlands. Whatever may be thought of his ability to handle a fleet in battle, he was definitely a leader. He had to cope with a quarrelsome fleet. The Genoese and Italians were old rivals, and trouble broke out when shortages of manpower in the Venetian ships were replaced by Italians and Spaniards – the latter coming to blows. It needed diplomacy and firmness on the part of Don John to weld the fleet into a fighting machine, and to keep it so. His briefing of commanders and ships' captains was thorough and shrewd, and he used a blackboard to explain his methods and the tactics to be used in varying contingencies. Finally, he sailed round his squadrons in a fast brigantine to show himself to his men and raise their morale – which he certainly did, being cheered by the crews as he passed.

Lepanto was a negative victory; it preserved the western Mediterranean from complete Turkish dominance, but it was followed up by no strategic offensive by the Christian powers. A new Turkish fleet was rapidly built, and until the English and Dutch fleets began to operate in the Mediterranean in the 1650's the Turks continued to terrorize those waters. Turkish seapower was, however, in decline, the principal reason being a failure to keep abreast with technological development in Europe. The Turks and the Italians continued to use galleys right up to the beginning of the nineteenth century.

Far more serious was the decline of the Turkish army, which was marked by the same feature of technological backwardness. For example, as firearms developed in western Europe with the introduction of good field artillery and the bayonet, the Turks failed to follow suit. They retained their old weakness for enormous and unmanageable cannon. There was also a failure of leadership. Selim the Drunkard (1566–74) lacked ability; after him, too many sultans abandoned their responsibilities as rulers and commanders-in-chief, and gave themselves over to pleasure, allowing the system to decay. A significant moment came in 1582; in that year Murad III forced the Janissaries to admit to their ranks the acrobats and wrestlers who had delighted the people at the festivities occasioned by the circumcision of his son. The result was that discipline, morale and efficiency declined.

At St Gotthard (Hungary) in 1664 the Germans under Montecucculi, a commander who had learned all the lessons of the Thirty Years' War, inflicted a defeat on the Turks which was the decisive turning-point in their military history. Their last serious aggressive demonstration in Europe was the unsuccessful siege of Vienna in 1683. By the eighteenth century the Ottoman empire was hard put to defend its frontiers. The distinctive Turkish military system finally died in 1826, when the Janissaries mutinied and Sultan Mahmud II himself, carrying the sacred Banner of the Prophet, led the people of Constantinople to destroy them. The descendants of Ertughrul continued to occupy his throne until 1922; but from 1826 the Turkish army was of the same kind as the other armies of Europe. Here we will leave the Turks for the time being, but we shall meet them again.

Armies now increased greatly in size. An Imperialist army on the march during the Thirty Years' War

12 European War in the Seventeenth Century

The subject of this chapter is warfare in the period of the Thirty Years' War, the English civil war, and the Anglo-Dutch wars at sea. It is not a self-contained phase, for there was a continuous development from the warfare of Maurice of Nassau to that of the age of Marlborough; but these years are rewarding to study by themselves. The period produced one outstanding figure, Gustavus Adolphus, king of Sweden, one of the 'great captains'. It was also rich in soldiers and sailors who were little less notable – Wallenstein, Pappenheim and Rupert, Condé and Turenne, Cromwell, Tromp and Blake. It was the age in which modern tactics originated, in that tactical systems involving the use of firearms were at that time first successfully developed. Furthermore, a great widening of the scale and scope of warfare took place – in strategy, organization, and the political, economic and social impact on national life.

A striking development of the seventeenth century was the increase in the size of armies. Those with which Philip II had dominated western Europe had seldom comprised more than 40,000 men, whereas Louis XIV needed 400,000 for the same purpose. This increase was originally a result of the enlarged range of strategy and the growing wealth of states. All states which did not wish to go under had to join in the race for quantity, and even a small one like Brandenburg increased the number of men under arms from 900 to 80,000 within a hundred years. Besides becoming larger, armies were beginning to be permanent. In order to garrison frontiers and to be ready for winter campaigning, it became the practice of most states to keep their best troops on a regular basis all the year round, for two reasons – the new tactics required longer training, and it was more economical.

As the scale of war increased, its economic implications became greater. In the first place it was now much more expensive to be an effective military state: Gustavus Adolphus allocated over a half of his budget to military expenses. The area in which an army was quartered, whether or not it was hostile, was likely to be sucked dry of its resources of food, fuel and other needs. But there were benefits. The necessity of feeding great armies was a stimulus to agriculture, and the demand for armaments provided a field for industrial expansion. Sweden, for example, found a profitable use for her natural endowments of copper, tin and iron ore, her vast charcoal-producing forests, and her rivers which could provide power and transport. The Crown played an active part in developing the armaments industry, and foreign technicians became interested. Between 1626 and 1646 exports of Swedish cast-iron guns rose from 22 metric tons a year to 1,000. This export also assisted Swedish shipping to develop. Furthermore, war provided a major source of employment, both in the fighting forces and in the attendant bureaucracy;

War became a profession. Throughout Europe the poorer nobility and the gentry annexed the officer corps and created a tradition of leadership in battle

and smaller and poorer countries, such as Switzerland and Scotland, could sell manpower to the great states.

There were interesting social implications. War now became one of the chief occupations of the masses, with cavalry regiments open to all who could sit a horse and operate a gun. Nevertheless the structure of armies hardly allowed any social mobility. Everywhere the poorer nobility and gentry of Europe saw an opportunity for self-preservation; they annexed the officer corps as the exclusive preserve of their caste, developing their fraternal code of honour and the duel, privileges and duties. Militarism was born.

The administrative and political implications of the growth of armies and navies were also significant. There could be no large armies unless the state had the power to raise a great deal of money. War Offices multiplied and the tentacles of bureaucracy became longer and stronger. As G. N. Clark writes, 'Just as the modern state was needed to create the standing army, so the army created the modern state, for the influence of the two causes was reciprocal.' The demands of finance, recruitment and equipment forced governments to interfere increasingly in the lives of their subjects; for example, the need for standardization in gunpowder and calibres made it necessary to institute arms' monopolies and state supervision. The strengthening of governments led, in most countries, to the suppression of democracy – in France, for example, and, most strikingly, in Prussia, where the *Intendantur der Armee* became the nucleus of the whole government. The Great Rebellion in England was, among other things, a successful attempt to check the tendency of kings in need of money to violate popular liberties. Most of the armies of the seventeenth century were state armies, not national armies; and in no country except England was the commander-in-chief of the army, the king, made responsible to the people.

In an age of developing absolutism the range of strategy, despite bad communications, increased. A greater mobility and range were in any case called for when the development of offensive tactics encouraged commanders to seek out the enemy and destroy him in battle. But this development was also linked with wider-ranging economic policies, and with the ambitions of absolute rulers in control of massive armies. Such armies could only with difficulty live off the country over which they were operating, and it became essential to guard one's own supply and trade lines. Conversely it was desirable to deprive the enemy of his. More positively, war was seen as a means to wealth. Economic theory persuaded most politicians in this period that the richest nation would be the one which, by fair means or foul, annexed for itself the largest share of the world's resources of materials and manpower. Logistical capacity now began to catch up with political imagination. The operations in the Thirty Years' War ranged all over central Europe: the Spaniards schemed to seize Göteborg, and Prince Piccolomini (an Austrian general) marched from Flanders to Bohemia. Gustavus Adolphus was a master at combining short-term strategy seeking a decisive battle with the longer-term strategy which sought to drive the enemy back on all fronts.

The Thirty Years' War, which began in 1618 in Germany, had its origin in religious disputes between Catholics and Protestants. But politics was interwoven with religion. France increasingly interfered (although she did not openly declare war till 1635), and as the war widened the political aspect became uppermost. It then developed essentially into a struggle to dominate Europe – between the Holy Roman Emperor Ferdinand II, supported by Spain and Bavaria, and France supported by various Protestant states as well as by the Pope. The details of the war, because of the political fragmentation of central Europe, were immensely complicated. But Richelieu, chief minister of France, produced a master-stroke when in 1630 he induced Gustavus Adolphus of Sweden to come into the war against the emperor Ferdinand II. As Richelieu no doubt knew, Gustavus was the best soldier in Europe.

In 1630 Gustavus Adolphus was thirty-six years old. He had become king at the age of seventeen, and since then had been frequently at war with Denmark, Poland and Russia to prevent any of them dominating the Baltic. Study of the science of war had been followed by practical experience in the art. His studies had included Xenophon's *Cyropaedia*, which Liddell Hart considers to be 'perhaps the greatest of all military text-books'. He had also kept in touch with scientific and technological developments. In fact, Gustavus was the first great soldier to approach the art of war with the mental attitude of the Renaissance. His ideas on organization, training and tactics were original and brilliant; furthermore he was energetic and efficient in applying them. As a man he was passionate and brave, being much liked and respected by his people, outstandingly humane, and motivated by high convictions without being bigoted. As was said, his great military achievements

were ever attended by devotion within and circumspection without. He first praised God, and then provided for man, at once having an eye on his enemies' next designs, and his soldiers' present necessities.

The underlying basis of Gustavus' success was his understanding of administration and organization. Sweden could not afford a mercenary army large enough to face the combined armies of her enemies, and Gustavus therefore introduced a system of conscription – eventually creating the first national army to be raised, paid, fed and equipped by the state. Using clergy and local juries as recruiting sergeants, he raised over 40,000 Swedes who were 'strong of limb, and, so far as can be ascertained, courageous – in years from eighteen to thirty'. Workers in 'reserved occupations' such as transport and munitions were exempted. Some men were paid in grants of land or tax remissions. Apart from being economical, it remained essentially a national army, and as a result its morale was higher than that of its predominantly mercenary opponents.

In composition and equipment the Swedish army differed from the others of Europe in that it corresponded with the king's tactical conceptions – the chief of which was the supreme importance of firepower and mobility. He made the musket the chief weapon and greatly increased the proportion of musketeers to pikemen. At the same time, following the example of Maurice of Nassau, he created smaller units and sub-units. Thus a company consisted of 72 musketeers and 54 pikemen; there were four companies in a battalion, eight battalions in a regiment, and two to four regiments in a brigade. The musket was shortened and lightened so that the rest was unnecessary; the loading drill was simplified; and the wheel-lock and paper cartridge were made standard equipment. The pike was shortened from 16 to 11 feet, and armour reduced. Cavalry consisted of cuirassiers armed with sword and pistol, and dragoons who were mounted musketeers.

Gustavus was the first great commander to recognize the importance of field artillery, and he made it a third essential arm. He was assisted by a brilliant general of artillery, Torstensson, who in 1630 was only thirty. Field guns were made shorter with lighter carriages to assist mobility, becoming distinct from siege guns. Calibres were reduced in number and standardized. Thus Swedish siege guns weighed from 15 to 63 cwt, while field guns weighed 12, 18 or 27 cwt. Smaller pieces were 4-pounders with fixed ammunition, called 'regimental' guns; these could be moved by one horse or three men, and fired eight rounds of grape or canister to every six shots of a musketeer. There was a corps of engineers, civilian experts being called in when necessary. Thus in Gustavus' army science and technology were closely linked with war; and standard equipment included new aids such as field-glasses and maps.

Drill was practised as an aid to discipline and efficiency in the junior ranks and for the soldiery. In a large army consisting of small units officers were naturally more numerous and important than in the past, and the concept of rank and hierarchy emerged. As Michael Roberts observes, the army was seen not as a brute mass nor as a collection of aggressive individuals, but rather as a complex organism each part of which had to respond intelligently to impulses from above. Senior officers had to have a working knowledge of science, geography, and even diplomacy; for these reasons several military academies were founded in Europe during the seventeenth century. Gustavus was intolerant of inefficiency, and ready to promote officers for their merit; while N.C.O.'s had never been given so much responsibility and initiative since Roman times. Tactics now demanded flexible manoeuvre and good fire-discipline, for both of which training was necessary – officers having to train their men by drill and exercises at all seasons of the year. A great step to achieving uniformity was the introduction of uniforms and badges, which also assisted morale and *esprit*.

rch   2 Prime your pan   3 Charge your piece   4 Ram your powder

d your piece   6 Guard your pan   7 Give fire   8 Give fire

pe your pike   10 Check your pike   11 dragoon   12 cuirassier

Drill was highly organized with standard equipment. 1 and 8 musket fire with the rest; 2 to 7 musket fire without the rest; 9 and 10 pike drill; 11 and 12 cavalry

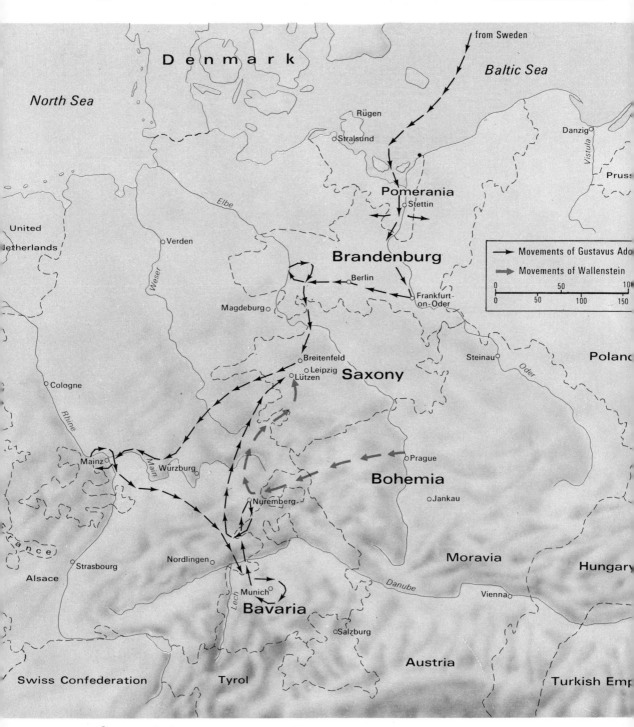

Germany at the time of the Thirty Years' War

Warm uniform, introduced by Gustavus, did much to ensure a good state of discipline and morale. This was likely to exist anyway in the Swedish army, in which the men were selected from the best of the national youth, led by bright young officers under an inspired commander. But such a vital matter was not left to chance, and in the *Articles of War* which he himself composed Gustavus forbade drunkenness, whoring and profanity. Punishments for small offences were humane, flogging being forbidden; but pillage, rape and 'despising divine service' were punishable by death. Church parades were held regularly, and these were intended to have a civilizing influence.

Because of the increased size of armies and the greater range of strategy, it became necessary to organize the commissariat on more business-like lines. Standardization of weapons meant that they had to be provided by the state rather than, as in the past, by individual soldiers. As I have said, it was practically impossible for a seventeenth-century army to live off the country, and for reasons of humanity it was obviously undesirable. Gustavus' reforms included an intelligent system of requisitioning, with supply depots at appropriate centres. In principle, too, he quartered his army in fortified camps, like the Romans. These reforms cut down wastage and atrocity; they did away with the need for the army to disperse over the countryside in search of forage and quarters; and mobility was gained by reducing the huge numbers of camp followers. In practice the system did not always work, and the Swedes were often reduced to pillage and forced billeting. But the system was a great step forward in the principle of military administration. Gustavus also made valuable innovations in the medical services; he provided a surgeon for each regiment, and allocated a tithe of all captured material for the maintenance of military hospitals.

The twin objects in the foreign policy of Gustavus were the strengthening of Swedish power and the defence of Protestantism. By 1630 he had to enter the Thirty Years' War, for the two 'Catholic' Imperialist armies of Wallenstein and Tilly now occupied all Germany up to the Baltic, and savage measures were being taken against Protestants. To defend the Baltic, Gustavus decided to take the offensive, in order to carry the war away from Sweden. Her long coasts would be difficult to defend, and the king did not wish his people to suffer. In the wide expanses of Germany the numerical superiority of the enemy would count for less. As Gustavus reckoned:

> He has an extensive country to occupy, and many cities to guard, which requires a large number of troops. It is not well to lose sight that the power of the enemy is more in fame than in the reality, and that the loss of a single pitched battle would render his position very critical.

He was to be proved right; but it was a bold calculation, for Gustavus landed at the mouth of the Oder in the summer of 1630 with only 13,000 men to oppose combined enemy forces totalling 100,000. At that moment the emperor, overconfident and possibly beguiled by Richelieu, dismissed Wallenstein – whose power he feared. Half of Gustavus' enemies were thus removed from the scene without a blow, and the Swedish army was actually able to recruit numbers of Wallenstein's out-of-work soldiers. Fortune generally favours the bold.

The Protestant princes in Germany remained too cowed and pessimistic to help him, and Gustavus' strategy was to progress cautiously and methodically – adjusting his strategy to his resources. He spent the first year in operations on the southern Baltic

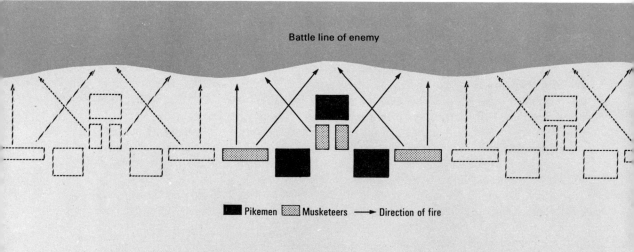

Battle line of enemy

■ Pikemen ▦ Musketeers ⟶ Direction of fire

Infantry formation used by the army of Gustavus Adolphus

coast, securing his base and communications and gradually bringing more men over into Germany. In May 1631 he was ready for battle, and then moved south to relieve Magdeburg, which was being besieged by Tilly. With a firm administrative foundation, the well-disciplined Swedish army marched quickly. But the Protestant elector of Saxony at the last moment upset this strategy by refusing to let it pass, and Magdeburg fell to the Imperialists. Tilly's gain, however, was instantly offset when his troops destroyed the city which they had captured. The Swedish army set out again in July by another route, towards Leipzig. By this time Gustavus had the support of the Saxons, and in September his allied forces met Tilly's army at Breitenfeld, five miles north of Leipzig.

Tilly had hoped to defer battle, but he had been more or less forced into it by his impetuous second-in-command, Pappenheim, who had gone forward to reconnoitre, and reported, untruly, that the enemy were approaching so fast that battle was inevitable. This contrasted with the Swedish king's careful and efficient reconnaissance. On important occasions Gustavus did his own reconnoitring; he had a system by which subordinate commanders passed information to him and to each other quickly and clearly. The orders of the Swedish army were a model in form, each numbered paragraph covering one point concisely, clearly, and in a logical sequence. This system helped to secure mutual protection, and economy and concentration of force in attack. The Swedish reconnaissance and preparation before Breitenfeld was as efficient as ever, and Gustavus joined battle at his own time and when the enemy was ill prepared.

He had 47,000 men, of whom 10,000 were Saxons and untried. But the rest were his own Swedes in whom he had every confidence; during their long service together he had instilled in them his own tactical conceptions, at training and in battle. In many respects Gustavus took over where Maurice of Nassau had left off, since he adopted Maurice's smaller units, and eliminated all infantry weapons other than the musket and the pike. But in his dislike of battle Maurice had been a commander of the sixteenth century, and

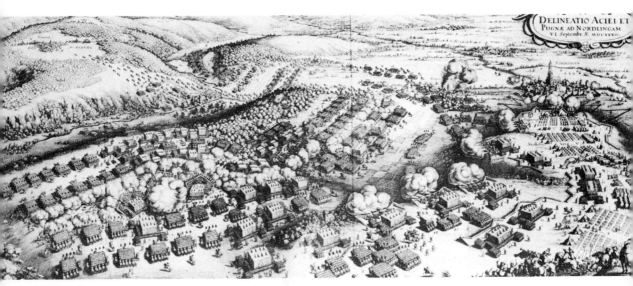

The battle order consisted of units of pikemen and musketeers, supported by artillery

this was as far as he had got. The problem of finding an offensive tactical system for the age of firearms still remained, and its solution was one of the great contributions of Gustavus to the development of the modern art of war.

Firearms were to provide the chief striking power of infantry, and the number of musketeers had been accordingly increased. The pike again became an offensive weapon, but the chief function of pikemen remained to cover the musketeers from attacks while loading. An efficient and flexible T-shaped formation was devised for the infantry brigade (which is illustrated in the diagram). This formation combined musketeers and pikemen most economically in their proper functions. The advanced central block of pikemen formed a breakwater in defence and a spearhead in attack, while the other units of pikemen covered the flanks of the musketeers. The latter, while fully protected, could assail the enemy front with volleys at any point, and bring converging fire to bear from different angles. As was remarked, the brigade was thus like 'a little movable fortress with its curtains and ravelins'. Besides musketry fire, Gustavus could employ shock in two other forms. His mobile field artillery with its rapid rate of fire supplemented the missile shock of musket fire, and was highly effective against massed formations. Furthermore, the smoke from the guns could to some extent obscure the movements of the troops behind. The cavalry arm was reorganized – the caracole of pistoleers being abandoned and replaced by a charge at the gallop, with the sword as the cavalryman's chief weapon and the pistol used as a supplementary weapon in the *mêlée*. This was a return to the proper use of the speed and weight of cavalry. Cavalry fulfilled a twofold tactical function: the preliminary clearing work in front to make way for the infantry assault, and delivering the decisive shock attack.

Realizing that a mass formation is a waste of manpower and is unmanoeuvrable, and that it is particularly vulnerable to gunfire, Gustavus used a linear disposition – repeating the T-shaped infantry formations and small cavalry squads, and backing them with

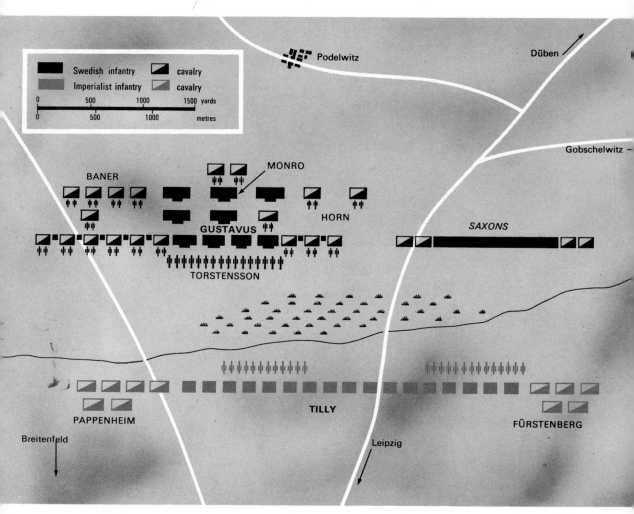

The battle of Breitenfeld

reserves. The pikemen were arranged six deep, the cavalry four deep with intervals
between the files, and the musketeers three deep. Firepower, movement and shock
could be adjusted and directed economically and freely.

The battleground at Breitenfeld was a slightly undulating plain, bare of trees. On the
far left Gustavus placed the Saxons, whose formation is unknown. Next came the
Swedish left, under Horn, consisting of three regiments of cavalry interspersed with
detachments of musketeers, and backed by two more cavalry regiments in the second
line. In the front line of the centre, where he himself commanded, Gustavus placed four
T-shaped brigades of foot; in the second line two brigades and one regiment; and in the
third line three brigades of foot and behind them two regiments of cavalry. On the right,
commanded by Baner, there were six regiments of cavalry interspersed with musketeers
in the front line, one regiment behind them and four more in a third line. Every regiment

had its two regimental 4-pounder guns in front. The heavier field artillery, under Torstensson, was massed in front of the centre. To face the 47,000 strong allied army, the Imperialist army of Tilly consisted of 40,000 men: 30,000 foot and 10,000 horse. Tilly was a good commander in the conventional Spanish tradition, a man of over seventy, and an impressive figure with his sunken cheeks and dark green velvet doublet. He drew up his army in one or two lines of 'tercios', seventeen solid squares fifty men deep, with the infantry in the centre and the cavalry on the wings. The armies, thus deployed, would face each other on a front of over two miles.

The emblem of the Swedes was a green twig, that of the Imperialists a white riband. Although there was little difference between the two armies in numbers, the Imperialists were at a clear disadvantage in artillery – having about 26 guns to their enemy's 54 or so. Both commanders were experienced and confident. The outcome of the battle would depend upon which of two different tactical systems proved to be superior. One relied on mass and the other on mobility; once again, the phalanx was challenged by the legion.

Gustavus spent the night before the battle in his carriage, discussing the coming action with his senior officers. Early on 17th September 1631, after prayers had been said and Gustavus had addressed his officers, the Swedish army advanced to attack. A marshy stream had first to be crossed, but Tilly failed to take advantage of this moment to fall on the Swedes and, apart from a small clash between some of the Imperialist cavalry and Gustavus' Scots, the crossing was made without incident. The first main phase of the battle was a cannonade, which began at noon and lasted for over two hours. The Swedes gained an advantage here as their artillery fired about three rounds to every one of their enemy. Eventually the Imperialist cavalry on the left became so galled by this fire that Pappenheim, in command on that flank, could restrain himself no longer; without any orders from Tilly, he moved with 5,000 men a little farther to his left, and then launched a charge against the Swedish right flank. The value of their training for manoeuvre and their flexible formation now paid a dividend for the Swedes. Gustavus quickly wheeled up his reserve line of cavalry to form a right angle with the front line. In seven vain charges against this bastion of mingled horsemen and musketeers, Pappenheim's cuirassiers disintegrated. Then Baner counter-attacked, and drove the Imperialist left wing of cavalry from the field.

Meanwhile, fortunes at the other end of the battle were swaying in the opposite direction. Fürstenberg's cavalry on the Imperialist right wing attacked and within half an hour had put the Saxons to flight; the situation then was that the remaining Swedes were outnumbered and their left was exposed. So far Tilly can hardly be said to have been in control of his army, but now he realized his advantage. Observing that his right overlapped the enemy whose left was weakly formed, he ordered it to move round and attack the Swedish rear, while his centre of heavy infantry moved to their right to attack the Swedish left in flank. But as this massive Imperialist manoeuvre began, Gustavus demonstrated both that he could react in a developing battle at least as well as Tilly and that his articulated formation was undoubtedly superior to his enemy's masses. He immediately ordered Horn to wheel his men left to face Tilly's new front; at the same time he brought across two brigades of infantry from the second line in the centre to reinforce the left. Since Gustavus' small units manoeuvred a great deal faster than the Imperialist squares, Tilly lost what had momentarily seemed to be a definite advantage.

Monro, the Scots commander of one of the Swedish central brigades brought over to the left, describes how the fighting now took place:

> The enemies Battaile standing firm, looking on us at a neere distance, and seeing the other
> Briggads and ours wheeling about, making front unto them, they were prepared with a firm
> resolution to receive us with a salvo of Cannon and Muskets; but our small Ordinance being
> twice discharged amongst them, and before we stirred, we charged them with a salvo of muskets,
> which was repaied, and incontinent our Briggad advancing unto them with push of pike . . . fell
> on the execution.

This was the hardest phase of the fighting, and the outcome of the battle hung on its
progress. Gustavus decided to risk all in a decisive blow. His right wing had been secure
since the defeat of Pappenheim; he now brought across four cavalry regiments and
himself led them in a great charge up the slope towards the enemy's artillery, sweeping
through the guns and round into the Imperialist left. The enemy's artillery being
captured, Torstensson turned it against them, thus bringing converging fire to bear
from the right and from the Swedish guns in the centre. While this was going on, the
attack by the Swedish left against Tilly's centre continued. Assailed on their front and on
their left simultaneously by infantry, artillery and cavalry, the close-packed mass of the
Imperialist infantry fought on bravely – but in the end were defeated, and broke. The
pursuit by the Swedish cavalry did not last long. The final losses of Tilly's army were
13,000, and the whole of its artillery and baggage train.

The battle of Breitenfeld was as significant politically as it was militarily, northern and
western Germany being saved from Jesuit and Habsburg domination. Gustavus did not
follow up his victory by marching through perilous country to the distant Imperial
capital of Vienna; instead he consolidated the situation nearer home by occupying the
Rhineland, thus breaking the Spanish link with the Netherlands and checking the
schemes of Richelieu. By the spring of 1632 Tilly had a new army. Gustavus caught him
at the River Lech, brilliantly assembling his forces and screening the crossing, and in the
ensuing battle Tilly's army was beaten and he himself was killed. Gustavus then marched
on south of the Danube. In alarm Ferdinand recalled Wallenstein, who drew the
Swedes back to the vicinity of Leipzig. The second great victory of Gustavus Adolphus
and the Swedish army was at the battle against Wallenstein's army at Lützen in November 1632. But the value of this victory was negatived, for in the battle Gustavus himself
was killed.

In a career which began at the same age as that of Alexander the Great and lasted very
little longer, Gustavus performed deeds hardly less spectacular and influential. He was
the founder of modern military organization, particularly in his system of conscription
and commissariat, and of modern military training – with the establishment of the full
officer hierarchy and battle drill. While others may have had greater strategical wisdom
and been more brilliant tacticians, Gustavus goes down in history as the foremost
maker of an army of his times. He forged the weapon to his liking and then used it in
battle with great effect – as we have seen. His army, with its linear formation of small
units of mixed arms, was the first in the age of firearms to combine security with a
successful offensive formula – power to guard with ability to move, and power to hit.
The development of modern European armies was to stem in direct descent from the
Swedish army created by Gustavus Adolphus.

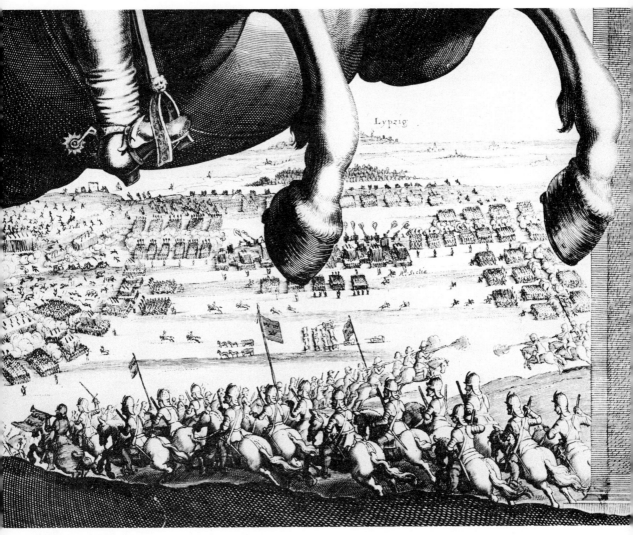

Swedish cavalry delivered the knock-out blow at Breitenfeld

Wallenstein, although defeated in battle, was now left as the most powerful man in northern Europe. He is a most interesting figure. By vigorous social intrigue and a gift for seizing his opportunities, this man of humble origins and immense ambition had won the emperor's favour and the grant of a dukedom. Early in the war when things were going disastrously for Ferdinand, Wallenstein had made an offer to raise and equip, at no charge, an army of 50,000 men for the Imperial service. Having gained a good military reputation in south-eastern Europe and being known as a generous landlord, in a short time he gathered together the promised number of mercenaries. By 1627 the Protestants of northern Germany had virtually disarmed, and Wallenstein overran the country up to the Baltic. He then saw that Sweden was likely to enter the war, and he did not underestimate her strength. In his attempt to build up an Imperial fleet in the Baltic he showed his remarkable strategical vision. This was the threat which Gustavus had faced when he landed in Germany with his small army in the summer of 1630, and it was thus a remarkable stroke of fortune for Sweden when Ferdinand dismissed Wallenstein at that moment.

Wallenstein accepted his dismissal without question and returned to the business of running his estates and civilizing Moldavia. He sent Ferdinand his plan of an alliance with Denmark in order to strike by sea at Gustavus' base, but it was rejected. Wallenstein bided his time. By 1632 all that he had gained for the Imperialist cause had been lost, and he was recalled to service. For a second time he raised 40,000 men at his own expense, and this time insisted that he should have supreme command of all the Imperial forces – above the emperor himself.

Wallenstein's Lützen campaign was a brilliant strategical operation. In the summer of 1632 the Swedes were occupying Bavaria, and the Saxons Bohemia. Wallenstein did not strike directly at his main enemy, but concentrated first on dealing with the Saxons. They were driven out of Bohemia and the elector was forced to come over to the Imperialist side. Having deprived Gustavus of his chief ally, Wallenstein still did not attack him, but moved north against his communications. Gustavus was forced to leave Bavaria and follow, with Maximilian of Bavaria tailing him. At Nuremberg the two armies entrenched opposite each other, each seeking to starve out the other. Gustavus wanted a battle, but Wallenstein refused. Finally Gustavus, desperately short of supplies, launched a heavy attack on the enemy's entrenchments. The Swedes were repulsed, and yielding to hunger and superior willpower Gustavus retired – Wallenstein remarking that 'the king has blunted his horns'. Gustavus now moved south to the Danube. But the battle of wills was renewed, and once more he lost. Wallenstein turned north and headed for Saxony, seeming to threaten the source of Gustavus' communications on the Baltic coast. The plan worked: Gustavus was again drawn right away from the Imperialist territories in the south, and doubled back. Then he made up for his failure; he brought Wallenstein, when he did not expect it, to battle at Lützen.

By 1633 Wallenstein had reconstructed his army, making good the losses of Lützen, and a complete Imperialist victory seemed certain. He defeated the Swedes at Steinau, and would have cut them off from the Baltic; but Ferdinand nervously recalled him to protect the south. In 1634, alarmed at being overshadowed personally, jealous of his success and mistrusting his puzzling character, Ferdinand dismissed Wallenstein for the second time – and shortly afterwards Wallenstein was assassinated.

Wallenstein is not easy to evaluate. He was a poor tactician, and although a good military organizer he was not in the class of Gustavus. But he was a very able strategist; and he had a clear political object: to bring about a peace which could last. He is possibly less interesting as a soldier than as a character, and as an outstanding military and political adventurer. It required a powerful personality to outwill Gustavus Adolphus, to attract thousands of followers with ease, to make the Holy Roman Emperor accept a humiliating contract, and in Richelieu's words 'by his sole presence and the severity of his silence' to make men obey him – all of which he did. He went into the war to make money, and succeeded – becoming a sort of military tycoon. He was something of an idealist, practising religious tolerance and urging the unification of Germany; but he also believed in the stars, and it was perhaps this fantastic streak which brought him to ruin.

The battle of Montjuic. French and Spanish forces clash outside Barcelona, 1641. A detail from a painting by Pandolfo Reschi

Either Gustavus Adolphus or Wallenstein, had they lived, might have brought the war to a quick end one way or another. But neither Richelieu nor Mazarin (who succeeded him in 1642) would end it until France had control of the left bank of the Rhine. Fortunes swayed, but from 1639 France and Sweden slowly got the better of Austria and Spain. France had not been at war since the time of Henry IV, but from 1643 the modernization of the French army was undertaken by Le Tellier, minister for war, along the lines of efficient state control. In 1643 the 21-year-old Duc d'Enghien, later Prince of Condé, dispelled what remained of Spanish military prestige and made an important strategical gain by his victory at Rocroi near Sedan in the western Ardennes. Under Condé's command French soldiers continued to learn the new tactics of fire and movement. France had another fine commander in Turenne, whose ability as a strategist complemented Condé's tactical brilliance. The Swedish army also remained formidable, now under the command of Torstensson – who won an important victory at Jankau in 1645. After long negotiations and more battles the Thirty Years' War was ended by the Treaty of Westphalia in 1648.

When peace was established France had probably gained most, with her frontiers fixed along the Pyrenees and part of the Rhine, and her army the most powerful in Europe. Sweden and Brandenburg also emerged as major powers. The political history of Germany was henceforward to be the history of her leading states, for the Holy Roman Emperor was now practically no more than ruler of Austria, and the Habsburgs in the next years were to turn their attentions increasingly eastwards – compensating themselves for their decline in western Europe at the expense of the decadent Ottoman empire.

The fate of the people of Germany was perhaps the gravest consequence of the Thirty Years' War, because this had been fought over their country by great armies in which administrative capacity could not cope with their commanders' intentions: in spite of the efforts of Gustavus and Wallenstein, devastation had for thirty years been a logistical necessity. Before ever the war had begun Hugo Grotius had foreseen this situation and had written his *De Jure Belli ac Pacis*, putting forward a code of international conventions which might to some extent mitigate the horrors of war. But even the limits of conduct that he suggested were appallingly wide; for example, he accepted the necessity of killing prisoners of war and even civilians. Human life was bound to be, as Thomas Hobbes observed, 'nasty, brutish and short'. Religious passion was not necessarily a civilizing influence as Gustavus had hoped, and no moral sanctions prevailed against political and logistical necessity. The sack of Magdeburg, during which 30,000 people were burned to death, was the single most horrifying episode of the war. But the cumulative horror was even worse. Eight million people in Germany perished. In Bohemia only 6,000 out of 35,000 villages survived. The richest areas suffered most. German Protestantism was preserved, but in other respects German civilization suffered deeply, perhaps ruinously.

England had, happily for her, held aloof as far as she could from the Thirty Years' War. But in August 1642 her own civil war began. An antagonism had long been developing between King Charles I and certain prosperous and articulate sections of his subjects – Puritans who demanded liberty for their own conscience and a state Church which was less Catholic in tendency, and Parliamentarians who demanded a more liberal and

An Anglo-Dutch naval engagement. A detail from 'The Four Days' Fight, 1666' by Abraham Storck competent regime than the inefficient absolutism which Charles was setting up. Charles found most of his support in those areas of England farthest from the capital; the supporters of the Great Rebellion were mostly in the manufacturing centres and sea-ports, particularly London. The majority of the English people committed themselves in advance to neither side.

Both sides regarded control of London as the key to victory. At the outset of war neither side could raise more than a handful of good quality troops. The Parliamentarians had an advantage in material resources, which lasted; the Royalists had an initial advantage in their cavalry, commanded by Prince Rupert of the Rhine – but this advantage was soon to be offset by the rise of Oliver Cromwell.

Cromwell was a country squire from East Anglia. In 1642 he was forty-three years old. He had not been a leader in Parliament and had no previous military experience. He was a Puritan, energetic, hot tempered and forthright. He joined the Parliamentary side as a cavalry captain, and was present at Edgehill in October 1642. His experience in that clumsy and bloody battle gave him furiously to think.

Cromwell saw that Parliament must raise a cavalry force capable of beating that of the king. Rupert had followed Gustavus in substituting the charge of cavalry, sword in hand, for the caracole of pistoleers, and he himself was a fine leader – courageous, headstrong, and flamboyant with his scarlet coat, his black horse, and the pet monkey which the

The Thirty Years' War brought terrible devastation to Germany, not only in the set battles, as at Lützen *below*, but from marauding armies *right*

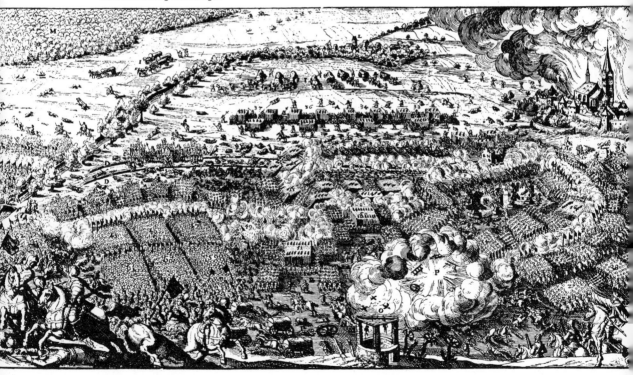

Puritans called 'the little whore of Babylon'. In the winter of 1642–3 Cromwell raised a regiment of cavalry in East Anglia, being highly selective in his recruitment. No 'decayed servingmen and tapsters and such kind of fellows' would do, nor 'that which you call a gentleman and is nothing else'. His principle was that

> a few honest men are better than numbers . . . I had rather have a plain russet-coated captain that knows what he fights for, and loves what he knows.

Religion was the foundation of his discipline, and training was rigorous. The men were armed with a sword, a 2½-foot carbine, and a pair of pistols – being taught to use them all with the utmost proficiency. Their defensive armour consisted of back and breastplates, a helmet and a buff coat. They were regularly paid, and strictly disciplined – swearing and all marauding (except damaging churches) being severely punished. The regiment had its first blooding in a clash at Grantham in May 1643, when, in Cromwell's words,

> We . . . came on . . . a pretty round trot, they standing firm to receive us; and our men charging fiercely upon them, by God's providence they were immediately routed.

Afterwards he wrote to a friend, 'I have a lovely company . . . , they are honest, sober Christians: they expect to be used as men!' Sir Winston Churchill once referred to me as a Cromwellian figure, because, as he said, I always tried both to praise the Lord and to pass the ammunition.

The real test of Cromwell's 'Ironsides', as they came to be known, did not come until July 1644 at Marston Moor. The battle had hardly opened before Rupert's charge swept three-quarters of his enemy off the field. But Rupert led the pursuit too far, and that quarter of the Parliamentary army which had stood firm included Cromwell's regiment. Charging knee to knee at a fast trot rather than at a wild gallop, the front rank holding their fire till the last moment, they fell on the flank of the king's infantry, and after a long, hard fight destroyed them. If it was Rupert who had introduced Swedish cavalry tactics to England, Cromwell was able to put them to better use.

Cromwell's reputation, both as a trainer and as a leader of cavalry, was now made. Indecision and intrigue prevented the Parliamentarians from exploiting the victory of Marston Moor to end the war, but in the following winter Cromwell persuaded Parliament to overhaul its forces. Fairfax, not Cromwell, was to be commander of the New Model Army, formed on the pattern already laid down by Cromwell in East Anglia. The cavalry consisted of eleven regiments, each 600 strong, armed, equipped and trained in the same manner as the Ironsides, except that the carbine was generally discarded. There was also one regiment, 1,000 strong, of dragoons; these were equipped with musket and sword, mounted for transport and skirmishing but generally fighting on foot.

The infantry force was twelve regiments, each over 1,000 strong, the proportion of musketeers to pikemen being two to one. The musket used was the new shorter and lighter weapon, and the match-lock was replaced by the wheel-lock and flint-lock. The latter, the detonation of which was caused by the spark from a piece of flint striking a metal plate, became the most common: being cheaper, safer and more reliable. The range of the musket was at least 400 yards, but in battle it was used at closer quarters.

His
Excellencie
Thomas Fairfax K.
Generall of the forces
raised by the
Parliament.

for John Partridg. Edua: Bowers Pinxit. W. Marshall sculpsit.

The New Model Army, commanded by Sir Thomas Fairfax, was formed to fight against the English Royalists.

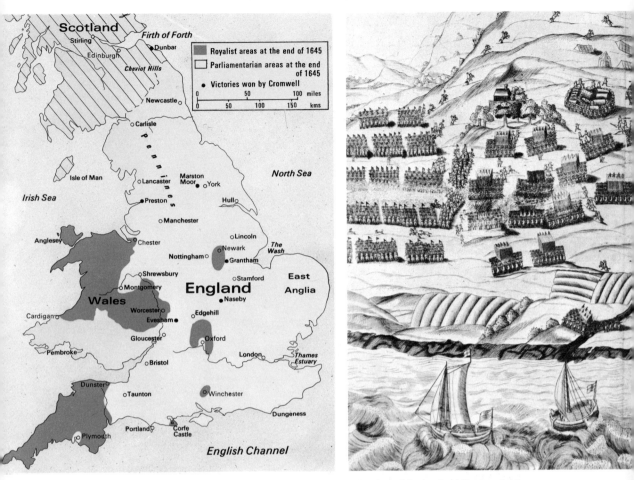

England at the end of the Civil War *left*. A contemporary engraving of the battle of Dunbar *right*.

The musketeers of the New Model Army wore no defensive armour; they had red tunics, which were to remain the uniform of the British army until the end of the nineteenth century. The metal helmet was gradually abandoned for a broad-brimmed felt hat. The defence of the musketeers was afforded by the pikemen, who used a 16-foot long weapon with a lozenge-shaped head; they also had swords and heavy defensive armour. The infantry of the New Model fought in linear formation usually six deep.

Regarding artillery reorganization, there were four grades of field guns, ranging from the 'culverin' which discharged an 18-pound ball to an extreme range of 2,100 paces once every six minutes, to the 'drake', a 3-pounder which could be fired every four minutes. The English field artillery was probably less mobile but more accurate than the Swedish. A powerful siege-train was also built up. Each gun crew consisted of the gunner and two assistants who attended to the powder and shot.

The authority of the commander-in-chief of the Parliamentary army was absolute. Officers were considered for promotion by seniority but the unfit were ruthlessly rejected, and for the only period in the history of the British army before the late nineteenth century it was possible for a good man of humble birth to rise to officer rank. Recruitment was almost entirely voluntary; Sergeant-Major-General Skippon was in charge of training; discipline retained its religious character. The post of 'Scout-Master-General' (head of intelligence) was upgraded, and sound administration was considered of first importance. William Clarke, who began as secretary to General Monck, became so indispensable in the running of the administration of the army that after the Restoration he was kept on as 'Secretary at War' – the office from which the later ministry developed.

In June 1645 the New Model Army defeated the Royalists decisively at Naseby. The course of the battle was a repeat of Marston Moor, Rupert sweeping the field initially, but Cromwell in a mood of religious excitement standing his ground – then charging at the right moment and retaining control of his troops to the end. From the evidence of Marston Moor and Naseby Cromwell emerges as a fine cavalry commander. His development into a successful general belongs to the period after the defeat of Charles I – the period when fighting continued against Scots and Royalists, Cromwell being commander-in-chief.

At Preston in 1648 Cromwell defeated a larger but unprepared and very poorly led enemy. The remarkable features of the battle occurred before and after it. In twenty-six days Cromwell had marched 250 miles through rough country in filthy weather in order to catch the enemy off balance. Having beaten them, he then pursued them relentlessly to ensure that they would never reform as an army.

At Dunbar in 1650 Cromwell was caught at a disadvantage: hemmed into a valley by the sea, and opposed by an able commander, Leslie, whose forces outnumbered his own by two to one. His men were becoming demoralized by foul weather and the Fabian tactics of the Scots. But Leslie also had his problems – in the weather and the very unmilitary-minded Scots churchmen who all the time urged him to 'fall on'. Allowing himself to be bullied into it, Leslie abandoned his position on the brow of a hill, and moved his army down to stretch in a three-mile arc from the foot of the hill to the sea. Cromwell reckoned that this development gave him a chance to attack and fight his way out. The Scottish army presented a straggled target; the compact and disciplined English army might be able to catch the enemy right wing nearest to the sea by surprise, and then turn inwards and roll up the centre – and that was the plan. Unsuspicious, the Scots passed a stormy night in no state of preparation for battle. At dawn the English van, six regiments of cavalry and some three brigades of infantry, fell on them. For a minute or two the Scots could not even reply to the English fire because their matches were not alight. Hard fighting followed and the first two waves of English foot were repulsed; then Cromwell threw in his reserves. They came 'seasonably in', and a witness commented, 'I never beheld a more terrible charge of foot.' It proved decisive. The cavalry rallied, and the Scots were, as Cromwell said, 'made by the Lord of Hosts as stubble to our swords'. The whole battle was over in an hour; 3,000 Scots were killed, 10,000 taken prisoner, and 15,000 arms captured on the field. The victory was a brilliantly calculated surprise operation – a triumph of nerve and of discipline.

Probably the most remarkable of all Cromwell's military feats was the strategy which led to the battle of Worcester in 1651. In June that year he found Leslie with his Scots very strongly positioned in the hills south of Stirling. He was anxious to move him, and this he did by abandoning his own base, and crossing the Firth of Forth to cut Leslie's communications with the north. Leslie was thus faced with the alternative of fighting in his now weak position at Stirling, or of moving south. He fell into the trap designed for him, and invaded England. Cromwell had calculated that the Scots-Royalist army would gather little if any popular support as it marched south, while he himself could call on large reserves of troops in England. The Royalists advanced as far as Worcester, their forces gradually dwindling until they totalled only about 12,000. Cromwell, moving southwards, took a more easterly route, concentrating other forces on the Worcester area from various directions. The Royalists were harried from behind by Lambert and Harrison with 12,000 men, blocked in front on the London road by Fleetwood, and finally trapped when Cromwell reached Evesham, a few miles east of Worcester. There by the end of August he had assembled 28,000 men. The battle which took place a few days later was stiff, but its result was a foregone conclusion.

Worcester ended Royalist armed resistance, and from then until his death in 1658 Cromwell was ruler of England. His political career turned out to be extraordinarily self-defeating, for, while he desired to give his country acceptable constitutional government, the only basis of his power remained the army. Strained by this dilemma he dissatisfied both soldiers and civilians. His military courage and caution turned to political blustering and hesitancy. Absolute conviction of his own rightness and a passionate desire for righteousness had served him as a soldier, but betrayed him now. It is sad that Cromwell should be remembered more for his unfortunate dictatorship than for his idealism, his courage, and his genius as a trainer and commander of cavalry and as a strategist. But one feature, at any rate, of his rule was to prove enduring and beneficial. This was the development of English seapower and imperialism.

The leading maritime people of the first half of the seventeenth century were the Dutch, who had exploited an advantageous geographical situation and a native flair for commerce and seamanship. By 1650 they were at the height of their prosperity, with a virtual monopoly of the international carrying trade, and with colonies in many parts of the world. The success of the Dutch, however, had been built during the time when England and France were concerned with checking the power of Spain, and therefore supported the Dutch. When Spain ceased to be a menace the Dutch found themselves facing competition, above all from England. Strategically England had an unrivalled position for the pursuit of an ambitious maritime policy. France had to concentrate primarily on problems inside Europe. The Italians still went to sea in galleys. The Dutch were a small, rather disunited people, and they also had to protect their land frontiers. But England was an island, well placed off the coast of Europe to keep an eye on her northern rivals, and from an interior position able to intercept their fleets. She also happened to have exceptionally good harbours and safe coasts – although these would have to be defended.

The English challenge to the Dutch began in the reign of Charles I, with the creation of his notorious 'ship-money' fleets in the 1630's. After the distraction of the civil war the aggressive naval policy was resumed by Cromwell, supported by commercial opinion. The principal points of contention with the Dutch were their monopolistic attitude and the question of fishing rights in the North Sea. Incidental clashes had built up considerable bitterness. Between 1650 and 1652 the English passed three Navigation Acts, excluding the Dutch from their trade and in the hope of making inroads on their rival's monopolies. Fearing a retaliatory threat to English ship-building supplies from the Baltic, Cromwell opened up the timber trade with North America and sent an expedition to seize Jamaica. At the same time a big ship-building programme was launched. By 1652 thirty new ships had been added to the fleet of thirty-six inherited from Charles I.

The design of warships in this period was a development of the Armada galleon. Charles I's *Sovereign of the Seas* differed from it essentially only in size; it was the first English three-decker, and carried 102 guns, almost three times as many as Drake's ship. The *Sovereign* turned out to be overgunned for her size, and she sailed badly. In the 1650's smaller ships were built, with between 30 and 60 guns. But then the three-decker came to stay, and between 1660 and 1670 nine ships of over 1,000 tons were built in England. Because of the shallowness of their coastal waters the Dutch had to build ships with less draught. They thus had no three-deckers, their ships could not support more than 80 or 90 guns at the most, and they sailed less well to windward. The Dutch had developed rigging considerably since the sixteenth century, increasing sail area by adding mizzen topsails and fore and aft staysails. Rig was to alter very little thereafter until Trafalgar.

Guns, too, reached by 1670 the form which they were to keep for nearly two hundred years. They were now cast in one piece, with a smooth bore and the outside of the barrel tapering from breech to muzzle. Trunnions projected from the barrel to fit into bearings on the carriage, and the gun was elevated or depressed by levering the breech of the barrel upwards with spikes, and then inserting underneath it a wooden wedge marked in degrees. The gun was trained right or left by levering the whole carriage round.

The rivalry between the English and the Dutch was now plain and fierce, and in 1652 war broke out. Each side mobilized about eighty sail. The English fleet had better ships and better weapons; the Dutch ships with their shallow draught could use the lines of sandbanks in the Channel for refuge. The Dutch admirals were probably the two best seamen in the world – Marten Tromp, a fine leader and a quick, cool thinker, and Michael de Ruyter, a resourceful seaman, and a cartographer and mathematician. While most of the Dutch officers were merchant captains of great experience, in the English fleet the senior officers were soldiers by training, good fighters but inexperienced at sea. The English commander was Robert Blake, a colonel of artillery, who took to naval warfare at the age of fifty. The object of England in the war was expressed simply enough by George Monck: 'What we want is more of the trade which the Dutch have.' The strategy of the English was therefore to gain naval control in the English Channel, and at the same time to protect their own merchant convoys. The Dutch had to deal with this challenge. Both sides therefore sought simply to destroy the enemy's fleet in battle.

The English fleet in theory used the line-ahead formation for tactics, but seamanship and discipline were not yet good enough for this to work; therefore in practice their ships fought like the Dutch, in squadron clumps, relying on each other for mutual support and seeking to isolate one of the enemy, then to bombard and board. Both sides recognized the advantage of the leeward position in battle but the Dutch, being better seamen, usually managed to get it. They exploited their advantage by firing on the upward roll to damage the enemy's rigging, making it impossible for him to escape to windward. These Dutch tactics paid off in the early battles of the war, for example in November 1652 when Tromp with a superior fleet defeated Blake off Dungeness. After the battle he hoisted a broom to his masthead to indicate that he had swept the seas clean

Naval engagements of the Anglo-Dutch wars. The battle of the Gabbard *top* ; the battle of the Texel *bottom*

of the enemy. But in February 1653 Blake reversed the situation with his victory off Portland. Tromp with 75 ships was convoying a merchant fleet when Blake intercepted him with 55. The English were outnumbered, but their warships were better and they were not hampered by a merchant convoy. A running fight took place between Portland and Gris Nez. The first day was indecisive as the English fleet was still scattered, but by the next morning the English had assembled and the Dutch began to run short of powder. Tromp fought a masterly retreat, his warships putting up a stubborn rearguard action, until eventually ammunition ran out and the retreat became a rout; he avoided total disaster only by brilliant seamanship, extricating himself with the loss of only 11 warships and 30 merchantmen. From now on the English became better trained in their line-ahead tactics and two more English victories and the death of Tromp forced the Dutch to sue for peace early in 1654.

The English now realized that naval warfare required a modernized administration, the right ships and professional seamen. This meant state control. The ship-building programme was pressed forward and by 1660 the fleet consisted of 230 ships. The state appointed commanders, provided dockyards, and became responsible for maintenance and recruitment – the latter being chiefly by the press-gang method. Conditions for seamen were improved, their pay was put on a monthly basis, and official care introduced for the sick, wounded and disabled. Meanwhile the Dutch navy remained comparatively decentralized for two main reasons – the confederate political structure of the United Provinces, and commercial preoccupation which was not compatible with specialization for war.

When Charles II became king of England in 1660 he carried on Cromwell's maritime policy, giving his fleet the title of 'Royal Navy'. In 1673 Samuel Pepys assumed control of administration as Secretary of the Admiralty Office. He introduced important reforms, including examinations and a minimum period of service for officers – thus laying the basis for a full-time professional corps of naval officers. Sir Arthur Bryant, his biographer, calls Samuel Pepys 'The Saviour of the Navy'.

England was again at war with the Dutch in 1665, the strategy being the same as in the war of 1652–4. The admirals were James, Duke of York, the king's brother and Lord High Admiral, and George Monck, a soldier. De Ruyter commanded the Dutch fleet. In 1667 de Ruyter in a brilliant operation sailed up the Thames and captured or destroyed the best part of the English fleet which was laid up. The Treaty of Breda followed; but this did not satisfy England, although by the cession of New Amsterdam (renamed New York after the admiral) she gained the whole Atlantic coast of America. A third Anglo-Dutch war took place between 1672 and 1674, in which France was allied with England. After four drawn naval battles, England made peace, but the Dutch and French fought on from 1674 to 1678 – during which years of neutrality England overtook the Dutch as a maritime and commercial power. But now she had to face France.

The battle of Blenheim, Marlborough's greatest victory

13　Marlborough and his Times

John Churchill was born in 1650, the son of Sir Winston Churchill, a Dorset landowner;
he died in 1722 as 1st Duke of Marlborough. Of all the military personalities who pass
across the stage during his times, some of whom we shall discuss, Marlborough was the
greatest – a military genius with great diplomatic skill. I have always considered that it
was he who was responsible for the rise of the British army to become one of the foremost armies in Europe. In Chapter 12 we saw Sweden emerge as a major power under
Gustavus Adolphus, and the French army become the most powerful in Europe; in this
chapter we shall see the eclipse of Sweden under Charles XII, and the temporary
decline of France. We shall also see the effect on warfare of fortification, as developed by
Vauban; it was Marlborough who prevented this factor from paralyzing generalship. It
was an age of cavalry; but the introduction of the ring and then the socket bayonet in the
second half of the century raised the status of the infantry soldier and caused the end of
pikemen.

The central factor in the politics of Europe after the Thirty Years' War was the
aggressiveness of France under her king, Louis XIV. Of the various individuals who
have set out to dominate Europe, none ever made a more long-standing nuisance of
himself than Louis XIV. Between his accession to full regal powers in 1660 and his death
in 1715 he unleashed four major wars: the War of Devolution (1667–8), the name
given to the war arising from his claims to certain Spanish territories; the Dutch War
(1672–8); the War of the Grand Alliance (1688–97); and the War of the Spanish Succession (1701–13). In the intervals of fighting, Louis' diplomatic activity was still
concentrated on achieving his war aims of *gloire*, wealth, the expansion of France to her
'natural frontiers' on the Rhine, the Alps and the Pyrenees, and the breaking of the
Habsburg ring. All the other states of western Europe united to resist the French, but in
the first three of these wars before 1700 they were unable to succeed. France had a
larger population and more natural resources than any other country; she also had
interior strategic lines, and centralized absolute government. Furthermore, some of
Louis' servants were exceptionally able: Colbert and Louvois were first-rate administrators, Condé and Turenne were the leading commanders of the time, and Vauban was an
outstanding military engineer.

Colbert and Louvois were Louis' ministers, who performed for him the vital services
of rationalizing his policy and of providing the means for its realization. Colbert concerned himself chiefly with finance and the navy. After the Dutch wars, warships did
not change in basic design. A nation could gain naval superiority only by increasing its
numbers of ships and bases, and by improving its organization. Colbert developed the

French navy from the 20 warships which he found in 1661 to over 270 by 1690, and these defeated the combined Anglo-Dutch fleet in June 1690 off Beachy Head. In May 1692, however, the allies got their revenge at the battle of La Hogue, near St Vaast on the east coast of the Cotentin peninsula in Normandy. From then on England was the leading naval power, and in the War of the Spanish Succession she had absolute command of the seas.

The speciality of Louvois was the administration of the army, and here he followed the tendencies, begun in the time of Gustavus, towards increased size, centralization, uniformity and professionalization. Condé had won the battle of Rocroi against the Spaniards in 1643 with an army of 23,000 men; in 1672 Louis XIV invaded the Netherlands with 120,000. Of these, 75 per cent were now infantry, with their own field artillery. In recruitment and organization, corruption and feudal traditions were as far as possible eliminated. Inspectors, such as the famous Martinet, saw to this, as well as supervising training and the enforcement of strict discipline. A system of magazines was set up for supply. The army was intensively drilled. The match-lock was replaced by the flint-lock as the standard infantry weapon. Corps of grenadiers were organized, the status of engineers was upgraded, and the artillery integrated more closely with the rest of the army. The real basis of power at this period was military, the security of a dynasty being closely related to the size and strength of its standing army. It was the efficiency of the French War Office which made possible the successes of French armies in the field before the 1690's.

Finally, the generalship of Condé and Turenne achieved these successes. The talents of these two commanders balanced each other well, for Condé was an outstanding tactician whereas Turenne was exceptional as a strategist and organizer. Enterprising, yet cool and comprehensive in his judgment, Condé inspired his men on many battlefields for thirty years after Rocroi. However, in the warfare of this age, when communications were poor and strong fortifications favoured the success of another type of general, it was the man of more patience and forethought, Turenne, who rose to greater distinction. In the civil wars of the 1650's, when he fought against Condé, he emerged as the better soldier.

The supreme ability of Turenne lay in manoeuvre. His object always was to produce a battle situation on the most favourable terms, and at the time and place of his choosing; with this end in view he trained his men to march long distances. His plans were always made with care and imagination; his soldiers knew this and trusted him, because his victories were won with a minimum expenditure of human lives. Between 1653 and 1658 in the civil wars, opposing an army commanded by Condé and superior in numbers and equipment, he succeeded in keeping his army together and made up for weakness in numbers by mobility, keeping touch with the enemy and hampering his activities until he should be strong enough to beat him in battle.

Later Turenne increased his range; his 'audacity', as Napoleon observed, 'grew with years and experience'. With the wide expanses of Germany in which to operate he could make fuller use of time and space. His greatest achievement was the Turkheim campaign of 1674–5. Turenne's role in 1674 was to hold the enemy allied forces on the German Rhine front while the French offensives were launched elsewhere. Having won two minor battles he was forced to withdraw in November, because the enemy had received heavy reinforcements. While he moved back into Lorraine, the enemy forces went into winter quarters, scattered through Alsace. The weather was bad, supplies were short, and neither among the enemy nor at Paris was any further fighting expected. But Turenne saw an opportunity for a surprise victory. Scraping together additional forces he brought his own numbers up to 33,000 to face the enemy's 57,000. Then at the end of December he moved through the mountains to outflank the enemy, and debouched from the Belfort Gap into Alsace. The allies could concentrate only a small part of their forces in haste near Colmar, and Turenne fell on them at Turkheim. The result of his victory was that within ten days not a single German remained on the left bank of the Rhine. That was Turenne's last successful exploit, for he was killed in the later campaign of 1675.

This was a time, however, when limitations were imposed on positive generalship by the power of fortification. After the disappearance from the scene of Condé and Turenne by 1675, the leading military figure was an engineer, Sebastien de Vauban. In an active career of over forty years, until 1707, Vauban was responsible for the systematic fortification of the vulnerable parts of the frontiers of France. In the gap between the Jura and the Vosges, Belfort, Neuf Brisach and other places were strengthened. During my ten years in the Western Union Defence Organization and in NATO, I carried out many reconnaissances of the Jura and Vosges mountains and motored across the Belfort Gap – getting to know the area well. In the times of which I am writing, and of course earlier, it was a definite avenue of approach from the east and had to be well defended. Today it has no strategical value, because of air power, the range and power of modern weapons, and, generally, twentieth-century means of waging war. Thionville and Metz were the chief elements in another defensive system along the Moselle and in northern Alsace. The area which it was most important for the French to bar was Flanders, a fertile plain where the maritime enemies of France could converge their forces and operate unimpeded by natural obstacles. Here by 1702 more than thirty large fortresses of the first class and some fifty lesser fortified towns and citadels in the hands of France made a formidable barrier.

Vauban developed several recent ideas in fortification. One of these was to build ramparts of earth, rather than of stone which shattered and shot off dangerous fragments; earth walls were safer and cheaper, and large ones could be built more easily. Secondly, bastions became angled rather than rounded, for thus all parts of the walls could be covered by enfilade fire against attackers. These ideas had to some extent been applied in the wars since the mid-sixteenth century, but nobody so far had thought them out and applied them to their fullest extent. Vauban's methods transformed this branch of warfare into a geometric exercise, and he made the defence too formidable to allow frontal assaults by irreplaceable soldiers. He always made the best use of ground to assist the defence.

Vauban adhered to simple basic principles in his fortifications, but followed no set design. He retained the traditional groundplan for a fortress: inner enclosure, rampart, moat and outer rampart. A fortress could last intact only until the main body of its fortifications had been breached, and the result of a siege was thus in large part a question of which side could best hold out. Where there was space, and time and money were available, Vauban liked to extend the outworks as far as possible. He thus compelled the enemy to begin his siege operations at a distance, and multiplied the ob-

Vauban brought fortification and siege warfare to a fine art. A model of Neuf Brisach *above*; the plan of a typical fort *below left*; the attack on a fort *below right*

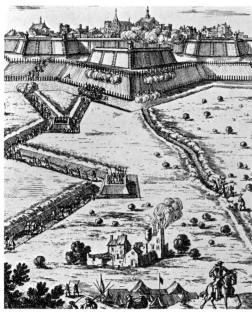

stacles in his way so that the difficulties in gaining ground never ceased. If the outworks should fall to the enemy, they were still commanded by fire from the main central works.

Vauban's geometrical skill and practical eye for ground enabled him to design fortifications in such a way that every face was flanked and supported by the works behind and beside it. The basic element in the design, multiplied and varied in scale, was an outward-pointing triangle with its inner side missing. The outward point made a difficult target for the enemy and forced him to concentrate his forces vulnerably, while each face was so angled as to cover the area of wall between it and the face of the next salient. This was the principle of the great bastions on every angle of the main polygon. The large bastions were interspersed with smaller ones along the curtain, close enough together for each to be able to cover the next with small-arms fire. Other triangles, widely varying in size, called 'ravelins' (or 'demilunes' if they were actually crescent-shaped) stood in a dry moat, projected farther forward, covering each other, and covered from behind. Repeated complexes of fortification of this type often extended 300 yards from the central rampart and made powerful obstacles to a siege. The best examples of Vauban's work are Neuf Brisach and Lille.

Vauban was also a master of offensive siegecraft. Before his time the usual method of investment had been to approach the walls with zig-zag trenches until the guns were in range. Since the enemy could concentrate their fire on the sap-head, this was costly of life and ineffective. Vauban's innovation was the use of parallel trenches connected by zig-zags. The besiegers could now converge their fire against points in the defence, and more simultaneous separate assaults could be launched. He also introduced the use of ricochet fire, plunging shot over the first parapet to drop on to the defenders behind. It was still the custom, once a breach had been made, to invite the defenders to surrender with the honours of war. If they did not, the place was stormed, and generally no quarter was given. From a study of Vauban's fortifications it would seem that an attack against them in those days would be best placed in the hands of engineers, who, through the application of mathematics, could bring their trenches and batteries to such positions that the defending commander would be 'caught in the toils of Euclid'.

Vauban's methods of fortification and siege remained standard until the later nineteenth century, when the increasing range of artillery changed the problems of defence and attack. Fortifications of this type could, on the whole, be overcome, but a successful siege would always require a lot of time – and a certain mathematical skill as I have suggested. The result was that by the end of the seventeenth century the intensive fortification of the French frontiers tended to slow down the pace of warfare: movement was hampered, refuge was made accessible, and manpower was absorbed. In the War of the Grand Alliance (1688–97) there were few open battles of significance, but many sieges. The French strategy seemed to be successful and in the next war, which began in 1701, they set out to repeat it. But in this, the War of the Spanish Succession, the armies of the allied enemies of France were commanded by a military genius, capable, when he was given the chance, of transcending the contemporary limitations of warfare. This man was Marlborough.

Marlborough had seen a wide range of professional service since the beginning of his career in 1667, including the benefit of serving as a colonel of infantry under Turenne in 1674–5. As a man he was reticent, and somewhat difficult to get to know. His private moral record has certain blemishes, but against this can be set his devoted care at all times for the men under his command, and the tireless service of his country. Outwardly he was serene, self-controlled, unfailingly courteous and charming. As a soldier he had a complete mastery of his profession, and while he saw the problems of the war in perspective as a whole, he also overlooked no essential detail, tactical or administrative. Furthermore, he possessed an equable temperament.

This was a time when the art of command was meeting increased complications. While the size of armies and the range of strategy continued to increase rapidly, the organization of the administrative machine did not keep pace. Furthermore, communications in Europe were slow and politics complex, so that a commander, particularly of an allied army, had many responsibilities as a diplomat. At the same time he had to deal with politicians in the home country. In the exercise of command, Winston Churchill, Marlborough's famous descendant, has written of the dynamic sum of numerous constantly shifting forces which had continually to be comprehended:

> . . . all the factors which are at work at the time; the numbers and quality of the troops and their morale, their weapons, their confidence in their leaders, the character of the country, the condition of the roads, time, and the weather: and behind these the politics of their states, the special interests which each army has to guard . . .

Command was personal and direct; corps and divisional commanders and staffs were to come later. A commander-in-chief could survey his whole battle area, and transmitted his orders by a system of gallopers and orderlies. In battle, he sat his horse in the thick of the activity and often under fire, keeping in mind the position and fortunes of every unit on a four or five-mile front, studying the enemy, and adjusting his dispositions to the developing tactical situation. To be in full control of all these factors with the means available in those days needed a supreme practitioner in the art of war.

Armies were cosmopolitan. Of the 40,000 men voted by Parliament as England's contribution to the allied force at the beginning of the war only 18,000 were British. Anti-military feeling was strong in England where, after the experience of the seventeenth century, a standing army was regarded as a threat to liberty. By contrast, French society was militaristic. The English Parliament jealously scrutinized the ordering of the armies which it authorized, and recruitment was difficult. Even the glorious successes which her armies were to gain did not alter England's attitude. There was only very limited conscription, and its object was generally regarded as the provision of suitable employment for criminals and ne'er-do-wells. Regiments were raised and equipped by proprietary colonels after whom they were named, and normally consisted of a single battalion of 700 to 900 men. There was frequently a good deal of fraud in administration – as officers drew pay, provisions and equipment for non-existent troops while those which did exist were often cheated of their due. Indeed, in 1712 Marlborough's enemies in Parliament brought charges of peculation against him, when he had fallen from power and been dismissed by Queen Anne from all his offices. But it was later proved that all such charges were utterly false, and as G. M. Trevelyan has declared, 'no one ever gave better value to England than Marlborough for every guinea he received'. In fact, he did much to eliminate such peculation in his armies.

The War of the Spanish Succession is interesting economically, since in those years the institutions of banking and credit were undergoing rapid development. The Bank of England had been founded in 1694, and in this respect the English and the Dutch were at an advantage over France (the *Banque de France* was not founded until 1800). The war provided a stimulus to financial development, as well as to diversification of trade, and to industries such as clothing, horse-breeding, mining and munitions. It was not unduly destructive either, for the memories of the Thirty Years' War caused men to mitigate horror as much as possible. Some plundering took place, but there was very little systematic destruction. Discipline was strict, although pay was generally in arrears; but supply magazines were now efficiently organized and careful attention was given to the provision of good quality equipment such as boots and warm uniforms. The army formed a very small proportion of the total population of a nation, and was divorced from it. G. M. Trevelyan wrote:

> Europe was too ill-organized and too poor to pay a heavy blood-tax, and her credit system was too primitive to draw large drafts on the wealth and happiness of future generations.

This period was very much the heyday of cavalry, even although open battles were comparatively rare and commanders put their main trust in infantry. The French

The French cavalry still relied upon firearms as much as on the sword

cavalry (as at Blenheim) still clung to the remnant of the sixteenth century tradition of the caracole, relying on firearms as much as on the sword. But the English cavalry as trained by Marlborough perfected the tactics of Gustavus and Cromwell, being trained to charge in a line three deep, advancing at a 'full trot' rather than at a gallop, and using only the sword. Pistols were issued, but were to be used only when foraging or when attacked by surprise. At first the cavalrymen wore no body armour at all, but in 1707 Marlborough introduced a cuirass in front. Dragoons might charge as cavalry, or ride only to the scene of action and fight on foot as musketeers.

Two important changes had recently taken place in the equipment of infantry. Since 1650 the flint-lock musket had replaced the match-lock as the standard infantry weapon; having a more reliable detonating device, it functioned better in wet weather and gave a higher rate of fire. Secondly, since about the same date the bayonet had been developed. At first the knife was plugged in to the muzzle of the musket. The vitally important change came with the invention of the ring bayonet in 1678; this clipped on to the outside of the barrel, allowing the soldier still to fire his weapon. Pikemen then became redundant because the musketeer could now perform their function for himself, and by 1704 they had disappeared from the British army. The French, although they had introduced the bayonet, adopted it rather more slowly. For the next hundred and fifty years infantry soldiers were to fight armed only with flint-lock muskets and bayonets, carrying leather pouches holding between 40 and 60 paper cartridges, and wearing no defensive body armour.

The new battalions, unencumbered with match and clumsy pikes, had a greater mobility than before. Mobility, and the reliance on firepower rather than shock, increased the possibility of good troops winning against numerical odds. Marlborough fully appreciated this, and he paid great attention in the six winter months outside the campaigning season to training his infantry in efficient firing, in marksmanship and volley firing by platoons of fifty men. Regiments were also drilled to form hollow squares when attacked by cavalry. Besides musketeers every regiment contained a company of grenadiers, who were selected for their physical qualities, and were to some extent storm troops. Linear formations were now normal, being designed to exploit the new firepower to its fullest extent. To train a soldier to excel in linear tactics took time, it demanded courage, experience and practice. As extensions became wider in the face of the increased power of small-arms fire, so the soldier might often be separated from his comrades; when this happens fear appears; hence the importance of discipline, the object of which is the conquest of fear.

Marlborough furthered the integration of artillery with other arms begun by Gustavus. Colonel Blood, who commanded his artillery, and his other officers and gunners performed outstanding services for him. The problems of ground which they surmounted in 1704 when marching through the Black Forest to the Danube and fighting among the marshes of Blenheim indicate that they were expert at their job. At long range field artillery fired cannon balls, and at closer quarters grape or 'partridge' shot as it was then called. The heavy siege trains were distinct from the field artillery and were usually transported by water. Marlborough placed great value on the tactical use of field artillery, selecting his battery sites with care.

In the War of the Spanish Succession when he was Captain-General of the Confederate Armies of Britain, the Dutch United Provinces, Austria, Baden and other

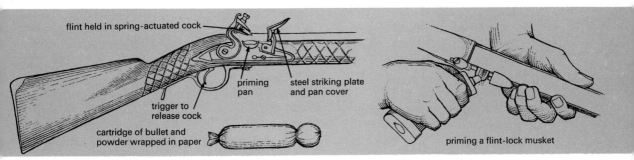

flint held in spring-actuated cock

priming pan

steel striking plate and pan cover

trigger to release cock

cartridge of bullet and powder wrapped in paper

priming a flint-lock musket

The area of Marlborough's campaigns *below*. During this period the flint-lock replaced the match-lock as a means of firing the musket *above*

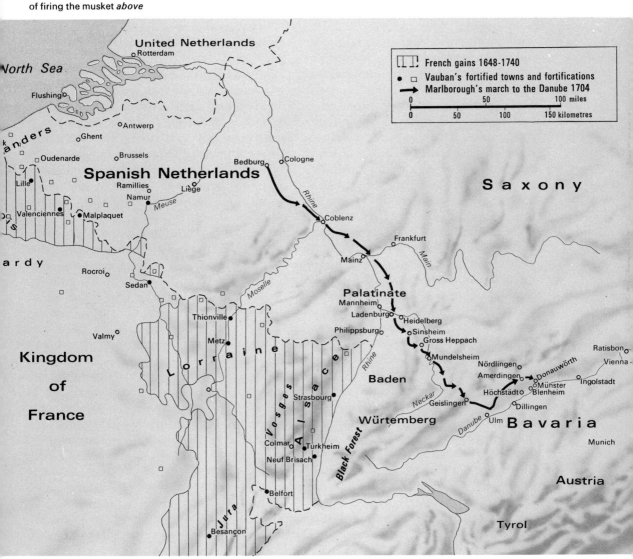

French gains 1648-1740

● ☐ Vauban's fortified towns and fortifications

→ Marlborough's march to the Danube 1704

0   50   100 miles

0   50   100   150 kilometres

North Sea

United Netherlands

Rotterdam

Flushing

Antwerp

Ghent

Brussels

Bedburg

Cologne

Oudenarde

Spanish Netherlands

Lille

Ramillies

Liège

S a x o n y

Valenciennes

Namur

Malplaquet

Meuse

Rhine

Coblenz

Frankfurt

Main

Mainz

Rocroi

Sedan

Moselle

Palatinate

Mannheim

Ladenburg

Heidelberg

Philippsburg

Sinsheim

Gross Heppach

Ratisbon

Thionville

Mundelsheim

Nördlingen

Vienna

Valmy

Metz

Amerdingen

Donauwörth

Ingolstadt

Kingdom

Lorraine

Rhine

Baden

Neckar

Münster

Höchstädt

Blenheim

of

Strasbourg

Geislingen

Danube

Dillingen

France

Vosges

Alsace

Würtemberg

Ulm

B a v a r i a

Colmar

Turkheim

Black Forest

Neuf Brisach

Munich

Belfort

Austria

Jura

Besançon

Tyrol

minor German powers, Marlborough faced a difficult strategic situation. France and Spain were united, able to operate on interior strategic lines, and in 1703 were joined by Bavaria. On the northern front France had possession of the great barrier of fortresses in the Spanish Netherlands, guarded by an army of 90,000 men. In the south the Spaniards were in Italy. In the east by 1703 there was nothing except their own disagreements to prevent the Bavarians and the French, under Villars their ablest general, from marching on Vienna with overwhelming force.

The allies were split into two widely separated blocs, and disagreed over policy. Marlborough's first difficulty was with the Dutch politicians and generals who wanted to keep their army close to their own home country. Time and again throughout the war his projects were viewed with alarm and even vetoed. This handicap, combined with occasional lack of support from the British politicians, placed Marlborough at a disadvantage compared to the enemy commander-in-chief, Louis XIV, who had absolute authority and a centralized war-machine. The strategy adopted in the south was to send a military expedition to Spain, and a British fleet into the Mediterranean in order to command the seas around the theatre of war and confine the enemy to a land strategy. Gibraltar was captured in 1704, and from that time forward British strategy never ignored the Mediterranean. Marlborough himself in the Low Countries planned to draw the war farther east, in order to remove the immediate threat to the Dutch, to co-ordinate operations with the Austrians, and to attack France on her more vulnerable north-east corner. Despite the obstruction of the Dutch, in 1702–3 Marlborough succeeded in manoeuvring the French out of the valleys of the Maas and the Lower Rhine. But by this time Austria was in extreme danger. Marlborough's strategy now was to seek a decision with the French on the Danube, and thus defeat their threat against Austria.

The idea of a campaign on the Danube had everything to recommend it. Vienna was threatened from Ulm (on the Danube) by a combined Franco-Bavarian army of 45,000 men (soon to be brought up by reinforcements to 57,000) under the elector Max Emanuel and Marshal Marsin. It was vital to save Vienna, for if Austria were to be knocked out of the war the French would be able to concentrate their whole effort on the northern front. Since a defensive or slow moving war suited Louis XIV, in his powerfully entrenched central position, the allies must clearly take the offensive. But there were two practical difficulties. The Dutch politicians were immensely timid, and Marlborough had to overcome their doubts and hesitancies. Secondly, if the allied armies were to reach the Danube they had to march across the French centre with their flank exposed. Marlborough's method of achieving his object was to act fast, and to deceive both friend and foe. He told the Dutch that his campaign was going to be on the Moselle (which flows into the Rhine at Coblenz) and with the greatest reluctance they gave him a contingent. His true destination was a secret known only to a few top political figures. The Margrave Lewis of Baden promised his support, and from Vienna Prince Eugene set out to meet Marlborough.

The march officially began on 16th May 1704 at Bedburg, twenty miles west of Cologne. Marlborough's forces totalled 40,000 men. Thanks to the work done in 1702–3 the allies had a clear run through the Meuse valley below Namur, and along the Rhine as far as its junction with the Neckar near Mannheim. But the operation of transporting the army to the region of Heidelberg was dangerous, for it was here that it would have to cross the front of the French army commanded by Villeroi – not a good general, and later heavily defeated by Marlborough at Ramillies (May 1706). Speed was the secret of success, and it was much aided by sending the heavy artillery and supplies by water. 'There were', as Trevelyan writes, 'two stages in the deception of Europe.' The first was as far as Coblenz, where the army was expected to turn up the Moselle, and enormous stores had been collected to give this impression. But when Coblenz was reached the army marched on south and the stores were sent after it up the Rhine. Even now its apparent destination was not the Danube, but Alsace. To assist this part of the deception Marlborough had caused a bridge of boats to be thrown across the Rhine at Philippsburg, some twenty miles south of Mannheim.

The reactions were immediate. Villeroi removed his army from the Netherlands, first to cover the Moselle, and then to join Marshal Tallard in the defence of Alsace. The Dutch in relief sent reinforcements to Marlborough. Only on 3rd June did the secret come out. On that date the cavalry crossed the Neckar at Ladenburg, halfway between Mannheim and Heidelberg, and instead of moving on Philippsburg continued south-east to Sinsheim, and on towards the Danube – which rises in the Black Forest mountains. The whole march was superbly carried out, and it has always interested me. I have flown over the whole length of the march and examined the route from the air, getting a good bird's-eye view of the ground. Certain parts of the route I know very well, having reconnoitred them by steamer on the Rhine, and by car – particularly the areas near Coblenz and Mannheim, and the Neckar river. It was a tactic which certainly puzzled the French marshals!

This great march, of large numbers of men over long distances, was a fine example of administrative ability. Marlborough had worked at top speed since the early spring to make the diplomatic and administrative arrangements for his campaign. The permission and assistance of all the German rulers concerned had been assured. Bridges were all in good condition at the right points, and provisions were ready where they were needed. Credits had been arranged with German bankers, everything being paid for on the nail – with the result that the army was well received by the people of the country. New boots awaited the army on the threshold of Bavaria. The good order of the men was assured by rigorous discipline, but still more effectively by this very careful forethought for their needs in the way of food, clothing and comfort.

As the army moved it was joined at intervals by contingents from German allies. At Mundelsheim, mid-way between the Rhine and the Danube, on 10th June, Prince Eugene rode into Marlborough's camp, and the two great companions-in-arms met for the first time. Eugene was a Savoyard, brought up at the court of Louis XIV. Having been snubbed by that king he transferred his services to the Holy Roman Emperor, and in a military career of fifty years his overriding object was to humble France. A skilled tactician and a gallant leader, his reputation was probably at this time higher than that of Marlborough, since he had for many years fought against the Turks and by his victory of Zenta in 1697 had driven them out of Hungary. He was to prove an ideal second string to Marlborough, for while he had great military skill and experience, and a welcome spirit of enterprise, his imagination was somewhat limited and he was ready to defer to the superiority of genius. A day or two later, at Gross Heppach, Marlborough and Eugene were joined by a third commander, the Margrave Lewis of Baden, already mentioned – also an experienced soldier, but unenterprising and obstinate.

The strategy concerted between the three commanders was that Eugene should move to the Rhine to hold Villeroi and Tallard in play, while Marlborough and the Margrave advanced eastwards on Bavaria to make the elector Max Emanuel change sides. Marlborough and Lewis were to exercise command over their combined army on alternate days – a curious plan and hardly likely to commend itself to Marlborough. However, according to Sir Winston Churchill: 'There was a definite understanding that the prevailing direction of the campaign lay with Marlborough, who had the largest army and had come at great personal risk to rescue the Empire.' We shall see later in any case how he got rid of Lewis before Blenheim.

Eugene departed towards the Rhine and the main army went on its way south and east, through pleasant undulating country towards the Danube. The only difficult part of the march was at the watershed in the steep defile beyond Geislingen some twenty miles north of Ulm, where the rain poured down on sliding horses and men struggling to move guns and wagons in the mud. At the end of June 70,000 men came down into the valley of the Danube. On 1st July, Marlborough was at Amerdingen, while Marsin and the elector were on the south bank ten miles farther upstream at Dillingen. Marlborough was now to the east of his enemy, and the nearer to Vienna.

Marlborough had already made up his mind that his first move must be to capture Donauwörth, on the Danube about fifteen miles downstream to his east, because the possession of it would secure for him a new line of communications northwards through Nördlingen into the friendly and secure area of central Germany, as well as placing him astride the Danube, with a bridge into Bavaria. He had no time to lose. Tallard with his 60,000 men was on the point of advancing eastwards across the Rhine from Strasbourg, and Eugene with only 30,000 could not hold him. Even more urgently, Marsin had seen the crucial importance of Donauwörth; already on 30th June some 14,000 men had been sent ahead to hold the place, and the main army was ready to move. Marlborough had a ten-mile start over Marsin, and on 2nd July, at dawn, he set out eastwards to capture Donauwörth.

The troops had fifteen miles of appalling road to cover, and at the end of it formidable fortifications to storm. The key to Donauwörth was the Schellenberg, a high-domed fortified hill by the wall of the town. It was taken at the end of the day after an hour-and-a-half's very bloody fighting: men, it was said, were 'slaying or tearing at the muzzles of guns and the bayonets which pierced their entrails'. The advance guard went straight into the assault on a steep and narrow front, forcing the defenders to concentrate at that spot while the remainder of the army moved round to attack from behind. The plan worked. It was a most costly victory, but Marlborough knew when the potential gains were big enough to be worth the casualties; he also knew that soldiers will accept casualties provided they win victories. But there are limits to the sacrifice of men's lives. Some of the so-called 'good fighting generals' of the 1914/18 war seemed to me to have a complete disregard for human life, and I will deal with that subject more fully in Chapters 20 and 21. Roads were now open where Marlborough wanted, behind and in front, and he was firmly placed between the French and Vienna.

The information of Tallard's crossing the Rhine was reported to Marlborough within two days of the event. It was urgently necessary to detach Max Emanuel from his alliance with the French, and to achieve this the allied army systematically devastated Bavaria in July. But the elector was prepared to let his people suffer for a while as he

The Duke of Marlborough gives orders to an aide-de-camp at the battle of Malplaquet. A tapestry at Blenheim Palace

expected relief from Tallard, and this unpleasant war measure, which Marlborough intensely disliked, served no useful purpose. By early August Tallard had joined forces with Marsin and Max Emanuel, and on the 10th they set out northwards to cross the Danube at Dillingen. Tallard, the commander-in-chief, was intelligent and much respected, but was a diplomat rather than a professional soldier, and he did not have the firm control over his army which is so necessary in war. The next day, the 11th, Eugene, who had come east at the same time as Tallard, wrote to Marlborough from Münster outlining the situation and advising him to rejoin him as soon as possible. Marlborough hastened to comply: for three years he had desired the opportunity of meeting the French in full battle.

By 12th August the French and Bavarians were encamped at Blenheim, on the Danube to the east of Höchstädt and some five miles upstream from Münster. They did not want a battle, nor did they expect the allies to seek one for their position was strong. Furthermore, as they knew, Lewis was away besieging Ingolstadt with 15,000 men. But in fact Marlborough had purposely disembarrassed himself of his slow colleague to give himself the freedom to fight. During that day Marlborough and Eugene surveyed the situation from the church tower of Tapfheim, a village between Münster and Blenheim, and made their plans.

The two armies, French and Bavarian, were encamped on an open plain recently harvested, just behind a marshy stream called the Nebel which flowed into the Danube from the north. They were spread across a front of four miles: Tallard's own army was positioned in the two miles between the village of Blenheim on the bank of the Danube and the village of Oberglau, while from Oberglau northwards to another village called Lutzingen lay the army of Marsin and the elector. North of Lutzingen were wooded hills. With both flanks thus protected, the villages forming bastions, and the Nebel marsh in front of them, the armies were in a strong defensive position. They also had a superiority in artillery. Otherwise the opposing forces were more or less equally matched, each being between 50,000 and 60,000 strong.

It seemed to Marlborough and Eugene that the dispositions of the enemy armies were unsound. They were disposed separately, each with its cavalry according to normal practice on the wings, except that Tallard, having no room on his right because of the river, had placed all his cavalry on his left. This meant in effect that the centre of the combined armies around Oberglau was predominantly composed of cavalry. It was admittedly perfect ground for a cavalry battle, but the relative dispositions of the French cavalry and infantry did not make sense. A second weakness in the French layout was that Tallard was about 1,000 yards back from the Nebel.

It will be of interest at this stage to consider in some detail the dispositions of the Franco-Bavarian force because Tallard's thinking requires comment. Some authorities state that his army was encamped 1,000 yards back from the river Nebel because he did not expect to be attacked on 12th August, nor indeed on the 13th – and therefore reckoned that no precautions were needed against surprise – a most potent factor in war. Two basic tactical principles have always formed part of my military thinking:

1. A force within striking distance of an enemy must be suitably disposed with regard to its battle positions, being ready *at all times* to fight quickly if surprised.
2. An obstacle loses 50 per cent of its value if you stand back from it, allowing the enemy to reconnoitre the approaches and subsequently to cross without interference.

The battle of Ramillies. A detail from a fresco by Laguerre at Marlborough House

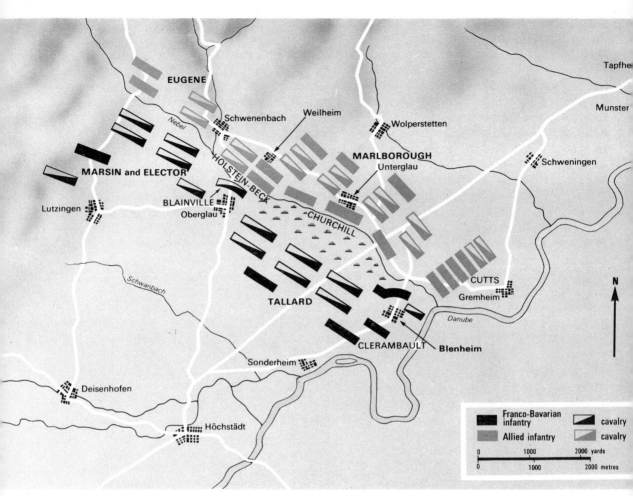

The battle of Blenheim

These two principles have stood me in good stead on more than one occasion in war. Two examples may be of interest. The first was in Africa. The Eighth Army under my command had fought its way from Alamein and in March 1943 was facing up to the famous Mareth Line on the borders of Tunisia. Rommel held us there while with strong forces he harried Eisenhower's army farther to the north, inflicting a severe defeat on an American corps in the Gafsa area. Now we considered Rommel to be an opponent not to be regarded lightly; he had strong forces to the north within easy striking distance of my army, and it was possible that he might turn south and deliver a surprise attack against us – which if successful would have delayed the end of the war in Africa. This is precisely what he did. But we were suitably disposed and ready to fight quickly. Rommel was seen off.

The second example was in north-west Europe. In December 1944 the Allied armies were on the threshold of Germany, planning to cross the Rhine. Hitler had managed to build up and refit a strategic reserve of armoured divisions; this we knew, but we were unable to ascertain where this force was located. On the northern part of the Allied front the British and Canadian armies under my command were well balanced tactically, and I had no fears. But this was not the case on the American front, because their armies were disposed in two main concentrations, each deploying for attack, with a gap in between of about 100 miles across the Ardennes held only by a corps of four weak divisions. Hitler, having considered the problem, selected this gap for a heavy attack. The American armies were surprised, their front was cut in two, and they suffered 80,000 casualties.

A word about obstacles. During the withdrawal operation in Belgium back to Dunkirk in May 1940, I was commanding the 3rd British Division. I always took the greatest care to ensure that the Germans were prevented by fire and patrols from reconnoitring closely the various river obstacles held by my division; as a result we had no difficulty in holding our positions until the time came to withdraw farther.

But to resume the story of the events leading up to the battle of Blenheim. Tallard's French army was within easy striking distance of the allied armies of two formidable generals, Marlborough and Eugene; he took no precautions against surprise. If he had pushed his leading troops forward to the river bank on 12th August, the bridging operations by Marlborough's army and the subsequent crossing would have been rendered very difficult. I have said he was intelligent; on this occasion he was downright stupid. Marsin and the elector acted far more sensibly on the northern part of the front; they held the firm ground close to their edge of the marshy river, so as to destroy the enemy before they could form up after wading across.

Marlborough and Eugene noted this and, being eager for battle and confident in the skill of their men, they decided to attack the enemy by surprise the next morning, 13th August (the date on which I assumed command of the Eighth Army in the western desert of Egypt in 1942, this curious coincidence being recorded in my autograph book by Sir Winston Churchill when he was staying at my headquarters a week later).

The advance of the allied armies began before dawn, and when the sun rose nine columns of soldiers debouched into the plain, and fanned gradually out into their battle formation. The Danish and Prussian infantry and the Austrian cavalry, all under the command of Eugene, moved northwards towards Lutzingen to form the right wing. The main force of British, Dutch, Hanoverians and Hessians, under Marlborough's command, advanced straight on down to the east bank of the Nebel. If Tallard had not expected an attack, by 7 o'clock he could no longer doubt that it was coming. Hastily the French aroused themselves to activity, their minds thrown into confusion by the urgency of the crisis.

The surprise had been successful, and the enemy dispositions were found to be dictated, as Marlborough had hoped, by the positions of their tents. Blenheim was strongly defended by 9 battalions of infantry, with 7 in support, and a further 11 in reserve. Between Blenheim and Oberglau the French had 44 squadrons of cavalry in two lines, supported by 9 infantry battalions and 4 squadrons of dismounted dragoons. Oberglau was defended by 32 cavalry squadrons and 14 infantry battalions. On the left there were 32 cavalry squadrons and 17 infantry battalions, and then at Lutzingen 51 cavalry squadrons and 12 infantry battalions.

While Eugene's columns made their way over the wooded and broken ground

towards Lutzingen, Marlborough watched the Franco-Bavarian dispositions unfold.
The enemy's right was particularly strong, with great strength deployed in the two
villages of Oberglau and Blenheim. While Eugene was to engage the enemy vigorously
in the north and turn that end of their line if possible, the decisive part of the battle was
clearly to be fought out between Marlborough and Tallard farther south. Marlborough
expected Tallard to dispute his crossing of the Nebel and he deployed for attack accordingly in an unusual formation of four lines. In front, 17 battalions of infantry were to
cross the Nebel and gain the west bank; behind them, two lines of cavalry, the first of 36
squadrons and the second of 35, were to make the main assault; the last line of 11 battalions of infantry were to wait east of the Nebel to cover a possible cavalry withdrawal.
At the outset of the battle the chief effort of the attack was to be made against the two
villages. This would surprise the enemy, in the same way as the attack against the
strongest part of the Schellenberg had done; and if the garrisons of the villages could be
contained, they would be unable to counter-attack in flank the advance of the cavalry to
break the centre of the Franco-Bavarian line.

The first action of the battle, at 10 o'clock, was the advance of Lord Cutts's column of
infantry over the Nebel opposite Blenheim, where the banks of the stream were comparatively firm. But the main attack could not begin until the right, under Eugene, was in
position. For four hours, until noon, an artillery duel was carried on causing considerable casualties, while the allied sappers worked to produce six passable bridges over the
stream, and prayers were held among the men. Marlborough inspected the lines, and at
one point was hidden from view by the dust of a cannon ball falling near him. The sun
was hot, and all waited tensely. At last, shortly after noon, a messenger arrived from
Eugene reporting that he was ready, and Marlborough ordered the attack forward.

On the left the first of Cutts's brigades moved forward against Blenheim, with orders
not to fire until they reached the French palisades. A third of them were destroyed by a
French volley from 30 paces, but two more brigades reinforced the attack. The Marquis
de Clérambault, in command of the French in Blenheim, had already called up the 7
battalions to support his first 9. The fighting went on, as bloody as it had been at the
Schellenberg, and with as good effect. Then Clérambault lost his head, and called in
his last reserve of 11 battalions. The allies continued to assault, but could not penetrate
into the village. Nonetheless they were carrying out their appointed function – of
containing the enemy. With the 12,000 additional soldiers who had joined the original
garrison, the French were so congested in the village that freedom of movement was
impossible. Marlborough now ordered that the enemy forces in Blenheim were to be
held there, so that they would be unable to take part in the battle elsewhere.

While this was done on the left with hard fighting all day, Eugene was playing a
comparable part on a broader front on the right. The whole day long he fought his
fierce containing action between Oberglau and Lutzingen, at the same time watching
the primary battle farther south, and ready if necessary to feed into that area any troops
which Marlborough might need – even though he himself could ill spare them.

The decisive developments were taking place in the centre, at Oberglau and south of
that village. Marlborough himself commanded here, keeping an eye on the events at
Blenheim but concentrating his attention on the centre. He was excellently served by his
subordinate commanders, notably Lord Orkney, and his own brother, Charles Churchill. Tallard, by contrast, moved to and fro to the different parts of the battle front,

without being fully in control anywhere, and not really comprehending what was going on.

It was now clear that Tallard had made a serious mistake at the very outset of the battle in allowing his enemy's first lines of infantry and cavalry in the centre to cross the Nebel unmolested except by artillery fire. His idea may have been that the more of the enemy, up to a certain point, that crossed the marsh, the more would be destroyed and driven back into it when he released a charge of his more numerous cavalry. If that was in his mind he bungled the tactic in practice, for he did not launch the charge until the allied troops had formed up on his side of the stream; and while the fighting was hard and at points the allies had wavered, they were not driven back. Indeed, more troops then crossed and the allies began to gain ground, with their superior numbers and better tactics – infantry and cavalry working in a close combination developed in previous training. The cavalry charged in front; the infantry were in reserve behind them, drawn up with spaces in their lines through which the cavalry might withdraw to re-form for the next charge, while they poured volleys by platoons into the oncoming enemy horsemen. Practised in the use of their bayonets, these infantrymen could also stand up to cavalry at close quarters more successfully than any had ever done before. The French infantry in this part of the battle did not perform well, being 9 battalions of young recruits who, as Trevelyan says, 'knew nothing of battles except how to die at their post'.

The high point of the battle came when, in the early afternoon, 10 battalions of allied infantry under the Prince of Holstein-Beck advanced to storm the village of Oberglau. Nine defending French and Irish infantry battalions commanded by the Marquis de Blainville made a desperate counter-attack from the village and drove their assailants back to the Nebel. The right flank of Marlborough's centre was suddenly open to attack, and his army in danger of being split. Marsin, spotting this, immediately gathered a force of cavalry near Oberglau. Marlborough, seeing the danger, sent an urgent call to Eugene for a cavalry reinforcement. As Marsin's men began their charge down towards the Nebel, the cavalry brigade duly sent by Eugene came up in the nick of time to hit them in flank and turn them away. Holstein-Beck's infantry now rallied, and returning to the attack forced their opponents back into Oberglau and penned them there. Marlborough was probably the only man present to understand that as a result of this action the allies now had the winning of the battle in their hands. Large numbers of the enemy were bottled up in Blenheim and in Oberglau, the enemy's left was held by Eugene, and it now only remained for the allies to concentrate overwhelming strength in the centre to gain a complete victory.

But Marlborough bided his time, holding the situation in the centre so as to let his men get their breath, reorganizing the tactics of the whole battle front, and drawing up his formation for the decisive blow. Eugene still had a lot of hard work to do on the right, but soon after 4 o'clock his men were working round and beyond Lutzingen. Meanwhile Marlborough had brought the last of his troops across the Nebel, and on the front between Blenheim and Oberglau he drew up first two lines of cavalry totalling 90 squadrons, and then 23 battalions of infantry in another two lines. In front of him Tallard had only 60 squadrons at the most and 9 battalions. When at last he realized Marlborough's tactics he brought up his infantry and sent them forward to the south of Oberglau to block the attack. Marlborough, not yet having completed the deployment of his cavalry, sent 3 battalions and some artillery against them. Momentarily the French infantry had the better of the encounter; but their cavalry did not charge to use the advantage. At 5.30 o'clock Marlborough was ready. Almost the last of the 9 brave French battalions were blasted out of the way by the artillery, and the allied cavalry launched their charge.

From the higher ground at Lutzingen the combatants of both sides could see the scene on the plain. As the allied cavalry moved forward in a great line, thigh to thigh at a medium trot but gathering pace, the French cavalry came forward to meet them. Even had they not been outnumbered they would have been beaten, for their charge was a dash of individual squadrons pausing at the last moment to fire their *fusils*. As the French paused the allied cavalry increased their speed, hitting their opponents with all the shock of speed and combined weight, relying on the sword to kill. Such gaps as appeared in the allied front line were instantly filled from behind. The French were borne back, at a speed which soon rose to the gallop of flight.

The fugitives from the French centre were driven to the Danube, being hurled over precipices and into marshes. Marshal Tallard, dutifully making his way to Blenheim, was captured and brought to the allied commander-in-chief. Marlborough at that moment scribbled a note from the saddle, on the back of 'a bill of tavern expenses', to his wife Sarah:

> I have not time to say more, but to beg you will give my duty to the Queen, and let her know Her Army has had a Glorious Victory. Monsr. Tallard and two other Generals are in my coach and I am following the rest.

At the moment when the French centre had broken, Lord Orkney had wheeled off his English and Scots, and joined Cutts and Churchill in the investment of Blenheim, sealing the village round to the banks of the Danube. Clérambault panicked and leaped into the river, being drowned, and at 9 o'clock in the evening the French officers in Blenheim capitulated. The 9,000 unwounded troops of the enemy in the village were gathered in. Oberglau had already been deluged in the great advance. Seeing what was passing, Marsin and the elector, themselves far from beaten yet, had by 7 o'clock begun an orderly retreat westwards. They were not pursued; Marlborough had no reserves, it was almost nightfall, and he had to deal with many prisoners. His army itself had lost about 4,500 killed and 7,500 wounded, or 20 per cent of its strength. The French losses were about 40,000, including 14,000 prisoners, say 70 per cent, and 60 guns.

The battle of Blenheim was profoundly decisive in its consequences. At the beginning of 1704 Louis XIV had been within an ace of achieving his ambition to dominate Europe; Spain, the Spanish Netherlands and Italy were in his pocket, and the emperor of Austria seemed doomed to bow before him. But after the campaign of that year he stayed on the defensive, knowing that his army was now outclassed and his economy exhausted – and seeking only an honourable peace to preserve his frontiers. By his campaign to the Danube, and particularly in those three hours when he rallied the situation at Oberglau and then launched a decisive cavalry charge, Marlborough dispelled a shadow which had hung over Europe for more than forty years. British soldiers, for the previous two and a half centuries almost unknown on the Continent, had now gained their reputation as the best in the world.

But the war was not yet over. From 1705 to 1711 Marlborough had to fight in the Low Countries, with all the old problems of Dutch timidity and French fortifications. Battles were hard to bring about, although he won three more great victories, at Ramillies (1706), Oudenarde (1708) and Malplaquet (1709). For the most part it was a war of sieges and small manoeuvres. But even in this uncongenial warfare Marlborough's genius excelled. In 1708, for example, he proposed to follow up his victory of Oudenarde with a direct advance on Paris, but the other generals would not have it and insisted on besieging Lille. While Eugene conducted the actual siege Marlborough covered his operations, protecting him from a larger force commanded by the Marshals Vendôme and Berwick. From July to December he held off the French relieving army, manoeuvring with extraordinary economy and foresight, every time parrying the enemy's next move before it was delivered. Not long after this Marlborough's relations with his political chiefs began to deteriorate, since his strategy for ending the war did not accord with the policy of any political party in England, and at the end of 1711 he was relieved from his command.

Marlborough absorbs the attention of the military historian as the giant of his times, but there are two lesser commanders of the War of the Spanish Succession who are worth noting. The first is the Earl of Peterborough, who went out in command of the

Marlborough's army broke into the French entrenchments at Malplaquet

The Swedish army defeated the Russians at the Dvina in 1701

British expedition to Spain in 1705. In the next two years he reduced Barcelona, Valencia and the east coast, opening the way to Madrid. These dramatic successes, achieved with a handful of troops, were due to boldness and effrontery, fertility in stratagem, and, more than anything, to the prodigiously bad generalship of the other side. Peterborough captured Valencia without firing a shot, having induced Las Torres, the Spanish general, with 7,000 men to retreat for the best part of a month before a force which never numbered more than 1,300 and at one point was as little as 150 men: Las Torres was allowed to 'capture' certain officers who 'warned' him of the imminence of Peterborough's huge army. Peterborough's feats made cheering news in London at a time when the war in the Netherlands was proceeding very slowly, but they were really something of a freak.

A more important figure is Marshal Villars, by far the ablest general that Louis XIV had after Condé and Turenne. It was he who placed Vienna in peril by his victories in

Germany at Friedlingen in 1702 and at Höchstädt in 1703. Villars, however, was a professional soldier rather than a courtier, and his hot temper and bluntness endeared him more to his men than to his political masters. For some time he was forced into obscurity. But from 1709 he held the major command on the northern front. He could not actually get the better of Marlborough, but he put up a very strong defence. He was audacious and willing to fight battles, yet cautious to the right degree. In 1709, when his army was the last French line of defence before Paris and considerably outnumbered, and although he was badly wounded in the battle himself, he managed to make Malplaquet a Pyrrhic victory for Marlborough and the allies. In 1710 the enemy were still held off, and again in 1711, when Villars constructed his famous *Ne Plus Ultra* line of earthworks across from the coast of Picardy to Namur, and Marlborough took most of the campaigning season to penetrate them. When Marlborough had departed from the scene Villars definitely got the better of Eugene in 1712, defeating him at the battle of Denain (in France, south-west of Valenciennes), and pushing the allies back. Having lost every campaign of the war, the French thus won the last. Thanks to the holding power of Vauban's fortifications and to the generalship of Villars, France secured very reasonable terms at the final Treaty of Utrecht in 1713.

Contemporary with the War of the Spanish Succession, and outlasting it, was the Great Northern War (1700–21) between Sweden and Russia. The Muscovite state was bound to expand, if only to find defensible frontiers, and already in the 1650's there had been a clash with Sweden – the established great power of the north.

The only military figure I will discuss in this war is Charles XII, but briefly since I have never held him in great regard. He became king of Sweden in 1697 at the age of fifteen and certainly had exceptional personal qualities; also he was heir to a military tradition which had been maintained since the time of Gustavus Adolphus. He loved war with all its rigours and perils and, having great powers of endurance, was willing to perform himself all the unreasonable feats he demanded of his soldiers. But he was so unwise as to engage in war with Russia. Peter the Great adopted the time-honoured strategy of evading battle and luring his enemy on into the vast open spaces of Russia, thus making him face up to the problems of distance, climate, devastation and the harrying of lengthy communications. As Napoleon commented, Charles violated most of the principles of generalship. The winter of 1708–9 was exceptionally severe and the Swedish army suffered terribly. The final disaster came in June 1709 when the Swedes were besieging Poltava in the Ukraine; Peter closed in on them with a greatly superior force; Charles himself was wounded and fled south to the protection of the Turks, and his army surrendered. In due course he made his way back to Sweden, alone. But he went on fighting until he was killed by a sniper during his campaign in Norway in 1718. The Great Northern War ended in 1721 with the Treaty of Nystadt; this marked the eclipse of Sweden, and the emergence of Russia as a new great power in Europe.

So much for Charles XII. Some writers have considered him to be one of the great captains, because of his leadership and victories in the field. I do not agree. He never seemed to have any clearly defined strategy. He overestimated the military value of his allies, and underestimated the great powers of resistance of the Russians – as both Napoleon and Hitler were to do later. He did not understand international politics, and he lacked wisdom and intelligence. My final comment on him would be that he had little regard for the lives of his soldiers, and he brought Sweden to the brink of ruin.

Colonial expansion led to an increase in sea warfare between the great powers. The escort of a Spanish treasure ship intercepted by an English squadron in 1708

14 European War in the Eighteenth Century

Three broad subjects are to be covered in this chapter on warfare in the eighteenth century. We begin with the competition for empire between Britain and France which was predominantly a question of naval strategy and economic warfare – for the first time on a world scale. The leading figures are George Anson, an outstanding sailor and naval organizer; William Pitt, a great political war leader; and James Wolfe, a soldier. The second subject is Prussia. The development of the Prussian military state and society will be traced and the qualities and ideas of Frederick the Great (1740–86) analyzed, particularly by reference to his victory of Leuthen in Silesia (1757). Lastly, we shall investigate the transition from dynastic to nationalistic war – as in 1792 at Valmy, in the French revolutionary wars, the citizen army of France fought the Prussians and Austrians as a nation in arms defending its democracy.

The Treaty of Utrecht in 1713 ended the French attempt to dominate Europe, but left wide open the other great source of friction, the question of trade and colonies. The chief competition was between Britain and France, with Spain for a time also involved as an ally of France; the Dutch now preferred to keep out of trouble. The years between 1713 and 1739 were years of general expansion in ships, trade and bases – and a time theoretically of peace. But tension steadily arose in certain key areas: Gibraltar and Minorca, West Africa, North America and India. A succession of incidents led to the first outbreak of war, the war of Jenkins' Ear (1739–44) in the Caribbean, which merged with the wider War of the Austrian Succession (1740–8). After a pause to gather strength the struggle was reopened in the Seven Years' War (1756–63); and again carried on in the War of American Independence (1775–83) (although this war was virtually ended by the capitulation of Cornwallis at Yorktown in 1781). All these wars had other political aspects to them as their names indicate, but a major feature of each was Anglo-French imperial rivalry. William Pitt recognized this, as well as the advent of the era of world war, when he spoke of 'winning Canada on the banks of the Elbe' – literally by using his Prussian ally to divert so many French troops that the French were weak in America.

In Chapter 1 the question was asked – 'Why do wars happen?' Various causes were examined and we considered certain qualities of human nature and circumstances which make men resort to war. But that a man's *ear* should be the cause of a war was not considered; nevertheless that is what happened in the war of Jenkins' Ear. The story may not be known to some readers. In 1731 an English brig, the *Rebecca*, returning home from the West Indies, was boarded by a Spanish guardship whose commander rifled the holds and cut off an ear of the English captain, Robert Jenkins. On arrival in England Jenkins complained to the king, who took little notice. But seven years later Jenkins repeated his story before a committee of the House of Commons; much political excitement was caused, and the Press added fuel to the flames to such an extent that the incident became a contributary cause of war between Britain and Spain in 1739, which ultimately merged into the War of the Austrian Succession.

France had a population in the eighteenth century of around 20 million, whereas England's was only five, although the advantage of Britain's geographical position out-weighed this numerical disadvantage in the oceanic struggle. France had always to give her primary diplomatic and military attention to Europe. Britain, on the other hand, could be content in that theatre with subsidizing diversionary allies – Austria and then Prussia. Marlborough's army was allowed to decline, only small forces being sent to the Continent – where often they played an undistinguished part. The navy was the chief strength of Britain in the eighteenth century, and her situation as an island on the westerly ocean gave her an immense strategical advantage from the start.

As so often happens in years of peace, Britain's navy had been allowed to fall into bad condition before 1739. In that year, although in theory she had 124 fighting ships, in fact only 80 were fit for service, and of these not more than 35 were actually in commission. The French had 51 warships, which had all been constructed fairly recently and were technically superior to the British. An English artillery expert wrote in 1744 that 'it is pretty apparent our 70-gun ships are little superior to their ships of 52 guns'. There was little progress in ship design in the eighteenth century, except for the disappearance of the high forecastle and the introduction in 1761 of copper sheathing for the ship's bottom to increase speed and sea-endurance. Until half-way through the nineteenth century the French in fact were the best builders of ships in the world, and there was much competition among English naval officers to command French prizes – such as the *Terrible* of 1,590 tons, captured in 1747, which had two decks, three masts and 74 guns. The frigate was introduced in this period as a fast cruiser.

The naval strategy of the French derived directly from their numerical inferiority. They aimed to avoid battle while protecting their commerce and extending their colonial possessions on land. In contradistinction, British strategy was offensive, being aimed at cutting the enemy's communications and destroying his fleet at sea. Tactically both sides adhered to the line-ahead formation, and the British Admiralty's 'Permanent Fighting Instructions' actually laid down that no ship should in any circumstances break the line to seek a *mêlée* with the enemy. In battle the British tended more often to take the offensive. The rigid tactics of the line, however, precluded the possibility of a decisive victory, and British naval victories between 1692 and 1782 were won by men who dared to ignore the official rule, and broke the line to hunt down and destroy the enemy.

In 1739 the French and British naval personnel seemed about equally bad in quality. The high command in both navies was vitiated by the system of purchasing commissions and by appointments through social influence. The crews were largely recruited by press-gangs; the best men were those stolen from the merchant navy, and the worst were criminals and idlers. Dr Johnson considered that a man who would voluntarily go to sea would as voluntarily go to hell. However, when the test of war came British sailors proved to be of better quality than the French or Spaniards. In 1739 Admiral

Edward Vernon captured the castle and harbour of Porto Bello on the Panama isthmus in a fine amphibious operation. And between 1740 and 1744 Commodore George Anson made his great voyage.

Anson was sent in 1740 as commodore of a squadron of six ships to harry the Spaniards in America and the South Seas. The voyage was very much in the tradition of Drake. By his personal powers of leadership Anson surmounted the handicaps of poor quality men and equipment. Much damage was done to the Spaniards, including the capture of the enormous Manila treasure galleon. Eventually, after great hazards, he returned to England by way of the Cape, with one ship, having circumnavigated the globe and bringing back the richest prize cargo in history. This voyage was the training ground of several sailors of future fame, including Keppel, Hyde Parker and Saunders. In 1747 Anson commanded at the first battle off Cape Finisterre, when he gained a victory by breaking his line at the right moment. His strategic conception was to destroy the enemy at sea combined with the blockade of his main ports – a new idea.

From 1745 until his death in 1762 Lord Anson was at the Admiralty. He introduced important reforms and under his guidance the British navy emerged from its decayed state. The dockyards were reorganized, and the conditions of the ships improved – their number being raised to 100, almost double that of France and equal to the strength of the combined navies of France and Spain. The recruitment of seamen was assisted by the introduction of bounties, and discipline was tightened. Corruption by vested interests was to a great extent removed, and numerous able young men were given the chance to rise to the top of the service. The French were at this time also building ships, but the other necessary reforms in their navy did not take place.

When the Seven Years' War began in 1756 Britain was thus strongly placed against France at sea. Yet because of ministerial bungling the first developments of the war were disastrous for Britain. Minorca was lost by a weak British fleet, and a scapegoat was made in Admiral Byng, who was tried by court-martial and shot – it was suggested by Voltaire *'pour encourager les autres'*. If his death encouraged his brother admirals to disregard Admiralty regulations when the need arose, Byng did not die in vain. Indeed, I have myself in war disregarded War Office regulations, and survived; but in each instance victory in battle resulted, and maybe that makes a difference!

The real encouragement to Britain came, however, with the accession to power in 1756 of William Pitt (later Earl of Chatham), a great war leader and statesman. Like Churchill, Pitt came to power at a dark hour in England's history, and like Churchill he rallied and led the British people by his superb oratory. As he said with arrogance but accuracy, 'I know that I can save this country, and that no one else can.' Some may say that he was even greater than Churchill as a strategist of world war, but that I would dispute. He saw that Britain's true interest in this war lay in commercial empire, that trade must be the 'last entrenchment'. The chief importance to England of the war in Europe was that it might divert France's attention and resources from the war in the rest of the world, and to this end Pitt subsidized Prussia with money but gave the minimum of direct military intervention. Thus Britain's strength was saved, and her great effort could then be made in India and above all in North America. The warfare in India will be described in a separate chapter, and it is enough to record now that the British there were immensely successful under the leadership of Robert Clive. Attention now focuses on North America.

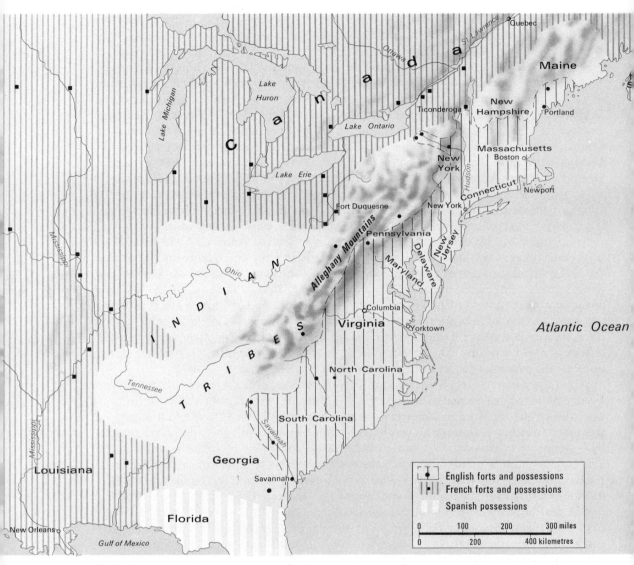

North America in the eighteenth century. The French aim to unite Canada and Louisiana was countered by the British drive to conquer Quebec and bring Canada under British rule

The strategical situation in North America at that time must be understood. The English colonies were confined to a narrow north-south strip between the Alleghany Mountains and the Atlantic. To the north the French had Canada and to the south Louisiana. It was their aim to occupy the valleys of the Ohio and the Mississippi in order to connect their colonies and prevent English expansion to the west. The British sought to upset this strategy by cutting the Atlantic communications of the French, and by forcing their way westwards. But up to date they had not been successful. In 1754 an expedition from Virginia to the Ohio led by George Washington was defeated, and in the following year a still larger force suffered the same fate. It was clear to Pitt in 1757 that a major effort must be made in America, and he decided to conquer Canada. The French navy was as far as possible put out of the war by the blockades of Brest and Toulon, and by raids all along the French Atlantic coast. A three-pronged attack on the French in America was planned by Pitt and his two able subordinates – Lord Anson (First Lord of the Admiralty) and Lord Ligonier (Commander-in-Chief of the Army).

Of these operations, the chief one was to be an amphibious attack on French Canada from the north up the St Lawrence River. The approach was guarded by Louisburg, fortified in the Vauban style and with 400 guns. The expedition of 1758 was led by relatively young officers of great ability: Amherst and Wolfe in command of 11,000 troops, and Boscawen commanding 22 ships. Louisburg fell to a first-rate inter-service operation. The second simultaneous attack in that summer was an expedition of regular troops and provincials led by John Forbes to capture Fort Duquesne and open up the Ohio valley. After feats of epic endurance the expedition succeeded, and Fort Duquesne was renamed Fort Pitt, and later Pittsburg. The third prong of the attack, however – Abercromby's expedition from the south towards Ticonderoga and Quebec – was a failure.

Enough had been achieved in 1758 to make it well worth pressing forward the conquest of Canada in 1759. In this year the whole British effort was concentrated on the advance up the St Lawrence towards Quebec, and the command was entrusted to Major-General James Wolfe, aged thirty-two. He had been commissioned at the age of fourteen in the Marines, was transferred as an ensign to the Suffolk Regiment at the age of fifteen, when sixteen saw active service at Dettingen, and was eighteen at the battle of Culloden. At the age of twenty-three he commanded the Lancashire Fusiliers. He was a dedicated soldier; he had been a serious student of the science of war and had had considerable experience in the art from an early age. He was also cultivated in other fields, and was a writer of good prose. Although loyal to his superiors and deeply patriotic, he was inclined to be outspoken and critical. Fortunately he was generally right, and, equally fortunately, Pitt was sensible enough not to allow his advance to be blocked by resentful senior officers.

The capture of Quebec in 1759 ranks among the most brilliant amphibious operations in history. Not the least brilliant part of it was the first passage of the fleet, commanded by Charles Saunders, through the currents and shoals of the St Lawrence. At the end of June, Wolfe and 9,000 soldiers disembarked on the south side of the river. Quebec was opposite them on the Heights of Abraham, defended above and below by 16,000 men under Montcalm, a fine commander, and with powerful artillery support. Wolfe's great assets were command of the river and hence the possibility of surprise. The French sat tight, maybe wisely. For weeks Wolfe looked for a way of taking Quebec which should not be obviously suicidal, and by the end of July he began to despair. His personal health was extremely bad. In August he received a reinforcement of 1,200 men, and at the beginning of September he decided to risk an attack by a small, winding path which climbed the cliffs a mile and a half up-river from Quebec, and which seemed so inaccessible that the French had defended it only by a small piquet. On the night of 12th–13th September the army was floated across the river and made a surprise landing; at dawn it appeared on top of the Heights. The battle, and the fate of Canada, was decided briefly by one perfectly timed volley. Wolfe himself was killed.

Wolfe was a great soldier. I would find it difficult to include him among the 'Great Captains' because his fame rests on a single year of achievement; as Liddell Hart has written, 'he flashed across the sky of human history' like a meteor. However, the student of war and of human nature will find much of value in Wolfe's early years of striving and preparation to fit himself for the opportunity whenever it might come – and when it did come he was ready. At Westerham in Kent, where he was born in 1727, his statue stands on the green near the church, and I always paused to look at it on my visits to Chartwell, the home of Sir Winston Churchill a short distance farther on. Wolfe was never very robust; indeed, like Nelson, he was frail in body but completely fearless in action. He proved that a great spirit can be found in a frail body. I often discussed generalship with Wavell and would say you cannot win battles if you are not feeling well. Wavell would reply that Napoleon often felt unwell (he suffered from dysuria) but he would sooner have a sick Napoleon on his side than some of his opponents whole! I would say the same of Wolfe. A minister commented to George II on his choice of a young colonel age thirty-two, made a local major-general for the operation, to command the most important expedition of the war – adding that Wolfe was mad. The king replied: 'Mad, is he? I wish to heavens he would bite some of my other generals!'

Wolfe cannot be compared with great commanders like Marlborough or Wellington because he never fought a battle on that scale. The battle which resulted in the capture of Quebec was fought between forces which, if added together, would hardly equal in numbers a division of the mid-twentieth century. The real battle lasted only some fifteen minutes, and the result was never in doubt after the British had fired their first tremendous volley; the casualties were light – the British 650 and the French about 1,500. Yet in spite of its minor scale and short duration, the battle changed the allegiance of Canada from France to England and was therefore one of the great battles of the world. It is particularly interesting to study the three or four months' campaign which led up to it, and the qualities of the commanders on both sides – Wolfe chief of all, but also Bougainville who was A.D.C. to Montcalm, and James Cook the future circumnavigator.

The capture of Quebec was only one aspect of the success of British arms in 1759. In that year Pitt's strategy bore fruit not only in the conquest of Canada but in a series of victories all over the world. At Minden in Europe the English infantry contributed to an allied victory. Boscawen defeated the French Toulon fleet at Lagos and Hawke shattered the Brest fleet at Quiberon Bay, with the result that for the rest of the war the French were left with no naval strength. Guadeloupe in the West Indies and Goree in West Africa were taken. Early in 1760 the battle of Wandewash dealt a heavy blow to the French position in India. The rest of the war until 1763 was, from England's point of view, a mopping up operation, and the exclusion from office of Pitt in 1761 by a new king and jealous politicians made no difference. By the Peace of Paris in 1763 almost all the English gains of the war were confirmed, except in the West Indies, and Britain emerged as the leading imperial power of the world.

Britain, as usual after winning a great war, then neglected her military and naval strength. Her conduct of the War of American Independence (1775–83) is in marked contrast to the record of the Seven Years' War. The logistical problems of fighting at such a distance were considerable, but no worse than they had been against the French. It was above all the complete lack of good military and political leadership which prevented England from quickly crushing what began as a thinly supported revolt. It is a nice point which were the worse equipped and the worse led: the American troops or the British. However, George Washington matured as a leader although he was never more than a mediocre soldier, and the Americans adapted themselves better to fighting in the type of country involved. Whereas the British troops fought in red coats and drill formations, the Americans camouflaged themselves in green and fought largely as irregulars.

The decisive factor in the war was the intervention against England in 1778 of France, followed by Spain and the Dutch United Provinces. The reconstructed French navy with its allied fleets could not be contained by the British navy. The war was now another world war, and Britain was desperately pressed to preserve her far flung colonial possessions. With his sea communications cut and Washington's large army behind him, General Cornwallis in command of the main British force in America was compelled to surrender at Yorktown in 1781. Admiral Rodney salvaged the situation to some extent by his victory over the French fleet off Dominica in 1782 which saved Jamaica and destroyed French naval prestige. But England was fortunate that by the Treaty of Versailles in the next year she lost little more than her American colonies.

The British troops, cut off in North America, marched in good order to surrender at Yorktown

The eighteenth century art of war was normally as limited on land as it was at sea. War was remarkably passionless: this was the age of reason and complacency which fell between the religious fanaticism of the seventeenth century and the nationalist fanaticism of the nineteenth. Most wars in Europe were fought for dynastic reasons, and their objectives were thus limited. The conduct of war was restricted by convention, and the strategical and tactical emphasis was on manoeuvre and the avoidance of overmuch fighting – not on seeking out the enemy to destroy him. Siege warfare took up a great deal of time. Armies, growing ever larger, were immobile and expensive. As far as possible war was prevented from affecting civil life. Armies were recruited from nobles and vagabonds, the only willing and available classes, and nationality made little difference to allegiance. Hard training, and discipline and rigid rules, were necessary to instil just a minimum of competence and to prevent desertion. The officer corps was permeated by corruption and the avoidance of work, and was separated from the men by the gulf of snobbery and incompetence. With such limitations eighteenth-century war was, on the whole, mediocre. It was not, however, impossible for genius to achieve something in these conditions, as the careers of Maurice de Saxe and Frederick the Great amply demonstrate.

Saxe, having served under Eugene and Peter the Great, made his first reputation by his surprise night attack and capture of Prague, and became the leading French commander in the War of the Austrian Succession (1740–8). In 1745 he won his most famous victory, over the British at Fontenoy, and in the following year he overran the Netherlands. In 1750 he died, leaving numerous illegitimate children, of whom one was to be the great-grandmother of George Sand. The study of his military career has been generally neglected, possibly because historians have tended to direct their attention to Frederick the Great, king of Prussia, who was his close contemporary. But in the 1740's, during the years he held high command in the field, he was considered to be one of the first generals of the age. He should be chiefly remembered for a remarkable work on the art of war, a classic, published seven years after his death – *Mes Rêveries*. I gave my view earlier in this chapter that you cannot win battles if you are not feeling well. Saxe, as well as Wolfe, would seem to disprove that statement because his health was precarious and he suffered a great deal from dropsy; indeed, he was so incapacitated by this disease at Fontenoy that he was unable to mount his horse and had to inspect his troops from an open wicker vehicle. I have read that amorous adventures in earlier days contributed to his poor health – an example to all who aspire to high command in the profession of arms!

In *Mes Rêveries* Saxe condemned almost every one of the weaknesses of eighteenth-century war, and advocated sound principles which had been all but forgotten since classical times, and which were not to be applied in practice until Napoleon. He condemned slavery to conventions, and above all immobility. He declared that too much time was wasted over the fortifications of cities, it being better to defend strong natural sites. He laid down that mobility, that is to say rapidity of movement, ease of manoeuvre and efficiency of supply, was the precondition of decisive success – 'The principal part depends upon the legs and not the arms.' His ideal army in the eighteenth century would consist of 46,000 men, for 'multitudes serve only to perplex and embarrass'. Such an army must be flexibly organized, on a legionary or divisional system, use being made of light-armed troops. The commander must create his opportunities and not

At the battle of Fontenoy the French, under Maurice de Saxe, defeated a British-Hanoverian army by superior manoeuvre. The parade-ground advance of the British forces came under heavy fire from both flanks, and a counter-attack put them to flight

wait for them to appear, he must concentrate strength against weakness, and he must pursue the enemy to destruction. Saxe clearly understood the factor of morale, and the delicate balance between the will to go forward and the instinct to go back. He urged that simple things could be great aids to morale: the use of armour, music, badges, the naming of regiments after something permanent rather than the colonel at the time, national service, and promotion by merit. The fact that all these things are now common-place, but were then extraordinary, testifies to the rare quality of Saxe's military mind.

In 1740 Frederick II, known as 'The Great', became king of Prussia. The essential background to Frederick's military achievements lies in the work of administrative and social organization carried out by two of his Hohenzollern predecessors, the Great Elector Frederick William (1640–88) and King Frederick William I (1713–40). The original scattered lands of Brandenburg and Pomerania were economically poor and had no natural defences, and if the Hohenzollern rulers were to retain the strong political position left to them by the decline of the Habsburgs in the Thirty Years' War they must construct a strong state and an army. This was done. The Great Elector made himself absolute master of a single administrative machine, centred on the army supply organization – the *Kriegskommissariat*. This process was made possible by a bargain

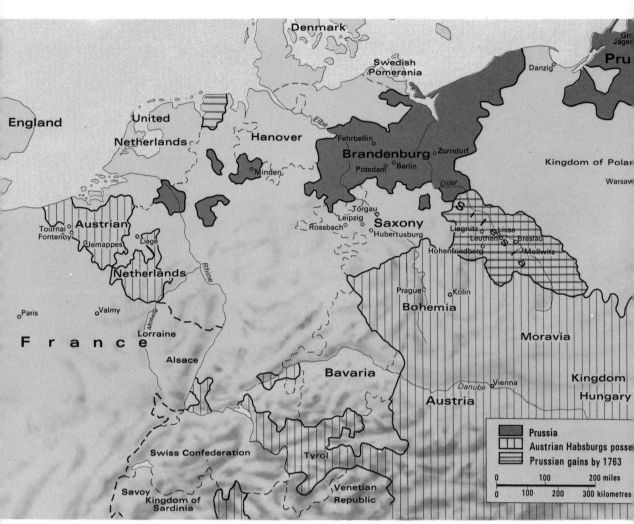

Central Europe at the accession of Frederick the Great *above*. By this time the musket with socket bayonet *below* had replaced the pike and given the infantryman a double-purpose weapon

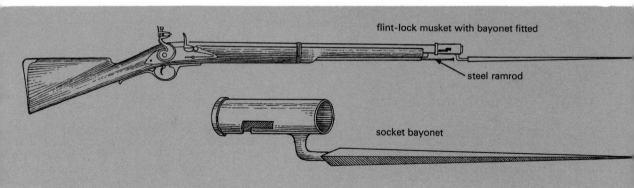

struck between the ruler and the nobles or 'junkers'. In 1653 the junkers gave the elector absolute power and the financial means to maintain a standing army, on the conditions that the officer corps should be their exclusive preserve and that the peasants on their estates should be reduced to serfdom. The middle classes east of the Elbe were too weak to oppose this. Such was the origin of Prussian absolutism and militarism.

The new Prussian army emerged to European significance with the victory against the Swedes at Fehrbellin in 1675. The Prussian state increased enormously in strength in the reign of Frederick William I, who doubled the budget and increased the size of the army from 38,000 to 80,000 men. Frederick II before his accession in 1740 had been more interested in French literature and flute playing than in battle drill, but as king he quickly became a hard realist in the already established Prussian tradition.

Prussia's trump cards were her army and her king. Her population was only twelfth among the states of Europe, and although the nuclei of the regiments were conscripted from the provinces of Prussia the majority of the men in the army had been raised abroad, if necessary by kidnapping. The first function of the Prussian bourgeoisie and peasantry was economic production. In the army the officers were mostly Prussians of noble birth, and Frederick relied on them more than on his men. In return for their privileges the junkers were glad to serve; every family sent at least one son to the cadet school; the officers were inculcated with *esprit de corps* and patriotism as well as discipline, and were given a practical military education. Frederick considered that the best he could do with the men was to drill them until each man was a highly efficient automaton, 'more afraid of his officers than of the dangers to which he is exposed'. This ruthless military training had two valid objects. First, in an army composed largely of foreigners lacking in goodwill and morale, it was only compulsion which could produce discipline, alertness and cohesion. Secondly, Frederick knew that mobility was the key to victory in the conditions of the time, and that battle drill alone would produce it. The formations and evolutions of the parade ground were those of the battlefield. It is true that discipline was savage and their life was hard, but Frederick himself got on well with his soldiers. The chief weapon of the Prussian army was the bayonet-carrying musket of Marlborough's time which had altered only in very minor respects, such as the introduction of the iron ramrod.

As time went on Frederick was to improve the quality of the Prussian army tremendously, but the instrument he inherited in 1740 was already good enough for him to feel confident to use it, and in that year he invaded the neighbouring Austrian territory of Silesia. His only excuse was that Silesia would be an invaluable economic and strategic acquisition for Prussia. This aggression began the War of the Austrian Succession in Europe. The political implications rapidly widened, but Frederick kept his eye on his main objective. By the victories of Mollwitz (1741) and Hohenfriedberg (1745) Prussia held on to Silesia. Peace came in 1748. But it was no more than a truce, for Austria was not content, and in 1756 Prussia was again at war, subsidized by England but opposed by Austria, France, Russia and Saxony. This was the Seven Years' War (1756–63).

In this war Frederick was again his own commander-in-chief. In the formulation and execution of his strategy he had the immense asset of being absolute master of a highly efficient and militarily orientated government. Unlike his contemporaries, except for Saxe and Wolfe, he believed that the aim of strategy was the destruction of the forces of the enemy, not just the occupation or defence of a piece of territory. Forcefulness and

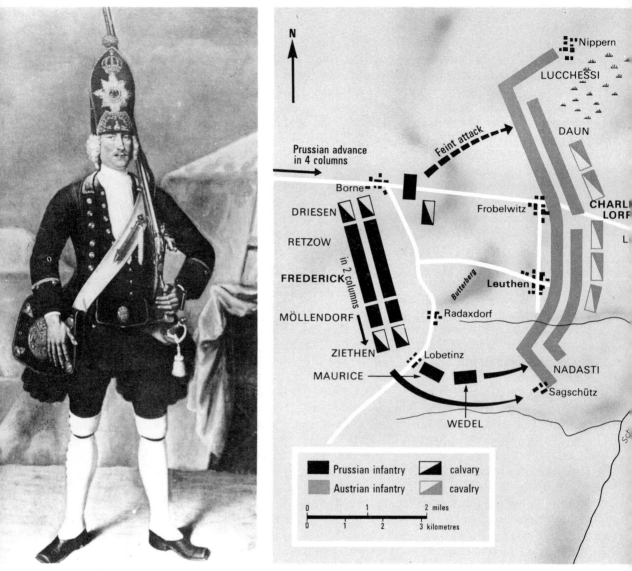

The battle of Leuthen *right* was won by the superior training of the Prussian soldiers, such as the famous regiment of exceptionally tall guardsmen *left*

mobility were the essence of his strategy. A resolute offensive on enemy soil would give Prussia the initiative and force the enemy commander to subordinate his movements to Frederick's. Besides, Frederick had so many enemies in this war that if he waited for them all to attack him in concert he was even more likely than ever to be ruined. Having the advantages of interior lines his method was to move fast and strike hard at one enemy, and then move again quickly to face the next. Thus he opened the war himself by invading Saxony without a declaration, and then in 1757 he defeated the Austrians at

Prague. But later in that year he was beaten by the Austrians with greatly superior numbers at Kolin, and then again by the Russians at Gross Jägersdorf. By the late autumn of 1757 the Prussians appeared to be doomed. But the quality of their government and army, and the courage of their king, kept them going. In November Frederick, still on the offensive, won a great victory over the combined Austrian and French army at Rossbach in Saxony, and in December he turned on the other Austrian force under Field-Marshal Daun and Charles of Lorraine and defeated them at Leuthen in Silesia.

Frederick's tactics as well as his strategy were always offensive because he believed that, given the initiative, his troops, being highly trained in the movements of battle and in the use of their weapons, could beat any number of the sluggish troops of his enemies. As a result of battle drill, he could write, 'a Prussian battalion is a moving battery . . . the rapidity in loading is such that it can triple the fire of all other troops. This gives to the Prussians a superiority of three to one.' Frederick used the 'oblique order' of battle a good deal, but there is no evidence to prove that he invented this tactic; it is more likely that he improved on the method of Epaminondas, the Theban general (Chapter 4). Its success depended on mobility. He explained it as follows:

> You refuse one wing to the enemy and strengthen the one which is to attack. With the latter you do your utmost against one wing of the enemy which you take in flank. An army of 100,000 men taken in flank may be beaten by 30,000 in a very short time . . . The advantages of this arrangement are (1) a small force can engage one much stronger than itself; (2) it attacks an enemy at a decisive point; (3) if you are beaten, it is only part of your army, and you have the other three-fourths which are still fresh to cover your retreat.

In practically all of his battles Frederick was outnumbered; indeed, during the Seven Years' War virtually the whole continent was in arms against him. When he attacked a huge enemy army in a strong position, as at Kolin, he could not achieve the impossible. But the victories of Rossbach and Leuthen proved his methods to be sound and were great tactical feats.

The odds at Leuthen were stacked heavily against Frederick's army. Since the battle of Rossbach early in November two other Prussian forces had been defeated and Austrian morale had considerably recovered. The Austrian army of Daun and Charles of Lorraine consisted of 84 battalions of infantry, 144 squadrons of cavalry and 210 guns: in all between 60,000 and 80,000 men. Frederick had only 36,000 men: 24,000 infantry in 48 battalions, 12,000 cavalry in 128 squadrons, and 167 guns. But when in early December he arrived in the enemy's vicinity in Silesia, country he knew well, he was determined to seek battle, even, as he admitted to his officers, 'against all the rules of the art'. On 4th December the Austrians took up a position in two lines in front of the Schweidnitz stream, on a five and a half mile front stretching from the bogs of Nippern in the north through the village of Leuthen, and thence south to Sagschütz. It was a strong defensive position, although somewhat long.

At 5 o'clock in the morning on 5th December 1757 Frederick advanced from the west straight along the Breslau road. His plan was to feint at the Austrian right but in fact to refuse his own left, and then march across the enemy's long front and hit him with great force on his left flank. The Prussian advance guard under his own command, 10 battalions and 60 squadrons, made contact with the enemy at the village of Borne in a dawn mist. The Prussians attacked straightaway, uncertain whether they were fighting the enemy's advance troops or his right wing. It turned out to be an advance formation of five regiments, which were rapidly scattered. Borne was captured, and from the village as the day dawned Frederick could see the whole line of the enemy's dispositions. The ground, sloping down behind Borne, concealed from the Austrians the advance of the four main Prussian columns.

As his main army came up, Frederick sent the advance guard to pursue the first Austrian fugitives and to feint at the enemy's right wing. The Austrian commander there, Lucchessi, thinking that he was about to receive a full attack, called urgently for help from his left. Daun sent him the reserve cavalry and some of the cavalry from the left. The preliminaries having been so successful, Frederick now put the main part of his plan into operation. Forming the four columns into two, he wheeled them away southward to the right, still covered from view by the lie of the ground. One who was present described this manoeuvre of the Prussian army:

> It was impossible to witness a more beautiful sight; all the heads of the columns were parallel to each other, and in exact distances to form line, and the divisions marched with such precision, that they seemed to be at a review.

The Austrian commanders had expected a direct frontal assault, and when this did not happen they came to the conclusion that the Prussian army had decided not to attack. Suddenly they were disillusioned; the heads of the Prussian columns became visible, marching round towards their left flank, between Lobetinz and Sagschütz. Nadasti, the commander of the Austrian left, sent desperately for help when, soon after midday, the Prussian van under Wedel, supported by a battery of 6 guns and followed by Prince Maurice of Dessau and 6 infantry battalions, stormed the defences of Sagschütz. Nadasti charged the first of the Prussian cavalry, 43 squadrons led by Ziethen, but after a swaying fight the Austrian left was routed. The field between Sagschütz and Leuthen was covered with fugitives pursued by the Prussian hussars, the infantry and artillery following behind.

Charles of Lorraine in the Austrian centre, much dismayed, recalled the forces he had sent to the right, and sent forward his infantry battalion by battalion to defend Leuthen. The defenders of the village were overcrowded and their dispositions chaotic; nevertheless they resisted the Prussian attack with the courage of desperation. Frederick had to throw in more troops than he would have wished at this juncture, but a fine charge by Möllendorf's guards at last carried the village.

The next advance of the Prussians northwards was still harder, for during the defence of Leuthen the Austrian right had had time to establish a battery on the ridge above the village, and under its fire their infantry formed up in a suitable direction at right angles to their original front. Frederick ordered forward his left column, the infantry under Retzow and the cavalry under Driesen, but the artillery fire blocked them. His counteraction was to organize his own artillery fire, including ten extra heavy guns, from an eminence slightly to the west of Leuthen, called the Butterberg. The effect of this artillery fire, supported by the charge of the Prussian troops, forced back the Austrian right.

By 4 o'clock in the afternoon the Austrians were giving way, and Lucchessi made his last effort. Retzow's infantry had been temporarily checked and Lucchessi prepared to launch his cavalry at their right flank. But Driesen's forty squadrons of cavalry were hidden behind the village of Radaxdorf. At that moment, under cover from the Butter-berg, they rode out, and Lucchessi's remaining troops taken simultaneously on three sides were routed. The rest of the Austrian infantry were then similarly attacked from all angles. By the time it was dark the Austrian army was in headlong flight. Frederick pursued his victory that night only as far as Lissa. On 6th December he rested his army, and then for three days mopped up the remnants of the enemy in the nearby country-side. On 19th December Breslau surrendered, and the possession of Silesia by Prussia was secured.

Napoleon described Leuthen as 'a masterpiece of movements, manoeuvres, and resolution'. 'Alone,' he said, 'it is sufficient to immortalize Frederick, and place him in the rank of the greatest generals.' But although tactically brilliant this victory was not strategically decisive, for the war lasted another five years, during which Prussia fought alone against odds greater than ever. At one stage in 1759 the Russians actually occupied Berlin. But by his indomitable courage, and by the further victories of Zorndorf (1758), Liegnitz (1760) and Torgau (1760), Frederick staved off defeat. In 1762 Russia changed sides, and at the Peace of Hubertusburg the next year Prussia retained Silesia – one of the largest enduring conquests ever made in Europe.

After the Seven Years' War the Prussian army, exhausted but complacent, maintained its established methods and traditions. In France, on the other hand, many were shocked at the events of the war, and a good deal of important rethinking and reorganization began.

Frederick's use of horse artillery had been a highly important innovation; this reflected the technical improvements in heavy guns which had been made in recent years as well as the new concern for mobility. Before the war of 1740 Jean de Maritz had developed a new method of boring cannon with a drill, making the barrel stronger and the calibre more accurately related to the circumference of the projectile. The English mathematician, Benjamin Robins, had subsequently proved that a smaller charge and a lighter gun could still project shot the same distance. Both these discoveries allowed a diminution in the size of guns without a loss of efficiency. Gribeauval, Inspector-General of the French artillery after 1765, applied these lessons, shortening the gun barrels and aiming to make artillery more mobile. Gun-carriages were also made to run more smoothly, and horses replaced bullocks. Thus on the march artillery could now keep pace with infantry, and need not lag far behind cavalry; furthermore, it was now more manoeuvrable in battle. The numbers of guns also tended to increase; this development was helped by the discovery of coke-smelting, which made improved and cheaper iron guns available, instead of bronze as previously.

There was no comparable technical development in small arms, but firepower increased due to experience and drill. The lessons of the War of American Independence suggested to Europeans the advantages of lightly-armed infantry. It was realized that such troops, if highly trained in manoeuvre and the use of ground, would be com-plementary to the close-drilled columns of the main force – adding greatly to the efficiency of the army in battle.

These developments in artillery and light troops suggested departures from the

The lightly-armed infantryman was playing an increasingly important part on the battlefield

traditional eighteenth-century tactical ideas. In 1778, in his pamphlet *Sur l'Usage de l'Artillerie Nouvelle*, Du Teil proposed a system of mobile artillery and infantry working together. The artillery was to begin the battle, opening fire at a range of 1,000 yards, and, from a flank, bombarding along the length of the enemy line. General Gribeauval also argued in favour of the new short-barrelled light guns which, though they might be less accurate at a distance, would be more mobile and effective at close quarters. There was considerable discussion regarding the right point of compromise between mobility and firepower, and this raised the question of concentration of force. Folard suggested that the line should be abandoned for parallel columns, which by concentrated attacks would penetrate the enemy line at varying points – the spaces between the columns being filled with light infantry. Column formations required a new battle drill, and Guibert's *Essai Général de Tactique* in 1772 set forth a system of simple basic movements by which troops could form quickly and without confusion from line to column and *vice versa*.

The new tactical principles of offence and mobility suggested a strategy of seeking battle rather than manoeuvre. With improved firepower, holding operations could be performed by smaller numbers of troops. It would thus be possible for a commander to divide his main forces into separate offensive columns, a converging net of detachments, which, if they could move fast enough, should be able to trap an enemy and force him into battle. Guibert suggested that the enterprising general should ignore the fortresses which had obsessed so many eighteenth-century commanders, and march straight on the enemy's capital: that being the main objective. The idea of such a strategy was made more realistic by the great improvement in communications during the second half of the eighteenth century, particularly roads and canals. Agriculture and industrial productivity were also increasing, and armies could once again expect to live off the country in which they were operating, thus largely dispensing with cumbrous baggage-trains. These more ambitious and complicated strategical concepts, on the other hand, demanded an ever improving administrative organization in peace time.

Until the French revolutionary war began in 1792 these new military principles remained mostly debatable and untried theses. The French revolution broke down conservatism in every way, and particularly in the armed forces by purging the officer corps. At least two-thirds of the officers in the French army before the revolution had been nobles, which was itself an important cause of revolutionary discontent. But in 1789 noble privileges were abolished, and by 1794 five-sixths of the noble officers had left the army. The upper ranks were thus opened to the ablest of the soldiery. As the revolution fired the French nation with democratic enthusiasm, the character of the whole army changed. The voluntarily recruited new National Guard became its hard core, and in due course the majority of all recruits were volunteers. The new and special quality of this voluntary, national army was that the soldiers in it followed their officers rather than being driven by them. War broke out in April 1792 between France and Austria and Prussia, because the rulers of the *ancien régime* feared the revolution and the French revolutionary leaders hated the *ancien régime*. For the people's crusade against despotism the French would rise voluntarily to arms.

In the early stages of the war the French had few successes. Their politics were chaotic, inflation was rampant, and the army lacked leaders, discipline, training and supplies. The first force sent against the enemy at Tournai and Liège turned tail and fled. But the French had courage, enthusiasm, and the right ideas, and they quickly improved. The thinking of Gribeauval, Guibert and Du Teil had largely passed into the official drill-book issued to the army in 1791. The test between the new and the old came when the French army of Dumouriez faced the Prussians and Austrians under Brunswick at Valmy on the Aisne in north-eastern France in September 1792.

The commander of the Prusso-Austrian army, the Duke of Brunswick, was widely considered by soldiers of the old school to be the best general of the day, on the strength of his bloodless and successful manoeuvring campaign in 1787 in Holland. Dumouriez, an opportunist but a man of courage, progressive ideas and leadership, considered that the title should rather be his. Neither in fact ought to have been able to claim it. For almost a month the enemies manoeuvred against each other. The operations of the French were characterized by impetuosity, disagreement, inefficiency, and sudden brief panics. The Prussian movements were extremely slow, subordinated to a useless supply system, and Brunswick missed at least three opportunities to get past or destroy his enemy. By 20th September, however, Dumouriez achieved a battle situation at Valmy more or less as he desired. Both armies were in some disorder. The battle of Valmy was in fact no more than a tremendous cannonade. After a morning's artillery duel Brunswick ordered his infantry to advance, but he soon withdrew them from the fire of the French batteries and in the afternoon broke off the battle before the fighting had ever really begun.

Valmy, though not a major battle, was a French victory, for Brunswick had decided quite rightly that with an army and communications such as he had, and at that time of year, he could not push on to Paris. The revolution gained a vital respite, and the success in checking the enemy was a factor of enormous psychological importance for the French. A second victory shortly afterwards at Jemappes added to the new confidence. By 1793 almost all the significant powers of Europe were ranged against the French. Their response was the Law of August 23, 1793, the declaration which announced the era of total war:

> The young men shall fight; the married men shall forge weapons and transport supplies; the women will make tents and clothes and will serve in the hospitals; the children will make up old linen into lint; the old men will have themselves carried in to the public squares and rouse the courage of the fighting men, to preach hatred against kings and the unity of the Republic.
> The public buildings shall be turned into barracks, the public squares into munition factories . . .
> All firearms of suitable calibre shall be turned over to the troops: the interior shall be policed with shot-guns and cold steel. All saddle horses shall be seized for the cavalry; all draft horses not employed in cultivation will draw the artillery and supply wagons.

I would like to close with a few notes about Frederick the Great, the outstanding military commander in this chapter. It is interesting to reflect whether Frederick was influenced in any way by the writings of Saxe, who was sixteen years older; the answer is probably not, since *Mes Rêveries* was published in 1757, the year of Leuthen, some seven years after Saxe died and seventeen years after Frederick had become king.

In the eighteenth century there was little difference between European armies as regards weapons, tactics and the organization of supply; the conduct of war therefore put a premium on generalship. In these conditions military strategy demanded a leader of great intellectual qualities and only two generals of those times possessed these qualities – Marlborough and Frederick the Great; both combined skill in manoeuvre with a belief in battle as the decisive element in war. The stature of Frederick as a general is linked to the rise of the military power of Prussia and to the decline of French arms; it was due to the success of the army of Prussia, and to the fact that her rulers considered the chief duty of a king was to be a soldier. His achievements can be explained, anyhow partially, by his varying of the normal eighteenth-century strategy. He agreed that 'hunger exhausts men more surely than courage', and he emphasized the importance of starving the enemy (troops, not civilians) by manoeuvring them away from their sources of supply. But he also saw that manoeuvre alone can never produce a decisive verdict – 'War is decided only by battles and it is not decided except by them' – and his willingness to give battle was what set him apart from other military leaders of his age. In a time of limited war he gained early success because he was different from

At the battle of Valmy the French revolutionary army halted the advancing Prussians by a tremendous cannonade

others; he was ready to take risks, and to commit his soldiers to battle whenever it seemed advantageous. This was similar to the Napoleonic approach to war, to be dealt with in the next chapter.

It can be said that Frederick's 'thirst for battle' would have been suicidal if his soldiers and armament had been inferior to those of his opponents – or even equal to them. But the Prussian emphasis on battle drill and discipline paid a great dividend; it produced soldiers who could march faster, change from column to line more quickly, and load and fire more rapidly and effectively than the men of any other armies. This mobility and precision gave Frederick great scope for generalship. Unlike Napoleon, he had no blank cheque on human lives. Forced to fight on several fronts in the Seven Years' War, and not being equal to any one of his three opponents in money or man-power, he had to move rapidly from point to point, dealing a series of blows to prevent a fatal junction of the armies opposing him. That he succeeded is a tribute to his energy and strength of mind, and to the capacity of his soldiers. He fought a defensive war within the guise of the offensive. We can end by stating that he was the supreme general of the period we have discussed in this chapter.

Napoleon, at the height of his military career, receives the surrender of Ulm after an almost bloodless victory

15 The Era of Nelson, Napoleon and Wellington

Not content with driving their enemies out of France, the revolutionary French carried their war for democracy, plunder and glory into all Europe – and the continent continued to experience war from 1792 till 1815. During that period there were pauses and shifts of alliance, but the fundamental disposition of the fighting was that four countries, Britain, Austria, Prussia and Russia, in combinations of two or three at a time, formed a league against the French – Britain being the chief. All the strategy of the French, under their great political and military leader Napoleon, on land and sea was ultimately concerned to defeat Britain. The warfare was notable more for individual genius than for systems or technical factors. Many brilliant individuals appeared, but in our study we shall concentrate on three of them: Nelson, Napoleon and Wellington.

In the war against her enemy across the Channel, Britain's main effort naturally began at sea – particularly since her navy was in much better condition than her army. Indeed, the British navy had rarely been better prepared. There were 55 ships of the line in good fighting trim, and corruption and inefficiency in the administration had been greatly reduced. By contrast the French navy, which in the American war had been a stiff rival to the British, by 1793 had never been less fit for war. The revolutionary purge had deprived it of its best elements, and mere enthusiasm and numbers, which were enough to carry the army through the time of crisis, were no substitute in the navy for well-maintained ships, good seamen and trained leaders. The French had only 42 ships of the line and lacked competent officers.

The French used their navy to damage British shipping and to threaten invasion. British naval strategy in the war had three aspects. Besides the usual functions of her seapower – the protection of British shipping and damage to the enemy's, and the protection of her shores from invasion – Britain also attempted to use seapower to confer mobility on her army. Several overseas operations were thus conducted, in Flanders, in the West Indies, and on the coast of France. But since they were unsuccessful this policy was abandoned for the time being and the British concentrated on blockading the coast of France, in order to stifle French trade and to force into battle any French fleet which dared to leave harbour.

Between 1794 and 1805 the British navy won six major victories. This period thus contrasted with the previous two hundred years since the defeat of the Armada, when full-scale and decisive naval engagements had been rare. The old warship remained technically much the same, but now at last British sailors discovered the most effective way to use it. One reason for this was the introduction of a comprehensive signalling system, devised by Kempenfelt and Howe. Efficient signalling enabled commanders to progress from pre-set and rigid formations to elaborate, flexible, yet controlled naval tactics. A second reason was the outstanding ability of some of the British seamen, notably Howe and Nelson.

The first British victory was won by Richard Howe on the 'Glorious First of June', 1794. Howe with 34 ships sighted the French with 25 far out in the Atlantic. Using his signalling system Howe gained the initiative and attacked on an entirely new principle – that of breaking the enemy line from windward. Having secured the windward position he was then able to choose his moment to bear down upon the enemy in an oblique formation, and cut their line at successive points; after this, each of the British ships engaged one of the enemy vessels at close quarters from leeward, the position which prevented the enemy escaping downwind. Howe's signalling system facilitated the perfect co-ordination of the fleet which his manoeuvre demanded. The battle of the First of June was a break-through in sailing tactics: Howe successfully combined the formal line approach with the ship-destroying *mêlée*. Six prizes were taken and one of the enemy ships was sunk. As a result of this action and of two lesser ones in 1795, the French conceded British dominance at sea and thereafter for the most part kept their fleets in port and on the defensive.

Nevertheless, by 1797 Britain's morale and war prospects were low. The French were completely successful on land in the Low Countries and Italy, and no British troops were left in Europe. Spain had joined France, and Britain was forced to evacuate the Mediterranean. In the winter of 1796–7 the French Brest fleet evaded the blockade, and was only prevented by storms from invading Ireland. Admiral Sir John Jervis retrieved the situation in February 1797 with his victory over the Spanish fleet off Cape St Vincent. But then came a moment of extreme danger for Britain, when mutiny broke out in the navy – in the Channel fleet at Spithead, and then in the North Sea fleet at the Nore. The dissatisfaction among the seamen arose from injustices in recruitment, bad pay and savage discipline; their reasonable demands for better pay and treatment were met, though the press-gang and prisons continued to provide most naval conscripts. The mutinies were concealed from the enemy long enough for the blockade of the Texel (West Frisian Islands) not to be broken, and in October Admiral Duncan won the third major victory of the war off Camperdown (Jutland), repeating the new tactics of Howe.

Jervis, now Lord St Vincent, became First Lord of the Admiralty in 1801 and devoted himself to reforming the dockyards and making the administration simple and economical. He provided the essential basis of Britain's naval strength in this way until 1806. Jervis was a great naval officer, a fighter, strategist, leader and administrator. He was also a good judge of men, and it was he who first recognized and promoted Nelson.

Horatio Nelson was born in 1758 and joined the navy when he was thirteen. He soon became conscious of ambition, and by 1793 he was a captain. In 1797 he took part in the Battle of Cape St Vincent. Jervis's plan in that battle was to cut through the enemy line and then turn about to attack before it could close again. Nelson's position in the British line was near the back, and he was able to see that the British van would be unable to tack back before the gap closed. Should he leave the line without orders, and attempt to prevent the junction? He decided to do so. He flung his ship alone into the gap, and the 74-gun *Captain* engaged seven of the enemy single-handed until the rest of the fleet

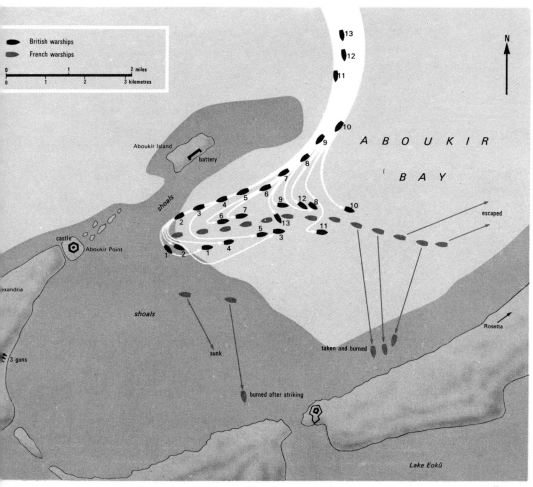

British warships
French warships

N

13
12
11

ABOUKIR

BAY

Aboukir Island
battery

shoals

10
9
8
7
6
5
4
3
2
9
12
8
13
11
10
5
3

escaped

castle
Aboukir Point
1 2 1 4

Alexandria

shoals

3 guns

sunk

taken and burned

Rosetta

burned after striking

Lake Eokū

The battle of Aboukir Bay

came up. The result of Nelson's brilliant, realistic and brave decision was a complete victory, and he won the congratulations of Jervis.

Early in 1798 it was reported that Napoleon was preparing to launch an expedition from Toulon. After the successes of the previous year the British decided to return to the Mediterranean, and a squadron of 13 ships was sent there under the command of Nelson, now a rear-admiral. Taking advantage of a storm, Napoleon with an army of about 35,000 and the Toulon fleet of 13 ships evaded Nelson and sailed to Malta and then on to Egypt. After chasing to and fro half the length of the Mediterranean, Nelson discovered and bore down on the French fleet in Aboukir Bay late on the afternoon of 1st August.

Nelson decided to attack that very evening. The manoeuvres leading to battle were carefully planned, and all his captains were taken into his confidence. He could rely on their ability, and he wanted them to use their own initiative within his broad tactical

Nelson is shot down by a sharp-shooter in the French rigging at Trafalgar

scheme. The French line of 13 warships was anchored across the bay, its head so near the rocks and shoals off Aboukir Point that the admiral, Brueys, considered that nothing could pass between it and the shore. The British thought otherwise. As night was falling Captain Foley led four ships through the shoals to the French rear; Nelson remained outside with the rest of the fleet. The immobile French ships were simultaneously engaged from both sides; the French were completely confused in the darkness and could only wait to be attacked. At dawn only two French ships escaped: the enemy fleet had been sought out and destroyed. As a result of the victory a large number of French troops were trapped in the Levant and the Mediterranean became a British sea. The capture of Minorca (1798) and Malta (1800) reinforced this dominance.

Nelson's next action was at Copenhagen in 1801. Britain depended to a large extent for her naval stores and materials on Scandinavia. Realizing this and being dominant on land, Napoleon attempted to seal off Scandinavia to English shipping. An English expedition was sent to Copenhagen, with Sir Hyde Parker in command and Nelson his second. The enemy were caught ill-prepared, and Nelson persuaded Parker to let him lead a squadron of lighter-draught ships against the Danish fleet – which was lying at anchor and unrigged, but under the guns of the fort of Copenhagen. Finely judging tides, currents and times, Nelson sailed in and poured accurate gunfire into the enemy. At the height of the action Parker lost his nerve and signalled to Nelson to withdraw. Putting his telescope to his blind eye Nelson declared that he saw no signal, and coolly went on to take the surrender of the entire Danish fleet.

The military successes of the French on the Continent continued, but everything remained vitiated for them by the unsuppressed menace of British seapower. Between 1803 and 1805 Napoleon devised a succession of schemes for the invasion of England, and a large army was encamped at Boulogne. But he could not touch London unless he could be master of the Channel – for six hours, as he put it, though six days would have been more like the time required to conduct a full-scale invasion. By the summer of 1805 he had abandoned the hope of actually invading England, but he still saw the importance of breaking the British control of the seas, and he kept the naval part of his invasion plan. This was to try to break the blockades of both Toulon and Brest, and to converge the two fleets on the Channel fleet – a very unrealistic plan. The French Toulon fleet under Villeneuve did break out, and Nelson chased it and brought it to battle on 21st October at Trafalgar. The battle of Trafalgar was fought by the then established tactics of cutting the enemy line and turning on their ships in a *mêlée*. It was the most perfectly co-ordinated and thoroughly successful application of those tactics: 18 out of the enemy's 30 ships were captured or destroyed. In this type of fighting the sharp-shooting and broadsides of two ships engaged at the closest range inevitably caused a great deal of slaughter, and Nelson himself was killed in the battle.

As an inspiring leader, a brilliant seaman, and a most original, intelligent and courageous fighter, Nelson's reputation is secure. Joseph Conrad said of him: 'He brought heroism into the line of duty.' Trafalgar, which was one of the last major battles of the age of sail, was also the most perfect. Its great consequence was that Britain became totally dominant at sea, not only then but also for the rest of the nineteenth century, and her commerce was secured and increased. More immediately, with a sound backing of supplies and communication she was able at last to make a full contribution to the military effort of Europe against Napoleon, who was now confined to a land strategy: his final doom, in consequence, being certain.

In November 1792, two months after Valmy and Jemappes, the Convention of France declared that it would 'grant fraternity and aid to all peoples who wish to recover their liberty'. Thus the French, motivated by a desire for national security and aggrandisement as well as by idealism, declared war on Europe. The assets of France were a population of over 25 million (equal to the combined populations of Austria, Prussia and England), 730,000 muskets of the 1777 model, more than 2,000 pieces of artillery of Gribeauval's design, much confused mass enthusiasm, and a number of devoted and able leaders.

From 1792 to 1797 the most valuable of these leaders was Lazare Carnot, the member of the Committee of Public Safety who saw that 'the popular frenzy must be organized'.

An administrator of genius and willing to work sixteen hours a day, he tackled the major problems: the merging of the new citizen-soldiers with the old regulars into one national army, and the organization of the whole by units; the training of officers, particularly in specialist arms; and the harnessing of industry and agriculture to war. The numbers under arms rose from 300,000 at the beginning of 1793 to over three quarters of a million in 1794. National Service was introduced in 1798 for all single men aged between twenty and twenty-five. Such was Carnot's success in organizing the forces that these great numbers were from the start an asset rather than a hindrance. The instruction of the army followed the new principles of Guibert and Bourcet, there were enough weapons, and the problem of supply was met by a system of living off the country. Carnot was also responsible for strategy in 1793–4, concerting the movements of twelve armies. It was his belief that 'it is the national characteristic of a Frenchman to attack all the time'. Full advantage was taken of French numbers and *élan*, and of the mobility which derived from the absence of supply trains.

From March 1793 there was a continuous series of French victories. Relief turned to heroic exultation. 'We marched' wrote Marmont long afterwards, 'surrounded by a kind of radiance whose warmth I can still feel as I did fifty years ago.' And a grenadier wrote: 'We suffered, but we were proud of our sufferings and tried to laugh at them. Our officers, with their packs on their backs, shared our meagre rations.' The tactics of this time were simple and costly of life, but well suited to numerically strong and enthusiastic troops commanded by young officers – of more energy and courage than experience or skill. A loose swarm of sharpshooters opened the attack; the artillery then prepared and covered the main advance; the infantry, formed in deep columns with their officers at their heads, dashed forward with fixed bayonets, shouting to keep up morale. A galaxy of brilliant commanders emerged, most of them in their twenties or thirties – Hoche, Jourdan, Augereau, Murat, Masséna, Napoleon and others. The career of Hoche is symbolic of these times. Noticed early by Carnot, he won victories at Froeschwiller and Wissembourg following his own maxim of 'prepare with caution, strike like lightning'. In 1797 he was commander of one of the most famous armies of the republic, the Army of Sambre-et-Meuse, and pushed the Austrians back to Frankfurt. But in that year, aged twenty-nine, he died. The death of Hoche marked the end of the revolutionary era and the opening of the Napoleonic era.

Napoleon Bonaparte was born in Corsica in 1769. Between 1779 and 1785 he attended military colleges in France and after that he served as a lieutenant of artillery at Auxonne and Valence. He was a student of the writings of Robins, Bourcet, Du Teil, Gribeauval and Guibert. To the last named he was greatly indebted – for ideas on the military significance of nationalist feeling, on mobility, on column tactics, and many other matters. Napoleon was an enthusiastic student of military history, and a firm believer in the value of its study. He also read the works of Rousseau, and supported the most radical party in the revolution. His first military distinction was at the relief of Toulon in 1793, where he attacked a battery occupied by the English, receiving a bayonet wound in the thigh. After some time in Italy he went to Paris, making the right friends and avoiding the wrong jobs. There in 1796 he married Joséphine de Beauharnais, the widow of a revolutionary general.

Two days after the wedding Napoleon left to command the Army of Italy. He was then twenty-six. At the outset of his campaign he had 38,000 troops with which to face

An Anglo-French naval engagement. A detail from the painting of the action off San Domingo by Nicholas Pocock. *Overleaf* The battle of the Pyramids. A detail from the painting by General Lejeune, an artist who served with distinction in the Napoleonic armies

47,000 Austrians and Sardinians; besides being inferior in numbers his army was also ill equipped. Six weeks after the opening of hostilities the general could say to his soldiers without much exaggeration:

> You have won battles without guns, crossed rivers without bridges, made forced marches without boots, encamped often without food.

A dozen victories in fact were to be won in twelve months, the most notable of which were Lodi, Castiglione, Bassano, Arcola and Rivoli. The Austrians were cleared out of central and northern Italy, and Napoleon marched within eighty miles of Vienna before peace negotiations began. The elements in his success were rapid marches, flexibility in manoeuvre, and the ability to concentrate force and make the maximum thrust at the enemy's weakest point. Unbroken victory raised French morale to fantastic heights, as well as turning Napoleon's head in no small way. At St Helena he recalled:

> It was only on the evening after Lodi that I realized I was a superior being and conceived the ambition of performing great things.

The next phase in his career, the Egyptian expedition of 1798, fitted this mood. Strategically it made no sense, and any value in the victory of the Pyramids was offset by Nelson's victory of Aboukir Bay. In 1799 Napoleon deserted his army and hurried back to France, where by a political coup he was established as First Consul. This was to mean, in effect, that Napoleon Bonaparte was the military dictator of France. As Consul, he was in fact an extremely able and enlightened ruler. Among many other achievements, work of enduring value was done in making just and more efficient the French civil administration and law, education and the Church. The defeat of the Austrians at Marengo and Hohenlinden in 1800 closed the war of the Second Coalition on the Continent, and in 1802 a truce was made with England.

Napoleon was a man of outstanding intellect, energy and willpower. He dominated all around him, and was totally self-centred. Caulaincourt, for ten years a close companion, said of him:

> He always applied all his means, all his faculties, all his attention to the action or discussion of the moment. Into everything he put passion.

Napoleon was a master of strategy: the range, speed and co-ordination of his operations were unique. Since his armies lived off the country and roads were becoming good, he could move fast. He himself was a great builder of roads. He formulated his plans on the basis of information supplied by his staff – headed by his chief of staff, Berthier, and Count Daru, another brilliant army administrator. Information was kept up to date and immediately accessible on every relevant subject. Minute research preceded the organization of a campaign, and Napoleon himself issued the final orders on everything, even the length and route of the marches of each corps. Weapons, uniforms, supply, finances, and the administration of conquered territory all came under his scrutiny. He would dictate to several secretaries at a time, and go short of sleep for days on end. He regarded the long-term preparation and administration of a campaign as vitally important.

The battle of Borodino. A detail from the painting by General Lejeune. Marshal Berthier receives the surrender of a Russian general; in the foreground a messenger from Napoleon brings the cross of the Legion of Honour to a dying officer and a grenadier guarding prisoners kicks a live shell out of harm's way

His strategy was always offensive. The campaigns of his early career in Italy were conducted in relatively small areas and with relatively small numbers. In Italy 35,000 men might be spread over a front of twenty miles, while Napoleon manoeuvred to concentrate superior strength at the weak point of the enemy's yet more extended front. He always kept his eye on developments in neighbouring areas, and he planned his campaigns to unfold in such a way that the maximum political advantage could be seized immediately the actual fighting ended successfully – although his foreign minister Talleyrand felt that he exploited his victories too thoroughly to be diplomatic. After 1805 Napoleon developed a new strategical technique suitable for armies of 200,000 men and commensurate with the increased range of his political concerns. The army corps, a self-contained formation consisting of two or three divisions, had been introduced. Part of the secret of his success remained rapid and accurate movement. He would use a strong army corps as an advance-guard to pin down the enemy, while the other corps manoeuvred with precision to prise the enemy forces apart, outflank or encircle them, or deliver the final shattering blow.

Napoleon's tactics were also offensive, and long prepared. He did as much as possible in advance to determine the course of the battle, but he also had a perfect sense of timing in a fight. As he said, 'the fate of a battle is a question of a single moment', and 'there is a moment in engagements when the least manoeuvre is decisive and gives victory; it is the one drop of water which makes the vessel run over'. His eye for ground was outstanding. Caulaincourt wrote that 'he seemed to extract men, horses and guns from the very bowels of the earth'.

Infantry was the chief arm of Napoleon's armies. In principle the infantry was deployed in *ordre mixte*, a formation of some battalions in line and some in column. The advantage of a line formation, which most other armies used exclusively, was that it produced the maximum firepower from the troops, whereas only the first two ranks or so of a column could use their muskets. But on the other hand inadequately trained troops would not fire steadily, and the psychological impact of massed troops in column was considerable. Columns had been advocated in certain circumstances by Guibert, and had already proved their worth in the revolutionary wars. From the Italian campaigns onwards the French armies used the *ordre mixte* with great success, varying their tactical combinations according to the terrain and opposition. The basic pattern was that skirmishers harassed the enemy; then battalions in line formation contained them, weakening them to some extent and preventing them from concentrating; the column then broke through the disorganized and depleted enemy line. These tactics constantly proved successful in battle.

The weapon of the infantry was the smooth-bored, muzzle-loading flint-lock of the eighteenth century. It was not very efficient since the flint had frequently to be replaced, the barrel became fouled by the coarse powder, and the powder itself was useless when damp. The most highly-trained soldiers could fire two rounds a minute. In fact, Napoleon bothered very little about developing the army's firepower by training. The ball would carry effectively not much more than 200 yards, at which range it was subject to an error of 9 feet. The more accurate rifle had been invented, but it was slow to operate and expensive, and therefore was little used.

Himself a gunner, Napoleon's most original contribution to tactics was in his use of artillery. He was fortunate in that now for the first time technological and industrial

volutionary infantryman

Revolutionary officer

Napoleonic grenadier

goon of the Imperial Guard

Officer of the Imperial Guard

Napoleonic hussar

Napoleon bolstered the morale of his troops by providing magnificent uniforms for the enthusiastic volunteers of the Revolutionary armies.

advance made it possible for a commander to use artillery lavishly. Hitherto artillery had merely been scattered along the front of a formation, to hamper the enemy troops as they formed up and to weaken their front before the real battle began. Napoleon reorganized the artillery into regiments, and exploited the mobility of Gribeauval's horse artillery. In battle he concentrated his guns – 200 of them at Borodino – and used them to blast holes in the ranks of the enemy before launching the infantry columns. As he continued on his career, and the quality of his troops began to decline, so Napoleon used ever more artillery and attached increasing tactical importance to it. There was nothing new about the guns themselves. They were smooth-bored, muzzle-loading and fired by coarse powder, and their fire was neither very rapid nor accurate. Two rounds a minute was possible, and a 12-pounder could carry 3,500 yards.

Cavalry retained its previous functions of reconnaissance, providing cover in advance and retreat, and conducting minor operations at a distance from the main army. It took time to build up a strong cavalry force after the revolution, since it was expensive and the cavalry regiments had been *par excellence* the aristocratic ones. Napoleon changed the organization of the cavalry, and gave it an important function in battle. With the development of the division, an independent unit of all arms 6,000 to 9,000 strong, cavalry was needed in smaller units than in the past, and in a more intimate and flexible relation to infantry. The light cavalry, the *chasseurs* and hussars, were the divisional and army corps cavalry. The number of heavy cavalry regiments was reduced by almost half; the *cuirassiers*, armed with sabre, breast-plate and back-plate, were not divisional cavalry, but were kept in massed formations to deliver heavy charges at the appropriate moment in battle. The medium cavalry were the dragoons, who ceased to be just mounted infantry. They, and some of the light cavalry, formed the main cavalry reserve, the function of which was to follow up victory with an energetic pursuit to ensure that the defeated remnants of the enemy army were completely destroyed – as happened in the Ulm and Jena campaigns. Napoleon's greatest cavalry officer was Joachim Murat, his own brother-in-law whom he later made king of Naples. Murat was impetuous and temperamental, but he was an inspiring leader.

One of the principles of the revolution was *la carrière ouverte aux talents*, and Napoleon's own career bears out the reality of this. Every man in the French army was said, if he was good enough, to carry a marshal's *bâton* in his knapsack. Of the twenty-six marshals created by Napoleon only two were of noble birth. However, while Napoleon was interested in talent rather than origin, he soon ceased to believe in *égalité*. The marshals were loaded with honours, from the new *Légion d'Honneur* to kingdoms. The military schools such as Saint-Cyr were for an *élite*. Crack regiments were formed, most notably the Imperial Guard. No one was eligible to be a guardsman who had not served in four campaigns, been wounded twice, or distinguished himself by some outstanding deed. But he was then paid more than the men of any other regiment, he had the best barracks and rations, and he escorted the emperor. Distinctions and ranks were multiplied in the army. There were gorgeous ceremonial uniforms. All this offended the pure principles of the revolution, but it was good for morale.

Some of the marshals, and many others too, were able soldiers. Apart from Berthier and Murat already mentioned, four others are worth particular notice: Davout, Masséna, Ney and Soult. Davout first fought with Napoleon in Egypt, where he became totally devoted to his master; his qualities were those of a regimental officer, a first-class

organizer and disciplinarian, feared but also respected by his men. But besides that he
was a tough fighter, and he understood Napoleon's mind to the full. In 1806 he won a
valuable victory against heavy odds over the Prussians at Auerstädt, and he did outstandingly well in Russia.

Masséna, according to Napoleon, possessed 'military qualities before which one
should kneel'. He was a useful assistant to Napoleon in Italy in 1796, he checked the
terrible Russian army of Suvorov in Switzerland in 1799, but he was beaten by Wellington in the Peninsula.

Ney was another great cavalry leader, and when commanding the rearguard in the
retreat from Moscow in 1812 he justified Napoleon's accolade of 'the bravest of the
brave'. But Waterloo was to show up Ney's weakness; when all was lost his judgment
vanished; he was later tried by court-martial, convicted, and shot in Paris on 7th
December 1815. Soult was an able and reliable tactician and organizer. Others, such as
Marmont, the artillery expert, and Augereau, a brave, dashing and brutal leader,
deserve also to be mentioned. All these men, however, were under the shadow of Napoleon; without his mastery and inspiration they would have been lesser soldiers.

By 1805 Napoleon was set on building an empire, and in the summer of that year the
Third Coalition – Britain, Austria and Russia – was formed against him. It was clear to
him by then that he had no hope of invading England, and he therefore turned his
attention eastwards. By August vast forces were assembling against him, but they were
still scattered. The main axis of the conflict was to be the Danube valley, running
through Austria and pointing to Russia. Eighty-four thousand Austrians in Italy, under
the command of the ablest enemy general the archduke Charles, could be barred off by
50,000 men under Masséna. Otherwise Napoleon had to deal with an Austrian army of
58,000 men on the Danube under Mack, and two Russian armies – one about to advance
through Galicia under Kutusov and the other mobilizing in Poland. Further operations
were threatening in the Low Countries and southern Italy, but these were not the main
concern and could be held in control. If Napoleon did not strike first his enemies were
likely by the early winter to assemble 140,000 men at Ulm, at the head of the Danube,
pointing into France. He calculated that he had less distance to travel from Boulogne,
where his army was still massed, to Ulm, than the Russians had. He decided therefore to
strike early and fast, and deal with his enemies singly, first wiping out the Austrian army
at Ulm and then moving on down the Danube to deal with the Russians.

Napoleon's staff system served him at its best as he planned the march of 150,000 men
from the English Channel to the Danube in the late summer of 1805. To conceal his
strength and intentions from the Austrians he rejected the most direct route through the
Black Forest, and moved through Würtemberg and Franconia south-eastwards, striking
the Danube beyond Ulm and taking the Austrians in rear. The *Grande Armée* marched
dispersed in seven columns. Besides the marching infantry there were 22,000 cavalry
and 1,000 horse artillery, under the overall command of Murat. Seven thousand men of
the Guard under Bessières, with the emperor, set out ahead with the cavalry. The
departures of the various forces were graduated so that in twenty-four marches all
should converge along the Rhine from Mannheim to Strasbourg, and then move north of
the Black Forest, marching altogether on an 80-mile front. Supplies were laid on at
scheduled halting places.

A diversion by the French in the Black Forest lured Mack up the Danube so that he

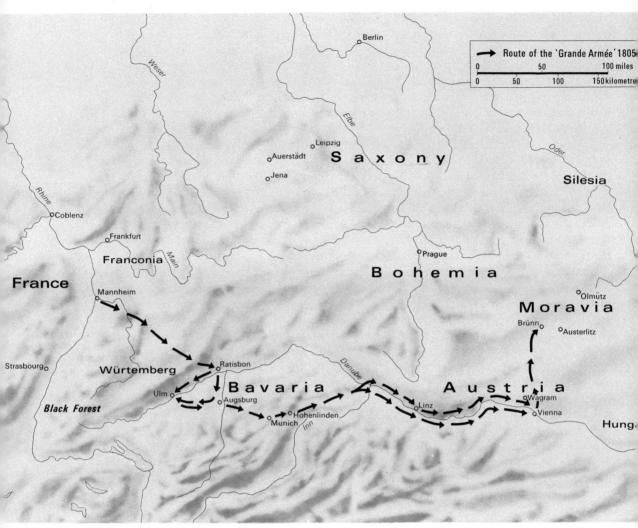

The Austerlitz campaign, 1805

could be cut off from behind. The *Grande Armée* followed its marching programme precisely. The daily pattern of the march was much as it was when Marlborough's army had marched to the Danube in 1704: starting at dawn, doing between eight and twenty-five miles a day, and stopping in the middle of the day at a prepared camp. Morale was high in the army until the last stages, when supplies became less regular and the weather turned bad. On 7th October the first four corps crossed the Danube. On the 9th Ulm was invested. Eighteen thousand Austrians who tried to break out were hounded down by the French cavalry, and after ten days Mack surrendered with his remaining 30,000 men. The first phase of Napoleon's strategy had culminated in a bloodless and complete victory.

It now seemed likely that the Prussians would also mobilize against the French. This reinforced Napoleon's view that bold and swift offensive action was the best plan, and on 26th October the army once more pressed down the Danube towards Vienna. But the men were tired, the weather was wintry, and Kutusov's 65,000 Russians were in front of them. The campaign was now a fight rather than a promenade. Napoleon wanted to encircle Kutusov, but the Russians, while slowing the advance of the French, kept dodging backwards out of reach. At one point Mortier's corps was all but cut off by the Russians. Vienna was entered on 14th November, and yielded valuable military stores. But Napoleon received the news of Trafalgar at about this time; his army was in the centre of a hostile Europe; it seemed that he would be unable to catch Kutusov before he should be reinforced by the second Russian army, and possibly a Prussian army. It looked indeed as if Napoleon was trapped.

But he laid his counter-trap in Moravia. It was defensible country and he halted there to rest his army, while devising a way of provoking the enemy to attack him. He was aware that the Russo-Austrian army, now at Olmütz, was continually increasing in size. It already numbered 85,000, with the expectation of 60,000 more from Poland, and with the possibility of 80,000 Austrians breaking through the Alps to aid them. But the Prussians were hardly beginning to get under arms. Napoleon had a month or so to play with. His plan was to lure the Russians to attack him by showing a weak front. Kutusov was allowed to see no more than 50,000 men at Brünn, the corps of Lannes and Soult, the Guard and three divisions of cavalry. But in fact more than 20,000 others under Bernadotte and Davout were in reserve, scattered in corps forty or sixty miles back but ready to move up at twenty-four hours' notice. The enemy would think that they had a numerical advantage of two to one, whereas in fact the numbers were not far short of equal.

From about 21st November Napoleon was sure of his ground and had decided in his mind the general tactical approach to the battle which he was planning to bring about. Between Brünn and Olmütz was a quadrilateral. The north of this area was bounded by a straight line of wooded heights, known as the mountains of Moravia. Just south and parallel with the hills ran the main road, and a turning to the south-east ran off it to the village of Austerlitz three miles away. Two streams descending from the mountains converged a little south of the road, to form a marshy rivulet called the Goldbach, which flowed on southward until marshy lakes bounded the southern end of the area. There were seven villages on the Goldbach whose names are marked on the map. The stream was not an obstacle, but it delimited the two halves of the terrain. West of it was a flat plain stretching to the well-fortified town of Brünn, which was in French hands. East of the Goldbach was a plateau called the Pratzen, rising gradually 350 feet from the stream and dropping more steeply the other side. Napoleon decided to station his forces, based on Brünn, on the eastern side of the Goldbach. The allies, concentrated at Olmütz, would hardly be able to resist the temptation to try and cut off the French from Vienna and from their retreat to the south-west by attacking their right. Napoleon deliberately exposed his communications with Vienna, and bunched his forces together on the road and at the foot of the mountains so as to increase the temptation for the allies to envelop his right with their larger forces. He was confident that if they would only swallow the bait he could defeat them overwhelmingly on ground of his own choosing.

There was much debate in the allied camp, where the tsar Alexander I had now taken supreme command, on the advisability of attack. Kutusov argued that everything was

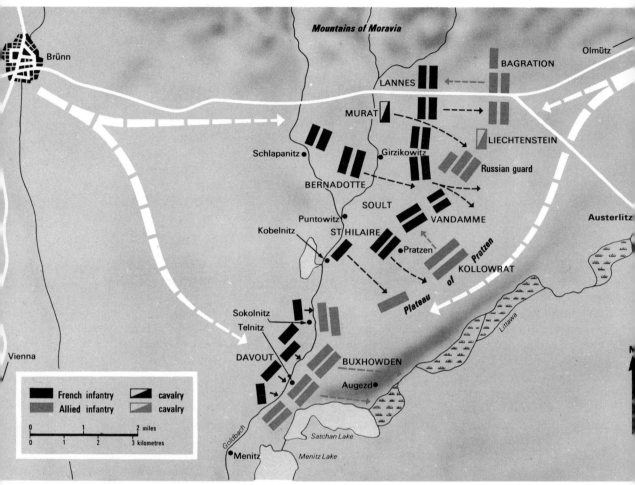

The battle of Austerlitz

to be gained by delaying until they were reinforced and the French were further depleted. But Alexander, young, vainglorious and urged on by sycophantic courtiers, was persuaded that he really did have Napoleon in a trap. The Russian troops were in poor physical shape after months of continuous marching, but they were fine soldiers all the same – in 1799 under Suvorov's command the Russians had cleared northern Italy, fighting in masses like battering-rams. Unfortunately the best commander on the allied side, the archduke Charles, was not present. The detailed planning of the attack fell to Weirother, the Austrian chief of staff.

The allied advance began on 1st December, and in the evening Weirother outlined his tactical scheme. The allies had nearly 90,000 men, most of whom were Russians, and 278 cannon. The plan was to approach the French right from the north-east, the head of the army crossing the Goldbach between Telnitz and Sokolnitz and then wheeling

Austerlitz as depicted by a contemporary artist. Napoleon took advantage of the hilly country to force his opponents to fight on ground of his own choosing

round in three columns to attack the French in flank from the south. A fourth column was to engage the French front from the Pratzen, and further north another corps would hold the French on the line of the road. On the night of 1st December, Kutusov and several other senior Russian officers were drunk – hardly a good beginning to a battle.

By 1st December, when Napoleon was certain that the enemy were moving, Bernadotte's corps had already joined him and Davout was on his way. During the afternoon the emperor inspected his army, riding at the head of a group of divisional commanders and staff officers, dressed in the green, white and red uniform of a colonel of the *chasseurs à cheval* of the Guard, his *redingote gris* blowing in the breeze. No doubt he was consciously the picture of his legend. He ignored the scruffy appearance of his men, but he repeatedly checked that weapons were in working order. He might have been anxious that Davout's corps had not yet arrived, but in fact he could rely on the co-ordination and mobility of his army, for at 4 o'clock it was reported that Davout was completing a march of ninety miles in two days. The French forces numbered altogether 61,000 fit men, and 139 cannon. Although inferior in numbers Napoleon's forces were soundly positioned for the coming battle, and he had the great advantage of knowing the enemy plan, and knowing that it was bad – because he had forced it on them. Soult commanded the centre, opposite the Pratzen, with great strength in reserve. Lannes was on the left, together with Murat and most of the cavalry. Davout was on the right. That evening Napoleon published a proclamation to his army in which he revealed his scheme: 'The positions we occupy are strong, and as they advance to turn my right, they will expose their flank to me.' During the night, when it was reported that the Russians were still moving south, he moved some of his troops in the centre slightly to the right.

A curious incident took place after dark. Some straw caught fire, and a few French soldiers spread the fire – thinking it was part of a fireworks demonstration to celebrate the anniversary of the emperor's coronation. For a few minutes the flames burned fiercely, and in a great surge of enthusiasm and devotion 30,000 men acclaimed Napoleon.

As Napoleon later wrote, 'the Battle of Austerlitz was nothing but the outcome of the plan of campaign in Moravia'. The battle on 2nd December went as he had willed. The allied attack was strong and persistent, though it was clumsily organized and throughout the day the allied command was lamentable. With a minimal force, Davout held the right all day. A mist concealed the French centre until, in *ordre mixte* – skirmishers, artillery, line and column – Soult's men attacked the Russians in flank at the Pratzen, gaining complete surprise. During the morning the allies pressed the French right; but the French consolidated themselves better in the centre and cut the enemy army in two. The last area in which battle was joined was the north, and there an equal and hard struggle took place. Murat's cavalry, operating between the left and the centre, cut the allied right off from their centre by midday, and the Russians there began a slow with-drawal. Napoleon himself by this time was on the Pratzen, and two divisions of his centre under St Hilaire and Vandamme were exerting a cross pressure on the defeated remnants of the Russian centre on the eastern slope. All which now remained was to relieve the French right, and to ensure that the allies were thoroughly beaten at all points. A last desperate charge of the Russian Imperial Guard was repelled from the Pratzen. The French centre then turned to destroy the allied left. Some of the Russian infantry fought their way out to the south; others were drowned as the ice on the lakes broke beneath them; most were captured. Although the enemy left was caught, their right was not prevented from getting away in good order – Murat, having received no orders, hesitated to leave the centre altogether and encircle the enemy's wing. By 5 o'clock firing ceased. All told the allies had lost 27,000 men and 180 guns. The French losses were about 7,000.

The immediate consequence of Austerlitz in December 1805 was that Austria fell out of the Coalition. In 1806 Prussia attempted to prevent Napoleon finally dominating all Germany, and mobilized an army of 130,000, still complacent in the dated glory of Frederick the Great. In a three weeks' campaign the Prussians were crushed, by the double defeat of Jena and Auerstädt and by Napoleon's rapid pursuit and occupation of Berlin. The next year the French, fighting now in north-east Europe, snatched a narrow

During 1809 the Napoleonic armies consolidated their conquest of central Europe. They cross the Danube by an improvised bridge before Wagram *above* ; they take Ratisbon by storm *below*

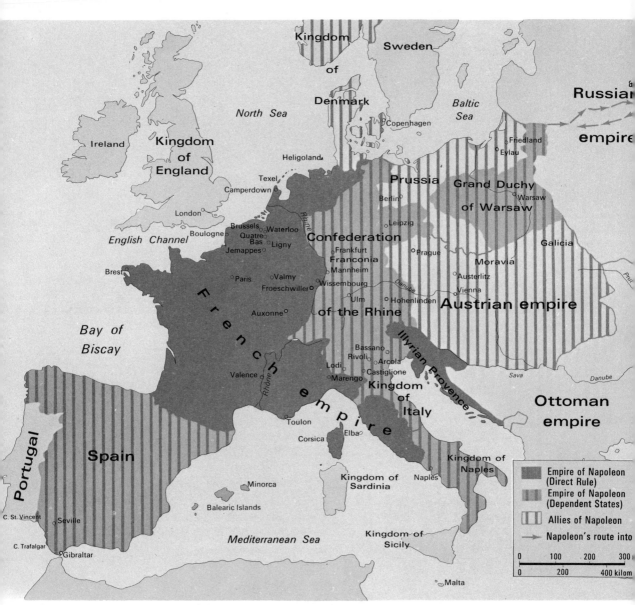

Napoleon's empire

and bloody victory over the Russians at Eylau. In June 1807 Napoleon defeated them again at Friedland, inflicting a loss of 25,000 men, and the tsar thought it best to come to terms.

The victories of 1805–7 raised Napoleon to the pinnacle of his fortune. From then till 1812 he was master of all western Europe. His empire stretched from Seville to Warsaw and from Naples to the Baltic – half a million square miles containing 44 million subjects. In much of that area valuable and enduring reforms were introduced: equality before the law, the abolition of serfdom, religious toleration, civil rights for Jews, secular education, unified systems of justice, road-building, single customs' areas, national armies – to mention a few.

The problem of Britain, however, still remained unsolved, and in November 1806 with Europe under his sway Napoleon opened a full-scale economic war against his arch-enemy. His intention was to seal off the continent from British ships and commerce. The Berlin Decree declared the British Isles to be 'in a state of blockade'; all commerce with them was forbidden and all goods in transit between Britain and her colonies were to be seized. If he could do it no other way Napoleon would 'conquer the sea by the power of the land'. As the English retaliated Napoleon extended the operation of this 'Continental System'. But so long as Britain ruled the sea there was no possibility, in fact, of Napoleon starving her into defeat by cutting off supplies of food and raw materials from her colonies.

The beginning of Napoleon's downfall can be sought at almost any stage of his career. It can perhaps be attributed to the fatal moment of excessive ambition on the evening after Lodi in 1796. The mistake may have been made in 1801 when he imposed the humiliating Peace of Lunéville on Austria instead of coming to terms with her and joining forces to defeat England. Possibly, considering his genius, nothing was un-reasonable until his head was turned by the victories of Austerlitz and Jena, and he set out on the deluded path of mastering the world, and so to Spain and Moscow. He was driven back from Russia ignominiously in 1812, but by 1813 he had another army. In 1813 he suffered his first major personal defeat in battle at Leipzig, and in 1814 he had to defend the frontiers of France herself. By then the demands of conscription and the evident selfishness of his ambition had lost him the support of the French nation. But Austria still offered good terms, and even at that stage he was not ruined. His campaign of that year was one of his most brilliant: he repeatedly divided his enemies and defeated them in detail. Napoleon's military genius did not fail until 1815, and there is no clear path of political decline. But Napoleon himself attributed his ruin to the 'Spanish ulcer'.

One small flaw in the triumph of 1806 set in movement a train of events which sapped Napoleon's strength and gave encouragement to his enemies. In 1806 Portugal refused to accept the Continental System. Like most other countries of Europe she did not want to be dominated by France, and she wished to trade with England. Unlike most, she resisted. In 1807 Napoleon sent an army under Junot into the Peninsula and in the following year the king of Spain was treacherously deposed. The hatred of the Spanish and Portuguese peoples was aroused, and French armies from now on were harried by guerrillas and priests. Europe was astounded when two French divisions surrendered to the Spaniards at Baylén, and this surrender sapped the morale of the *Grande Armée*. Such was the situation in the Peninsula in 1808 when the British expeditionary force landed there under Sir John Moore.

At first Napoleon took command in Spain, and almost succeeded in trapping Moore's contingent at Corunna. But events elsewhere in Europe called away from the Peninsula the man whose presence at the head of an army was estimated by Wellington to be worth 40,000 troops, and he never returned. So far the only effective contribution of England to the military efforts of her continental allies had been monetary subsidies.

But now, with strong popular support against the French and backed by secure communications at sea, the British were at last able themselves to get a real foothold on the continent. In August 1808 Sir Arthur Wellesley, later Duke of Wellington, landed in Portugal with 13,000 men and defeated the French at Vimeiro – though by the stupidity of Wellington's seniors Junot was able to extricate his army by the Convention of Cintra.

Wellington was born of an aristocratic Irish family in 1769, the same year as Napoleon. He was educated at Eton where he showed some promise at mathematics and music, but he left that school when he was fifteen. In 1787 he entered the army, not out of vocation or ambition, but because he had family interest and it was the normal career for the less bright younger sons. He did little regular service in his regiment, but in 1796 he went to India. He was by then almost thirty, and he set about mastering his profession, studying all the best authorities on military science and on India. At this time he was said to be 'cheerful, free of speech and expansive among his particular friends but rather reserved in general society'. He always remained witty, but increasingly he was to conceal his sensitivity beneath a somewhat crusty exterior. His natural lethargy and strong emotions were unfailingly controlled by the strongest self-discipline.

In India he received a sound military training, building up a considerable local reputation. No British commander had previously worked out a tactical technique for dealing with the hordes of Maratha horsemen, but Wellington found the answer with a line formation. His supply lines were well organized to give him a long line into the heart of the enemy country and mobility once he got there. His most notable engagements were the storming of Ahmednagar, one of the strongest fortresses in southern India, and his victory in the very bloody battle of Assaye in 1803. Shortly afterwards peace was made on terms advantageous to the British, due principally to Wellington's victories.

In 1805, after nine years in India, he returned to England. Although the reputation he had gained in India counted for nothing at home, he had accumulated very valuable experience – in pitched battles against heavy numerical odds, the organization of supply, forced marches, sieges, and the coaxing of difficult allies. Between 1805 and 1808 he occupied himself with politics, becoming Chief Secretary for Ireland. It was his political interest rather than his position in the army which secured him his next appointments – to take part in the abortive expeditions to north-west Europe in 1806 and 1807, and then in the expeditions to the Peninsula. There, following his success in 1808, Wellington returned in April 1809 to command 21,000 men.

The British army of this period differed in many ways from the French. Most notably it was not a national army but an old-style small professional army, of the type which military theorists were then writing off as obsolete. The contrast between the careers of Wellington and Napoleon is characteristic. Officers' commissions in the British army were obtained by purchase and interest, and were normally available only to men of gentle birth. Apart from six months' drill and the optional reading of a few War Office pamphlets, most officers were untrained. It cannot be said that the soldiers were recruited from the criminal classes, but they were not on the whole the best elements of the population. Yet the system worked, despite the element of amateurism and the social gulf. Officers and men for the most part got on well, discipline though sometimes savage was generally secured by good will, and the army was an efficient fighting force. This was an improvement on the situation in the past, and was the achievement of General Moore, the Duke of York, and Wellington.

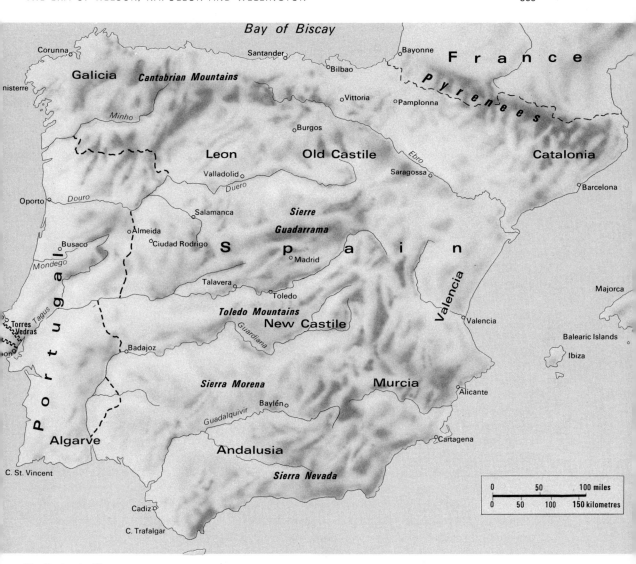

The Peninsular War

In 1803, in his camp at Shorncliffe, Moore had revolutionized discipline and training, by deliberately relying on cooperation rather than coercion, and proving by the resultant high morale and efficiency that this was the better way. The administrative head of the army was the Duke of York, an able man who founded a military academy and a staff college, and encouraged the rise of young officers of ability. Wellington himself, in the Peninsula, attached great importance to the care and training of his troops. Finance, transport and supply were the domain of his able Commissary-General, Kennedy, who rarely failed to provide adequate supplies of clothing, food, cooking utensils, tents, blankets, boots and pay. Unlike the French, the British used a magazine system of supplies and paid for the products of the country; this was sound policy since it gained the support of the native populations of the areas of operation, even that of south-western France in 1814. Part of the purpose of Wellington's tough discipline was to prevent excesses among the soldiers, such as drunkenness, which might be harmful to their health. The Surgeon-General, McGrigor, could rely on his commander's full support (unlike Napoleon's Baron Larrey). Again, unlike Napoleon, Wellington thought it worth while to give his soldiers thorough training in the use of their weapons.

Before the Peninsular War the basic unit of the British army had normally been the brigade or regiment. Pride in long-standing regimental traditions was a most important factor in maintaining good morale – a problem since the army had achieved so little success in the field since the Seven Years' War. But Wellington established the divisional system. The division was a formation of all arms and services, self-sufficient and detachable if necessary from the main force and, with training, capable of extended manoeuvre. To raise the numbers of his troops in the Peninsula, Wellington incorporated Portuguese troops into the British divisions, usually in a ratio of one Portuguese brigade, which included some British officers, to two British brigades. He had one division composed only of Portuguese. The training and organization of the Portuguese forces was ably taken in hand by General Beresford. Occasionally Wellington formed army corps, but this was exceptional; the division was the basic unit. Eventually there were ten of them; among the better known of his divisional commanders were Hill, Graham, Picton and Craufurd. Wellington was also responsible for the introduction of the first British corps of sappers and military police.

As he gained in experience in the Peninsula, Wellington's staff and intelligence system became more efficient. He had a close understanding with his Quartermaster-General, Murray, who not only attended to the organization of encampments and troop movements, but was responsible for topographical intelligence and was an invaluable assistant to Wellington in strategical and tactical planning. Other members of the staff whom Wellington probably saw daily were the Commissary-General, the Adjutant-General, the Inspector-General of Hospitals, the Commanding Officer of Artillery and the Commanding Royal Engineer. Wellington did not differ much from Napoleon in his attention to the important details of preparation, and in his capacity for getting through quantities of work. He was perhaps better at delegation, and his team was happier and more loyal than Napoleon's. But Wellington, unlike Napoleon and Blücher, had no chief of staff. The staff work, normally supervised and directed by one man, was shared amongst three officials – a Military Secretary, the Adjutant-General, and the Quartermaster-General. This would not have suited me at all; but apparently it was adequate a hundred and fifty years ago when war was not so complicated as it has become in the mid-twentieth century.

Besides preparation behind the lines Wellington attached great importance to intelligence information about the enemy, and he later said that he thought much of his success was due to his care in studying what was happening 'upon the other side of the hill'. Accordingly he built up a good intelligence organization. At the beginning of the Peninsular War no reliable maps of the area existed, but Murray's staff gradually remedied this situation in the areas that mattered. Efficient reconnaissance preceded the army's movements. Cavalry patrols and individual officers were sent forward every day; their function was not only to examine the ground but also to discover the enemy lay-out.

News travelled fast and accurately in the native population, and good information could generally be had, at a price, from the guerrilla bands and in the villages. A network of 'confidential persons' was built up over the Peninsula. The bulk of the intelligence thus gathered was received personally by Wellington, who required the highest standards of accuracy.

Wellington's strategy in the Peninsula was conditioned by the numerical superiority of his enemies. He began with 21,000 men, and his army at no time exceeded 80,000. The French rarely had less than 250,000, commanded by Masséna, Marmont or Soult. Wellington depended on Portugal as his essential base of operations. Portugal must be held and then, if possible, he could advance from there. Moore had regarded Portugal as indefensible, but Wellington disagreed. There were five gaps in the mountain frontier of Portugal, but with the support of the Spaniards and Portuguese he reckoned a strong defensive area could be organized. The first necessity was to clear the French out of the country, at any rate for the time being, in order to give him time to prepare the defences. Soult was attacked and beaten at Oporto, and Wellington advanced into Spain. His Spanish allies stupidly got themselves defeated and lost southern Spain, but at Talavera Wellington won a victory, and then retired back into Portugal.

By the winter of 1809–10 it was more than ever likely that the French, triumphant in Spain and Austria, would concentrate massive forces to finish off Wellington's army in Portugal. Some 10,000 reinforcements were sent out to him from England, but no more were available. He decided to make his stand in 1810 near the frontier, but he also prepared an immensely powerful defensive position to protect Lisbon – the Lines of Torres Vedras. Portuguese labourers supervised by English engineers constructed the defences: two lines of mutually supporting batteries and redoubts running for thirty miles through the hills between the Tagus and the sea. In 1956, while serving in NATO, I reconnoitred the whole length of the Torres Vedras position and well appreciate its great natural strength.

In May 1810 Masséna took command of the French *Armée du Portugal* and began the advance to drive Wellington into the sea. Wellington resisted the temptation to try and save the Spanish frontier fortresses of Ciudad Rodrigo and Almeida, and in September, as Masséna's 72,000 men advanced into Portugal along three routes, Wellington retired before him with his 49,000. At the Mondego river he reckoned that he could afford to give battle, and there on the ridge of Busaco he defeated Masséna.

Wellington was as good at tactics as he was at other aspects of generalship. Napoleon and Wellington were both believers in firepower, and their troops used virtually the same musket and bayonet, which the British called the 'Brown Bess'. The difference was that Wellington's troops were well enough disciplined and trained to stand up in line against the French columns. That being the case it was an easy calculation that they would win, since they could bring to bear at least four times the firepower of their enemy. Wellington's normal tactics were to base his main strength on a double line of infantry, drawn up on the reverse slope of a ridge, since this screened his forces from the eyes and artillery of the enemy. In front of the line there were skirmishers, and the flanks were protected by cavalry and artillery. This was his lay-out at Busaco. He used no massed artillery in the Napoleonic style, though the mobility of the English horse artillery impressed the French. Since his cavalry was not numerous he did not generally follow up his victories by pursuit.

The impact that Wellington's army in battle made on its enemies was described by Bugeaud, later a French marshal:

The English generally occupied well chosen defensive positions having a certain command, and they showed only a portion of their forces. The usual artillery action first took place. Soon, in great haste, without studying the position, without taking time to examine if there were means to make a flank attack, we marched straight on, taking the bull by the horns. About 1,000 yards from the English line the men became excited, spoke to one another and hurried their march; the column began to be a little confused. The English remained quite silent with ordered arms, and from their steadiness appeared to be a long red wall. This steadiness invariably produced an effect on the young soldiers. Very soon we got nearer, shouting '*Vive l'Empereur! en avant! à la baionnette!*' Shakos were raised on the muzzles of the muskets; the column began to double, the ranks got into confusion, the agitation produced a tumult; shots were fired as we advanced. The English line remained silent, still and immovable, with ordered arms, even when we were only 300 yards distant, and it appeared to ignore the storm about to break. The contrast was striking; in our inmost thoughts each felt that the enemy was a long time in firing, and this fire reserved for so long, would be very unpleasant when it did come. Our ardour cooled. The moral power of steadiness, which nothing shakes (even if it be only appearance), over disorder which stupefies itself with noise, overcame our minds. At this moment of intense excitement, the English wall shouldered arms; an indescribable feeling rooted many of our men to the spot; they began to fire. The enemy's steady concentrated volleys swept our ranks; decimated, we turned round seeking to recover our equilibrium; then three deafening cheers broke the silence of our opponents; at the third they were on us, pushing our disorganized flight.

After the victory of Busaco, Wellington astonished both his own army and the enemy by continuing to retreat. Masséna followed him up to the Lines of Torres Vedras; but there he was finally held. Through the winter of 1810–11 the armies faced each other. The British were secure and well supplied; the French were far from their bases and they could make no impression on the Lines. In March 1811 Masséna retreated, and Wellington began the long, slow advance which was to lead in three years to victory in 1814. The frontier area of Almeida, Ciudad Rodrigo and Badajoz was gained in 1811 and 1812, not without much manoeuvre, and with constant attention still to the preservation of the Portuguese base of operations. Disagreements among the French marshals in Spain and misguided instructions from Napoleon, sent from as far away as Moscow, assisted the British, but the success of the operations was, most positively, the achievement of Wellington and his soldiers. His defensive genius and his skill in manoeuvre did not mean that he would not strike hard when the favourable moment for battle came. With two great victories, at Salamanca in 1812 and at Vittoria in 1813, he eventually cleared the Peninsula of its invaders.

The effect on Napoleon's fortunes of what he long tried to convince himself was a Spanish sideshow was profoundly damaging in various respects. It was a serious drain on his troops; for example, if he had not detached troops to the Peninsula in 1809 he might have avoided the repulse at Essling. It was also a training-ground for his marshals in disobedience and acceptance of defeat. The penetration of Wellington's army into south-west France by 1814 came at the same time that Napoleon was pressed back within his frontiers in the north-east. Furthermore the courage and success of the Spanish and Portuguese peoples gave courage to Europe. The Germans had been subjected by fear and force, but from 1808 a powerful surge of nationalism rose up against the alien French – epitomized by Fichte in Prussia and by Hofer in Austria. Alexander also quarrelled with Napoleon, and in 1812 the Russians inflicted a defeat of the greatest magnitude on him in the Moscow campaign, destroying most of the original *Grande Armée*. Leipzig followed in 1813. In 1814 came abdication, and in May of that year the fallen emperor arrived in Elba; there his sovereignty was recognized: the former master of Europe ruling over a few square miles. He was then only forty-five. Paraphrasing the words of Sir Winston Churchill in the second volume of *The World Crisis 1911–1918*, the nations of Europe might well have said: 'Surely, Frenchmen, for history it is enough!' But it wasn't.

In 1815 Napoleon came back. He suffered his final decisive defeat at the hands of allied armies under Wellington and Blücher at Waterloo, near Brussels. It was the first time the two great commanders had faced each other in battle, and neither was at his best in this campaign. The battle was a very equal affair, but the outcome was, as Wellington put it, that 'Napoleon . . . just moved forward in the old style, in columns, and was driven off in the old style'. Peace came to Europe after twenty-three years, and Napoleon was exiled to St Helena where he died in 1821. Wellington continued his political career; he became prime minister from 1828 to 1830 and won civil rights for the Catholics. Like his vanquished and dead enemy, Wellington became more and more of a legend. He died in 1852.

In this chapter we have dealt with three commanders whose names will live in history. It is curious that the two most famous generals of their time, Napoleon and Wellington, were born in the same year, 1769; it is also remarkable that in the long struggle between British and French arms in their time, the two never met in battle until Waterloo in June 1815 – the last battle each was to fight. I have studied both of them deeply since my days as a cadet at the Royal Military College, Sandhurst, in 1907, and to conclude this chapter will give my personal opinion on certain aspects of their careers. I will keep Nelson until last, since I can speak of him, a sailor, only from the viewpoint of a soldier – who although he has had naval forces under his command in peace has never commanded them in war.

NAPOLEON

Millions of words have been written in an endeavour to explain the secrets of his success; many writers have been severe critics. But when all is said, it has to be admitted that he had few equals – and no betters. He had a magnetic personality and all who came into contact with him were immediately impressed by the energy and penetrating intelligence of their commander. When he received command of the French Army of Italy in 1796, aged only twenty-six, he found that army unpaid, poorly clothed, ill shod, hungry, nearly mutinous, and disillusioned. Within the short space of seven days sullen discontent was transformed into willing cooperation. Napoleon had given the army back its soul. The campaign in Italy which followed in 1796–7 was probably the most brilliant the world had then seen. In those years a great military genius was loosed upon the world, and the world has never been quite the same since.

The retreat from Moscow

He was a master of strategy, with a wonderful tactical eye for ground. His methods were, in essence, simple – mobility, concentration, morale; these are all evident in his campaigns in Europe with the *Grande Armée*. Although continually outnumbered in the theatre of war, he seldom fought a battle without local superiority at the point of conflict. Marshal Saxe wrote in *Mes Rêveries*: 'War should be made so as to leave nothing to chance.' From my own experience of high command in war I would not agree with that statement. Napoleon was wiser; in one of his maxims he wrote: 'Secure yourself *all possible chances of success* when you decide to deliver an important engagement' (my italics). The problem really amounts to this – having taken all reasonable measures to ensure victory, how much can be left to chance? And that is where 'luck' comes in – but you must not expect luck if you are not bold.

Napoleon's judgments were not always sound. He made his first major mistake by invading Spain in 1808. Long before, a French king had said of Spain that 'it is a country where small armies are beaten and big ones starve'. He entrusted the campaign to a series of marshals, but he must be held responsible for at least some of the tragedy which was to fall on French arms. What defeated the *Grande Armée*, apart from Wellington and his soldiers, was the heat, the sun-baked countryside, and the fanatical resistance of the Spanish irregulars who killed about a hundred French soldiers daily. The emperor was always too busy in northern Europe to intervene personally in Spain; he had over-extended himself. The French left Spain in 1813.

Then consider the tragedy of 1812 in Russia. I have never understood Napoleon's reasoning at that time. In my view one of the basic rules of war is – don't march on Moscow. Hitler broke that rule and lived to regret it. It was not only the weather which led to Napoleon's defeat in Russia; it was the blunders of the man himself, and the consequent failure of discipline in the *Grande Armée*; looting began the day Moscow was entered and a rapid decline in morale set in – the French soldiers being quick to take advantage of the decline of their general, due primarily to the onslaught of the disease – cancer – which was ultimately to take his life. In Russia, Napoleon found conditions with which he was unfamiliar – a vast country with few good roads and without supplies, and a sprawling organism of state with no heart at which he could aim a decisive blow. His failure to adjust himself to these conditions is considered by many of his critics as proof that his genius was not creative; he could take over a military machine, improve it, and manipulate it with incredible skill – he could not invent a new one.

In Sir Walter Scott's life of Bonaparte published a few years after his death, an amusing story is told of his journey to Elba. It seems that he tipped the crew and the bo'sun got up to thank him, adding 'and I'm sure we all wish you better luck next time'. But it didn't work out that way!

And finally we come to Waterloo. Napoleon by that time was only occasionally his former self. It is anybody's guess as to what might have happened if he had met Wellington in battle when he was in full possession of all his vigour and drive. I will deal with Waterloo when we come to Wellington.

Many judgments have been passed on Napoleon and his deeds. It has always seemed to me that he was too ambitious. He was determined to be known as the greatest general ever, and this ambition drove him on to final defeat. But one thing can be said for certain – his victories have not been surpassed, and so long as there are soldiers he will be remembered as one of the greatest of the captains.

WELLINGTON

Wellington was a very different man from Napoleon. Whereas the latter was driven by a selfish ambition, the great principle of Wellington's life was 'duty'. Of personal ambition he knew nothing; the desire to win applause or to advance himself to positions of honour and power seems never to have moved him. As a soldier, he was a cautious and supremely able strategist; he had learned the art of warfare in India on a bullock-cart standard, and was sure and steady rather than brilliant. As a tactician he was both sure and brilliant. Above all he was a master of defence, but when opportunity offered he could be bold and aggressive – for example, as at Salamanca in July 1812.

It is curious why, at times, he made so many disparaging remarks about his soldiers – for instance, before Waterloo he wrote, 'I have an infamous army.' He is also *supposed* to have said after Waterloo – 'the battle of Waterloo was won on the playing fields of Eton'. To attribute this statement to him is wrong and ungenerous; in fact, the words were first used by the French writer Montalembert in a work published some years after Wellington's death – and have done much to harm his reputation. In any case it is inconceivable to me that he could ever have used such words after the battle, because nobody knew better than he the contribution to victory made by the young rank and file soldiers of Britain.

I would agree with John Laffin when he says in *Links of Leadership* that it was the British army that won the many battles which brought Wellington from Spain across the Pyrenees and into France – and I say this without in any way seeking to detract from his own tactical genius, leadership, and soldierly qualities which sustained him through the campaign. Laffin's is a fine tribute to the British soldier of those days.

I will conclude with a few remarks about Waterloo. No student of history should study Waterloo on 18th June 1815, without consideration of the events at Ligny and Quatre Bras on 15th and 16th June. One might just as well study *Hamlet* without the Prince. I cannot imagine a campaign being fought in the mid-twentieth century in the way Waterloo was fought. It is a nice point as to who made the worse errors – Wellington or Napoleon.

On the night of 15th June, Wellington was dancing at a ball in Brussels given by the Duke and Duchess of Richmond – his army not being deployed for battle and ready to fight effectively if surprised, although Napoleon and *his* army were within striking distance, having crossed the Belgian frontier *that morning*. Napoleon had gained complete surprise, and had placed his army between those of Wellington and Blücher – whose armies were too widely scattered to offer effective combined resistance if the initiative gained by Napoleon had been acted upon swiftly. But it wasn't. If ever victory was in the grasp of a commander, it lay on a plate on 15th June ready to be taken by Napoleon. Wellington had only himself to blame for allowing this situation to develop. To me, such neglect is almost unbelievable in a very great soldier. And yet, in spite of all, three days later overwhelming French success had been transformed into disaster, due to a series of blunders and omissions, the blame for which must be laid on Napoleon. I often wonder what he thought about it all at St Helena, where he had plenty of time for reflection! I have read that he said, 'in spite of everything I should have won that battle'. And he might well have won if he had followed up the Prussians after Ligny with his whole army, and had hammered Blücher's army to such an extent that it could not have appeared again on the battlefield as an effective fighting force for some time – and certainly not on 18th June to help Wellington at Waterloo.

And what would Wellington say if I could speak to him today and put to him the situation on 15th June as seen by me, and say to him that he had been completely misled by Napoleon's strategy ? A backhander ? Probably.

However, in spite of my comment on his errors at Waterloo, I have always considered Wellington to be the best soldier Britain has produced for many a long day – and I still think the same today as I write this book.

NELSON

From my earliest days Nelson has been one of my heroes, and when I myself began to study war it was brought home to me how much that sailor did for England. The secret of Nelson's strength was that he understood plain men and was, in turn, understood by them. He knew how to win the hearts of men. He seemed to have a magnetic influence over all who served with him; he led by love and example. There was nothing he would not do for those who served under him; there was nothing his captains and sailors would not dare for him.

Great victories on land and sea call forth admiration and respect for the victorious commander-in-chief; but they do not always evoke affection or love. The power to draw loyalty and whole-hearted service from subordinates has not always been regarded as a necessary quality for a naval commander; I have read that there have been successful admirals who have commanded through their subordinates' fear of the consequences of failure. But Nelson's amazing influence over his fellow men was perhaps as much responsible for his unique record of success in battle as were his brilliant actions. The moment he stepped on board ship some magnetic power radiated from him, a motley collection of men with no common purpose became a band of brothers, and this power radiated far beyond his own ship – being felt in every ship in the fleets he commanded. The qualities of leadership in Nelson have always appealed to me enormously.

Naval command is, in one respect, similar to that of armies on land in that the raw material of the admiral's trade is men; it is basically a great human problem, to win the hearts of the sailors. That was my problem in command – to win the hearts of the soldiers, beginning when I commanded a platoon of thirty men in battle in 1914. But in other respects naval command was vastly different in Nelson's day. Once his ships were locked in deadly combat he could do no more; no signals could be seen through the smoke of battle; no ships with broken spars and tattered sails could respond even if a lull gave a glimpse of the flagship's masts. Nelson had a more difficult task than his successors who commanded fast-moving ships in the era of steam; if his plans of approach had been faulty he could not remedy them by signal. We who live in the days of oil fuel and wireless communications are apt to forget how different conditions were in the days of sail.

Of Nelson's victories at sea, others are more competent to write in depth – and I will not attempt it. If he had to die in battle there could have been no more fitting place than in the ship wearing his flag as Vice-Admiral of the White. He died knowing that the fleet he had led in battle and the men he loved had won a great victory. When he fell on 21st October 1805, the day of his annihilating victory at Trafalgar, he left Britain a command of the world's seas so absolute that Napoleon's doom was certain – although it took another ten years to consummate – because from then on he was confined to a land strategy.

I would acclaim Nelson as the greatest naval commander of all time.

Japanese warriors of the sixteenth century in their highly decorated protective armour

PART FOUR

16 The Mongols, the Chinese and the Japanese

So far our study of warfare has not taken us beyond what today we call the Near East. We now move away to the Far East, and as the title of this chapter indicates we shall study the history of the warfare of three Asiatic peoples – all racially related but nonetheless very different from each other. I have travelled extensively in China and Japan and have been able to observe at close quarters the peoples who today live in those countries, and will say more about them shortly. A study of the map will enable the reader to see the country of the Mongols whom we shall study first. I do not know it. But I have travelled in Inner Mongolia and flown along the Great Wall and the southern edge of the Gobi Desert, and observed a portion of Outer Mongolia from the air.

The Mongols were once totally a warrior society – and perhaps the most successful the world has seen. They produced in Jenghiz Khan one of the few really great captains and conquerors. The Chinese, by contrast, were a naturally unwarlike people who waged war reluctantly under the compulsion of historical circumstances. They made no major contribution to the art of war, except for the thoughts of one great military theorist – Sun Tzu; it is, all the same, interesting to study them as a uniquely pacific people. Japanese society has, on the other hand, almost always been intensely militaristic. The Japanese developed a distinctive and outstanding warrior type, the *samurai*; they also produced at least one general of considerable note, Hideyoshi.

It is an interesting fact that after the sixteenth century, when they had encountered the newly developed superior military technology of Europe, each of these peoples, the Mongols, the Chinese and the Japanese, more or less abandoned war. Their distinctive military systems lingered in decadence into the nineteenth century, up to which point we shall deal with them here. The study of the military history of the Asiatic peoples from the middle of the nineteenth century onwards, when they began to westernize their warfare, will be examined in Part 5.

The Mongols came from the steppe-lands of Central Asia. The inhabitants of that vast area with its pastoral economy were necessarily horsemen. They were toughened by the rigour of the climate, with its extremes of heat and cold, and by living all their lives in tents and on horseback. They were bound to be fighters, since the land was poor and in the continual search for new territory the different tribes and peoples had to compete for survival. From the eternal welter of nomadic movement and conflict a leader occasionally emerged, so strong that he overshadowed the other chieftains and unified the Turkish and Mongol tribes – the Keraits, the Naimans, the Merkits and others. In the fourth century Attila was the leader of the Huns or the Hiung-nu, as they were known at opposite ends of the world. The Magyars of the ninth century were their descendants.

The most complete and sinister unification in the history of these nomads was the achievement of Jenghiz Khan (1162–1227). When born, his father, a minor Mongolian chief, called him Temuchin. When he succeeded his father at the age of thirteen he had to fight for his inheritance. Physically he was as tough, brave and resourceful as any of his race. He had confidence, ambition and eloquence, and he soon developed an exceptional ability to win devoted followers and to compose differences within his vision of a larger unanimity. In 1206, when forty-four, after incessant work and fighting he gained the title of 'khan' over the tribes, and he then assumed the name of Jenghiz Khan.

It is interesting to reflect how very few of all the commanders of the past have been 'great captains', notwithstanding that the human race has been waging wars throughout its history. Deprived of intelligent leadership, in Europe in the Middle Ages fighting men took to armour; mobility was forgotten, firepower neglected, and surprise made virtually impossible. But just at that time in Asia a great military genius appeared – Jenghiz Khan, in the front rank of great soldiers, a *grand chef* if ever there was one, whose campaigns are models in the art of war. We shall now see how he went about his business.

The Mongol peoples were primitive and barbarian. In the past the victory of one tribe over another had normally been followed by destruction and slaughter. Jenghiz Khan quickly showed the superiority of his conceptions by using his victories constructively: to unify the peoples. He elevated his victims to be his subjects, and such was his leadership that they were proud of their new status. He unified the nomads by his willpower and the fear of his strength, but also by offering the prospect of greater rewards. He organized the whole nomad fraternity for war.

Vassalage of a tribe to Jenghiz Khan was not a formality. The great men of the tribe came to serve on his staff or in his guard, tribute was paid to his treasury, and the tribe prepared itself to be a unit in the great fighting force. The tribes were numbered by tents, and allotted to their pasture grounds. Authority within the tribes was upheld, and the security of the individual was protected, by the just and inflexible *Yassa* – the legal code which Jenghiz Khan promulgated in 1206. Princes, chieftains and headmen of tribes were, for purposes of war, commanders of 'toumans' (a unit of 10,000 and the strongest in the army), of thousands and of hundreds. The decimal system prevailed from the touman down to the file of ten men. The head of the tribe was responsible for keeping his men permanently trained and equipped according to the regulations laid down, and he had to answer the khan's summons to war instantly. The khan had his own touman *d'élite*. The most senior officers of all, the commanders of armies, were the 'orloks', who numbered usually about eleven. When the nomads were unified in 1206 Jenghiz Khan ruled an empire which stretched 1,000 miles from east to west, from the Khingan Mountains (east of the Gobi Desert) to the Altai Range (north-east of Lake Balkash), incorporating in all thirty-one tribes. To this people, peace was nothing but a time in which to prepare for war.

Every man in the Mongol army was a cavalryman. Some were more heavily armed than others, and the equipment of all improved as they became more experienced and richer. There was little protective equipment. The men wore sheepskins, loose tanned leather jackets, and armour of lacquered leather plate. Some wore a shirt of raw silk – which was not penetrated by an arrowhead but was driven by it into the flesh, thus making the

The Mongols fought on horseback with a hooked lance or a bow, and made effective use of the Parthian tactics of shooting while in simulated flight

wound less serious. A round shield was used by all on sentry duty, but in battle only by the shock-troops of the front line and the khan's guard. The main weapons of the Mongols were a hooked lance, a curved scimitar with a sharpened point which was suitable for both thrusting and cutting, and two bows – one for use on horseback and the other for more precise firing on foot. There were three types of arrow, suitable for different ranges and against different armour. Besides these, each man had an axe hanging from his belt; a lariat, a length of rope which he might use for tethering his horse, lassooing his enemy, or hauling heavy equipment; a kit which included wax and spare bow-strings, files for sharpening the arrows, and needle and thread; and a water-tight skin to carry spare clothes, which could be inflated for crossing rivers. Finally he had equipment for food – a nose-bag for his pony, his own cooking-pot, and basic rations of smoke-cured meat and dried milk-curds.

Jenghiz Khan ordained that it was the responsibility of the wife in peace time to see that her husband's provisions and uniform were in readiness. In the intervals of peace the men were kept fit and trained in the use of their weapons by hunting wild beasts. The Mongols gradually learnt from their city-dwelling enemies the art of siegecraft, and their later armies carried missile-throwing machines, mangonels and catapults, in pieces on pack-animals.

The distinctive qualities of Mongol fighting were mobility and co-ordination. When describing the campaigns of these horsemen who swept through unmapped lands from China to the Mediterranean it is difficult to measure distances in miles. Part of the secret of their co-ordination was the nomad's instinct for landmarks and direction; there was also a well organized system of intelligence and communication. General information was continually sent to Jenghiz Khan from his subject rulers, and special messages and intelligence were relayed by the khan's own messengers, the 'Arrow Riders' – who everywhere received priority and also assistance in the form of the best available horses and provisions. The messengers could cover distances in days which normally took weeks; their bodies were bandaged for support in their long rides, and they slept in the saddle. As the Mongol conquests extended it was an important part of the khan's policy to maintain and protect roads – the old caravan routes which he knitted into an Asiatic network with regular posts. In wartime an army on the march was preceded by scouts moving several days in advance. Jenghiz Khan also made full use of spies, and here itinerant merchants were useful.

The urge of Jenghiz Khan to dominate, and the need to provide his peoples with war, led him to pit the Mongols against the Chinese. The Kin emperors in China were politically weak and they had not, as had always been Chinese policy in the past, inter-vened to prevent the unification of the nomads of the north and west. However Jenghiz Khan was a careful strategist; he had no sure intelligence of the strength of China, but he discovered that her armies were composed of vast numbers of foot-soldiers and that she depended very much for defence on powerful fortifications. Chinese warfare was unfamiliar to the Mongols, and in 1207 the khan experimented by leading a strong Mongol army into the state of Hsi-Hsia, a semi-independent part of the Chinese empire in the north-west. In the field the Mongol horsemen carried all before them, but they were checked by the fortified cities. Profiting from the experience, in the next few years Jenghiz Khan trained some Mongol officers in siege-warfare: in the use of catapults, naphtha, ladders, sandbags and so on. By 1211 the Hsia were conquered; his army had learned a good deal, and since his flanks were then clear he launched his great enterprise against China proper.

A pattern had by this time developed for Mongol invasions – though this one was to be the greatest yet. A council was called at the headquarters of the khan. All higher officers attended and the situation was discussed, the objective made clear, routes chosen, the grouping of divisions settled, and the plan of campaign outlined. The intel-ligence service had been studying the problem for some time. The Horde, as the Mongol invaders were called, then began to move. The first troops to set out were the scouts,

some 200 riders in pairs, dispersed over the countryside. Then came the advance-guard –
three toumans, or 30,000 picked warriors well mounted and each with a spare horse. The
touman commanders in 1211 were Muhuli, Sabutai and Chepé Noyon – of whom the
two latter received high command before they were twenty-five years old. Behind came
the main body in three divisions, totalling about 160,000. Jenghiz Khan commanded the
central division of 100,000. His personal standard was nine white yak's tails. Throughout
the campaign the commander-in-chief was constantly in touch with all his divisional
commanders by 'Arrow' couriers.

The country of the doomed enemy was normally entered simultaneously at several
points. In 1211 the Great Wall was penetrated in this way and the divisions advanced
along separate lines through Shan-si and Chih-li – on the Peking axis. There was no
provision for supplies except what could be found on the way, but that was enough. Each
divisional commander had authority to manoeuvre and engage the enemy at his discretion, but the main objective was clear and paramount, and a message from the
commander-in-chief might at any moment call him to particular action. With their
mobility and co-ordination the separate columns could very rapidly converge and
support each other. The Mongol army perfectly exemplified the principle of 'march
divided, fight united' – a maxim of von Moltke, possibly the greatest military brain
Germany has produced, who was chief of staff of the army under Bismarck.

The tactics of the Mongols were simple, but very effective. They planned to surprise
the enemy, marching rapidly by day and night and converging their toumans with
absolute precision. If this did not bring victory, they would seek to encircle the enemy by
moving round one of his flanks. They also used the old Parthian tactics of simulating
flight, sometimes retreating for days while they fanned out before turning and outflanking the enemy. The Mongol cavalry charged in formation under cover of their own
arrow and javelin fire. The movement of the formations was controlled by signals –
flags in the daytime and lamps when it was dark – and their battle drill was good. The
troops were in five ranks, the men in the leading two being more heavily armoured. After
the first shock the *mêlée* itself was loose and disorderly, each man fighting for himself,
wielding his sabre, and pulling down his opponent with his lariat or the hook of his lance.

The first rapid advance into China proceeded in this style, all resistance being overcome. But the weakness of the Mongols against fortifications still remained, and as
the masses of the Chinese population barricaded themselves into their cities the war
slowed to a stalemate. Some cities fell to ruses, in which the Mongols were experts. But,
like Hannibal before Rome, Jenghiz Khan and his converging Horde were stopped at
Yen-king, the capital (later called Peking). This was the situation which prevailed for
five years, from 1211 to 1216. Every autumn the Mongols withdrew, and in the following
spring they returned, sweeping in separate columns through the open country. Each year
their devastation was more terrible and each year they captured more towns, but the
major cities, despite domestic political disorder, continued to hold out. But at last in
1216 the Kin emperor humiliated himself to buy off the Mongols. A vast tribute was
paid, Jenghiz Khan received a wife of the Chinese imperial blood, and Muhuli, a
touman commander, was left as viceroy and military governor of China. Jenghiz Khan
returned to his capital of Karakorum, north of the Gobi Desert, taking the rich booty
promised to his warriors and also Chinese craftsmen, technologists and scholars – and
slaughtering his useless prisoners.

Siberian Taiga

Hokkaido

Amur

Lake Baikal

MERKITS

Japan Sea

Japan

Kamakura

KERAITS

Khingan Mountains

Sekigahara

Karakorum

Yamato

M o n g o l i a

Chin Empire

Pyong-Yang

Gobi
Desert

Peking
(Yen-king)

Seoul

Korea

Shimonoseki

Hsi-Hsia

Great
Wall

Chih-li

Kyushu

Shan-Si

Tsinan

Yellow Sea

Huang-ho

Nanking

C h i n a

Formosa

tains

Yangtse-Kiang

Brahmaputra

Pacific Ocean

Assam

Canton

Arakan

Burma

Cochin-China

Philippines

Hainan

of

Irrawadi

gal

Siam

Mekong

China Sea

ANS

i Mountains

200   400   600   800 miles

400   800   1200 kilometres

Having overrun and humbled the East and made sure of good order in the heart of his domains, Jenghiz Khan then turned his attention to the West: to the great Islamic power, the Khwarizmian empire which lay beyond the Himalayas. The shah, Ala-eddin Mohammed, was himself a conqueror who ruled from the Persian Gulf and Baghdad to the Himalayas. This was the highest moment of Islamic power: in the far west the crusaders were everywhere retreating. Jenghiz Khan knew little of the Islamic world, except that merchants occasionally brought from it rich goods – fabrics, horses, and fine metalwork such as swords and armour. Mohammed knew even less of the Mongols, but he did not fear them for he had an army said to be 400,000 strong.

In the spring of 1219 Jenghiz Khan, now aged fifty-six, ordered the Horde to assemble in the south-west, on the upper waters of the Irtysh river. A quarter of a million men are supposed to have assembled, better equipped than ever before, each man with three horses, and there was an artillery train carried on yaks. To divert attention from his main concentration the khan sent a force under Juji towards the lower reaches of the Syr Daria river (the Jaxartes of Alexander), which laid waste the trough of country between the Akkum desert and the Alatau range. The shah supposed this to be the main invasion, and sent his son Jelaladdin to deal with it. The Mongols skirmished and then disappeared behind the burning grass of the plain. Mystified, the shah posted troops along the whole line of the Syr Daria. The Khwarizmian defences were thus strong nowhere, and this gave Jenghiz Khan the advantage when his real operations began. The Mongol troops began to move in the autumn. A direct advance was blocked by the mountains which are the highest in the world. The main army set out westwards on the long and arduous march to the Zungarian Gates, the pass into northern Turkestan. The men were wrapped in sheepskins and kept their insides warm with *koumiss* or fermented mare's milk. To mislead the enemy and as the first part of his pincer strategy, Jenghiz Khan detached a column of 20,000 men under Chepé Noyon to march round the mountains the opposite way and approach the Khwarizmian domains at a south-easterly point – from Kashgar on to Khojent. So perfect was the timing and co-ordination of the Mongol operations that both forces reached their different frontier points in January and February 1220.

Chepé Noyon's column posed an immediate threat to two major Khwarizmian cities, Tashkent and Samarkand in the north-west area of Turkestan, and the shah reacted by moving additional forces into the south. But this was the very moment when Jenghiz Khan with the main body was advancing across his northern frontier in three columns. In February two of the columns of 30,000 each, under Juji and Jagatai, appeared on the shah's left flank, and began to work down the Syr Daria river, destroying the scattered Khwarizmian forces in detail, and moving to join Chepé Noyon's force. At the same time the remaining column of 40,000 under Jenghiz Khan moved due south on Bokhara. Masked by Juji's and Jagatai's columns, Jenghiz Khan's force can hardly have been noticed as it passed into the desert of Kizylkum. The first the shah knew of it was when at the beginning of April Jenghiz Khan emerged from the desert in the south, took Nuruta, and approached Bokhara. On 11th April Bokhara was taken.

The shah had been surprised. His line was turned, his available troops were trapped by columns converging from three directions, and communication with his westerly domains was severed. He himself fled westwards, while the Mongols reunited at Samarkand. Complete success had crowned this campaign of Jenghiz Khan. Extraordinary mobility and endurance, and the brilliant co-ordination of the movements of four columns, each covering and complementing the movements of the others, was the essence of this strategy. At every successive point the enemy had been surprised by superior forces.

It took longer to finish the conquest of the shah's empire, he himself being hounded night and day by Sabutai and Chepé Noyon and finally driven on to an island in the Caspian Sea – where he died. The rest of the conquering Mongols advanced more slowly westwards, capturing the cities one by one. Terror was the policy. Jenghiz Khan proclaimed himself in the mosques to be the scourge of God, and the faithful had good reason to believe him. In the Khwarizmian empire only those individuals, technical experts and the like, who might be useful to the Mongols were spared. Otherwise the whole population and its civilization was annihilated. When there were no people to kill, the animals were hunted down and slaughtered. Yet resistance was desperate, and it continued until December 1221, when Mohammed's braver son Jelaladdin lost the last of his troops in a battle by the Indus. Sabutai and Chepé Noyon meanwhile rode on round the Caspian, through the Caucasus towards the Dnieper and Europe before they were recalled by Jenghiz Khan. They completed the greatest cavalry campaign in history by fighting their way back home, passing eastwards and south through the lands of the Russian nomads.

Having conquered from Tibet to the Caspian and the Persian Gulf, Jenghiz Khan was ready to return to his homelands. He might have supposed there was nothing left to conquer, and in fact he fought only one more war, moving against the rebellious Hsia and then into southern China. He died in 1227. He had made himself by personal force the ruler of a martial race, and then at their head he had conquered the greatest empire of the world, stretching from the Persian Gulf to the Pacific, from the Siberian Taiga to the Himalayas. There is no flaw in his military record, and it can certainly be claimed that he was as great as any commander and leader in history. But he was a ruthless barbarian, the most brutal figure in the history of his times, and it is useless to try and hide the fact. He was interested in domination but not in civilization, and when he saw no use in something he destroyed it. On the other hand it was fine to be a Mongol in the time of Jenghiz Khan. As he himself said: 'The greatest joy a man can know is to conquer his enemies and drive them before him.' His political qualities were in some way creative, for he unified the tribes of a savage race and gave them just laws, and the horrible wave of Mongol conquest was at any rate followed by a peace in Asia of religious and racial tolerance, of easy communication and economic security.

In the reign of Jenghiz Khan's son Ogotai, Sabutai returned to Europe and in campaigns of a brilliance which almost match those of Jenghiz Khan he overran Europe to the Adriatic and Poland. After 1241 the Mongols withdrew from Europe, except from Russia. The reign of Kublai Khan, Jenghiz Khan's grandson, marked the furthest extension of Mongol dominion. But then the Mongol empire began to disintegrate. In the second half of the fourteenth century one more great Mongol conqueror arose, Timur, who recovered the domination of southern Asia west of the Himalayas. But thereafter the Mongol horsemen never produced another leader, and they returned, little less suddenly than they had appeared, to their original obscurity.

We now come to the Chinese. Before examining their methods of warfare we ought to know something of the teeming millions who have their being in that vast country. It is a race which numbers today nearly a quarter of the inhabitants of our planet, which occupies a territory greater than Europe, which comprises many different peoples, and which speaks as many different dialects as there are cities and districts in the land. And it has a civilization which was a thousand years old before Christ was born. The real China is not the China of the former great Treaty Ports, which foreigners made virtually their own, nor of the cities – but is rather of the land, and of the thousands of villages scattered throughout the length and breadth of the country. The family is the unit, and then the village.

The political history of China in bygone days is a long story of internal dissension and rebellion, which weakened the state in its continuous struggle to protect the frontiers against nomadic tribes from the north and west. But centuries of frontier fighting produced considerable changes in military organization and a certain military skill, and this we shall see as the story unfolds.

If any satisfactory generalization can be made about this vast and diverse people, it is that their past history has shown them to be, in essence, a peace-loving nation. They have had good reason to prefer peace, for they possess in China a useful and habitable area of Asia. There have been many wars in the 3,000 years of their recorded history, but these were the result either of the presence of covetous enemies on the border of China, such as the Mongols, or of rebellions due to political instability. The Chinese have been abundantly creative in the arts of peace, but not in warfare. Their great religions, Confucianism, Buddhism and Taoism, are all fundamentally pacific. Indeed their tradition of pacifism gradually strengthened, and they have cared to remember only very little of the history of their warfare.

The earliest period of which any reliable history is known is that of the Chou dynasty (1122–256 B.C.). Ancient Chinese society was feudal, in that great nobles commanded the allegiance and service in peace and war of the masses of peasants on their land. The warfare which is heard of before about 500 B.C. was 'heroic' in character, reminiscent of the earliest Greek warfare pictured by Homer. The aristocracy had leisure to play war-games, and a particular junior class of nobles known as the *shih* were closely comparable to Homeric heroes, medieval knights and Red Indian braves. The existence of a code of military etiquette known as *li* indicates that much so-called war was not serious, but fought for amusement, honour and prestige. Mean tactics such as attacking the enemy while crossing a river, or picking an opponent much older than oneself, were condemned! A Chou general challenged the Chin ruler in 632 B.C. with the words: 'Will your Excellency permit our knights and yours to play a game?' The actual method of fighting reminds one of Homer. The aristocratic champion went into battle, clad in leather armour and riding in a four-horsed chariot. His weapon was a powerful bow, and he was accompanied in the chariot by a driver, and sometimes a lancer also. A company of foot-soldiers, lightly armed, followed each chariot.

Important changes began possibly as early as the sixth century B.C. The failing strength of the Chou dynasty led to a struggle for power among the greater nobility, and nomadic incursions also had to be repelled. This sort of situation was to be recurrent in Chinese history. The period from 403 to 221 is known as the 'period of the warring states'. Warfare was now in deadly earnest. Chariots remained for some time the most powerful striking force. But infantry, tough peasants, became exceedingly numerous and

火籠箭式

The Chinese, although not naturally a martial race, developed ingenious weapons, such as extendable scaling ladders *left* and fire rockets *right*

of far more tactical significance. The foot-soldiers fought with javelins, short swords and bows and arrows. The appearance of iron at about this time brought an improvement in weapons and armour.

In 249 the Chou dynasty fell and the Chin dynasty assumed control. It had now become essential that China should present a united front to external foes, and to this end feudal particularism had to be overcome. The Chinese then became a nation in arms, the different parts of the country being united into an empire in 228 by the emperor Shih Huang Ti.

The people of Chin, on the north-western frontier, had learned many lessons from their nomad neighbours, and had been given an infusion of nomadic blood. Thus cavalry, on the nomadic model, appeared in Chinese warfare and then chariots gradually disappeared.

In the same period there was also development in fortification and siegecraft. The instruments of siegecraft were catapults, scaling ladders, and so on – essentially the same as in early European warfare. Fortifications of outstanding strength were developed, the most famous example being the Great Wall, which runs, in parts over mountains and gorges, for 1,600 miles along the nomad frontier south of the Gobi Desert. It is generally some 25 feet wide at the base and 17 feet at the top, being 25 to 30 feet high; crenellated parapets stand 5 feet above the walk, and there are regular towers. Tradition ascribes its building to the policy of the Chin emperor, Shih Huang Ti (246–10 B.C.). Being great builders of cities and being usually on the defensive in their wars, the Chinese built many great fortifications; it was these which, as we have seen, succeeded in checking the Mongols a thousand years later. The city walls built in the period of the Ming dynasty (A.D. 1368–1644) dwarf contemporary European fortifications. The walls, for example, of Nanking, Sian and Tsinan are 50 to 70 feet thick, and in places 70 feet high. The gateways were not so strong, but they were defended by large numbers of soldiers. I have explored parts of the Great Wall on foot, and have studied the fortifications of Nanking and Sian.

As early as about 500 B.C. the military experience of the Chinese was expressed in a notable military treatise, *The Art of War* by Sun Tzu. The author was a career officer who probably rose to senior rank, but was not himself an outstanding soldier. His book survives as thirteen chapters, each composed of a number of maxims or precepts. It is worth remarking that, apart from its military value, *The Art of War* is regarded as one of the great works of Chinese literature. For 2,500 years it has fascinated the best minds of China, and among the many who have written commentaries on it are not only certain Chinese commanders but also Tu Fu, one of the major poets of the Tang period. The sentences are terse, sometimes obscure, sometimes deceptively simple, but always full of mature military wisdom – much of which Europeans were not to learn for themselves until the Napoleonic era.

Sun Tzu's treatise deals with the fundamentals of strategy and command. It discusses the considerations that a commander must have in mind when he begins a campaign, the wider political factors as well as administration and the opening moves. It teaches that the proper object of strategy is the speedy attainment of the political object of the war and a secure peace, not lengthy and destructive warfare. Victory must be gained at the minimum cost in lives and destruction. Intelligence, or 'foreknowledge', is therefore extremely important.

If stratagems will serve to attain the objective they ought not to be despised. The Chinese, like the Mongols, appear to have been particularly fond of tricks involving the use of fire, such as setting fire to animals and sending them against the enemy. Sun Tzu valued integrity in a commander, but he recognized that, ultimately, 'all warfare is based on deception'. This quotation reminds me of Napoleon's policy of mystifying and misleading the enemy, which was well brought out in his tactics at Austerlitz in December 1805. I can, however, find no evidence that he had studied the writings of Sun Tzu.

Sun Tzu devoted considerable space to movement over different types of country, to the use of ground, and to 'the science of weak points and strong'. He saw war very much as a struggle between commanders:

> The clever combatant imposes his will on the enemy, but does not allow the enemy's will to be imposed on him.

A Japanese mounted warrior: a model representing the armour and weapons of the late sixteenth century

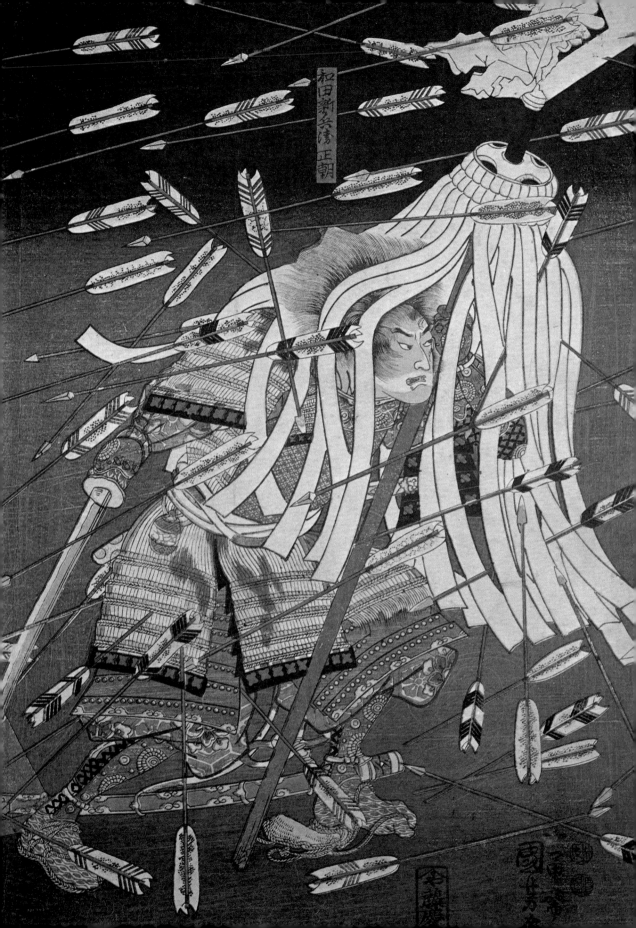

Sun Tzu made some perceptive psychological observations about the relationship between officers and soldiers in the ranks – such as how the general should recognize signs which indicate the state of morale and the condition of his troops. Characteristic of Sun Tzu's style and wisdom is this extract from the advice he gives to the commander: 'The quality of decision is like the well-timed swoop of a falcon which enables it to strike and destroy its victim'.

I should like to have talked with Sun Tzu; it would appear that on the subject of the conduct of war we would have much in common, and he understood the human factor. Wavell had studied the thinking of Socrates (470–399), and often discussed with me the emphasis that wise man laid on administration which he (Wavell) reckoned was the real crux of generalship – coming before tactics. I don't think he had studied Sun Tzu. To me these views of Socrates and Wavell are of intense interest. I used to think in the desert in 1942 and 1943 that Rommel was unfortunate in that he often had to fight when his administration in rear was not commensurate with what he wanted to achieve in battle in the forward area – because of Allied bombing which sank ships carrying supplies and oil for him across the Mediterranean.

The 1,400 years after the decline of the Chou dynasty is reputed to have produced some good soldiers in China, particularly in the periods of civil strife which broke out during the fall and rise of dynasties. But the difficulties of historical research into what went on in those days make it impossible to write of them satisfactorily. Po Chi is said to have served the Chin dynasty as a regular soldier for thirty-five years, between 294 and 260 B.C. The climax of his career was his victory over a Chou army of 450,000 men at Chang-ping. He was later reduced to the ranks for refusing to command an invasion which he knew would fail. Other famous individuals were Chang Chien, Han Hsin and Tsao Kung. Under the Han dynasty, and particularly in the brilliant reign of Wu Ti (140–86), and then again under the Tan in the seventh century A.D., China was a unified and strong imperial power.

But there is no evidence that Chinese warfare developed significantly beyond the stage it had reached under the Chin. The general tendency to pacifism was hardening, and expansion is likely to have been as much a matter of alliances and cultural conversion as of force of arms. When the Mongols invaded and conquered China in the thirteenth century the military resistance they met was weak. Once the Mongols were established in China, even their military character seems to have been subdued by the deep-rooted aversion to things military which was inherent in Chinese civilization. Although in the time of Kublai Khan (1259–94) the combined Mongol and Chinese arms touched Japan, Burma and Java, these expeditions were not finally successful. The Mongol dynasty was expelled by the Ming in 1368.

The advent of the Mongols opened the first communication between medieval Europe and China. But the first important contacts from the point of view of military history came with the arrival of the Portuguese in the China Seas towards the end of the fifteenth century. In 1517 a Portuguese fleet arrived at Canton and fired a salute with guns. As early as the tenth century the Chinese themselves had used gunpowder, and they are known to have used guns in 1356. But in the fifteenth century the great European technological breakthrough in guns and sails, discussed in Chapter 10 (The Greatness of Spain), set Europeans far ahead of Asiatics in the conduct of war. The Chinese reacted somewhat doubtfully. Recognizing their military impotence against the outside world,

The last stand of the Kusunoki. A print by Kuniyoshi depicting the battle of Shijo Nawate, 1348

they emphasized their pacifism and did their best to ignore the new situation, securing themselves behind a screen of xenophobia and cultural *hauteur*. On the other hand, they also desperately sought to discover the military secret of the Europeans and to compete with them; they would pay almost any price for guns. For a time it was the policy of the Europeans not to reveal their techniques. But men could always be found to sell the secrets, and it was eventually the Jesuits who instructed the Chinese in the manufacture and use of firearms. The Italian Father Alfonso Vagnoni (1566–1640) taught Han Lin, who wrote two treatises on the use of firearms; and in the 1640's a German Jesuit, Schall, operated a cannon foundry near the Imperial Palace: on condition that he was allowed to pursue his missionary work.

Yet the Chinese were slow to understand and adopt western techniques of warfare. This peace-loving and conservative society of scholars and peasants would not industrialize itself merely for the sake of military strength. The pacific reaction to contact with the Europeans intensified; in the seventeenth century Father Ricci wrote that 'the military is one of the four conditions which are considered mean among them'. The same applied at sea as on land; the Chinese junk was a highly seaworthy and navigable vessel, but it was not a ship of war and never became one. At the end of the sixteenth century the Chinese were persuaded to put cannon on to their junks, but they did not make the necessary mental adjustment. Geronimo Roman, a Portuguese, commented:

> Their arquebuses are so badly made that the ball would not pierce an ordinary cuirass, especially as they do not know how to aim.

This situation lasted until the mid-nineteenth century. The Chinese were not only unwilling but even incapable of making modern war. But then at last the avaricious aggression of European powers, particularly Britain, compelled the Chinese to westernize their warfare. It required the humiliation suffered by the Chinese in the Opium War of 1839–42 against the British to bring realism and to awaken China to the West.

One last word about the Chinese of today. It has always interested me to read to what extent warfare has featured in their history, they being naturally an unwarlike people. For a nation which traditionally held the warrior caste in low esteem, they seem to have devoted tremendous resources, time, and energy to fighting. From my personal observation of the Chinese there is in their make-up a curious combination – an industrious and very pleasant people on the whole, but some are inclined to be cantankerous. I doubt if the historians of any country have ever before recorded the swimming in a big river of their leader as being a factor in leadership! King John may have lost his baggage in the Wash; but did Cromwell swim the Thames and at nine miles an hour? It is interesting to reflect why Chinese newspapers should make a fuss about Chairman Mao's swimming – a form of exercise which does not figure prominently in Chinese thought as an accomplishment or sign of virility in a leader? I have myself been on a swimming excursion with Mao Tse-tung in the Yangtse (in September 1961); insofar as I am aware he swims entirely for pleasure, it being a form of exercise which is about all he can do at his age. He actually does little arduous swimming, but merely floats down stream with the tide. There is an odd inconsistency somewhere. Whither China? It is a real Chinese puzzle!

Lastly, we come to the Japanese. Whereas Chinese civilisation is half as old as time, and it is not known for certain where that nation had its origins, we are on surer ground when considering the Japanese. They came from the high plateau of the Asiatic continent and found the islands occupied by the Ainu, a primitive race of hunters and fishermen. A struggle with these people began in the south, which ended in their final subjugation and flight to their present home in the northernmost island of Hokkaido – the strange race not being finally subdued until about A.D. 800. This heavy and continuous fighting over the years resulted in a Japanese military race imbued with a strict code of discipline and loyalty, probably the outcome of their Mongolian blood and teachings.

Throughout Japanese history relations with Korea have been close, and a series of migrations from that country brought into western Japan families and groups who were dissatisfied with life in their own land. In due course Chinese culture reached Japan by way of Korea, bronze culture and later iron – the nation thus acquiring weapons and tools of iron, increasing its military strength and improving methods of cultivation.

With the introduction of feudalism, the study of the science of war spread rapidly; the Japanese people turned to China for much of its instruction in warfare, but gradually improved on the teaching it received. Being an island people, strong seafaring instincts were developed.

The history of Japan contrasts with that of China in that warfare has always been a prominent element. This was largely the result of environment. The Japanese archipelago stretches for over 1,000 miles, but a great part of the land is mountainous and infertile, and the high incidence of war among its inhabitants can largely be attributed to competition for the sparse areas of good rice land. The pacific influence of Buddhism was not enough in Japan to counter the need felt to fight. A second basic physical factor is that the islands abound with good natural harbours. The Japanese people have thus become tough mountaineers and seamen. The prevailing winds and currents in the China Sea generally made it difficult for them to make contact with the Asiatic mainland although the Japanese have always been concerned with the Korean peninsula, to maintain their influence there and to prevent its occupation by hostile powers: notably China. On the whole Japanese society developed in seclusion and distinctively, with a strong militaristic orientation.

In the first century B.C. there were about a hundred tribes in Japan. At that time ambitious chieftains began to import iron swords and armour from China. The competition between the tribes continued, but in the fourth century A.D. the people of Kyushu succeeded in subduing the other clans, and a centralized government was established at Yamato – in the main island. In 369 southern Korea was successfully invaded, and in 391 Japanese forces penetrated as far north as Pyong-Yang. This was the peak moment however, and shortly afterwards the Japanese withdrew from Korea, not to reappear there in force for 1,200 years. During the next few centuries the Yamato rulers sought to extend their rule over all the peoples of the archipelago, and legend recalls this time as a long age of disorder.

By the end of this period a distinctive Japanese military system had evolved, and in 702 specific laws were promulgated to produce an efficient state army. The early Japanese warrior was an aristocratic knight, elaborately armoured and mounted on horseback. Although attended by a retinue he fought as an individual. His chief weapon was the bow, but he used a sword for close fighting. Later, in the eighth century, under Buddhist influence there was a pacifist movement among the upper classes, and an attempt was made to organize the peasants as a huge reserve for national defence – on the Chinese model. But this did not work because the conscript peasants resented it and lacked equipment, and the system was dropped. Instead, each province was required to maintain a force of trained regular soldiers. Then, as previously, the fighting men were drawn from the upper classes. The separation of the peasant and the warrior classes in Japan was to become increasingly marked.

In the ninth century Japanese society entered a long phase of typical feudal development. A weak central government meant independence among the aristocracy and insecurity among the peasantry. At the same time land reclamation was going on, and the strongest men carved out for themselves personal territories. Dependence and loyalty focussed on the great estates, including the monasteries, and on the clans. Private armies were formed, and rivalries were let loose. Two particular clans emerged as the leading contenders, the Taira and the Minamoto, and for 250 years of incessant private wars and rebellions the struggle between these two continued. The Minamoto became supreme on land, but the Taira held the seas. Eventually in 1185 the Minamoto succeeded in defeating the Taira at sea, at the battle of Dan-no-ura in the Shimonoseki Straits: the Minamoto collected many more ships and their commander Yoshitsune made clever use of the turning tide. The Taira by this time lacked leadership, and the Minamoto swept all before them. After 1192 their leader Yoritomo set up the *Bakufu*, a military form of government, at Kamakura. He assumed the title of 'shogun' or 'barbarian-subduing generalissimo', and the emperor at Kyoto remained only as a puppet figure.

In two and a half centuries of endless, desperate fighting over wild country the Japanese had learned much about war, and the warriors had emerged as a privileged class – known as *samurai*. The chief weapon of the *samurai* was the bow; its size varied according to the height of the individual, but the maximum length was about $7\frac{1}{2}$ feet; it was made of boxwood or bamboo, and bound round with cord. Next in importance for fighting purposes was the sword, single-edged and slightly convex. By the tenth century the art of sword-making had already reached a high level and in the thirteenth century it was carried to perfection by two famous swordsmiths, Masamune and Hoshimitsu, who produced perfectly balanced blades of finely tempered steel. The *samurai* devoted much time to acquiring skill in swordsmanship. They had two types of sword, a long sword of 3 feet or so for fighting, and a shorter one used for decapitating a victim or committing suicide. The sword was regarded as the soul of the warrior. The *samurai* also developed *jujutsu*, the art of injuring or killing an enemy by using one's bare hands with the most economical application of muscular force, turning the opponent's weight and strength to his own undoing. The protective armour of the *samurai* was a garment of iron and leather held together with silk or leather cords, and a horned metal helmet. Some armour was decoratively inlaid with precious metal. The Japanese never had a proper war-horse; they rode to battle on small, sturdy ponies, which were sometimes also armoured.

Tactical conceptions often involved surprises and ambushes, but for the most part the opposing armies simply sought open battle. Every campaign was initiated by a human sacrifice to the God of War. The battles of the *samurai* had a strong ceremonial character. For instance, notice of intention to attack the enemy was given by firing a single arrow and raising a special chant. Signals were given by means of flags emblazoned with figures such as dragons, and by the beating of drums and gongs. Before the fifteenth

The *samurai* acquired great skill in fighting with their single-edged slightly convex swords

century a battle resembled a gigantic multiple fencing match. Each *samurai*, selecting an individual opponent, would proclaim his name, titles and achievement, and would probably insult his enemy. The duellists would then fight to the death without interference. There was particular honour to be the first *samurai* into battle, and at the end each warrior submitted the heads of his victims to his commander. At this stage in their development there does not appear to have been any organization into divisions, nor any tactical manoeuvre by units. The individual warrior was all, and it is therefore not surprising that the era produced no commanders of note.

A code of individual etiquette, and of solidarity and feudal obligation, developed in the *samurai* class. This was known as *Bushido*, or 'the Way of the Warrior'. It differed from chivalry in that there was not the same emphasis on courtesy. The *samurai* had to die for his lord. He was bound also to fight to the death rather than surrender, and if he

因寅刻ニ信死ウ婦小路西洞院乃至常四追捕
志く火を放川ニみ三四年ハ参伐禁制なと
あつて玉下静證ありつ木まに王る乱せ
弟を禁中を宣車を筆を三らくた王こ
ちけくなるまれ手まふつを貴賤ウ不三あら

The chief weapon of the Japanese was the bow

did surrender he was an object of utter contempt, unworthy of treatment as a human being – hence, perhaps, the Japanese treatment of their prisoners in the 1939/45 war. If a *samurai* was dishonoured he must commit suicide by the form of *hara-kiri*, disembowelling himself with his own sword. From the twelfth century *hara-kiri* became an increasingly frequent phenomenon, and there were instances of hundreds of *samurai* committing mass suicide rather than surrender.

Yorimoto, the Minamoto victor in 1185, proved himself to be a considerable soldier-statesman, for he succeeded in establishing a strong central government while maintaining Japanese feudalism in its military character. In the next century Japan was strong enough to face the Mongols, and the nation was well prepared when Kublai Khan launched the first Mongol invasion in 1274. For one long day the Mongol landing on Kyushu was desperately opposed, and when a storm blew up next day the Mongols retired to Korea. The experience was not however encouraging, for the Mongol forces

Marching to battle had a marked ceremonial character

had been more numerous and had proved the better fighters. Another invasion was inevitable, and for seven years the Japanese prepared to meet it. A stone wall was built along the shore of Hakozaki Bay, and when the Mongols reappeared in 1281 the Japanese forces and their needs were concentrated in that area. For seven weeks the obstacle was resolutely held while the Japanese warships did much damage to the enemy offshore. Finally, as before, the Mongols were forced to withdraw and their fleet was destroyed by a storm. Since this favourable wind had twice saved Japan it was called the *Kamikaze* or Divine Wind; and the Japanese suicide pilots who attacked American ships in the Pacific in the 1939/45 war were also called *kamikaze*.

The Mongols did not again molest Japan, but another period of domestic anarchy began. A new line of shoguns took power in 1338, but they had no claim to the loyalty of the feudal and military lords and internal warfare was renewed. As in other times of general insecurity weaker men lined up with the more powerful, and large private armies of *samurai* were built up. The history of the fourteenth, fifteenth and sixteenth centuries in Japan is a monotonous record of strife, with no outstanding incidents or individuals. The one interesting development was the re-emergence of a class of peasant soldier, the *ashigaru*. Many of these fought in bands simply for themselves. Being poor they had little armour, and one weapon only, a sword, spear or halberd – and they were mostly inclined to burn and loot.

Turmoil was thus the condition of Japan when she first made contact with the western world. In 1543 three Portuguese were blown off course in a Chinese junk and landed in Japan. They had muskets with them, and these caused great excitement – although the Japanese undoubtedly had already some knowledge of Chinese guns and gunpowder. But these people had none of the pacifism and conservative cultural pride of the Chinese, and they were eager to learn any effective way of fighting. Mendes Pinto observed that 'they are naturally addicted to war, and in war they take more delight than any nation that we know'. The Japanese, and the Koreans also, quickly appreciated the superiority of European firearms over their own bows and arrows. One chieftain, Iyeyasu, wrote bluntly to the king of Siam that 'guns and gunpowder are what I desire more than gold brocade'. In a short while Portuguese and other merchants were selling weapons to them, and before the end of the century the Japanese themselves were manufacturing arms.

The long period of internal disorder and strife gave the opportunity for able men of obscure birth to rise to power. By the second half of the sixteenth century the political pattern of Japan was again resolving itself into a number of major feudal blocs, and eventually the country was brought under one strong political authority. The progress from anarchy to unity was the work of three men, Nobunaga, Hideyoshi and Iyeyasu. Born in 1534, Nobunaga began his career by defending his own small estate. He then carried the war into his enemies' lands, and by 1559 he had gained mastery over the province of Owari. The courage and ability of Nobunaga so impressed two men, Hideyoshi the son of a woodcutter, and Iyeyasu a chieftain of eastern Japan, that they entered his service. Together they gained control of the country, and in 1573 Nobunaga became shogun. He himself had no exceptional military talent, and Hideyoshi and Iyeyasu were his generals. But he was prepared to learn intelligently from the Europeans, and it was he who began the main development of the Japanese firearms industry as well as introducing fortification and ship-building in the European style.

In 1582 Nobunaga was assassinated. The progress already made towards unification was then imperilled, but Hideyoshi and Iyeyasu set out to avenge his murder and complete his work. Hideyoshi now emerged as an outstanding soldier and statesman, his particular qualities being patience, organization and leadership. The key moment of his success came in 1587 when he crushed on Kyushu the chief dissidents – the Shimazu family who were head of the Satsuma clan. The Shimazu then asked for peace, and Hideyoshi, showing remarkable magnanimity and constructive political sense, allowed them to submit reasonable terms.

But Hideyoshi's ambition was not yet satisfied. His dream was now to conquer China, and in 1592 he began this project by invading Korea. The land operations were notably successful, the Japanese forces covering 200 miles to Seoul in three weeks. But while they were successful on land the Japanese suffered a disastrous blow at sea. The Koreans were a seafaring people and they had an outstanding admiral in Yi-sun, who besides being a strategist, tactician and leader of exceptional qualities, had a remarkable talent for mechanical invention. Asiatic naval tactics were still a matter of archery bombardment, ramming and boarding; cannon were not mounted on ships. Yi-sun had invented a vessel which could resist all these methods of attack and yet had great offensive power. The hull of his ship was designed for speed and manoeuvrability, and the deck was covered with a tortoise-shell of iron plates, impervious to fire, arrows and bullets, with spikes on top to hamper boarders. The prow was strengthened so that it could be used offensively as a ram, and there were archery ports all round. The Japanese sailors fought bravely, but Yi-sun's ironclad battleships wrought irresistible destruction among their fleet.

The effect of the Korean victory at sea was to paralyze Hideyoshi's land offensive. In 1597 he again invaded Korea, but this time the Koreans and Chinese fought more effectively on land and the same misfortune befell the Japanese at sea. Hideyoshi died in 1598. His military and administrative achievement in his own country was great, although the senseless and unsuccessful ventures into Korea sadly spoil the end of the story.

After Hideyoshi's death there was a brief struggle for power, but in 1600 Iyeyasu won the battle of Sekigahara, and established the Tokugawa shogunate. The strange policy of the Tokugawa, who remained in power until 1867, was to freeze Japan's social and political institutions and to isolate her from the rest of the world. This gave her 250 years of peace. But during that time her technology fell further and further behind that of the rest of the world, and her army of *samurai* became an increasingly outdated and ineffective fighting force. In 1853, however, a squadron of American ships, commanded by Commodore Perry, appeared, and the Japanese also were compelled to make a positive response to the modern world of the West.

What can we learn from this short study of Asiatic peoples? The Mongols in bygone days (and the Japanese in the twentieth century) have reminded us that courageous and well-trained troops can come from the Orient. The lesson all must learn is that Asiatic forces are not to be despised; what has happened before can happen again. From the vast areas of Asia could once more come an invading force with which the Western world would have to deal. But this need not happen if the Western nations apply wisdom and common sense in handling world problems in the twentieth century – and particularly learn to understand the great Chinese nation.

A sixteenth-century Moghul painting for the Akbarnama, illustrating the Turko-Islamic conquest of India

17 India

The Indian sub-continent comprises an area of $1\frac{1}{2}$ million square miles, inhabited in historical times by peoples of at least eight distinct races, professing many different faiths, and speaking some 200 different languages and dialects. It would therefore be pointless to attempt to write a general history of warfare in India within the space of one chapter. Instead I propose to highlight certain types of warfare which were prominent in particular periods. I have chosen the warfare of the ancient Hindus between 500 B.C. and A.D. 1200, that of the Turko-Islamic peoples who conquered Hindustan between 1000 and 1600 and set up the Moghul empire, and that of the Marathas of the eighteenth century. The story of Indian warfare after the eighteenth century, like that of the rest of Asia as European influence became predominant, will be resumed in Part 5.

Certain recurring general factors should be understood. The course of warfare in India has been dictated to an exceptional degree by the natural factors of geography, population movement, and climate. Between the Himalayas and the Vindhya range in central India lies Hindustan, a vast fertile plain with no natural defences. Possibly because of inadequate communications Hindustan was almost continually the scene of confused political struggle between small states. Kingdoms usually decayed for internal reasons, but an important additional factor making for political instability was the perpetual movement of population from north to south. Before the British assumed control no power took responsibility for guarding the north-west frontier, and from earliest times immigrant peoples crossed the passes. In due course Greeks and then Turks, Huns, Mongols and Persians came the same way. Between 2400 B.C. and A.D. 1500 the actual inhabitants of India were everywhere defeated by the foreign invaders and pushed southwards, the invading movements being generally halted by the Vindhya mountains. Certain areas in southern India, notably the Deccan and Vijahanagar, are hilly and dry – unsuitable for the movement of considerable bodies of people. This country lends itself to resistance against both invasion and internal government by loose-fighting warriors such as the Marathas.

The last major pre-condition of war in India is the climate. In the times of which I write the monsoon rains between June and September rendered the movement of armies virtually impossible. The best season for campaigning was always October and November – when the crops were ripe, the herbage green, and it was possible to live off the country. It is also worth mentioning that the native breeds of horses in India have always been inferior to those of western and central Asia.

War was most prominent in the politics and literature of the ancient Hindus. There

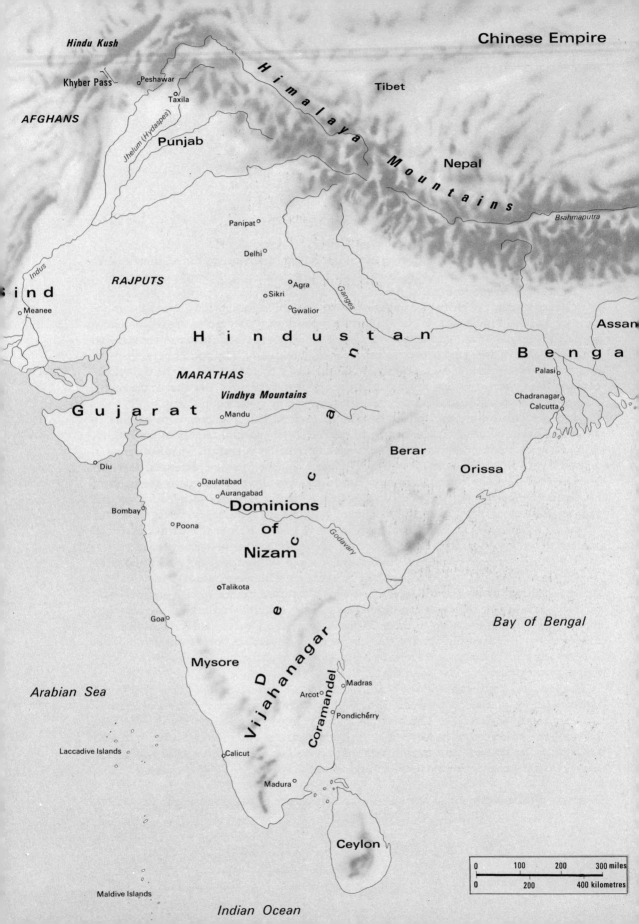

appears to have been an endless struggle between the various powers in Hindustan. Occasionally one man, a Maurya, a Gupta or Harsha, succeeded in subduing and unifying all the peoples of the land – but never more than briefly. The political history of India in the period from 500 B.C. to A.D. 1100 has not been written – nor can it be, for the Hindus were not historians. Occasional moments are illuminated by foreign writers, for example Hsuan Tsang, a Chinese Buddhist pilgrim (c. A.D. 635). Notwithstanding this difficulty, it is possible to discover a certain amount about Hindu attitudes to war and the methods used. Manuals of statecraft, such as the *Arthasastra* of Kautilya (relating to the period 300 B.C.–A.D. 100), indicate the prominence of war.

The army is called the sixth of the seven essential elements in the state. The doctrine of *mandala*, epitomizing the Hindu concept of relations between states, is essentially a doctrine of strife and struggle. A peaceable king is almost a contradiction in terms. It was written: 'No respect is due to a king who does not . . . subdue his enemies. He sinks like a cow in the mud.' And again: 'There is absolutely no rule but conflict for one of the warrior caste.'

Kautilya is a useful authority for, significantly, he includes a military treatise of some merit within his political theory. Of more doubtful reliability are the Sanskrit epics, such as the *Mahabharata*. The difficulty is to distinguish between what is historically authentic and what is literary fantasy. The *Mahabharata* is comparable to the *Iliad* and the *Nibelungenlied*, a great epic poem on the theme of war.

It is likely that there was an 'heroic' period in Indian warfare similar to the periods of Greek and Chinese warfare when battles were multiple duels between aristocratic charioteers accompanied by retainers on foot. But champions had been subordinated to the commander-in-chief of an organized army by the time of the first definitely recorded fact in Indian political history: the invasion by Alexander the Great in 327–5. Alexander crossed the Hindu Kush, captured the city of Taxila, and defeated King Paurav (Poros) at the battle of the Jhelum (Hydaspes). Chariots were still a considerable force in the army of Paurav, the earliest being light cars, made of wooden struts bound together with thongs, and drawn by two horses – each chariot with a driver and a bowman. Later, the chariot had four horses and carried six men – of whom two were shield-bearers, two were archers, and two were drivers who dropped the reins in the *mêlée* to become javelin-men. The Indian chariots at the Jhelum got stuck in the mud, but in any case the Macedonians would have disposed of them as they had those of the Persians. Small and large chariots, ranging in eight sizes with crews of from 2 to 12 men, remained in service in India until the eighth century A.D.

King Paurav came to battle mounted upon an elephant. It was at about this time that elephants first came to be regarded as the chief offensive power in Indian armies. They were to retain that honour, among the Hindus and later among the Moslems, until the impact of firearms in the seventeenth century caused serious doubts on their usefulness. The Indian front line at the Jhelum was composed of 85 elephants, deployed 100 feet apart, the spaces between being filled by picked infantry. Chandragupta Maurya (322–298) had an elephant corps 9,000 strong, and the numbers continued to increase. Each elephant carried a driver, and generally three warriors armed with bows and arrows – although javelins, knives, pots of oil and stones might also be used. The animals themselves were elaborately equipped with mail armour and carried bags for ammunition, as well as necklaces, rugs, heraldic devices and so on. The best elephants were bred in eastern India. There was an elaborate and formally prescribed programme of taming and military training, which proceeded from the basic stages of lying down, sitting, being ridden and jumping, to *samyana* (moving forward and sideways, or making serpentine movements), *vadhavadha* (trampling down and killing), *hastiyuddha* (fighting in formation) and other methods as might be needed.

Paurav was undoubtedly a leader of courage and possibly the ablest Hindu commander; however he was opposed by a veteran victorious army under a commander of supreme genius (Alexander), and could hardly hope to win. But he founded a bad tradition in Indian warfare – reliance on elephants for success. Since Paurav lost the battle of the Jhelum it is curious that his successors relied so much on elephants – which had obviously made a poor showing in that battle.

Elephants certainly had strength and a terrifying appearance. They could trample men under foot, batter down obstacles, and strike terror into the hearts of inexperienced soldiers and untrained horses. The Greeks, after Alexander, used them in western Asia and Europe, where we have traced their inglorious career. But while they may have had some value, they had too many defects for them to be trustworthy as the chief offensive force in battle. They were always difficult to control, and there are numerous instances, from the Jhelum onwards, of wounded or panic-stricken elephants turning and causing chaos in their own forces. We have seen in Chapter 5 how, because of panic, Hannibal's elephants caused confusion in his army at the battle of Zama in 202 B.C. It is possible that a commander mounted on an elephant could be better seen by his men and thus be an inspiration to them; but he would also be very conspicuous and vulnerable to enemy action – particularly with the advent of firearms.

The great mass of Hindu armies was composed of foot soldiers. Obviously there must have been wide differences in equipment and tactical conceptions between the professionals of the warrior caste and the savages and brigands of the jungle tribes. Inferior infantry soldiers were probably posted to special units which were used as labour forces to carry equipment, to gather food and to make entrenchments. In the 'heroic' era the infantry appear to have been little more than lookers-on, but maybe the poets were interested only in describing the fighting of the heroes. However at a later date greater reliance was placed on the infantry arm in hilly country, for the defence of fortifications, and in battles where numbers alone might be decisive.

From the dimmest periods of the fourth millenium B.C. until the nineteenth century A.D. the bow was the chief weapon in India. The earliest bows were made of wood, usually bamboo which was readily obtainable and reasonably strong and flexible. Later a composite bow appeared, made of metal, horn and wood, with a string of hemp, silk, hide or sinew. The arrow was of reed or wood, feathered, and tipped with horn, bone, wood or metal in a variety of shapes – such as *ardha-candra* (crescent-shaped head), *sucimukha* (needle-shaped head) or *kaka-tunda* (head-shaped like a crow's beak). Fire-arrows were occasionally used. The length of the bow varied; there is evidence of quite short bows, while on the other hand Arrian describes the Indian bows in 326 B.C.:

> The Indian infantry have a bow equal in length to the man who carries it. Placing this down to the ground and stepping against it with the left foot, they discharge the arrow, drawing the string far back. Their arrows are little less than three cubits long, and nothing can withstand one shot by an Indian archer, neither shield nor breastplate.

The Indians relied largely upon elephants in battle. A suit of eighteenth-century elephant armour, worn in the battle of Plassey

A Hindu army consisted of infantry, cavalry, elephants and chariots

Needing both hands free, the archer carried no shield. The hazard which the English surmounted at Agincourt, of rain dampening the bowstring, incapacitated the Indian longbowmen at the Jhelum.

Apart from bows Hindu foot soldiers had other weapons. The sword came gradually to rival the bow in esteem, and in Arabic literature Indian swords were renowned and coveted – many types existing with different regions specialising in their manufacture. According to Arrian, in the fourth century B.C. short, broad swords were in general use. Kautilya distinguishes three varieties: one a precursor of the *kukri*, incurved with the cutting edge on the inner side; another a long straight sword; and a third, with a leaf-shaped head. The sheaths were usually of leather. Swordsmanship was raised to the level of a fine accomplishment, and in the *Mahabharata* twenty-one special movements are described.

Numerous different types of spear and javelin existed, such as the six-edged iron *kunta* and others with polygonal heads. The Indian spear was probably never as long as the Macedonian *sarissa* or the seventeenth-century European pike. In the early period the mace and club were as important as the sword; they might be hurled, used for jabbing, or smashed downwards. The battle-axe developed as an aristocratic weapon, while slings, quoits and discusses were occasionally used. Shields were carried by all except

archers and the very poor; they were made of the skins of oxen or tigers, and of bamboo or matted creeper – being decorated with emblems, and varying widely in shape and size. Only the rich had body armour; others had some form of chain armour, but wadded coats of quilted cotton were in more general use.

Cavalry was regarded by the ancient Hindus as somewhat superior to infantry, but inferior to chariots and elephants: the basic reason being the lack of good horses in India. The cavalrymen of Paurav were probably mounted on ponies, and could thus be defeated by superior physical strength. Kautilya enumerates among the functions of cavalry:

> Disturbing the enemy's halt; gathering the troops; curving, circling, miscellaneous operations; removal of the rear; protection of the broken army; and falling upon the broken army.

It is clear that as recognition of the proper use of cavalry developed, so the standard gradually rose. There were two types of cavalry, heavy and light – the one to be positioned in the centre of the line to deliver charges, and the other on the wings for scouting, flanking, encircling and pursuit. Long lances were used for the charge and swords for the *mêlée*, but mounted archery was never developed by the Hindus. The poor quality

of their cavalry was their greatest weakness; the disasters at the hands of the Greeks and
the Turks can be described basically as the defeat of armies having a poor cavalry element
by armies consisting essentially of good cavalry well commanded.

Six categories of Hindu recruitment are distinguished: hereditary troops, mercenaries, gild levies (municipal guards), contingents from feudatory chiefs and allies, troops captured or seduced from the enemy, and men of the jungle tribes. But all things considered, the real distinction is likely to have been between the regular corps of professionals kept by rulers of any power, and the additional feudal and other levies raised as necessity demanded. In practice, members of any caste might serve in an army but men of lower castes tended to have lower functions. It is noteworthy that the Brahmans, the priestly caste, furnished a number of notable commanders – for example, Pusyamitra, the commander-in-chief of the last Mauryan monarch, Brhadratha. The army was divided into units on a decimal basis. Kautilya emphasises that spirit can be infused even into the timid by 'discipline and training'. Regular and fairly high pay was normal, and occasionally awards of land, money and decorations were made. In principle the state undertook to support the dependants of a soldier who was killed or disabled.

The most common time for beginning a campaign was the month of October, after the monsoon, though political conditions might alter the timing. Espionage, both diplomatic and military, was highly organized. Kautilya describes how spies were used to investigate enemy positions and numbers; he also mentions the sending back of messages in cipher by carrier pigeon, demoralising the enemy by circulating false information, and attempting to seduce the allegiance of important individuals in the army and in the harems. There are many instances in Indian history of wholesale desertion and the changing from one side to another. Before a march there would be elaborate consultation with astrologers, the king or commander then performing propitiatory rites to the God of War.

For transport the army used elephants, camels, pack-ponies, bullocks and bullock-carts. There was a large and motley body of camp-followers, such as priests, prostitutes, traders and minstrels. A Hindu army on the march was a spectacular sight, with majestic elephants and noble cavaliers equipped with gorgeous panoplies, precious metals, feathers, silks, rugs and parasols. The whole mass moved slowly, with a great deal of music and shouting. The author of the *Kalingattu Parani* describes how:

> The conch-shells sounded, the big drums thundered, and the reeds and pipes squeaked till the ears of the elephants . . . were defeaned. Rows of umbrellas and banners were unfurled, crowded so that the daylight was hidden.

There was probably no fixed plan for military camps, but ground near a river was generally chosen – the tents being laid out in rows, and sentries posted.

It is extremely difficult to determine from the various authorities the deployments and tactics used in battle. The poet of the *Mahabharata* gives free rein to fantasy in describing successive formations called 'heron', 'rhomboid', 'hawk' and 'crocodile', and in remaining consistent in his metaphors to the most minute detail. Kautilya talks a little more realistically of four basic formations, the 'staff', 'snake', 'circle' and 'detached order' – each with its own variations. There appear to have been numerous theoretical battle deployments, and it is probable that considerable time and ingenuity was spent in

A Hindu army on the march moved to the music of a band

forming troops into the order needed. But once the fighting began little discipline seems to have been retained. We read that champions rushed at each other, while masses of men locked themselves in conflict with their opponents. Doubtless the elementary tactics of flank attacks, the concentration of strength against weakness, and so on, were understood; but there is no direct evidence, and I have found no account of a Hindu battle written by a soldier. Musical instruments were used to arouse the ardour of the fighters, to beat time in marching, and to signal orders. A high regard for the virtues of courage and patriotism is expressed in such sentiments as 'victory is the root of religious merit and every kind of happiness'. But if the commander of one side fell, as happened to King Dahir of Sind in A.D. 712, his army was liable to disintegrate. We know that surgeons accompanied the army; also that prisoners of war were, in principle, decently treated.

It will be understood from what I have written that the warfare of the ancient Hindus left a good deal to be desired. They were interested in war, and liked it, but reached no high standards. The main weaknesses in the composition and organization of their armies were excessive reliance on elephants, poor cavalry, and a feudal method of recruitment which militated against unity of command and standardisation in equipment and organization. The Hindu soldiers and their commanders were not lacking in courage, but even the greater individuals, such as Chandragupta Maurya who drove out the Greeks, and Skandagupta and Yasodharman who repulsed the Huns, seem to have lacked vision and had little strategical or tactical sense. For example, the passes of the

north-west frontier were not held, and armies moved sluggishly. There was never a
single enduring empire of Hindustan; none, even among the major figures, achieved the
secure overall dominion which was necessary for real unity, military strength and an
outward-looking policy. Hindu wars were petty affairs, fought with reserve – affairs of
politicians, which were ignored by the peasants cultivating the fields. Hindu civilization
by A.D. 1000 was complacent and conservative. All these weaknesses were exposed by the
Islamic invaders.

The Turko-Islamic conquest of India developed in a definite pattern. It was a gradual
process which began in the tenth century and was completed only in the seventeenth – the
wild Turkish tribesmen being continually lured to invade a rich and disunited country.
The Turks would begin by making raids across the frontier; these developed into invasions, in which the nearest Hindu king was defeated in pitched battle. The first conquest
was the springboard for the next advance, and the Hindu territories were gobbled up one
by one as the forces of Islam progressed south and eastwards. The process went on into
the seventeenth century, when the tribesmen of the Assam jungles halted the then
decadent Moghul forces. As the invaders of the earlier waves settled and became Indians,
they themselves were swamped by succeeding waves from the north-west – the sequence
of invasion and conquest being uninterrupted for eight centuries. Each separate advance
was usually short, but occasionally an outstanding Moslem conqueror swept all before
him in a devastating tide. Four names stand out.

The first and possibly the greatest Turko-Islamic conqueror of India was Sultan
Mahmud of Ghazni (997–1030), who is said to have led seventeen campaigns in India.
It was he who took the Moslems over the Indus, the only potential barrier to the rich
plain of Hindustan. His greatest victory was gained over the forces of Anandpal between
Und and Peshawar in 1008. Eventually his empire extended from Persia to the Ganges;
he was a notable leader, capable of inspiring his men and gaining their devotion – and he
himself was a stout-hearted fighter.

The second great fighter is Shihabuddin Ghori. In 1190, having advanced to Tarain
near Delhi, his Turkish army being greatly outnumbered was defeated by the Hindu
king Prithviraj. But, characteristically, the Hindus did not follow up their victory
energetically or with any strategic sense, and after eighteen months Shihabuddin was
able to get his revenge at the second battle of Tarain. Eventually he conquered the whole
northern plain of India.

Two centuries passed before another great conqueror appeared from the north-west.
This was Timur, the Mongol, who swept through Hindustan in five months during 1398,
sacking Delhi but then returning to his capital at Samarkand. Finally, Timur's sixth
descendant, Babur the Tiger, descended upon India in 1525. He defeated the Afghan
sultan of Delhi at Panipat in 1526, and subsequently destroyed the Hindu Rajput
Confederacy at Sikri near Agra. Before his death in 1530 Babur's dominions extended
from the Oxus to the frontier of Bengal, and from the Himalayas to Gwalior. Babur laid
the basis of the Moghul empire which was to be formed by his grandson Akbar.

The Turks were able to defeat the Hindus because they possessed in outstanding
measure those essential martial qualities which the Hindus lacked. They found complacency and tolerance, and opposed these with the vigour of a barbaric people fired by
fanatical devotion to the faith of Islam. Apart from the proselytizing zeal of their religion,

they also possessed the characteristics of social solidarity, a fatalistic contempt of death, and sobriety – all of which the Hindus lacked. The Turks had energy. With it they also had mobility, being mounted on fast, tough Turkoman and Arabian horses. Their armies were in fact hordes of mounted archers, in the old and effective tradition of the Parthians, the Huns and the Mongols. Their composite bow was as good as any weapon of the Hindus, and they used it to better effect. They had as much courage as the Hindus, but, unlike them, they were also able to produce senior officers of high military intelligence, and occasionally commanders of genius.

The essence of Turkish strategy was controlled mobility over large areas. Their tactics, as in the West, were normally to harass and exhaust the enemy by means of clouds of encircling, elusive mounted archers, and then to clinch the victory by a charge of heavier cavalry. The Turkish tactics at second Tarain were identical to those at Manzikert. This style of fighting has already been analyzed fully in the chapters on the fall of the Roman empire, on the Ottoman Turks and on the Mongols. It was the same process in the time of Timur, and just as effective.

But as the Turkish peoples settled in India so they lost the original *élan* of the steppes, and to some extent became absorbed in the ancient, unchangeable ways of their new land. Furthermore, the advent of firearms affected their warfare. Already Babur's army at Panipat was different from those of his predecessors. He had fewer Turkish horsemen, although these remained the *élite* troops; he had contingents of native Indians, fighting with their traditional bows, swords and spears; and he had infantry armed with match-locks and falconets mounted on carts. The use of elephants was adopted, and although cavalry became more highly regarded than previously, mobility declined. By the eighteenth century a Moghul army on the march was not unlike the old type of Hindu army.

The story of firearms in India differs somewhat from that of China and Japan; incendiary substances, such as naphtha, had long been known. Rockets were an old Hindu weapon, which remained in use in the Moghul army and also in the Maratha armies of the eighteenth century. The rocket – an iron tube about a foot long and one inch in diameter, fixed to a bamboo stick – had a range of up to 1,000 yards and was almost as dangerous to the man who fired it as to the enemy; but if with luck it exploded on impact it might frighten raw troops, stampede horses, or start a fire. Real guns were imported into southern India at an early date; in the 1360's they were used in the Deccan by the rajah of Vijahanagar – being manned by Turks and Europeans. Guns were brought into India thereafter in considerable numbers by both the Portuguese and the Turks. The Indians, like other Asiatics, did not succeed in mastering the proper use of guns in naval warfare. (So little is known of early Indian naval warfare that it is not worth attempting to discuss it.)

In the use of guns in land warfare the Indians followed the methods, and the weaknesses, of the westerly Turks. Babur, whose guns were probably the first seen in northern India, used them skilfully – particularly at the battle of Sikri where he drew the Rajputs to dash their forces against a strongly entrenched position defended by infantry and guns. (This tactical plan is reminiscent of the method of Gonzalo de Córdoba.) But already in 1526 Babur had a huge mortar, which was fired only three times in the battle and later burst. The Turks in India shared the liking of their westerly cousins for enormous guns; some cannon later manufactured in India weighed 40 and even 50 metric

The Turko-Islamic invaders pursued the Hindus across the Ganges with guns in 1565

tons. On the other hand the Indians did eventually succeed in manufacturing service-able guns, and they absorbed into their tactical systems the use of handguns as well as swivel-guns mounted on elephants and camels. Yet as late as the Mutiny of 1857 some Indian troops were using the bow and arrow as effectively as the handgun.

After Babur's death there were still native Hindus (such as the Rajputs), and Moslems (such as the Afghans), who were not demoralized and were ready to fight for independence whenever the Moghul power seemed weak. In time, with the assimilation of races and variation of political alignment, the opposing armies came to resemble each other closely. When the Turko-Moslems were true to their distinctive tradition their superiority remained evident. But when they lacked intelligent tacticians, and relied too much on elephants and main force, they were in trouble.

The battle of Talikota in 1565, which caused the downfall of Vijahanagar and established the power of the Moslems over the Hindus in the Deccan, shows a Moslem Indian army at its best. Husain Nizam Shah, a fine general, was undismayed by the fourfold numerical superiority of his enemy. His artillery was greatly superior and he positioned it forward, screening it with Turkish horse-archers who lured the enemy towards them. His cavalry was well equipped and trained, being formed into divisions with a powerful reserve to deliver a final decisive charge. The three victories of Aurangzeb in 1658–9 which won him the Delhi throne were against armies similar to his own, but each time his superior artillery and tactical sense decided the issue. The victories of Nizam-ul-Mulk (Ratanpur and Balapur 1720, Shakar Khera 1724) shows the strengths and weaknesses of the opposing types of army. Nizam had good artillery, efficient organization, and excellent cavalry – the best of which were actually foreign Moslems – and seasoned and intelligent officers. He himself was an able tactician; at Ratanpur he turned the position of Sayyid Dilawwar Ali's army before the fighting began, and laid a clever artillery trap.

The Rajputs were tremendously brave – but equally stupid. Their only tactic appears to have been a rush forward in mass. Furthermore, their equipment was often primitive. For all their fury and courage, by advancing thus against well-prepared artillery they were merely sacrificing their lives 'like moths in a flame'. Such was the impact of a Rajput attack that their enemies usually needed all the defensive strength of their artillery, elephants and armour. When generalship was lacking on the other side, the balance might long be in doubt. But ultimately superior arms and tactical sense were bound to prevail.

Even the army of Nizam-ul-Mulk had absorbed too many traditional Hindu characteristics; this was shown when the Nizam's forces were defeated by the Marathas, who fought much in the style of the Mongols and the original Turkish invaders of India. They were Hindus from south-western India, hardy frugal people, unlike the dwellers of the rich north – and they had been forged into a new military force by Sivaji in the mid-seventeenth century. When Wellington fought the Marathas in 1803 they were not what they had been (though this is no reflection on the brilliance of Wellington's generalship). They were at their best in the eighteenth century, and the Palkhed campaign of 1727–8, in which Baji Rao I outgeneralled Nizam-ul-Mulk, is a masterpiece of strategic mobility. Baji Rao's army was a purely mounted force, armed only with sabre, lance, a bow in some units, and a round shield. There was a spare horse for every two men. The Marathas moved unencumbered by artillery, baggage, or even handguns and defensive armour. They supplied themselves by looting.

Baji Rao resented the Nizam's rule over the Deccan and feared his diplomacy, and it was he who struck the first blow. In October 1727, as soon as the rainy season ended, Baji Rao burst into the territory of Nizam's supporter, Asaf Jah. The lightly equipped Marathas moved with great rapidity, avoiding the main towns and fortresses, living off the country, burning and plundering. They met one reverse at the hands of the Nizam's able lieutenant, Iwaz Khan, at the beginning of November, but within a month they had fully recouped and were off again, dashing east, north, west, with sudden changes of direction. The Nizam had mobilized his forces, and for a time pursued them, but he was bewildered by the swift and unpredictable movements of the enemy, and his men became exhausted.

At the end of January the Nizam changed his strategy; he gave up the pursuit of the elusive Maratha forces and instead made direct for their heartland around Poona, which he captured and ravaged. Baji Rao received urgent calls to come back. But with good strategic sense he resisted the call, and instead countered the Nizam's move by in turn threatening his capital, Aurangabad. Nizam predictably evacuated the Poona district and returned to rescue Aurangabad. Baji Rao had not actually captured the capital, but he had pillaged the neighbouring area. As the Nizam once again endeavoured to catch Baji Rao, the Marathas harried and circled round his forces. The Nizam preserved his army intact, but in March 1728 he gave up. The Marathas returned home laden with plunder, and by the peace terms some of their territorial claims were conceded.

Mention should be made of fortification in India, for some Indian forts were as powerful as the best in medieval Europe. The most remarkable are some of the hill forts, of which Mandu (in Gujarat) will serve as an example. The hill on which Mandu stands rises 1,000 feet above the plain. Its scarped sides, crowned by powerful walls, bastions and gates, present a formidable sight from below, particularly on the precipitous southern side. The fortifications were built by Shah Hoshang Ghori (1406–35). The difficulties of construction were immense, on account of the height of the hill and the irregularity of the ground.

The basic strength of Mandu was a powerful crenellated wall of grey basalt built round on the edge of the cliff above the escarpment, strengthened at points by bastions and with a number of strongly defended gateways. A wide and deep gorge runs up from the east side into the centre of the city; this was defended by a causeway, called the Seven Hundred Steps, built across its mouth. The main entrance was on the north side, where a path, barred by three successive gates, wound up the moderately steep slope. The topmost, the Delhi gate, is a magnificent vaulted structure of reddish limestone. The gates on the south-east and south-west are also particularly strong; the passage of Tarapur gate is narrow and steep, with the defence assisted by right-angled turns within the gateway. The doors were plated with iron and protected against the assault of elephants by rows of iron spikes. An assailant who forced the passage would come under attack from the rear by the defenders of the west wall.

The citadel of Mandu itself contained many fine palaces and mosques. Its greatest period was in the fifteenth century. It was taken by Bahadur, ruler of Gujarat, in 1567, and by the seventeenth century the buildings of Mandu began to fall into disrepair.

The capture of Bakadur Khan, 1567. A Moghul painting for the Akbarnama

Among the numerous other notable fortifications in India are those of Agra, Daulatabad and Madura. Indian siegecraft was a matter of catapults and later of heavy artillery, but the most successful strategists generally skirted round and avoided the great strongholds.

Finally, we must deal with the early Europeans in India. The Portuguese were the first to arrive in force, and in the early years of the sixteenth century Albuquerque established wide Portuguese influence – based on maritime supremacy. In the seventeenth century the Dutch replaced them as the leading European power in India. Meanwhile European adventurers were taking service in increasing numbers under Indian native rulers, particularly as gun-founders and gunners. In the mid-eighteenth century the stage became clear for the imperial struggle between Britain and France. The Dutch were now weak; the Moghul army had become too massive and cumbersome, and lacked leadership; and the Maratha system of war was losing its purity and could not avail against trained troops equipped with the most modern firearms. The French and the British in competition exploited the political disunity of India.

The chief British bases were Madras, Bombay and Calcutta – the chief French base being Pondichéry. A Frenchman, Joseph Dupleix, was the first European to train Indian troops in the European method of war in any numbers and with any success. He was also clever at diplomacy among the Indian native rulers, gaining allies and setting one ruler against another to the advantage of the French. The War of the Austrian Succession in Europe (1740–8) gave the French the excuse to attack the British in India, and Dupleix captured Madras. However the British East India Company very quickly learned to play the same game as the French. Stringer Lawrence began to raise 'sepoys' – the name given to Indian troops trained by Europeans and retained in their service – and Robert Clive emerged as a diplomat and soldier even abler than Dupleix.

Peace in Europe did not interrupt the imperial struggle in India. Dupleix and de Bussy were for a while successful in the Deccan. But in 1751 Clive gave evidence of his courage and generalship in his heroic defence of Arcot with only 200 English and 600 sepoys. By 1756 the situation had altered. Dupleix had been recalled to France, and the French were without a good commander. A threat, which was also an opportunity, arose with the accession in Bengal of Suraj-ud-Dowlah, who was rabidly anti-British; he seized Calcutta with an army 50,000 strong, imprisoning his captives in the notorious 'Black Hole'. Clive led a relieving expedition. War had again been declared in Europe, and Clive determined to follow up his advantage. Having attacked and captured the French fort of Chandranagar, he set about undermining the position of Suraj-ud-Dowlah in Bengal, sowing dissension in his *entourage* – with the result that one senior commander, Mir Jafar, was induced to promise support to the British.

Clive met Suraj-ud-Dowlah's army at Palasi (Plassey). Clive had about 800 Europeans, some 2,000 sepoys, and 8 pieces of artillery to set against 34,000 foot, 15,000 horse and 53 cannon. The odds seemed hopeless. But the British were well positioned in the shelter of a mango grove, and by chance a heavy fall of rain put the Indian artillery out of action. Suraj-ud-Dowlah suddenly panicked and fled, and Mir Jafar, having sat on the fence, then led the prearranged retreat. The generalship on the Indian side was so bad that the battle of Plassey was little more than a skirmish and a rout. Two subsequent victories by Admiral Pocock and Sir Eyre Coote sealed the ruin of the French and opened the way for the expansion of British dominion over the native peoples of India.

Akbar's forces besiege Rauthaubhor Fort, 1568. A Moghul painting for the Akbarnama

The thin red line of the British infantry advances at the battle of the Alma in the Crimean War

PART FIVE
WARFARE 1815–1945

18 The Beginnings of Modern War

In our study of warfare we have now reached the stage when war is to become highly complicated and professional. By the nineteenth century signs pointed to an intensification of warfare with an increased impact on society.

The Industrial Revolution and massive populations caused whole societies to organize themselves for the function of war in a more complete way, and armies were equipped with weapons far more powerful than ever before. This kind of war was developed mainly in Europe and America, but it penetrated in due course to all parts of the world. Actually the years between 1815 and 1848 saw a period of relative peace in Europe. However, during that time general developments were taking place which had a direct bearing on the emergence of modern war. The ideas of imperialism and nationalism were hardening; revolutionary changes in armies and equipment were born with the growth of populations and new industrial techniques; new methods of communication increased the pace of life in general; and military theorists and politicians arose who rationalized and exploited these factors. Before 1848 these developments were only experimental; but a great deal was experienced in the fighting of the next decade or so. Finally in the two major conflicts of the nineteenth century, the American Civil War (1861–5) and the Franco-Prussian War (1870–1), the new techniques pointed the way to what was likely to happen in major clashes between great powers – and which actually did happen – in the first half of the twentieth century.

Perhaps the most important of the background developments was the rise in population – that of Europe rose from 140 to 170 million between 1750 and 1800, and reached 274 million by 1850. Between 1830 and 1870 it increased by 30 per cent; as Disraeli remarked, the invasions of a few hundred thousand barbarians into the Roman empire were trivial compared to this. Enormous pressures were thus imposed on national life. There was a steady flow of emigration out of Europe – westwards to North America where the population grew threefold between 1830 and 1870, and eastwards into Asia. This undoubtedly eased the strain in Europe, but, on the other hand, it gave an impulse to imperialism. The masses which remained in Europe provided the labour for the new factories, and mass production came into existence to revolutionize the manufacture of armaments. Furthermore, immense numbers were available for conscription, where that principle was accepted. Vastly increased numbers would, however, be a mixed blessing, in that they created problems in transport and supply and also in the tactical movement of armies. The increasing influence of public opinion on the conduct of affairs was yet another new factor which had to be taken into account by military commanders and policitians.

The relative peace in Europe between 1815 and 1848 provided the opportunity for peaceful pursuits. The continent was run by conservative statesmen, notably Metternich, who conspired to preserve the diplomatic settlement reached by the Congress of Vienna and to damp down the fires of nationalism, liberalism and social change. The first concern of the major nations was the development of their industry and trade. Free trade replaced the mercantilist system in economic affairs, and it seemed to be in the material interest of all peoples to remain at peace with each other. Interdependence as much as competition characterized economic relations between states, and Prince Albert, opening the Great Exhibition in Britain in 1851, declared his conviction that the 'unity of mankind' would shortly be realized. Followers of the philosopher Saint-Simon planned the *Réorganisation de la Société Européenne*, and hailed engineers and financiers as the pillars of a new and naturally pacific society. In more real political terms Britain was the strongest power, having emerged victorious from the Napoleonic Wars besides being the leader of the Industrial Revolution, and it suited her well that the world should be at peace. The British navy, unchallengeable since Trafalgar, undertook to keep a *Pax Britannica*, policing the seas and intervening to support approved causes, for example the abolition of slavery in Brazil.

Fighting was not, however, altogether avoided between 1815 and 1848; nationalism, allied with romanticism and liberalism, found outlets in numerous revolts – most of which were suppressed by the great autocratic powers. For example, a rising in the Papal States was put down by Austria in 1831, and in the same year the Poles, after desperate resistance, were crushed by the Russians at Ostrolenka. There was a great outburst of revolutionary activity in 1848 and barricades reappeared in the streets of many European cities. But Marx's expectations of class war and Lamartine's republican ideals were trampled down decisively by the forces of reaction – after much bloodshed. Nevertheless some movements were tolerated – the Greeks were supported in their struggle for independence from the Ottoman empire not only by Byron but also by a British fleet under the command of Sir Edward Codrington, the naval power of Turkey and her ally Egypt being destroyed in Navarino Bay in 1827. The movement of the South American countries to free themselves from Spanish and Portuguese bonds was also tolerated.

There were fifteen years of war in South America, during which the high plateaux of Peru and modern Bolivia were heavily fought over. In 1816 Spain seemed to be on the point of regaining control. However the two great 'Liberators', José de San Martin and Simon Bolivar, were preparing their armies. After more than two years of training and planning, San Martin invaded Chile from across the High Andes. The operation was carried out in the most arduous conditions and on a front of 500 miles. Concentrating his forces with precision he surprised his enemy at Chacabuco in February 1817. Peru was then liberated, with the aid of a fleet commanded by an intrepid and erratic British seaman, Thomas Cochrane. In the north at the same time Bolivar, with a mixed force of foreign legionaries, marched through the hot and flooded plains of the Orinoco, and over bleak paramos of the Andes. A gripping story could be told of these adventures, and the heroism of the 'Liberators' recalls that of the *conquistadores*. But the fighting was remote from that of modern war.

The same, on the whole, is true of the imperialist wars – as the following outline indicates. The 'manifest destiny' of extending the U.S. frontier to the western edge of the North American continent was pursued throughout this period, and much fighting took place – chiefly against Red Indians and Mexicans. The defence of the Alamo in Texas (1836) and the stand of the U.S. 7th cavalry under Custer against the Sioux and the Cheyenne at the Little Big Horn river in Montana (1876) are famous episodes. In southern Africa during the 1830's and 1840's the Boers were driven northwards from the Cape by the British, and became involved with a welter of warring Bantu tribes. The Zulus had been welded into a terrible military power by Chaka, but his successor Dingaan was eventually crushed at the Blood River by the Boers under Piet Retief. Bloody fighting took place before the British were able to conquer the Maoris in New Zealand in the 1860's. British forces in India were constantly occupied and in 1837, with the First Afghan War, a new phase of war and conquest began which lasted for twenty years. The north-west frontier had to be secured; Sind was brought under control in 1843 when Charles Napier with 3,000 troops crushed 20,000 Baluchis at Meeanee, in what was possibly the most brilliant feat of arms in Indian history; and the Sikhs were defeated at Gujrat in 1849. The British position in India was then imperilled by the mutiny of the native army of the East India Company in 1857–8. The campaigns to suppress the mutiny occasioned some notable military feats, particularly the clearing of central India by Sir Hugh Rose. The British also took the lead in the general competition of the European powers to exploit China, where the Opium War took place between 1839 and 1842, and the Taiping rebellion between 1850 and 1864. While the British and French preyed on China in the south and east, the Russians grabbed what they could in the north and west. Russia had been held up by her preoccupation with the Balkans, and by the tenacious resistance of the Moslem guerrillas of the Caucasus under their remarkable leaders Kazimullah and Shamyl; but she too was now following a manifest destiny of expansion into Turkestan and Siberia.

The story of the imperialist wars of the nineteenth century provides plenty of incidental interest, and not only in outstanding personalities and feats of valour. The clash between European and primitive warfare showed clearly that numbers and bravery could not prevail against superior weapons and discipline. It is interesting to watch the native peoples of the rest of the world beginning to learn by their unpleasant experiences, and then to Europeanize their warfare – for example, Li Hung-Chang's training of the Huai army to deal with the Taiping rebels. These wars were also opportunities for Europeans themselves to try out new techniques and ideas. But the mainstream of development was in Europe and in the old part of the United States.

In Europe the era of peace was over by 1848, when the statesmen of the Vienna settlement fell from power. The conduct of affairs was now to be in the hands of men such as Palmerston, Napoleon III, Cavour and Bismarck, and nationalism was once again in the ascendant. The diplomatic balance was upset as the powers looked jealously at the decaying Ottoman empire, and as the unification of Italy, and also of Germany, challenged the position of France. Four important wars took place within seventeen years: the Crimean War (1853–6) between England, France and Turkey allied against Russia; the Italian war of 1859 in which the main contenders were France and Austria; the war between Prussia and Austria in 1866; and the Franco-Prussian War of 1870–1. European warfare was by now feeling the impact of the military theories of Jomini and Clausewitz, of the Industrial Revolution, and of the population explosion.

Military theory in the nineteenth century had to take account, as I have said, of new developments of fundamental importance: massive populations and nationalism, speedy communications, technical inventions and mass production. The years after 1815 were in fact a period of original and fateful military thinking. The first edition of his book *Vom Krieg* by von Clausewitz was published in 1832 (after his death), and the *Précis de l'Art de la Guerre* by Henri Jomini appeared in 1837. These two outstanding thinkers had both pondered upon what they had seen in the Napoleonic wars.

Jomini, a Swiss by birth, had produced his first book on military theory at the age of twenty-five, and he joined Ney's staff in 1805, being present at Austerlitz. His arrogance and brilliance provoked the jealousy of Berthier and he went over to the Russians, in whose service he remained for some years. After 1829 he lived in Brussels where he wrote his major work. He died in 1869.

Clausewitz joined the Prussian army in 1792 at the age of twelve. He became a *protégé* of Scharnhorst at the Berlin Academy for Officers, and after Jena (1806) took a leading part in the reform of the Prussian army. He served with the Russian army in 1812, was a staff officer in the Waterloo campaign, and then from 1818 until his death in 1830 he was Director of the Prussian War School. Though their experiences were comparable, Jomini and Clausewitz derived from them different theoretical approaches to war.

Since the views of these two had a profound influence on military thinking in their times, and in the early years of the twentieth century, it may help the non-military reader to have some knowledge of their different attitudes to war.

Jomini's work is essentially a technical analysis of the conduct of war, based on a study of the campaigns of Frederick the Great and Napoleon. But he failed to realize that with the revolution and Napoleon a new age had dawned in warfare; he lacked understanding of those factors which were new and he put military thought back into the eighteenth century – an approach which many professional soldiers of the nineteenth century found comfortable and safe. The emphasis of his book is too much on 'mathematics' to the exclusion of psychology and the human factor; you cannot conduct war successfully like that, as I have myself learned. My view would be that he failed to allow for the factors of the unknown and the unexpected, and by so doing he didn't grasp the fact that in war only one thing is certain – that is, that everything will be uncertain.

Clausewitz took the opposite approach. Though he deals with 'mathematics', he is more concerned with war as a social and psychological phenomenon, and he had a profound understanding of those factors. Human feelings seemed to him more interesting and more important than lines and angles. He realized that war could not be understood if isolated from its economic and social background, from the motives of politicians, and from the impulses of human beings. He held that the destruction of the enemy's armed forces is the first aim of generalship, and that the best method of bringing this about is by direct attack. 'Let us not hear of generals who conquer without the shedding of blood'. He emphasized the importance of mass and concentration in Napoleon's methods, but missed the importance of elastic deployment – so well understood by Napoleon. Many authorities have attributed to Clausewitz's thinking the bloody slaughter in the 'mausoleums of mud' (Liddell Hart's words) on the western front in the 1914/18 war.

Like Jomini, Clausewitz also missed some important points in his practical analysis of operations. Possibly because he was writing from the point of view of Germany, his own country, he overlooked the factor of seapower. Also, he failed to consider the movement of forces in terms of potential concentration rather than of actual mass. He wrote that 'there is no more imperative and no simpler law for strategy than to keep the forces concentrated'. On the eve of the mechanized age this observation, taken together with the remark that 'superiority in numbers becomes every day more decisive', pointed the disastrous way forward to the bulldozing methods of the 1914/18 war.

But when all is said and done, I consider Liddell Hart is right when he points out that much of the blame should be laid on those military leaders who misinterpreted Clausewitz's thinking, and took his startling sentences out of their context – and without the qualifications which invariably accompanied them. But it must be remembered that his language is exceedingly difficult to understand; indeed, I pointed out in Chapter 2 that I couldn't understand him myself, and turned to historians of my own nation and language. Clausewitz certainly understood that military strength is, in part, a product of economic forces. In the modern state, military strength and economic strength are both necessary, the two being nicely balanced – a fact which I frequently had to point out to my political masters when I was chief of staff of the British army in 1946–8, and when I served in the Western Defence Organization during the years 1948 to 1958.

With the Industrial Revolution there came a flood of inventions in weapons, armour and communications. In naval warfare the nineteenth century saw the transition from sail to steam. The British, in other ways the world's leaders in the application of steam technology, resisted this transition because they had the most powerful fleet in the world and thus stood to lose by any change. And so the new trends were pioneered by lesser naval powers, France and the United States. John Ericsson, a Swedish engineer, tried unsuccessfully to interest the British Admiralty in the screw propeller; but it was taken up in America, and in 1843 that country launched the first screw warship, the *Princeton* – a 10-gun sloop fitted with a 6-bladed screw, with steam engines developing some 400 horsepower and giving a speed of 13 knots. Following this, in the 1840's and 1850's, naval opinion in Britain and France was converted. The British navy's first screw ship, the *Dauntless*, was launched in 1844, and in 1850 both Britain and France launched screwdriven ships of the line. The early steam warships were single-screw vessels with inefficient engines which consumed great quantities of fuel, leaving them still semi-dependent on sail. With the development of ironclad ships more powerful engines were required, and in the 1850's compound engines of two or more cylinders came in. By 1870 horsepower had almost doubled, and in that year the British navy abandoned sail altogether.

In the 1820's a French artillery officer, Colonel Paixhans, realized that the best way to render the British wooden fleet obsolete was to arm ships with guns which fired shells instead of solid shot. The shell was like a mortar bomb, filled with gunpowder and detonated by means of a time-fuse; it was fired on a flat trajectory by a cannon, and thus more accurately. Trials showed the effectiveness of the shell-gun and in 1837 it was adopted by the French navy, the British and American navies following suit. The counteraction to the introduction of shell-guns was to protect ships with armour. Shells proved so effective against wooden ships at Sebastopol in 1854 during the Crimean War that the French and British were induced to construct floating batteries covered with iron plate. In 1857 the French went further and started to build an ironclad seagoing fleet. Four ships of the *Gloire* class were built – wooden steamships converted into iron-clads by a belt of iron 5 inches thick covering the hull. Thereafter France continued to set the pace in the development of ironclad steamships, and Britain followed her lead.

Since shell-guns had led to ironclads, gun fire had to be made more powerful. Ericsson therefore designed a rotating gun-turret, and by 1870 a 7-inch cannon had been developed. The tactics of the days of sail were now obsolete, and two actions between ironclads pointed the way to new tactics. The fight in Hampton Roads in the American Civil War in 1862 between the *Merrimac* and the *Monitor* showed the value of the rotating gun-turret in making possible all-round fire. In 1866 the ironclad fleets of Italy and Austria met at the battle of Lissa in the Adriatic; their armour rendered gunfire ineffective, and the battle was reduced to an old galley-type ramming match. As a result of these two actions the French adopted the rotating gun-turret and the ram, other navies shortly doing the same. The problems of rusting and fouling were overcome. The result of a quarter of a century's evolution in fighting ships was the British *Devastation*, commissioned in 1875 – a ship described as 'an impregnable piece of Vauban fortification with bastions mounted on a fighting coal mine'. Her tonnage was 9,330, of which 27 per cent was armour; she had a prominent ram, carried four 35-ton guns in two turrets fore and aft giving all-round fire, and had a speed of 15 knots. The *Devastation* presented a small target and was a very stable gun platform.

Three other inventions in naval warfare are worth mentioning. In 1855, in the Baltic, Russia made the first serious use of floating mines. In 1863 the submarine invented by Brun, *Le Plongeur*, was launched; and in 1864 in the American Civil War the small semi-submersibles of the South, called 'Davids', inflicted damage on Northern shipping. Americans on both sides also experimented with torpedoes, the earliest 'fish' torpedo being developed in 1866. These inventions were all exploited initially by lesser naval powers, and were then taken up by Britain. While naval warfare was thus being transformed in the mid-nineteenth century, Britain kept her position as the strongest naval power. But changes in naval tactics had not yet been fully tried out in any major conflicts.

On top of all this, a military arms race took place. Much of the nineteenth century, like the twentieth, was, in Oswald Spengler's words, a time of 'war without war, a war of overbidding in equipment and preparedness, a war of figures and tempo and techniques'. Advances in metallurgy, precision-engineering and ballistics made possible improvements in handguns. The muzzle-loading, flint-lock muskets of the eighteenth century and the Napoleonic era had been slow to load, were unreliable in wet weather, and inaccurate. The first stage in improvement came with the switch from the flint-lock to the percussion cap, which was weatherproof. Most countries had adopted it by 1842. At the same time the greater accuracy gained by rifled barrels was appreciated, and experiments were made everywhere to produce a conical bullet which could be fitted into a muzzle-loading handgun so that it gripped the rifling. In 1850 Captain Minié, a French officer, designed a bullet with a deep recess at the base filled with an iron cup. When the rifle was fired the bullet expanded to fill the rifling of the barrel and create a gas-tight fit; this was easy to load since it required no ramming. In 1853 the British army adopted a muzzle-loading Enfield rifle firing a modified Minié bullet, which was used in the Crimean War. One of the provocations of the Indian Mutiny in 1857 was a rumour that the cartridges of the newly issued Enfield rifle were lubricated with the fat of cows, animals sacred to Hindus.

Naval warfare saw many technical advances, some of which were developed during the American Civil War. Semi-submersibles were designed capable of launching torpedoes *above*; at Hampton Roads *below* the rotating gun turret of the *Monitor* (right) was pitted against the armour plate of the *Merrimac* (left)

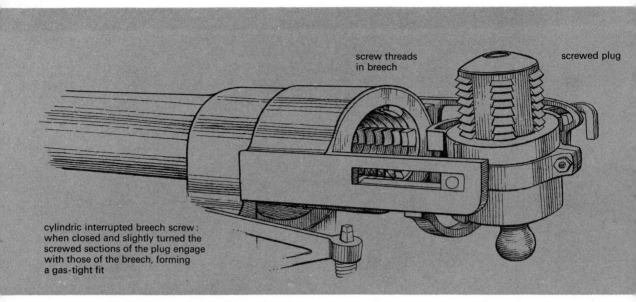

screw threads
in breech

screwed plug

cylindric interrupted breech screw:
when closed and slightly turned the
screwed sections of the plug engage
with those of the breech, forming
a gas-tight fit

In artillery, breech-loading was gradually introduced *above*; mortars continued to be used for siege operations, as at Sebastopol *below* during the Crimean War

Rifles had by now been given increased range and accuracy, but so long as they were muzzle-loaders the rate of fire remained slow. The invention of a breech-loading system by Johann Dreyse in 1839 was therefore a most important break-through. In 1842 the Prussians adopted a modified version of Dreyse's 'needle-gun' (so called after its method of detonation), and tested it to their satisfaction in the war with Denmark over Schleswig-Holstein (1848–9). The important asset of the breech-loader was that it could be fired much more rapidly and be operated easily from a lying-down position. Its development was completed with the addition of a magazine, pioneered in America in the 1860's, and by the solution of the problem of gas escaping from the breech. In 1866 the French adopted an improved breech-loader named after its inventor, M. Chassepot, which gained extra range from its smaller calibre and more gas-tight breech. Colonel Boxer, an Englishman, then invented a brass cartridge which expanded to seal the breech entirely. This was adopted by Britain for the Martini-Henry rifle in 1871, and within a short time it was used by most European countries. By the time of the Franco-Prussian War armies were normally equipped with rifles which were accurate to 600 yards, had ranges of up to 2,000 yards, and could be fired at a rapid rate by men lying down or from trenches.

Major advances in repeating weapons were also made during this period, mostly in America. In 1832 Samuel Colt patented his design for a revolver in which a multi-chamber cylinder was rotated by cocking the hammer, the upper chamber being automatically locked in line with the barrel. The advantages of this weapon were demonstrated in 1835 in fighting against the Seminole Indians in Florida. Colt showed his various revolvers at the Great Exhibition in London in 1851, and sold some to the British navy for the Crimean War. A machine-gun, the Montigny *mitrailleuse*, was designed in Belgium about the same time, and France adopted it shortly before the Franco-Prussian War. It was really a descendant of the 'infernal machine', consisting of several weapons mounted together, being loaded simultaneously by the insertion of a perforated iron plate fitted with cartridges into a common breech-block. A better machine-gun was designed in America in 1862 by Richard Gatling, consisting of a number of barrels around a central axis. The magazine was a hopper above the gun which fed cartridges into the reloading and ejecting mechanism; the gunner turned a handle to rotate the barrels, and it could fire 600 rounds a minute. This was used by both sides in the American Civil War (1861–5).

Artillerymen were impressed by the improvement in handguns which resulted from percussion, rifling and breech-loading. After 1815 experiments were made in Europe and America with rifled, breech-loading artillery weapons, but by 1850 no satisfactory design had been made. The problems of breech-loading mechanisms were threefold – they made artillery heavier and hence less mobile, it was difficult to devise a gas-tight fit at the breech, and a radical re-equipment in artillery was enormously expensive. In the second half of the nineteenth century these difficulties were gradually overcome, and by 1900 guns had been developed which were virtually the same as those used in the 1914/18 and 1939/45 wars. The story of this development is not one of progressive advance, but of a series of hesitant steps which were often retraced.

In France, Napoleon III, for reasons of expense and mobility, retained his old bronze muzzle-loading guns and modified them to Colonel de Beaulieu's system for large-grooved rifling and studded shot, developed in 1842. These were used successfully at the battles of Magenta and Solferino in 1859. Most continental countries followed by adopting muzzle-loaders instead of breech-loaders. In England, William Armstrong at last devised a system of manufacturing cannon which gave increased strength without adding weight, and this made breech-loading feasible. A heated, cylindrical iron jacket was fitted over the barrel; as it cooled it brought the barrel under compression, thus allowing it to withstand a greater charge. This invention was adopted by the British government in 1859, and Armstrong's 9-pounders and 12-pounders were used in action in China in 1860. Prussia and Russia preferred cast steel breech-loading guns manufactured at the Krupp works in Essen. Prussia's artillery, weak in 1866, had been entirely re-equipped with these guns by the Inspector-General, von Hindersin, by 1870; but even these Krupp guns did not prove reliable, and in the same year the British, after concluding that breech-loaders were too expensive and complicated, reverted to muzzle-loaders. Their decision seemed justified when faulty breech mechanisms caused a great many Prussian guns to fail during the Franco-Prussian War.

The nineteenth century was thus a period of inventiveness in arms and armour; furthermore the new inventions could be made available in Europe more readily than ever before. Mass production in factories for mass markets was a basic feature of the new industrial age, and the output of coal, iron and steel was soaring. Samuel Colt was a good example of the new type of manufacturer. He mass-produced his goods and was a master salesman; the North in the civil war in America bought from him 35,000 revolvers, 113,980 muskets and 7,000 rifles.

Another feature of the Industrial Revolution was the development of communications. The improvements in roads which had begun at the end of the eighteenth century was continued, as more and more people travelled for business and pleasure. By the middle of the nineteenth century railways were being constructed apace in Europe and America; most of the trunk lines were completed in France by 1859; by 1855 in Germany, 5,410 miles had been built under strict state planning; and in America 30,000 miles of railroad were laid down between 1830 and 1860. The telegraph, invented by Morse in 1832, was taken up by the railway companies, and in the 1850's the cable networks in Europe and America were rapidly developed.

When a new era of war began in the middle of the nineteenth century practical answers thus had to be found to certain basic questions. With the great increases in numbers of men, what were to be the principles of recruitment and training? Should all these men be equipped with the new weapons, and if so, what was to be the tactical role of infantry armed with rifles, and of artillery? What was to be the role of cavalry? How should officers be trained? How should the new communications, particularly railways, affect strategic planning?

The military leaders of Europe faced these questions and moved into the modern age slowly and reluctantly. Before 1848, when the main threat was from within in the form of liberal revolts, and when the function of armies was to keep the peace domestically, virtually nothing happened. Armies were better kept small in case they themselves should become permeated with revolutionary ideas, and so the great national forces of the Napoleonic period were reduced to small professional armies. Of the great powers, only Russia and Prussia retained the principle of massive armies; and they believed, as I do, that you cannot have a good army without good infantry.

The defence of Chateaudun: an incident in the Franco-Prussian War. A detail from the painting by Felix Philippoteaux. *Overleaf* The Battle of the Alma by Felix Philippoteaux

Furthermore, so long as the old type of army continued to be in any way successful in the field conservatism could be justified. The years between 1830 and 1860 were not barren of able soldiers. Field-Marshal Radetzky, the Austrian commander in the Italian war of 1848–9, showed himself and his army to be extremely competent. When the revolt broke out in northern Italy in 1848 Radetzky had relatively few troops and these were scattered in different areas. But by rapid and energetic movements he avoided the encircling tactics of the enemy, collected his own forces, and struck successive blows at the hostile forces. Having evacuated Milan to avoid being trapped, he held the Piedmontese forces at the 'Quadrilateral' of fortified towns: Mantua, Peschiera, Verona and Legnano. When he had been reinforced, he kept the Piedmontese in check while he moved eastwards to destroy the Papal and Neapolitan forces established on his line of communications near Vicenza. Then he cleared the Brenta valley. Next, he turned back against the Piedmontese and rapidly concentrated superior force to pierce their front at Custozza. Quickly following up his victory, he drove the Piedmontese back into their own territory, and reoccupied Milan some four months after he had left it. In the following year the revolt broke out again, and Radetzky performed a comparable series of resolute and effective manoeuvres, culminating in his victory at Novara. And all this at a time when the Austrian field-marshal was eighty-two years old! At the time of the publication of this book, I am conscious that I myself am about to become eighty-one!

What could still be done without mass armies was also shown by the achievements of Giuseppe Garibaldi and his red-shirted Italian legion: the victories of Cerro and Sant' Antonio in 1846 which assured the independence of Uruguay, his skilful retreat through central Italy in 1849, and the conquest of Sicily and Naples in 1860.

The French army had the legend of Napoleon and a record of thirty years' success in Africa to convince itself that it was invincible. The first expeditionary force sent to Algeria in 1830, cumbrously organized in columns, had run into trouble against the nimble native forces led by Abd-el-Kader, emir of Mascara. But the tide turned in 1836, with Bugeaud's six weeks' campaign in western Algeria. His method was to make swift offensive thrusts with flying columns, lightly equipped and carrying their supplies on pack-animals. After 1840, when governor-general, he applied his technique more extensively and very successfully. His thoughts on war provided a handbook for generations of French imperialist soldiers. New regiments were born in Africa – *zouaves* and *turcos, spahis* and *chasseurs d'Afrique* – and the soldiers of France kept their reputation for *élan*. The lively approach of commanders such as Bugeaud, Canrobert, MacMahon and Bourbaki also contrasted with the mentality of the average British or German general of the day – which lacked inspiration. The French forces in the Crimea acquitted themselves better than those of other nations. In the Italian war of 1859 the French infantry, in their skirmishing *chasseur* formations, showed impressive mobility and intelligence. Despite confused generalship at Solferino, the charging French infantry swept the Austrians away before they could bring their rifle-fire to bear.

Nonetheless the Crimean War, and the Franco-Austrian war of 1859 in Italy, revealed an unsatisfactory state of affairs in all armies – which could no longer be ignored. The Crimean War really provided an object-lesson in how not to make war. The administrative organization on both sides was disastrous. The allies despatched a naval expedition to capture Sebastopol without discovering beforehand that the water on either side of the isthmus was too shallow for their ships to berth. The British brought

The battle of Gettysburg. A detail from the Cyclorama by Paul Philippoteaux, depicting the climax of Pickett's Charge

no transport for their food and ammunition, and the troops lacked practically all the equipment necessary for a winter campaign. The Crimean War was the first in which the telegraph was used, but it did not mitigate the confusion in logistics and strategy.

That war exposed the astonishing weaknesses in the professional armies of the great powers. Tactical blundering led to one of the most famous military disasters of all time, the charge of the British Light Brigade at Balaclava, which brought the observation from General Bosquet of the French army who watched the charge – *'c'est magnifique mais ce n'est pas la guerre'*. The Crimea was one of the most ill-managed campaigns in all recorded history.

The French under Napoleon III did not do much better in 1859, moving their troops into Italy with speed by rail but without arranging proper supplies. The first units were without blankets, cooking equipment or ammunition; shirts had to be torn up to bandage the wounded at Solferino while medical equipment was piled up in the docks at Genoa. One of the reasons for the heavy loss of life at Solferino was that it was an encounter battle pure and simple, a rare event in military history, neither side expecting to have to fight immediately.

The appallingly high casualty rate in these wars provoked a revolution in medical services. In the Crimea, of 405,000 men sent out by the British and French armies, 25,600 were killed in action and 38,800 died of disease. Florence Nightingale left the seclusion of Harley Street with thirty-eight trained nurses to go and nurse the troops in the Crimea, and it was not the least important consequence of this war that the emancipation of women was considerably advanced. Every war since then has seen a marked gain for women in social emancipation and public responsibility. Mainly as a result of the work of Henri Dunant, a Swiss banker and philanthropist who had been impressed by the work of Florence Nightingale as well as being appalled by the slaughter at Solferino, the International Red Cross Committee was set up and the first Geneva Convention was agreed by twelve powers in 1864. In the Franco-Prussian War the Red Cross was to care for over half a million sick and wounded.

The army which was most rapidly, efficiently and thoroughly reformed after 1859 was that of Germany. Prussia was not involved with the war of 1859 in Italy, but she watched the course of events with interest, for she stood to gain diplomatically by the weakening of either of the main contenders, France and Austria; and many Prussians were becoming aware that the condition of their army would not do. Her professional army was too small, and the *Landwehr* or militia was politically disaffected and militarily only half-trained. However in 1858 Prince William became regent for his mad brother, and he brought to the government of Prussia a professionalism and single-minded enthusiasm for military matters which bears comparison with that of Frederick William I. Under Prince William three men rose to eminence, and these between them secured Prussia as an autocratic and militaristic state and gained for her political supremacy in the German Confederation. The three were: von Roon, minister of war after 1859; von Moltke, chief of the general staff; and their political chief von Bismarck, minister-president from 1862. Prince William and Roon decided to professionalize the forces available to Prussia, by making long-term service compulsory and by spending more money on equipment and training. 'Discipline, blind obedience, are things which can be inculcated and given permanence only by long familiarity', the regent considered. It took them some years to

The most disastrous blunder of the Crimean War was the suicidal charge of the Light Brigade at Balaclava down a valley with Russian guns on three sides

get their way with the public. Bismarck used war deliberately as a tool of policy. The outcome of his premeditated wars with Denmark (1864), Austria (1866) and France (1870) was the unification of Germany under Prussian leadership; she also became a major industrial power.

By 1868 the army of the North German Confederation had emerged. The various nominally independent states of the Confederation were persuaded to toe the Prussian line: albeit with uneven enthusiasm, but satisfactorily enough. Universal obligation to military service was laid down, and the army was described as 'the training school of the entire nation for war'. Service with the colours was for three years from the age of twenty; conscripts then served with the reserve for a further four years; they then passed into the *Landwehr*. The regular army, in addition to particular cadres, thus consisted of seven annual intakes – or eight if necessary, since men could be called up with the reserve during their first year in the *Landwehr*. Service with the *Landwehr* was for five years, and the force was supervised so closely by the regular army that it constituted in effect a second reserve. When the test came in 1870, Roon put into the field well over one million officers and men. The infantry were equipped with the Dreyse needle-gun, the effectiveness of which had been well demonstrated in 1866, when the Prussians firing six shots to every one fired by the Austrians swept the enemy from the field of Sadowa. The army was also equipped with the most up-to-date breech-loading Krupp artillery.

Size would not however be an advantage without efficient organization. The training, mobilization and deployment of troops, and their supply, presented immense problems;

efficient staffs were vital in a way they had not been before. The organization for command and control had now to take account of the increased areas over which operations would take place, due to the size of armies and to the strategic dispersal of forces made possible by railways, and to tactical dispersion made necessary in battle by rifled fire-arms. Greater responsibility had to be delegated to subordinate commanders, and it was essential for these to be responsive to the ideas and methods of their seniors without initiative being cramped. The problems of supply and of communication had now become highly technical, and experts were needed in every field. But the Prussian army had, in its general staff, a body of skilled experts capable of dealing with these related problems of training, planning and communications.

Von Moltke was appointed chief of the Prussian general staff in 1857. His intellect was brilliant, and his understanding of staff functions was highly developed. He brought to his work personal dedication and the highest standards; his subordinates regarded him with the reverence of disciples. He was a man of wide culture but rigorous self-discipline, and had made himself, as Michael Howard puts it, 'the most exact and exacting of specialists'. He trained the staff officers of the German army in his own image. Twelve of the best graduates of the *Kriegsakademie* were selected each year for special training, and they worked under Moltke's personal supervision. Any who proved unsatisfactory were quickly returned to regimental duty, and in any case all staff officers did a spell with their regiments before each step in promotion. The staff were thus kept in touch with the soldiery, and Moltke's ideas and standards permeated the army, which by 1870 was largely orientated as he had planned; most of the brigade and divisional commanders had been trained under him, and each corps and army commander had a chief of staff at his elbow.

Training the staff and the army command was Moltke's supreme contribution to the wars his country was to fight, and was of the greatest value when it came to drawing up war plans. These included the smooth and efficient mobilization of the army, the efficient functioning of the railway service, and plans for the deployment of the army to meet any international crisis. By 1866 Moltke had achieved an efficient degree of decentralization in the mobilization plans, and by 1870 the machinery was perfect. The commanders of corps areas had been well briefed, and every unit in the regular army, the *Landwehr*, and the communications and supply departments had orders which needed only a code word and a date to be put into operation. The Prussians had long been aware of the military importance of railways, and much of their railway network had been constructed with strategic considerations in mind. In the campaign of 1866 in Austria they made some of the mistakes which the French had made in 1859 in Italy in failing to co-ordinate the movement of troops and supplies by rail. But Moltke learned from those mistakes. A special 'Line of Communication Department' of the general staff was set up under one of his principal assistants. The mobilization by means of the railways in 1870 was highly successful, although it is true that the supply lines became congested at some points. From 1858 to 1880 Moltke was continually bringing his plans up to date, crystallizing the work of his staff and departments. At any moment Prussia was capable of mobilizing and deploying her army to deal with any of her three chief potential enemies – France, Austria and Russia.

Military reform in France began later than in Prussia. After their Italian campaign of 1859 the French tried to persuade themselves for a while that all was well enough, though the weaknesses of the French army in that campaign were very apparent to German eyes beyond the Rhine. In due course disillusionment came when it was seen what the Prussians could do against Austria in 1866, and with the more ignominious aspects of the military intervention by France in Mexican affairs between 1861 and 1867. From 1866 Napoleon III and Marshal Niel, minister of war, worked to bring the French army more into line with Prussian standards. But the reformers had to fight against opposition even stronger than that in Prussia, for the regime in France was more liberal and public opinion could not be overridden in the same way. Gay uniforms and romantic passages of arms in far corners of the world had led to some revival of the sentiment of an earlier Napoleonic era, but French public opinion was still cautious. The middle classes were interested above all in prosperity and peace, and the army was acceptable only if it cost no extra money and so long as those who wished could avoid military service. Since 1818 conscripts in France had been permitted to send substitutes; the result was that the army had developed as an element apart from the nation, and the officer corps was socially despised. In 1866 the French authorities considered the problem and calculated that, while Prussia might be able to raise 1,200,000 trained men, the military strength of France could produce only 288,000 – from which contingents must be drawn to meet commitments in Algeria, Italy and Mexico. But when Niel proposed the adoption of universal military service on the Prussian model he was accused in the Legislature of wanting to turn France into a barracks. His reply was that if the French were not careful their country would be turned into a cemetery.

In January 1868 a new law was passed. Under this, 172,000 men were to be called up annually, to do five years with the colours and four in the reserve – which by 1875 should provide a mobilized strength of 800,000 for the army. Another 500,000, drawn from those who escaped the call-up, were to be trained in the *Garde Mobile*. This was to be the French equivalent of the *Landwehr*, but Niel's proposal had been so watered down by the deputies that the resemblance was slight. Service was for five years, but the annual training period lasted only two weeks; even this could easily be evaded, and to avoid the taint of militarism it was laid down that the men were to be trained only for one day at a time, and in conditions which would enable them to get home by the evening. After Niel's death in 1869 his successor, General Leboeuf, discarded the *Garde Mobile* altogether.

By 1870 the professional army of France consisted of nearly half a million men, and it was certainly well equipped – there being ample quantities of clothing, food and ammunition. A million *chassepot* rifles had been manufactured, and although the artillery had not been re-equipped, that which existed was by no means bad. On the other hand, despite incessant warnings from the French military *attaché* in Berlin, hardly a start had been made in those areas of staff work in which the Prussian army by now excelled: for example, the training of officers, the organization of supply and railway communications, and machinery for mobilization and deployment. The French soldiers were known to be courageous, but also to be indisciplined. The standard of teaching at the military colleges of Saint-Cyr, Metz and Saumur was poor, and only a few intelligent or wealthy officers attended them. Most French officers were elderly, brave men who had risen in the colonial wars by virtue of their qualities of courage, dash and *coup d'oeil*, rather than for technical expertise in their profession. In 1870 the French army was better prepared for war than it had been at any time since the Napoleonic wars, but it was not prepared for modern war.

The outbreak of war between France and Prussia in July 1870 was due ostensibly to diplomatic irritation about the succession to the Spanish throne. But in fact the two powers were more deeply antagonized than that, and Napoleon III and Bismarck needed only an excuse to resort to war. Napoleon feared Prussia as the leader of a united Germany, while Bismarck saw war with France as an opportunity to rally Germans to his programme. Moltke and Roon were confident that the German army could beat the French, and here was the opportunity.

Napoleon III declared war on 19th July, and a week later at Metz he personally ordered the advance of French forces across the Rhine near Strasbourg in order to prevent the junction of the south and north German contingents. But the mobilization of the French did not keep pace with their strategy; at first there were *no* armies in Alsace and on the Moselle, and a concentration of 300,000 men was achieved only when it was too late. The Prussian mobilization had been brilliantly organized by Moltke in advance, and in the opening phase each formation and unit followed precise directives. The First Army, only two corps and a cavalry division under General von Steinmetz, was pushed forward on the right over the Rhine and towards the Moselle between Trier and Wittlich. The Second Army, under Prince Frederick Charles and comprising four army corps and two cavalry divisions, assembled on the Rhine between Mainz and Mannheim and shortly afterwards was moved up to connect with the left flank of the First around Homburg. The Third Army commanded by the Crown Prince of Prussia and consisting of four corps, the divisions of Würtemberg and Baden and a cavalry division, assembled farther up the Rhine on the left wing. Two additional corps were held in reserve for the Second Army. The three armies, totalling 384,000 men, were mobilized and transported to the forward zone west of the Rhine in eighteen days. Rail transport would be available in three weeks to bring up three more army corps. Moltke had at one time been apprehensive of a French attempt to dislocate his mobilization, but the superiority of his strategic and administrative foresight completely obviated that danger and gave the Prussians the opening initiative.

The detailed advance plans of Moltke ended at this point, with his troops facing the enemy's capital and so deployed as to be able to attack the enemy in strength as they appeared. His arrangements were simple and fluid. He hoped to fight a decisive battle in the area of the Saar, concentrating the weight of the three German armies to crush the outnumbered French. But he thought it wrong to attempt to lay down precise plans too far ahead, since the situation beyond the first clash with the enemy was bound to contain unknown factors. His army commanders knew his broad plan and had operational directives, but they were given latitude in their detailed operations and were expected to display initiative.

The French had been foiled in their first plan, and were in some doubt about what to do. But when they had concentrated some 200,000 men in the forward area they opened the fighting – a reconnaissance in force on 2nd August at Saarbrücken, which achieved little. Moltke now thought that the French were about to launch a strong offensive. He therefore closed the Second Army in the centre on to its advance posts; the First Army on the right, the weakest and the farthest advanced, was ordered to halt; and the Third Army, not quite completely assembled, was moved forward over the frontier into northern Alsace at Wissembourg – where the first serious engagement of the war took place on 4th August. Two days later the German Third Army, pushing on forward to

Wörth, enveloped part of the French right wing commanded by MacMahon. The battle was fiercely contested, each side returning to the attack again and again and both suffering heavy casualties. There were two gallant but unavailing French cavalry charges. Eventually the superior handling of their artillery and the better fire-discipline of the Germans caused the French to break off the action and retreat.

Central Europe in the nineteenth century

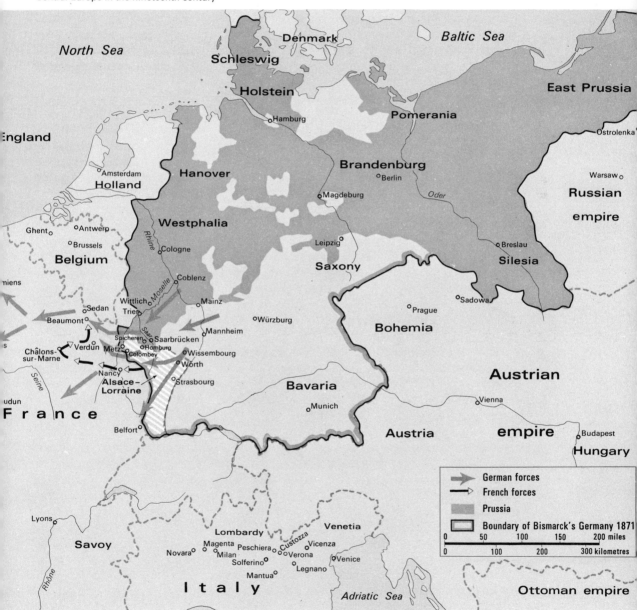

But at this stage matters ceased to go altogether as Moltke had ordained. On 6th August, the same day as the battle of Wörth, Steinmetz rashly engaged the First Army against French forces strongly entrenched at Spicheren, thirty-five miles to the north-west. The commanders of neighbouring German formations quickly came to the assistance of the leading attacking division, and by the evening the French were forced to withdraw. But the German losses in men at Spicheren had been heavier than those of the French. The German reconnaissance now lost sight of MacMahon's movements, and Moltke supposed that the French right was moving north-westwards to join the forces of the French left under Bazaine near Metz on the Moselle – whereas in fact MacMahon was moving back south-westwards. Moltke also assumed that Bazaine was retreating from Metz, which was not the case. The German reconnaissance was not too well handled by the cavalry, the net result being that their forces were experiencing the fog of war as they moved forward.

On 14th August a second unexpected battle took place at Colombey, east of Metz, which the Germans just won as before. By the evening of 15th August Bazaine was definitely retreating from Metz, but he had not gone as fast towards Verdun as Moltke supposed when, on the 16th, the German Second Army pressed across the Moselle south of Metz to pursue Bazaine – whose forces were strongly concentrated less than ten miles to the west. The Second Army was strung out and isolated, and Bazaine had a golden opportunity to attack it in flank with superior forces – but he allowed events to drift. The first German corps collided with a stronger French force at Mars-la-Tour – across the Moselle to the west of Metz. The same pattern unfolded as at Spicheren; the Germans fought desperately until additional forces came to their help, and by the end of the day they had gained some ground. Each side lost about 16,000 men.

Bazaine now decided to stand and fight, and he ordered his forces to entrench in a strong position just west of Metz – the ridge that runs for about seven miles between the villages of Gravelotte to the south and Saint-Privat to the north. The ridge sloped gently to the west and dropped steeply to the east. By 18th August the French defences were completed – fire and communication trenches had been dug, many of the batteries protected by emplacements, and some farmhouses had been converted into small forts. In the battle which was about to take place both sides would actually face their own strategic rear. The German push since 6th August had brought their forces round on a wide south-westerly movement and, when the French did not retreat as expected, the German First and Second Armies found that they had completely enveloped the right flank of Bazaine's forces. On 18th August as dawn broke, Prince Frederick Charles still imagined that Bazaine was retreating westwards, and he marched his army northwards in strong parallel columns west of the ridge – thereby exposing them to a situation of great potential danger. But as at Mars-la-Tour Bazaine failed to attack when the advantage was his. This time the Germans intended to fight when they should find the enemy, and for the first time the bulk of the forces of both sides were to be engaged in one battle. The Germans, having removed the original right of the French from the picture by the victory of Wörth, had 188,300 men and 732 guns to oppose 112,800 Frenchmen and 520 guns.

The leading corps of Prince Frederick Charles's Second Army came into contact with the French at Amanvillers. The Germans at first supposed this to be the extreme right of the French position, and shortly before midday Manstein's IX Corps attacked the

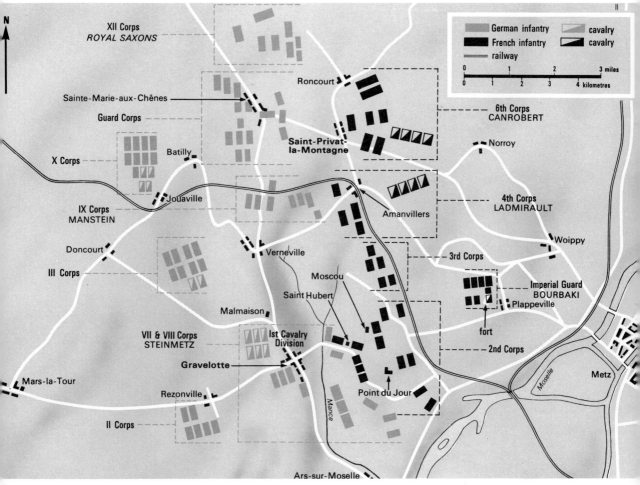

The battle of Gravelotte-Saint-Privat

French positions commanded by Ladmirault beyond Verneville. By the time it was realized that the French were holding Saint-Privat in force, and might attack the German forces in flank, it was too late for Moltke to alter the orders for attack – which orders had been given on the assumption that the French position based on Gravelotte could be turned from the north. In the initial fighting around Amanvillers the Germans were checked by the fire of the French *chassepots* in the open fields, and they lost some artillery to a counter-attack. The battle in this area was then reduced to an artillery duel which the troops on both sides endured passively, while more troops of the German Second Army were brought up to support their left. By 3 o'clock Manstein had been reinforced and the Germans soon drove the French out of the village of Sainte-Marie-aux-Chênes. By 5 o'clock the French infantry was thickly bunched about Saint-Privat and their artillery did its best to protect them from the concentrated fire of 180 German guns.

Prussian troops storm the cemetery of Saint-Privat after a desperate defence

Meanwhile around Gravelotte from the north and south the artillery of the German VII and VIII Corps had at midday opened continuous fire from 150 guns on the French positions – the fire continuing until dark came. The Germans were to see the effect of this fire the next day:

> In Moscou and Point du Jour some French were found burnt in their defensive positions, and a large number of the wounded showed marks of the flames. All around there lay rifles and swords, knapsacks and cartridges, the remains of limbers which had been blown up, broken gun-carriages and wheels, and a large number of hideously torn and mangled horses.

Nevertheless neither artillery fire nor infantry attacks could move the French from the positions opposite Gravelotte on 18th August. All assaults against that area were repulsed except at the outpost of Saint-Hubert, which fell in the middle of the afternoon – the only gain made by the German First Army (commanded by Steinmetz).

A little farther south, in the ravine of the Mance, Steinmetz made a series of flagrant mistakes. Assuming the fall of Saint-Hubert to be a sign of French disintegration, he ordered all the available infantry and artillery of VII Corps to attack along the axis of the narrow road into the ravine and, for a *coup de grâce*, sent with them the 1st cavalry division which was to chase the defeated French as far as Metz. A very few Germans fought their way through to Saint-Hubert, but the rest were blocked in bloody chaos in the ravine. By 5 o'clock it was clear that the First Army's attack had been a failure, and a withdrawal was beginning. Within an hour the German advantage at Saint-Privat was also to be prejudiced – when Prince Augustus of Würtemberg ordered the Guard Corps to advance on Saint-Privat before the Saxons could co-ordinate their attack farther to the north. When the skirmishing lines of the Guard advanced up the slope towards the French line of *chassepots* a massacre ensued. The field-officers were shot from their horses, and then the men were mown down as they struggled on; finally, when the attack came within some 600 yards from Saint-Privat it was halted – having suffered 8,000 casualties in twenty minutes.

By 6 o'clock the French had thus checked the Germans along the whole length of the line from Gravelotte to Saint-Privat. The moment was now ripe for a French counter-attack, which might well have been successful. But for the third time in four days Bazaine neglected to seize his chance; his will-power and energy appear to have been paralysed by the weight of responsibility, and, as he claimed, he was exhausted. Refusing to come forward from his headquarters at Plappeville, he was aware only that the defence was succeeding – which seemed to him enough. When subordinate commanders asked for new orders he displayed hesitation and indecision, and they themselves lacked the initiative necessary to complete the victory.

Even although the French did not launch a counter-attack, the German situation in the south was about to deteriorate further. When Steinmetz's own troops had all been thrown into the chaos of the Mance ravine, he appealed to royal headquarters for permission to throw in fresh troops from II Corps, which was just arriving in the battle area. Steinmetz had misled the king with a report that he had all but carried the heights, and, since Moltke remained silent, permission was granted. The French could see the helmets of their enemies glinting in the evening sun, and they were ready. The assault was met with murderous fire at point-blank range, and the German infantry fell back in disorder. Then some of the horses began to bolt, and suddenly the tension broke in VII and VIII Corps. Cavalry and horse artillery careered in flight back through Gravelotte, and the German infantry ran back down the ravine – yet still the French did not counter-attack. II Corps resisted the tide of panic, but in the darkness the soldiers found them-selves firing into disordered German troops; they did no more than hold the position and at 9.30 o'clock they ceased fire.

The king and his staff made their way back to Rezonville, to contemplate the defeat of the First Army. Their gloom was not lightened until after midnight, when at last Moltke learned from Prince Frederick Charles that the French right wing had collapsed. The tremendous pressure of the Guard Corps had actually helped the German situation in no small way, for when the Saxons made their flank attack from the north the French were not ready to face them. At the same time the artillery fire broke up all French attempts to move forward between Amanvillers and Saint-Privat, and Canrobert, commanding on the right, decided that he must fall back, requesting Bourbaki, com-manding the Imperial Guard in reserve, to cover his retreat – which he was unable to do. A last charge by cavalry was quickly broken up by German rifle fire. Soon after 8 o'clock the Germans, 50,000 strong, had gained Saint-Privat at the point of the bayonet, and the French right withdrew in a straggling column down the Woippy road. Farther to the French left, at Amanvillers, Bourbaki in a rage refused to support Ladmirault in the centre, and there too the French started to retreat.

The retreat of the French right was an orderly affair compared to the rout of the Germans at Gravelotte, and the Germans were too disorganized to pursue. But it was enough to decide the verdict of the battle of Gravelotte-Saint-Privat in favour of the Germans. On 19th August the rest of Bazaine's Army of the Rhine retired into the defences of Metz. The Germans had suffered some 20,000 casualties, considerably more than the French, but they gained a decisive strategic advantage at the conclusion of the battle because they were able to bottle up Bazaine's army in Metz – thus eliminating it altogether from the rest of the war. Bazaine's failure in generalship needs no further discussion; it is sufficient to add that the French troops had displayed a fighting quality which deserved better leadership. Moltke was lucky to have gained such a victory, for he had not really been in control of events at any time since 6th August, the day of the battles of Wörth and Spicheren, and on 17th August the Germans no more deserved to win than did the French. The battle showed that Moltke's qualities were those of a trainer and organizer of large armies rather than those of a commander-in-chief in the field. But his years of work were triumphantly vindicated in the instinctive mutual understanding which German subordinate officers showed in this campaign; the blunders of Steinmetz and Prince Frederick Charles were repaired repeatedly by the speed, intelligence and loyalty with which the commanders of lesser German formations and units helped each other out, as well as by the discipline and courage of the troops – born of confidence in their officers.

Meanwhile MacMahon, following his defeat at Wörth, had retreated in the direction of Paris as far as Châlons-sur-Marne. There he had time to build up his army to four corps, and on 23rd August he was ordered to advance north-eastwards to relieve Bazaine. As Liddell Hart observes, Moltke now reaped the benefit inherent in wide manoeuvre. The German Third Army had continued after Wörth on a southerly circuit and had thus passed well out of the focal centre of the phase of operations which had culminated at Gravelotte-Saint-Privat; but this manoeuvre placed it in a perfect position from which to wheel north on to the flank and rear of MacMahon's army as it advanced. MacMahon was at the same time headed away by part of the German forces moving from Metz, and by the end of August he was trapped against the Belgian frontier; a battle took place at Beaumont on the 30th. Even now the German command was operating somewhat in the dark. On 1st September the Battle of Sedan (on the Meuse) took place; the French were surrounded in a cup of land, and the Germans used their artillery to defeat them from beyond the range of the *chassepot*. The next day the French forces surrendered – the Germans taking 104,000 prisoners, including Napoleon III, while losing only 9,000 men themselves.

The Germans had effectively defeated the French in two months of operations, for France did not have another organized army. The war was, however, drawn out a further six months before its final conclusion. A republic was declared in Paris, and Gambetta, minister of war, inspired the resistance. The sieges of Metz and Paris were prolonged. The French hurled themselves against the besieging Germans with ferocious courage, and in the countryside the *francs-tireurs* assailled them with guerrilla warfare. Gambetta escaped from Paris by balloon to organize an army of the Loire. Only in

January and February 1871 did the last of the French surrender in Paris, the Loire and the Jura. William proclaimed himself German Emperor in the Hall of Mirrors at Versailles, and on 1st March the Germans marched in triumph through the streets of Paris. The French then fought and massacred each other in Paris during the Commune – watched by the Germans.

Another great 'modern' war had taken place in North America. The origins of the American Civil War (1861–5) lay in the growing tension between two completely different types of society bound together under one government, and the issue of slavery sharpened hatreds during the 1850's. In the presidential election of 1860 victory went to the republicans, whose programme was tied to the economic interests of the North; eleven southern states in consequence seceded from the Union. Jefferson Davis was, in February 1861, elected the first 'president' of the new 'Confederate States of America', the South, with the capital at Montgomery, Alabama – of which city I am a Freeman. In the North, Lincoln took office as 'president of the United States of America' in March 1861, the capital being, as always, Washington.

The North had a population of over 18 million to pit against the South who had half that, 9 million – one third of which were negro slaves. The North possessed 90 per cent of the country's manufacturing capacity, two thirds of its railway mileage, control of the seas, and most of the mineral resources. The South was particularly badly off for weapons: of 135,000 handguns seized from government arsenals at secession, only 10,000 were rifles, the rest being old-fashioned smooth-bores and some of them flint-locks. In time enterprising Southerners were able to capture and improvize more modern weapons, but they remained at a grave disadvantage. But the South was fighting to protect its way of life and its homes from invaders, whereas the troops of the North were fighting only for an abstraction – the principle of the Union. For this reason the South found it easier to raise enthusiastic fighters. Moreover a much higher proportion of Southerners were countrymen – good horsemen and used to an open air life.

Certain facts should be understood. Lincoln considered that slavery was an issue which time and common sense would solve. But once the Union was split in twain, unity would never return; North America would become like Europe, a continent torn with disunity, jealousy, economic rivalry, and war. He fought to preserve the Union, and after he had taken office as president he delayed the issue of slavery as long as he could. The war broke out in April 1861 when the United States garrison at Fort Sumter in South Carolina was attacked by troops of the 'Confederate States of America'; the Union flag, the Stars and Stripes, was fired on, and then hauled down as a white flag was hoisted and the garrison surrendered. That was too much! The North sprang to arms; the South followed suit. The American Civil War, or as many prefer to call it in that country 'The War between the States', had begun.

A great deal has been written about this war and it certainly repays study. I propose to deal with it somewhat differently than in our other studies, examining personalities, the generalship, the armies, rather than the conduct of the war and details of the battles which were fought. This approach has often been neglected, and it is likely to be of particular interest to the non-military reader.

Let us take the two presidents first. Davis in the South was well qualified to handle the material at his disposal; he was a graduate of West Point and had served several years in the regular army. He had been secretary of war in Washington and after that was chairman of the Senate committee on military affairs. He knew the army of the United States inside out, and he was well able to select the right men for the more responsible posts. Not only did he select the right men, but he supported them in adversity and did not at once remove a general because he met with a reverse. Thus the same generals who were in command at the beginning of the war were still in command at the end – with the exception of any who were killed, such as Johnston and Jackson. Furthermore, he had in General Lee possibly the best American military thinker and organizer of those days, and during the first year of the war he retained Lee as his chief of staff in the capital, a decision which in my view had much to do with the initial success of the South. Later, in June 1862, Lee was given command of the Army of Northern Virginia.

In Lincoln the picture is very different. He was a lawyer, and a good politician. But he had no practical military experience, knew nothing of the army, and was personally acquainted with very few of its officers. His appointments were too often made on political grounds; when popular outcry demanded the recall of a defeated general, Lincoln generally yielded; a general who failed once was rarely allowed a second chance. None of the generals commanding the main armies at the end of the war had held a high command at the beginning. A ruthless process of elimination eventually brought the best men to the top, and some were good, but in the process several good men had disappeared, and the North was the poorer for their loss. To me it is intensely interesting to study his attempts to find a general who could win battles, which, after all, is what generals are meant to do. He began with Scott, a sick man aged seventy-four. Then we see the following pass across the military stage – McDowell, McClellan, Halleck, Pope, Burnside, Hooker, Meade.

The general whom Lincoln eventually found, Ulysses Grant, came up the hard way, beginning as a commander of a regiment and ending as General-in-Chief. He was a soldier's soldier, a general's general, thoughtful of his subordinates and fitting his orders to their experience and skill. Of all the generals on either side in the war, he alone demonstrated the capacity to command small forces as well as large ones in battle under a great variety of conditions – and finally to command and direct the operations of several armies. And he did not believe in large staffs; in 1864 he commanded five armies operating in an area half the size of Europe, and his headquarters staff consisted of fourteen officers. Lincoln had at last found a general, but not until February 1864 – and then with a thankful heart he appointed Ulysses Grant to command the armies of the North. He and Sherman were the two best field commanders produced in the War between the States – both serving under Lincoln.

When the war began both sides had to create an army, and in each case it was bound to be an army of volunteers. In 1860 the regular army of the United States totalled only some 16,000, the greater part being scattered in small detachments on the Indian frontier which could not be withdrawn. Both in the North and South there were many militia units, but these lacked training and discipline. It was a great advantage for the South to be able to cut loose from the red tape of the War Department in Washington; and Davis had Lee to help him in organizing his forces during the first year of the war, Lincoln having no such advantage.

Geography, the strategic use of railways, tactics and generalship played a large part in the war. In the western theatre the war was more fluid and mobile than in the east, being

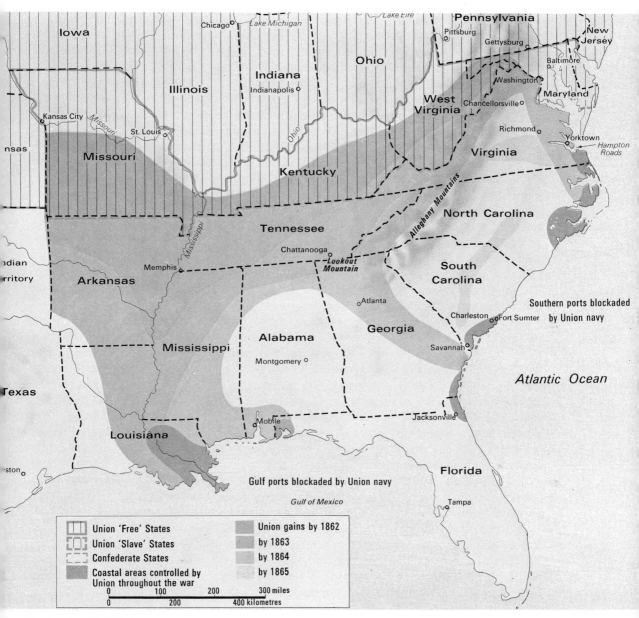

The American Civil War

fought over vast areas. The control of rivers was a major strategic objective, particularly for the North as it had most of the steamboats, the trained river men, and the building and repair organizations.

When Virginia joined the Confederacy, Davis made Richmond the capital of the South. It was a major error to choose for the capital a city which was so near the frontier and accessible from the sea – particularly since the North had the navy. Atlanta would have been a better choice, or the capital might have remained at Montgomery. The two capitals were now within 100 miles of each other, and much of the effort of each side was directed to capturing the other's capital. If either had succeeded it would have been of great moral importance. If Washington had fallen at any time, the will to victory in the North might well have collapsed; Lincoln realized this; he also realized that the destruction of Lee's army, even more than the capture of Richmond, would have had a similar effect on the South. As events turned out, Washington was threatened more than once. But the North had in Lincoln a real man, one of tremendous courage, determination and singleness of mind; it may be that without Lincoln the North would probably have given up the struggle. Richmond finally fell in the closing weeks of the war.

Earlier in this chapter we saw the tremendous improvements in firearms which took place during the fifty years or so after Waterloo. These improvements in weapons revolutionized tactics; the solid infantry formations of earlier years disappeared; the old type of cavalry warfare, shock action against infantry, went out of business; the spade and the axe became necessary articles in battle; breastworks and rifle pits were used to give cover and protection. The civil war in America produced all these lessons; yet the professional soldiers of Europe refused to take them seriously because they said the war was fought by amateurs! They had to learn the hard way, and this they most certainly did as we shall see in the next two chapters.

We have summarized the different personalities of Davis and Lincoln, the two political leaders. I will conclude with a few remarks about Lee and Ulysses Grant, the two military leaders. My view of Lee is that he wasn't sufficiently firm with his corps commanders, and he was not a good picker of men. After Jackson had been killed at Chancellorsville, he had three indifferent corps commanders (Ewell, Hill and Longstreet) all of whom failed to measure up to their responsibilities at Gettysburg. His own judgment was generally sound, but he didn't like to give firm orders to unwilling subordinates; this was brought out very clearly at Gettysburg, in which battle he was at his worst. I agree with the American historian, Douglas Freeman, who wrote that the army of the South at Gettysburg had no commander-in-chief. Later, the odds were heavily stacked against Lee when he was called upon to confront Grant, the greatest general of the victorious North – at a time when he, Lee, was the champion of a lost cause. In any case he couldn't successfully take on two such generals as Grant and Sherman at the same time.

It is difficult to understand why Lee hung on so long to Richmond. Grant reckoned it was a point of honour with Lee that the last stand should be made in the defence of the Southern capital. Against this, Fuller is reported to have said that Lee was afraid to withdraw his soldiers from their entrenchments lest the soldiers should desert; so long as they faced the enemy they would fight, but once the hostile pressure was relaxed the temptation to break might prove too strong. I find that view difficult to believe. My own study of the war has revealed that whereas the generalship was not too good, what might be called 'the soldiership' was first class – the men in the ranks on both sides being magnificent natural soldiers, ready and willing to fight for the cause in which they believed and, if necessary, to die for that cause. My final word on the War between the States is that it well repays study by soldiers of the present day.

The victory of the North in the American Civil War was a victory for nationalism, liberalism and industrialism. From the military point of view it produced many of the same experiences and lessons as did the Franco-Prussian War. The effect of rifle fire, at Saint-Privat and Gettysburg equally, indicated the new strength of the defensive. The fate of cavalry charging in the old style, as at Wörth, showed that it must devise different tactical functions; this had not apparently been appreciated in Europe so well as in America – where the Southern cavalry commander, Nathan B. Forrest, adapted his forces to use them mainly as mounted infantry. The defensive power of the machine-gun had yet to be gauged, but the paralysing and destructive power of modern artillery had been felt. It had been shown that the existence of railways could be an advantage or a disadvantage, depending on their use. The swift Prussian victory in 1870 was due to Moltke's brilliantly efficient mobilization by means of railways as much as to any other factor. On the other hand one of the reasons why the North was unable to make any decisive breakthrough for so long was that it became tied too rigidly to fixed lines of supply; the North won quickly only when Sherman broke free of his dependence on railheads. The growing size of armies rendered mobility much more difficult, and gave increased importance to staffs, and to commanders of corps and divisions: matters which the Germans appeared to have understood better than the French. The signifi-cance of the technical developments in naval warfare could not yet be judged, for it had hardly entered into the Franco-Prussian War; but the blockade of the Southern States from the sea had undoubtedly helped the North in what was partly a war between two economies. The Civil War was in fact a powerful stimulus to economic growth in the Northern States. By 1871 modern war, in its various aspects, had been widely ex-perienced. It remained to see whether the lessons of those experiences would be drawn – and that did not happen quickly.

Federal troops, under Grant, launched a surprise attack in mist and rain on Lookout Mountain

The British army, adopting traditional tactics, was at first unable to cope with the guerrilla warfare and accurate marksmanship of the Boers

19 Learning the Hard Way

I decided to give this chapter its present title because the great powers had much to learn after the close of the three wars referred to in Chapter 18 – the Crimean War, the American Civil War and the Franco-Prussian War. During the last quarter of the nineteenth century they were so occupied by the scramble for territory in Africa and Asia, which involved them in 'limited wars' in those continents, that they neglected to study seriously the lessons of the major conflicts referred to above (by limited wars I mean conflicts which are restricted in objective or in area by the inability of the contestants to engage the whole of their national strength). Furthermore the great powers failed to understand the lessons of the Boer War, as it was popularly called – which should have already been made clear during the American Civil War some thirty-five years earlier.

I call to mind the words of Maeterlinck: 'The past is of use to me as the eve of tomorrow; my soul wrestles with the future.' In other words, to plan the future wisely nations must learn from the past. Neglect of this principle means that the path to success in the future has to be trodden the hard way – and the cost is then paid in men's lives.

The years between 1870 and 1914 were years of armed peace in Europe and of frequent small wars throughout the rest of the world. Peace was kept at first in Europe through Bismarck's positive diplomatic policy. After his fall in 1890 the tensions within Europe grew; peace, however, was still kept, though only through the deadlock created by the balance of power between two armed camps. All this time the European powers furthered their interests and found outlets for their tensions in other areas of the world – those of most direct competition being East Asia, North Africa and the Balkans. As long as there was plenty of space the European imperialists largely managed to avoid fighting each other, and engaged in operations against native peoples. Within this period, however, the emergence on the international scene outside Europe of two new industrial and mass powers indicated that imperialism might have to be curbed. In 1904–5 Japan defeated Russia in a war which involved more men than any previous war in history. Similarly, when the United States of America in the war of 1898 over Cuba deprived Spain of the last of her significant colonial possessions, it was indicated that European powers would no longer be able to relieve their tensions by expressing them in a vast imperial arena; the world outside Europe was beginning to be crowded with people and with industrial and military power.

It is remarkable that large-scale war was so successfully avoided in this period, considering how great were the strains set up in Europe by economic and social factors. The population of Europe rose by 10 per cent each decade, and industrialization continued to grow, with world production rising four times between 1870 and 1900. The cumulative interaction between population growth, industrial methods, and pure science produced entirely new industries such as the electrical and chemical industries, and new sources of power such as the internal combustion engine. Aluminium, the pneumatic tyre and wireless made their appearance. In particular the armaments industry entered a phase of growth which controlled politics at least as much as it was influenced by them. The world's leading manufacturers of arms were the great firms of Armstrong, Krupp and Creusot. No power would willingly allow another to grow stronger than itself and, with new inventions and the increase in productive capacity, the international arms race moved quickly – as did competition in strategic railway building and rivalry in the size of armies.

Universal service on the German pattern was adopted everywhere after 1870, except in Britain and the U.S.A. Between 1870 and 1898 the German war establishment trebled to over 3 million men, while that of France rose to the same mark, that of Russia to 4 million and that of Austria to over 2 million. Altogether the number of men which the great powers of Europe could put into the field rose in twenty-five years by 10 million. The principle of conscription was scarcely modified by fear of popular politics or by concession to the feelings of the middle classes. Indeed the armed forces became the focus of intense patriotic emotions in all nations, as was evinced in France by the Dreyfus affair in the 1890's. A practical objection to mass armies was that they were not suitable for imperialist wars, and for this reason Britain preferred to maintain smaller long-service professional forces. But Britain was no less fiercely nationalistic than the other powers; her navy was as potent a national symbol to the British as their armies were to the continental peoples.

The total expenditure of the European powers on defence increased between 1874 and 1896 by 50 per cent, and the pace of the arms race caused sufficient misgivings for a conference on disarmament to be held at The Hague in 1899. (The conference was called by the tsar who had been influenced by a work written by I. S. Bloch about the horrors of future war. His book is discussed at the end of this chapter.) Some small regulations to mitigate the horrors of war were accepted, but no agreement was made on the restriction of armaments. Instead the American representative observed that his government did not 'consider limitations in regard to the use of military inventions to be conducive to the peace of the world'.

As in numbers and equipment, so also in organization the armies of continental Europe increasingly tended to match each other – the differences which remained being matters of detail, or small concessions to tradition and *esprit de corps*. The French infantry kept their red trousers, but most troops in the field now wore khaki, first used by the British on the Indian frontier in 1848. The necessity for efficient staffs was universally recognized. The German staff was the model, with its formalized yet flexible procedure, its control over training and its powerful chief. The Nicholas General Staff Academy in St Petersburg and the Staff College at Camberley were the counterparts of the Prussian War Academy. Standards in these institutions became far higher than before, with stiffer entrance requirements and a wider syllabus. Armies were increasingly professionalized, and drew more and more on the middle classes for their officers. In Britain the abolition of the purchase of commissions was one of many reforms which made the army more efficient during the time when Edward Cardwell was at the War Office, and then later when Sir Garnet Wolseley and Lord Roberts were commanders-in-chief.

In European armies the basic unit was the corps, a force of some 30,000 men, so organized and self-contained that it could fight efficiently if detached from the parent army. The corps was usually linked to a particular territorial area, its commander then being responsible not only for the organization and training of his units, but also for recruitment, supply and mobilization. A typical corps might consist of two divisions, each containing two infantry brigades, one cavalry brigade, and a regiment of field artillery. Under direct corps command was a regiment of heavy artillery, as well as engineering and supply services, medical units, telegraph units, railway and balloon detachments, cyclists, bridge trains, and other administrative or ancillary services. Armament was by the turn of the century more or less uniform: infantry being armed with 8 or 9 mm. magazine-rifles, field artillery with 8 cm. steel guns, and siege and heavy artillery with guns, mortars and howitzers of 15 and 21 cm. calibre.

The arms race during the years between 1870 and 1914 ensured the continued development of military and naval technology. By 1900, rifles, pistols, carbines and

Magazine-loaded rifles *left* and automatically re-loading machine guns *right* enabled the rate of fire to be greatly increased

Breech-loaded guns with hydraulic buffers to check recoil were now standard equipment. Their range was greatly increased by firing from rifled barrels

machine-guns had reached the stage of development in which they were to be used during the 1914/18 war. The principal developments in the rifle were the magazine system of loading invented by James Lee, and smaller calibre bullets which, being lighter, travelled faster and with a flatter trajectory. A rifle incorporating these two features was adopted by Britain in 1887, and by other powers shortly after. Smokeless powder, the chief ingredient of which was nitrocellulose in granular form, was adopted by the French in 1884 – a development which was literally to transform the face of battlefields. There were also major developments in explosives, with the invention of dynamite in the 1860's by Alfred Nobel and the manufacture of cordite in 1890. The most significant development in pistols was Borchardt's automatic of 1893, which was the forerunner of modern pistols in its utilisation of the gas from the explosion to operate the automatic mechanism. A simpler version was developed by Mauser in 1898, and this was the first reliable and popular automatic. A longer-barrelled version with a 10-shot magazine was used extensively by the Boers in South Africa as a carbine.

Various machine-guns were developed and tried, until in 1883 Hiram S. Maxim patented the one finally adopted. With his gun the recoil was used to load, fire and eject continuously so long as the trigger was held back. The cartridges were stored in a flexible belt, the barrel being cooled by a water-jacket. The qualities of the gun were recognised immediately, and in 1891 the British army adopted a special light model which weighed only 40 lb and fired 650 rounds a minute. With slight modifications Maxim's gun became the Vickers machine-gun, which was used in both 'world wars'. More than any other weapon it was responsible for the character of trench warfare, and probably no other type of weapon has killed so many soldiers.

In 1870 opinion was divided as to whether muzzle-loading or breech-loading artillery was best. But by the 1880's there was no longer any doubt: muzzle-loading was found to be unsatisfactory, both on land and at sea, because of the risk of accidentally loading twice and because long barrels were needed to gain velocity and range. The British field artillery adopted 12-pounder guns; these weighed altogether 38 cwt and were drawn by six horses. In 1890 carriages with a hydraulic recoil were adopted. The French had a similar but more refined 75 mm. field gun. By 1890 most European armies were equipped with the guns which they were to use, with only minor modifications, in the 1914/18 war.

In this period, war for the first time took to the air. The value of observation from the air was recognized; balloons and airships were built in Britain, France and Germany, and the first Army Balloon School was founded at Woolwich in 1878. The Germans developed the Zeppelin, and from 1909 the arms race was extended in earnest into the sphere of air warfare. Following the aeroplane flight by the Wright brothers in 1903, France was the first power to recognize the potential value of the aeroplane for military purposes. Progress in speed, range, and reliability was rapid from 1908, and by 1914 aeroplanes reached speeds of 75 m.p.h. and could remain airborne for two or three hours. They had not yet been used in war, but military opinion inclined to the view that they would be useful chiefly for reconnaissance. The British air force was divided in 1914 into a naval wing, the Royal Naval Air Service, and an army component, the Royal Flying Corps.

During the 1870's as the penetrating power of shells increased so the tendency in ship building was to cover ships with thicker iron armour, sometimes up to 24 inches. However by the next decade the process of steel manufacture had so advanced that thin steel armour-plating became available which was lighter, but sufficiently tough. The demands of security and mobility at sea ceased to be mutually opposed. With the *Royal Sovereign* of 1890 the British navy abandoned the floating platform and returned to a high free-board, and other navies followed suit. By 1900, with the stimulus of the international arms race, battleships displaced some 15,000 tons, had a speed of 18 knots, and mounted 12- or 13-inch guns with a high muzzle velocity. Britain took alarm at the alliance of France and Russia, since their combined fleets were larger than her own, and by adopting a huge building programme in 1899 she intensified the naval race. The *Dreadnought* was laid down in 1904, and with her all-big-gun armament of ten 12-inch guns this ship outmoded all previous battleships, and remained the model for capital ships until the 1939/45 war. The introduction of the steam turbine and the change from coal to oil increased speeds from 18 to 25 knots, and made it possible for ships to remain at sea and run at high

Artillery in the Boer War *left*. Observation balloons in the Spanish-American War *right*

speeds for longer periods. In the years before 1914 Britain and Germany became the foremost rivals in the naval race. In one single year Britain laid down eight new ships. The powers had also to compete for bases in all parts of the world, a requirement which fitted well with their imperialist tendencies.

In 1877 the Russians used torpedoes effectively against stationary Turkish ships, and thereafter torpedo boats became a normal element in naval war. The real development of the submarine began with the invention in 1877 of the horizontal rudder, which made

The *Dreadnought* created a model for capital ships that was widely followed

possible a controlled drive. The accumulator battery and the petrol engine finally made the submarine a weapon of great potential effectiveness. The French were the pioneers here: in 1899 the submarine *Gustave Zédé* travelled at 8 knots 60 feet below the surface. In 1901 France had twenty-three submarines built or under construction; Britain ordered five in that year; Germany did not immediately adopt them. But by 1912 the experience of submarine manoeuvres had convinced naval opinion in all countries of their value as offensive craft, and no major navy was without them.

In the profusion of military literature which appeared during this period one outstanding work was Major-General Sir Charles Callwell's *Small Wars: Their Principles and Practice* (1896) – a consideration of the numerous campaigns undertaken by the imperialist powers. These were mostly in the nature of irregular operations. The latest military equipment and the material resources of industrial societies were pitted against the forces of primitive peoples. Set-piece operations were rare, because whatever the courage of the natives, the ultimate issue in such fighting could not be in doubt. The problems and the interest in this type of warfare arose from its irregularity; terrain such as jungle, swamp or desert presented difficulties in supply and transport, and climate alone could be a formidable enemy. When the enemy avoided open fighting and relied on elusiveness and invisibility, ambushes, sniping and raiding, it was difficult to keep morale high. In particular it was not easy to find a worthwhile objective: there was no main body of the enemy to seek out and destroy, and it was probably not worth while to strike at his capital. Thus regular troops were compelled to forget their formal tactical training for European war, and to adopt the methods of guerrilla and savage warfare.

One solution to the problem of the objective in this type of war was to strike at the enemy's sources of refuge and supply. Laying waste his crops and villages and impounding his herds and stores was effective; on the other hand these methods made war savage and resentful, and military commanders of the proconsular type, such as Lyautey and Kitchener, with an eye to the future administration of the subjugated territory, were reluctant to resort to them. The enrolment of natives on the European side could be helpful, since they would know the country and the characteristics of the enemy – though they might be treacherous. Otherwise, in loose formations the tactical advantage lay with the side which had good horses, light field artillery and repeater rifles with their long range. Strategically an important rule was to maintain the offensive, because a bold bearing would gain the initiative and discourage the enemy – whereas he would attribute delay to fear.

The ablest single commander of this period was the Russian conqueror of Turkestan, Mikhail Skobelev (1843–82). By 1877 Skobelev had served for seven years in this area, and the conclusion he drew from his experience was that 'in Asia he is the master who seizes the people pitilessly by the throat'. In 1880 he conducted a campaign against the Tekke Turcomans with the numerical odds heavily against him and in country which was no more than a desert from the supply angle. He moved slowly and patiently, but never gave the enemy any respite, and the campaign was a total success. Similarly, in 1898 Kitchener never abandoned the strategic offensive against the Dervishes.

Tactically the offensive was not essential: when Kitchener reached Khartoum he adopted the defensive against the wild charges of the Dervishes, who were shattered by the fire of the Anglo-Egyptian troops. Against such brave fighters as the Maoris or the Dervishes, or against the mountaineers of the Indian frontier and the highly disciplined and tactically minded Zulus, a disaster was always possible. Rock-like defence which tempted the enemy forces to dash themselves to destruction, or resolute attack, would both be suitable – but indecision was fatal. At Maiwand in India in 1880 a British force moved forward from a defensive position but then failed to attack, and was annihilated. The Italian commander made every mistake against the Abyssinians at Adowa in 1896, underestimating the enemy's strength and allowing his own forces to straggle; the result was that his 15,000 men were routed. The Zulus were superb warriors, combining

The Zulus were superb warriors but were eventually defeated by concentrated rifle fire

organization, drill and discipline comparable to that of Frederick the Great's army; they had terrific mobility – because they moved on foot with their tireless lope almost as fast as cavalry and had a wonderful sense of ground. Their battle horde, the *impi*, attacked with its centre moving relatively slowly to allow time for the horns to envelop the enemy. In 1879 a British force of some 6,000 men under Lord Chelmsford was all but wiped out at Isandlwhana by a much larger Zulu army, whose main body had completely concealed its presence.

Later that same year at Ulundi, Chelmsford avenged his defeat: the rifle proved too much for the *assegai*. What could be done with the combination of modern arms and resolute offensive tactics was demonstrated in 1865 when 2,000 Russian troops successfully stormed Tashkent against 30,000 defenders. On the whole, however, the defensive was a better tactical approach, being surer and less costly.

Although the Boer War of 1899–1902 was on a scale which transcended the category of small wars, it nonetheless contained many of the features which had marked previous irregular imperialist wars. The Afrikaans-speaking inhabitants of southern Africa had been unified and become violently anti-British – because of the imperialist drive, inspired principally by Cecil Rhodes, to paint the map red from the Cape to Cairo. There had been some hostilities before, in the Boer War of 1881 and the Jameson Raid of 1895. Full-scale war began in October 1899.

The Boers, hardy farmers and excellent marksmen with their Mauser rifles, were unhampered by traditional military methods. Knowing their own country intimately they were a stubborn foe – even for a nation with the resources of Britain – and they resorted to guerrilla warfare on a large scale. It was a concept of the nation-in-arms, carried out to the limit. 85,000 names were inscribed on the Boer Commando lists. All were tough fighters, first-class horsemen and with a natural sense of minor tactics. Although nearly all were mounted, they fought on foot. They were unexpectedly strong in artillery, and in this and other fields they were assisted by a number of European adventurers and experts. Their weakest feature was indiscipline: they disliked being organized and their officers could never count on all the men on the muster-roll being present to go into action. Fighting over their own country they had no problem about supply.

The British forces in South Africa in 1899 did not exceed 10,000 men; in small arms these were well equipped, but the Boers had the better artillery. The British soldiery were inadequately trained to deal with fighters so well armed and so capable as the Boers. British army training was not conducive to intelligent initiative; as one staff officer wrote:

> We make the soldier in many cases a fool because we start with the assumption that he is a fool, and gradually teach him that he is thus to regard himself.

The Boers adopted the offensive and by the autumn had met with quick success, driving the British troops to take refuge in the towns of Ladysmith, Kimberley and Mafeking. The British commander-in-chief, Buller, attempted to force the Tugela river, and he might have succeeded but for the short-sighted estimate that his losses in casualties were too high. In December he was defeated by Botha at Colenso, and on 24th January 1900 suffered a disaster at Spion Kop. Professor Cyril Falls calls that day 'the supreme day in the history of the rifle'. The Boers pushed home their attack to close quarters entirely by rifle fire, overwhelming the British troops without even having to make a final charge. Such a success is a credit to the weapon they were using, but even more it is a tribute to their skilful marksmanship. The Boers shot down their man if he exposed for a moment so much as a limb.

In the early days of 1900 reinforcements from Britain at last reached South Africa. Cardwell's organization of the army had been designed to supply relatively small contingents for imperial garrisons, and it had not been possible to raise quickly a substantial force suitable for fighting such an elusive and redoubtable enemy. Britain's chief lesson from the war was to be the need for keeping a larger and better trained reserve, and by 1914 she was in a reasonable position to undertake a major war. Besides the reinforcements a new commander-in-chief arrived: Field-Marshal Roberts, the veteran commander of the north-west frontier of India. Roberts brought with him as chief-of-staff a first-class organizer, General Kitchener, and a brilliant railway engineer, Colonel Girouard (a Canadian). The transport was reorganized, and in February Roberts began his campaign, feinting and eventually concentrating to the west, south of the Modder river. The beseiged towns were relieved, and by the end of the summer the main Boer centres had been taken and their troops defeated at Diamond Hill and Belfast. Kruger, the Boer president, fled to Europe; the war seemed virtually over and Roberts returned to England, leaving Kitchener to finish it off.

The war was in fact far from over. Under an outstanding guerrilla leader named Christian de Wet, the Boers carried on an irregular war for nearly two more years. Moving secretly and rapidly they executed highly skilful raids, sabotaging the railways, cutting off British detachments, and evading pursuit. Kitchener had repeatedly to call for reinforcements, which came from the dominions as well as from Britain. To gain mobility he mounted his infantry in the Boer fashion, but still he could not pin them down. To strike at the enemy lifeline Kitchener instituted the hated system of destroying the farms and interning the civilian population in camps, where inevitably the living conditions were terrible. Even that did not end the Boer resistance. Eventually Kitchener found the solution; he systematically partitioned the country into great enclosures enclosed by barbed wire, with garrisons in block-houses in selected areas. Slowly but thoroughly, British columns drove through each enclosure, and flushed out the enemy. At the peace of Vereeniging in May 1902 generous terms were given – and kept. The determination had been equal on both sides, but in the end Kitchener's skill and thorough organization got the better of the Boers.

As the Ottoman empire entered the last stages of decay the Balkans became an increasingly dangerous flashpoint. The vacuum of power caused by the failure of Turkey disturbed the diplomatic balance of nineteenth century Europe. Nationalism animated the Balkan peoples, and while Russia and Austria looked covetously at the decaying empire, Germany sought to extend her sphere of influence, and Britain was concerned to protect her interests in the Dardanelles and Suez Canal. A characteristic crisis was that of 1876–8. The Bulgars revolted against the Turks; they were quickly crushed, but the atrocities committed by the Turkish irregulars were intensely disliked throughout Europe. Serbia and Rumania also revolted, and in May 1877 Russia took the opportunity to strike at Turkey. The Russians crossed the Danube, but were held by the Turks at the town of Plevna.

As the Russians advanced they were unaware that a corps twice their own local strength, commanded by Osman Pasha, was blocking their way. Osman reckoned that the enemy could be held at Plevna while Turkish forces were concentrated for the main defence of the empire, for example at Adrianople. He had chosen a good defensive position which he strengthened by field fortifications. The Turkish troops, with the Martini-Peabody rifle and the Krupp breech-loading field gun, were better armed than their enemies, and the size of their forces soon increased considerably. The first Russian assault against Plevna on 20th July was repelled, their casualties amounting to 35 per cent of the attacking force. The second assault was more cautious, but, though bravely carried out, it was clumsy in conception; the Turks coolly held their entrenchments. By September, Osman had 56,000 troops and had built eighteen redoubts. The Russians now had 84,000 men, and preceded their attack by a four-day bombardment. Only one section of the Russian assault was successful: that commanded by Skobelev in the Green Hills sector. He himself organized the reconnaissance. His losses in the assault were heavy, but he fed in reserves skilfully, and then at the crucial moment personally led his

The Balkans, 1876–8

men to their objective. Plevna, however, did not fall yet. Only when still more Russian forces arrived and established a complete blockade did Osman consider he could do no more, and by December the Turks had to fall back. An armistice was signed at the end of January 1878, the Russians then being close to Constantinople.

This war presents various interesting features. One was the skilful and inspiring leadership of Skobelev. Once before in Turkestan he had disguised himself as a Turcoman, and had fearlessly reconnoitred through hostile territory the route his men were to take. Now, following his own task in the assaults on Plevna, in January he crossed the Balkan mountains in snowstorms, defeating the Turks at Senova, and capturing 36,000 men and 90 guns. Dressed in white uniform and mounted on a white horse, and always in the thickest of the fighting, the 'White General' was adored by his soldiers. Skobelev died of heart disease in 1882 at the age of thirty-nine. Besides his leadership, the courage of the Russian soldiers deserves to be praised; they returned again and again to the assault of the strongest entrenchments and would march all night over mountains under snow.

The success of the resistance put up by the Turks astonished contemporary Europe. Osman Pasha's field fortifications pointed to the character of future fighting between armies armed with rifles. The Russians learned from the Turks that the rifle must be supplemented by the spade. The duration of the Turkish stand made it seem worthwhile to Russia's rivals, principally Britain, to give eleventh-hour diplomatic support to the Ottoman empire, and, as a result, final chaos in the Balkans and Europe was deferred.

The situation in the Far East was upset as far as the European powers were concerned by the emergence of Japan. Following her awakening after the arrival of Commodore Perry's squadron in 1853 (described in Chapter 16), the pace of Japan's modernization was rapid. In 1871 feudalism was abolished and two million *samurai* were pensioned off. A national army was established in 1873, and conscription of the whole male population was introduced, in place of the *samurais'* exclusive privilege of military service. Equipment and training were provided for the Japanese army by Germany, and for the navy by Britain. Industrialization proceeded rapidly; by 1903 Japan's population stood at 45 million. With the development of her capacities Japan's ambitions also grew, and she began to seek power in eastern Asia. Her first interest was naturally Korea, the stepping-stone to the mainland of Asia. She tried her strength with considerable success in the Sino-Japanese war of 1894–5. But at this time Russia was just extending the Trans-Siberian railway through to the Far East, and China was made to lease the Liao-tung peninsula to her. Russia and Japan found themselves in direct competition. The Japanese were able to get some measure of the inefficiency of their rival by observing the Russians' part in the handling of the Chinese Boxer uprising of 1900 – aimed at ousting the foreigners from China once and for all. Relations worsened over the issue of 'spheres of influence' in the peninsulas, and eventually in February 1904 the Japanese opened war with the Russians – without a formal declaration.

It was astonishing that a fledgling power such as Japan should take on single-handed the most massive of all the old European powers. But the Japanese had calculated the odds well. A treaty of 1902 guaranteed that Britain would come to Japan's assistance if a third power intervened against her. The Japanese were fighting for a strictly limited aim: the security of a certain area of hegemony. The location of the war was to Japan's advantage; it was more than 5,500 miles between the two Russian bases of Moscow and Port Arthur. The Russians of course possessed far greater resources of men and materials, but they had a tremendous problem in getting them to the theatre of war. When hostilities began there was a gap in the Trans-Siberian railway around Lake Baikal, and, although the Russian engineers did remarkable work on the railway, throughout the war it took about a month to transport a battalion from Moscow to Port Arthur.

In 1904 Japan could put into the field immediately 300,000 troops in 13 divisions and 400,000 trained reserves, whereas Russia's available force had risen from 83,000 to only 250,000 combatants by the end of that year. The equipment on each side was more or less equal in standard, but, as the fighting was to show, the Japanese command, based on the German model, was better, and their troops had a higher morale. Seapower was a vital factor, for the Japanese communications with the mainland depended on their control of the seas. The Japanese fleet was slightly superior in size and quality to the Russian Far Eastern fleet, which was based on Port Arthur with a detachment at Vladivostok. But the Russians had another fleet in the Baltic which could reach the theatre of operations – though the long sea voyage would take time.

The aim of the Japanese was to knock out Port Arthur, thus removing any threat to Japan herself and securing the free movement of her land forces – and then to win a major battle which would convince Russia that she must respect Japan in the Far East.

The first operations to be considered were at sea. At the outset of war the main Japanese fleet, commanded by Admiral Togo, took the initiative. On the night of 8th February his torpedo-boats surprised the Russian squadron in Port Arthur, seriously damaging two battleships and a cruiser; and on the same night in the Korean harbour of Chemulpo one Russian cruiser was sunk and another damaged. The Russian ships in Vladivostok were still icebound. The Japanese established a tight blockade at Port Arthur and this allowed their forces to land unimpeded in Korea and drive back the Russians on the Yalu. The blockade of Port Arthur in winter conditions tested both fleets; the Japanese battleships engaged the shore batteries and each side attempted to damage the other by means of torpedoes and mines. In March, Admiral Makarov took command of the Russian fleet, and in a series of sorties caused Togo considerable anxiety. But in mid-April the Russian flagship was blown up by a mine, Admiral Makarov being killed; his loss was a disaster for the Russians. A sortie by the Russian fleet in August produced a battle which, being fought at very long range, was not decisive tactically; but since the Russian fleet withdrew back to Port Arthur it was a strategic victory for the Japanese. The Japanese maintained their blockade and held on to their advantage in keeping Russian seapower out of action – which to Japan was vital.

By June 1904 enough Japanese troops had been transported for the siege of Port Arthur from the land to begin. The commander of the Japanese land forces, Oyama, was a most able soldier; he was bold and encouraged his army commanders to use their initiative within the broad limits of his directives – one general, Nogi, being a gifted leader in battle. The Russian land commander, Kuropatkin, a former staff officer of Skobelev, was intelligent but inclined to be unduly cautious and to lack confidence. The long siege of the fortress was a grim struggle. By using dynamite and incurring a loss of 52,000 men the Japanese at length prevailed, and on 1st January 1905 the Russians surrendered Port Arthur, losing 24,000 prisoners and 546 guns – together with what was left of their fleet.

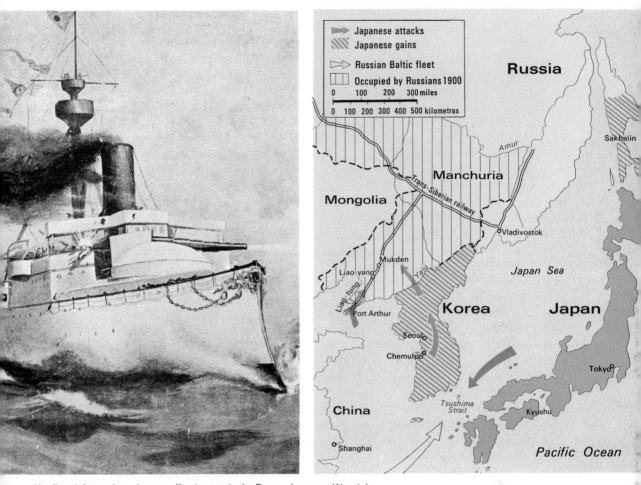

Her fleet *left* was Japan's most effective arm in the Russo-Japanese War *right*

Meanwhile the Japanese had already been seeking the great battle which was to make the Russians give up the struggle. After the two weeks' battle of Liao-yang in August and another great encounter in the battle of Sha Ho in October, Kuropatkin had decided to withdraw on Mukden. The battle of Mukden in March 1905 was the last of the war on land, and in the size of the operations it was the greatest which had ever been fought. The opposing forces were each some 310,000 strong, being extended on a strongly entrenched front of over forty miles. The Japanese began the pressure. Their tactic was to open rifle fire at a distance of about half a mile from the position attacked; the soldiers would run forward in bursts, bodies bent low, then fall to the ground at a hand signal – maintaining strict discipline. A battalion could take over three hours to get within a quarter of a mile of the objective, at which distance the assault was launched. At Mukden, Nogi succeeded in forcing back the Russian right; a powerful enemy counter-offensive failed and the Russians then conducted a well-controlled retreat.

The Russian Baltic fleet, under Admiral Rozhestvenski, was on its long voyage half way round the world, much distracted by incidents to do with neutrality and coaling. On the fall of Port Arthur Togo had taken his ships back to Japan to refit. The Russian fleet was formidable on paper – 38 ships, including 7 battleships – and, although rumours of inefficiency and indiscipline had been heard, Togo was apprehensive. When the Russians approached the Straits of Tsushima on 27th May 1905 Togo's fleet awaited them; he had only 4 battleships, but this was offset by a superiority in cruisers. The Japanese ships had an advantage in quality, since some of the Russian ships were archaic and the fleet had to go at the pace of the slowest.

The Russian ships steamed into action with coal piled so high on their decks that they were low in the water and deprived of much of their manoeuvrability; all in all, the fleet was in some disorder. The fighting began with a cruiser action. Because of superior speed the Japanese line was able to steam across the head of the Russian line, in the tactic known as 'crossing the T'. The leading Russian ships were enfiladed by each Japanese ship in turn while the Russian ships behind were not in a position to reply. The gunnery of the Japanese was brilliant, and within forty minutes two Russian battleships and a cruiser were practically out of action. After a little over one hour the fleets became separated, but Togo again attacked in the evening, and three more Russian battleships and a cruiser were sunk. The enemy fleet was thus all but annihilated, and its remnants were beset by destroyers during the night and relentlessly pursued on the following day.

The battle of Tsushima was the first major sea battle since Trafalgar (for Navarino, and the American bombardment of the Spanish fleet at Santiago in Cuba in 1898, were too one-sided to be called battles). Togo's 'crossing of the T' was an outstanding achievement in the history of naval tactics. It was this absolute defeat at sea rather than the situation on land after Mukden which persuaded the Russians to give up the war and accept the mediation of the American president. By the Peace of Portsmouth (September 1905) Japan gained her precise aims in Korea, the Liao-tung peninsula and the southern half of Sakhalin, but no more. Diplomatically little was altered as a result of the Russo-Japanese War; but the defeat of Russia by Japan was felt as an omen. In Russia the revolutionary movement of 1905 caught a mood of discontent, further disturbing the people and weakening the tsarist regime – while not only in Japan but all over Asia it was said that the peasants 'tingled' with the news and with the desire that European predominance might be overthrown.

Certain conclusions stand out from the wars which took place in the world between 1870 and 1914. In fighting at sea, the mine, the torpedo and the submarine were clearly to be most important. Togo had given an idea for a new pattern in tactics, suitable for the age of steam propulsion and long distance gunnery. In a book which received wide attention, *The Influence of Sea Power on History* (1890), the American naval historian A. T. Mahan made a profound analysis of the strategic role of seapower. The strength of the modern state depended on wealth, which was to a large extent founded on trade and colonies; every part of the world was linked economically to Europe. For this reason every ambitious state must maintain a powerful navy and frame for itself a maritime strategy which was world-wide in its scope. European war in the modern age could only be world war.

The situation with regard to land warfare was not so well appreciated. The most significant characteristic of the wars of this time was the tactical power of the defensive.

Rifle and artillery fire, machine-guns and hand grenades, all operated from the cover of entrenchments and earthworks, protected by barbed wire, were making it difficult and costly for attacks to be brought to close quarters; the spade had now become an essential article of military equipment; the only defence against machine-guns and artillery fire was to dig in.

For some time after 1870 military thinkers attempted to build theories on the basis of what had been experienced in the Franco-Prussian War. The tendency in France and Germany was to abandon the 'mathematics' of Jomini and think in Clausewitzian terms of force tempered by Moltke's more practical approach. Tactics received more attention than strategy. Then, as technical change progressed and the experience of actual war in Europe receded, theory became less realistic. In Germany the chief of the general staff from 1891 to 1905, Count von Schlieffen, produced the Schlieffen Plan for the invasion of France, which will be discussed in Chapter 20. In France nationalistic pride caused the emphasis to be laid on the offensive, and when Foch wrote, 'Whatever the circumstances . . . it is the intention to advance with all forces to the attack', then, as Dr Luvaas puts it, 'indiscretion had become the better part of valour'. More than ever before it seemed that the way to victory must be sought by turning a flank, and when this became impracticable a stalemate followed.

The best work in England was Callwell's book, but his subject did not come within the main line of European development. In the British army concern for vested interests produced an unrealistic approach to war: the *Cavalry Journal* was founded in 1906 by certain regiments of the British army, the aim being to propagate the idea that the shock action of cavalry was still the essential tactical counterpart to infantry firepower. Because the Boers were mounted riflemen an excuse was ready to hand for the retention of mounted troops for a generation – long after they had outlived their usefulness in battle.

Instead of noting the effect of entrenchments, barbed wire, and modern small arms, most European soldiers chose to ignore Plevna, to regard South Africa as irrelevant guerrilla war, and to congratulate themselves that the Japanese victory was a triumph for Moltke's system. Meanwhile south-eastern European countries were at war with each other again in 1885, 1897, and from 1911 to 1913. The industrial competition and the armaments race between the great powers intensified, and the strains on the diplomatic fabric increased.

A clear indication of what was to come was given in a work published in 1898 by I. S. Bloch, a Warsaw banker, which made a pretty accurate forecast of the nature of total war. He clearly had in mind that a great war could not be long delayed. He argued that in the event of large-scale war in Europe a stalemate between the armed forces of the contending nations was inevitable – due to technical development of weapons, and to the harnessing of all the political and economic forces of powerful states to war. The only result would be the most fearful distress to civil populations, the victor suffering as much as the vanquished – with the ultimate collapse of social organization. Bloch's warnings were largely put aside by military commanders in Europe because he was not a professional soldier; they said much the same about the lessons of the civil war in America, on the ground that it was fought between amateurs – a startling statement to make!

Anyhow there was at least one man, Bloch, who was not afraid to point the finger to what was likely to happen to the world – and which actually did happen, as we shall see in the next two chapters.

The 1914/18 war developed into a deadlock of trench warfare, with appalling casualties from gunfire and poison gas. French troops in gas masks stand ready to repel an attack

20 The 1914/18 War

The conflict which began in August 1914 in Europe developed into the bloodiest war in history. The only impressive results in that theatre were the casualties, and these had a profound influence on my military thinking. A large number of those killed had no known grave, being merely blown to pieces by artillery fire; in some cases corpses formed part of trenches, being finally devoured by rats. As the story unfolds we shall examine carefully the leadership, political and military, because when all is said and done it is there that the responsibility lies in war. The generalship on the western front in Europe seems to me to have been tragically dominated by the philosophy of the French general, Foch – 'to make war means always attacking'. In fact, whatever the circumstances or conditions it was correct to attack; this was almost the only answer of the generals to the great power of the defensive given by machine-guns, barbed wire, entrenchments, and artillery – to attack with infantry in close formations in a direct charge across no-man's-land, each soldier carrying almost half his own body weight. Of all this I was a witness: I suffered from it. I saw clearly that such tactics could not be the key to victory.

The reader will understand that to write an intelligent and readable story of the 1914/18 war in a single chapter is a colossal task – indeed, most authors have devoted a whole book or even several volumes to the war. That is my problem. Therefore I shall merely try to present a picture of that war which will fit into its right place in our study of the history of warfare throughout the ages. It will be a dismal canvas, with a very few bright spots. I myself fought in the war side by side with splendid young men who did not know what they were in for but who offered their lives because we were all told by political leaders that it was to be 'a war to end war'. Let us first examine why the nations fought at all, and whether the tragedy could have been avoided.

On 28th June 1914 the Archduke Franz Ferdinand, Inspector-General of the Austro-Hungarian army, was assassinated in Bosnia. Austria, rightly supposing that pro-Serbian feeling in Bosnia accounted for the incident, delivered an ultimatum to Serbia on 25th July, and the following day declared war on her. Russia, the self-styled patron of the Slav peoples, mobilized against Austria on 30th July. Germany was an ally of Austria; France and Britain were allies of Russia. Taking alarm at the quick succession and turns of events, one by one each of these powers chimed in. By early August Germany and Austria (the 'Central Powers') were aligned in war against France, Belgium, Britain and Russia (the 'Entente Powers'). Turkey emerged from secret into open alliance with the Central Powers in September. Other countries entered the war later.

The 1914/18 war was caused by a murder in the Balkans. None of the statesmen or peoples of Europe positively desired war. Nobody consciously engineered it. A succession of diplomatic interchanges took place, in which the true object of national political leaders – Berchtold (Austria), Sazonov (Russia), Bethmann Hollweg (Germany), Viviani (Italy), and Asquith (Britain) – was to preserve the security of their countries. But they all miscalculated. Gestures intended to bluff and to deter provoked violent reactions which were not anticipated: the politicians were playing with diplomacy in an atmosphere which was in fact highly inflammable.

First, rivalries existed between the various powers. Britain was acutely conscious of the challenge by Germany to her commercial and industrial power, and had been actively engaged in building up her naval and merchant fleets. In the General Election campaign of 1911 the Conservative Party had exploited anti-German feeling. In France there was resentment at the events of 1870–1 and at Germany's possession of Alsace and Lorraine. Germany and Russia were rivals for influence in the Balkans. The Ottoman empire in its ramshackle state had nothing conceivable to gain from being hostile to anybody; but the Germans had been wooing the Turks – who had a score to pay off against Britain and Russia, the two powers which had patronized or bullied them all the way through the nineteenth century. While these antagonisms were by no means enough to make war inevitable, they did mean that there was a highly charged atmosphere in which war might break out.

The situation was made still more dangerous by the fact that none of those responsible, and indeed few men in any nation, had any understanding of what war would mean. Nothing on a bigger scale than the recent small Balkan wars was imagined, and therefore the idea of war was generally taken lightly and irresponsibly. The fatal step was the ordering of mobilization. From this point events got out of the control of individuals and became dictated by the war plans of the general staffs. These plans, because of the military doctrine of the time, were all offensive. Military escalation followed diplomatic insanity, and, as A. J. P. Taylor writes, the great armies which had been accumulated to provide security 'carried the nations to war by their own weight'.

Thus it was that a Balkan incident provoked widespread alarm, and extreme measures were taken. But if any of the political leaders involved had had a true perception of the consequences of what they were doing, and if a clear warning had been given in time, the terrible catastrophe of 1914 could have been averted. Cyril Falls writes:

> Britain accepted no commitments up to the last moment in 1914, and only limited ones then. It is probable that the British Government which took office in 1906 could have prevented war by a bolder policy and a stronger stand by the side of France.

I often discussed this question with Sir Winston Churchill. His view was that once the chain of events had begun to unroll in the Balkans and then Germany had become involved, no human power could prevent war: it became inevitable. Those are interesting reflections. As it seems to me, nobody *tried* to prevent the war.

The mobilization plans, once set in motion, removed the control of events from individuals. Among the plans of the various countries, that of Germany was outstanding because of its bold and offensive conception. With this plan Germany hoped to gain the initiative; and in fact the German war plan dictated the main course of events in the whole opening phase of the war during the autumn of 1914, and fixed the main theatres in which the remainder of the war was to be fought. The plan had originally been formed by Count von Schlieffen, chief of the general staff from 1891 to 1906, who in 1914 was dead. His idea was to attack France quickly with strong armies and knock her out in six weeks, before dealing with Russia. There was no question of a direct invasion of France, since the Franco-German border was barred by a line of fortresses, strongly manned. Schlieffen's own original plan was to draw the French forward and hold them with the German left wing in Lorraine, while the main force on the right was to carry out an enveloping offensive sweep through Belgium and then turn south-eastwards. But his plan had been modified by his successor, the second Moltke, who strengthened the German left. Schlieffen's dying words are reported to have been: 'It must come to a fight. Only make the right wing strong.'

I have discussed the plan at length with Liddell Hart. His description of the plan as a 'revolving door' conception is exactly right – 'the harder the French pushed on one side in their initial offensive, the more sharply would the other side swing round and strike them in the back'. In his foreword to *The Schlieffen Plan* by a German author, G. Ritter, he wrote as follows, and I quote: 'It was a conception of Napoleonic boldness.' He then goes on to point out that, while the plan was possibly suitable for Napoleonic times, the advent of the railway enabled the French to switch troops across the chord of the Schlieffen 'scythe-sweep', giving the plan small prospects of success in more modern times. In fact, the Schlieffen plan failed in 1914 for logistic reasons. The sweep of the marching German infantry and horse transport, their advance in any case slowed up by demolished bridges and rail tracks, was countered by more speedy French movements by rail. Some may not agree, but it is a most interesting comment, and worth considering.

None of the other powers which found themselves at war in 1914 had anything more than sketchy plans ready. Austria hoped to crush Serbia quickly and then advance against the Russians in the north-east. In France, Joffre said:

> There was never any plan of operations set down in writing . . . I adopted no preconceived idea other than a full determination to take the offensive with all my forces.

The French, unlike the Germans, intended to respect Belgian neutrality. Britain did not have a mass army; but she could carry out a naval blockade of the enemy, and a small British army would cover the French left. The Russian plan was to attack, sending two armies into East Prussia, and more troops farther south to envelop the Austrians north of the Carpathians.

Events inevitably began to unfold in the direction determined by the Schlieffen plan. The Germans were off the mark quickly; 350,000 troops moved into Lorraine and 400,000 into the Ardennes. On 4th August three German armies, totalling 750,000 men, were launched in the enveloping attack through Luxembourg and Belgium. The French launched their main offensives, just as their enemy had hoped, in north-eastern France: 450,000 men in Lorraine and 360,000 in the Ardennes. By 24th August the French had suffered very heavy losses in these areas, and were forced to retire behind the frontier. Meanwhile the Belgians had not been able to prevent the German advance through their territory. The Germans swung round through Brussels (20th August), and fell upon the

French forces on the Franco-Belgian frontier commanded by Lanrezac, who, finding his forces outnumbered two to one, attempted to hold a position on the Sambre – but without success. He was falling back under intense pressure when by 21st August the British Expeditionary Force, some 100,000 strong under Sir John French, reached the Mons area and came under attack from German forces.

The Allies fought hard and retreated only slowly. The Germans were held up at Mons on the 23rd, at Le Cateau on the 26th, and at Guise on the 29th. The Germans were now behind on their programme, and were taken aback at the strength of the resistance they were meeting. The German advance, already slowed, wavered before Paris, and on 30th August von Kluck turned his First Army – the right-wing army of the German movement – south-eastwards, passing to the east of Paris instead of enveloping the city. The Allies now rallied, and French forces issued from Paris and struck the flank of von Kluck's army – which on 5th September began to withdraw north-eastwards. From that moment things definitely ceased to go according to the German plan. By this time Joffre had moved himself and considerable forces back from Lorraine, and he attacked Bülow's army on the Marne. The two armies held each other in deadlock, until the British army advanced into the gap which had been caused in the German front on Bülow's right by von Kluck's retreat, whereupon Bülow was also forced to withdraw. This fighting, which forced the Germans to retreat behind the Aisne, constituted the 'battle of the Marne'. It was one of the very few battles of the 1914/18 war to have a decisive strategical value, though this was not then realized. It had, in fact, prevented the Germans from winning the war.

Behind the Aisne the Germans reorganized their front and dug in. The French assault was checked by 17th September. Both sides then raced to turn their opponents' open northern flank. The opposing lines were extended north from the Aisne, past Amiens and Arras, and were still neck and neck when they reached the sea at Nieuport in Flanders. There, in an attempt to roll up the Allied front, the Germans launched what came to be called the first battle of Ypres. But heavy and repeated attacks by superior numbers could not move the Allies. The fighting to the south-east in the Nancy area reached a similar stalemate.

By the end of 1914 a deadlock existed on the western front in Europe. As winter descended on the tired soldiers, the western front congealed into trench warfare. Barbed wire and machine-guns dominated the battlefield. From now on generals on both sides would try to smash through the opposing front – but in vain: they knew not the answer and merely destroyed more lives.

A curious incident took place on Christmas Day, 1914. Soldiers of both sides fraternized in no-man's-land, exchanging cigarettes and playing football. But this was not approved and the friendly fraternization stopped – never to happen again.

The Germans had not defeated their enemies in the west in six weeks, which meant that the original plan for the eastern front could not be carried out. Things here had not begun as anticipated. The Austrians had actually been driven back from their invasion of Serbia, and the Russians had begun to move quickly. These first operations by the Russians exhibited two characteristics which were to continue: loyalty to their allies, and inefficiency. In response to French pleas the Russian commander-in-chief, the Grand Duke Nicholas, pushed forward two armies towards East Prussia in August, although these were as yet quite unprepared. This theatre of operations was divided by

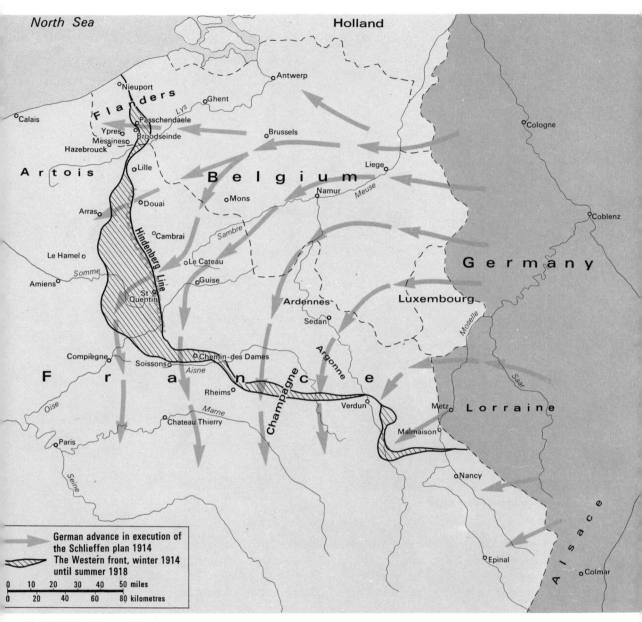

North Sea   Holland

Nieuport

Calais   Flanders   Ghent   Antwerp

Passchendaele   Brussels   Cologne

Ypres Broodseinde   Liege

Messines

Hazebrouck   Lille

Artois   Belgium   Namur   Coblenz

Arras   Douai   Mons   Meuse

Cambrai   Sambre   Germany

Le Hamel   Hindenberg Line   Le Cateau

Somme   Guise   Luxembourg

Amiens   St Quentin   Ardennes   Sedan   Moselle

Compiègne   Soissons   Chemin-des Dames   Argonne

France   Aisne   Metz   Lorraine

Oise   Rheims   Champagne   Verdun   Malmaison

Chateau Thierry   Marne

Paris   Nancy

Seine   Alsace

Epinal   Colmar   Saar

Legend:
German advance in execution of the Schlieffen plan 1914
The Western front, winter 1914 until summer 1918

0 10 20 30 40 50 miles
0 20 40 60 80 kilometres

The Schlieffen Plan and the Western Front

the Masurian Lakes; one army under General Rennenkampf, which set out first, passed north of the Lakes, and the other, under General Samsonov, moved more or less parallel but south of them. When Rennenkampf crossed the border the Germans had one army, under General Prittwitz, in East Prussia. Rennenkampf did not push forward vigorously, and his army was in a chaotic condition; for example, his staff had compasses but no

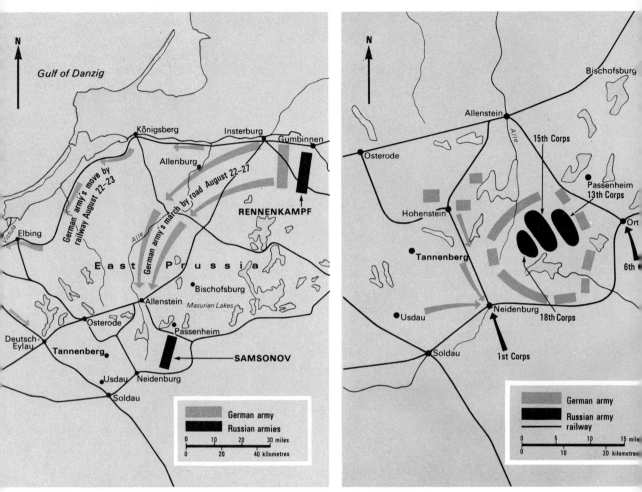

The battle of Tannenberg

maps. However, when he came in contact with a German corps on 20th August at Gumbinnen his advantage in numbers was very great and he gained a victory. There was no communication between the forces of Rennenkampf and Samsonov, due mainly to the fact that these two commanders disliked each other intensely. Samsonov, a man of impetuous temperament, leaped to the conclusion that the whole German army had been routed and decided to push forward at top speed.

At this stage Prittwitz proposed to the chief of the general staff that the Germans retire behind the Vistula. Thereupon he was dismissed from his command, being replaced by General Paul von Hindenburg – about whom a few notes may be of interest since he and his chief of staff are to appear a good deal in our story. He was born in 1847, entered the Prussian Cadet Corps, and when eighteen was commissioned in the Foot Guards – seeing active service in 1866 in Austria and in 1870-1 in France. During the next forty years of peace he rose in rank from captain to general, not because he was in any way outstanding, which he definitely was not, but because he was a decent and conscientious officer. He retired in 1911 aged sixty-four. On 22nd August 1914 he was recalled from retirement, being then sixty-seven, and given command of the German Eighth Army in East Prussia. He was given as his chief of staff one of the most brilliant officers in the army – General Erich von Ludendorff, aged forty-nine. Hindenburg at once saw in Ludendorff an officer of great intellectual powers (which he himself lacked), and decided to give him a free hand and wide scope so as to get the utmost value from his military gifts. The two travelled together to Eighth Army Headquarters at Marienburg, arriving there on 23rd August. Some ten days later the battle of Tannenberg had been fought and won; Hindenburg, as Army Commander, naturally got the credit; he leaped from obscurity to fame and became an idol in Germany. From then onwards he never parted with Ludendorff until shortly before the war ended in 1918 – which shows he had considerable wisdom!

On their arrival at Marienburg Ludendorff found that the situation had been taken in hand by a member of Prittwitz's staff, Lt-Col. Hoffman, and preliminary moves were already under way in a scheme of operations which corresponded very closely with his own ideas. Rennenkampf had done nothing to exploit his success at Gumbinnen and was hardly moving; on the other hand Samsonov was advancing dangerously. The Germans therefore decided to leave only a screen to bar Rennenkampf's northern army, and to move all possible strength southwards and fall upon Samsonov. It was a bold plan in that it was always possible that Rennenkampf would galvanize himself into activity. However, a copy of his orders had been found on a captured Russian officer, and these confirmed that he had no immediate plans which would endanger the German plan; and in any case the Masurian Lakes prevented him from going directly to help Samsonov. Samsonov's immediate intentions were also known to the Germans because of the Russian habit of sending wireless messages *en clair*. The speed of his advance was already widening the gap on his unprotected right. Ludendorff could go ahead, and did.

The stealthy transference southwards of the units facing Rennenkampf proceeded between 24th and 27th August. Three corps were moved, two by road to Allenstein and one in a wider sweep by rail. By the 27th only two German cavalry brigades were left to screen the whole of Rennenkampf's forces. Meanwhile, during the few days in which these movements were taking place, the German forces opposite Samsonov were critically placed, having to hold the Russian advance against odds of more than six to one.

On the 26th some of the reinforcements had arrived and Ludendorff could set in motion his tactical plan. His intention was to hold Samsonov's advance in the centre, and drive his wings right back in order to clear the way for the main envelopment of the centre. Some progress was made by hard fighting on the 26th. Samsonov was not unduly disturbed; he himself, exercising direct command in the centre, appears to have been ignorant of what was happening to his flanks. On the 27th the plan was pressed relentlessly, the Russian right being forced back farther from Allenstein to Bischofsburg, and their left from Usdau towards Neidenburg.

On 28th August the decisive movement of the battle began. The German right pressed on to Neidenburg, and the left turned inwards on Passenheim. A heavy attack was launched in the centre. On this day and the next two the Russian wings, after some ups and downs, were finally driven off the scene, and the Russian centre was hemmed in and surrounded. All the time, as Ludendorff wrote, 'Rennenkampf's formidable host hung like a threatening thundercloud to the north-east'. But his daring plan had been well judged and Rennenkampf did not move. The 31st was the day of 'harvesting', as Hindenburg called it, and he wrote in his dispatch to the Kaiser:

> The ring round the larger part of the Russian army was closed yesterday. The 13th, 15th and 18th Army Corps have been destroyed. We have already taken more than 60,000 prisoners . . . The guns are still in the forests and are now being brought in. The booty is immense . . . The Corps outside our ring, the 1st and 6th, have also suffered severely and are now retreating in hot haste through Mlawa and Myszaniec.

Samsonov committed suicide. Ludendorff named this battle 'Tannenberg' (the name of a hill in the area held initially by the German centre). Tannenberg was the most brilliant tactical feat of the 1914/18 war.

Hindenburg and Ludendorff, now reinforced, crowned their victory by turning against Rennenkampf; the Russians were driven back in the battle of the Masurian Lakes and 30,000 prisoners were taken. Thus the Germans recovered their position in East Prussia which had been in danger. But elsewhere the Russians were doing well: Galicia was taken from the Austrians, and far to the south the Turks were being driven back from the Caucasus. Had Hindenburg been beaten in East Prussia it would have been a total disaster for Germany. As it was, the Russians had received a heavy blow.

By the winter of 1914–5 the impetus of the German war plan had run out. Its legacy remained in the position of the battle fronts, which were now more or less settled. The political leaders and military chiefs on both sides sought to get a grip on events. Let us outline the overall strategical picture of the 1914/18 war after the initial clashes of the mighty forces.

The Germans had gained considerable advantages in the first phase, now over. In the west they were in possession of enemy soil, which included important industrial regions of France. In the east they had dealt a heavy blow at the Russians. On the other hand it had always been the nightmare of the general staff that Germany might have to fight a war on two fronts. Now she had to do so. Furthermore, so did Austria and Turkey; these two allies could fight well, but it was already clear that the Germans would have to stiffen the effort of each with economic assistance, military ideas and manpower.

The chief of the German general staff was now Falkenhayn, who had succeeded Moltke. His strategy for 1915 was to stay on the defensive in the west, holding the German gains, while making a major effort to settle the issue in the east. The Germans would then be able to concentrate all their strength in the west to finish off the war victoriously. Having interior lines between the western and the eastern fronts, and a good railway system, so long as their resources lasted it was possible for the Germans to switch pressure from point to point at will and quickly meet new threats. To counter the blockade by the British fleet, Germany embarked on a policy of submarine warfare.

There was little co-ordination in strategy between the Allied powers – the first military conference of all the Allies not being held until December 1915. The only way for the Allies to win the war was to defeat Germany decisively on one of her own main fronts. The Russians were unlikely to achieve this, therefore the Allies must seek to win on the western front. The French, much of whose soil had been occupied by the Germans, naturally accepted this as the main task, and viewed all other ideas with grave suspicion. The Russians were, on the whole, willing to co-ordinate their operations with those of the Allies in the west, so that the maximum pressure could be brought to bear on both fronts of the Central Powers at the same time; but this ideal of synchronization rarely operated satisfactorily in practice.

Britain, the great naval power, considered her major task to be the strangling of Germany by a blockade of her commerce and supplies from the sea. Regarding the war on land, Britain recognized that the key theatre must be the western front; but the implications of this fact were not generally agreed among those who had to formulate British policy. Asquith, the prime minister, and Sir William Robertson, who became C.I.G.S. at the end of 1915, were in favour of doing as the French wished: concentrating on building up the British forces on the western front. But this school of thought, which included most of the military experts, was regarded by another as being merely blind to other possibilities. The second school considered that the Germans could be defeated on the western front only by a force as large as theirs; but Britain had only a small army, and she did not want to raise and commit such vast numbers of men. Even if she were to raise a great army, would the 'military experts' know how to use it? Would it not be better to leave the western front to the French, and for Britain to make her contribution to the war on land by an indirect strategy which would have great value and be more economical in manpower?

These two schools of thought became known as the 'Easterners' and the 'Westerners'. The Easterners, headed by Lloyd George, considered the war could be won by 'knocking away the props' – in other words, by defeating Germany's allies. The Westerners considered the war could be won only by defeating Germany decisively on the western front.

The chief advocates of the idea of knocking away the props were two politicians, Winston Churchill and Lloyd George, and the area in which they wanted to see Allied strategy developed was south-eastern Europe. If the Allies could achieve domination in that theatre valuable results would follow – Turkey would be knocked out; Russia would be strengthened for her effort on the eastern front by being free of having to fight the Turks, and also by receiving supplies from the west; Austria would be forced to fight on two fronts, and the Germans would have to divert yet more troops to bolster her up; and if Austria could be knocked out, Germany herself would have to fight on a third front. All these ideas were attractive. Accordingly in 1915 the British sent an expedition to the Dardanelles. In this and the next year the Central and Entente Powers competed in bidding for the favour of the various countries of south and south-eastern Europe. Italy entered the war on the side of the Allies in 1915, and Rumania in 1916. Serbia was already fighting against Austria. Bulgaria on the other hand joined the Central Powers in 1915.

The strategy of the Allies in south-eastern Europe had much to commend it. While it was wishful thinking to suppose that the war could actually be won by any 'side shows', nonetheless it was true that extremely valuable advantages would accrue if the Allies could definitely gain the upper hand in this theatre. But, as we shall see, this was not in fact achieved quickly. And the longer it took, the greater was the drain of troops that might have been used elsewhere. In the end a great army did have to be raised in Britain, and most of the troops were sent to the western front, as demanded by the 'Westerners'.

The British also opened up another separate theatre of war: the Middle East. The intention behind the operations in Egypt, which were extended into Arabia, Palestine and Syria, was to safeguard British economic interests, particularly in the Suez Canal, and to deliver a blow from behind at the Turkish empire. The armed intervention in Mesopotamia was justified by the need to protect oil supplies from the Persian Gulf – though the French suspected shrewdly that a good part of the motive was British imperial greed.

To complete the strategical picture we must mention the war in other parts of the world. In 1914 the Japanese moved into the German territory of Shantung, and between 1914 and 1918 they succeeded in extending their influence in China very considerably. Their motive was undoubtedly imperial ambition. Similarly, where colonies of the belligerents were neighbours, as in parts of Africa and the south Pacific, they took the opportunity to 'have a go' at each other. From the German point of view these 'side shows' were valuable as a nuisance to the enemy; their effect was to divert troops of both sides from the central theatres, but many more British and French were so diverted than German. However, all in all, it can be said that the war in theatres outside Europe was of minor strategical importance. The 1914/18 war was essentially a European war. It came later to be called a 'world war' because contingents from many parts of the British empire served in Europe, and because the United States joined the Entente Powers in 1917. But in reality, since the role of seapower was mostly passive, this was less of a 'world war' than some previous conflicts such as the Seven Years' War.

Having glanced at the picture of the war as a whole, I now propose to look more closely at certain parts of the canvas which are of interest – taking the theatres one by one, and analysing in particular the nature of the fighting and the leadership.

The war on the western front congealed into immobility at the first battle of Ypres, as has already been described. The German line ran between Flanders and Switzerland, bulging in a broad salient with its blunt apex at Compiègne. The fighting in this theatre in 1915 consisted mainly of two big Allied offensives in Artois and two in Champagne. The casualties in the autumn offensives alone were 190,000 French, 50,000 British and 140,000 Germans. The net result of this carnage was that the German positions were slightly dented.

The great battles of 1916 were Verdun and the Somme. The battle for Verdun lasted in all nearly ten months; a French estimate placed the total losses on the two sides as 420,000 dead, and 800,000 gassed or wounded – nearly a million and a quarter in all; at the end the front was almost exactly where it had been when the battle began. Alistair Horne wrote in *The Price of Glory*:

> Neither side 'won' at Verdun. It was the indecisive battle in an indecisive war; the unnecessary battle in an unnecessary war; the battle that had no victors in a war that had no victors.

The battle of the Somme, from 1st July to 18th November, cost each side about 500,000 men killed, wounded or taken prisoner; the Allies gained thereby a wedge of muddy ground, at no point more than about nine miles deep on a front of some twenty miles or so – and of no strategic value.

The man responsible for the conduct of operations on the German side during these two years was Falkenhayn. He took over from Moltke in September 1914 and prevented the failure of the Schlieffen Plan from becoming a disaster. He recognized that on the whole the defensive was now the best posture for the Germans in the west; and the only major offensive by the Germans between 1914 and 1918 was the attack at Verdun – a frontier fortress which became a symbol to the French, who allowed their manhood to be bled almost white in its defence. Falkenhayn was replaced by Hindenburg and Ludendorff in August 1916. Shortly afterwards in Rumania he proved himself to be a good fighting general in the field. He was the only prominent strategist on either side to urge that it would be wise to aim ultimately for something less than total victory.

There was no one supreme commander of the Allied forces on the western front before 1918. In 1915 and 1916 the French commander-in-chief, General Joffre, was the guiding force for all. The British commanders – French was superseded by Sir Douglas Haig in December 1915 – although theoretically independent did not yet have enough troops of their own to be in a position to dictate a strategy themselves, and on the whole they fell in with that of the French. Joffre was tough and brutal. He would not give in, no matter what the suffering. He was also stupid. He won the battle of the Marne by pure luck; as Liddell Hart observes, he had launched a million Frenchmen against a million and a half Germans in the wrong place, and it was only because he failed in Lorraine that he was able to halt the Germans at the last moment after they had marched almost round to the back of his forces. Since the German front in 1915 offered no exposed flank to turn, Joffre set about hammering frontally at either end of it – the offensives in Artois and Champagne – in an attempt to cut off the salient. This could hardly be called strategy. In a life which has seen much fighting I have learnt that what is strategically desirable must be tactically possible with the resources at one's disposal. Joffre did not seem to understand this fundamental truth.

It was beyond question that the Allies did have to operate offensively; the Germans were on French and Belgian soil and public opinion demanded that they be removed. Furthermore, if the Germans were left undisturbed on their western front they would be all the stronger to deal with the Russians in the east. But the method of the offensive to be adopted was open to question, and several possibilities existed. One was to entice the enemy forward into a 'sack' which could then be closed by an envelopment from both flanks, as was almost to happen by accident in 1918. Alternatively, the German front might have been turned by the use of British seapower in full combination with an assault on land on the Flanders flank. But the method chosen was simple frontal bludgeoning in repeated assaults. It was a basic miscalculation to suppose that such a method could prevail: all commanders underestimated the power of the tactical defensive. If the Allied commanders had been serious students of history, and had been truly professional soldiers, they would have realized early in 1915 that such frontal assaults were not going to achieve positive results. But this did not happen. They decided to continue the same policy on a more massive scale for the next year – which was not war as I understand it.

The strength of the defensive consisted essentially in men firing rifles and machine-guns from the security of entrenchments and supported by artillery. How could assailants even reach close quarters? Trench warfare was in fact siege fighting rather than open battle. That was the problem; it had been clearly indicated, not only in the Russo-Japanese and recent Balkan wars, but also in the engagements at Mons, Le Cateau and

Guise where a very few troops had seriously checked the great German sweep forward. At one time in the initial clashes in the Mons-Le Cateau area two British divisions had held off two German army corps. Quite apart from logistical factors, the tactical strength of the defensive alone made it practically certain that the Schlieffen plan would fall behind in its timing and would therefore fail.

A rifleman in a stationary position could fire fifteen rounds per minute accurately across the normal no-man's-land. The machine-gun fired a continuous stream of bullets. The number of machine-guns was soon stepped up; Haig at first considered two per battalion enough, but Lloyd George disagreed; by the end of the war there were machine-gun battalions each of forty-eight guns. Barbed wire entanglements made another obstacle to approach. As time went on refinements were added to defence. The Germans introduced gas of various types: asphyxiating, lachrymatory and vesicant (blistering). Mustard gas, in the last mentioned category, was the worst, because it was the most unpleasant and disabling and took a long time to clear. The trench systems consisted of several lines in depth, so that if the first line should be penetrated the assailants were little better off. With rail and motor transport fresh defenders could always be brought up from behind to fill a gap faster than the attackers could keep pushing forward. For example at one point in the first battle of Ypres the Germans penetrated right through the British fighting lines into the back area of administrative services, but they did not succeed in using the advantage. During the winter of 1916–17 the Germans prepared a reserve trench system, the 'Hindenburg line', to which they fell back in the early part of 1917. The site was chosen for its natural and strategic advantages. The trenches contained deep dug-outs in which men would be secure from practically all forms of artillery fire; concrete emplacements were built for machine-guns; and a network of light railways could carry men and materials up to the forward area.

The fact was that, with the weapons available, the advantages in battle were heavily stacked on the side of the defensive. But a theory at odds with this had been formulated before the war – summed up in the words of Foch that 'to make war means always attacking'. It was supposed that modern artillery and small arms fire would give such power in attack that the enemy could be attacked successfully at his strongest point. Foch wrote:

> A battle cannot be lost physically . . . it can only be lost morally . . . A battle won is a battle in which one will not confess oneself beaten.

I would agree that no battle is ever lost until the general in overall command thinks it is. But a well-balanced judgment is essential; although a commander will always aim to force his will on his opponent, he must know when discretion is the better part of valour; his desire to dominate his opponent must not outweigh his judgment of the actual possibilities of the situation. Furthermore, the good general wins his battles with the least possible loss of life. A blind offensive at all times is not the best way to operate this philosophy; the strategical defensive is often advisable while a favourable tactical objective is sought. When that is found, then is the time for boldness: everything having been done to ensure success which reason can dictate. Foch did not seem to understand this.

The normal pattern of an attack was a preliminary bombardment by artillery, followed by assaulting waves of men armed with rifle and bayonet. Machine-guns and gas were less useful in assault than in defence.

Attacks on the western front were preceded by an artillery bombardment lasting several days, the main purpose being to cut lanes in the barbed wire and put located enemy machine-guns out of action before the infantry assault began. The German artillery was at first superior both in quantity and quality, but later the types of artillery became much the same in all armies. During the war the proportion of medium and heavy artillery greatly increased. The British guns most used were the 25-pounder and 6-inch, 8-inch, and 9.2-inch howitzers, with ranges rising to over 10,000 yards. Motor transport came to be used to some extent, but guns were mostly moved by horses; larger weapons were often on railway mountings. Some very large guns, such as the famous 17-inch 'Big Berthas', were used for long-range bombardment, mostly by the Germans. Mortars, which had long been discarded, reappeared for this siege type of warfare; high explosive shells gradually replaced shrapnel; smoke and gas shells were also used. The bombardments which took place were on a tremendous scale and required a high degree of organization. The command of artillery along wide stretches of front came to be more and more centralized, so that the bombardment could be co-ordinated and fire concentrated at the right time and place. This was assisted by improved methods of communication – telephone, wireless and observation aircraft – and by means such as sound-ranging and flash spotting. By 1916 and 1917 these artillery techniques were well developed.

The disadvantage of such artillery bombardments was that they removed all possibility of tactical surprise. Moreover, in wet weather they churned up the ground to such an extent that movement became very difficult for soldiers who had to advance on foot carrying equipment which weighed some 66 lbs. When the bombardment was finished, sometimes with a smoke screen to conceal movement, waves of attacking infantry left the trenches, threaded their way through the wire on their own side, formed up and advanced at a walking pace behind a creeping barrage.

The process of a fairly characteristic assault and its fate is described by an officer of the German 180 Regiment facing the British 8th Division in the Battle of the Somme:

The intense bombardment was realized by all to be the prelude to an infantry assault sooner or later. The men in the dugouts therefore waited ready, belts full of hand-grenades . . . gripping their rifles and listening for the bombardment to lift from the front defence zone on to the rear defences. It was of vital importance to lose not a second in taking up positions . . . to meet the British infantry which would advance immediately behind the artillery barrage. Looking towards the British trenches through the long trench periscopes held up out of the dugout entrances there could be seen a mass of steel helmets above the parapet showing that the storm troops were ready for the assault. At 7.30 a.m. the hurricane of shells ceased as suddenly as it had begun. Our men at once clambered up the steep shafts leading from the dugouts . . . and ran singly or in groups to the nearest shell craters. The machine-guns were pulled out of the dugouts and hurriedly placed in position, their crews dragging the heavy ammunition boxes up the steps and out to the guns. A rough firing line was thus rapidly established.

As soon as the men were in position, a series of extended lines of infantry were seen moving forward from the British trenches. The first line appeared to continue without end to right and left. It was quickly followed by a second line, then a third and fourth. They came on at a steady

German machine-gunners take advantage of a shell hole after a heavy bombardment.

easy pace as if expecting to find nothing alive in our front trenches . . . The front line, preceded by a thin line of skirmishers and bombers, was now half way across No Man's Land. 'Get ready' was passed along our front from crater to crater, and heads appeared over the crater edges as final positions were taken up for the best view, and machine-guns mounted firmly in place. A few moments later, when the leading British line was within a hundred yards, the rattle of machine-gun and rifle broke out along the whole line of shell holes. Some fired kneeling so as to get a better target over the broken ground, whilst others, in the excitement of the moment, stood up regardless of their own safety, to fire into the crowd of men in front of them. Red rockets sped up into the blue sky as a signal to the artillery, and immediately afterwards a mass of shells from the German batteries in rear tore through the air and burst among the advancing lines. Whole sections seemed to fall, and the rear formations, moving in close order, quickly scattered. The advance rapidly crumpled under this hail of shells and bullets. All along the line men could be seen throwing up their arms and collapsing, never to move again. Badly wounded rolled about in their agony, and others, less severely injured, crawled to the nearest shell hole for shelter.

The British soldier, however, has no lack of courage, and once his hand is set to the plough, he is not easily turned from his purpose. The extended lines, though badly shaken and with many

British infantry go forward from their trench to an attack across no-man's-land

gaps, now came on all the faster. Instead of a leisurely walk they covered the ground in short rushes at the double. Within a few minutes the leading troops had advanced to within a stone's throw of our front trench, and whilst some of us continued to fire at point-blank range, others threw hand grenades among them. The British bombers answered back, whilst the infantry rushed forward with fixed bayonets. The noise of battle became indescribable. The shouting of orders and the shrill cheers as the British charged forward could be heard above the violent and intense fusillade of machine-guns and rifles and bursting bombs, and above the deep thunderings of the artillery and shell explosions. With all this were mingled the moans and groans of the wounded, the cries for help and the last screams of death. Again and again the extended lines of British infantry broke against the German defence like waves against a cliff, only to be beaten back.

Such was the general pattern of war on the western front in Europe. With the weapons available, and within the existing strategical situation, there was little opportunity in trench fighting for variation of the set pattern and the exercise of tactical skill.

Nonetheless there were periods of well-managed fighting which indicated that something a little better than the normal was possible. The Germans in their tactics at

Verdun continually sought to achieve surprise and to attack the enemy in force at his weakest rather than his strongest point. Reconnaissance parties, daringly and intelligently led under cover of darkness, would probe the enemy front for weak spots. If they found the French at some point especially alert and strong, they would switch their attack elsewhere, or postpone it while continuing further artillery preparation. In their minor attacks they reinforced success rather than failure, demonstrating that it was possible to penetrate an enemy line; and they exploited the loops of the Meuse and the suitability of the ground in searching for possibilities of envelopment. Detailed co-operation between artillery and infantry was achieved by signals with yellow, red and green rockets, in a way which the Allied troops had not achieved. The German soldiers were also very hard working and thorough in their entrenching techniques. On the whole, and particularly at Verdun, the Germans made better use than their enemies of such scanty tactical opportunities as existed. But in the end they were unable to break the French resistance at Verdun: the conception of tactics generally applied in trench warfare could yield no decisive results.

The scene on the front, in the Passchendaele area during the third battle of Ypres in 1917, is described in the British Official History:

> The shelled areas near the front became a barrier of swamp . . . The margins of the overflowing streams were transformed into long stretches of bog, passable only by a few well-defined tracks which became targets for the enemy's artillery; and to leave the tracks was to risk death by drowning.

Fatigue and boredom in these ghastly conditions were as demoralizing as filth and danger. But if ardour gradually lessened, courage and self-sacrifice remained constant. Comradeship was sustaining above all. Sidney Rogerson wrote:

> Life in the trenches was not all ghastliness. It was a compound of many things: fright and boredom, humour, comradeship, tragedy, weariness, courage and despair.

A remarkable, and disgraceful, fact is that a high proportion of the most senior officers were ignorant of the conditions in which the soldiers were fighting. It was normal for orders to be given that attacks were to be delivered *'regardless of loss'* – often for several days in succession. The quality of the men who had to do the fighting contrasts with the quality of the generals who gave the orders. A. J. P. Taylor justly observes: 'The unknown soldier was the hero of the First World War.' It can well be said that the soldiers were worthy of better generalship; on the whole they were better than their generals, though among these there were a few notable exceptions.

If both sides persisted in fighting by this method of frontal attack, then the war on the western front must become a war of attrition – a trial of each side's endurance and resources.

But amazingly, the soldiers on both sides showed no sign of flagging. The Germans after all were succeeding reasonably well in fighting a war on two fronts; everywhere they were holding their ground and killing greater numbers of their enemies than they were losing themselves. Because of their pre-war territorial system of recruitment with its long training period, the fronts could still be supplied with high-grade troops. The

French also were holding out, their morale actually heightened by the saving of Verdun; their losses had been the worst so far, both in numbers and the quality of the men killed; the best of their regular soldiers had gone, but the French spirit was not broken. The British were just coming in to their own on the western front. After the 100,000 or so of the original B.E.F., 500,000 civilians had volunteered for the 'New Army' in the first month of the recruiting drive launched by Kitchener, secretary of state for war. They were somewhat haphazardly trained and equipment was in short supply, but by 1916 the British felt ready to take an equal share of the burden with the French. The Allied forces at the Somme in 1916 were nearly all British: mostly men who had volunteered for the duration of the war. During the experiences of 1916 the original cheerfulness of the volunteers only changed to a grim determination.

Both sides in the war could draw on immense resources of population and materials. In 1910 the populations were: Germany 65 million, France 39 million, Britain 45 million. Britain also drew, to a much greater extent than the other powers, on the population of her overseas empire. Britain and Germany were, apart from the U.S.A., the two greatest industrial and commercial powers of the world. The German economy was run during the war by a brilliant capitalist, Walter Rathenau, who kept it going remarkably. The Germans could draw on the agricultural lands of central Europe for food; the French relied on their own farming; the British could import. The mobilization of millions of men inevitably affected the nature of society in the countries involved, making the conflict 'total war', and giving the 'home front' an importance it had never had before. David Lloyd George emerged as a great war leader in Britain, rallying enthusiasm with his oratory. He persuaded trade union leaders and business men alike to give support in the reorientation of manufacture to meet war needs. To fill the places of the men who were away fighting he encouraged women to work in factories and offices. In this way the war left a permanent mark on home life, as it did in many others, such as the institution of British summer time and set closing hours for public houses – the purpose of both being to make people do more work. Careful censorship and propaganda in all countries kept the public unaware of what was really happening at the front, and generally speaking people were enthusiastic for the war. Bombing raids made no serious impact on national life; that was to come in Hitler's war.

The Central Powers and the Entente were thus well matched in manpower and well supplied materially; morale on the home fronts was reasonable; and as things stood in 1916 a war of attrition could continue for some time. At the end of 1916 Ludendorff told the Germans that there was no question of a compromise peace: the war must be won. Lloyd George became prime minister in Britain in December of that year, and declared the same. In France a new figure came into prominence at this time, General Robert Nivelle, promoted commander-in-chief in place of Joffre. Nivelle had achieved at Verdun what was regarded as a spectacular success, actually gaining an extent of ground with relatively few casualties, and he now proclaimed that he knew 'the secret of victory'.

Lloyd George was an excellent leader of the British people on the home front, but his intervention in the military conduct of the war was less satisfactory. He disliked the war on the western front and had a poor opinion of Haig. His first scheme was for a major effort in 1917 on the Italian front, but the Allies would not have it. Then he became impressed by Nivelle. He decided to commit the British effort in support of Nivelle, and intrigued to ensure that Haig would be subordinated to the French high command.

Nivelle never divulged in so many words what his 'secret' was, but his actions when in command soon revealed that he had no new formula. Once again in 1917 the Allies hurled an even greater weight of men and metal against the Germans than in the previous year. In two offensives in the spring of 1917 – the battles at Arras and on the Aisne – the French losses were heavy. Then in May the French army began to crack up. Nivelle was removed from his command and replaced by Pétain, the real hero of Verdun. It was a black time for the Allies: Russia was in the throes of revolution, and German submarines were devastating Allied shipping.

At this point Haig took the lead in the planning of Allied operations on the western front. His idea was to make a heavy frontal assault against the Germans in Flanders. Here the British might draw off pressure from the French and, more importantly in his view, avoid being entangled with them; furthermore a victory could turn the flank of the German front, and assist British seapower to prevent enemy submarines from operating from ports bordering on the North Sea – for example, in the Netherlands. The Messines Ridge was taken in June 1917. A pause followed, and then the third battle of Ypres took place from 11th July to 10th November. The rainfall in August happened to be double the normal average, and from 3rd October onwards the rain came down almost ceaselessly. Men fought and died in the mud, and were drowned in shell holes; many British soldiers today recall the word 'Passchendaele' with horror. This offensive culminated in the capture of the Passchendaele ridge and no more, the British having lost 240,000 men and the Germans the same number.

Farther to the south-east Pétain launched an offensive in October at Malmaison, which merely removed a few ragged edges on the battle front. The Allied strategy of 1917 had proved to be completely sterile.

To point to the futility and horribleness of this trench warfare is not, however, to deny that the fighting spirit of the men was still bearing up; moreover some operations were ably conducted and it was possible under skilful command to make real if limited gains in ground.

The 1917 season of slogging in 'mud and blood' all but broke the French, who had been dashing themselves in suicidal attacks against entrenchments for so long, and mutinies occurred after Nivelle's offensives. But Pétain weeded out the bad elements and nursed the rest back into condition, so that by the autumn of 1917 the French army had achieved a good recovery. The British were still hopeful and were glad to be reinforced by splendid contingents from the dominions and by the first Americans. The endurance of the German soldiers was the most remarkable, for they bore the burden on their side of the western front for four years without any outside assistance.

Looking back on the third battle of Ypres it is interesting to reflect that while the rain, the mud, and the cold have earned a terrible reputation for 'Passchendaele', which was one part of the whole battle, yet it was here, as John Terraine observes, that the science of the persistent application of sheer weight in order to breach the enemy front was brought to its highest level.

The man who achieved this was the commander of the British Second Army, General Herbert Plumer, in whose army I was then serving. Plumer was one of the very few commanders in the war who was a soldier's soldier, held in trust and respect by his men – also being a high-class professional soldier, with all that this implies. He had been planning and preparing for two years the mining operation which gained the Messines

Ridge in June 1917. Nineteen deep mines had been dug more than 100 feet below the surface and filled with a million pounds of explosive. They were all set off together at dawn on the morning of 7th June, and the British troops merely had to walk in and take possession of the ridge. When after the end of August his Second Army became the spearhead of the battle, Plumer conducted its operations with the same thoroughness. Terraine writes:

> Plumer's method was the carefully prepared, limited advance, step-by-step, approximately 1,500 yards at a time, of which 1,000 yards would be saturated by the initial barrage. He was a firm believer in guns. He asked for three weeks to prepare his first attack, and for over 1,300 guns and howitzers to carry it out. These, with 240 machine-guns, laid down five belts of fire along the whole front of attack . . . When Plumer's first attack came, it was a model of forethought and precision. At the Battle of the Menin Road Ridge on September 20th, four divisions, two Australian and two British, attacked on a 4,000-yard frontage.

The enemy positions were taken with little struggle. Twice more, by the same technique of delivering a massive and concentrated artillery preparation beforehand, Plumer's men gained ground on a limited front, at Polygon Wood and Broodseinde: the casualty rate being far lower than at the Somme, or, for that matter, at Waterloo.

Ground could be gained. But at the rate of 1,500 yards in three weeks it would take a long time to drive the Germans back to their own country. But then at last there came an indication of how the war might really be made to move again. On 20th November 1917 the British used tanks in an offensive at Cambrai. Without any preliminary bombardment over 300 tanks went forward in massed formations. That day they made a hole in the Hindenburg Line four miles wide, and for a loss of 1,500 men took 10,000 German prisoners and 200 guns. The tanks penetrated altogether five miles – a distance which it had taken four months and 300,000 lives to gain at Ypres. The impact of their immediate onset in the battle is described by Captain D. G. Browne, who was present:

> The triple belts of wire were crossed as if they had been beds of nettles, and 350 pathways were sheared through them for the infantry. The defenders of the front trench, scrambling out of dug-outs and shelters to meet the crash and flame of the barrage, saw the leading tanks almost upon them, their appearance . . . grotesque and terrifying.

The advantage gained was in fact then lost by the inefficiency of the high command; the only reserves available to exploit success were horse cavalry, whose tactical mobility in the face of modern weapons had long disappeared. On 30th November the Germans staged a surprise counter stroke on the flank and rear of the British penetration, and wiped out the British gains. Nonetheless the battle was a landmark in the history of warfare.

On my birthday in 1953 Sir Winston Churchill gave me a copy of his *World Crisis 1911–1918*. In Vol II, page 1220, I found he had written the following about the Cambrai battle:

> Accusing as I do without exception all the great ally offensives of 1915, 1916, and 1917, as needless and wrongly conceived operations of infinite cost, I am bound to reply to the question, What else

Tanks represented the only means of breaking the stalemate

could be done ? And I answer it, pointing to the Battle of Cambrai, '*This* could have been done'. This in many variants, this in larger and better forms ought to have been done, and would have been done if only the Generals had not been content to fight machine-gun bullets with the breasts of gallant men, and think that that was waging war.

It seems unnecessary to say anything more on the subject. The best account of Cambrai will be found in Liddell Hart's brilliant book *The Tanks*.

In the strategy of the Allies at sea the main role was taken by the British navy, while the French played a useful part in the Mediterranean and Russian fleets operated in the Baltic and the Black Sea. As usual, Britain's naval policy was to secure the lines of sea communication upon which she and her allies depended for survival, and to damage those of the enemy. In 1914, thanks to Admiral Fisher's pre-war *Dreadnought* programme, British naval strength was 20 battleships and 7 battle-cruisers as opposed to 13 battleships and 3 battle-cruisers of Germany. The British set about sweeping the seas clear of the enemy. A German squadron under Admiral Von Spee was on the loose and ran into an inferior British force under Cradock off Coronel on 1st November, sinking two cruisers. But when Von Spee met the British a second time – by accident – at the Falkland Islands in December, four out of the five German ships were sunk. The German High Command then made the decision not to risk its High Seas Fleet against the British navy, but, instead, to keep it in operational order in the Baltic – where it would be a perpetual threat and possibly a bargaining factor in later armistice negotiations. The British were thus left to carry out their traditional policy of blockade – to confine the enemy fleet to its harbours and destroy it should it venture out.

This was not, however, to be the old method, as in the days of sail, of cruising outside enemy harbours, since mines and submarines made this too dangerous. Instead, an invisible blockade was established, the operations of the Grand Fleet being based on Scapa Flow in the Orkneys, facing the Baltic at a distance. The main activity of British ships was in arresting German merchant shipping, in checking neutral shipping, and in waging war against submarines. Various actions were fought in the North Sea between battle-cruisers, but there was only one full-scale confrontation of the two fleets – off Jutland in 1916. The German admiral, Scheer, had ventured out, but with no intention of engaging in full battle. Jellicoe, the British admiral, was aware of the danger from torpedoes, and considered that as things were Britain had little to gain from a naval victory and everything to lose in a defeat. The fleets were slightly engaged during the night of 31st May–1st June. But then both sides were content to draw off. Thereafter the German fleet remained almost entirely inactive, and in 1918 the sailors mutinied from sheer boredom.

Germany accepted more or less without challenge that Britannia ruled the waves. But the sea beneath the surface waves was a different matter. The British blockade would be countered by submarine warfare.

Research and experiment had recently developed the submarine into a weapon of great effectiveness. Its striking power lay in torpedoes, launched by compressed air from tubes in the bows. The biggest submarines had four tubes and carried two torpedoes for each tube; 500 lbs of T.N.T. could be launched at 36 m.p.h. for 7,000 to 8,000 yards. While cruising at a depth of some 25 feet the whole horizon could be observed through a periscope. In 1914 Britain actually had more submarines than Germany: 36 to 28. But when the Germans committed themselves at the end of 1914 to large-scale submarine warfare they rapidly built a large number of U-boats (as they were called) of increased size, striking power and endurance. As well as the cruiser type such as the U.140, small submarines for harbour protection and for mine-laying were built.

The Germans opened their submarine campaign early in 1915. They hoped at first to strike at the Grand Fleet, but, despite alarms, no U-boat ever succeeded in penetrating the base in Scapa Flow. They did however become devastatingly effective in their attacks on merchant shipping. The German policy in 1915 was 'unrestricted submarine warfare': striking at sight and without warning at all merchant shipping of enemies and neutrals. This was contrary to international law, and strong protests from neutral America caused the Germans to limit their U-boat campaign. Nevertheless immense quantities of Allied shipping continued to be sunk in the North Sea, in the Western Approaches between Ireland and Ushant, and in the Mediterranean. By the spring of 1917 it seemed as if the operations of U-boats might almost win the war for Germany. In April alone more than a million tons of British and neutral ships were destroyed. One ship in every four sailing from British ports failed to get home, and crews of foreign ships were refusing to sail to England. The Germans at that point resumed unrestricted submarine warfare in the hope of finishing things off.

It took a long time to discover the best anti-submarine measures. Mines were laid extensively; ships could sail in zig-zags and drop depth charges; and towards the end of the war 'asdic' was invented, a device which detected nearby submarines by sending out a supersonic wave. But none of these methods was really effective. The answer was discovered only in the nick of time by Lloyd George. It was convoys. Against the advice of the Admiralty, which itself could produce no solution, Lloyd George ordered the convoy system to be instituted at the end of April 1917. Although the number of U-boats in operation rose to 140 by October, the rate of loss in Allied shipping had by that time fallen sharply and the rate of destruction of enemy submarines increased. A convoy was harder for the U-boats to attack than isolated ships, since the herd of merchant ships could be defended by ships of the navy with all the means available. The success of the convoy system against submarines was a gleam of light for the Allies in 1917. Further hope was given to the Allied cause by the decision of the United States of America to enter the war on the side of the Allies in April – that nation being provoked by the renewal of unrestricted submarine warfare by the Germans.

The contribution of British seapower to the whole war effort of the Allies was of crucial importance, since command of the seas made it possible to transport troops to the various theatres; it also ensured the continual flow of supplies; and in this respect her seapower complemented another role of Britain, that of banker to the Entente Powers. Furthermore, although the Central Powers possessed immense domestic resources of food and materials, eventually the blockade seriously weakened them. For more than two years the U-boats were a serious menace, but they were dealt with in the end, and the entry of the Americans was a heavy blow to Germany.

Air power was never of more than minor importance during the 1914/18 war. Aeroplanes were used as adjuncts to army and naval operations. They were most useful for reconnaissance and attacking supply lines, but until the last year of the war they played only a minor part in the tactics of land warfare. The exploits of some of the air aces, such as Immelmann, became celebrated, but really they hardly mattered. Nor did bombing make any real material impact, although the raids by Zeppelin airships over British cities caused a flurry of alarm. The R.A.F. was, however, developing into a considerable force by 1918, and air power was to become a mighty weapon during the 1939/45 war, as we shall see in the next chapter.

The eastern front was another area where victory by one or other of the belligerents might influence the war decisively. The tactics were the same as those on the western front, but more movement took place – the front moving backward or forward often fifty miles, and sometimes more. In those vast spaces the troops were relatively thin on the ground; furthermore, many of the Austrian and Russian troops were inadequately equipped and trained; thus it was often possible for attackers to send the defence reeling back. The quality of command in this theatre ranged, more extremely than in the west, from abysmal to brilliant. The war on the eastern front was even more murderous than the war in the west: Russia alone is said to have lost two million men in 1915, and a further million in 1916.

Instead of following up their victory at Tannenberg by an advance into Poland, the Germans had to go to the relief of the Austrians in Galicia. There the Russians resumed the offensive in the spring of 1915. Undeterred by Joffre's offensives in the west, Falkenhayn switched large numbers of German troops eastwards by rail for a great effort against the Russians. The German campaign of 1915 succeeded as far as it was possible to succeed against that particular enemy. In May combined German and Austrian forces commanded by Mackensen attacked on a 28-mile front at Gorlice. Many of the Russian soldiers did not even have rifles. For the only time in the war a front was broken through so widely and deeply that the defenders were unable to seal off the gap. The Russians were driven out of Galicia and then forced to abandon most of Poland. Ten million civilian refugees trailed along in the retreat. Yet the defeat was not decisive, because the Russians were falling back on to their home territory, with its infinite

U-boats nearly brought Britain's overseas supplies to a halt *above*, but their attacks on merchant shipping were eventually countered by the convoy system *below*

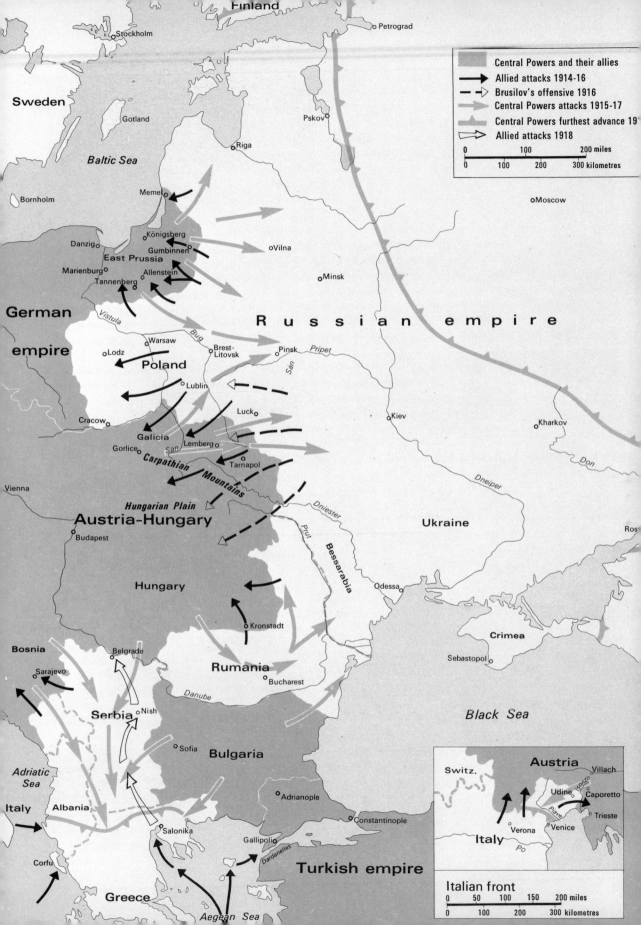

Finland

Stockholm

Petrograd

Sweden

Pskov

Baltic Sea

Riga

Gotland

Bornholm

Memel

Moscow

Königsberg

Danzig

Gumbinnen

Vilna

East Prussia

Marienburg

Allenstein

Minsk

Tannenberg

German

Vistula

R u s s i a n   e m p i r e

Warsaw

Bug

empire

Lodz

Brest-Litovsk

Pinsk

Pripet

Poland

San

Lublin

Cracow

Luck

Kiev

Kharkov

Galicia

Gorlice

Lemberg

San

Tarnapol

Don

Carpathian Mountains

Dneiper

Vienna

Hungarian Plain

Austria-Hungary

Dniester

Ukraine

Ros

Budapest

Prut

Hungary

Bessarabia

Odessa

Crimea

Kronstadt

Sebastopol

Bosnia

Belgrade

Sarajevo

Rumania

Black Sea

Serbia

Nish

Bucharest

Danube

Sofia

Bulgaria

Adriatic Sea

Italy

Albania

Adrianople

Greece

Corfu

Salonika

Constantinople

Gallipoli

Dardanelles

Turkish empire

Aegean Sea

Legend:
- Central Powers and their allies
- Allied attacks 1914-16
- Brusilov's offensive 1916
- Central Powers attacks 1915-17
- Central Powers furthest advance 19..
- Allied attacks 1918

0   100   200 miles
0   100   200   300 kilometres

Inset:
Switz.
Austria
Villach
Udine
Caporetto
Italy
Verona
Piave
Venice
Trieste
Po

Italian front
0   50   100   150   200 miles
0   100   200   300 kilometres

reserves of population; furthermore their production of armaments was actually improving. In September a new front was established 300 miles farther east; this was easier to defend, being shorter and with no vulnerable flanks. The Germans made overtures for a compromise peace, but the tsar, Nicholas II, in personal command of his armies, refused to contemplate the idea of sacrificing Russian territory and abandoning his western allies.

Kings and emperors in modern times are not trained to command great armies in battle, and Nicholas proved a thoroughly bad commander. Under him the Russian forces were given no coherent strategy. Morale was still reasonably good and the supply situation continued to improve, but the chaos in the staff system became even worse than before. In March 1916 masses of men were thrown against the strongest parts of the German front in the north: the Russian losses being five to every one German. Shortly after this failure Italy appealed to Russia to relieve her by attacking Austria. The commander of the south-western group of Russian armies, Brusilov, responded.

General Alexei Brusilov was one of the few exceptional fighting commanders whose ability shone out in the gloom of the military misconduct of most of the 1914/18 war. He had a remarkable record of success in command before 1916. In the early months of the war his army had swept into Galicia and made possible the taking of Lemberg thirty days after the declaration of hostilities. Later he was penetrating into the plain of Hungary, causing panic among the enemy, when the destruction of the neighbouring army on his right necessitated a general retreat; with his right flank exposed to attacks by greatly superior numbers of Germans and being short of ammunition, Brusilov withdrew his army through difficult country in good order, and was actually able to deliver a check to the Germans on the San. He was a man of humour and humanity, qualities which contributed to his military ability. His first act after taking over command in 1916 was to make a personal inspection of his troops at the front, thereby getting to know them and thus being able to judge what to expect from his soldiers. He always made a careful study of ground, built up an efficient staff, and studied the ways of his enemy. He was, in fact, a good professional soldier.

Brusilov decided to launch the offensive at several points simultaneously, calculating that the value of the surprise thereby gained would be great. The offensive would be delivered in particular weight in two main sectors: on the right opposite Luck and on the left in the valleys of the Dniester and the Prut. On his whole front he had a considerable superiority in numbers: 40 of the larger Russian divisions against 38 Austrian.

His campaign against the Austro-Hungarian forces was a fine example of generalship and the conduct of war, and is worthy of further study than I have space for in this chapter. It began on 4th June 1916.

After swaying backwards and forwards Brusilov's offensive finally petered out high in the Carpathians in October 1916. German reinforcements made the resistance stronger at the same time as the Russian communications were becoming strained to breaking point. The Russian armies at last came to a halt, having captured 400,000 prisoners and 500 guns; then the retreat began. Brusilov later gave it as his opinion that if Nicholas had insisted on a major offensive in the north at the same time as his own the Central Powers would have been defeated everywhere on the eastern front. That is improbable, but his resentment was justifiable. Two years later Brusilov was serving another master – Trotsky.

The fronts in eastern and south-eastern Europe

The Russian effort in 1916, the product of the tsar's determination at the beginning and Brusilov's at the end, may well have saved France and Britain, since it forced Germany to keep large forces on the eastern front. It was certainly a calamity for the Austro-Hungarian empire, where utter demoralization set in among the people as well as in the army. But it was also the ruin of Russia. The million casualties in 1916, the strain on production, and the rottenness of the government were cumulatively having their effect. During the winter the shortage of food caused riots in the cities, and in March 1917 the tsar was forced to abdicate. Ludendorff took the opportunity to put the cat among the pigeons by allowing Lenin to travel from Switzerland through Germany in a sealed train on his way to Russia. Russia had still not quite dropped out of the war, but discipline in the army was crumbling when, in July, Kerensky launched it once more against the Germans. This last offensive destroyed the Russian army and opened the way to the Bolshevik revolution. On 8th November the Soviet Congress established itself as the government in Petrograd, and Lenin read out a 'Decree on Peace'. The Bolsheviks hoped for a peace which would be 'fair for all nationalities without exception', but the Germans were not so obliging. In effect the terms they dictated at Brest-Litovsk in March 1918 removed from the former Russian empire a quarter of its population and of its arable land, three-quarters of its iron and coal resources, and half its industrial plant.

The general strategical purpose of the operations in south-eastern Europe has already been outlined. But the best known of these, the British expedition to the Dardanelles in 1915, is worth examining in some detail.

After the fighting of December 1914 the Russians asked their western allies to give them some relief by carrying out operations against the Turks, and in Britain the idea was enthusiastically received by Kitchener, Fisher and Churchill. There were many strategical advantages to be gained by the Entente Powers from domination in south-eastern Europe, and success of any kind was desirable at that stage. The Turks, it was attractive to suppose, were the least formidable of the Central Powers.

A German military mission, headed by Liman von Sanders, had recently effected a considerable improvement in the training and organization of the Turkish army, and its soldiers were notably brave and disciplined. But they were poorly equipped, only the crack troops being armed with the modern Mauser rifle. What is more, in the winter fighting against the Russians in the Caucasus the Turks had lost 53,600 men out of 66,000; and they still had to keep troops on the Russian front and garrison the extensive Ottoman empire. So at the beginning of 1915 the approach to Constantinople through the Dardanelles was guarded only by two divisions and a few dilapidated forts.

After some hesitation the British War Council decided in January 1915 that the expedition against Constantinople should be purely naval. But by 19th February, when ships of the British navy bombarded the outer forts of the Dardanelles, the plan had been changed; orders had been given that an army should be formed in Egypt, and under General Sir Ian Hamilton take part in an amphibious operation to open a passage through the Dardanelles. Hamilton's army should have been ready to start operations by 18th March, but it was held up when the transport vessels were wrongly loaded – certain essential equipment being loaded at the bottom of the holds. Nonetheless the warships entered the narrow straits a second time – though when three were sunk by mines Admiral de Robeck would take no further risk and withdrew. In fact the Turks had practically run out of ammunition and the squadron could have steamed up to Constantinople. But the opportunity was lost. Instead, the two uncoordinated naval operations merely sacrificed surprise and gave the Turks warning to strengthen their defences guarding the straits.

During March and April the German mission increased the Turkish forces on the Gallipoli peninsula to 6 divisions, and the Turks worked hard at digging trenches and preparing the beaches for defence. The Allies built up their force to 84 ships, 5 divisions, and quantities of animals and vehicles. But there was only one regular division in the force, the rest being inexperienced dominion troops and territorials – none of whom had ever studied or rehearsed the operation of an opposed landing on a hostile coast. Hamilton had left London without a staff, without proper maps, and with no information about the Turkish defences more recent than 1906.

At any rate the initial landing on 25th April went well, taking the Turks by surprise. But the first impetus quickly ran down, and the operation degenerated into the stagnation of trench warfare. One Turkish commander, Mustapha Kemal, later to be known as Ataturk, distinguished himself in repelling the Australians and New Zealanders north of Gaba Tepe. Repeated frontal assaults were made against Turkish defensive positions. These attacks were as hopeless and costly as those on the western front – and the physical conditions were possibly worse, since the men had no secure rear area and no shade from the hot sun. The Turks continued to bring up reinforcements and supplies. They had 15 divisions in July by the time the Allies had increased their strength to 12.

On 6th August Hamilton launched a double assault. In a thrust from Anzac Cove to Sari Bair Ridge the troops made a difficult advance by night over mountainous country, only to be shelled on the last stretch by their own ships which mistook them for the enemy. The other thrust, at Suvla Bay, was commanded by General Stopford, who had previously commanded the Tower of London but no forces in war. His 20,000 men landed almost without loss, whereupon they were congratulated and told to relax. Stopford himself did not go ashore, but settled down for his afternoon nap. Hamilton woke him up and remonstrated politely. But when the advance tried to move again the Turkish defence had been alerted and was too strong. Stopford was relieved of his command and I remember seeing him in London in plain clothes later in the month – which gave me a clue to what was going on in the Gallipoli area.

All through the autumn the British forces remained frustrated on the Gallipoli peninsula. The politicians at home pondered the question of withdrawal, but were worried lest Britain should lose prestige if such action was taken. Meanwhile men at Gallipoli went on dying. At Joffre's demand more British troops were thrown into the autumn offensive on the western front. Eventually the expedition was evacuated at the turn of the year, and this operation at any rate was well carried out. But a brilliant strategic idea had been thrown away because of every conceivable mistake in its execution by the commanders.

In 1915 the Allies opened a second area of operations in the Balkans, from Salonika. The Germans were preparing to deal with Serbia and give effective aid to Turkey, and had drawn Bulgaria in on their side. In October an Allied force landed at Salonika with the object of going to the help of the Serbians, but it was driven back by the Bulgarians. Although few believed it could have any further value, the force was kept at Salonika for the rest of the war. It grew to nearly 500,000 men – who were serving no useful function.

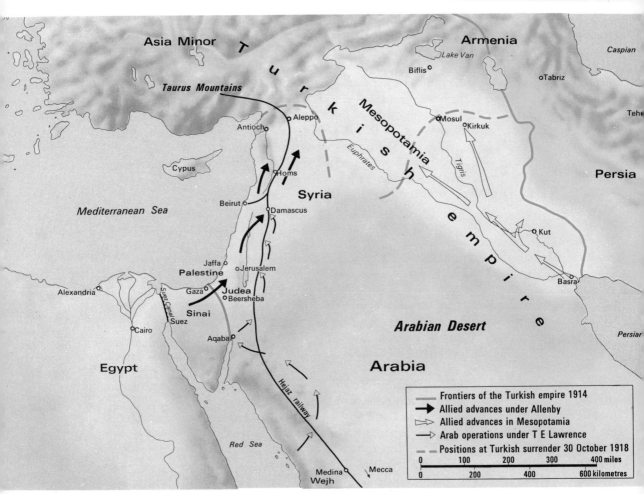

The war in the Middle East

Clemenceau called them 'the gardeners of Salonika', digging trenches against an attack the Germans and Bulgarians had no intention of launching; and music-hall comedians in London in 1917 used to sing 'if you want a holiday go to Salonika'. The Germans called Salonika 'their largest internment camp'. Only in September 1918 did this force, under General Franchet d'Espérey, launch a serious offensive; this penetrated into Bulgaria and split the Bulgarian army in half. But the whole war in Macedonia was misconceived.

One other country entered the war in south-eastern Europe: Italy. The Allies reckoned the Italians might usefully attack Austria-Hungary by the 'back door', and the Italians thought they should play the part of a great power. As it turned out the Italians were not of much use to the Allies, being a considerable economic burden to the British who were already giving supplies to France. The Italian navy cooperated in the Mediterranean; but the army was short of equipment after the Libyan War of 1911–12. The 'back

door' of Austria was in fact a barricade of mountains, and the Austrians easily held it
against the Italians, who in repeated battles of the Isonzo failed to drive the Austrians
from their mountain positions. In October 1917 the Germans intervened, and a strong
counter-attack was launched at Caporetto. The Italians were driven back seventy miles,
losing 200,000 men; many more deserted before a shorter front could be stabilized on
the Piave. Caporetto was one more dismal episode for the Allies at the end of 1917.

The war in theatres outside Europe was of minor strategical importance, but it did
produce some good generalship – notably in the Middle East against the Turks.

By 1916 the British had 250,000 men in Egypt commanded by General Murray, the
original purpose of the force being to keep the Turks away from the Suez Canal. In the
winter of 1916, in order to gain elbow room, Murray advanced into the Sinai Desert.
Meanwhile plans had been made with Hussein, Sherif of Mecca, that he should start an
Arab rising in the Hejaz which would draw the attention of the Turks away from the
British force. The Arab revolt broke out in Mecca in June 1916. When the Turks with
their superior weapons drove southwards from Medina towards Mecca the Arab forces
scattered. However the atrocities perpetrated by the Turks caused the revolt to spread,
and late in 1916 the British gave support to the Arabs, sending to them Captain T. E.
Lawrence, aged twenty-nine, a man who knew a great deal about the Arabs from
previous study and travel.

The Arab forces were primitively armed and indisciplined, their military virtue lying
in their mobility. Lawrence quickly saw how to use them as an independent irregular
force. Instead of directly opposing the Turkish regular forces, his strategy was to make
tip and run raids on their long communication lines, particularly against the Hejaz
railway, and to spread the revolt northwards to Damascus by propaganda. His first
operation with Feisal, Hussein's son, in January 1917 was a striking success. Skirting
250 miles round the flank of the Turkish force which was advancing on Mecca, he
threatened their communications from Wejh. He then moved on to Aqaba, again riding
round in a great loop to enlist tribesmen and avoid the Turks. Aqaba was not fortified
against an attack by land, and Lawrence captured the town in July.

Meanwhile the British force had twice been repulsed by the Turks at Gaza. Murray
returned to England and the new British commander, Allenby, saw that the Arabs might
play an important part in another offensive at Gaza which he was preparing; so arms,
ammunition and aircraft were sent to their new base at Aqaba. Lawrence and the Arabs
then pushed northwards, raiding the Hejaz railway and threatening the Turkish rear.
They succeeded in diverting considerable Turkish forces from the front at Gaza, and at
the same time they protected Allenby's flank. Lawrence's military skill and personal
endurance in these operations made him a hero among the Arabs, and earned him a place
among the great guerrilla leaders. I have often wished we had met.

The British force now planned to progress northwards into Palestine. When General
Allenby took over command in June 1917 the force was halted in front of the Gaza-
Beersheba line. The troops – British, Australians, New Zealanders, Indians and French,
many of them survivors of Gallipoli – were dispirited by heat, dust and lack of progress.
Allenby immediately went to the front himself to raise the morale of his troops. He reorganized the force into three corps: the XX under Chetwode, the XXI under Bulfin,
and the Desert Mounted Corps under Chauvel. The Turks were commanded by the

German General Kressenstein; their line was well fortified with entrenchments, barbed wire entanglements and machine-guns.

The plan which Allenby made for breaking the Gaza Line embodied the principles of deception and surprise. Blows were to be delivered alternately at either end of the line, so as to confuse the Turks as to where the main thrust would come. A final feint at Gaza would lead them to suppose it was there, but the real break-through would be at Beersheba, because in that area were the water wells which were necessary for the further advance to Jerusalem.

The offensive was well prepared. False papers were allowed to fall into Turkish hands to mislead them about the real intentions of the British, and to reinforce the deception elaborate movements of troops and supplies were staged at Gaza. The Turks were deceived. Meanwhile the army was thoroughly equipped and thousands of water-carrying camels assembled. The offensive opened in the last week of October with a massive artillery bombardment at Gaza from land and sea. The Turks, who were concentrated at that end of the line, sat under the storm while XX Corps and the Desert Mounted Corps moved by night on Beersheba. The infantry delivered a direct surprise attack on the town at daybreak, while the cavalry drove in on the flank – the precious water wells being safely captured. The Turks were thrown into confusion and two days later Gaza fell.

This breaking of the Turkish line was immediately followed by a tremendous push of the Mounted Corps beyond Beersheba towards Jerusalem. On the coast XXI Corps drove the Turks back relentlessly, and by the second week in November an advance of forty miles had been made. Despite fatigue and casualties the offensive was pressed on continuously so that the Turks should never have time to settle into new defensive positions. Jaffa was taken on the 16th. Then Allenby drew his forces together in the foothills of Judea. The assault of Jerusalem was rendered difficult by bad weather and the undesirability of harming the city. But an encircling movement broke the Turkish defences, and Jerusalem was occupied on 9th December 1917 – after four centuries of Moslem rule. Ten miles beyond Jerusalem the British offensive was brought to a halt by heavy rain.

A long delay now followed before Allenby resumed his advance into Syria. Some of his troops were removed to the western front, and the new troops in his army needed training. His plan for breaking the new Turkish front was similar to his previous one, but in reverse: he feinted at the Turkish left in the hills and broke through along the coast, the operations beginning on 19th September 1918. The Turks were taken off balance, one army was pushed back, and the other two encircled and destroyed. This was one of the best cavalry operations in history, and virtually the last by horsed cavalry. Lawrence and Allenby raced for Damascus, which Lawrence reached first on 1st October. Only a remnant of the Turkish forces survived to be chased beyond Damascus, and on 30th October Turkey signed an armistice of surrender.

There is one other individual commander in the war outside Europe who deserves mentioning – Colonel von Lettow-Vorbeck, who conducted German operations in East Africa for four years, causing a nuisance to the Allies out of all proportion to the size of his force. Through his understanding of the nature of war in a tropical climate and in the vast hinterland of East Africa without roads and railways, he defied all attempts to put an end to his activities and did not surrender until after the armistice in November 1918.

A large scale combined operation was conducted by General Smuts in 1916, but Lettow-Vorbeck still eluded his enemies. He never had more than 3,500 Europeans and 12,000 natives under his command, and there was no question of his defeating the British forces in Africa. His achievement lay in having diverted, by the end, 130,000 enemy troops from the war elsewhere at a cost to Britain of £72 million. For his personal qualities of military skill, presence of mind, determination and leadership, Lettow-Vorbeck deserves to be remembered as a master of irregular warfare.

The more sober and pessimistic school of strategists were right: whatever happened elsewhere, the ultimate resolution of the war could be reached only on the western front, as the 'Westerners' had said. Ludendorff decided that Germany must go all out for victory in the west in 1918. Russia was out of the war and there was no danger from Italy; at last Germany could concentrate her whole strength on a single front. But it was important to strike quickly. Austria was tottering; American troops were beginning to pour into Europe; and although Germany could find a reasonable supply of food in the recently secured territories of the eastern front, British mastery of the seas was causing her to run dangerously short of industrial materials. Finally, Ludendorff hated the idea of a compromise peace. Between 21st March and 15th July 1918 a major German offensive in several phases was launched on the western front. I was myself involved in the first three attacks – 21st March on the Somme, 9th April on the Lys, 27th May on the Chemin des Dames and at Soissons.

The Germans had no particular advantages for the offensive. The opposing forces were more or less equal, even after the Germans had moved fifty-two divisions from the eastern front. Nor did they have a new weapon, since the general staff had not recognized the value of tanks. Ludendorff now at any rate intended to rely on the principles of deception and surprise which had been practically forgotten in the tactics of trench warfare. The enemy was to be misled as far as possible by continual movements of troop-trains behind the lines, and attacking forces were to take up their battle dispositions by night. There was to be no heavy preliminary bombardment. The infantry were to probe to find the weakest spots in the enemy line, instead of just hurling themselves *en masse* against the front. Ludendorff's strategy was to feint in the south, in some force in the Somme area, where the British and French lines joined. The real breakthrough would be sought just south of Ypres, with the object of turning the Allied front from the north.

The Germans achieved a considerable measure of success in this ambitious strategical programme. They opened the offensive with an attack against the British on the Somme on 21st March, using their new tactics, and being helped by a dense fog. The British defence crumbled and was driven back some distance before the German onslaught. Pétain made ready to cover Paris while Haig was concerned for the Channel ports, and there was a brief danger that the French and British might themselves open a gap in their front. The alarm at this development caused the appointment at last, on 14th April, of a 'Commander-in-Chief of the Allied Armies in France': Marshal Ferdinand Foch. Even then Foch was not empowered to give orders to the commanders of the fighting forces – Haig, Pétain and Pershing (the American) – who continued to fight without full coordination to the end. However he did control the reserves.

The impetus of the German advance on the Somme ran down, as the defenders brought up reserves by train faster than the attacking troops could fight their way forward on foot. But Ludendorff broke his own rule of not attacking the enemy where they were strong, and ordered the offensive to be continued, expanding it on 28th March northwards towards Arras, where it met strong resistance and suffered heavy losses. The German blow in the north was then not delivered until 9th April on the Lys, by which time they had only 11 fresh divisions instead of the 35 originally envisaged. However the attack broke into the front at Hazebrouck, which was held only by one Portuguese division, and Ludendorff threw in all the reserves he could find. Haig abandoned Passchendaele and moved back on to the ports, requesting reserves from Foch, who sent 4 divisions – and the defenders held firm. The Germans had not discovered the secret of how to crown initial success in an offensive – the secret which had also eluded the Allies.

The Allies now tried out some new methods: enemy troops were bombarded with propaganda urging them to desert, and the Czechs were encouraged to break away as an independent nation from the Austro-Hungarian Empire. Meanwhile Ludendorff was developing new plans. During May well concealed preparations were made for a second diversionary offensive against the French in the south. On 27th May the Allies were surprised by an attack in the Chemin des Dames area on the Aisne, and by 3rd June the Germans had reached the Marne – bombarding Paris with long-range artillery. But for the second time Ludendorff was tempted by success to neglect the main part of his plan elsewhere; again all available reinforcements were thrown in, and again the Germans were halted. Foch used his reserves skilfully, ensuring that adequate troops should be available if needed elsewhere. Nerves were on edge in Paris, but Foch knew what he was doing and the French prime minister, Clemenceau, supported him. In June Ludendorff again rejected the idea of a compromise peace, and on 15th July he launched an offensive astride Rheims – which brought the Germans nearer to Paris than they had been before. But Foch had foreseen the attacks and the enemy was halted. Ludendorff's strategy had been thwarted.

Then the tide turned. On 18th July the French attacked the Germans with tanks west of Rheims. Ludendorff called off his projected blow in the north and ordered his forces to retreat to a front behind the Marne. On 24th July Foch concerted plans with the Allied commanders for a general offensive. Joffre's old idea of cutting off the salient was adopted, but with better tactics. The British were to attack in the north and the Americans in the south, while the French held the centre. On 8th August the British took the offensive at Amiens, using tanks in considerable numbers.

It was the British who first produced the tank, and who first used it in war. When trench warfare began Lt-Col. Ernest Swinton conceived the idea that the tank provided the solution to the problem of dealing with barbed wire and trenches defended by small arms fire. The tank Mark I, which he had a part in designing and which was the prototype of all tanks later used in the war, first appeared on the battlefield in 1916. But nobody in high command at that stage properly appreciated its tremendous potentiality. Swinton was a Royal Engineer officer. I often wished we had met, because he was the author of two superb books on war which I still read today – *The Green Curve* and *The Defence of Duffer's Drift*. Churchill became interested in his ideas and in November 1915 in a memorandum on the use of tanks in battle he wrote: 'None should be used until all can be used at once.' Unfortunately this advice was not followed; they were used at the Somme in 1916, badly in small packets instead of *en masse*. The first proper use of tanks was made only in November 1917 at Cambrai, as has been described on an earlier page.

After November 1917 a number of senior officers at last realized that the problem of deadlock in trench warfare might be resolved. Sir John Monash, the Australian Corps Commander, formed the theory that:

> The true role of the infantry was not to expend itself upon heroic physical effort, not to wither away under merciless machine-gun fire nor to impale itself on hostile bayonets . . . but on the contrary, to advance under the maximum possible protection of the maximum possible array of mechanical resources, in the form of guns, machine-guns, tanks, mortars and aeroplanes.

Based on this view, it was decided to go in for tank production in a big way.

Tanks were used in a number of minor operations in the first part of 1918. Monash tested his ideas in a small operation at Le Hamel on 4th July. There was no preliminary artillery bombardment; instead infantry and tanks advanced in cooperation. Four carrier-tanks were used, which took forward loads that would have needed 1,250 men to carry, and aircraft were also used for the first time on the western front to lift supplies on the battlefield. Monash insisted that his master plan for the battle, carefully worked out with his commanders and staff in advance, was not to be departed from during the fighting. The operation at Le Hamel was a success, and the same principles were applied in the planning of the battle of Amiens on 8th August, in which Monash advised General Rawlinson – another convert to tanks. For the coming battle Rawlinson had 13 infantry divisions and 3 cavalry divisions, 2,070 guns, 800 aircraft and 540 tanks, consisting of 324 heavy Mark V's, 96 lighter 'Whippets', and 120 supply tanks. The British forces were well supplied, thanks to a great effort by Lloyd George to boost production in Britain during 1918. Every precaution was taken to conceal from the enemy the dispositions of the troops, and to confuse them as to British intentions.

The mist on the morning of 8th August assisted surprise. There was a brief artillery bombardment, then the long lines of tanks and infantry swept forward. The dovetailed plan unfolded as intended, except on the left where the Germans had been alert during the night and the ground was steep. The Australians in the centre reached their first objective at 7 o'clock, and their second by 10.30; the Canadians on the left were up alongside them by 11 o'clock. By this time there was more noise of movement than of firing, and a little over two hours later the main fighting was finished, the Australians having gained almost all their objectives and the Canadians having advanced over seven miles. It was the use of tanks which had achieved these results. They had passed with ease through the barriers of barbed wire, trenches, machine-gun and rifle fire; the enemy artillery knocked out a considerable number, but those which got right through went on to cause havoc among the Germans.

The battle of Amiens did not yield the full promise of its opening; the infantry fell behind and the attempt to co-ordinate cavalry with tanks did not work. Nonetheless Ludendorff called 8th August 'the black day of the German Army in the history of the war'. The Allies pressed forward their offensives. As September went on the German resistance stiffened. The British reached their former Flanders battle area, where mud, the old enemy, again bogged them down. On 26th September the Americans launched an attack in the Argonne, in the old style of trench warfare, suffering very heavy casualties for an advance of eight miles in one week. Then on 4th October Germany requested an armistice. During the negotiations fighting still continued, the Germans being driven from western Belgium and almost out of France. The fighting on the western front ceased on 11th November 1918.

The war came to an end at about the same time in all the theatres, but there was hardly any strategical connection in this. The collapse of the Turks and the Bulgarians made no difference to the Germans and Austrians beyond discouraging them. The fact was that the Austrians and the Italians had had enough, and so had the Germans. The war was lost for Germany in Ludendorff's 1918 offensive rather than in the Allied counter-offensive or in the blockade. The spirit of the German soldiers at long last broke as they smashed themselves against defensive positions which they had not the means to over-come – in the manner of the Allied forces in previous years. It was this which really broke them at last, although 8th August was indeed a black day for the Germans psychologically. When the Germans asked for an armistice their front was still intact on the old ground of the war, and although they lost ground during the month after they admitted defeat the Allies even then did not succeed in breaking up their armies. The deadlock, which was the accidental product of the technology of the time, remained the prime factor in the warfare of 1914 to 1918. Even the use of tanks did not resolve the deadlock enough to make decisive tactical victory possible. The 1914/18 war could not be won; it could only be lost in a final failure of endurance by the men of one or other side. The men on both sides fought with tenacity and courage, but in the end the Germans broke.

The war defied the attempts of the generals to master it, but the generalship was by no means all poor. If the war produced no soldier of genius, Falkenhayn, Ludendorff, Mustapha Kemal, Plumer, Monash, Allenby and Brusilov were all outstanding fighting commanders. Lawrence and Lettow-Vorbeck had their special abilities. I would name Sir John Monash as the best general on the western front in Europe; he possessed real creative originality, and the war might well have been over sooner, and certainly with fewer casualties, had Haig been relieved of his command and Monash appointed to command the British armies in his place. Haig was unimaginative. Maybe he was competent according to his lights, but these were dim; confidence of divine approval appeared to satisfy him. Nothing can excuse the casualties of the Somme and Passchendaele. Furthermore, he intrigued against his commander-in-chief and his political masters, which in my view is unforgivable, even though he was himself intrigued against.

In the realm of strategy, my comment would be that the Entente Powers dissipated too much strength in minor theatres, and conducted the war in the main theatres crudely and without imagination. The Russians were admirably loyal to their allies, but they handled most of the war on the eastern front inefficiently. Joffre began the crude strategy in the west. Foch, because of his theory of tactics, must bear much responsibility for the carnage of the war, although his handling of the reserves and the counter-offensive in 1918 indicate that latterly he had begun to see the light.

On the German side, the two chiefs of the general staff, Falkenhayn and Ludendorff, deployed their forces wisely to meet requirements on the various fronts, and were right to maintain a defensive strategy in the west for most of the war. But Ludendorff threw everything away in the end by refusing a compromise peace, and by going over in 1918 to the type of offensive which had all but lost the war for the Allies in previous years – and which finally lost it for Germany.

In Chapter 2 I paid a tribute to the British soldier. Before closing the story of the 1914/18 war I would like to express my admiration for the soldier of France.

All armies have their periods of high success and also times of depression. Our study of warfare has shown how difficult it is for the armed forces of a nation to give success to a government which vacillates, lacks courage, and is unable to call forth the fighting spirit of its people in a crisis. But if all is well in these respects then generalship can avail, and victory goes to the nation whose forces are best commanded at all levels, are best equipped, and have the highest standards of discipline, physical fitness, training and morale.

All these factors are well exemplified in the case of France. We have seen French soldiers fighting valiantly in spite of the drain of the 'Spanish ulcer' and the terrible toll of the retreat from Moscow. The 'Old Moustaches' were magnificent soldiers, and so were their young successors at Verdun, Dien Bien Phu and in Algeria.

I myself have fought in battle alongside the French army. Under good generalship and given courageous leadership in the junior ranks, which are necessary for all armies, the soldier of France is second to none in communities of fighting men. I salute him – being myself *Caporal d'Honneur 1re Compagnie 11e Bataillon de Chasseurs Alpins*, and having the rare honour (for a British soldier) of the *Médaille Militaire*.

The fighting was done, but it was no easier to make a satisfactory peace than it had been to win the war. As a last manoeuvre against France and Britain the Germans sent their request for an armistice to President Wilson of the United States. Wilson had long seen himself as a mediator and in January 1918 he had put forward fourteen Points for an idealistic peace (Clemenceau is reported to have said 'The Lord God only had ten'!) which would respect national self-determination and which would by the institution of a 'League of Nations' make war impossible in the future. This seemed to the Central Powers to offer the best chance of not losing too much. But France and Britain would not be done down. In the discussions of the peace terms which took place in Paris between January and June 1919 the Central Powers were not represented, and idealism and the soothing of bitterness had to give way to the interests of the victorious powers.

Peace was *dictated* from Versailles on 28th June. Alsace and Lorraine were returned to France; the British empire and France acquired considerable territories under the guise of 'mandates'; a new Poland was created with a free and secure access to the sea. The former Austro-Hungarian and Ottoman empires were abolished by the recognition of new national states. Germany lost comparatively little territory in Europe, but was disarmed and ordered to pay reparations. Russia, after the Bolshevik revolution, was not accepted in the comity of civilized nations, and the territorial settlement of Brest-Litovsk was left in effect to stand. The League of Nations was set up, but Germany was not allowed to join for some years, and the United States after all chose not to. The lasting and dangerous effects of the 1914/18 war were a humiliated and resentful Germany and an outlawed and mistrustful Russia. The economic stability of the pre-1914 world was never quite restored. The conditions of the peace of Versailles were to prove most unsatisfactory.

The 1939/45 war was total war — for civilians as much as for fighting men. Allied troops advance through the ruins of a German town

21   Twenty Years After : 1939/45

When Foch heard of the signing of the Peace Treaty of Versailles he observed: 'This is not peace; it is an armistice for 20 years.' He was right. Twenty years after the great war described in the last chapter the nations became involved in a second struggle which lasted for six years. Whereas the 1914/18 war could hardly be called a world conflict, there can be no such thoughts about the war brought on by Hitler in 1939.

The folly of the political leaders of the victorious Allies in 1918–19 caused a second conflict to be highly probable. Hitler made it clear in *Mein Kampf* that peace was merely a period of preparation for total war, and the Nazi state became a war machine tuned for action. The former corporal himself took over the leadership of the state and of the high command, and those Germans who did not accept guns as well as butter were ruthlessly dealt with. In Spain the civil war of 1936–9 was a preview of the 1939/45 war; it was a conflict during which communists and fascists tried out new weapons and methods of warfare; the terror and frightfulness of that war were symptoms of what was to come later.

The principles held by the new German leaders – total war and *blitzkrieg* tactics – were in utter contrast to the defensive attitudes that were prevalent in the western democracies, where the belief was maintained that war would be avoided. In reaction to Nazi policies Britain eventually began to rearm, but she also worked to appease the dictators – which was a futile policy to adopt against Hitler and his military state. When Hitler attacked Poland on 1st September 1939 the world war began – ending a series of peace time aggressions which had started with the occupation of the Rhineland in 1936.

I had many discussions about Hitler's war with Sir Winston Churchill when it was all over. Whereas he considered that the 1914/18 war became inevitable once the chain of events had begun to unroll in the Balkans and Germany became involved (as I wrote in Chapter 20), he was very much of the opinion that the tragedy of the second conflict could have been prevented. He wrote in *The Second World War*, 'the malice of the wicked was reinforced by the weakness of the virtuous'.

Somebody once wrote, 'thrice armed is he who hath his quarrel just'. But Hitler knew well that 'four times armed is he who gets his blow in *fust*'. And that is exactly what he did in the east and in the west. The *blitzkrieg* burst on Poland in September 1939, and then on the west in May 1940. The war which thus engulfed the world was totally different from the conflict of 1914/18; trench systems, barbed wire, siege warfare, all disappeared; I who fought in both can truly say that it would be impossible to find two wars against the same enemy which were more different.

During the war, crimes were committed by the Germans and Japanese which have, I think, no parallel in scale and wickedness in history. Moreover, the mighty weapon of air power brought destruction and misery to non-combatants on the home fronts by the 'hideous process' of bombarding open cities and industrial centres from the air – begun by the Germans, but well and truly repaid by the Allies as the war progressed.

This was an immensely complicated war, and one which does not fall naturally into clearly defined parts as did the 1914/18 conflict. The scene is constantly changing and covers the entire planet except for the land mass of the American continents. It was, I suppose, the greatest tragedy in the history of mankind. According to the military editor of *The New York Times* with whom I once discussed it, the total number of people killed from all causes was nearly 40 million – of whom at least 17 to 18 million were civilians. The amount of human suffering was beyond all belief. But enough of that for the moment. Let us first examine the causes of the tragedy, beginning from the Treaty of Versailles signed in 1919.

A peace which had been dictated to humiliate and avenge could not be stable or satis-factory, and this fact came to be recognized in the 1920's soon after the Treaty of Ver-sailles had been signed. Reasonable neighbourly relations had to be found with the country which had (apart from Russia) the greatest population and the greatest indust-rial potentiality in Europe – namely Germany, left intact in 1919 except for the removal of a few minor scraps of territory from her borders. Diplomatic manoeuvres to find a new settlement for Europe finally led to mistakes which brought the world to war in 1939.

Russia and America ignored the German problem, while France was inclined to take a negative line; thus it was largely left for Britain and Germany to work out a new solution. British policy towards Germany from the time of the first premiership of Ramsay Mac-donald moved increasingly towards conciliation. There were various arguments in favour of 'appeasement', as this policy came to be called. The 1914/18 experience had produced a horror of war; many argued that the Germans had a good case in desiring the return of the territories they had lost; the alternative to the power of fascism in central Europe was an advance of communism; a tough line, it was thought, would merely antagonize the Germans and lead to further trouble, whereas if they were treated decently they would surely behave decently. The fallacy of the appeasement policy lay in this last assumption: the ruler of the Germans was not the gentleman foreign statesmen thought he must be.

Adolf Hitler, who became Chancellor of Germany in 1933, played the diplomatic game less decently than other statesmen as he sought to restore Germany to the status of a great power. He became Führer in 1934, and was thereafter in practice dictator. He used the Spanish Civil War which began in 1936 to try out new weapons and tactics. In 1936 he marched into the Rhineland, and in 1938 annexed Austria and the Sudeten district of Czechoslovakia. Chamberlain and Daladier, the leaders of Britain and France, thought that these German gains must be accepted as the price of a secure and lasting peace, and in a meeting with Hitler at Munich they condoned what he had done. How could Germany be denied her legitimate revival? How could politicians start a second major war for the sake of a scrap of territory? Gauging her chances, Germany got away with one coup after another. Hitler was no fool in those early days, whatever he became later. He proclaimed a protectorate over Bohemia and Moravia, and gained the cession of Memel early in 1939.

It has been said that Hitler did not seek the war which began in 1939; that, in so many words, may be true. But I find it impossible to believe that he thought he could trouble the nations of Europe in the way he was doing without it ending in a fight.

When Britain and France became alarmed and guaranteed the integrity of Poland in March 1939, surely he could not think that these peoples would not honour their word – in spite of Munich? Yet six months later he invaded Poland, deliberately unleashing the hounds of war. No! To gain his ends he was prepared to embark on war if necessary. Furthermore, the Nazi regime was based on the emotional appeal to the German people of militarism, racialism, and a nationalism which was embittered and arrogant. An interesting point to me is: when did Hitler decide in his own mind actually to risk war to gain his ends? That presumably we shall never know. What we do know is that he was an irresponsible gambler, and when he invaded Poland he overstepped the mark.

The guarantee by Britain and France to preserve the integrity of Poland was a strategical objective impossible to implement without the armed assistance of Russia, which was not forthcoming because in August 1939 Hitler had obtained a non-aggression pact with Russia – a very cunning tactic. But Britain and France sought to honour their word and both declared war on Germany on 3rd September – the nations of the British empire rallying to the support of the mother country. Italy sat tight for the moment. The United States of America decided to avoid commitment. Belgium, Holland, Denmark, Norway and Luxembourg remained neutral (though they were totally unprepared to defend their neutrality).

Maybe a tougher policy in the 1930's than that of decent conciliation could have averted war; maybe Hitler would in any case have been too reckless. But so it came about that in 1939, as in 1914, war broke out as a result of miscalculation on all sides.

Neither Britain nor France was satisfactorily prepared for war in 1939. How about Germany? In numbers of trained men she was better off, since Hitler had introduced conscription early in 1935, and in the theory of warfare the Germans had moved far ahead of the victors of the 1914/18 conflict. It was realized in Germany that a new warfare of vastly increased mobility and striking power was possible with the application of the new weapons, the tank and the aeroplane (both of them stemming from the development of the internal combustion engine). Working on this basis the German army had developed a new tactical doctrine, the *blitzkrieg* – the essence of which was to achieve a break-through and deep penetration by an armoured force, supported from the air. Aircraft would create havoc among the enemy communications and installations, would assist the field artillery during the advance by attacking ground targets, and would keep the attacking force supplied with men and materials. Tanks, supported by infantry, would achieve the break-through on the ground. The essential tactical principles in the *blitzkrieg* were concentration, surprise and speed – the enemy being overwhelmed and shattered with ruthless thoroughness.

Except in aircraft there had been little technical inventiveness between 1918 and 1939. The weapons of the 1914/18 war had been further developed, though without urgency. The speed, armour and armament of tanks improved; anti-tank guns emerged; mortars were adapted for use in the field, and a sub-machine-gun was developed which could be carried by hand; gas-masks, camouflage and dispersion techniques were improved; and transport was mechanized.

Since 1918 the only other power apart from Germany to have adopted new ideas on the conduct of war was Russia, where tanks and airborne troops were highly esteemed. The victorious powers of 1914/18 hardly altered their ideas at all; the complacency of having won the last war and the expectation of future peace stultified military development. The ideas and theories of a few soldiers, such as Liddell Hart and Fuller, who argued that the fighting of the future would not be dominated by the defensive, were ignored by those in authority in Britain and France; in both countries equipment and training were at a very low ebb in 1939. The French built the Maginot Line to protect their frontier with Germany, a defensive line of fortification which would have been impregnable in the 1914/18 war but which had no place in the new tactical conceptions. Only in Germany were the writings of Liddell Hart carefully studied by those in authority and then put to good effect – as the nations of Europe were to learn to their cost in the spring of 1940, when the *blitzkrieg* came west.

The German invasion of Poland gave a first and most convincing demonstration to Europe of the power of *blitzkrieg* tactics. The initiative was gained by striking without a declaration of war. First the German air force, the Luftwaffe, destroyed the Polish air force within two days – much of it never even getting off the ground to meet the enemy. The undefended railways were paralyzed by attacks from the air so that the Polish army could not properly mobilize. To add to the chaos and demoralization, towns, villages and columns of refugees were bombed and strafed from the air. The Poles brought up what forces they could to resist the ground invasion, but Marshal Smigly-Rydz handled them in the 1914/18 manner – deploying them all along the frontier so that they were weak everywhere and strong nowhere. The German forces advanced in three massed columns from north, north-west and south, and armoured spearheads penetrated the Polish front with ease. By 7th September the two northern armies under Bock were converging near Lodz; and large Polish forces were enveloped in the triangle Lodz-Warsaw-Torun. Farther south, forces from the Carpathians under Rundstedt crossed the San, and on the 17th Stalin moved Russian forces in behind the Polish army from the east. Poland was again partitioned. The conquest of Poland, a country of 33 million people, had been carried out by the Germans in eighteen days for a loss of 10,500 men killed and 30,000 wounded.

Britain and France, having embarked on war for the purpose of preserving Poland, could do nothing for her, as I have already said. Britain sent her expeditionary force of four regular infantry divisions, organized in two corps, to France in September, where it occupied its time extending the defences of the Maginot Line northwards along the Belgian frontier (which country was neutral). My division, the 3rd, was on the left of the British front in the area to the south of Lille. On my left were divisions of the Seventh French Army which prolonged the front to the North Sea. A Royal Air Force component was sent to France in support of the expeditionary force. Possessed by the theory of the defensive, the British and French forces did not even attack Germany on her western front when her armies were engaged in eastern Europe. Instead, they bombed her with propaganda leaflets! If this was war, I did not understand it. With the British army in France was one Army Tank Brigade, but I never saw it. And we were the nation which had invented the tank and had first used it in battle in 1916.

The inactivity on the western front lasted from September 1939 to May 1940, a period which became known as the 'phoney war'.

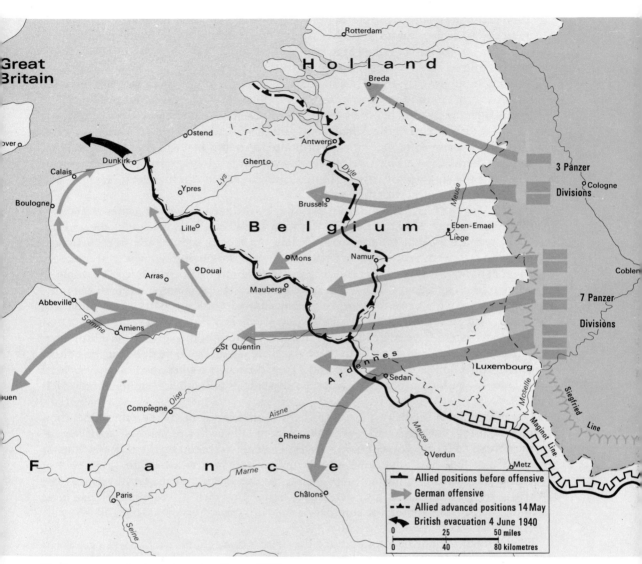

The German campaign in north-western Europe, 1940

During that time the Russians conquered Finland for themselves, and German forces gained control of Denmark and Norway. The phoney war ended on 10th May 1940 with the German invasion of the Low Countries and France.

The French had mobilized eighty divisions. The British had ten in France by May 1940, but some of the Territorial divisions lacked equipment and training and were unfit to take part in major war. Hitler adopted a plan made by General von Manstein. This was to overrun neutral Belgium and Holland, thus outflanking the Maginot Line and securing North Sea ports and air bases. France was then to be attacked immediately. Anticipating that the British and French would have directed their forces to meet an invasion through Belgium, the Germans decided to deliver their main armoured thrust through the Ardennes towards the Meuse at Sedan, on the hinge of the Allied wheel towards and into Belgium. All went as had been planned. The *blitzkrieg* offensive overwhelmed Holland in five days. A combat team of parachutists and assault engineers captured the supposedly impregnable Belgian fortress of Eben-Emael in thirty-six hours. The thrust to the Meuse went faster even than the Germans had expected, as the French artillerymen were demoralized by the attacks of Stuka dive-bombers. A breach fifty miles wide was torn in the Allied front, and then General Guderian thrust on westwards towards Saint-Quentin with his armoured group – motorized divisions moving up to form 'hedges' on either side of the passage blasted by the armour. The German command of the air was virtually absolute – and the Allied commanders, Gamelin and Gort, were unable to deal with the German army.

By 20th May the Germans were in Abbeville; by the 23rd they had reached Boulogne. At midnight on 27th May the Belgians capitulated. This was awkward for me and my division, because by that time we had become the left division of the Franco-British forces, with a Belgian army of over twenty divisions prolonging our left to the sea. At dawn on 28th May I learned that the king of the Belgians had surrendered the whole of his army to the Germans. I decided in my own mind that it is not suitable in the mid-twentieth century for kings to command their national armies in battle. One thing was fortunate – there were so many Belgian soldiers between my division and the sea that the Germans would have some difficulty in getting through, thus giving me a little time to think out what to do about it! But there was little which could be done for the British force. By 4th June the British troops and 120,000 French soldiers had been evacuated from Dunkirk with their personal weapons, all vehicles and other equipment being left behind.

The evacuation of the British forces from the Dunkirk beaches (code name 'Operation Dynamo') lasted nine days, and saved 338,000 men. This was a remarkable achievement by the British navy which assembled 887 vessels of all sizes, and by the R.A.F. which in one period of four days shot down 179 enemy aircraft for the loss of 29. The relief in Britain at the extrication of the troops countered the shock, but the truth was that the British army had been thoroughly defeated in battle. So much of its equipment had been abandoned in France that in the summer of 1940 only one division in England (the 3rd) was respectably equipped.

The German armour had not pursued the British up to Dunkirk; this was because of the orders of Hitler, who decided to turn south and finish off the French. French morale cracked, and on 16th June the French government under Pétain surrendered. The Germans occupied northern and western France. At this stage Italy declared war on Germany's side.

The German conquest of the Low Countries and France was due to superior tactical methods and leadership. The Allies actually had a slight superiority in numbers and equipment: 146 to 126 divisions; but many of the French and British divisions were of little fighting value. Some of the Allied tanks were individually stronger than those of the Germans, for example the British Matilda. The decisive factor was the difference in approach. Whereas the Allied dispositions were faulty, with their strength dispersed on a wide front with no reserves, the Germans struck in a column, fast and hard. Seven of their ten panzer divisions were concentrated for the break-through between Sedan and

Namur. Manstein's overall plan and the panzer tactics by which it was carried out, particularly Guderian's strong westward thrust, altogether constituted a very remarkable military achievement.

By 17th June France was out of the war. In the following years the partisans of the French resistance movement and agents of the British Special Operations Executive were of particular value, harassing the German forces of occupation, and organizing escape routes for soldiers who had escaped from prisoner-of-war camps and for airmen shot down over France. Commando raids were a nuisance to the Germans, and Free French units served in Britain and Africa. But the fact had to be faced that in June 1940 Britain and her empire stood alone against the Axis powers, Germany and Italy.

The British people prepared for invasion; for nearly 900 years no foreign enemy had set foot on the soil of Britain, and although nobody in the country knew how the Germans were to be beaten, nobody thought of giving in. Even Winston Churchill himself did not see at that time how it was to be done, as he told me when I discussed it with him in June 1940; but he was in no doubt about the final result; nor was I, because I saw in him the leader we needed, the man who had rallied a defeated nation, and was prepared to lead it through further troubles if they should burst upon us – which was soon to happen.

Churchill had been Prime Minister since May, and after the disaster of Dunkirk he called forth the spirit of the British people by his courage and oratory:

> We shall not flag or fail. We shall go on to the end. We shall fight in France, we shall fight in the seas and oceans, we shall fight with growing confidence and growing strength in the air; we shall defend our island whatever the cost may be. We shall fight on the beaches, we shall fight on the landing-grounds, we shall fight in the fields and in the streets, we shall fight in the hills; we shall never surrender.

A Home Guard sprang into being. Britain's productive capacity was turned over to the war effort, and much material aid came from neutral America. The re-equipment and enlargement of the army, and the adaptation of training to up-to-date methods got under way. Great things from now on were achieved in the organization of the British army by Sir Alan Brooke, C-in-C Home Forces and later C.I.G.S. But there was much to be done, and I myself, commanding a corps on the south coast of England, was not sure how long we had before Hitler would strike. The armed forces of Germany were in occupation of the whole of western Europe from Norway to France; Churchill told us that Hitler knew he must conquer Britain or else lose the war, so we all reckoned it would be our turn next.

We will now examine the war in the air in Europe between the summer of 1940 and May 1941. To prevent the Germans in 1940 from crossing the Channel, Britain had to rely on her strength in the air and at sea. The essential preliminary for a German invasion against the shores of an enemy who was immensely superior at sea was command of the air. Without it, the German troops and supplies would never be able to cross *la Manche*.

The aeroplane had been of small importance in the 1914/18 war. But between the two wars aircraft had developed enormously. During the 1939/45 war air power became a mighty weapon which transformed the concception of war at sea, as well as ground

The Battle of Britain was Hitler's first check. Fighter pilots of the R.A.F. run to take off

tactics, enabling land battles to be won in less time and with fewer casualties than would otherwise have been the case. Strategic bombing played a large part in warfare and Allied air power was a decisive factor in the war in Europe. When I myself rose to high command in 1942, I laid it down as an axiom that you must win the air battle before embarking on the land or sea battle. But as the war progressed and my experience grew, I decided that was not quite right; it was necessary to gain, so far as possible, 'mastery in the air' over the area of operations – and that principle saw me through to the end of the war.

The task of the Luftwaffe in the summer of 1940 was to gain that air mastery over England and the Channel as a prelude to invasion. The head of the German Air Ministry and C-in-C of the Luftwaffe was Hermann Göring. By August he had concentrated two *luftflotten* between the Netherlands and Brittany, one commanded by Kesselring at Brussels and the other by Sperle at Paris. A third, small *luftflotte* commanded by Stumpff was based in Norway. The two main *luftflotten* had a first line strength of about 2,000 serviceable aircraft. These consisted of Junker 88 bombers, the fastest and best yet made, Junker 87 dive-bombers, Messerschmitt 109 fighters and Messerschmitt 110's.

To oppose this force, the British Fighter Command under Air Chief Marshal Dowding had 50 squadrons of Hurricanes and Spitfires – a first-line strength of about 900 aircraft. There were also 1,700 anti-aircraft guns. With a numerically inferior force the British had to defend a whole coastline, whereas the Germans could choose the areas in which to concentrate their attack.

There was little to choose between the British and German fighters. The Spitfire and Hurricane, armed with eight machine-guns, were slightly slower than the Messerschmitt 109 (358 m.p.h.) but made up for it with greater manoeuvrability. The German bombers were slow and vulnerable, and consequently had to be escorted by fighters – which limited the activities of both. Furthermore Fighter Command was well organized, the system having been set up under Dowding in 1936 at Bentley Priory near London. The essence of the system was the centralization of an early warning complex at Bentley Priory, and the decentralization of tactical control to subordinate Groups throughout the country. Information of the approach of enemy aircraft was collected from the twenty or so radar stations on the coast. (Radar, a device which detected objects at a distance by bouncing radio waves against them, had been developed in the 1930's by R. A. Watson-Watt.) The information was then passed on to the relevant Group Headquarters whose responsibility it was to engage the enemy, bringing into operation its fighters, search-lights and anti-aircraft guns. The system worked well.

On 2nd July Hitler ordered his armed forces to prepare for the invasion of Britain ('Operation Sea-Lion'), and Göring launched the Battle of Britain in the air with a limited preliminary offensive against shipping in the straits of Dover. Dowding refused to be drawn. The first main phase began in mid-August. The R.A.F. was to be smashed by the destruction of aircraft in the air, while at the same time the offensive against shipping was to continue. Kesselring and Sperle concentrated their Groups on south-eastern England, and Stumpff from Norway on the Midlands. During the first big battle, 13th August, British fighters in the south-east Group under Air Vice-Marshal Park destroyed 45 German planes for the loss of 13 of their own. In the next major clash Stumpff lost one sixth of his force, and thereafter could only play a minor part in operations. Between 16th and 18th August the Germans again suffered heavy losses: 236 for 95 British planes. The R.A.F. had the advantage that the pilots of their destroyed planes were not necessarily lost to them, but might parachute to safety. Also, aircraft production in Britain was proceeding rapidly.

Göring now saw that he had made a mistake in not first concentrating his whole force on defeating the R.A.F. in the air. From 19th August to 6th September – the second phase – this was his main object; Kesselring's fighters came over by day, and Sperle's bombers by night. Park would not be drawn to risk all his strength against the fighters, but continued to pick off the German bombers.

The third phase began early in September, when the whole German attack was concentrated on London. Hitler spoke, characteristically, of 'extermination'. On 7th September Kesselring attacked London with 300 bombers and 600 fighters. Most of the bombs were dropped, causing heavy damage and casualties in the docks. But 21 fighter squadrons of the R.A.F. engaged the enemy, and again the Germans suffered many more losses in aircraft than they inflicted. The German raids continued, culminating in the fighting of 15th September. On that day Kesselring threw in all his strength, making one raid in the morning and another in the afternoon. Park, reinforced by neighbouring

Groups, committed practically his whole force. Kesselring's bombers were decimated and the German fighters definitely repulsed.

The Luftwaffe admitted defeat by Fighter Command, and on 12th October Hitler cancelled his invasion plan. Churchill's tribute to the men of the R.A.F. who won the Battle of Britain was:

> Never in the field of human conflict was so much owed by so many to so few.

The Luftwaffe continued night bombing through the following winter and spring, not now to clear the way for invasion but with the object of dislocating production and breaking civilian morale. Most of the main cities of Britain suffered greatly, Coventry in particular, yet the Germans did not achieve these strategic objects. In mid-May 1941 the Luftwaffe began to look towards Russia, since Hitler had decided to strike down that people in June.

The Battle of Britain had been a rebuff to Germany, but, despite that, the Axis powers thereafter widened their strategy. The roots of British strength were attacked. Manufacturing centres and bases were bombed, and British maritime communications everywhere attacked by air and sea. In September 1940 the Italians started an offensive in North Africa, and in October they invaded Greece. The Germans quickly had to support them in both these areas. Mussolini's motive was probably envy of German success, but the war in the Mediterranean theatre had a true strategic value for the Axis in that it was a further blow to the communications of Britain's empire. Axis strategy thus far was bold, also temporarily realistic and successful.

Then on 22nd June 1941 Germany attacked Russia – a major strategic error about which I shall have more to say. On 11th December 1941 she declared war on the United States of America. Hitler's motive in thus pitting Germany against the two most powerful states in the world simultaneously is unfathomable. Maybe he feared attack, or maybe megalomania overtook him. As it turned out, the war in the west and the war which began in the Far East when Japan attacked the United States at Pearl Harbour on 7th December 1941 were little related. Germany and Japan had a pact, but in practice they did not concert operations as allies. Since they had common enemies, each did to some extent divert the other's opponents, although Russia and Japan never fought each other. Hitler now had to fight not only the British empire but also Russia and the U.S.A.; his service chiefs could hardly view the problem with any great hope, particularly since one of the Axis powers, Italy, was already proving a broken reed.

The Italians had strong naval forces and an air force in the Mediterranean, also a large army in Libya. On 13th September 1940 the Italian forces began an advance from Cyrenaica towards Egypt and having occupied Sollum pressed on to Sidi Barrani, where they came to a halt. The British C-in-C, General Wavell, decided, even although his forces were greatly inferior to those of the Italians, that the enemy threat to Egypt must be met with boldness. The Western Desert Force took the offensive under the efficient command of Major-General O'Connor. During the night of 8th–9th December the offensive cut through the line of Italian forts, capturing them one after the other, and two nights later had cut across the desert to the sea west of Sidi Barrani to block the

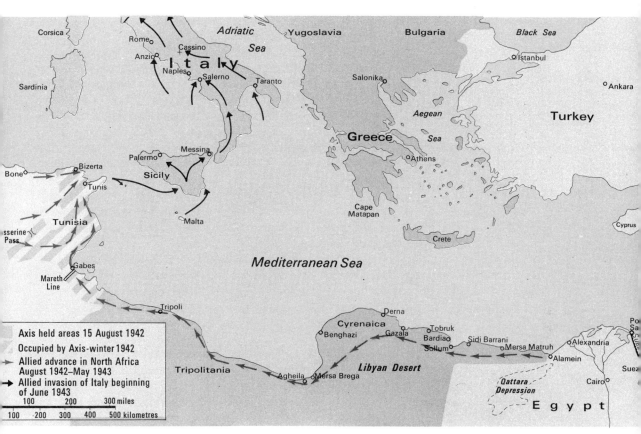

The war in the Mediterranean

retreat of the main Italian force. What had begun as a raid was pushed on as a campaign. Tobruk was captured on 22nd January 1941, and the British again pushed forward boldly; on 8th February Mersa Brega and Agheila were captured. The British force of two divisions had destroyed the Italian force of ten divisions, taking 130,000 prisoners, 380 tanks and 845 guns for the loss of 500 dead and 1,400 wounded. Boldness, mobility, and above all the generalship of O'Connor together with inter-service cooperation were the elements in this success. The Italians in East Africa, Eritrea and Abyssinia were also defeated by virtue of the great mobility and driving force of much smaller British armies.

During the same period Admiral Cunningham's fleet, based on Alexandria, inflicted serious damage on the Italian navy. On 15th October three Italian destroyers were sunk; on 11th November the Fleet Air Arm torpedoed and sank three battleships in Taranto harbour; on 9th February the docks of Genoa were bombarded; and on 19th March in an engagement off Cape Matapan Cunningham destroyed three cruisers and two destroyers for the loss of only two aircraft.

These were heartening successes. But on 12th February 1941 General Rommel arrived in Tripoli with advanced elements of his Afrika Korps and events began to turn against the British once more. At the end of March the Western Desert Force was attacked at Mersa Brega by Rommel's armoured force and had to retire, having been weakened by the withdrawal of troops for operations in Greece. Most unfortunately, during the withdrawal O'Connor was taken prisoner. By 13th April Rommel had encircled Tobruk, which was besieged but held out, and by 28th April he had crossed the Egyptian frontier and occupied Halfaya Pass and Sollum. It was during this period of British reverses that the first steps were taken to reconnoitre defensive positions in the Alamein area – in case the worst should happen. General Wavell launched various offensives but to no avail, and Rommel continued to dominate the desert scene. On 1st July 1941, Wavell having been appointed C-in-C India, Auchinleck took over as C-in-C Middle East.

In October 1940 the Italians had invaded Greece, but failed there too; so the Germans had to intervene – overrunning Yugoslavia and Greece in the spring of 1941. On 20th May the Germans invaded Crete. After bombing out the anti-aircraft installations they dropped paratroops and followed them by glider-borne troops. It was a bold and skilful though costly operation, and Crete fell to them. The Greek and Cretan operations had diverted troops from the desert, and also air power. I have always considered the British intervention in Greece to have been a strategic error; it weakened the British front south of Benghazi; and in the end the British forces were driven out of Greece, Crete and Cyrenaica.

We must now examine the attack by the Germans on Russia, called 'Barbarossa' and launched on 22nd June 1941, in which they soon made great advances. The design of the operation was that the Germans should envelop the Russians in a series of pockets by means of convergent thrusts made by columns, and not be drawn into the great open spaces of the country. The Germans had 145 divisions, 20 of them armoured, as well as some forces from their satellite countries, with which to attack 158 Russian divisions and 55 armoured brigades near the frontier. The convergent thrust method was highly successful, and Russian troops were captured during 1941 in enormous numbers. Guderian with his armoured divisions conducted one of the most brilliant operations of the war in his thrust to Smolensk and the encirclement of enemy forces in that area. The Russians had not the equipment nor the ideas with which to oppose *blitzkrieg* tactics. Major battles took place at Kiev, Viazma-Briansk and the Azov Sea. But after covering 700 miles and getting within 15 miles of Moscow before winter fell, the German generals were not permitted by Hitler to make a final thrust on the centre of Russian communications and the capital of communism. Hitler took over direct overall command from Field-Marshal von Brauchitsch, and the Germans fell back somewhat and fortified a winter front. The German troops were not equipped for the terrible Russian winter, and they also suffered considerably from Russian counter-attacks. But they endured great hardships with remarkable fortitude.

In the spring of 1942 the eastern front ran from Leningrad to Rostov-on-Don, some of Russia's best corn lands and her chief industrial areas being thus in German hands. At first the Russian people rather welcomed the Germans as liberators from Stalin's rule. But Hitler failed to take advantage of this; instead, he decided that the best method of pacification was cruelty and destruction – mass depopulations being carried out by the 'Security Service' run by Himmler. From then on torture and murder became all too

The war in eastern Europe, 1942-4

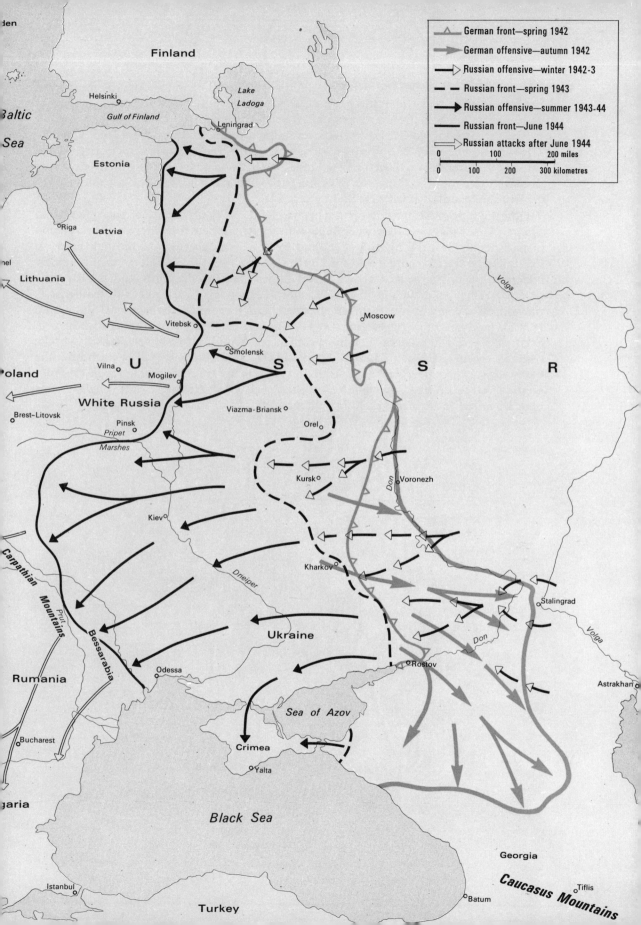

	Germanfront—spring 1942
	German offensive—autumn 1942
	Russian offensive—winter 1942-3
	Russian front—spring 1943
	Russian offensive—summer 1943-44
	Russian front—June 1944
	Russian attacks after June 1944

0   100   200 miles

0   100   200   300 kilometres

Finland

Helsinki

Lake Ladoga

Baltic

Gulf of Finland

Sea

Leningrad

Estonia

Riga

Latvia

Lithuania

nel

Vitebsk

Moscow

U

S

S

R

Vilna

Smolensk

Poland

Mogilev

White Russia

Viazma-Briansk

Brest-Litovsk

Pinsk

Pripet

Orel

Marshes

Kursk

Voronezh

Don

Kiev

Dneiper

Kharkov

Carpathian Mountains

Stalingrad

Volga

Prut

Bessarabia

Ukraine

Don

Rumania

Odessa

Rostov

Astrakhan

Volga

Bucharest

Sea of Azov

Crimea

garia

Yalta

Black Sea

Georgia

Istanbul

Tiflis

Batum

Caucasus Mountains

Turkey

common in German dealings with those they conquered or imprisoned. A murderous partisan warfare was the natural consequence of this policy in the occupied areas of eastern Europe – and the Germans suffered severely from it.

They resumed the offensive in 1942, confining it to the southern front from Kursk to Kharkov. Some fifty-one German divisions, with complete air superiority, swept forward to Voronezh on the left and to Stalingrad in the centre – bracing themselves for a decisive drive into the Caucasus to capture the oilfields. But before that could happen the Russians counter-attacked at Stalingrad.

Offering fierce resistance the Russians had held out against the German offensive at Stalingrad. At this time they were being rapidly strengthened by increased production in factories behind the fighting area, and by American and British aid delivered via Persia and by the sea route round the North Cape of Norway. The ablest men were now coming to the top in the Red Army. In November 1942, heavily reinforced, the Russians under Marshal Zhukov, a good soldier whom I know well, went over to the offensive, the pincers closing in on eighteen German and Rumanian divisions at Stalingrad. Hitler would not allow retreat, and on 31st January 1943 the remnants of the German Sixth Army under General Paulus surrendered. Simultaneously the Russians broke through the investment of Leningrad. Field-Marshal von List had to withdraw the German army group in the Caucasus to prevent it being trapped, and to repair the front on the Don; this retreat, through Rostov, was conducted with great skill. The Russians now advanced in strides, reaching Kharkov, 350 miles west of Stalingrad, by mid-

German troops stumble through the snows of Russia to a disastrous defeat

February 1943. The advance was checked for a while, as Manstein stabilized the front in that area and the spring thaw rendered movement difficult. In July the Germans launched the most powerful armoured assault of the war at Kursk. But the Russians held firm.

During this time the Russian army was gradually growing stronger in equipment and numbers, under able new commanders – notably Koniev and Rokossovsky, both of whom I know. The Germans were not the force they had been in 1941. In September the Russians reached Smolensk in the north, and, by the end of 1943, Kiev in the south.

The turn of the tide on the Russian front was matched elsewhere. In the six months from October 1942 (the battle of Alamein) the Germans were driven out of North Africa, and the Allies followed up that victory by conquering Sicily and invading Italy. The Americans were now making headway in building up their great strength, which was badly needed. The Allied bombing attack on Germany was stepped up during the winter of 1942–3 and in the summer of 1943 the war in the Atlantic turned decisively in favour of the British and Americans.

Confident of victory, Churchill met Roosevelt at Casablanca in January 1943 to formulate strategy. Together they declared that the policy of the Allies was to force the 'unconditional surrender' of Germany, Italy and Japan. I have always considered this decision to have been a tragic mistake. What it led to was well summarized by the late Lord Hankey, in his book *Politics – Trials and Errors*:

> It embittered the war, rendered inevitable a fight to the finish, banged the door on any possibility of either side offering terms or opening up negotiations, gave the Germans and Japanese the courage of despair, strengthened Hitler's position as Germany's 'only hope', aided Goebbels' propaganda, and made inevitable the Normandy landing and the subsequent terribly exhausting and destructive advance through North France, Belgium, Luxemburg, Holland and Germany. The lengthening of the war enabled Stalin to occupy the whole of eastern Europe, to ring down the iron curtain . . . By disposing of all the more competent administrators in Germany and Japan this policy . . . retarded recovery and reconstruction . . . Unfortunately also, these policies, so contrary to the spirit of the Sermon on the Mount, did nothing to strengthen the moral position of the Allies.

But from the time the war turned in favour of the Allies the unconditional surrender of all their enemies was their strategic objective. (Insofar as Hitler's Germany was concerned, when the war ended there was no government which could surrender – only a high command!)

I now propose to look more closely at certain of these strategical developments, taking them one by one.

Hitler's fatal mistake was to attack Russia. It was doubly stupid of him to do so before the Germans had successfully finished off the war against the British in the Mediterranean and northern Africa. Had a proportion of the troops and equipment used against the Russians been sent to Africa, and particularly armoured divisions, it is reasonable to presume that the Germans would have gained Egypt, the Suez Canal and possibly established a stronghold in the Middle East.

As in all war, success in the war in the African desert depended of course on general-ship. But it also depended to a remarkable degree on the factors of equipment and supply, and it is this problem that I now want to discuss. Important changes in the balance of these two factors were the chief reason for the shuttling of the two sides backwards and forwards across the desert. With smaller numbers but better equipment Wavell defeated the Italians in 1940. Then Rommel arrived with his Afrika Korps and the balance switched back in favour of the Axis. In 1941 and until autumn 1942 the Germans had superior equipment. Their tanks had a better armament than the British ones, which were under-gunned. The British 2-pounder anti-tank gun, and even the 6-pounder, were less powerful for example than the German 88-mm. gun, which could pierce thick tank armour at 2,000 yards; this was, in fact, an anti-aircraft gun, but Rommel found it to be a very effective anti-tank gun and often used it as such. Other examples of superior German equipment were their petrol containers, known as 'jerrycans', and their tank-transporters which saved wear of tracks. Equipment which gave any superiority in mobility and fire-power counted for much in war in the open desert, with its independence of fixed defences. Rapid and wide manoeuvre, and superiority in gun-power and armour, were the best methods to win battles. Wavell once compared the tactics of war in the desert to war at sea; minefields were laid in the desert very much as they were in the sea.

The Germans had the advantage in equipment but not always in supply – which also counted for much. The British retention of Tobruk after the reverse of March 1941 deprived Rommel of an important base. Malta was also a crucial supply point for the British, as well as being a base whence submarines and aircraft could attack the enemy supply lines. The Germans did not pay enough attention to Malta in 1941, and in August of that year 35 per cent of German and Italian supplies and reinforcements were lost when trying to cross the Mediterranean; in the autumn the figure rose towards 75 per cent. When Rommel was relatively short of supplies between October 1941 and early January 1942, Auchinleck was able to drive him back to Agheila – causing him many casualties in men and armoured vehicles. The Germans then realized how essential was the supply factor. In the winter of 1941, twenty-five U-boats were diverted from the Atlantic to the Mediterranean, and in December the Axis began an intense air attack on Malta, the result being that in January 1942 they did not lose a single ton of supplies in the Mediterranean, while British naval losses in that period were severe.

It was then the turn of the British to be short of supplies. Auchinleck had advanced a long way and his army was at the end of communications stretching back to Egypt. Late in January 1942 Rommel hit back, but was held on the Gazala line. He attacked again towards the end of May, took Tobruk on 21st June, and Malta became in great danger. Rommel pressed on with brilliant and daring rapidity. The British were bounced out of Mersa Matruh before they could collect themselves, and by the end of June 1942 they were back at the Alamein position. Here, between the sea and the impassable Qattara Depression, a position was established – some thirty miles in a straight line. During the winter of 1941–2 Auchinleck had had to send away some of his forces for the war against Japan, and this did not help in his efforts to deal with Rommel. But the Alamein position held against Rommel's assaults; it had no open flanks.

Again, with the Germans only sixty miles from Alexandria, the supply pendulum swung. It was now Rommel's army which found itself at the end of a long supply line.

Auchinleck and the air C-in-C, Tedder, very intelligently took advantage of this fact and bombed the German supply points along the coast, Mersa Matruh, Bardia and Tobruk, leaving Rommel with no proper base nearer than Benghazi – 680 miles to the west. Furthermore, Hitler deferred the final reduction of Malta, which staged a recovery, and the British supply situation began to improve. Additional troops arrived, and the Americans sent 300 Sherman tanks and 100 self-propelled guns – equipment at last to match that of the Germans. Such was the situation in mid-August, when General Alexander replaced Auchinleck as C-in-C Middle East, and I took over command of the Eighth Army.

My determination to deal firmly with Rommel and his army once and for all was clearly expressed to the Eighth Army: to hit the Axis forces right out of Africa. But I was equally determined not to begin the attempt until we were fully prepared, and I said as much to officers and men. We must have enough supplies not only to defeat Rommel at Alamein but also to pursue him westwards until we could open up the ports of Tobruk and Benghazi. Accordingly I spent two months building up the army and its morale. I instituted a system of command which was efficient and novel, whereby the detail of staff work was handled by a chief of staff, I myself being free to concentrate on the main problem of defeating my famous opponent.

On 30th August Rommel attacked the Eighth Army – a gambler's last throw to get to Cairo and Alexandria. His objective was the Alam Halfa ridge, the real key to the Alamein position. I was expecting such an attack. I had pondered deeply over Rommel's previous successes in the desert, and had observed that his favourite tactic was to induce the British tanks to attack his armour which he protected by a screen of anti-tank guns; he thus knocked out most of the British armour – having done which he launched his own armour and won the *mêlée*. I decided to play this tactic with him, and did so in the Alam Halfa battle; his forces had a good hammering from my anti-tank guns and tanks in dug-in positions, and he gave up the contest and withdrew. So I won my first battle with Rommel, a defensive one.

I had not been long in the desert, but already one point was very firmly fixed in my mind – desert warfare was not suited for remote control. I decided to give a clear lead and to take a firm grip on the Eighth Army from above; there must be no uncertainty about anything.

After Alam Halfa I continued with my own preparations for a large scale offensive which I was determined would be the beginning of the end for Rommel in Africa. We had a considerable superiority in troops and tanks, and air superiority of three to one. The Germans were desperately short of petrol. Strategical surprise was not possible; I therefore planned for tactical surprise.

By an elaborate cover plan, with dummy installations and diversionary operations, we conveyed the impression that our main attack would be launched in the south. Actually, the essence of the plan was to punch two corridors through the enemy front *in the north*. Engineers would clear the corridors through the mines with detectors, assisted by flail tanks. The infantry divisions were to lead through the corridors, followed by armoured divisions. I then reckoned that Rommel's armoured divisions would have to attack mine in position, and while this conflict was going on my infantry divisions would defeat the enemy infantry by what I described as 'crumbling' operations on their flanks and rear.

So it worked out. But the battle of Alamein, which began on 23rd October 1942, was a stern fight; our offensive met desperate resistance and the counter-attacks of the enemy armour were formidable. Since the German resistance was particularly strong in the north, where our break-in had originally been made, I decided to put in the final break-out thrust a little to the south – on the Italian part of the enemy front. This knock-out blow was launched on 2nd November – 'Operation Supercharge'. A great deal has been written about the battle; indeed, few modern conflicts have received so much attention from British writers. Space will not allow me to discuss it more fully. By 4th November the battle was definitely won, and insofar as the British were concerned it was the turning-point of the war. It had lasted twelve days; we took 30,000 prisoners, including nine generals; our casualties (all kinds) were just over 13,000. The pursuit then began.

Rommel had often before been forced to break off a battle and withdraw, generally for administrative reasons; he had never before at any time during the war in the desert been smashed in battle. That had now been done. The driving of him and his forces out of Africa remained. He was so short of petrol that he would be unable to carry out any major manoeuvre for the time being; but he was a very good general and had several times hit back when it was least expected. I was determined not to have any more set-backs in the desert war, and was not prepared to run undue risks during the long march to Tripoli and then on to Tunis. Moreover, I wanted as few casualties as possible.

Such was the state of confusion in the break-in area after the battle, and the delay caused by rain, that it took some time to develop the pursuit. But when the Eighth Army got going it moved fast, with its eye always on the essential supply points of Tobruk, Benghazi and Tripoli. Tripoli was reached on 23rd January 1943, and once we had opened the port there was no further danger of our losing the advantage for lack of supplies. Meanwhile in November an Anglo-American force under General Eisenhower had landed in French North Africa, and Rommel, in Tunisia, was thus caught between two fires. In February he dealt some stinging blows to the Americans in the region of the Kasserine Pass. But on 30th March the Eighth Army attacked him at the Mareth Line, turning the German right flank and forcing a withdrawal. This was the beginning of the end. On 13th May 1943 the Axis forces in Tunisia laid down their arms.

The clearing of the Mediterranean for Allied shipping was completed by the conquest of Sicily, which was overrun between 10th July and 16th August. The invasion of Italy began on 3rd September. The Italians quickly capitulated, but the German forces in Italy resisted strongly. The progress of the Americans on the west coast and of the British on the Adriatic side became slowed up as the Italian winter set in.

The reader should now know something of the bombing of Germany. The British had begun a strategic bombing offensive against that country in May 1940. The purpose of it was later defined at the Casablanca Conference in January 1943 as being

> the progressive destruction and dislocation of the German military, industrial and economic system and the undermining of the morale of the German people to a point where their capacity for armed resistance is fatally weakened.

Bombing was intended to complement the naval blockade, in striking at the basis of Germany's economic strength. Bombing, even more than concentration camps, made the 1939/45 conflict 'total war'. The first raid took place on the night of 15th May 1940,

Tanks and infantry fought in close cooperation to achieve victory at Alamein

when a British force of ninety-nine bombers attacked oil and railway targets in the Ruhr. The offensive was kept up all through 1940 and 1941, but the results were not what had been hoped. Daytime bombing was out of the question because of German anti-aircraft guns and fighers. So the raids had to be launched at night, but even then the Germans made it very dangerous, with the aid of radar, and accuracy could not be achieved on selected targets. All in all, the bombing had little effect on full production in Germany at that time.

Then in 1942 the bombing offensive was intensified, the Americans now being in the war. In March the first Lancaster bombers came into use – strong and reliable four-engined aircraft. In February, Air Marshal Harris took command of the whole British bombing offensive, and by his energy and drive he improved the system. The training of navigators and bomb-aimers was stepped up; and in August the 'Pathfinder' force was introduced: a force of light, fast, manoeuvrable Mosquito bombers which went ahead of the Lancasters, Stirlings and Halifaxes to mark the target accurately. In 1943 several radar devices were introduced to assist navigation and aiming. Large-scale destruction was caused in the Ruhr, and the breaching of the Möhne and Eder dams in May 1943 by

German cities were reduced to rubble by Allied bombing. The centre of Stuttgart

Gibson's 617 Squadron was a spectacular feat. Nine thousand tons of bombs were dropped in four major attacks on Hamburg, and then attention was switched to Berlin. The British raids by night were complemented by American raids in daylight. The Americans, insisting on daylight raiding, had lost a great many of their Fortresses and Liberators during 1942 and 1943; but the development of the P51 Mustang, a very long-range fighter, altered that situation.

By 1944 the Allies had gained command of the air over Germany. But even in 1943 and 1944 the achievement of the bombing offensive fell very far short of the paralysis of the enemy which had been hoped for. However it did at any rate cause the Germans to concentrate on the production of fighter aircraft, and to give up almost all bombing themselves.

We will now turn to the war at sea. On 17th August 1940 Hitler declared a total blockade of Britain. The war against the Germans at sea was of crucial importance, since Britain was not able to supply herself adequately with food or arms except by imports. Hitler had, however, neglected to build up sufficient seapower before he began to implement his intentions. In 1940 German naval strength was not enough to maintain an effective blockade, and the Germans had no hope of dominating the Channel by seapower for the projected invasion of Britain. The German strategy at sea was threefold: submarines went out in packs, surface vessels in sorties, and bombers attacked shipping within reasonable range of land. The British navy was employed in defending convoys and seeking out the German surface raiders; but it was handicapped by the fact that many of its ships were out of date, and by a shortage of submarines and aircraft.

From the start the struggle on the surface of the seas was evenly matched. In January 1941 Admiral Lütjens left Kiel with *Scharnhorst* and *Gneisenau* for a two month cruise during which he sank or took twenty-two ships (115,600 tons). Similar destructive forays were successfully made by the pocket-battleship *Scheer* and the heavy cruiser *Hipper*. But the British also struck. In December 1939 the German pocket-battleship *Graf Spee*, which had sunk nine British ships, was brought to battle outside the River Plate by three cruisers under Commodore Harwood and so damaged that she was scuttled by her captain. Admiral Cunningham overwhelmed the Italian fleet in the Mediterranean. Later *Bismarck* and *Scharnhorst* were sunk – to mention two notable incidents. German commerce was very hard hit from the beginning.

The operations of the German U-boats were extremely effective, and serious for Britain. In 1942 the Allies lost 1,664 ships (7,790,697 tons), of which 1,160 were sunk by U-boats. For a while in 1942 Britain ran perilously short of oil. Most of the submarine operations took place on the trans-Atlantic routes, but there were other vital areas: the Indian Ocean, the convoy route to Malta, and the route to Archangel – a terrible sea route for the sailors; few survived from ships that were sunk in those icy waters.

The whole war at sea began to move in favour of the Allies in the autumn of 1942. The key factor in this development was air power. The direct use of aircraft in sea warfare, particularly against submarines, was highly effective. Coastal Command had hitherto been kept short of aircraft, priority being given to the bombing offensive against Germany. But that bombing had not been particularly fruitful, and even when it was concentrated on the U-boat yards and bases between January and May 1943 it did little good. But from the autumn of 1942 Coastal Command had more aircraft at its disposal, capable of patrolling 800 miles out to sea; aircraft were also used from convoy escort carriers. Further factors in the Allied recovery were short-wave radar to detect nearby submarines and heavier depth charges. In late 1942 the Arctic convoy PQ.18 lost 13 out of 43 ships, but the convoy fought its way through; 41 German aircraft based on Norway were shot down and the escort carrier *Avenger* played a decisive part in that effort. The struggle remained desperate throughout the winter, and Admiral Doenitz kept 100 U-boats on patrol. Some 108 Allied ships were lost in March 1943. But then the new system began to yield results. In May, convoy SC.130 from Canada, supported by Liberators from Iceland, got through unscathed in a battle which cost the enemy 5 U-boats. During that month Allied losses in merchant shipping fell greatly, while the Germans lost 41 U-boats.

The U-boats however did not give up their operations and no reliable way of destroying them was ever discovered; but at least patrolling aircraft forced them to stay submerged, thus reducing their mobility and preventing them from getting at convoys. Germany's grip on Britain's lifeline now progressively weakened, and although there was often fierce fighting at sea the strategic danger was practically removed. Altogether by the end of the war the Germans lost 785 out of 1,162 U-boats. The U-boats had sunk 2,828 Allied ships (14,687,230 tons), most of which were British, and Britain lost about 82,000 men at sea.

Air power gained the final mastery for Britain over Germany's surface fleet as well. On 19th November 1944 thirty-two Lancasters bombed and wrecked the battleship *Tirpitz*. German maritime trade had ceased to exist, while Britain's survived.

By the beginning of 1944 success in the Mediterranean, in the Atlantic and on the eastern front was clearly in sight. Some twenty-three German divisions were being contained in Italy – though Kesselring's able generalship, for example at Anzio and Cassino, prevented the Allies from progressing before mid-1944 as well as had been hoped. Tito's partisans in Yugoslavia were diverting other German troops. In the east the Russians began the year by bursting out from the salient west of Kiev, and in the south by May 1944 they had passed the upper Prut. The next task of the Allied strategists was clearly the recovery of France, followed by the invasion of Germany itself from the west. The Americans indeed had urged this in preference to the conquest of Italy in 1943. The Russians were pressing for the opening of a second major front in Europe in order to take some of the German pressure off them.

Stalin, unlike some other statesmen of the Alliance, seeing that victory was certain, had a far-sighted political strategy. He was determined to confine the operations of the British and Americans to western Europe, so that he could conquer eastern Europe for communism. At a conference between Stalin, Roosevelt and Churchill, held at Teheran in November 1943, Stalin agreed with the Americans that divisions from the Italian front should be used to land in southern France and develop an offensive up the Rhône valley and thence towards the Vosges and the upper reaches of the Rhine. Churchill disagreed with this strategy, and I consider rightly; it removed ten divisions from Italy and thus made it impossible for an offensive from that country to be developed northwards through the Ljubljana Gap towards Vienna. The war in Italy then became senseless; as Fuller wrote, it became 'a campaign with inadequate means, with no strategic goal and with no political bottom'. The invasion of southern France was, of course, exactly right for Stalin: it would keep the British and Americans well away from the Balkans and eastern Europe. I argued fiercely against it with Eisenhower when we were preparing the invasion of Normandy, but to no avail – the Americans were set on it. In my view it was one of the great strategic mistakes of the war, and I said so to the Americans in no uncertain voice. What it made clear to me was that Russia was now fighting not only to defeat Germany, but also to win the peace from her allies. It was impossible to make the American leaders understand this.

It was further agreed at the Teheran conference that the main task of the British and Americans in 1944 should be the invasion of north-west Europe, and these two powers then planned to concentrate for that offensive. The experience of the raid on Dieppe in August 1942 by Canadian troops not adequately supported from air and sea had taught the Allies the absolute necessity of making an opposed landing on a hostile coast – one of the most difficult operations in all warfare – a fully combined operation by all three services. The supreme commander was an American general, Eisenhower; his deputy was a British airman, Tedder. The air forces were commanded by Leigh-Mallory, and the naval forces by Ramsay – both British. I had been appointed by the British government to command the British armies to take part in the invasion – the 21st Army Group. But Eisenhower, under whom I had served in the Mediterranean theatre, ordered me to take operational direction of the American armies as well, so as to have all the land forces under one commander for the landing and subsequent break-out from the lodgment area. In fact, he made me his land force commander for the invasion of north-west Europe – the operation being given the name 'Overlord'.

The area selected for the landing of the Allied forces was that part of Normandy in the Bay of the Seine between Cabourg and Valognes. This plan was disguised from the Germans by full scale dummy preparations for an invasion of the Pas de Calais area. At my request, during some months before D-day railways, bridges, and other means of communication were intensely bombed; the object was, first, to dislocate the German supply organization, and secondly to isolate the battle area and make it difficult for divisions from other parts of France to intervene quickly in the bridgehead battle – and this second object was maintained once we were ashore in Normandy, so much so that the first arrivals of reinforcing German divisions generally appeared on bicycles!

The Germans, having lost hope of winning on the eastern front, put a great deal of

The battle of Normandy

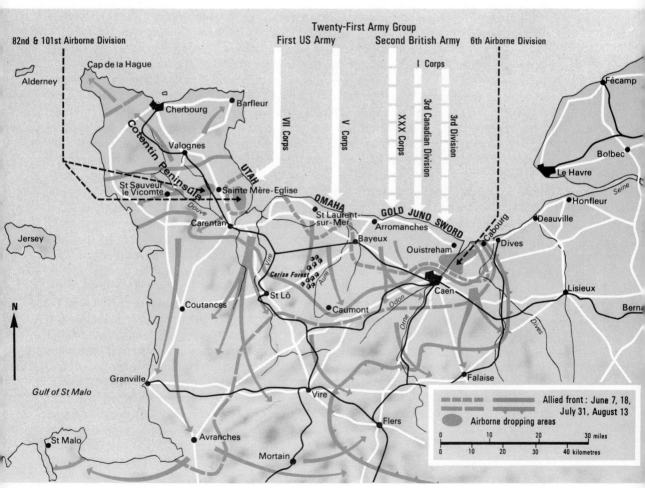

what they had into the west. Field-Marshal von Rundstedt, C-in-C West, had under his command 60 divisions, 11 of them armoured, organized in two army groups. These were stretched from Holland via Antwerp, Normandy, and the Biscay coast to the Mediterranean; and a proportion of them were poorly equipped. My opponent of the desert days, Rommel, commanded Army Group B, in the area from Holland to Normandy. The Germans were very weak in air power, having only 90 bombers and 70 fighters fit for action. They were also, ironically, somewhat as the French in 1939 – strung out along a line of defences uncertain when or where to expect the enemy to strike. Furthermore there was disagreement between Rundstedt and Rommel as to the tactics of opposing the invasion. Rundstedt favoured holding the forces slightly inland, and then counter-attacking before the Allies could consolidate a beach-head; Rommel wanted to position his forces well forward to prevent any landing on the beaches – although he did not know where the attempt might be made. Hitler agreed with Rommel, and a compromise was adopted, with most of the infantry well forward and most of the armour back. Hitler had frequently intervened to bad effect in the conduct of the war in the east; he was to do the same in France.

The forces I proposed to use for the first wave of the landing were 5 seaborne divisions and 3 airborne (150,000 men in all), and I planned to have 18 divisions on shore in Normandy by the end of the first week or so. We also had 5,300 ships and craft, 12,000 planes and 1,500 tanks. For the actual invasion we had the advantages of surprise and concentration of effort; the Allied armies were a balanced force of all arms; finally we had complete air superiority, thus ensuring that the enemy concentration and subsequent movements would be greatly hindered. A number of the tanks, called 'funnies', had been specially converted for invasion purposes: amphibious tanks, flail tanks for exploding land mines, mat-laying tanks for crossing soft patches on beaches, and several other varieties. Old ships were to be sunk to make breakwaters; there were two artificial harbours (code-named 'Mulberries') built of concrete caissons; and a cross-Channel pipe-line, called 'Pluto', was ready to supply petrol to the shore of Normandy. Preparations for invasion had begun in 1943, and the expedition was very well equipped.

D-day was 6th June 1944. The landing in Normandy was a truly combined operation. The Americans were on the right and the British and Canadians on the left. In the early hours of 6th June three airborne divisions were dropped to secure the flanks of the lodgment area, engaging the Germans to prevent them attacking the seaborne troops as they were landing on the beaches. Gliders brought in anti-tank equipment. The airborne landings were more scattered than had been intended, but this in fact helped to confuse the enemy, and they succeeded in their tactical function. The landings on the beaches were preceded by bombardment from ships, and by intensive air bombing on radar stations, airfields, gun positions and beach defences generally. The hardest resistance was met by the Americans on Omaha beach; the exits from the beach were steep, and the Americans had declined to accept any of the British 'funnies' or specialized armour, which I had offered. Also, they made the mistake of transferring to their landing-craft too far off shore, and the troops were exposed to rough seas and gunfire for a considerable time. Nevertheless, fighting with great gallantry and *élan*, the Americans gained their bridge-head. The British landings were very well supported by the Royal Navy, with accurate navigation and bombardment; the run-in in the landing-craft was quite short; and the specialized tanks proved their worth.

Battleships in action. A detail of the painting of H.M. ships *King George V* and *Duke of York* bombarding the coast by Richard Eurich. *Overleaf* Rocket-firing Typhoons at the Falaise Pocket by Frank Wootton

The Allies were assisted by a certain dislocation in the German command – Rommel and two other commanders were absent; certain armoured units were not to be used without Hitler's personal order; and, it has been said, the Führer was in bed at Berchtesgaden and it was not permitted to awaken him. Rundstedt wondered for some time whether the landings might not be just a feint for a real invasion farther north, so the German counter-attacks got off to a slow start and, thanks largely to Allied air action, were badly co-ordinated. The Allies secured bridge-heads at all landing points on 6th June, with 9,000 casualties. The counter-attacks built up during the next week, but they were fought off, and by 11th June the beach-heads had all been linked and some elbow-room gained. By 12th June, 326,547 men had been landed, with 54,186 vehicles and 104,428 tons of stores. More delay was caused to the Allied landing programme by bad weather than by the Germans.

My plan, after establishing a firm lodgment area, was so to conduct the land battle that the British would draw the main German strength, and particularly the enemy armoured divisions, on to our left flank in the Caen area, to fight it and keep it there, so that the Americans might the more easily gain territory on our right or western flank – and then to make the ultimate break-out on that flank. So, more or less, the battle developed. With total air superiority our attacks on the ground were more effective than ever before, and the army and air co-operation became highly developed. General Arnold describes the advance of American troops towards St Lô:

> Fighters and fighter-bombers in closest communication and under common direction ranged ahead of them destroying military targets . . . Fighters in direct communication with tanks by radio flew constant alert over our armored columns. Ground officers called on the fighters to bomb or strafe artillery or armor in their path. Pilots warned tank commanders of traps.

In spite of the magnificent part played in battle by aircraft, artillery and tanks, to my mind in modern war it is the infantry soldier who in the end plays the decisive part in the land battle. I do not say this just because I happen to be an infantry soldier myself; I believe it to be true. The infantry is the most versatile of all the arms; it can operate in any weather, in any type of ground (mountains, forests, jungle, swamps, desert). The infantry soldier remains in the battle day and night, with little rest and without adequate sleep. He can use very expressive language about the way he has to bear the main burden in battle, but he does it! I salute him. You cannot have a good army without good infantry. I would add that land forces cannot win battles without the assistance of a good air force – and this is particularly true in warfare against the well-armed guerrillas or irregular forces of the mid-twentieth century.

The German soldiers, with no air support, fought hard against the Allies in Normandy. The disorganization in the German High Command added to their disadvantages, and the crisis came (on 20th July) when a number of generals made an unsuccessful attempt to assassinate Hitler. In my view they were wrong; it is not the job of generals to 'bump off' political leaders; if it ought to be done it is best done by the politicians themselves! Rommel knew about it, but refused to have anything to do with it – rightly I think. Hitler replaced Rundstedt by Kluge as commander in France, and later Kluge by Model; Rommel's car was strafed by fighters on 15th July and he was so badly wounded that his part in the battle in Normandy was ended. Hitler then intervened, and, being ignorant

American troops landing on Iwo Jima, as seen from the Japanese defences. A painting by Takaeo Terada

of the fact that the Germans had lost the battle in Normandy, or maybe not wanting to believe it, he ordered on 7th August an armoured thrust from Mortain westwards to the coast at Avranches in the hope of cutting the American armies in two. Such a thrust could achieve nothing; without air support it was madness; and in any case the battle was already lost. The only imaginable hope for the Germans was to withdraw quickly over the Seine and try to form a new front behind that obstacle. But Hitler refused to allow any withdrawal, and even if he had, in fact by 7th August it was too late. In the event, the armoured thrust to Mortain was penned into a pocket, known as the 'Falaise Pocket', by the American, British and Canadian armies, and was there pounded for several days. I visited the pocket when all was over; the carnage was terrible.

Allied bridge-heads over the Seine were soon established. On 19th August Paris rose in revolt, and six days later the capital was liberated by French forces. Normandy and Brittany had been conquered, and the Germans had lost half a million men. I issued orders for further operations designed to push home the advantage we had gained, and to end the German war by Christmas. But on 1st September Eisenhower assumed direct command of the land armies himself, in addition to his responsibilities as supreme commander of all the Allied forces in western Europe; he had different ideas, and fresh orders were issued.

The precise details of German losses in Normandy were not known. But General Bradley considered that

> by the first of September the enemy's June strength on the western front had been cut down to a disorganized corporal's guard. The total of all German remnants north of the Ardennes equalled only 11 divisions.

Clearly the Germans had been severely beaten, and the task of the supreme commander of the Allied forces then was to drive the enemy back into Germany and end the war as quickly as possible. The right military action could yet have averted some of the political implications of the Teheran agreement – had these been understood by the American command. I therefore urged that the Allied forces should be concentrated for a thrust in overwhelming strength, first to seize the Ruhr and then to move on Berlin: the political heart of Germany. German military opinion, according to Liddell Hart, admitted after the war that 'such a break-through, coupled with air domination, would have torn in pieces the weak German front and ended the war in the winter of 1944'. But the Americans considered such a policy to be militarily risky and politically unnecessary. Roosevelt was not alarmed at the idea of Russian forces overrunning eastern Europe. The Americans now provided far more strength than the British, and they had to have their way. The American method was to form up on the Rhine from Switzerland to the North Sea, and then to decide what should be done. All the armies were to advance simultaneously, on a broad front. I pointed out the three main disadvantages of a 'broad front' strategy:

1. Our administration was becoming very stretched, and could not support an advance of all the armies.
2. Nowhere would we be strong enough to get decisive results quickly, and this was necessary if we were to finish the war by the end of the year.
3. The advance would gradually peter out and the Germans would be given time to recover.

American troops go ashore on the Normandy beaches for the invasion of Europe

To get decisive results quickly we must concentrate somewhere – left, centre, or right, whichever the supreme commander considered most suitable. It was as simple as that, and the British chiefs of staff supported my view. But the American generals did not agree. The Germans recovered.

In mid-September, the Germans, having been given breathing space to recover, delivered a repulse to airborne forces at Arnhem who were fighting for a bridge-head over the Neder Rhine, having already gained valuable bridges over the Meuse, and over the Rhine at Nijmegen. Later, in December they gathered enough armour for a strong offensive, thrusting through the Ardennes towards Antwerp. This started successfully, but broke down under attacks on the flanks and from the air. The German 'secret weapons' for the second half of 1944, the jet-propelled V1 and V2 'flying bombs' or missiles, caused some terror but insignificant damage in Britain. After the Ardennes battle the Germans gave no serious resistance. The Rhine was crossed at various points in March 1945, and the Allied armies advanced as far as the Elbe.

Meanwhile on the eastern front the Russians wasted no time. At about the time of the
Allied break-out in Normandy they had launched a massive offensive from Vitebsk to
the Pripet Marshes, and by early August 1944 the Red Army had reached Memel and
Warsaw. The German S.S. had time to wreak savage punishment on a Polish rising in
Warsaw. Then the Russians pressed on to shatter German Army Group North and
reach the Baltic. From the point of view of defeating the Germans they might then have
continued their offensive into Germany in 1944 – but that could come later: Stalin's

The defeat of Germany, 1944–5

Legend:
- Allied fronts—June 1944
- Western Allied advance by the end of 1944
- Russian advance by the end of 1944
- Western Allied advance by 5 May 1945
- Russian advance by 5 May 1945
- Areas occupied by Germans at surrender

0   100   200   300 miles
0   200   400 kilometres

first concern was to overrun the countries of south-eastern Europe. The Russians were in Rumania in August, Yugoslavia in October, and Hungary in December. Only in January 1945 did the armies of Koniev, Zhukov, Rokossovsky and Cherniakovsky sweep into Germany. On 4th February Stalin, Roosevelt and Churchill met again, at Yalta in the Crimea.

The leaders of the democratic nations behaved to the communist dictator at Yalta much as their despised predecessors had to the Nazi dictator at Munich. They persuaded themselves that Stalin was a gentleman, and agreed to the partition of Germany. But by that time there was nothing else they could do. Stalin had outwitted his allies; he had won the peace for Russia at Teheran; Yalta merely crowned his victory.

Events now moved rapidly. On 30th April Hitler committed suicide in Berlin. On 4th May a delegation from Admiral Doenitz, the new German leader, arrived at my headquarters on Lüneburg Heath and signed a declaration of unconditional surrender of all German armed forces from Holland to Denmark – a total of nearly two million fighting men. On 7th May Germany's unconditional surrender of all her armed forces on all fronts was signed at Eisenhower's headquarters in Rheims. The German war thus ended, with the Russians in possession of the great political centres of mid-Europe – Berlin, Prague, Vienna, Belgrade – and all capital cities east of that general line. The Japanese war remained, and we will now look at that.

Japan was a more natural enemy to the United States than was Germany. After her mushroom growth to economic maturity Japan had become ambitious, and planned to weld the area of eastern Asia and the Pacific into one sphere under her economic and political domination. In March 1933 she formally announced her withdrawal from the League of Nations, thereafter invading Manchuria and making substantial progress towards her goal. Taking advantage of the fall of France, the Japanese had called up over a million conscripts and in July 1941 announced a protectorate over Indo-China. General Tojo, who had been war minister, became premier of Japan in October 1941, and the country came under the grip of a military autocracy. The progress of Japanese ambitions and particularly the aggressive declarations of the new regime alarmed America, with her established interests in the Pacific. When in 1941 the American government applied oil sanctions to Japan, and warned that nation to cease aggression, war became inevitable. Japan resolved to strike when the moment was favourable.

Late 1941 was, all in all, an opportune time for Japan to make war against the imperial powers of the Far East. Her leaders certainly made a miscalculation in supposing that the Germans had as good as won the war in the west, but nonetheless at that time the Dutch were powerless, and the British had no strength they could afford to spare. The best troops of the British imperial possessions, Australia, New Zealand and India, were engaged in the Middle East. The British navy was strained to its utmost, and the R.A.F. in Asia was equipped with obsolete aircraft. America had greater armed force than Japan, but the Americans at this time were looking westwards and had transferred ships from the Pacific to the Atlantic.

Between 1936 and 1941 Japan had doubled the tonnage of her navy, and modernized her older ships. She had 10 battleships, 10 aircraft-carriers, 38 cruisers, 112 destroyers and 65 submarines. Japanese warships were not basically different in design from those of the western powers (though their torpedoes were more reliable than those of the

Americans). Their aircraft-carriers could each carry some 63 fighters, torpedo-bombers and bombers. The number of divisions in the Japanese army in 1941 was 51. The strength of a division varied from 10,000 to 18,000 men: the army totalling about 750,000 men. There was no independent Japanese air force, but the navy and army each had its own air arm. Five air divisions, comprising some 1,500 aircraft, were attached to the army, and the navy had an operational strength of about 3,300 aircraft. Since the invasion of China the Japanese had gained valuable experience in modern warfare, and their equipment was highly developed. The Japanese people fought with an intense ferocity and a fanatical courage alien to the peoples of the West.

The Japanese plan was to strike fast and hard. The American fleet in the Pacific was to be destroyed, and the Philippines, Borneo, Malaya, the Dutch East Indies and Burma overrun. Beyond the southward advance an impregnable ring of ocean fortresses was to be established, running through Wake, the Marshall Islands and the Archipelago north of Australia. On 7th December 1941, without a declaration of war, simultaneous attacks were launched on Pearl Harbour, the Philippines and Malaya.

Although the Americans knew that the Japanese were hostile to them they were, in fact, taken completely by surprise by the attack on their Pacific Fleet in Pearl Harbour, Hawaii. The Japanese naval striking force of six carriers, with a total of 450 planes, under Vice-Admiral Nagumo, approached Hawaii from the north-west and launched its aircraft at daylight on 7th December. Of the 94 American ships, the main Japanese targets were 7 battleships at their moorings. All were hit; only one escaped serious damage and 2 were lost completely. Very heavy damage was also inflicted on other ships and on installations, and 200 of a total of 400 American aircraft parked close together were destroyed. The Japanese lost 30 aircraft. The success of the raid was due to complete surprise and to the skill of the Japanese air arm, particularly in shallow-run torpedo attacks.

Simultaneously with Pearl Harbour the Japanese launched air attacks against the Americans in the Philippines, destroying a third of their fighters and half their bombers, and on 10th December the naval base of Cavite was smashed. By these quick, devastating air blows at Pearl Harbour and the Philippines the Japanese gained that period of complete superiority at sea and in the air which they needed to give security to their invasion operations. They confirmed the advantage in December by overrunning the enemy bases of Guam, Wake and Hong Kong. The Philippines were not finally overrun until the following May – because of the resistance organized by General MacArthur, who finally left in March 1942 for Australia in order to take command of the American offensive against Japan to be launched from that country.

The invasion of the Malay Peninsula, under General Yamashita, also began on 7th December, with Japanese forces landing in Siam and crossing the frontier. On 10th December shore-based Japanese aircraft sank the British battleship *Prince of Wales* and the battle-cruiser *Repulse* off Kuantan on the east coast of Malaya. Using captured British shipping the Japanese advanced down the coast by means of combined operations against the flanks of the defence. Their numerical superiority was not great, but the Japanese troops were more enterprising and more highly trained in jungle fighting than the defending British, Australian and Indian troops. British air power was quickly written off and then unopposed bombing of towns destroyed the will to resist. On 11th January 1942 the Japanese were in Kuala Lumpur; their advance continued rapidly,

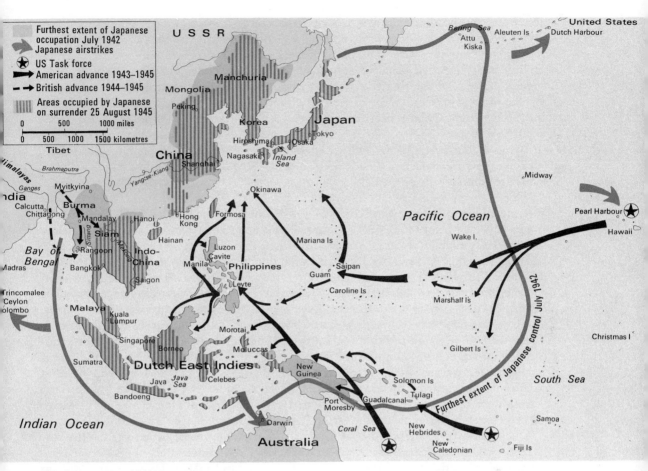

The Japanese war, 1941–5

and at the end of the month the defenders retired to the island of Singapore, cutting the causeway. They were now without sea or air power, and had weak artillery. After only four days of bombardment the Japanese landed on the island, and in less than a week they were in possession of the reservoirs which supplied the city. Britain's foremost commercial and naval centre in the Far East surrendered to Lieutenant-General Yamashita on Sunday, 15th February 1942 – together with its garrison of over 70,000 troops.

This was a humiliating defeat for British arms. There is no doubt that much ought to have been done in training and other matters; but nobody had seen that it was done. My view has always been that Singapore was lost in London, in Whitehall, before the war ever began, because of the lack of true inter-service cooperation in planning the defence of a major strategic base – in fact, because of bad peace-time planning.

The Dutch East Indies now lay exposed. Since January the Japanese had gained footings in Borneo and Celebes, and they were now ready to strike at Java, the strongest of the islands. On 27th February 1942 the Dutch Allied commander, Rear-Admiral Doorman, learned that a Japanese convoy of 30 transports escorted by 3 cruisers and 7

destroyers was heading for Java. Doorman mustered a force of 5 cruisers and 10 destroyers and engaged the Japanese under Vice-Admiral Kondo off the north coast of Java.
A long and complex battle took place, largely in darkness; it ended with the Japanese
sinking half the Allied ships without losing any of their own. In gunpower the Allies
were superior, but the battle was won by superior Japanese tactics, communications,
torpedoes and air power. This battle of the Java Sea decided the fate of the Dutch East
Indies. During the night after the battle the Japanese landed at three positions on the
north Java coast. On 8th March some 90,000 European and Indonesian troops surrendered at Bandoeng. The remaining islands were quickly conquered, and isolated
pockets of guerrilla resistance made no strategic difference. All remaining Allied shipping
in the area was sunk.

We now move to Burma. Simultaneously with their campaign against the Dutch East
Indies and even before the fall of Singapore, the Japanese had turned westwards against
Burma. They aimed ultimately to cut the Burma Road, the route by which assistance was
reaching Chiang Kai-shek in China, and with the help of Indian nationalism to remove
the hold of the British on India. Bangkok provided the advanced base for the invasion,
and their first objective was Rangoon. The defence of Burma was weak, since Wavell, in
command, had only two incomplete divisions – later reinforced by a similar Chinese
force, commanded by Lieutenant-General Stilwell, chief of staff to Chiang Kai-Shek.
There were not enough resources in Burma to nourish a campaign and supplies had to
come from India – but communications were extremely difficult. The Japanese controlled the normal sea routes from India and there were no roads across the mountains;
communication and supply had therefore to be by air. The communication routes inside
Burma were the valleys of the Chindwin, Irrawaddy and Sittang rivers, and a single
railway track which ran northwards from Rangoon through Meiktila and Mandalay.

The Japanese, commanded by Lieutenant-General Kawabe, opened the attack on
Burma by bombing Rangoon in January 1942, and this had the effect of greatly lowering
the will of the population to resist – as had happened in Malaya. Then, moving in from
Malaya and Siam they quickly reached the Gulf of Martaban. By mid-February they
had advanced to the Sittang valley, and on 7th March Rangoon was abandoned. The
new British commander, Alexander, decided he must get his troops back to India
before the monsoon broke and establish a defensive front on the Assam frontier.

In the retreat the British and Indian troops suffered severely; against this, the Japanese
never seemed to tire. They brought into action three divisions and three armoured
brigades with light tanks. There had never before been war between modern armies in
that type of country; but the Japanese had trained in similar country in Hainan and
Formosa, and had become really first-class fighters. They fought in small, lightly equipped detachments, armed principally with light machine-guns and mortars. They made
skilful and daring manoeuvres to infiltrate, envelop, and cut communications – fighting
their way up the parallel valleys of the Irrawaddy and Sittang and continually outflanking
resistance.

As the British withdrew, the weight of the Japanese attack was transferred to the
Chinese front in the north-east, where resistance soon petered out. They then pushed
rapidly towards the Burma Road at Lashio, reached it at the end of April, and operated
up that axis – crossing the Chinese frontier on 15th May. The British, accompanied and

hampered by many thousand native refugees, struggled through jungle and over mountains to reach Imphal just inside the Indian frontier. By the end of May 1942 Alexander had succeeded in extricating most of his men, but much equipment was lost.

By mid-1942 the Japanese, travelling as fast and fighting as efficiently and ruthlessly as any of the Mongol hordes of history, had gained all their immediate objectives, not only in Burma but also in Indonesia and in the Pacific. After conquering Burma they did not penetrate into India, but established themselves in strong defensible country. From the Dutch East Indies they extended their conquests east to New Guinea and to the Gilbert and Solomon Islands. In April a Japanese squadron under Nagumo had entered the Indian Ocean, and was able to roam at will; the British bases of Colombo and Trincomalee were damaged and two cruisers and an aircraft carrier sunk. Nagumo then turned north and inflicted immense damage to merchant shipping off Madras and in the Bay of Bengal. Without seapower the Allies could not begin to assail the ring of Japanese positions.

The war at sea in the Pacific is a story of tremendous interest. The problem for the Japanese now lay in the air and naval power of her enemies. The raid on Pearl Harbour in December 1941 had crippled the Americans in the Pacific, but only temporarily; it did not prove, in fact, to be the decisive success for Japan which she had hoped. The Americans had lost their battleships – but with the advent of the aircraft-carrier the era of the large battleship was really over. The American Pacific Fleet had four carriers, capable of operating between them 350 aircraft. This was what mattered. The damage to installations at Pearl Harbour was repaired and, with ten times the industrial capacity of Japan, America was able to build up her relative strength rapidly. The Americans reckoned they could be ready to launch a counter-offensive by 1943. The Japanese saw the weakness in their situation and realized they must destroy the enemy naval strength in the Pacific during 1942. Admiral Yamamoto, head of the Japanese navy, considered that Pearl Harbour was too distant for the Japanese to be able to strike there immediately in sufficient strength; he therefore evolved a double plan to bring the American carrier fleet within striking range. First, he planned to gain command of the Coral Sea and mount a threat to Australia – which would entice the Americans to the rescue. Secondly, he would capture Midway, a small atoll half way between California and China, and 1,100 miles north-west of the Hawaiian Islands.

The advance of the Japanese into the Coral Sea began in late April 1942. They aimed to seize two points. One, Tulagi in the southern Solomons, was captured as planned on 3rd May. A second naval group moved on Port Moresby on the south coast of New Guinea. But Japanese security measures were poor, and Admiral Nimitz, in command at Pearl Harbour, learned what was afoot. The carriers *Lexington* and *Yorktown*, commanded by Admiral Fletcher, had been positioned near Samoa to prevent the enemy capture of Port Moresby.

On 7th May the Japanese covering force, the light carrier *Shoho* and a screen of light cruisers, was located by Fletcher. A swarm of 193 bombers from *Lexington* and *Yorktown* attacked *Shoho* and sank her in half an hour. The main striking force under Admiral Takagi still continued steaming westwards through the Coral Sea. On the next day, when the opposing forces were 200 miles apart, their scouts sighted each other. American bombers attacked the Japanese carriers, and *Shokaku* was left blazing and *Zuikaku* damaged. Japanese torpedo-bombers scored six hits on *Lexington*, which blew up during the night.

Strategically the battle of the Coral Sea was an American victory, since it thwarted the Japanese plans both against Australia and against the American Pacific Fleet. Tactically the battle is of great interest, marking a revolution in naval warfare. Both sides had a considerable force of conventional warships, but these were not engaged. The battle was fought out between aircraft-carriers, and the fleets never even sighted each other. Aircraft-carriers were not battleships but *mobile bases of air power*, and their strength was offensive – carrying torpedo-planes, dive-bombers and fighters.

At this stage, the Japanese aircraft were rather more powerful than the American. But later the Americans introduced the Avenger torpedo-plane and the Hellcat fighter with greatly improved performances; furthermore, American carriers carried more aircraft than the Japanese. An aircraft-carrier itself was not thickly armoured and constituted a huge target of oil and explosives. It relied for defence on its fighters, and on the firepower of a protective screen of light warships. Aircraft-carriers proved, in fact, to be extremely vulnerable to attack from the air.

The setback in the Coral Sea did not cause the Japanese to put off the second part of their programme, the attack on Midway. In May, Admiral Yamamoto assembled almost the entire Japanese navy, some ninety ships, in the Inland Sea and the Mariana Islands. But the Americans had broken the Japanese code (Japanese security and reconnaissance were often bad) and by mid-May Nimitz knew that an attack on Midway from the north-west was due in early June. Midway was reinforced, and the Americans

Naval warfare in the Pacific. Japanese aircraft attack the U.S. fleet

formed two task forces – the first under Admiral Fletcher in the carrier *Yorktown*, and the second commanded by Admiral Spruance with the carriers *Enterprise* and *Hornet*. There were no battleships; the nuclei of aircraft-carriers were screened by cruisers and destroyers. In late May the two task forces left Pearl Harbour for a point in the Pacific 300 miles north-east of Midway, where they were to cruise in ambush. The Japanese approached in two groups, the main striking force of four carriers – *Akagi*, *Kaga*, *Hiryu*, and *Soryu* – under Nagumo moving some 100 miles ahead. By dawn on 4th June Nagumo was at his launching point 240 miles from Midway. The American carrier fleet was approaching from 100 miles to the east. The Americans had an enormous advantage: the Japanese did not have radar and they did not know that the American fleet was at sea. But Yamamoto counted on complete surprise.

At 4.30 o'clock in the morning on 4th June the four Japanese carriers sent off 100 bombers and fighters. Two hours later Midway was flaming and smoking – though the bomber force suffered heavy losses. Petrol tanks, installations and aircraft were destroyed, but little damage was done to guns and runways and Nagumo decided that a second strike was needed. To shorten the journey of the returning aircraft the carriers steamed southwards. During the interval the torpedoes in other aircraft were replaced by bombs for the second attack.

At 6 o'clock Admiral Spruance had launched a strike of 100 bombers and fighters, and these headed to intercept the Japanese carriers on their south-easterly course. But Nagumo learned of their approach and altered course, warning his returning aircraft of the new pick-up position, and the bombers were safely taken on board. The Japanese fighters were then launched in time to meet the first squadron of 29 American torpedo-bombers which had no fighter cover, and when they attacked at 9.30 o'clock 25 of the 29 were shot down by fighters or from the ships, and none of their torpedoes went home. When the second wave of 12 bombers arrived they met the same fate. Of the first 41 American aircraft to locate the enemy, 35 were lost.

The initial sacrifice was, however, of great value, because following the torpedo-planes came 50 American dive-bombers, and while manoeuvring to avoid torpedoes, the Japanese carriers were unable to launch more aircraft. *Akagi*, *Kaga* and *Soryu* were in formation together, all with aircraft on their decks. The dive-bombers attacked them with devastating effect. Within a few minutes the three carriers were flaming furnaces, with their own torpedoes and bombs exploding in the hangar decks.

The fourth Japanese carrier, *Hiryu*, was some miles ahead, and had time to launch her dive-bombers in retaliation against the Americans. At about midday *Yorktown* was attacked. Six Japanese planes got through her screen of fighters, and she was hit by three bombs which set her on fire and damaged her boilers. The fire was brought under control, and after about an hour *Yorktown* was under way again. But a second attack of 32 torpedo-bombers from *Hiryu* was made, coming in low. *Yorktown* put up a splash barrage by firing her guns into the water, but five aircraft broke through and she was struck by three torpedoes. Badly damaged, *Yorktown* had to be abandoned, and two days later she was sunk by a Japanese submarine.

Meanwhile *Hiryu* had been located, and *Hornet* had launched her dive-bombers. By 5 o'clock the last of Admiral Nagumo's carriers was ablaze. Eventually all four sank. It was only late in the afternoon that Admiral Yamamoto in his flagship 100 miles astern gathered any clear reports of the battle. Fearing a carrier attack next on his own fleet he immediately started to withdraw westward. Spruance, with *Enterprise* and *Hornet*, pursued him, but no contact was made on 5th June. On 6th June American bombers sank the heavy cruiser *Mikuma*. This was the last episode of the Battle of Midway. Yamamoto continued steaming for safety, and as the American carriers were running short of fuel Spruance gave up the pursuit.

Strategically Midway in June 1942 was an immensely important battle. Had the American carrier fleet been destroyed the United States would have had no chance of defeating the Japanese in the Pacific for a considerable time. In the following years of the war seapower in terms of carriers was to be vital. The conquest of the island-studded western Pacific was impossible without air cover. The Japanese, having lost four carriers, were from now on at a serious disadvantage. They built only one more reliable carrier before the end of the war; otherwise they had to use converted battleships which were no proper substitute.

The Americans were now in a position to take the offensive. Their long campaign began with the struggle for Guadalcanal, lasting from August 1942 to January 1943. Guadalcanal, an island in the Solomon group on which the Japanese were building an airstrip, was an important strategic point. On 7th August an American fleet entered the area, and nearly 20,000 marines were successfully landed. But two days later a Japanese naval squadron came on the scene, and in a night action four American cruisers were sunk – half the American force. The ensuing struggle for Guadalcanal was very fierce. Besides numerous small actions and constant air attacks by both sides, six more naval battles were fought. The first three of these enabled the Japanese to bring in heavy reinforcements. On Guadalcanal itself there was much hard fighting, on roughly equal terms and with equal casualties. Then the American fleet got the better of the Japanese, and the last naval action was a covering operation by the Japanese for the evacuation of Guadalcanal. This American success finally stopped the southern advance of the Japanese, and provided a launching pad for the American counter-offensive. Its unofficial title of 'Operation Shoestring' indicates the narrowness of the margin.

By early 1943 heavy losses among Japanese ships and aircraft were limiting the support they could give to their outlying garrisons, and the Americans began to develop their campaign of reconquest. Their strategy brought the art of combined service operations to a high level. The advances on Japan had to be made along the various island chains in a series of hops, gaining one Japanese-held island before moving on to the next. From an advanced air base or carrier, air power was used in a preparatory strike against the enemy base; then a forward bound was made by seaborne and airborne troops to seize the point; a 'mobile base', composed of craft carrying all stores and equipment, was then established in preparation for the next bound. General Douglas MacArthur was in command of the line of progress along the north coast of New Guinea and on to the Philippines. Simultaneously Admiral Nimitz advanced from Hawaii to the Gilbert and Marshall Islands and on to the Marianas. Admiral Halsey mopped up the area south-east of New Guinea.

MacArthur's forces, mainly Australian, had a hard fight to gain the Finschafen Peninsula, which was captured in October 1943. By September 1944 he had reached the western end of New Guinea, and was poised at Morotai in the Moluccas for the invasion of the Philippines. Nimitz gained the Gilberts in November 1943 and the Marshall Islands early in 1944. Saipan and Guam in the Marianas were attacked in June 1944.

Japanese production of war material was failing badly, whereas the Americans were introducing new aircraft in large numbers, and their carrier superiority was vast. The Japanese used their submarines to attack American warships; American submarines more profitably concentrated on enemy freighters and tankers. The Japanese were rarely able to reinforce the islands, and the Americans bombed them very thoroughly before attempting to land. But the fighting was always fierce, with no quarter given by either side. The Japanese waited in the jungle and attacked the marines on the steeply sloping beaches. After several weeks of fighting, however, the Marianas were captured. Next, in the battle of the Philippine Sea, on 19th and 20th June, Spruance's fleet sank two of the best Japanese carriers and damaged another, while over 400 Japanese planes were destroyed by Hellcats.

MacArthur and Nimitz, both of whom I knew, fought brilliant campaigns in their war against the Japanese in the Far East. It was entirely an American war; they fought a novel war by novel means and saw it through to complete success. Alliances ride the waves of war uneasily. MacArthur had no inconvenient ally to suggest alternatives to him! A most profound impact was made on naval warfare in the 1939/45 war by the Americans. They developed new strategy, tactics and techniques suited to war at sea in the new age of air power, and in those four years of war rose to become the strongest naval power in the world. I am glad I was privileged to know Admiral Nimitz – a very great sailor.

We must now return to Burma, where we shall find General Slim fighting brilliant battles with his Fourteenth Army.

While the tide was turning against the Japanese in the Pacific, the Allies took up the offensive in Burma. Stagnation for a while followed the retreat of Alexander's forces in 1942; the British carried out a major retraining programme in India, and the Japanese reinforced their positions in Burma. But in January 1943 the British reopened operations – somewhat experimentally. A drive was made down the west coast belt of Arakan. The Japanese withdrew to a prepared position in the Mayu Peninsula, defended with a maze of bunkers. Here against odds of two to one they repulsed repeated attacks and the British eventually withdrew, having suffered heavy casualties and a further loss of morale. Meanwhile a British officer, Brigadier Orde Wingate, carried out an operation of his own conception approved by Wavell; his theory was that a small and highly trained force could operate in the interior of Burma, waging guerrilla warfare against the Japanese communications while avoiding their main forces – without ground communications but supplied by air. In February 1943 Wingate crossed the Chindwin river with 3,000 men and penetrated deep into Japanese-occupied territory. In March he cut the railway from Mandalay to Myitkyina in numerous places and killed hundreds of the enemy. Some 2,000 of his men survived to return to India in May. Materially Wingate's expedition was not of great value, and the necessity of abandoning his sick and wounded to the brutal Japanese made its value seem even more doubtful. But useful experience had been gained regarding air supply.

A new Allied command organization was set up in 1943, Admiral Mountbatten becoming supreme commander responsible for co-ordinating forces in south-east Asia. His deputy was Stilwell, who was in command of the American-Chinese force in the northern area, amounting to three Chinese divisions, three American battalions and a

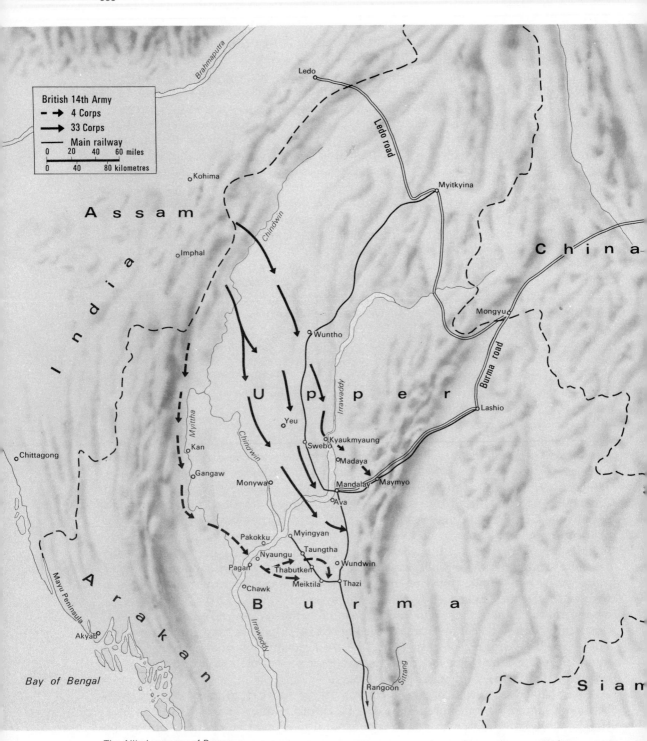

British 14th Army
- → 4 Corps
- → 33 Corps
- Main railway

0 20 40 60 miles
0 40 80 kilometres

Ledo

Kohima

Assam

Imphal

India

Chindwin

Ledo road

Myitkyina

China

Wuntho

Mongyu

U p p e r

Yeu

Irrawaddy

Burma road

Lashio

Chittagong

Myittha

Kan

Chindwin

Swebo

Kyaukmyaung

Madaya

Mandalay   Maymyo

Ava

Gangaw

Monywa

Pakokku

Myingyan

Taungtha

Wundwin

Nyaungu

Pagan

Thabutkon

Meiktila   Thazi

Chawk

Mayu Peninsula

Akyab

Arakan

B u r m a

Irrawaddy

Sittang

Rangoon

Siam

Bay of Bengal

The Allied recovery of Burma

small irregular force. The other main force was the British Fourteenth Army, consisting of about ten divisions of British, Indian, Gurkha, and West African troops with two brigades of tanks. Late in 1943 General Slim took command of the Fourteenth Army. The Japanese forces in Burma, under General Kawabe, totalled about nine complete divisions, divided into three armies: the 28th responsible for the Arakan front, the 15th for the central front and particularly the railway corridor, and the 33rd which held the north-eastern front.

The Americans considered the first priority to be the clearing of the route through northern Burma into China, and Allied strategy for the winter offensive of 1943–4 was framed around this principle. The offensive was to be renewed in Arakan, while Stilwell's force moved south on Myitkyina to cover the Ledo road. A second 'Wingate offensive' would cooperate with Stilwell's northern force. An essential feature of the campaign was the new use of air support, provided by the R.A.F. and the Americans. Communications were entirely by air; a division advancing rapidly through difficult country was supplied throughout from the air. The campaign went well. In Arakan the Japanese, attempting to envelop the British, were themselves enveloped when Slim flew in additional forces. This first British victory over the Japanese brought a great rise in morale. Stilwell's forces were opposed by only one division, and gained their objectives. Two brigades of Wingate's 'Chindits' landed by glider at different points while one brigade marched, and by attacking communications these succeeded in drawing Japanese forces away from Stilwell before they joined up with him. Wingate himself was killed in an air crash.

The Japanese launched, in March 1944, a major offensive against Assam. A three-month struggle took place in the area of Imphal and Kohima. Again Slim fed in troops by air, until the British had six divisions against the Japanese three. After a desperate assault on Imphal in June the Japanese broke and withdrew across the Chindwin. They had fought ferociously, themselves losing over 53,000 men. Many extra casualties were caused by disease, particularly malaria. It is a measure of the quality of the medical services that campaigns could be conducted at all in that type of country.

Following the crushing defeat of the Japanese in Assam, Slim's task was to occupy central Burma as far south as Mandalay. The total strength of the Japanese was now ten infantry divisions, two 'Indian National Army' divisions, one tank regiment, and numerous troops on the communication lines. Of this total, two divisions might be drawn off by the Allied northern force, now commanded by General Sultan, and three by the force in Arakan and the threat of amphibious landings. Thus an offensive into central Burma by the Fourteenth Army of six divisions could expect to face five enemy divisions. The Japanese had a new C-in-C, General Kimura. Slim divided his army into two corps: 4 Corps, commanded by General Messervy, consisting mainly of the 7th and 17th Divisions and the 255 Tank Brigade (Shermans), and 33 Corps, under General Stopford, comprising the 2nd, 19th and 20th Divisions and the 254 Tank Brigade (Grants and Stuarts). The 5th Division was held in reserve. Air transport was to be the means of supply to forward positions.

The Fourteenth Army offensive began on 3rd December 1944. Slim's six divisions crossed the Chindwin with the intention of bringing the Japanese to battle and defeating them in the Shwebo plain. However, after the battering at Imphal, Kimura decided not to risk battle in an open plain, and gradually withdrew his forces behind the Irrawaddy –

where he prepared for a 'battle of the Irrawaddy shore'. He hoped to cripple the Four-teenth Army as it attempted to cross the river, and then destroy it as it limped back to the Chindwin. But when it became clear that the Japanese were withdrawing, Slim formed a new plan for the destruction of the main Japanese forces beyond the Irrawaddy. 33 Corps (Stopford) was to force the crossing of the river north and west of Mandalay, drawing on to itself the greatest possible concentration of Japanese forces. Meanwhile 4 Corps (Messervy) would steal along the Gangaw valley and cross the Irrawaddy near Pakokku, and then without pausing would strike violently with armoured and airborne forces at Meiktila – the main administrative centre of the Japanese armies. In this area were their chief supply bases, ammunition dumps, hospitals, and several airfields; road and rail routes from the south-east and west converged there before spreading out again to the north. If Meiktila was taken the communications of the Japanese armies in an arc from the Salween to the Irrawaddy would be cut, and Kimura would be compelled to fight a battle off-balance to recover them. The British could follow up the victory by a dash to Rangoon.

By the second week in January 1945 Slim's army was approaching the Irrawaddy on a front of over 200 miles from Wuntho to Pakokku. The Japanese did not attempt to hold the entire river line, but concentrated defences at the likely crossing places – with reserves mobile and held well back until the British intentions became clear. On the night of 14th January 33 Corps began to execute its part of Slim's strategy. The 19th Division started the crossing of the Irrawaddy north of Mandalay at Kyaukmyaung, and a bridge-head was established. By the 17th the enemy had decided that this was the main British crossing operation, and Japanese forces were concentrated to make a heavy attack there. In the next three weeks heavy fighting built up. Kimura brought in more and more troops, including reinforcements from Meiktila, to beat back the British from the Irrawaddy. But the British bridge-head was steadily expanded, and another crossing was made west of Mandalay.

Meanwhile 4 Corps was driving southwards beyond the Chindwin towards the Irrawaddy at Pakokku. The deadline for crossing was 15th February. To forestall a hold-up by the Japanese rearguards, the advance was made beyond the Kan area on a wide front so as to outflank the enemy. On 28th January 4 Corps reached the Irrawaddy valley. Every man was set to work building airstrips and improving roads so that tanks and transport vehicles could be moved forward, together with material for the crossing. Messervy decided that the crossing was to be made near Nyaungu where the river was narrowest. To divert the enemy two demonstrations were mounted at other points of the river. Just before dawn on 14th February the first troops crossed by boat in complete silence about a mile north of Nyaungu, and established a defensible position on the far bank. A larger force followed in daylight with artillery, tanks and air support to expand the bridge-head for the remaining troops. Nyaungu was captured on the 16th. The Japanese had been taken completely by surprise, having formed no idea that a major force was in the area. Such an operation was possible only with the cover afforded to troop movements by the jungle and air superiority.

Kimura was completely deceived by Slim's plan. He still thought that practically the whole of the Fourteenth Army was in the Chindwin-Irrawaddy loop north and west of Mandalay; the activities in the direction of Pakokku he regarded as demonstrations by minor forces. Expecting that the British would make a major attempt to break out

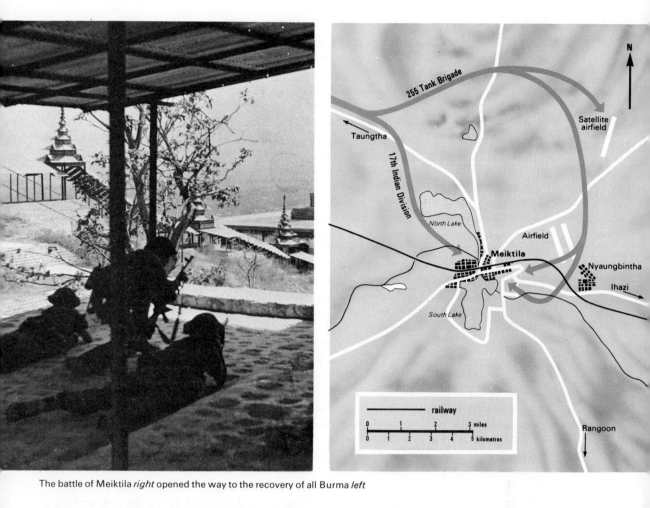

The battle of Meiktila *right* opened the way to the recovery of all Burma *left*

towards Mandalay, he continued to withdraw forces from all other sectors to concentrate them for the battle of the Irrawaddy shore. Towards the end of February reinforcements had brought Kimura's strength up to nine divisions as against the British five at Mandalay. The local odds against 33 Corps were thus heavy. Both corps were making heavy demands on a long supply line. It was necessary for 4 Corps to achieve a quick success in its attack on Meiktila, and one which would force Kimura to turn to its relief, thus exposing his forces to a double assault.

On 21st February the 17th Division and the Tank Brigade of 4 Corps began the advance on Meiktila. On the 25th they occupied the Thabutkon airstrip only ten miles from the town. Next day more troops were flown in. Attempts by the Japanese to block the road were quickly overrun by frontal assaults of massed tanks. Then five miles from the town 4 Corps stopped to regroup. The Japanese at Meiktila, under Major-General Kasuya, had spent several days digging defences. Kasuya disposed of a fighting strength of about 3,200 men, and large numbers of guns; all his available men, even hospital patients, were armed and established in strong points; anti-aircraft guns from the nearby airfields were set up as anti-tank guns and for perimeter defence. In any case Meiktila was a most difficult place to attack; on the north and south of the town were lakes which made the roads easily defended causeways, and the surrounding country was cut up by irrigation channels and ditches.

The first step in the attack was to seize the airfield on the eastern outskirts of the town, in order to fly in reinforcements and supplies. On 28th February, while an attack on the western defences held the attention of the Japanese, 255 Tank Brigade made a 10-mile sweep round Meiktila from the north and regrouped on the east. Then, with artillery and air support, a heavy armoured assault was launched and the British penetrated into the town – where the resistance of the Japanese was fanatical, pockets of survivors fighting desperately in the overrun area. March 1st was the day of bitterest fighting. As the advance was pressed in the east, further attacks were launched at western and south-easterly points. Savage in-fighting took place as the British pressed in from the outskirts towards the centre of the town, Japanese snipers and machine-gun nests being concealed in every house, water channel and heap of rubble. The Japanese never surrendered, but died where they fought. The progress of the British was slow but steady. By the evening they were well into the town, and on the 2nd the Japanese were confined to the southern end. On 3rd March 1945 the garrison was almost entirely wiped out, and Meiktila was in British hands.

Kimura was astonished at the fall of the town. He duly abandoned his projected offensive against 33 Corps at Mandalay, and diverted troops under Lieutenant-General Honda to recover Meiktila. The Japanese had large forces available for this operation, but they had to be assembled from different directions, and it was difficult for Honda to co-ordinate the movements. Furthermore, the Allies now had complete control of the air. As the Japanese forces began to converge on Meiktila from north and south 4 Corps struck out in all directions in a bold offensive. Infantry and tanks made daily sorties to a 20-mile radius to hunt and attack approaching Japanese forces. The first objective of the Japanese was the airstrip, the occupation of which would cut off British supplies. After a savage and continuous struggle, during which the Japanese reached its very edge, they were gradually beaten back. By the last week in March Meiktila was secure.

Meanwhile, at the moment Kimura turned to recover Meiktila, 33 Corps launched an all-out offensive from its bridge-head on to Mandalay. When the drive began on 26th February, the Japanese were swept back, leaving only pockets of resistance which could be dealt with later. But as the British moved nearer to Mandalay fanatical resistance was met. The Japanese used human mines – a soldier crouching in a fox-hole with a 100-kilo aircraft bomb between his knees and a large stone poised above the fuse; when a tank passed over his hole he was to drop the stone and the bomb, man and tank were to go up together. But in fact the human mines did little damage. By 8th March the Japanese resistance was isolated in two strongholds, Mandalay Hill and Fort Dufferin. Mandalay Hill was captured on the 11th, when the last Japanese defenders had been burnt out of the cellars. Fort Dufferin was bombed, and captured on 20th March.

By the end of March 1945 the Allies held both banks of the Irrawaddy from Mandalay to Chawk and the main road and railway to Rangoon as far south as Wundwin. From the firm position of Meiktila the Allied hold on the country could now be expanded. The subsequent campaign was as brilliantly managed by Slim as had been the Mandalay-Meiktila phase. An advance in Arakan opened up new airfields and sea supply routes.

Rangoon was recovered on 3rd May. The Japanese fled eastwards across the Sittang river, though tough fighting was necessary to round them up. Preparations then began for the invasion of Malaya. But this never had to take place.

By September 1944 both MacArthur's and Nimitz's forces were poised for the attack on the Philippines and Japan. On 20th October the 6th Army, supported by battleships, cruisers, destroyers and eighteen escort carriers, started to land on the island of Leyte. The Japanese decided that the Philippines must be saved, and all available naval forces converged from various bases. The struggle for Leyte Gulf was a series of battles, separated by hundreds of miles, over a period of four days, and was the largest-scale naval engagement of the war. The Japanese fought with desperation. Japanese pilots used *kamikaze* tactics, whereby they dived their bomb-laden planes directly into the decks of American carriers and other unarmoured vessels. This tactic accounted for thirty-three American ships. But, thanks principally to the American air superiority, the Japanese suffered a serious defeat, losing four carriers, two escort carriers, three battleships and much else.

The Japanese army continued, however, to defend the Philippines. General Yamashita had about 250,000 troops. By the end of 1944 General Krueger's 6th Army had gained all Leyte, and in January the 6th and 8th Armies invaded Luzon, the most strongly held island. By May 1945 the entire Philippines had been recovered by the Allies. The next main objective was the island of Okinawa, an important advance air base, and on 1st April a Marine Corps and the 24th Army Corps began to land. Besides a garrison of 120,000 Japanese troops, *kamikaze* pilots again operated. The fighting on Okinawa was the most savage of the war. It lasted until 21st June, when the Americans finally secured the island. Over 100,000 Japanese were killed, the American casualties (all types) being 39,000.

Aircraft operating from Okinawa now joined in the bombing offensive against Japan herself, which had begun in November and intensified between April and August 1945, in preparation for invasion. Previously carrier-borne aircraft had done most of the bombing, but now B.29 Superfortresses of the Army Air Force took over the main work. From Okinawa attacks were concentrated on Nagasaki, destroying the docks and aircraft production area. From bases in China and the Marianas planes bombed the industrial centres, night incendiary attacks supplementing daylight precision bombing. Tokyo and Osaka suffered immense devastation.

The bombing offensive reached its culmination in August. On 6th August the Americans dropped the first atomic bomb on Hiroshima, killing 80,000 people. On 9th August the second atomic bomb was dropped on Nagasaki, killing 40,000 people – more than the total killed in all the air raids of the war on London. The Americans felt justified in using this new weapon. The Japanese still had 250,000 troops in the Pacific Islands, with more established in the Dutch East Indies, Malaya and China. The nation which treated their prisoners as atrociously as the Japanese had done, which violated all conventions of war such as the Red Cross, which used human mines and suicide pilots – received no pity. On 10th August 1945 the Japanese government surrendered unconditionally, and the 1939/45 war was over.

REFLECTIONS

The war which began in 1939, often called by me 'Hitler's war', started slowly; it then flared up swiftly in 1940, finally raging over almost all the world and becoming very complicated. I have tried to present the story to the reader as simply as possible, and in such a way that he will see the whole wood without having his interest distracted by too many trees. I would like to conclude this chapter with a few reflections which may help my readers to understand some of the more complicated issues of this most modern war.

National leadership was immensely important. Many regard Hitler as merely an insane political figure. He was, indeed, an evil man, but he was a leader – enterprising and astute. He had no use for 'declaring' war and giving the victim time to prepare for the blow; he reckoned that was not the way to fight, and that view is logical if it is accepted that a nation fights only to win militarily. But that should not be the ultimate object in war. He imparted his evilness to others.

Who made the worst mistakes in the conduct of war? I think Hitler, and his mistakes have been pointed out in what I have written. It was a fatal error to attack Russia in June 1941; one of the first rules of war is: don't march on Moscow. He probably could not prevent the Japanese from attacking America, after which he declared war on the United States because of his pact with Japan. He then found himself fighting the British empire, Russia and America – and could not hope to win. Subsequently on the western front he made three major mistakes – to try to fight the battle of France south of the Seine after his defeat in Normandy in 1944, to launch a counter-offensive in the Ardennes in December 1944, and to stand and fight west of the Rhine in the hope of saving the Ruhr. He began well. From the viewpoint of sheer tactical efficiency one cannot but admire the cold-blooded assault of the Wehrmacht on western Europe in the spring of 1940; it upset the world balance of military power, and made Germany the dominant nation-in-arms. But in the end Hitler brought destruction on his country because he was driven forward by selfish ambitions.

Now consider Stalin. A great leader, ruthless maybe, and no kind of gentleman; but if it hadn't been for him the Russians might well have left the war early in 1942. Only Churchill realized that he would use the war to fasten his grip on eastern Europe and that this political strategy was uppermost in his mind before the conflict ever began. Indeed, he began to implement it the moment the ink was dry on his non-aggression pact with Germany in August 1939. Stalin made almost no mistakes; he had a clear-cut political strategy and he pursued it relentlessly. I first got to know him at the Potsdam conference in July 1945, and then stayed as his guest in Moscow in 1947. He had an amazing strategical sense and I cannot recall that he put a foot wrong in our discussions on strategical matters – though of course his political strategy, aimed to gather the peoples of eastern Europe into the communist fold, could hardly appeal to the West.

Roosevelt never seemed to me to be clear about what he was fighting for. He tried to woo Stalin, but the latter won the peace for Russia at the Teheran conference, and Yalta crowned his victory; he had no difficulty in fooling Roosevelt.

Churchill was a great leader of the British people in a crisis. Much has beeen written about him, and indeed I have written a good deal myself because I got to know him really well and he became chief among all my friends. One thing is quite clear – by standing firm against Hitler when all seemed lost, he saved not only Britain but Western civilization as well.

Besides being a national leader in a crisis, and, indeed, for a time the sole leader of the Western world against the Nazi tyranny, Churchill had the quality of vision – a quality which entitles him to a foremost place among strategists. There is no sealed pattern for national leaders or strategists, nor for generals; we are all human, and we all make mistakes. As a commander-in-chief in the field I often wished Churchill had not himself once been a soldier; he was so interested in the tactical conduct of a battle that he would occasionally try to interfere in matters which were outside his province – though he never pressed his point and would always accept my explanation. I would appraise him by saying that never has any nation found any leader who so matched the hour as did the British in Winston Churchill during Hitler's war; when weighed in the balance in 1940 he was not found wanting.

Science and technology is too vast a subject to explore at all deeply in the space of this chapter, but I would say this. Put very simply, war before 1918 can be said to have been concerned with fighting in two dimensions (land and sea) over short visual ranges, with weapons of small area coverage and a low degree of deadliness. Tremendous changes came during the 1939/45 war – extensions into a third dimension (the air), extension of the ability to 'see' the enemy (radar), extensions in the range at which battles are fought, improvements in the effect of weapons. To these must be added counter-measures of all kinds. I have always held the view that the most important impact on battle during the 1939/45 war was the rise of air power as a major factor. It revolutionized the strategy and tactics of war on land and at sea. Soldiers and sailors in many nations, particularly my own, are apt to forget what they owe to their air forces. Certainly the United States would not have become the strongest naval power in the world without recognizing the impact of air power on war at sea.

War in the nuclear age is discussed in Chapter 24, but let me say this now. In my view it was unnecessary to drop two atomic bombs on Japan in August 1945, and I cannot think it was right to do so. According to President Truman it was done to save 'hundreds of thousands of lives, both American and Japanese'. But the removal of the obstacle of unconditional surrender would of itself have saved those lives, because, I consider, Japan would then have surrendered earlier. The Japanese had already been defeated by conventional weapons. Conventional bombing had done such a thorough job of destruction in Japan that no targets would have been left for atom bombs if orders had not been given to save four cities for that purpose, including Hiroshima and Nagasaki. The dropping of the bombs was a major political blunder, and is a prime example of the declining moral standards of conduct in modern war. Maybe it was the first American blow in the cold war. I profoundly hope that the full potential of scientific warfare will never be used.

One last point. Some people seem to think that military actions need be based only on purely military grounds, without taking into account their political repercussions. But to think and act thus merely leaves the area of politics in danger. At the top level, can any decision in war be non-political? Because of muddled thinking on this matter, the six years of war from 1939 to 1945 did not give the Western nations the just and lasting peace for which they fought. Only Stalin got the results he sought, and that because his military decisions were taken against the background of a definite political policy – Russian domination in Europe and the stamp of communism as far to the west as possible.

22

The Ethics of War

Having taken our general study of warfare from 7000 B.C. up to the mid-twentieth century, it may be valuable to look more closely at the moral aspect of war. In all these ages of fighting, has mankind made any progress?

Sometimes in history principles of morality were translated into rules of conduct; at other times they remained as a climate of opinion. But it would seem, in fact, that as men have become more 'civilized', so their wars have become more horrible. In modern times it must be admitted that agreed rules of conduct have often been shamelessly and flagrantly violated. Crimes against humanity were committed during the 1939/45 war, and in later days, for example in the Congo, which force us to the conclusion that war and murder may be synonymous terms; passions can be aroused which turn men into fiends. Happily this tendency is not universal; but the past, and particularly the more recent past, has proved the need for political and military leaders to keep a firm grip on moral principles – which can so easily be lost.

We are now going to look back at history and try to discover the facts which concern progress and failure in this matter of the ethics of war. Let us consider some of the fundamental aspects of the question – such things as honour, methods in the taking of life, surrender and the treatment of prisoners and wounded, conduct in the area of operations and the idea of total war, and international regulations of war. We must then try and reach some conclusions which will help us to discern the future, however inscrutable it may seem.

During the years 500 to 400 B.C., in the early days of the Greek wars, treachery, poisoned wells and poisoned weapons were all used in warfare. Later, in medieval sieges, the carcases of dead animals would be thrown across the defence works so that putrefaction would spread disease; this might be called the first example of bacteriological warfare. This particular form of warfare was declared illegal at a conference in Washington in 1925 – which has always seemed to me a mistake. This was very much in my mind when the armies under my command had crossed the Rhine in March 1945 and were moving across the North German plain towards the Elbe and the Baltic Sea. Hamburg with its enemy garrison presented a problem, and I arranged with the British Bomber Command to bomb the city; a fleet of a thousand bombers was sent; thousands of Germans were killed and tremendous damage was done to buildings and public services. It would have been less horrible, and produced the same strategic results, to have put the entire population out of action for forty-eight hours with the use of suitable 'bugs' or even gas. To disable temporarily large numbers of the enemy is surely better than using weapons of mass-slaughter and destroying the inanimate property of non-combatants. There are great possibilities in the use of nerve gases to produce short-term disablement, without killing – and political leaders might well examine this question.

From the time of the Normans right through the Middle Ages the influence of the Christian Church gradually imposed on western Europe an elaborate code in which treason and treachery were regarded as contemptible crimes, and courage in battle and loyalty to one's feudal master were cardinal virtues. Within the narrow confines of the hereditary warrior class the ideal of chivalry, with its fidelity to vows, and magnanimity towards one's defeated enemies, took the place of what Sir Arthur Bryant has called 'the old suicidal law of tribal vengeance and the bloody anarchy of might is right'.

We learn that as the years passed there grew up, gradually, a sort of brotherhood of arms even between opponents, however savagely they had previously been fighting one another. In the eighteenth century a considerable degree of mutual esteem existed between European enemies. Generals exchanged courteous letters, ranging from the exchange of wounded prisoners of equal rank to the offer of domestic hospitality for commanders who had been captured. The Napoleonic wars show examples of fraternization – British and French in Spain, and French and Russian troops outside Smolensk and Moscow. Nicknames for the enemy, like 'Johnny Crappo' or 'John Bull', came into friendly use, and even in the 1939/45 war terms like 'Jerry' persisted (in the 1914/18 war it had been 'the Hun'). In 1810 we find a British captain in Portugal writing home: 'I was at our posts yesterday. The French *vedette* saluted us, not with a shot, but by kissing his hand. Is not this civilized warfare ?' One day, when the hounds belonging to another British officer followed a hare into the French lines, they were politely returned. This gentlemanly type of warfare was evident in the Macedonian campaign of 1915–18. In the upper Struma Valley the British 28th Division ran a pack of beagles; when hounds penetrated the enemy lines on several occasions, the Bulgars always returned them to their owners.

Codes of chivalry were not restricted to Europe. In Japan, from the eighth century onwards, a prolonged period of family feuds and civil war produced a recognized code of behaviour in the military class. Known as 'the way of the horse and the bow', it was based upon the unquestioned loyalty of a man to his superior. This Japanese equivalent of chivalry lasted for close on a thousand years. Then, in the eighteenth century, the government replaced it with the cult named *bushido*, meaning 'the warrior's way'. This ethical system, while retaining the traditional principles of fidelity in time of war, was adapted to the needs of a more peaceful society by the infusion of moderation, conservatism, and certain elements of Confucian teaching. However, this 'moderation' had little effect on the behaviour of the Japanese soldiery during the 1939/45 war, when their brutal treatment of prisoners of war in the Far East was past all belief and broke all accepted rules of civilized conduct – under the cloak of *bushido*.

As Christian principles spread, so to varying degrees they affected the customs of waging war. But morality, while requiring the courteous treatment of prisoners, for some time set no limits to the methods of taking life. However, in the eighteenth century, the age of 'enlightenment', endeavours were made to impose certain restrictions. Louis XIV of France and Louis XV both refused to employ 'infernal liquids' offered to them by chemists. And in 1855 when Lord Dundonald secretly proposed that asphyxiating smoke-clouds be used at the siege of Sebastopol, his plan was rejected by the British government; ten years later Napoleon III stopped trials with asphyxiating shells being made on dogs, declaring that such barbarous methods would never be used by the French army – being against 'the law of nations'.

Then came the first Hague Conference in 1899. This prohibited the use of poison and poisonous arms, but did not condemn gas warfare nor the emission of cloud gas, although it forbade 'the use of projectiles the only object of which is the diffusion of asphyxiating gases' – which presumably meant gas shelling, but overall left the issue far from clear. The Conference did, however, definitely prohibit the use of expanding bullets.

The seventeenth century saw the custom of allowing the defenders of a fortress to surrender with 'the honours of war' – to march out bearing arms, with flags flying and bands playing, and then to lay down arms. This custom remained a feature of the sieges in Marlborough's day and also in Wellington's – Flushing in 1809, San Sebastian in 1813 are examples. In the 1939/45 war there was the case, in May 1941, of the Italian garrison of Amba Alagi in Abyssinia and the viceroy of the Italian East African empire, the Duke of Aosta, being granted 'Surrender with Honour' as an inducement to hand over the battlefield without sabotage, booby-traps and destruction – a policy which saved many British and Indian army lives.

Some progress can be seen when we consider the treatment of wounded. For long it has been customary in Europe for opposing sides to arrange a suspension of hostilities to allow the wounded to be brought in and the dead to be buried; but when no such truce occurred arrangements for the wounded were generally inadequate, haphazard and partisan – the enemy's wounded being inevitably the last to be tended. In 1862 a Swiss philanthropist, Henri Dunant, published a book in which he described the sufferings of the wounded at the battle of Solferino so vividly that the subject aroused widespread public attention and concern. Dunant urged that voluntary aid societies should be formed and, as a result, sixteen European countries were represented at a conference assembled in Geneva the following year.

In 1864 the first Geneva Convention, since revised three times, was signed. An International Red Cross Committee was formed to improve the condition of wounded soldiers in the field, and later it became responsible also for the supervision of prisoner-of-war camps. In time of war sick and wounded combatants are now to be respected and cared for, whatever their nationality. The ambulances and hospital ships which transport them, the hospitals which shelter them, the doctors, nurses, chaplains and administrators who look after them, are to be respected and protected under all circumstances – provided they use the distinguishing marks of a flag and an arm-badge bearing a Red Cross. So in this matter all is now well, provided the Red Cross is respected. But it should be recorded that the Red Cross flag and badge were disgracefully abused by the Japanese soldiery in the Far East during the 1939/45 war.

For many centuries the lot of prisoners-of-war was, on the whole, terrible. At sea they were massacred or else turned into galley slaves; so long as small warships were in use, there was very little room in which to stow prisoners, and even less food and water to spare for them; the inducement to take prisoners was therefore small. But as ships became larger so accommodation was improved; the codes of reasonable treatment of prisoners which had gradually prevailed on land then came into use at sea. In 1587, a year before the defeat of the Armada, the Spanish commander-in-chief had orders to kill every man found on board an English ship. But the victorious Queen Elizabeth I sent home all Spanish sailors who had been wrecked on the coasts of Ireland and had been fortunate enough to fall into the hands of her soldiers rather than be killed by the Irish. As regards the treatment of prisoners by the Germans and Japanese in the 1939/45 war, I think I have already made my views clear.

In 1907 the Hague Regulations set out to codify some of the better principles which have prevailed, in the hope that all nations would adopt these principles of conduct towards prisoners-of-war.

It was laid down that all personal belongings of a prisoner, except his weapons, horses and military papers, were to remain his property. Prisoners-of-war had to be treated, in respect of food, quarters and clothing, on the same footing as the troops of the nation which had captured them. Opinions varied sharply as to what clothing was adequate, and several countries considered boots to be part of a soldier's military equipment rather than of his uniform. A belligerent state might use the labour of prisoners, except officers, but the tasks given to them must have nothing to do with military operations, must not be excessive, and must be paid for. These regulations were to be disgracefully contravened by the Japanese during the 1939/45 war, particularly on the notorious 'Railway of Death' in Siam. During the two great wars, 1914/18 and 1939/45, Britain and Germany reached agreement that neither side would employ prisoners within nineteen miles of the firing line.

Belligerents who took refuge in neutral countries such as Switzerland had to be interned, though officers could be granted parole. At a later date it was laid down that no prisoner was obliged to divulge to his captors any information except his number, rank and name. But a new treatment for prisoners called brain-washing has been introduced by communist peoples in the twentieth century, and in the Korean War which began in July 1950 British and American prisoners were subjected to varying degrees of this treatment.

In the seventeenth and eighteenth centuries the attempt to limit the general impact of warfare, begun as we have seen after the Thirty Years' War, was helped by the institution of disciplined standing armies. Looting was prohibited; this had always been one of the inducements held out to the adventurers who formed part of the fighting forces. For a time battles were avoided on account of the very high rate of casualties, and the overall aim of strategy tended to be to exhaust rather than to annihilate the enemy. But the mass levies of the French revolutionary wars led to a renewal of unlimited warfare. Hostilities against civilians resulted in reprisals in the form of partisan and guerrilla activities, as in Russia and Spain, and these led to more atrocities and sharply increased the savagery and the horror. One has only to look at Goya's series of etchings, 'The Disasters of War', to appreciate this. I have several times used the expression 'unlimited war', and that term was used in those days; in the mid-twentieth century we use the expression 'total war'.

Good conduct by troops has generally reaped handsome military dividends, whereas unbridled cruel behaviour against civilians can bring just the reverse. An example of the first is Wellington's army. The duke always insisted that his troops should behave themselves, and should pay for all they used; this had the result that when he led his men into southern France at the end of 1813, expecting to be faced with hostile French partisans, he found instead that his army was welcomed – because its conduct was so much better than that of France's own soldiers. An instance of the second dividend is the decision by Germany in 1917 to carry out a policy of unrestricted U-boat warfare; this aroused world-wide anger and horror, and eventually brought America into the 1914/18 war. The German invasion of Russia in 1941–2, Operation 'Barbarossa', shows the same. The leading troops were in many places welcomed by Russian villagers when they first marched in. But the follow-up 'occupation forces' behaved so abominably that the same Russians who had waved to welcome the leading German troops then disappeared into the woods, and fought as partisans and saboteurs against the 'liberators' – who were hated with a deadly hatred.

During the American Civil War, General Sherman's order for all private citizens to leave Atlanta, because he had decided to convert the city into a purely military base, aroused the outcry of 'barbarism'. But in reply to a local petition he wrote: 'You cannot qualify war in harsher terms than I will. War is cruelty, and you cannot refine it.' Sherman's famous 'march to the sea' left in its wake a belt of country, 300 miles long and 50 wide, swept clean of food and supplies. People likened it to the worst excesses of the Thirty Years' War, or even to those of Attila, the 'scourge of God' (fifth century A.D.). (In fact no non-combatants were harmed unless they actively interfered with the advance. Some soldiers exceeded their orders, but most private property was respected, beyond animals and supplies required by the Union forces.) This was an example of total war, ruthlessly conducted. 'If the people raise a howl against my barbarity and cruelty,' declared Sherman, 'I will answer that war is war.' He was waging war against the enemy's civilian population just as much as against the armed forces of that enemy. In 1914 the arrest as hostages of notables such as landowners, mayors and priests, was part of German policy to intimidate the hostile Belgian population. A whole community was held responsible for acts of hostility – although the principle of collective responsibility had been expressly outlawed by the Hague Convention.

The borderline between soldiers and civilians is further blurred in the instance of guerrilla warfare, for example the *francs-tireurs* of the Franco-Prussian War of 1870–1. Those peasants who fired on German troops were, if caught, hanged. The Crown Prince declared: 'Nothing is left for us to do but to adopt retaliatory measures by burning down the house from which the shots came or else employ the help of the lash and forced contributions.' And Bismarck said: 'They are not soldiers. We are treating them as murderers.' This is a pattern which has been repeated many times, since one side's resistance hero is the other side's terrorist or bandit. Anyone committing hostilities without belonging to the organized hostile army is not entitled to the privileges of a prisoner-of-war, in much the same way as spies in wartime.

It will now have become clear that in spite of efforts to make war more humane there have been cruel relapses into barbarism. Following the age of chivalry came the Renaissance, when the principles set forth by Machiavelli were a potent influence in politics. Nevertheless, factors have operated towards improvement, principally stimulated by the sufferings in war of non-combatants and civil populations. Perhaps the most important of these has been the development of international regulations of war. In Europe the appalling anarchy, destruction and starvation caused by the Thirty Years' War (1618–48), which cost the lives of, possibly, eight million people in addition to those killed in battle, led jurists, following Grotius, to urge that war's violence should be moderated, and that soldiers should be distinguished from civilians. Events such as the sack of Magdeburg horrified Europe. It was seen that some limits had to be set to war.

The Second Hague Conference in 1907 agreed resolutions for the 'humane conduct of war'. It was forbidden to declare that no quarter would be given, to kill or wound an enemy who had surrendered, and to attack or bombard cities, towns and villages which were not defended (the term 'open city' came into use).

The Conference of 1907 also laid down that no hostilities were to begin 'without previous and explicit warning in the form of a reasoned declaration of war or an ultimatum with conditional declaration of war'. This regulation was necessary because, as we know, in 1904 Japan opened her war with Russia without prior ultimatum or declaration, just as she had done against China in 1895 and was to do against America in December 1941 at Pearl Harbour. The 1939/45 war also saw various deliberately fabricated frontier incidents, designed to provide an apparently valid pretext for declaring war – when the victim-designate had inconveniently failed to furnish one.

In 1922 some 'Rules of Warfare' were agreed at the Washington Conference on the limitation of armaments. In particular, aerial bombardment for the purpose of terrorizing the civilian population, of destroying or damaging private property not of a military character, or of injuring non-combatants, was prohibited. So, too, in 1925, was the employment of asphyxiating and poisonous gases (and these were not used in the 1939/45 war). Bacteriological warfare was also declared illegal, as I have already mentioned. But in spite of these well-intentioned rules, both the Spanish Civil War which began in 1936 and the 1939/45 war saw many instances of terror bombing and the killing of civilians; even the most careful air raids were liable to damage private property, and all too many bombing raids were indiscriminate, inaccurate or wilfully destructive.

Lastly, I will consider neutrality. This is defined in the *Encyclopaedia Britannica* as

> the legal status arising from the abstention of a state from all participation in a war between other states, the maintenance by it of an attitude of impartiality in its dealings with the belligerent states, and the recognition by the latter of this abstention and impartiality.

That status of neutrality as defined above is of comparatively recent origin. By the seventeenth century it had become recognized that neutral states should afford no help to belligerents; but considerations as to whether neutrals could prevent their territory being used for hostile purposes were in those days ill-defined.

Neutrality gained nothing for Belgium in the two great wars of the twentieth century; that country was unable to defend its policy, and this is surely the acid test as to whether neutrality is worth while. Switzerland, for different reasons, has managed to maintain a neutral status. In the Spanish Civil War of 1936–9, Germany, Italy and Russia, all nominally neutral, sent troops or air forces to help one side or the other, in order to gain experience in modern techniques of waging war.

Under the Hague Convention of 1907 no neutral power may supply warships, supplies or war material to a belligerent, or refuse to one belligerent any facility which she had granted to another. However, the American Lend-Lease Act of 1941 authorized the manufacture or procurement of 'any defense article for the government of any country whose defense the president deemed vital to the defense of the United States', and to permit such articles, which included agricultural and industrial commodities as well as armaments, weapons, munitions and ships, to be sold, exchanged, leased or lent to such governments.

What lessons can we learn from this short examination of the ethics of war?

I have said that the Hague Convention of 1907 agreed certain resolutions for the 'humane conduct of war'. But we should get out of our heads once and for all that there is, or can ever be, anything humane about war. Unfortunately, the time has not yet arrived when we can say that war has been abolished and we have 'Peace on Earth'; therefore, political leaders and service chiefs must continue their efforts to make war less horrible. This chapter shows what has been achieved in that respect, but it has to be admitted that total war has brought about a decline in moral standards far beyond anything known before.

During the years immediately following the 1914/18 war, the slogan used to be, 'If you want peace, prepare for war.' Nations should learn that such thinking will not get them very far, because with all nations following this counsel the world must be an armed camp, with explosive situations liable to develop. A more positive slogan was coined by Liddell Hart: 'If you want peace, understand war;' this knowledge should prompt nations to avoid its inhumanity. Clausewitz taught that the destruction of the enemy's armed forces is the first aim of generalship – by which many thought that he meant the use of the utmost violence to achieve complete annihilation. That idea has been the cause of much unnecessary, tragic loss of life in warfare, and is responsible for a good deal of the unrest which exists in the distracted world of politics and war in which we find ourselves in the mid-twentieth century. But the remark was taken out of its context; Clausewitz also wrote that war is 'a continuation of political transactions intermingled with other means', and I read that statement to be a sound argument for the supremacy of political over narrow military policies, and for the exercise of moderation once victory has been ensured.

The responsibility of statesmen and politicians is very great. The higher direction of war is in their hands and they must see to it that they give clear political directives to the service chiefs. Unless they understand that the object of Grand Strategy must be a peace in which true values may be preserved, and unless they direct all military effort in war to the attainment of a favourable, controlling position at the end of it, they will throw away the fruits of tremendous sacrifices and all the slaughter will have been useless – more than ever in a nuclear age. In the 1939/45 war this principle was badly ignored, and the most humane intentions and sentiments about war cannot cover up the mischief that was wrought.

Military commanders who implement political policy carry a different responsibility. Success is vital; but battles must be won with the least possible loss of life. Nothing rots morale quicker than the suspicion that a commander is careless of his men, which can grow from such sensitive feelings as those aroused by indiscriminate burials of the dead and the sight of scattered graves neglected and bodies lying in ditches. No commander can afford to overlook the reverent and fitting burial of the dead – including enemy dead.

While the major conflicts of the twentieth century have shown that there is still much to be done in making war less horrible, most of mankind have, I hope, progressed some way since Blaise de Montluc, Marshal of France, wrote in the sixteenth century:

> Towards an Enemy all advantages are good, and for my part (God forgive me) if I could call all the devils in Hell to beat out the brains of an Enemy that would beat out mine, I would do it with all my heart.

23 The Iron Curtain and the Cold War

We have dealt in considerable detail with the history of warfare over a period of some 9,000 years. I propose to devote the last three chapters to a discussion of certain problems which are not yet part of history, but which our study of history may help us to understand. This is a realm of conjecture – and a realm in which decision and moral courage to face up to practical realities is sadly lacking, as an uneasy peace broods over our world.

It seems to me that a soldier with considerable practical experience of war, and of working with political leaders in many countries in peace, has a right to pose the problems which arise as he sees them, and to put forward his own opinion as to some of the answers – and this I now propose to do.

The two expressions contained in the title of this chapter are in common use today, but it is doubtful if we all understand their origin and what they mean. We had better get this doubt cleared up. 'The Iron Curtain' is an expression which owes its wide currency to Winston Churchill. He first used it in May 1945. He was disturbed at the victory Stalin had gained at the Yalta conference in February 1945, and at the way any agreements reached at that Conference were being deliberately disregarded by the Russians. President Roosevelt had died in April 1945 and his successor, Truman, had terrific responsibility suddenly thrust upon him – at a time when his vision was less wide than it later became. The German war had ended on 8th May 1945 with the Red Army in possession of all the main capitals of eastern and central Europe – notably Berlin, Prague, Vienna and Belgrade. In fact, Stalin had fastened his grip firmly on eastern Europe and was in a formidable negotiating position, practically unassailable.

Churchill warned Truman about what was likely to happen, but he was unreceptive. Nothing daunted, on 12th May 1945 Churchill sent Truman a telegram beginning in para. 1 with the words: 'I am profoundly concerned about the European situation.' He then analyzed the position of the Western Allies *vis-à-vis* Russia, and para. 3 begins with the words: 'An *iron curtain* is drawn down upon their front. We do not know what is going on behind' (my italics). The full text of the telegram can be read in Churchill's *The Second World War, Triumph and Tragedy*. Of that telegram he wrote: 'Of all the public documents I have written on this issue, I would rather be judged by this.'

Later, after I had been appointed commander-in-chief and military governor of the British Zone of Germany in 1945, I became very conscious of the truth of his words. Early in October 1945 I went to London and told the prime minister, Attlee, that on the Control Council for Germany we could reach no agreement with the Russians, and the Western powers must prepare for a continuous struggle with the communist East, which would last for many years. That prophecy at least has proved correct! On 5th

March 1946 Churchill made a speech at Fulton in the U.S.A. in which he said: 'From Stettin in the Baltic to Trieste in the Adriatic, an *iron curtain* has descended across the continent of Europe' (my italics). This was the first occasion on which he used the expression publicly.

'The Cold War' is not so easy to explain; nor do I know who coined the expression or when. Insofar as I am aware the expression came into common use in the autumn of 1945, a few months after the end of Hitler's war, being used to describe the state of tension which then began to develop between the Western nations and the Soviet bloc. Tension between peoples has always existed, as has been clear in this book, and in the past when the tension became unbearable the nation concerned resolved it by declaring war. But in the mid-twentieth century the destructive power of nuclear weapons and the perfection of delivery systems has made open war between powerful states, or groups of states, definitely a self-negating method of trying to enforce political ends. It would merely result in the utter destruction of life in the nations concerned, and no nation wants to commit suicide.

In the mid-twentieth century we live in a split world; there are two Germanys, two Berlins, two Europes, two worlds – 'capitalist' states and 'communist' states. As well as hostility between communist and democratic peoples, there is hostility between white and coloured peoples. Conflict between differing societies has come to be regarded as inevitable – but not necessarily armed conflict; it is considered preferable to gain objectives without open war. Communists have, instead, turned in so-called peacetime to what are, in effect, lesser forms of war – subversion, colonial rebellion, satellite aggression; they are experts at combining and operating non-military forms of war – political, economic, psychological; they incite small countries to armed aggression and support such activities financially and by providing weapons. All this activity, falling short of total war, is part of what has come to be called the 'cold war'. A shorter definition would be that the cold war is the policy of making mischief in the world by all methods short of war – that is, short of involving the communist states in open hostilities with the free world. The nations of the free world have found it difficult to combat the communist tactics in the cold war since it began in 1945.

Why are things in the world today in such a mess? Some may say that it just happened, and that the reason is inscrutable; I would not agree. Things don't just 'happen' in this world of politics and war; they take place because of national policies or lack of them – particularly in respect of wars. Anyhow, if the reason appears to many to be inscrutable, we should try to 'unscrew' the inscrutable.

Broadly, I hold that it has been due in a large measure to the decline of the white man in Oriental and African countries. The former submissiveness of Asiatics and coloured peoples to white European rule disappeared in the winter of 1941–2 when Japan entered the Second World War and her armed forces overran south-east Asia. The Japanese conquerors appeared at first as liberators to the peoples in that part of the world, in spite of their imperialistic intentions and their brutal and barbarous methods. When Japanese overlordship ended in 1945, as suddenly as it had begun, the peoples in that part of the world did not want to take their old masters back – who, in truth, had not on the whole done very much for the mass of the people but rather had used the natural resources of the countries to increase their own national wealth. Inevitably, movements of independence began, and these spread throughout the Middle and Near East. As it was in India, so it was then among the dark masses of Africa. The coloured peoples throughout the world began to be emancipated at a rapid rate. Everywhere the white man was being forced on to the defensive; and, of course, the process was hastened by Stalin's Russia promising freedom to all backward peoples and denouncing imperialism, colonialism and capitalism. Perhaps most important of all, the peoples of the West were unsure of any ideals themselves.

After the Yalta conference ended in 1945 it should have been clear to all that after Hitler's war ended the world would be split by two conflicting ideological doctrines or social systems – which in fact happened. If it had not become clear then, it was made crystal clear by the end of the Potsdam conference in July 1945 – at which I was present and where I first met Stalin and Truman. That was the last conference between the leaders of the three great nations which had formed the grand alliance in the fight for freedom and justice against the Axis powers. Since those days it has seemed to me that international affairs have degenerated into a kind of chessboard on which the mass of ordinary people are the pawns. The issues of move and countermove are of profound importance to ordinary people – but all they see is politics as a struggle for power by ambitious men. Nowhere is that struggle more evident today than in Asia and Africa, where government can be defined as subjugation of the masses – not merely to conform to the laws of the country, but to the enforced rule without question of the reigning hierarchy.

Having defined the cold war and discussed its immediate consequences, it is suitable to remind ourselves of how it has, on occasions, been brought near to boiling point. The first example we might quote was the blockade of West Berlin by the Russians, which began in June 1948 and continued all that year and well into 1949 – being defeated by the tremendous effort of the air-lift. This led to the creation of the North Atlantic Treaty Organization in April 1949. The communist planners, having been foiled in Europe by NATO, turned to Asia – where Japanese conquests during the 1939/45 war had caused the Western powers to lose 'face' and their traditional prestige. I must emphasize that in the eastern world 'face' is very important.

In Indonesia a struggle for independence wrested that country of 100 million people from the Netherlands.

In Malaya Chinese guerrillas took to the jungle to fight against the re-establishment of British control. At first they achieved some success. But then under the Templer regime in 1952–4 all the resources of the state – political, military, police, intelligence – were concentrated under the supreme command and direction of the High Commissioner, who had full powers in all matters granted to him by the home government in London. The war was then conducted by the man on the spot, intelligently, with determination and vigour, and with full regard to local conditions. The result was victory, definite and complete.

About the same time, and not far away, a similar type of war was being fought by France against Vietminh nationalists in the French-supported Vietnam state. The war began in 1946 with the French attempt to reconquer Indo-China, which had been part of their empire since the early 1880's. It ended with the armistice agreements signed in Geneva in 1954, which left Vietnam divided between North and South along the 17th parallel. In this war the French losses were 35,000 killed and 48,000 wounded. The campaign repays study. What stand out are the hesitation, vacillation, lack of clear political purpose, and the constant political and military interference on the part of the home government in Paris. It also highlights the utter incompetence and arrogant blindness of the French military command set-up in Indo-China, which conducted the war with a complete disregard for local conditions. The final disaster was the surrender of the French garrison of Dien Bien Phu on 6th May 1954, which was the death blow to the French empire, and threw that area open to the cold war. The lesson for the present is – do not hold an Asian enemy in contempt. There is an interesting book on the subject by a French author, Jules Roy, *The Battle of Dien Bien Phu*. When Roy returned to Hanoi in 1963, the Vietminh commander General Giap, said to him: 'You were defeated by yourselves.' That is very true.

And now the United States is fighting the same sort of war in the same country. The French realized in 1954 that they had lost their Indo-China war; at the time of writing, in 1967, the Americans have yet to be persuaded that they cannot win their Vietnam conflict on the battlefield. The best summing-up of the war in Vietnam which I have seen was written by Correlli Barnett in *Punch* of 1st March 1967.

There is no doubt that the rebellions in Indonesia, Malaya and Indo-China were communist-inspired. In 1950 a good example occurred in Korea of the communist method in Asia passing from the stage of supporting colonial rebellions to that of armed aggression by satellites. On the 25th July 1950 the Russian-trained North Korean army crossed the 38th parallel and invaded South Korea, from which country American forces had recently been withdrawn. In some ways the Korean war was a limited war, localized in that country. Although Chinese forces intervened later in the year, as the Peking government had warned Washington they would if United States troops crossed the 38th parallel, Chinese territory to the north of the Yalu was ruled 'out of bounds' to all United Nations forces, land and air. The Korean war did not end until July 1953; the total Allied casualties in killed, wounded, missing and prisoners were some 400,000. The Korean conflict led to the Western nations drawing closer together; it also led directly to the arming of Western Germany; a wave of fear swept over Europe.

In this close-knit world there is always a danger that war anywhere might spread and involve the whole world, and become total. Many people put forward proposals for disarmament. But all such proposals depend on a degree of confidence and trust between nations which does not exist. Nothing has happened since the end of the 1939/45 war to suggest that an enemy would refrain from taking advantage of a nation's military weakness – as enemies have always done throughout recorded history. Therefore military planning must continue, being directed to *preventing* war. One has a feeling today that there is a lack of long-term strategy; responsible leaders, and their officials, are preoccupied in coping with the complexity of day-to-day affairs with the result that too often short-term improvizations masquerade as policy.

Put simply, the issue is this: Is it possible to find some way by which states with different ideological doctrines and social systems can live peacefully together without interfering with each other's affairs ? This *could* be achieved given wise leadership on the part of both sides – East and West. But it is *not* possible so long as each side thinks the other is going to attack it, and so long as each side mounts threats of nuclear destruction at the other. It is *not* possible until the fear, suspicion, and mistrust each side has of the other are removed.

Political leaders must face up to practical realities. The greatest danger is to be a slave
to preconceived ideas and slogans of the past. For instance it is highly illogical, indeed an
illusion, to think as follows:

> That a united Germany is possible in any future we can foresee. The Russians will never allow a
> nation of 70 million Germans in the middle of Europe, with nuclear launching sites on the Polish
> border.
>
> That we can solve the German problem without first solving the European security problem.
>
> That the true government of China is in Formosa.
>
> That we can move towards a more peaceful world without bringing the biggest nation in the
> world to the conference table – China.

I must be honest in defining my own thinking about world peace. After serving for
ten years in the Western Defence Organization, I reached the conclusion that there
could not be any sound peace in this distracted world until the armed forces of all
nations could be got back into their own territories. This thinking was confirmed when I
withdrew from active employment in NATO in 1958, and was free to visit political and
military leaders in non-aligned countries and in the eastern bloc. And I said as much in a
book published in 1961, *The Path to Leadership*. Now I am not sure.

The trouble is that the two sides, East and West, have got into a log-jam and cannot
get clear. Some have the hope that one day a stage will be reached in the cold war when
one side will surrender and peace can be agreed. Prolonged thinking has made me
realize that this hope is a delusion – based on a misunderstanding of the nature of
international relations. Agreements and conventions, even wars and disputes, are like
passing milestones; they mark only stages along the road in international affairs. The
present confrontation between the ideologies of the free world and the communist is
not one of limited duration; it is a continuing struggle, sometimes diffuse and unob-
trusive and at other times very much in focus, which will go on for a generation or longer.
Like domestic problems, it will not suddenly disappear, and it is not likely to be solved
in a conclusive way. It is inseparable from other equally pressing international problems
– such as economic viability and social justice. We must reject any solution to our
problems of today which is based exclusively on *winning* the cold war. I do not believe
that total victory in that sense is possible. But by the patient exercise of diplomacy, and
by the determination to break down suspicion, fear and even hatred, the mutual relation-
ships between different social systems and ideologies can be made less liable to erupt
into war and more consistent with a true meaning of peaceful co-existence. There has
been a tendency in recent years in this direction, but not enough sincerity was behind it,
no determination to end the conflict. All will agree on one point: a permanent state of
peaceless co-existence will merely bring misery to millions of decent people, and must
therefore be prevented.

In the next chapter I will discuss the terrific problems of the nuclear age and the need
for a basic reorganization of armed forces.

24   The Nuclear Age

We must now examine more closely the nuclear deterrent which is what prevents all-out war today between the great powers. Many people, maybe, do not understand the power and implications of nuclear weapons, and in particular the hydrogen bomb. Let us consider the matter, to see if we can discover what policies are best suited to enable mankind to live peacefully on the earth.

Work on the theory of nuclear physics has been carried out by scientists for many years, but we need not go farther back than the early 1940's. The production of an atomic bomb would obviously give the Allies an advantage in the 1939/45 war; it was known in 1940 that German scientists were working on the project. Very secret work was pushed ahead urgently by British and American scientists, and it was agreed in 1943 by Roosevelt and Churchill that all research and development should be carried out in the United States because that country was beyond the range of German bombing. The first live test of an atomic bomb was made in New Mexico on the morning of 16th July 1945 and was completely successful. The German war was by then over, but the war against Japan remained.

The Potsdam Conference had opened in Berlin on 15th July, and the news of the successful test was received by the American delegation on the afternoon of the 16th; Churchill was at once informed – and he told me in the strictest secrecy. The question then arose as to whether Stalin should be told; some discussion took place, it being finally agreed he should be – by Truman – and this was done on the evening of 24th July. Stalin displayed little interest; of course he may have known all about it from the Russian secret service network, but this is pure speculation.

It was agreed unanimously by the British and American delegations that the bomb should be used against the Japanese. Churchill wrote in *The Second World War*, vol. VI:

> We seemed suddenly to have become possessed of a merciful abridgement of the slaughter in the East and of a far happier prospect in Europe. There was unanimous, automatic, unquestioned agreement around our table; nor did I hear the slightest suggestion that we should do otherwise.

In spite of this agreement by the British, American and Russian delegations at the Potsdam Conference, many people, including myself, considered it was unnecessary to use the bomb against Japan – because that nation had begun to sue for peace some weeks before. In any case, conventional bombs had done such a thorough job of destruction in Japan that little 'will' to continue the hopeless struggle was left in the Japanese people. However it was so used – the first atomic bomb being dropped on Hiroshima on 6th

August 1945, and the second on Nagasaki on 8th August. Six days later the 1939/45 war was over.

But the scientists continued their work to develop an even more powerful bomb. An underwater explosion took place at Bikini in the South Pacific in 1946, and in August that year an Atomic Energy Commission was established by Congress. The first H-bomb explosion took place in the Pacific in 1952, and three more at the same site in March and April 1954. Later, in September 1954, a Japanese fisherman died from jaundice brought on by radiation sickness caused by exposure to 'fall-out' – and public opinion throughout the world became alarmed, demanding a suspension of testing in the atmosphere – and this was agreed, in 1958.

We now come to a most interesting situation. In March 1962 President Kennedy announced that the United States would resume nuclear testing in the atmosphere because Russia had broken the then existing moratorium. The president's statement contained the following paragraph:

> We must test in the atmosphere to permit the development of those more advanced concepts and more effective, efficient weapons which, in the light of Soviet tests, are deemed essential to our security. Nuclear weapon technology is still a constantly changing field. If our weapons are to be more secure, more flexible in their use and more selective in their impact – if we are to be alert to new break-throughs, to experiment with new designs – if we are to maintain our scientific momentum and leadership – then our weapons progress must not be limited to theory or to the confines of laboratories or caves.

If this statement has validity, and I personally reckon it has, it is of interest to consider why President Kennedy agreed that the United States would join with Britain and Russia in signing the 'Treaty for a Partial Nuclear Test Ban' in the following year, July 1963, (the word 'Partial' was included because it was agreed that underground tests could continue). We shall probably never know what was in the president's mind because he was assassinated on 22nd November 1963; and Khrushchev fell from power one year after that – 14th October 1964. The Treaty was subsequently signed by many nations, but not by France or China – the only other countries with a nuclear strike potential.

Russia was not far behind the United States in developing nuclear weapons; Russian scientists had exploded their first atomic bomb in 1949, and had the H-bomb in 1953. Maybe the president was anxious about nuclear progress in China. The Chinese had already made certain atomic tests, and on 16th October 1964 – two days after Khrushchev's fall from power – they exploded a low-yield nuclear device in a remote area in Sinkiang. It is therefore not surprising that China did not sign the Test Ban Treaty. (The Chinese exploded a second nuclear device in 1965, and two more in 1966, May and December, both of which contained thermo-nuclear material.)

We should now consider the H-bomb in its relation to warfare. It is not merely just another weapon with greater destructive power. There are today in existence delivery systems which can take a bomb at ever increasing speeds to any target in the world; this amazing combination of firepower and mobility has revolutionized warfare. In bygone days offensive action to capture or destroy a military objective took many weeks; today, one single H-bomb could do the job in a fraction of a second. Of course no H-bomb has been dropped in wartime but tests have proved it to be unbelievably powerful. The total weight of bombs dropped by the Allies during the 1939/45 war both in the European and Pacific theatres was about $3\frac{1}{2}$ million tons; expressed in nuclear parlance this figure would be 3.5 megatons – which is less than the yield of one medium-sized H-bomb or missile warhead. We had better get an idea of the explosive power of a single multi-megaton H-bomb, using the figures published by the Atomic Energy Commission.

We will assume that the weapon has struck the centre of a large city. The explosion produces a crater about 350 feet deep, and 3,700 feet in diameter. Beyond this enormous crater a 'lip' of radio-active debris extends outwards for approximately 1,800 feet, and to a height of nearly 100 feet. The resulting fireball is about 4 miles in diameter and temperatures within it are around 8,000 degrees Fahrenheit. All matter within that area, living and inanimate, has been pulverized, and lingering radio-activity will make it impossible to rebuild this area – certainly within fifty years. Large buildings within 6 miles from where the bomb hit the centre of the city would be nothing more than shells of rubble and collapsing roofs and walls. In addition to the blast effects which have caused this damage, the terrific heat has started fires; widespread devastation, raging fires, electrical short circuits, and millions of casualties extend to some 18 miles from the centre of the city. Heavy radio-active fall-out starts raining down on this area within 20 minutes after detonation of the bomb, and it would last up to half-an-hour before subsiding. And for 48 hours after the time of burst, a lethal fall-out pattern some 18 miles wide would extend downwind for about 130 miles – resulting in further heavy casualties. All this would be caused by one single H-bomb, according to the Atomic Energy Commission of the U.S.A.

This, then, is the weapon the fear of which has caused the Eastern bloc to refrain from over-stepping the mark in the cold war and by so doing bringing on all-out nuclear war between East and West. It is the weapon which the Western world hopes will be a sufficient deterrent against any such action by the communist world. No matter how successful a surprise attack might be, an aggressor could not escape a considerable degree of retaliation. The stakes in all-out nuclear war are too high to warrant a gamble in the matter.

Since the Western world has decided to pursue the policy of nuclear deterrence, the first question to ask is – what does one mean by the expression 'a nuclear power'? From the strategical angle a nuclear power can be defined as one which has a minimum nuclear delivery capability, sufficient to deter any aggressor nation which is considering how to strengthen its own position by a sudden knock-out blow. The nation attacked must have the power to hit back, which power by its existence can avert the disaster of war. Hit back to what extent? I would suggest to hit back and utterly destroy an unacceptable number of major cities or vital areas. In the Concise Oxford Dictionary 'to deter' is defined as 'discourage or hinder by fear'.

There are only four powers in the world today which fit this definition: America, Russia, Britain, France. China has the atom bomb, but not the accurate delivery system; she is likely to achieve the fully developed H-bomb and its delivery system in due course – that is, the delivery system to strike at any selected targets in Asia.

The point to understand is that what might deter one nation, for instance, Russia, will not necessarily deter another – say China. Herein lies the 'deterrence dilemma'. The problem is to know exactly what a communist nuclear power would consider unaccept-able or unprofitable, and what is required from a nation in the Western world to convince the communist nation that aggression would gain less and cost more than it would be willing to accept. The Cuba crisis of 1962 gave a hint, but there is no conclusive answer to this question.

Furthermore, no means has yet been found to restrain satisfactorily the spread of nuclear weapons through disarmament, and thus provide by a different means the guarantees for a reasonable degree of national security which arms can no longer bestow. The United Nations has merely become a mirror of a divided world; as at present organized it can never be more than a forum for discussion; it has become a battleground of the cold war rather than the resolver of it.

War cannot abolish itself. In the simplest terms, nuclear weapons have given mankind a choice between either abolishing war or being abolished by it. *What has got to be achieved is a resolution of the political and ideological differences which divide the world*; unless this is first done, nuclear disarmament is likely to increase the likelihood of 'conventional' war. The crunch might come when a nuclear power waging a conventional war against another nuclear power finds itself likely to lose. Would it then, as a last resort, try to snatch victory by using a nuclear weapon at a decisive moment?

We must not run away from this question. It is probably best answered by posing another: Is it likely that in limited war a nation would resort to the use of relatively small-scale nuclear weapons? Today there are only two nations which could produce such weapons, the United States and Russia; later France and China may have the required *small-scale* nuclear capability – but not for many years. Both the United States and Russia could provide the weapons for smaller nations with which they were in sympathy, but to do so would involve the risk that weapons of greater yield might be demanded; the conflict would then expand rapidly and beyond control, and finally might escalate into all-out nuclear war between the great power blocs – the very kind of war the West is trying to deter, and which the East does not really want.

In my opinion the answer to the question is 'No'. No nation, whether in the Western world or communist world, would risk using any nuclear weapons in a limited conventional-type war unless it possessed a massive and credible war-winning nuclear capability for use should the conflict widen. The Western world has such nuclear power; so has Russia, the most powerful nation in the communist world. Neither nation will risk the consequences of using it, because the retaliatory damage to its own country would be too terrible to contemplate and neither could be certain of winning. Both sides will maintain the massive nuclear capability until statesmen can bring about some degree of peaceful co-existence.

The crisis over Cuba in 1962 may well be considered here. Photographic reconnaissance over the island made it clear to President Kennedy of the United States that Russian missile sites were being installed, thus imposing a nuclear threat to America. He decided to lay on a quarantine against arms shipments to Cuba, using sea and air power. If the Russian leader, Khrushchev, had chosen to start a nuclear war over the Cuban issue, the integrated war plans of the Strategic Air Command of the U.S.A. together with the navy's Polaris submarines would have brought about the destruction of the Soviet war machine. President Kennedy told Khrushchev to take his missiles back to Russia – or else! The Russian leader did the only thing he could – he took his missiles back to Russia. It was a classic example of 'dynamic deterrence', operated by a courageous leader. It succeeded because the United States had a proper combination of the three vital factors needed in such an emergency – military strength, courageous diplomacy, and public unity.

Unfortunately, we are faced with the ironical fact that while nuclear war seems capable of destroying society, the means to avert it consist in building up the means to wage it. What we must hope for is some measure of arms control; pending agreement on this problem, prevention of nuclear war will depend on the maintenance of a balance of political and military forces between East and West. This balance can be easily upset – a new weapon, a new defence system, a new method of attack, or any striking innovation which could disrupt the balance and give an advantage to one side.

Some have said that the chances of preventing nuclear war lie in the creation of some supernational authority or world government to control relations between states. The difficulties in any such solution to the problem are insuperable. The most which might be possible at present is to prevent the proliferation of nuclear weapons beyond the four nuclear powers I have named. (But even that will prove difficult because it has been stated by one Western political leader that only by being a nuclear power can a nation demand a seat at 'the top table'. Since every sovereign state wants to be at the top table, that statement was not helpful.)

So long as peaceful partnership between the nations of East and West is not possible, the only sound strategy for national security on the part of major powers is the maintenance of both deterrent and conventional forces. This, of course, makes the respite unstable and uncertain. And meanwhile scientists on both sides pursue their investigations to produce even more powerful weapons, while service chiefs wrestle with the almost insoluble problem of designing a strategy for their deployment in the nuclear age. The prospects for nuclear disarmament are dim; the destruction of all nuclear weapons would not destroy the knowledge of how to make them. As one writer has put it: 'Pandora's box, having once been opened, can hardly be closed.'

When all is said and done, it is only the statesmen of the world who, backed by the resolution of an informed public opinion, can find the path along which the world may escape disaster.

Statesmen have to learn by experience, and often by bitter experience – as has been the case in the mid-twentieth century. In 1943 the policy of 'unconditional surrender' reared its ugly head and committed the Western world to a policy which has 'boomeranged' on us all – although it suited the communist world very well at the time. The true object in war must be a secure and lasting peace; this will not be brought about if a nation or group of nations go all out for a complete military victory and slam the door on any idea of a negotiated peace – which was what happened in the 1939/45 war, and also in the 1914/18 war.

We must not rely on diplomatic relations standing still in the nuclear age. One has only to compare the relations between Germany, the British Commonwealth, the U.S.A., Russia, and China in 1941, 1950, and the late 1960's, to realize that the most unlikely and kaleidoscopic change is possible in the years which lie ahead.

It is difficult to prophesy with any certainty how armed forces are likely to develop in the nuclear age. But the following principles seem to me to stand out, and against that background I see the military future.

The progress of science has revolutionized strategical and tactical conceptions during and since the 1939/45 war. It is anybody's guess what the scientists may produce for us in the future; their contribution in the realm of research and development during the past twenty-five years has been fantastic. If progress in world disarmament makes any headway and defence budgets are reduced, the money and manpower allotted to the scientists must still be maintained.

It would be dangerous to reach definite conclusions for more than, say, fifteen years ahead. But the impact of science on warfare and on the organization of armed forces in the mid-twentieth century has been tremendous, and this impact has caused the big war, the all-out war with both sides using nuclear weapons, to be hardly likely. No nation will care to overstep the mark in the cold war, and by so doing commit suicide. During the next fifteen years, up to about the early 1980's, the military emphasis will be on small wars, limited geographically, and in which only so-called conventional weapons will be used; such conflicts will take place in the eastern hemisphere rather than in the western, and possibly in Africa.

The most important development in modern war has been the upsurge of naval and air power. It was stated in Chapter 1 that from ancient times the nation which has had control of the seas has, in the end, always prevailed – because the enemy was thereby confined to a land strategy. Air power, when developed to its full potential, has tremendously confirmed this truth; the skilful combination of sea and air power is a battle-winning factor of the first importance, and the same principle applies to land and air forces.

In any military organization there is no surer way to disaster than to take what has been done for many years, and to go on doing it – *the problem having changed*. This principle indicates that seapower will in future be operated differently from in the past, because of the impact of science on warfare. The day of the big warship is surely over. Navies will go increasingly under the sea, their main armament being the submarine – the Polaris, and the hunter-killer. If the Polaris submarine can gain greater depth than at present, it will be impossible to locate it by any means known to science at present. Surface ships will increasingly become fast, small vessels capable of launching missiles. Strike aircraft will give way to missiles. Until suitable V.T.O.L. aircraft capable of being operated from small ships can be produced, which is a vital necessity, aircraft carriers will be required; in the early 1980's the large carrier may well disappear from the navies of world powers.

The greatest asset of air power is its flexibility. Within the range limitations of their aircraft, air forces are able without change of base to be switched quickly from one objective to another throughout the area of operations. The whole weight of the available air power can thus be used in selected areas in turn. It follows that control of all available air power, land and sea based, must be centralized, and command exercised through one channel.

The more I consider the problem of defence the more I reach the conclusion that the answer lies basically in the ability to be able to use sea and air power freely, and to confine the enemy to a land strategy. Only in this way will the maximum flexibility be possible. The Western Alliance, to which my nation belongs, must plan to be so well and flexibly deployed that it can deal quickly and effectively with all situations, including the unlikely and the unexpected – in fact, an elastic deployment based on a maritime strategy. This demands unity and leadership. When planning defence, and deciding the best organization for armed forces, a *long-term* strategy is essential. I am doubtful whether the West is best served by a multitude of fixed land bases. They may in a crisis suddenly be found to be facing in the wrong direction. They tend to cramp force-mobility. They are hostages to fortune. Those which are considered essential must not be in territory where the local inhabitants are none too friendly, or may not be friendly for long – and in this last connection such bases make good propaganda for enemies of the West. Armies must go to sea. Where small forces are concerned the army must be sea-mobile, and tactically air-mobile with helicopters for movement, supply, and ground support.

The above points are merely the outline of a very big problem, the solution to which lies, I believe, in the general direction I have indicated. But when all is said and done, it is essential to remember that the true and ultimate strength of a nation does not lie in its armed forces, nor in its gold and dollar reserves. It lies in the national character, in its people – in their virility, in their willingness to work, in their understanding of the truth that if they want prosperity and economic strength they must get it for themselves or else go without it.

In 1946 I wrote these words:

> The most important single factor in war is morale. It is impossible to prosecute a war for long if the will of the people to fight is lacking; in such a case the national war machine will not function. In battle it is morale which counts; no strategy can succeed without it. Once morale has gone, defeat is inevitable.

These words are as true today as when they were written. I would add only five words – they apply equally in peace.

This brings me to the end of my thoughts on war. The Epilogue – the Ideal of Peace – remains.

25   Epilogue – The Ideal of Peace

When reading my Bible one night I came across the following in Jeremiah:

> From the prophet even unto the priest every one dealeth falsely saying, Peace, peace – when there is no peace.

These words were probably written nearly 3,000 years ago; they apply equally today. Many who read this book will have had their fill of war, and know how tempting it is to paper over the cracks in the concord of the world.

Something seems to have gone wrong in the world in which we live. Notwithstanding the progress in civilization, and the longing for peace in the minds of all decent people over the past 2,000 years or more, mankind has not been able to prevent the twentieth century from becoming the bloodiest and most turbulent period in recorded history. During the years of the Nazi regime in Germany things happened which could not find a parallel in the most debased days of the Roman or Mongol empires, crimes were committed which most people could not imagine – unless they had seen a place like Belsen, which I entered on the day of its liberation by my troops in April 1945. The wholesale liquidation of civilians was unprecedented.

A study of the German assault on Russia which began in June 1941 reveals scenes where 'the septic violence of German Nazism festered openly'. Mass murder, deportations, deliberate starvation in prisoner-of-war cages, the burning alive of school children, target practice on civilian hospitals – such atrocities were common under the warlike passions of German brutality in the Russian-German conflict.

All these things were the responsibility of one evil man – Hitler. Millions starved and died while he and his followers feasted. He parted the wife from her husband, the maid from her lover, the child from its parents. If he had lived he could never have given back what he had taken from those he had so cruelly wronged – years of life and health and happiness, wives and children, loved ones and friends. If he had had ten thousand lives they could not atone, even though each was dragged out to the bitter end in the misery which he meted out to others. The harnessing of the whole German national life to war ended, as it must, in the complete destruction of the vanquished state; and the problem then arose of feeding a starving nation, as I know very well because that problem became my responsibility in the British zone of 20 million Germans. Things were much the same in the Far East with the Japanese – whose brutality equalled that of the Germans.

Is it possible that such things could happen again? Can others such as Hitler arise? Are we to reach the conclusion that modern war between nations is merely a reversion to total barbarism ? These questions will have to be faced by responsible political leaders. My own view is that a study of warfare over the ages, with the many interlocking political and economic elements which erupt in armed conflict, will help to show us what to do to prevent it and find the answer we have not yet got.

We know that on the physical and material plane the keys of peace are in the hands of strength; the strong man armed keeps his goods in peace. But on the spiritual plane there is a stronger than he. The big battalions do not always win. Great occupying armies cannot for ever hold in check that which moves in the minds of people. The study of warfare brings to light spiritual values significant for the future.

What of the future ? This is in the hands of youth, and these hands are at present unsteady. Youth is saying: 'Our fathers have made such a mess of things, we must break away and go on our own and do better.'

What better to do, they do not know; they are all at sea. They tend to move towards materialism – 'Gather ye rose-buds while ye may' – and think that devotion to peace as the condition of a pleasant, happy life was what their fathers lacked. But their peace-loving fathers fought for freedom and justice, without which the peace of cowed and enslaved peoples would have been hell on earth. The peace we now enjoy is the peace of victory over the beast in men, and this victory will not survive if the virtues which gained and sustain it are lost. What worth is peace without freedom, or freedom without justice between one man and another ? The ideal of peace must not walk too closely with the temptress to a slack and easy life. We must marry the ideal of peace to the practice of virtue.

A nation must stand for something of spiritual and not only material value, and the key to the decline of the spirit is in religion. There is always a choice to be made, and for the British people I believe the Kingdom of God to be the right choice, and that those who choose it will never lack support – both human and divine.

I wrote this in my *Memoirs*:

> I do not believe that today a commander can inspire great armies, or single units, or even individual men, unless he has a proper sense of religious truth . . . All leadership is based on the spiritual quality, the power to inspire others to follow.

But this lead will be of no avail unless others are inspired to accept it. Much good as well as much evil is released in war. When men are inspired to offer themselves to a high and noble cause, the hardships of war draw out of them their best qualities – comradeship, endurance, courage, self-sacrifice, willingness to die. This was expressed in a poem found in the Western Desert during the onward march of the Eighth Army after Alamein:

> Help me, O God, when Death is near
> To mock the haggard face of fear,
> That when I fall – if fall I must –
> My soul may triumph in the Dust.

To that spirit I have unveiled many memorials. When I unveiled the Alamein Memorial in the Western Desert of Egypt in October 1954 and gazed over the scene, the crosses standing row after row, each one a life dear to someone at home, I could not but think that there is no merit in needless loss of life – indeed, nothing but shame and folly. The lives of his men should be precious to any commander in battle; they are not to be risked without cause, nor used when other means will serve.

But there are times in war when men must do a hazardous job, when a position must be held or taken whatever the cost, and when success and a nation's fate depend on the courage, determination and tenacity of officers and men. Then those who set duty before self give their lives to see the task committed to them through to its completion; they win the day and, in our Christian faith, a higher honour than mortal man can give. It is a free choice. And for the immortal virtue of that choice, the crosses stand – whatever the religion, faith, or form of worship.

Through the mists of years, through the gulfs of twilight, could we but listen hard enough, we might catch some message of hope and encouragement from those who gave their lives – a message which would help us to create a better world than that in which they lived:

> We are the Dead . . . .
> . . . .
> To you from failing hands we throw
> The torch; be yours to hold it high.
> If ye break faith with us who die,
> We shall not sleep . . . .

There must be no broken faith with the torch of Justice and Freedom which they threw to us.

The true soldier is the enemy of the beast in man and of none other; and it is a soldier's hope that one day will come a golden sunset when the Last Post will be sounded over enmity and strife, and a glorious sunrise when Reveille will waken the nations of the world to an era of goodwill and peace.

SELECTED BIBLIOGRAPHY

This list is necessarily limited to a few of the more important books used in the research for this book. Many general historical works, studies of individual campaigns and biographies of great commanders have had to be omitted.

GENERAL WORKS

R. A. Preston, S. F. Wise, H. O. Werner, *Men in Arms: A History of Warfare and its Interrelationships with Western Society*. 1956. (Has extensive bibliography)

Hans Delbrueck, *Geschichte der Kriegskunst im Rahmen der politischen Geschichte*. 7 v. 1900–36

Gaston Bouthoux, *Les Guerres: Eléments de Polemologie*. 1951

S. Andrzejewski, *Military Organisation and Society*. 1954

Konrad Lorenz, *On Aggression*. 1966

J. F. C. Fuller, *The Decisive Battles of the Western World and their Influence upon History*. 3 v. 1954–6

Cyril Falls (ed.), *Great Military Battles*. 1964

Oliver Warner (ed.), *Great Sea Battles*. 1963

E. M. Lloyd, *A Review of the History of Infantry*. 1908

G. T. Denison, *History of Cavalry*. 1913

J. W. Fortescue, *A History of the British Army*. 7 v. 1899–1912

Charles de Gaulle, *France and her Army*. 1945

C. H. Hermann, *Deutsche Militärgeschichte*. 1966

T. R. Phillips (ed.), *Roots of Strategy*. 1943
Incorporates texts of:
Sun Tzu, *The Art of War*
Vegetius, *The Military Institutions of the Romans*
Maurice de Saxe, *My Reveries upon the Art of War*
Frederick the Great, *Military Instructions for the Generals*
Napoleon, *Military Maxims*

E. M. Earle (ed.), *Makers of Modern Strategy: Military Thought from Machiavelli to Hitler*. 1948

Michael Howard (ed.), *The Theory and Practice of War*. 1965

Karl von Clausewitz, *On War* (trans. by Angus Malcolm in preparation)

B. H. Liddell Hart, *Strategy: The Indirect Approach*. New ed. 1954

A. H. Burne, *The Art of War on Land*. 1944

A. T. Mahan, *The Influence of Sea Power upon History, 1660–1783*. 1890

S. W. Roskill, *The Strategy of Seapower*. 1962

Michael Lewis, *The History of the British Navy*. 1959

W. L. Clowes, *History of the Royal Navy*. 7 v. 1897–1903

Otto Heilbrunn, *Warfare in the Enemy's Rear*. 1963

B. H. Liddell Hart, *Great Captains Unveiled*. 1927

John Laffin, *Links of Leadership*. 1966

Jac Weller, *Weapons and Tactics*. 1966

Dudley Pope, *Guns*. 1965

Philip Cowburn, *The Warship in History*. 1965

Sidney Toy, *A History of Fortification*. 1955

ANCIENT WARFARE

H. H. Turney-High, *Primitive War*. 1949

Yigael Yadin, *The Art of Warfare in Biblical Lands*. 1963

F. E. Adcock, *The Greek and Macedonian Art of War*. 1957

J. F. C. Fuller, *The Generalship of Alexander the Great*. 1958

W. L. Rogers, *Greek and Roman Naval Warfare*. 1937

F. E. Adcock, *The Roman Art of War*. 1940

H. M. D. Parker, *The Roman Legions*. 1928

R. E. Oakshott, *The Archaeology of Weapons*. 1960

W. L. Rogers, *Naval Warfare under Oars from the Fourth to the Sixteenth Centuries*. 1939

MEDIEVAL WARFARE

Charles Oman, *A History of the Art of War in the Middle Ages*. 2 v. 1924

Ferdinand Lot, *L'Art Militaire et les Armées au Moyen Age*. 2 v. 1946

J. B. Glubb, *The Great Arab Conquests*. 1963

Johannes Brønsted, *The Vikings*. 1960

C. H. Haskins, *The Normans in European History*. 1916

Henry Loyn, *The Norman Conquest*. 1965

R. C. Smail, *Crusading Warfare*. 1956

H. W. L. Hime, *The Origin of Artillery*. 1915

H. W. L. Hime, *Gunpowder and Ammunition*. 1904

A. H. Burne, *The Crécy War*. 1955

A. H. Burne, *The Agincourt War*. 1956

Edouard Perroy, *The Hundred Years' War*. 1951

EUROPEAN WARFARE

Charles Oman, *A History of the Art of War in the XVI Century*. 1937

F. L. Taylor, *The Art of War in Italy, 1494–1529*. 1921

C. M. Cipolla, *Guns and Sails in the Early Phase of European Expansion, 1400–1700*. 1965

Geoffrey Callender and F. H. Hinsley, *The Naval Side of British History, 1485–1945*. 1952

Michael Lewis, *The Spanish Armada*. 1960

D. M. Vaughan, *Europe and the Turk, 1350–1700*. 1954

H. Inalcik, 'Ottoman Methods of Conquest', *Studia Islamica*, 11. 1954

Michael Roberts, *The Military Revolution 1560–1660*. 1956

A. H. Burne and P. Young, *The Great Civil War*. 1959

C. H. Firth, *Cromwell's Army*. 1902

D. G. Browne, *The Floating Bulwark*. 1963

C. T. Atkinson, *Marlborough and the Rise of the British Army*. 1921

R. E. Scouller, *The Armies of Queen Anne*. 1966

G. A. Craig, *The Politics of the Prussian Army, 1640–1945*. 1955

J. S. Corbett, *England in the Seven Years' War*. 1907

Piers Mackesy, *The War for America, 1775–83*. 1964

Spenser Wilkinson, *The French Army before Napoleon*. 1915

J. L. A. Colin (ed.), *La Tactique et la Discipline dans les Armées de la Révolution*. 1902

D. G. Chandler, *The Campaigns of Napoleon*. 1967

Antony Brett-James, *Wellington at War 1794–1815*. 1961

Jac Weller, *Wellington in the Peninsular*. 1962

Cyril Falls, *The Art of War*. 1961

B. H. Liddell Hart, *The Ghost of Napoleon*. 1933

A. T. Mahan, *The Influence of Sea Power upon the French Revolution and Empire 1793–1812*. 1892

Oliver Warner, *Portrait of Lord Nelson*. 1958

Michael Lewis, *A Social History of the Navy, 1793–1815*. 1960

EASTERN WARFARE

Harold Lamb, *The March of the Barbarians*. 1941

Jadunath Sarkar, *Military History of India*. 1960

V. R. R. Dikshitar, *War in Ancient India*. 1948

Adam Watson, *The War of the Goldsmith's Daughter: The Moslem Conquest of Southern India*. 1964

William Irvine, *The Army of the Indian Moghuls*. 1903

Surendranath Sen, *Military System of the Marathas*. 1928

Sidney Toy, *The Fortified Cities of India*. 1965

WARFARE 1815/1945

Cyril Falls, *A Hundred Years of War*. 1953

W. C. Macleod, *The American Indian Frontier*. 1928

Henri Jomini, *Summary of the Art of War*. 1837

Cecil Woodham-Smith, *The Reason Why*. 1953

D. R. Morris, *The Washing of the Spears: Rise and Fall of the Zulu Nation*. 1965

Walter Goerlitz, *History of the German General Staff, 1657–1945*. 1953

Michael Howard, *The Franco-Prussian War*. 1961

Bruce Catton, *The Centennial History of the Civil War*. 3 v. 1962–6

Rupert Furneaux, *The Siege of Plevna*, 1958

Brian Bond (ed.), *Victorian Military Campaigns*. 1967

Rayne Kruger, *Goodbye Dolly Gray: The Story of the Boer War*. 1959

Reginald Hargreaves, *Red Sun Rising: The Siege of Port Arthur*. 1962

Richard Hough, *The Fleet that had to Die*. 1958

Cyril Falls, *The First World War*. 1960

B. H. Liddell Hart, *The War in Outline 1914–1918*. 1965

A. J. P. Taylor, *The First World War*. 1963

W. S. Churchill, *The World Crisis 1911–1918*. 1931

Corelli Barnett, *The Sword-bearers*. 1963

John Terraine, *The Western Front 1914–1918*. 1964

B. H. Liddell Hart, *The Tanks*. 2 v. 1959

A. J. Marder, *From the Dreadnought to Scapa Flow*. 3 v. 1961–6

W. S. Churchill, *The Second World War*. 6 v. 1948–53

Peter Young, *World War 1939–45*. 1966

H. A. Jacobsen and J. Rohwer (ed.), *Decisive Battles of World War II: The German View*. 1965

F. W. von Mellenthin, *Panzer Battles 1939–45*. 1955

Montgomery of Alamein, *El Alamein to the River Sangro*. 1946

Montgomery of Alamein, *Normandy to the Baltic*. 1946

Chester Wilmot, *The Struggle for Europe*. 1952

Telford Taylor, *The March of Conquest*. 1959

D. Fedotoff-White, *The Growth of the Red Army*. 1944

Basil Collier, *The Battle of Britain*. 1962

Noble Frankland, *The Bombing Offensive against Germany*. 1965

S. W. Roskill, *The Navy at War*. 1960

Donald Macintyre, *The Battle of the Pacific*. 1966

William Slim, *Defeat into Victory*. 1956

ACKNOWLEDGMENTS

Quotations on the following pages are quoted from the sources listed and are reproduced by courtesy of the respective publishers:

p. 113 Tacitus, *Germania*. Loeb edition, trs. Maurice Hutton. Harvard University Press, 1914

p. 114 Tacitus, *Annals*. Trs. Michael Grant. Penguin Books, 1963

pp. 177, 192–3 Sidney Toy, *A History of Fortification*. Heinemann Educational Books, 1955

pp. 473–5 M. Gerster, *Die Schwaben an der Ancre*. Trans. in A. H. Farrar-Hockley, *The Somme*. Batsford, 1964

p. 566 Gerald Kersh, 'A Soldier – His Prayer', included in *Poems from the Desert*. Harrap, 1944

Reference was made to the following works in the preparation of some of the weapon drawings: *Weapons: A Pictorial History* by Edwin Tunis, illustrated by Edwin Tunis. The World Publishing Company, Cleveland and New York, 1954

The Age of Firearms: A Pictorial History by Robert Held, illustrated by Nancy Held. Harper, 1957

ACKNOWLEDGMENTS FOR ILLUSTRATIONS

The producers wish to express their thanks to the trustees and staffs of the libraries, galleries and museums, and to the individuals, who have allowed objects from their collections to be reproduced in this book, and to the photographers who have supplied copyright illustrations, as listed below.

Page COLOUR PLATES

49 Copy from the rock temple of Ramses II at Beit El-Wali in Nubia. British Museum

50 Wooden figures from the tomb of Masahti, Assiut. Cairo Museum. Photo Roger Wood

75 Spink and Son Ltd, London

76 One of four mounted Amazons on the lid of a mixing bowl. From Capua. British Museum

173 Bibliothèque de Bayeux. Photo Michael Holford

174 Photo Alistair Duncan

199 The scene is intended to represent the battle of Hastings. MS Bodley 968. Bodleian Library, Oxford (Bodleian colour slide B.10)

200 The scene is intended to represent the battle of Issus. Pinakothek, Munich

225 Galleria di Capodimonte, Naples

226 National Maritime Museum, Greenwich

251 National Maritime Museum, Greenwich

252 Heeresgeschichtliches Museum, Vienna

277 Galleria Corsini, Florence. Photo Scala

278 National Maritime Museum, Greenwich

303 His Grace the Duke of Marlborough

304 By gracious permission of Her Majesty the Queen

341 National Maritime Museum, Greenwich

342-3 Musée de Versailles

344 Musée de Versailles. Photo Giraudon

381 Victoria and Albert Museum, London

382 Victoria and Albert Museum, London

407 Victoria and Albert Museum, London

408 Victoria and Albert Museum, London

421 Musée de Chateaudun

422-3 The Regimental Lieutenant-Colonel, Coldstream Guards

424 Gettysburg National Military Park

521 National Maritime Museum, Greenwich

522-3 Imperial War Museum, London

524 Department of the Army, Washington, D.C. Photo Time Life Inc.

Commissioned photographs in colour have been taken specially for this work by the following photographers: pp. 49, 76, 226, 303, 304, 381, 382, 422–3 Michael Holford; pp. 75, 407, 408, 521

Derrick E. Witty; p. 200 Theodor Heller; p. 225 Angelo Murale; p. 252 Werkstatte Meyer; p. 421 Georges Angeli; p. 424 the Lane Studio

Page MONOCHROME ILLUSTRATIONS

26 *Left to right* Archaeological Museum, Istanbul. Museo Nazionale, Naples; photo Mansell Alinari. Museo Nazionale, Naples; photo Mansell Anderson. Uffizi Gallery, Florence; photo Mansell Alinari. From *Portraits of Emperors and Empresses of Mongol.* From *Denckwürdiger Geschichten;* photo Radio Times Hulton Library. Rainbird Archives. Nationalmuseum, Stockholm. Radio Times Hulton Library. National Portrait Gallery, London. After Kneller, National Portrait Gallery, London. Radio Times Hulton Library. After Reynolds, National Portrait Gallery, London. By Fantin de la Tour, Dresden Gallery; photo Radio Times Hulton Library. By Anton Graff, Schloss Sanssoucci, Potsdam; photo Bildarchiv Foto Marburg. By F. P. Gérard, Musée Condé, Chantilly; photo Giraudon. By L. F. Abbatt, National Portrait Gallery, London. By Goya, National Gallery, London. By Lenbach; photo Mansell Collection. From *Battles of the Nineteenth Century,* 1896

28 Photo J. D. Lajeux from *The Rock Paintings of Tassili,* London, Thames and Hudson, Paris, Editions du Chêne

34 Royal Standard of Ur. British Museum

35 *Left* From Kish. Oriental Institute, University of Chicago. *Right* From the Palace of Nimrud. British Museum. Photo Mansell Collection

37 Stele of the Vultures. Louvre, Paris. Photo Giraudon

40 From the Great Temple at Abu Simbel. Photo Roger Wood

43 Wooden figures from the tomb of Masahti, Assiut. Cairo Museum. Photo Roger Wood

44 From the hypostyle hall in the Ramasseum, Thebes. Photo Roger Wood

Page

53 *Above* From the Palace at Nineveh. Louvre. Photo Bildarchiv Foto Marburg. *Below left* From the great bronze gates of Shalmaneser. British Museum. *Below right* From Nineveh. British Museum. Photo Mansell Collection

54 From Nineveh. British Museum

56 From Nimrud. British Museum. Photo Mansell

58 Kunsthistorisches Museum, Vienna

61 Hirmer Fotoarchiv

62 Frieze at Persepolis. Photo John Donat

66 British Museum

69 British Museum

72 The Alexander Mosaic, from Pompeii. Museo Nazionale, Naples. Photo Alinari-Giraudon

80 *Left* Staatliche Museen zu Berlin. *Right* Sarcophagus of Abdalonymos. Archaeological Museum, Istanbul. Photo Hirmer Fotoarchiv

84 Museo, Magonza. Photo Mansell Alinari

87 Villa Giulia, Rome. Photo Mansell Alinari

92 Soprintendenza alle Antichita della Campania, Naples

104 Museo Capitolino, Rome. Photo Mansell Alinari

106 Vatican Museum

108 Louvre, Paris. Photo Alinari

110 Sousse Museum, Tunisia. Photo Roger Wood

111 Museo Nazionale, Naples. Photo Alinari

112 Column of Marcus Aurelius, Rome. Photo Deutsches Archäologisches Institut, Rome

115 Column of Marcus Aurelius, Rome. Photo Anderson

119 Column of Marcus Aurelius, Rome. Photo Josephine Powell

120 Trajan's Column, Rome. Photo Mansell Alinari

121 Photo J. Allan Cash

128 Persepolis. Photo Josephine Powell

131 Landesmuseum, Halle. Photo Bildarchiv Foto Marburg

134 From Psalterum Aureum, ninth-century. Stiftsbibliothek St Gallen, Switzerland

140 Ivory casket lid, eleventh-century. Treasury of Troyes Cathedral. Photo Hirmer Fotoarchiv

147 From Utrecht Psalter, *c.* 830. Bibliothèque Nationale, Paris. Photo Giraudon

153 *Left* Universitas Oldsaksamling, Oslo. *Right* Lärbro parish, Gotland. Photo ATA

156 Drawing of Duke Robert of Normandy made for the choir windows of St Denis abbey church, 1097. From the Montfaucon Collection, Bibliothèque Nationale, Paris. Photo Bildarchiv Foto Marburg

158 Shrine of Charles, Aachen. Photo Bildarchiv Foto Marburg

162 Bayeux tapestry. Photo Percy Hennell, by courtesy of the Phaidon Press

164 Bayeux tapestry (see p. 162)

168 Photo A. F. Kersting

169 Photo Institut Géographique National

170 From William of Tyre, *History of Outrémer.* Bibliothèque Nationale, Paris

178-9 Linen wall hanging, north Italian fourteenth-century, from the bishop's palace, Sitten (Valais). Historisches Museum, Basel

181 From Matthew Paris, *Chronica Majora, c.* 1250. Corpus Christi College Library, Cambridge

182 Wallace Collection, London. Photo Mansell

185 *Left* Tower of London Armoury. *Right* Schloss Churburg, south Tyrol. Photo V. Oberhammer

187 'The Rout of San Romano' by Paolo Uccello. National Gallery, London

188-9 Casket painting, Florentine school. National Gallery, London

191 From the MS of Walter de Milemete. Christ Church, Oxford

192 Photo Aerofilms

196 *Left* The battle of Granson from the Schodoler Chronicles. Kantonsbibliothek Aarau, Switzerland. *Right* From *Les Chroniques d'Angleterre.* British Museum

202 From Harleian MS 326. British Museum

209 *Left* From MS 5090. Bibliothèque de l'Arsenal, Paris. Photo Bibliothèque Nationale, Paris. *Right* From Flavius Vegetius Renatus, *De Re Milltari,* ed. 1532. British Museum

210 By Juan de Borgogna. Mozarabic chapel, Toledo Cathedral. Photo Foto Mas

214 Sixteenth-century miniature. Musée Condé, Chantilly. Photo Giraudon

215 'Die Schweizerschlacht' by Hans Holbein. Kupferstichkabinett, Oeffentlichen Kunstsammlung, Basel

217 From Mateo Roselli, *La Vie de Ferdinand Ier de Medicis,* engravings by J. Callot. Victoria and Albert Museum, London

221 Sixteenth-century Flemish tapestry. Galleria di Capodimonte, Naples. Photo Mansell Alinari

222 'Schlafender Grabwächter' by Bernhard Strigel. Pinakothek, Munich

228 Photo Aerofilms

229 *Above* From Roselli (see p. 217). *Below* By Hans Sebaldus Beham. Photo Ullstein Bilderdienst

230 *Left* and *middle* By Jacob de Gheyn after Heinrich Goltzius, 1587. *Right* An engraving of 1598

237 From Roselli (see p. 217)

240-1 From P. Ubaldino, *Expeditionis Hispanorum,* 1588. British Museum

242 From Caoursin, *Relation du Siège de Rhodes.* Bibliothèque Nationale, Paris

246 Persian miniature, *c.* 1400. Library of the Palace of Topkapi, Turkey

249 *Above* Reconstruction by Cornelius Gurlitt. Photo Courtauld Institute, London. *Below* Photo Hirmer Fotoarchiv

254 From *Nusretname,* Add MS 22011, 1582. British Museum

255 From Caorsini, *Stabilimenta Rhodiorum Militium,* 1496. Photo Ullstein Bilderdienst

262 Detail from 'The Siege of Breda' by J. Callot, 1637. British Museum (Crookshank Collection)

Page

264 By Jacob Weier. National Gallery, London

267 1 to 10 from Jacob de Gheyn, *The Exercise of Arms for Calivres, Muskettes and Pikes*, 1607. British Museum. 11 from Lodovico Melzo, *Regale Militari . . . della Cavalleria*, 1611. British Museum. 12 from *Kriegskunst zu Pferdt*, 1616

271 Battle of Nördlingen, 1634. Photo Ullstein Bilderdienst

275 By J. v. d. Heyden. Kungl. Biblioteket, Stockholm

280 By Emil Hildebrand

281 By Jan Brueghel and S. Vrancx. Kunsthistorischen Museums, Vienna

283 From Joshua Sprigge, *Anglia Rediviva*, 1647. British Museum

284 By Payne Fisher. Ashmolean Museum (Sutherland Collection), Oxford

288 *Top* By Heerman Witmont. National Maritime Museum, Greenwich. *Bottom* By Van de Velde II. National Maritime Museum, Greenwich

290 Detail from engraving by Jan van Huchtenburgh in J. Dumont, *Batailles de Prince Eugene*, 1720. British Museum

294 *Above* Musée des Plans et Reliefs, Les Invalides, Paris. *Below* From Allain Manesson Mallet, *Les Travaux de Mars, ou l'Art de la Guerre*, 1685. British Museum

297 By Jan van Huchtenburgh. National Gallery, London

311 British Museum (Crookshank Collection)

312 By F. Lemke. Nationalmuseum, Stockholm

314 Detail from 'Action off Carthagena' by Samuel Scott. National Maritime Museum, Greenwich

321 Detail from the painting by Van Blarenbergh. Musée de Versailles

323 By Van Blarenbergh. Musée de Versailles

326 Photo Ullstein Bilderdienst

330 By J. B. Le Paon. Musée Condé, Chantilly. Photo Giraudon

333 By Horace Vernet. National Gallery, London

334 Detail from the painting by Charles Thevenin. Musée de Versailles

338 By Denis Dighton. National Maritime Museum, Greenwich

347 From P.-M. Laurent de l'Ardèche, *Histoire de l'Empereur Napoléon*, 1840. Illustrated by Horace Vernet

353 Bibliothèque Nationale, Paris

355 *Above* By Jacques François Fontaine. Wellington Museum, London. *Below* By Charles Thevenin. Musée de Versailles

364 By L. Marin. Bibliothèque Nationale, Paris

368 Models, early twentieth-century. Victoria and Albert Museum, London

371 From E. T. C. Warner, *Chinese Weapons*, Royal Asiatic Society, 1932

379 From *Chinese Weapons* (see p. 371)

387 By Kuniyoshi. Victoria and Albert Museum, London

388-9 'The Burning of the Sanjo Palace' by Heiji Monogatari. Museum of Fine Arts (Fenollosa-Weld Collection), Boston

392 Victoria and Albert Museum, London

397 Tower of London Armoury

398-9 Late eighteenth-century embroidery depicting the Mahabharata epic. Victoria and Albert Museum, London

401 Mahabharata embroidery (see p. 398–9)

404 Victoria and Albert Museum, London

410 By Caton Woodville. The Regimental Lieutenant-Colonel, Coldstream Guards

417 *Above* Photo Mansell Collection. *Below* Photo Radio Times Hulton Library

418 By W. Simpson. Victoria and Albert Museum

427 By W. Simpson (see p. 418)

434 By A. de Neuville. Musée d'Arras

441 From the painting by Thomas Nast. Radio Times Hulton Library

442 'An engagement on the Majuba mountain top' from Archibald Forbes, *Battles of the Nineteenth Century*, 1896

445 Details from *left* 'The Grenadier Guards at Biddulph's Berg', *right* 'Colonel Plumer's attempt to relieve Mafeking'. From *The Art Annual*, 1900

446 By Leon Abry. Musée de l'Armée, Brussels

448 *Left* 'A 4.7 naval gun in action in South Africa', from *The Art Annual*, 1900. *Right* 'US troops reconnoitering off Santiago', 1898, from A. Hilliard Atteridge, *The Wars of the Nineties*, 1899

449 Photo Imperial War Museum, London

451 'The battle of Ulundi' from Louis Creswicke, *South Africa and the Transvaal War*, 1900–2

457 From A. Hilliard Atteridge (see p. 448)

460 Photo Roger-Viollet

474 Photo Imperial War Museum, London

475 Photo Imperial War Museum, London

480 Photo Radio Times Hulton Library

483 Photos Imperial War Museum, London

496 Photo Camera Press

504 Photo Imperial War Museum, London

510 Photo Novosti Press Agency (A.P.N.)

515 Photo Imperial War Museum, London

516 Photo Ullstein Bilderdienst

527 Photo United Press

534 Photo Imperial War Museum, London

541 Photo Imperial War Museum, London

Endpapers Photo Ullstein Bilderdienst

Commissioned photographs in monochrome have been taken by John Freeman of the illustrations reproduced on the following pages: 26/5, /7, /20, 209 *right*, 217, 229 *above*, 230, 237, 240–1, 262, 267, 280, 283, 290, 294 *below*, 311, 347, 371, 379, 418, 427, 442, 445, 448, 451, 457; and by Michael Holford of the illustrations on pages 368 and 410. In all other cases the copyright of the illustrations rests with the institution owning the originals, except where a photographer's name is given.

INDEX

A.F.V's (armoured fighting vehicles) 14, 219; *see also* Tanks
Aaran ⨉ 179
Abbasid caliphs 145
Abd-al-Rahman 149
Abd-el-Kader 425
Abercromby, General 319
Aboukir Bay ⨉ 338, 345
Abraham, Heights of 319
Abstemiousness in generals 22
Achilles 31, 59
Acroinon ⨉ 141
Acropolis (Athens), siege of 250
Actium ⨉ 107
'Ad Decimum' ⨉ 132–3
Adad-Nirari II 51
Administration, military (logistics) 23, 39, 43, 45, 264, 265, 269, 279, 296, 331, 425; 'the crux of generalship', 383
Adowa ⨉ 450
Adrianople ⨉ ⨉ 125–9 *pass.*, 183, 244
Aegospotami ⨉ 67
Aeroplanes *see* Aircraft
Aerarium militare 122
Aëtius (Roman general) 130
Afghan War, first 413
Afrika korps 512
Agincourt ⨉ 194
Agricola (Roman general) 119
Ahmednagar, storming of 358
Ahmose (of Thebes) 38, 39
Air aces 482
Air bombing 15, 477, 482, 499, 506, 508, 514–16, 520, 532, 551, 559–61
Air mastery (*see also* Air superiority) 15, 504
Air power (*see also* Air bombing, Air mastery *and* Air superiority) 15, 482, 499, 504, 508, 517, 525, 536–7, 545, 563
Air superiority (mastery in the air) 15, 504, 516, 525, 530–1, 543

Air supply (and maintenance) 532, 539
Aircraft (*see also* Balloons, R.A.F., Zeppelins *and under their names*) 15, 447, 482, 493, 499, 500, 503–6, 517, 543, 563
Aircraft-carriers 533, 534–5, 563
Aisne ⨉ ⨉ ⨉ *1914*, 464; *1917*, 478; *1918*, 492
Aisne, River: Caesar defeats *Belgae* on 103
Ajax 59
Akbar (Moghul emperor) 402
Akbarnama 407, 408
Akkad & Akkadians 33–4, 38
Ala-eddin Mohammed, Shah 376
Alam Halfa ⨉ 513
Alamein ⨉ 15, 508, 512, 513–14, 566; Memorial, 567
Alamo, defence of the 413
Alaric (Visigoth general) 125, 129
Alesia, siege of 103
Alexander I, Tsar 351, 352, 363
Alexander the Great 29–33, 71–83, 97, 104, 161; appreciation of, 82–3
Alexander, General Sir Harold 513, 532, 533
Alexander of Parma *see* Parma
Alfred the Great 155
Ali Pasha 258, 260
Allenby, General Sir Edmund 41, 489–90, 494
Allia ⨉ 85
Alliances in war, disadvantages of 537
Alma ⨉ 422–3
Almeida (fortress) 361, 362
Almeida, Francisco de 233
Alp Arslan 146
Ambiorix (general of Gauls) 103
Ambushes 45, 105, 114, 123, 143, 144
Amenhotep: I, 39, 41; III, 38
American Civil War 24, 411, 416, 419, 420, 437–41, 443, 457
American Independence, War of 315,

320–1, 329
American Pacific Fleet 533–7
American troops: in W.W.I, 491–3 *pass.*; in W.W.II, 514–43 *pass.*
Americans on Omaha beach 520
Amherst, General 319
Amiens ⨉ ⨉ *53 B.C.*, 103; *1918*, 492, 493
Amorous adventures 322
Amphipolis ⨉ 70
Amphissa ⨉ 71
Amr ibn-al-As 135
'Anabasis', the 70
Anaxandrias (of Sparta) 60
Anglo-Dutch wars at sea 277, 286–9
Animals and human beings 29–30
Ankara ⨉ 245
Anson, Commodore George 315, 317, 319
Antioch: sacked (540), 133; captured (1098), 175
Anti-submarine operations (*see also* Convoys) 481–2
Anti-tank guns 499, 512, 513
Antony, Mark (Marcus Antonius) 107
Antwerp: mutiny at, 224; siege of, 227
Anzac Cove 487
Anzio, landing at 518
Aosta, Duke of 548
Appeasement, policy of 498
Aqaba, capture of (1917) 489
Arabs ('Saracens') 133, 135–45, 152, 211, 489
Arakan, the 539, 543
Archangel 517
Archelaus (Pontic general) 100
Archers & archery (*see also* Arrows *and* Bows) 35–6, 38, 42, 45, 50, 52–6 *pass.*, 61, 63, 70, 73, 76, 78, 79, 82, 104, 110, 124, 127, 130, 132, 133, 138–207 *pass.*, 247, 396–403 *pass.*
Arcot, defence of 409
Ardennes, German counter-offensive in

(1944) 307, 527
Argive force (of hoplites) 60
Armada, Spanish 211, *226*, 238–41
Armaments: industry, 263; development of (1918–39), 499
Armecy ✕102
Armée de Portugal 361
Armée Grande 349, 357, 363–5 *pass.*
Armies: growth of, 263–4, 322; and modern state, 263–4; in the time of Gustavus Adolphus, 274; in xvii & xviii centuries 296, 332
Arminius (German chieftain) 114
Armour (*meaning A.F.V's*) 14, 219; *see also* Tanks
Armour, body (in general, *see also* Helmets, Mail, Shields *and next three below*) 36, 42, 45, 55, 60, 90, 103, 104, 141, 147; development of, 186; transition (mail to plate), 201, 207; abandoned, 222
Armour, body (in detail): breast-plates (and back-plates), 60, 86, 103, 282, 348; caps, head (metal), 141, 184, 197 (*see also* Helmets); caps for knees, elbows and shins, 186; coifs, 178; cuirasses, 73, 85; 147, 186, 197, 298, 348; *gambesons*, 186; gauntlets, 141; greaves, 60, 85, 138, 141; jerkins, leather, 70; light, 195, 323; link (chain), 78, 178, 186, 399; plate, 186 (*see also* Mail); shoes, steel, 141; surcoats, 186; tunics, quilted, 197, 399
Armour, body: for elephants, 395; for horses, 52, 104, 141, 178, 386
Armour, body: of Byzantine cavalry, 132; of Cromwell's pikemen, 284; of crusading knights, 178; of Franks, 126, 146; of Janissaries, 247; of Japanese *samurai*, *381*, 386; of longbowmen, 197; of Mongols, 370; of Vikings, 154
Armoured fighting vehicles 14, 219; *see also* Tanks
Arms (*or* armaments) race 416, 443–4, 445–9, 458
Armstrong Whitworth & Co. 444
Armstrong, William 420
Army corps 346, 360, 445
Army Group, 21st 518
Arnhem 527
Arnold, General 525
Arnulf (king of Franks) 154
Arquebuses (handguns) & arquebusiers (*see also* Muskets *and* Rifles) 211, 213, 216–23 *pass.*, 231, 232, 247, 259
Arras ✕478
'Arrow Riders' 372, 373
Arrows & arrow-heads 29, 35–6, 42, 77, 105, 130, 132, 133, 253, 259, 371, 373, 395, 398; loopholes for, 168, 184; 'bolts' for crossbows, 184; for longbows, 197; feared by horses, 185, 206
Artemisium, Cape ✕64
Articles of War (Gustavus Adolphus) 269
Artillery (*see also* Cannon *and* Guns) 73, 183, 207, 208, 214, 216, 220, 224, 227, 230, 248, 256, 266, 271, 273, 284, 285, 292, 298, 308, 309, 329, 330, 346, 348, 361, 419, 420, 441, 445, 447, 452, 471, 472–3 (*subsequent chapters deal more with A.F.V's and aircraft than with artillery*)
Asaf Jah 406
'Asdic' 481

Ashdown (Berks) ✕154, 155
Ashigaru (Japanese peasant soldiers) 390
Ashurbanipal 52, 55, 57
Assam campaign (1944) 539
Assassination of political leaders 525
Assaye ✕358
Asses 34, 35, 38, 43
Assyria & Assyrians 51–7, 59
Athens 14, 61–70; fall of, 67
Atlantic, battle of the 511, 516–18
'Atmosphere' created by a general 15, 21
Atomic (& nuclear) bombs 543, 545, 558–62
Atomic Energy Commission 559
Atrocities & war crimes 498, 508, 546, 547, 565–6
Attila the Hun 129, 130, 369, 550
Auchinleck, General Sir Claude 508, 512, 513
Auerstädt ✕349, 354
Augerau, Marshal 340, 349
Augsburg, War and League of 295
Augustus Caesar (Octavian) 107, 109–10, 114–15, 118, 121, 123
Augustus of Württemberg, Prince 435
Aulus Plautius 115
Aurangzeb 405
Aurelian (Roman emperor) 118, 123, 124, 125
Austerlitz ✕351–4, 357, 380
Austria & Austrians 279, 298, 310, 316, 328, 335, 351–4, 461, 466, 468, 485, 488–9
Austrian Succession, War of the 315, 316, 322, 325
Austro-Hungarian empire & army 461, 486, 488
Auxiliae (Roman) 109, 110, 122, 124
Avaricum (Bourges), siege of 103
Avenger (escort carrier) 517
Avenger (torpedo-aircraft) 534
Awards, military 348
Axes, battle 35, 37, 39, 42, 141, 144, 150, 160, 161, 186, 247, 371, 398; for throwing, 126, 146; '*francisca*', 146
Aztecs 233, 234

B.S.O.E. (British Special Operations Executive) 503
Babur, 'the Tiger' 402–5
Babylon 51, 57; sacked, 52
Badajoz 362
Baecula (in Andalusia) ✕93
Bagradas ✕93, 96
Baileys (bailies) 167, 169, 192
Baji Rao I 405–6
Bakufu (Japanese military government) 386
Balaclava ✕426
Balance of political and military forces 562
'Balance of Power' in Europe 444
Balapur ✕405
Balkan wars 244, 453–5, 459, 487–8
Ballistae (*see also* Catapults) 139, 161, 184, 227, 248, 253
Balloons 437, 447
Barbarians 109–33, 124–7, 243
Barbarigo, Augustina 258
'Barbarossa' (Frederick I, H.R.E.) 181, 185
'Barbarossa, Operation' (1941) 508–11, 550
Barbarossa (Alan Clark) 21
Barbary corsairs 127, 255, 257
Barbed wire 219, 472, 473, 493
Bases, fixed 448, 564

Bashi-bazouks (Turkish infantry) 246, 247
Basil II (Byzantine emperor & general) 145, 155
Basra, Port of 257
Bastille, the 194
Battering-rams 38, 45, 56, 68, 73, 77, 170
Battle-axes *see* Axes, battle
Battles (in general) 17, 21, 219, 346, 472
Battleships 447, *521*
Bayezit: I, 253; II, 253
Baylén (in Spain) 357
Bayonets, 'ring' 209, 291, 298, 309, 325
Bazaine, Marshal 432
Bazan, Alvaro de 235
Beachy Head ✕292
Beaulieu, Colonel de 419
Beaumont ✕436
Beffrois see Siege towers
Bêlasitza ✕145
Belfort gap 293
Belisarius (Roman general) 131–3, 141
Benevento ✕185, 186
Beneventum ✕83, 85
Benghazi 513, 514
Berbers (of N. Africa) 135
Beresford, General 360
Berlin: blockade, 555; bombed, 516
Berlin Decrees 357
Bernadotte, Marshal 351, 353
'Berserks', Viking 155
Berthier, Marshal 345, 348, 414
Berwick ✕191
Berwick, Marshal 311
Bessières, Marshal 349
Bicocca ✕220, 221
Bismarck, Prinz Otto von 14, 21, 373, 413, 426–7, 430, 443, 550
Bismarck (battleship) 517
Black Death 17, 243
Black Prince 204, 206
Blainville, Marquis de 309
Blake, Colonel & Admiral Robert 263, 287, 289
Blanchetaque ford 203
Blenheim ✕305–10
Blitzkrieg 497, 499–502, 508
Bloch, I. S. 444, 459
Blood, Colonel 298
Blood River (S. Africa) ✕413
Blücher, Field-Marshal 363, 366
Boadicea 118–19
Boats, barbarian 126–7
Bock, General 500
Boer War 443, 447, 451–2, 459
Boers, the 451–3
Bohemund (crusader) 172, 173, 175, 179
Bokhara 376
Bolivar, Simon 412
Bomber Command, R.A.F. 546
Bombing, aerial *see* Air bombing
Booms across Golden Horn 139–40
Borchardt's automatic pistol 446
Borodino ✕344, 348
Boscawen, Admiral 319, 320
Bosquet, General 426
Botha, General Louis 452
Bouvines ✕166, 183
Bows & bowmen (*see also* Archers *and* Arrows) 29, 35–6, 38, 39, 42, 52–5 *pass.*, 59, 104, 124, 130, 132, 133, 141, 144, 151, 154, 161, 164, 168, 178, 180, 194, 247; longbows (English), 197
Boxer, Colonel 419
Boxer rebellion (in China) 455
Bradley, General Omar (*quoted*) 526
'Brain-washing' 549

Brasidas (Spartan general) 70
Brauchitsch, Field-Marshal von 508
Breda, siege & capture of 227
Breitenfeld ✕ 270–4
Bremûle ✕ 167
Brentford ✕ 103
Brest, blockade of 319, 336, 339
Bridges: of boats, 63; pontoon, 234
Brigantines, Cortes' 234
Britain and the Romans 103, 115, 118–21, 126
Britain, battle of 504–6
British army (see also under battles) 25, 310; Moore's reforms, 358; Cardwell's reforms, 444, 452
British navy 235–41, 286–9, 316, 317, 321, 335–9, 412, 415–16, 444, 480–2, 486, 502, 516–17
Broadsides (ships') 235, 239, 258
Broadswords 126, 132, 133, 141
Brooke, General Sir Alan (Viscount Alanbrooke) 503
'Brown Bess' (musket) 361
Brueys, Admiral 338
Brun (inventor of submarine) 416
Brunswick, Duke of 331–2
Brusilov, General Alexei 485–6, 494
Bryant, Sir Arthur 20, 289, 547
Bugeaud, Marshal 362, 425
Buhen (Egyptian fortress) 39
Bulgaria & Bulgars 135, 143, 145, 244, 453, 469, 487–8, 494
Buller, General Sir Redvers 452
Bülow, General Karl von 464
Burma Road 532
Burma wars 532, 537–43
Busaco ✕ 361, 362
Bushido 387, 547
Byng, Admiral John 317
Byzantine military system 138–46
Byzantium (see also Constantinople) 125, 135, 138, 173, 244

Cacafuego (Spanish treasure ship) 236
Cadiz harbour, Drake in 238
Caerphilly Castle described 192–3
Caesar Augustus see Augustus Caesar
Caesar, Julius 99, 101–7, 109
Caesar, Octavian see Augustus Caesar
Calais 206, 223; siege of, 191
'Calculated risks' 162
Calcutta, 'Black Hole' of 409
Callinicus (Syrian general) 139
Callwell, Major-General Sir Charles 450, 459
Camberley, Staff College 444
Cambrai ✕ 479, 480
Cambyses 60
Camels & 'camelry' 105, 124, 138, 180, 400
Camillus, Marcus Furius 85
Camouflage 321, 499
Camperdown ✕ 336
Camp-followers 141, 269, 400
Camps, military 87–8, 91, 114, 118, 126, 141–2, 400
Camulodunum (Colchester) 115
Cannae ✕ 91, 92, 94, 97, 105
Cannon (see also Guns) 13, 190–2, 205, 207, 214, 216, 227, 233, 234, 239, 248, 253, 329, 330, 419–20
Canute, King 152, 155
Cape St. Vincent ✕ 336
Caporetto ✕ 489
Captain, H.M.S. 336
Caracole (cavalry manoeuvre) 232, 271, 280, 297–8
Caractacus (Caradoc) 118
Caravans, the Author's 17, 24

Carbines (see also Rifles) 282, 445
Cardwell, Edward 444, 452
Caribbean, the 234–6 pass., 237
Carmel, Mount 41
Carnot, Lazare 339–40
'Carracks' 235
Carrhae ✕ 105, 243
Carrier task force 15
Carthage 14, 89–98, 133
Casablanca conference 511, 514
Cassino ✕ 518
Cassivellaunus (guerrilla) 103
Castles (see also Fortifications) 133, 155, 167–9, 175–6, 180, 183, 191–4
Casualties, acceptable (see also Economy of Lives) 302
Cataphracts, Saca 78, 80
Catapults (see also Ballistae) 68, 73, 77, 82, 132, 139, 155, 171, 372, 409
Caucasus, the 510–11
Caudine Forks ✕ 85, 105
Cavalry (see also Chariots) 34, 52, 55, 61, 63, 68–73 pass., 78–81 pass., 86, 91–9 pass., 104, 106, 109–66 pass., 178, 186, 195, 206, 208, 216, 221, 232, 243, 246–8 pass., 257, 263–86 pass., 291, 297–310 pass., 348, 369–80 pass., 399, 405, 489–90; charging (shock tactics), 71, 93, 104, 147, 199, 200, 216, 271, 280, 399, 405, 440, 441, 459; heavy (see also Cuirassiers), 73, 82, 124, 127–8, 132, 150, 183, 185–6, 194, 231, 348, 399, 403; light, 186, 216, 348, 399; medium (see also Dragoons), 348; tactics, 143–4, 145, 186, 399
Centuries & centurions (Roman) 89, 99
Cerignola ✕ 211, 218, 219
Chaeronea ✕ ✕ 388 B.C., 71; 87 B.C., 100
Chain (or link) armour see Mail
Chaldiran ✕ 254
Champions, battle of the 60
Chandragupta Maurya 395, 401
Chaplains (& medical staff) in Spanish army (1534) 231
Charge of the Light Brigade 426
Chariots & charioteers 34–9 pass., 42, 52, 55, 59, 61, 73, 78, 80
Charlemagne 149–52
Charles I (king of Spain, and H.R.E. as Charles V) 211, 212
Charles VIII of France 212, 213, 224
Charles XII of Sweden 291, 313
Charles of Anjou 185
Charles, Archduke, of Austria 349, 352
Charles the Bald 155
Charles of Lorraine 327, 328
Charles Martel 148, 150
Charles the Simple 152
Chassepot rifle 419, 429, 435, 436
Chasseurs 348
Chateaudun ✕ 421
Chatham, Earl of see Pitt
Chelmsford, Lord 451
Chemin des Dames 491, 492
Chepé Noyon 376–7
Cherusci, the 114
Chevauchée (raid) 207
Chiang Kai-shek 532
China & Chinese 377–84, 413, 455, 532, 555–6, 559, 560, 561
'Chindits', Wingate's 537, 539
Chindwin, River 537, 539, 540
Chivalry 189–90, 243, 546–8
Chosroes (Persian emperor) 139
Christianity 125, 547
Churchill, Charles 308, 310
Churchill, John see Marlborough

Churchill, Sir Winston 23, 29, 282, 296, 302, 307, 317, 320, 462, 469, 479, 486, 497, 503, 511, 518, 529, 544–5, 553, 558
Cimon (Athenian general) 67
Ciudad Rodrigo 361, 362
Cividale ✕ 191
Civil Defence 18
Civil War (in England) 279–86
Civilians and war 13, 15, 17–18, 549–51
Civilis (Batavian chieftain) 122
Civitate ✕ 159
Clarke, William 285
Clausewitz, Karl von 20, 414–15, 459, 552
Clemenceau, Georges 488, 492, 495
Cleopatra, Queen 105, 107
Clérambault, Marquis de 308, 310
Clive, Robert 317, 409
Clothar II (king of Franks) 147
Clovis (king of Franks) 146
Clubs (weapons) 126, 179, 398
Coastal Command, R.A.F. 517
Cochrane, Admiral Sir Thomas (Lord Dundonald) 412, 547
Codrington, Admiral Sir Edward 412
Cohorts, Roman 99, 109
Colbert, Jean Baptiste 291
'Cold War' 554–7
Colline Gate (Rome) ✕ 100
Colombey ✕ 432
Colonna, Prosper (Italian general) 213, 220
Colt, Samuel 419, 420
Columbus, Christopher 233
Combined operations 234, 520, 536–7
Comfort and military standards 141
Command and control of armies (see also General staffs) 17, 62, 296, 427–8, 441, 471, 472–3
Commando raids 503
Commissariat (see also Supply) 269, 274
Communications 14, 39, 73, 85, 176, 224, 236, 336, 420, 473, 539
'Companion Cavalry' (Macedonian) 73, 78, 80, 81
Comradeship 17
Condé, Prince de 263, 279, 291–3
Condottieri 212
Conduct of soldiery 549
Congo, the 546
Conquistadores 233
Conrad, Joseph 339
Conscription 124, 266, 274, 296, 340, 357, 411, 426, 429, 444, 455, 499, 529
Constantine, Emperor 125
Constantinople (Byzantium, q.v., now Istanbul) 125, 133, 138, 486; sieges of, 139–41, 145, 244, 245, 248–50
Continental System 357
Convoys, maritime 236, 289, 481; arctic 517
Cook, Captain James 320
Copenhagen ✕ 339
Coracesium ✕ 101
Coral Sea ✕ 15, 533–4
Corbulo, (Roman general) 122
Cordite 446
Corfe Castle (Dorset) 167
Cornwallis, General 315, 321
Coronel ✕ 480
Corps (army formation) see Army corps
Cortenuova ✕ 185
Cortes, Hernando 233–4
Corunna ✕ 357
Courtrai ✕ 194
Coutras ✕ 232

Cradock, Admiral 480
Crassus, Marcus Licinius 100, 104, 105
Crécy ✕ 194, 201–6
Creusot (armament firm) 444
Crimean War 415, 416, 419, 425, 426, 443
Cromwell, Oliver 263, 280–7, 289
Cross Lake ✕ 31
Crossbows & crossbowmen 161, 170, 172, 178, 184, 191, 197, 201, 214, 216, 217, 222, 247, 253; described, 184
Crusades, the 171–81, 183, 189, 244
Cuba: 1898, 443, 458; 1962, 561
Cudgels 197
Cuirassiers 266, 273, 348
Culverins 214, 227, 239, 284
Cunaxa ✕ 70
Cunctator (the delayer) 91
Cunningham, Admiral Sir John 507, 517
Cutts, Lord 308, 310
Cynoscephalae ✕ 98
Cyrus the Great 60, 70

Dabik ✕ 255
Daggers 86, 141, 146, 201, 247
Daladier, Edouard 498
'Dam busters', the 515–16
Damascus 41, 177, 490
Dan-no-ura ✕ 386
Dardanelles, attack on (1915) 469, 486
Darius I 60, 63
Darius III 74, 77, 78–82 pass.
Darts, feathered 132
Daru, Count 345
Daun, Field-Marshal 327, 328
Dauntless, H.M.S. 415
'Davids' (submersible warships) 416
Davis, Jefferson 437–40 pass.
Davout, Marshal 348, 351, 353, 354
D'Enghien, Duc see Condé
De Gaulle, Charles 25
De Robeck, Admiral 486
De Ruyter, Admiral 287, 289
De Wet, Christian 453
Deal (fortress) 227
Decebalus (Dacian general) 118
Deception in warfare 301
'Decimation' (in Roman army) 122
Declaration of war 551
Defence: expenditure on, 444; in the future, 562–4
Defensive in warfare 109, 143, 167–71, 183, 224, 227, 230, 441, 458–9, 461, 471–2
Delean League (naval) 67
Delium ✕ 68, 139
Delphi, oracle at 25, 74
'Demilunes' 295
Democracy and armies 263–4, 331
Demosthenes 68
Denain ✕ 313
Dervishes 450
Desert Mounted Corps 489, 490
Destriers 150, 178
Devastation, H.M.S. 416
'Devil's Wall' 118
Devolution, War of 291
Dien Bien Phu 495, 556
Dieppe, raid on (1942) 518
Diocletian (Roman emperor) 123, 124
Dionysius I (king of Syracuse) 68, 73
Disarmament 556, 561; conferences 444
Discipline 17, 269, 285, 298, 325
Discus (as a weapon) 398
Dispersion techniques 499
'Divided (split) world, a' 554, 560–2
Divisional system 348, 360

Doenitz, Admiral 517, 529
Domestic architecture (defensive) 194
Dominica ✕ 321
Domitian (Roman emperor) 118, 123
Donauwörth ✕ 302
Donjons (keeps) 167–8
Doorman, Rear-Admiral 531–2
Doria, Giovanni Andrea (Spanish admiral) 257, 258
Dorylaeum ✕ 175
Dover Castle 167
Dowding, A. C. M. Sir Hugh 505
Dragoons 266, 282, 298, 348
Dragut (Barbary corsair) 257
Drake, Sir Francis 211, 235, 236–41, 287, 317
'Drake' (a field-gun) 284
Dreadnought, H.M.S. 447, 480
Drepana ✕ 102
Drill 266, 274, 292, 325, 327
Dromons (see also Triremes) 132, 139, 253
Du Teil (tactician) 330, 331, 340
Duillius (Roman admiral) 102
Dumouriez (French general) 331–2
Dunant, Henri 426, 548
Dunbar ✕ 285
Duncan, Admiral 336
Dundonald, Lord (Thomas Cochrane) 412, 547
Dungeness ✕ 287
Dunkirk (1940) 307, 502
Dupleix, Joseph 409
Dupplin Moor ✕ 198
Duquesne, Fort (later Fort Pitt & Pittsburg) 319
Dutch East Indies (see also Indonesia) 531–2
Dutch wars: 223, 286–9, 291
Dyle ✕ 154
Dynamite 446
Dyrrhachium, siege of 105

Eagles, Roman 99, 124
East Indies, Dutch (see also Indonesia) 531–2
Ecnomus, Cape ✕ 102
Economy of lives 17, 292, 302, 333, 472, 552, 567
Eder dam 515–16
Edgehill ✕ 280
Edington (Wilts) ✕ 154–5
Edward I 183, 194, 195–8
Edward II 198
Edward III 191, 197–207
Edwin and Morkar 160
Egypt & Egyptians (ancient) 31–48
Eighth Army, Montgomery's 513–14, 566–7
Eisenhower, General Dwight D. 513, 526, 529
Elamites 55, 57
Elba, Napoleon in 363
Elephants 78, 82, 83, 90–6 pass., 115, 395–6, 403; horses fear 78, 82, 83
Elizabeth I 224, 236–38 pass., 240
Elk River ✕ 31
Enemy, courses open to the 16
Engineers, military (sappers) 29, 39, 56, 63, 73, 142, 247, 266, 292, 308, 360, 513
Engines of war, projectile-throwing (see also Battering-rams, Ballistae, Catapults, etc.) 168, 171
Enterprise, U.S.S. 535, 536
Entrenchments see Trench warfare
Epaminondas (Theban general) 70, 327
Equipment and Supply 512
Ericsson, John 415, 416

Esarhaddon (king of Assyria) 52
'Escalation' 462, 561–2
Eugene, Prince 300, 301–5, 307–9, 311, 313, 322
Eurybiades (Spartan admiral) 64
Eurymedon, River ✕ 67
Evesham ✕ 195–6
'Excalibur' 126
Explosives, development of 446
Eylau ✕ 356

Fabian strategy 97, 500
Fabius Maximus, Quintus 91
Fairfax, General Thomas 282
Falaise (Normandy) 157; Pocket, 522–3, 526
Falconets 403
Falkenhayn, General Erich von 468, 471, 482, 494
Falkirk ✕ 195, 198
Falkland Islands ✕ 480
Falls, Cyril 20, 452, 462
Fear in warfare 298
Fehrbellin ✕ 325
Feisal, Emir (later king of Iraq) 489
Ferdinand II (H.R.E.) 265, 274, 275, 276
Feudal levies (levée en masse) 39, 150, 186
Feudal system 135, 150, 155, 157, 161, 178, 186, 196, 245
'Fifth Column' strategy 63
Fighter Command, R.A.F. 505, 506
'Fighting Instructions' 316
Finisterre, Cape ✕ 317
Firearms (see also Arquebuses, Cannon, Carbines, Guns, Muskets, Pistols, Revolvers, Rifles, etc.) 183, 190–1, 201, 211, 224, 247, 248, 250, 259, 263, 271, 274, 298, 384, 390, 396, 403, 405, 415–20, 446
Firepower 14, 34, 198, 266, 271, 272, 298, 329, 361, 459; and mobility, 14, 233, 266, 272, 279, 298, 329, 330, 331, 361
Fireships 239
Fisher, Admiral Sir John 480, 486
Flails (as weapons) 247
Flint-locks 282, 292, 298, 346, 416, 437
Flores (in Azores) ✕ 240–1
Foch, Marshal Ferdinand 459, 461, 472, 491–2, 497
Foley, Captain, R.N. 338
Fontenoy ✕ 322
Forbes, General John 319
Formations, fighting: column, 330, 346, 354; crescent, 91, 143; 'hedgehog', 195; Hindu (various), 400; line (linear), 271–2, 274, 284, 298, 330, 346, 354, 358; line-ahead (naval), 287, 316; mass, 271, 273 (see also Phalanx); oblique, 70, 327; ordre mixte, 346, 354; phalanx, see Phalanx; square (hollow), 298; T-shaped, 271, 272; testudo (tortoise), 113; wedge (Herce), 204
Formigny ✕ 214
Fornovo ✕ 212
Forrest, General Nathan B. 441
Fortifications & fortresses (see also Castles, Maginot Line, Siege warfare and Walls) 29, 33, 38, 39, 45, 56–7, 87, 102, 118–19, 151, 155, 157, 167–9, 191–4, 207, 223, 224–5, 227, 248, 256, 291, 293–5, 300, 313, 372, 379–80, 396, 406–7, 453, 471
Fortresses (bomber aircraft) 516
Fortune favours the bold 269
Fosse Way 115, 118

Fourteenth Army, Slim's 537–43
France & French (see also Napoleon) 25, 135, 279, 291–311, 316, 318–19, 335–63 pass., 409, 429–37, 560; in W.W.I, 461–4, 468–80, 491–5; in W.W.II, 499–503, 519–26
France, battle of 501–3
Franchet d'Espérey, General 488
Francis I (king of France) 214
Franco-Austrian War 413, 425
Franco-Prussian (Franco-German) War 155, 411, 413, 419, 420, 427, 430–7, 441, 443, 459, 550
Franks, the (see also Charlemagne) 126, 129, 133, 135, 146–55
Fraternization in war 464, 547
Frederick I ('Barbarossa', H.R.E.) 181, 185
Frederick II, the Great 19, 315, 322, 323–9, 332–3
Frederick Charles, Prince 430, 432, 435
Frederick William (elector) 323
Frederick William I (king of Prussia) 323, 325
'Free French', the 503
French army (see also Napoleon) 279, 292–313, 339–40, 345, 425–6, 428–37 pass.
French, General Sir John 464, 471
French military academies 348, 429
French navy 291–2, 316, 317, 319, 321, 335–6, 415, 480
French 'Resistance' 503
French revolutionary wars 331, 335, 340
French soldiers, tribute to 495
French War Office under Louis XIV 292
Friedland × 356
Friedlingen × 313
Frigates 316
Führer, der see Hitler, Adolf
Fulford (York) × 160
Fuller, J. F. C. 20, 78, 87, 91, 103, 500
'Funnies' (converted tanks) 520
Fustae (light rowing boats) 258
Fyrd, the 160, 163

Gaillard, Château, siege of 169–71
Galba (general of Belgae) 103
'Galleasses' 236, 238, 253, 258, 259
Galleons 235, 236, 238, 239, 240, 287
Galleys 63, 77, 139, 253, 258–9, 286
Gallienus (Roman emperor) 123, 124, 125
Galliots 258
Gallipoli 250, 486–7
Gambetta 437
Gamelin, General Maurice 502
Garde Mobile 429
Garigliano × 219, 220
Gas masks 499
Gas warfare 472, 473, 547–8, 551
Gatling gun 419
Gaugamela × 78–82, 145
Gaza × × × 489, 490
Geiseric (Vandal general) 125, 127
Gelimer (Vandal general) 133
General staffs 349, 360, 428, 444
Generals & generalship 15–27, 70, 224, 291, 319–23 pass., 332, 366–7, 413–14, 461, 472, 476, 494
Geneva Convention 426, 548
Genitors 216, 217, 218
German air force see Luftwaffe
German (formerly Prussian) army 426–8, 463–94 pass., 497–529 pass.
German navy (see also Submarines) 480–1, 516–18
Germanicus (Roman general) 113, 114

Germany & Germans (see also Prussia) 113–15, 124, 279, 426–37; in W.W.I, 461–94; in W.W.II, 497–529, 544
Gettysburg × 424, 440, 441
Ghazis (Moslem warriors) 244, 250
Gibraltar captured (1704) 300
Gibson, Wg. Cdr. G. P. 515–16
Gloire (French warship) 416
'Glorious First of June' 336
Gneisenau (German cruiser) 517
Golden Hind (Drake's ship) 236
Gonzalo de Córdoba 216–20, 403
Goree captured 320
Göring, Hermann 504, 505
Gorlice × 482
Gort, General John, V.C. 502
Goths (Ostro- & Visi-) 125–9, 130, 131, 133
Graf Spee (German pocket battleship) 517
Grand Alliance, War of the 291
Grand strategy (see also Strategy) 14, 552
Grande Armée (Napoleon's) 349, 357, 363, 364, 365
Granicus × 74
Grant, General Ulysses 438, 440
Grantham × 282
Gravelotte-Saint-Privat × 432–6, 441
Great Exhibition (1851) 412, 419
Great Northern War 313
Great Rebellion in England (1642) 264, 280–6
Great Wall of China 33, 373, 380
Greece in W.W.II, 508
'Greek fire' 139
Greek (Athenian) fleet 63, 64
Greek Independence, War of 412
Greeks, the ancient (see also Athens and Sparta) 59–83
Green, V. H. H., on Wars of religion (quoted) 223
Gregory of Tours, Bishop 147
Grenadiers 292, 298
Grenville, Sir Richard 240
Gribeauval, General 329, 330, 331, 340, 348
Gross Jägersdorf × 327
Guadalcanal, campaign for 536
Guadelupe captured 320
Guard Corps (German) 435
Guderian, General Heinz 502, 503, 508
Guerrilla warfare & guerrillas 99, 103, 118, 119, 357, 361, 413, 450, 453, 459, 489, 490–1, 537–8, 550, 555–6
Guibert (tactician) 330, 331, 340, 345
Guicciardini 215, 220
Guiscard, Robert ('the Wary') 158, 159
Gujrat × 413
Gunpowder 34, 139, 190, 209, 227
Guns (see also Artillery and Cannon) 183, 190–2, 211, 214, 263, 266, 284, 287, 298, 329, 403, 416, 419–20
Gun-turrets, rotating 416
Gustave Zédé (French submarine) 449
Gustavus Adolphus 263–79, 291, 298, 313; appreciation of, 274
Guy de Lusignan 177, 180

Hadrian (Roman emperor) 118–23 pass., 126
Hadrian's Wall 119, 126
Hague Conferences: 1899, 444, 548, 549; 1907, 551, 552
Haig, General Sir Douglas 23, 471, 472, 477, 478, 491, 492, 494
Hair-cuts, military 197

Halberds 195, 390
Halifaxes (aircraft) 515
Halsey, Admiral 536
Hamburg bombed 516, 546
Hamilton, General Sir Ian 486, 487
Hampton Roads × 416
Handguns (see also Arquebuses, Muskets, Pistols, Revolvers and Rifles) 216, 437
Hannibal 89–91, 93–7, 102; and Scipio compared, 96–7
Harfleur, siege of 207
Harold II (king of England) 160, 162–6, 172
Harold Hardrada 160
Harpalus bridges Hellespont 63
Harris, Air Marshal Sir Arthur 515
Harwood, Commodore 517
Hasdrubal Gisgo (Carthaginian general) 93
Hasdrubal (another) 93
Hastings × 160–6, 173, 183
Hattin × 177, 180
Hattin, Horns of 180
Hauteville family 158–9
Hawke, Admiral 320
Hawkins, Admiral Sir John 236
Hector 59
Hejaz, the 489; Railway, 489
'Hellcats' 534, 537
Hellespont bridged 63
Helmets 35, 42, 52, 60, 85, 86, 103, 126, 138, 141, 146, 147, 150, 154, 160, 161, 178, 186, 190, 217; 'pot-helms', 178, 186, 190
Helots (slaves) in Sparta 59
Helvius, Rufus (Roman soldier) 122–3
Henry II (king of France) killed by Author's ancestor 188
Henry the Fowler (king of Franks) 152
Henry of Navarre (French general) 232
Henry the Navigator, Prince 233
Heraclea × 83
Heraldry 190
'Herce' (wedge) formation 204
Hideyoshi (Japanese general) 369, 390, 391
Himmler, Heinrich 508
Hindenburg, General Paul von 466–7, 468, 471
'Hindenburg Line' 472, 479
Hindersin, General von 420
Hindus, ancient 393–402
Hipper (German cruiser) 517
Hiroshima 543, 558
Hiryu (Japanese aircraft-carrier) 535
Hitler, Adolf (der Führer) 313, 365, 497–511 pass., 525, 526; criticism of, 544, 565
Hittites 41, 45–8 pass., 51
'Hobilars' 186
Hoche, General 340
Höchstädt × 313
Hohenfriedberg × 325
Hohenlinden × 345
Holstein-Beck, Prince of 309
Home Defence 18
'Home Guard' in Britain 503
Honda, Lieut.-General 542
Hoplites 60–4 pass., 68, 70, 73, 78, 79, 85
Horde, the (Mongol army) 372, 376
Hornet, U.S.S. 535
Horses (see also Cavalry and Chariots) 35, 38, 52, 61, 68, 78, 80–3 pass., 128, 130, 147, 150, 154, 185, 186, 206, 395, 399, 403; 'Destriers', 150, 178; armour for, 52, 104, 141, 178, 386; fear elephants, 78, 82, 83; fear arrows, 185, 206

Horseshoes 68
Hoshang Ghori, Shah 406
Hoshimitsu (Japanese swordsmith) 386
Houdan keep (in France) 168
Hounds returned by enemy 547
'Housecarls', Harold's 160, 162, 163, 165
Howard of Effingham, Lord 238
Howe, Admiral Richard (Lord Howe) 336
Human factors in war 16–18, 22
'Human mines' (Japanese) 543
Hundred Years' War 183, 186, 197–208, 216
Hungary (see also Austro-Hungarian empire) 529
Huns 125, 129–31, 369, 403
Hurricanes (aircraft) 505
Husain Nazim Shah (Moghul general) 405
Hussites, Bohemian 194, 208
Hydaspes (Jhelum) river crossing 82, 208, 395
Hyde Parker, Admiral Sir 317, 339
Hydrogen bombs 558–64
Hyksos (Shepherd kings of Egypt) 34, 38, 39
Hypaspists 72, 73, 77, 78, 81
Hysiae ✕60

Iceni (East Anglian tribe) 119
Idistaviso ✕114
Ilerda ✕105, 107
Ilipa ✕93, 97
Immelmann (German air ace) 482
'Immortals', the (Persian infantry élite) 78
Imperial Guard: French, 348, 351, 353; Russian, 354
Imperialism 233–5, 287–9, 317–21, 443
Imperialists, Tilly's 270, 273, 274
Imphal ✕539
Incas 233
Incendiary missiles and operations 68, 77, 132, 207, 253, 396
Indentures, military 197
India 82, 317, 320, 358, 393–409
Indian Mutiny 413, 416
Indian Ocean 517
Indians: Mexican, 234, 413; Peruvian, 234; Red, 30–1, 413
Indo-China 555
Indonesia 531–2, 554, 556
Industrial Revolution 411, 415–20
Infantry (see also Hoplites, Legions, Phalanx and all other foot-soldiers) – a selection of many references – 37, 38, 42, 52–4, 55, 60–81 pass., 85–96 pass., 113, 124, 126, 131, 132, 138–55 pass., 161, 163, 178, 185, 194, 195, 209, 216, 230, 246–7, 271, 292, 298, 309, 330, 340, 346, 379, 396, 420, 441, 445, 457; lightly armed, 68–9, 70, 73, 90, 106, 195, 329; mounted, 85, 459; in W.W.I, 463–93 pass.; Author's tribute to, 525
Initiative, importance of the 17, 22
Intelligence, military 16–17, 39, 55, 285, 360
Iphicrates 70
Iron Curtain: Roman, 118; modern, 553
Ironclads 416
'Ironsides', Cromwell's 282–6
Irrawaddy, River 539, 540
Irrawaddy shore ✕541–2
Isandlhwana ✕451

Isonzo, River ✕ ✕489
Israelites 48
Issus ✕74
Istanbul see Constantinople
Italy & Italians 212–14, 413, 425, 428; in W.W.I, 469, 488–9; in W.W.II, 506–8, 512, 514, 518
Iwo Jima ✕525
Iyeyasu (Japanese general) 390, 391

Jackson, General Thomas J. ('Stone-wall') 440
Jagatai (Mongol general) 376
Jamaica 287, 321
James, Duke of York 289
Jameson Raid 452
Janissaries 246–7, 250, 257, 261
Jankau ✕279
Japan & Japanese 15, 369, 384–91, 455–8, 470, 547; in W.W.II, 529–43
Japanese air arm 389, 530, 543
Java Sea ✕532
Javelins & javelin-men 34, 42, 68, 70, 73, 78–91 pass., 99, 114, 124, 141, 143, 144, 160, 216, 231, 247, 373, 379, 395
Jelaladdin 374, 377
Jellicoe, Admiral Sir John 481
Jemappes ✕332, 339
Jena ✕348, 354, 357
Jenghiz Khan (Temuchin, see also Mongols) 130, 370–7
Jenkins's Ear, War of (see also War of Austrian Succession) 315–16
Jericho 29, 48
Jerusalem, kingdom of 175, 181
Jerusalem (city): sieges of: 701 B.C., 57; A.D. 70, 118; 1099, 175; 1187, 181; surrendered to British (1917), 490
Jervis, Admiral Sir John (later Lord St. Vincent) 335–6
Jhelum River ✕395–8
Jihads (holy wars) 138, 177
Joan of Arc 207
Joffre, General Joseph 463, 464, 471, 477, 482, 494
John (king of England) 166, 170, 171, 187
John of Austria, Don 257–60; appreciation of, 260
John of Gaunt 257
John of Salisbury (quoted) 190
Jomini, Henri 20, 414, 459
Josephine de Beauharnais 340
Joshua (Israelite general) 48
Jousts (and tournaments) 187–9
Juji (Mongol general) 376
Ju-jutsu (or Ju-jitsu) 386
Junot, Marshal 357, 358
Justinian (Roman emperor) 131, 132, 133, 142, 155; his wife, Antonina, 132

Kablinu ✕57
Kadesh (city & fortress) 41
Kadesh ✕45–8
Kamikaze 389, 543
Kasserine Pass ✕514
Kasuya, Major-General 541
Kawabe, Lieut.-General 532, 539
Keeps (donjons) 167–8
Kemal, Mustapha (later Ataturk) 487, 494
Kempenfelt, Admiral 336
Kennedy, General (Wellington's) 359, 360
Kennedy, President John F. 559, 561
Keppel, Admiral 317
Kerensky, Alexander 486

Kesselring, General (later F.-M.) Albert 505, 506, 518
Khairredin Barbarossa (Barbary corsair) 255, 257
Khaki uniform 444
Khalid ibn-al-Walid 135
Khrushchev, Nikita 559, 561
Khwarizmian empire 376–7
Kimura, General 539–42
Kitchener, General Sir Horatio (later F.-M. Viscount Kitchener of Khartoum) 450, 452, 477, 486
Kluge, General Günther von 525
Knights 61, 85, 127, 133, 135, 150, 160–5 pass., 175–81 pass., 183–90 pass.; creation and initiation of, 189–90
Knights Hospitallers (of St John of Jerusalem) 175, 176, 180, 253, 255–7
Knights of St John: of Rhodes (1309–1522) and of Malta (1529–1798) see Knights Hospitallers
Knights Templars 175, 177, 180, 189
Knights, Teutonic 175, 192
Knives (preceding bayonets) 298
Kohima 539
Kolin 327
Kondo, Vice-Admiral 532
Kordyle, castle of 250
Korea 385, 389–91, 456, 458, 549, 556
Korean War 549, 556
Kossovo ✕1389, 245, 248; 1448, 245
Krak des Chevaliers 174, 176
Kressenstein, General 490
Kriegsakademie (Prussian War Academy) 428, 444
Kriegskommissariat 323
Krupp breech-loading field gun 453
Krupp's armament and steel works (Essen) 420, 444, 453
Kublai Khan 377, 383, 388
Kukri (Gurkha weapon) 398
Kunta (Indian spear) 398
Kuropatkin, General 456, 457
Kursk ✕510, 511
Kutna Hora ✕208
Kutusov, Marshal 349, 351, 353

La Hogue ✕292
La Motta ✕220
La Noue (French general) 224
Labienus (Caesar's second-in-command) 102, 105
Lachish, siege of 57
Lade ✕63, 253
Laelius 94, 96
Lagos ✕320
Lancasters (bomber aircraft) 515, 518
Lances & lancers 73, 86, 104, 124, 126, 132, 133, 138, 141, 144, 150, 161, 178, 185, 201, 207, 247, 371, 373, 378, 399, 405
Landsknechte 215, 223
Landwehr 426–9 pass.
Langobardi (Lombards) 126
Lannes, Marshal 351, 354
Lariats 371, 373
Larrey, Baron (Napoleon's Surgeon-General) 360
Las Torres, General 312
Lashio 532
Lassoes 130
Laupen ✕195
Law of 23rd Aug. 1793 332
Lawrence, Colonel T. E. ('Lawrence of Arabia') 21, 489, 494
Le Cateau ✕464, 471
Le Hamel, tanks at 493
Leadership ('Captaincy', see also Generals) 15, 24, 367, 565–7; national,

462, 544–5
Leboeuf, General 429
Lech, River ⚔ 274
Lechfeld ⚔ 152
Lee, General Robert E. 24, 438, 440;
  appreciation of, 438, 440
Legions, Roman 85–124 pass., 273
Legnano ⚔ 185
Leigh-Mallory, A.C.M. Sir Trafford
  518
Leipzig ⚔ 357, 363
Lemberg captured 485
Lend-Lease Act (1941) 551
Lenin, Nikolai 486
Leningrad ⚔ 510
Leo I, Pope 130
Leo the Isaurian (Byzantine general)
  139–41
Leo the Wise 142, 144, 145, 151
Leonidas (king of Sparta) 64
Lepanto ⚔ 63, 236, 251, 253, 258–61
Leslie, General 285
Lettow-Vorbeck, Colonel von 490–1,
  494
Leuctra ⚔ 70
Leuthen ⚔ 315, 327–9, 332
Levée en masse (feudal levy) 39, 150, 186
Levett, Rev. William (maker of iron
  cannon) 227
Lewes ⚔ 186
Lewis of Baden 301–2, 305
Lexington, U.S.S. 533, 534
Leyte Gulf ⚔ ⚔ 543
Li Hung-Chang 413
Liberators (bomber aircraft) 516, 517
Libyan War 489
Liddell Hart, Sir Basil 20, 96, 265, 320,
  414, 415, 463, 471, 480, 500, 526,
  552
Liegnitz ⚔ 329
Ligny ⚔ 366
Ligonier, Lord 319
Lille: fortifications at, 295; siege of, 311
Liman von Sanders, General 486
Limes Germanicus 118
Lincoln, President 437–40
Lissa ⚔ 416
List, Field-Marshal von 510
Little Big Horn River ⚔ 413
Lloyd George, David (later Earl Lloyd
  George) 469, 472, 477, 481, 493
Lodi ⚔ 345, 357
Logistics see Administration
London 280; bombed, 505
London, Tower of 167
Longbows & longbowmen 194–209
  pass., 214; described, 197
Loopholes (for archers) 168, 184, 192
Looting (and pillage) prohibited 230,
  549
Loredano, Pietro 250
Louis (king of Hungary) 257
Louis IX (king of France) 181
Louis XIV 263, 291, 300, 310, 547
Louis XV 547
Louisburg captured 319
Louvain 154
Louvois (French statesman) 291, 292
Lucchessi, General 328, 329
Luck in warfare 365
Lucullus, Lucius 100
Ludendorff, General Erich von 467–8,
  471, 477, 486, 491–4 pass.
Luftwaffe (German air force) 500,
  504–6
Lutjens, Admiral 517
Lutzen ⚔ 274, 275
Lutzingen village 308–10 pass.
Lyautey, Marshal Louis 450

Lysander (Spartan admiral) 67

MacArthur, General 536–7, 543
Macedonian army 71–3
Macedonian wars 96–8, 102 (see also
  Alexander the Great)
Maces (weapons) 35, 42, 161, 165, 172,
  247, 398
McGrigor, General (Wellington's Sur-
  geon-General) 360
Machiavelli, Niccolo 195, 212, 216, 550
Machicolations 169
Machine-guns 219, 419, 441, 447, 464,
  473–4, 480, 493, 499
Mack, General 349, 350
Mackensen, Field-Marshal August von
  482
MacMahon, General 431, 432, 436
Madras captured 406
Magdeburg, siege and sack of 270, 279
Magenta ⚔ 420
Maginot Line 109, 500, 501
Mago (Carthaginian general) 93
Magyars (of Hungary) 152, 370
Mahan, Admiral A. T. 458
Maharbal (Numidian general) 91, 97
Mahmud II, Sultan 261
Mahmud of Ghazni, Sultan 402
Mahomet Sirocco 258
Mail armour (see also Armour, body) 36,
  42, 43, 52, 53, 126, 132, 144, 150,
  160, 161, 178, 179, 184, 186, 247;
  chain (or link), 138, 147, 154, 178,
  186, 399
Maiwand ⚔ 450
Makarov, Admiral 456
Malaya 530, 532–3, 555, 556
Malplaquet ⚔ 303, 311, 313
Malta 256, 257, 338, 512, 513, 517
Mamelukes 254–5
Mandala (Hindu doctrine) 395
Mandalay ⚔ 539, 542
Mandu (hill-fort) 406
Manfred 186
Mangonels 372
Manila treasure galleon 317
Maniples, Roman 86, 89, 94, 99
Mannheim 300, 301
Manoeuvre 22, 332 (see also Mobility)
Manpower 17–18
Manstein, General von 501, 503, 511
Mantinea ⚔ 67
Mantlets 170
Manzikert ⚔ 146, 171, 244, 403
Mao Tse-tung 19, 384
Marathas 358, 405–6, 409
Marathon ⚔ 60, 64
Marcellinus, Ammianus (Roman
  soldier) 129
March discipline and timing 300–1, 349,
  350, 354
'March divided, fight united' 78
Marchfeld ⚔ 184
Marengo ⚔ 345
Mareth Line ⚔ 205, 306, 514
Marignano ⚔ 214, 216, 221
Maritz, Jean de (cannon maker) 329
Maritza, River ⚔ 245
Marius, Gaius 99, 100, 110
Marlborough, John Churchill, first
  Duke of 263, 291–311, 316;
  appreciation of, 291, 295–6, 311,
  332
Marmont, Marshal 349, 361
Marne ⚔ ⚔ 1914, 464, 471; 1918, 492
Marshes, warfare in 55
Marsin, Marshal 300, 302, 305, 309
Marston Moor ⚔ 282, 285

Martinengo, Gabriel (military engi-
  neer) 256
Martinet, General 292
Martini-Henry rifles 419
Martini-Peabody rifles 453
Masada (Jewish stronghold) 118
Masamune (Japanese swordsmith) 386
Masinissa (king of Numidia) 93, 94, 96,
  97
Maslama (Arab general) 139
Mass production of armaments 411, 420
Massena, Marshal 340, 348, 349, 361,
  362
Masurian Lakes ⚔ 465–8 pass.
Matapan, Cape ⚔ 507
Match-locks 282, 292, 298, 403
Mauriac Plain ⚔ 130
Maurice (Roman emperor) 128, 141,
  142
Maurice of Nassau 211, 223, 227–32,
  263, 266, 270, 328
Mauser pistols and rifles 446–7, 452, 486
Max Emanuel (elector) 300, 302, 305–10
  pass.
Maxim, Hiram S. 447; his machine-
  gun, 447
Maximilian (H.R.E.) 215
Maximilian of Bavaria 276
Mazarin, Cardinal 279
Medes 52
Median Wall 33
Medical services 39, 142, 231, 269, 539
Medieval warfare 135–209
Medina Sidonia, Duke of 238
Meeanee ⚔ 413
Megiddo (fortress) 41, 45, 57
Mehmed II, Sultan 245–56 pass.
Mehmet Ali (of Egypt) 39
Meiktila ⚔ 540–3 pass.
'Men-at-arms' 186–208 pass., 212, 216–
  18 pass., 222
Mercenaries 17, 45, 68–73 pass., 78, 79,
  90, 100, 129, 130, 132, 158, 161, 163,
  178, 184, 186–7, 196, 205, 212, 221,
  223, 266, 275; Swiss, 195, 212
Merrimac, U.S.S. 416
Mesopotamia (now Iraq) 31–8 pass., 470
Messervy, General 539, 540
Messines Ridge ⚔ 478–9
Metaurus ⚔ 125
Metz, siege of 432–4
Mexico 31, 233, 234, 413, 429
Middle East, the 31–57; in W.W.I, 470,
  486–7, 489; in W.W.II, 506–8,
  511–14
Midway Island ⚔ 15, 535
Migdol (square fort) 45
Milan ⚔ 125
Militarism, birth of 264
Military academies 266, 348, 359, 429
Military police 360
Militia see Feudal levies
Miltiades (Athenian general) 63, 67
Milvian Bridge ⚔ 125
Minamoto (Japanese military clan) 386,
  388
Minden ⚔ 320
Mines, floating and sub-marine 416,
  456, 458, 480, 481
Mines, land 479, 512
Minié, Captain 416; his bullet, 416
Mining (against fortifications) 170, 171,
  479, 512
Minorca 317, 338
Mir Jafar 409
'Misericords' 201
Mitanni (near Mosul) 39, 41
Mithridates IV (of Pontus) 100–1
Mitrailleuse, Martigny 419

Mobility (& movement) 14, 42, 78, 138, 233, 266, 269, 272, 273, 279, 292, 298, 322, 330, 332, 425, 508, 563–4; and firepower, see Firepower; *blitzkrieg (q.v.)*, 500–3
Model, General 525
Moghuls in India 402–5
Mohacs ✕257
Mohammed, the Prophet 135, 138
Möhne dam 515–16
Mollwitz ✕325
Moltke, Helmut Graf von 16, 373, 426, 428, 430–6 *pass.*, 441, 459
Moltke II 463, 468, 471
Monash, General Sir John 493, 494
Monck, General and Admiral George 285, 287, 289
Mongols (*see also* Jenghiz Khan) 244, 369–77, 383, 388–9, 402
Monitor, U.S.S. 416
Monro, Colonel *or* General 274
Mons ✕464, 471
Mons Graupius ✕119
Montcalm, General 319, 320
Montecucculi, General 261
Montgomerie, Lord 188
Montgomery (in Alabama) 437, 440
Montgoméry, Roger de 157
Montiuic ✕278
Moore, General Sir John 357, 358–9
Morale 15–18 *pass.*, 25–7, 60, 138, 201, 205, 208, 220, 266, 269, 323, 336, 348, 350, 359, 564
Morat ✕183
Morgarten ✕194
Morlaix ✕204
Morse, Samuel 420; his code, 420
Mortars 473, 499; Babur's 403
Moscow: in 1812, 357, 363, 365; in W.W.II, 508
Moses 48
Mosquitoes (aircraft) 515
Mottes 167, 168
Mountbatten of Burma, Admiral Earl (Louis) 537
Mukden ✕457, 458
'Mulberries' (artificial harbours) 520
Munda (in Spain) ✕105
Murad I, Sultan 245
Murad III, Sultan 261
Murat, Marshal Joachim 340, 348, 349, 354
Murray, General (Wellington's Q.M.G.) 360
Murray, General Sir Archibald 489
Music, martial 61, 195, 323, 400
Muskets & musketeers (*see also* Flint-locks, Match-locks *and* Wheel-locks) 230, 232, 266, 270, 271, 272, 282–3, 284, 298, 325, 390
Mussolini, Benito (Il Duce) 506
Mustangs (P.51, aircraft) 516
Mutallu (Hittite general) 45–8
Mylae ✕102

N.C.O's 266
Nabopolassar 57
Nagasaki 543, 559
Nagumo, Vice-Admiral 533, 535
Napier, Charles 413
Napoleon Bonaparte 15, 24, 41, 79, 292, 313, 329, 335–65; appreciation of, 340, 345–8, 363–5
Napoleon III (Louis-Napoleon) 413, 419, 426, 429, 430, 436, 548
Naram-Sin 33, 35
Narses (Roman general) 133
Naseby ✕285
National Guard (of revolutionary

France) 331
Nationalism 315, 363, 411, 412, 413, 441, 444, 453, 499
NATO (*or* 'Western Alliance') 62, 293, 555, 557, 563
Naval personnel (British and French), quality of 316
Naval race (1900–14) 445–9
Naval warfare 63, 64, 67, 101, 102, 139, 152–3, 211, 223, 233–41, 250–3, 257–61, 286–9, 316–17, 335–9, 345, 455–8, 480–2, 507, 516–17, 533–7, 543
Navarino Bay ✕412, 458
Navarro, Pedro (military engineer and artilleryman) 215, 220, 253
Navigators 232–5
Neckar, River 301
'Needle-guns', Dreyse's 419
Negroponte captured 253
Neil, Marshal 429
Nelson, Admiral Lord (Horatio) 320, 336–9; appreciation of, 367
Nets (for combat) 130
Neuf Brisach 293, 295
Neutrality 551
New Carthage 93, 97
New Guinea 533, 536
New Model Army 282–6
Ney, Marshal 348, 349, 414
Nicholas II, Tsar 485, 486
Nicholas General Staff Academy in St Petersburg 444
Nicholas, Grand Duke 464
Nicknames for the enemy, 547
Nicopolis ✕245
Nieuport ✕223, 231, 232, 241
Nightingale, Florence 426
Nile (or Aboukir Bay) ✕338, 345
Nimitz, Admiral 533–7 *pass.*, 543
Nineveh (capital of Assyria) 51, 57
Nissa ✕125
Nivelle, General Robert G. 477, 478
Nizam-ul-Mulk 405–6
Nobel, Alfred 446
Nobunaga (Japanese unifier) 390
Nogi, General 456, 457
Nombre de Dios 236
Non-combatants, treatment of 548–50
Non-commissioned officers 266
Nore, the naval mutiny at 336
Norman society 166–7
Normandy, the Cotentin peninsula 292
Normans, the 157–71
Norsemen *see* Vikings
North Atlantic Treaty Organization *see* NATO
North German Confederation, army of 426–7
Northampton, Earl of 201, 204
Novara ✕ ✕1513, 214, 215; 1849, 425
Nuclear warfare 543, 545, 558–62
Numantia (in Spain) 99
Numidia, war in 99
Numidian troops 91, 93, 94
Nur ed-Din 177
Nuremberg ✕276

Oberglau village 305–10 *pass.*
Obstacles in warfare 307
O'Connor, Major-General Sir Richard 506
Odovacer (Herul) 125, 131
Officer hierarchies 73, 89, 99, 142, 264, 266, 274, 322, 325, 331, 340, 358
Okinawa Island 543
Omaha beach (Normandy) 520
Oman, Sir Charles 143, 212
Omar, Emir (Arab general) 145

Ommayad caliphs 145
'Operation Barbarossa' 508–11, 550
'Operation Dynamo' 502
'Operation Overlord' 518–25
'Operation Sea-Lion' 505
'Operation Shoestring' 536
'Operation Supercharge' 514
Opium War 384, 413
Oporto ✕361
Oran captured 253
Orchomenus ✕100
Ordre mixte (Napoleon's infantry formation) 345, 354
Orewin Bridge, ✕197, 198
Orkhan (Turkish general) 244, 246
Orkney, Lord 308, 310
Orléans, siege of 207
Osman (*or* Othman, Turkish general) 244
Osman Pasha 453, 455
Ostrogoths (East Goths) *see* Goths
Otto the Great (king of Franks) 152
Ottoman Empire (*see also* Suleiman the Magnificent, Turkey *and* Turks, Ottoman) 243–61, 279, 453–5, 486, 489–90, 495
Oudenarde ✕311
Oyama, General 456

Pacific theatre of war (W.W.II) 529–32, 533–7, 543
Pack animals 105, 141
Paixhans, Colonel 415
Palermo, siege of 159
Palestine, revolt in (A.D. 66–73) 118
Palkhed campaign 405
Panzerati 186
Pappenheim, General 263, 270, 273, 274
Paris: sieges of: *1885–6*, 155; *1870*, 436–7; liberated (1944), 526
Park, A. V.-M. Sir Keith 505
Parker, Admiral Sir Hyde 317, 339
Parma, Alexander Duke of 211, 223, 224, 227, 232, 238
Parmenion (Alexander's cavalry commander) 78, 81–2
Parthia & Parthians 104–5, 373, 403
'Parthian shots' 104, 179, 373
Passchendaele ✕ ✕ 1917, 476, 494; 1918, 492
Path to Leadership, The (Montgomery) 557
'Pathfinder' force 515
Paulus, Aemilius 99
Paulus, General F. 510
Paurav, King 395, 396, 399
Pausanias (Spartan king & general) 62
Pavia ✕221, 222, 225
Pax Britannica 412
Pax Romana 123
Peace Conference in Paris (1919) 494, 495
Peace: ideal of, 564–7; insidious dangers of, 25, 41; prospects of world-wide, 557, 562, 564–7
Pearl Harbour 15, 530, 533, 535
Peking 373
Pelopidas 68
Peloponnesian League 60
Peloponnesian War 67–70, 237
Peltasts (javelin-men, *q.v.*) 70
Peninsular War 15, 349, 357–8, 359–62
'Penteconters' (Greek warships) 63, 64
Pent-houses 73
Pepys, Samuel 289
Pericles 62, 67
Pershing, General John J. 491
Persia & Persians 60–83 *pass.*, 510; their

army, tactics and strategy, 62–3, 78;
their navy, 74
Peru 233, 234
Pétain, Marshal Henri 478, 491
Peter the Great 313, 322
Peterborough, Earl of 311–12
Phalanx, the (see also Formations) 35,
37, 42, 60, 63, 70, 73, 77–86 pass.,
98, 113, 273
Phalerum ✕ 63
Pharsalus ✕ 105
Pheidon (king of Argos) 59
Philip Augustus (king of France) 169,
170, 171, 181, 183
Philip II (king of Macedon) 70–1
Philip II (king of Spain) 211, 224, 238–
41, 263
Philip VI (king of France) 201–5
Philippine Sea ✕ 537
Philippines, the 530, 536, 543
Philippsburg, bridge of boats at 301
Phocas, Nicephorus (Byzantine em-
peror & general) 138, 142, 143, 145
'Phoney war', the 500
Piccolomini, Prince (Austrian general)
265
Pikes & pikemen 73, 81, 161, 183, 195,
201, 209, 213–22 pass., 230, 247,
266, 270, 271, 272, 282, 284, 291,
298
Pinnaces 235, 238
Pinto, Mendes 390
Piraeus, the (port of Athens) 63, 64, 67
Pirates, Mediterranean 100–1, 102, 127
Pistols & pistoleers 232, 266, 271, 280,
282, 298, 446–7
Pitfalls (trous de loup) 204
Pitt, William ('the Elder', Earl of
Chatham) 315, 317–20
Pizarro, Francisco 233–4
Plague, bubonic see Black Death
Plassey (Palasi) ✕ 409
Plataea ✕ 60, 68
Plate, River ✕ 517
Plevna ✕ 453, 455, 459
Plongeur, Le (French submarine) 416
Plumer, General Herbert (later F.-M.
and Viscount) 478–9, 494
'Pluto' (sub-marine oil pipe line) 520
Plymouth 238, 239
Poitiers ✕ 194
Poland & Poles 349, 351, 495, 499, 500
Polaris submarines 561, 563
Politics & politicians 13, 19, 24, 27, 99,
264, 291, 296, 544–5, 552, 565
Poltava, siege of 313
Polybius (Greek historian) 16, 89, 91,
96, 97
Pompey (Gnaeus Pompeius) 100–7
'Popinjays' 197
Poppenruyter, Hans (Flemish cannon
maker) 227
Population, pressure of 30–3 pass., 411,
443–4
Porphyry (a whale) 132
Port Arthur (1904–05) 456
Port Moresby 15, 533
Portland ✕ 289
Porto Bello (Panama) 317
Portsmouth 235
Portugal & Portuguese 233, 257, 357,
360, 383, 390, 409
Pot-helms see Helmets
Powder, smokeless 446
Praetorian Guard 109–10
Prague ✕ 322, 327
Praise, value of 23
Press-gang 289, 316
Preston ✕ 285

Prevesa ✕ 257
Primitive peoples, bellicosity of 30
Prince of Wales, H.M.S. 15, 530
Princeton, U.S.S. 415
Pripet Marshes 528
Prisoners-of-war, treatment of 51, 77,
99, 100, 114, 546, 548–9
Prittwitz, General 466, 467
Professionalism, military (see also
Mercenaries) 183, 187, 196, 292,
429, 444
Proliferation of nuclear weapons 561
Prussia & Prussians (see also Germany)
264, 315, 317, 322–9, 332–3, 335,
354, 420
Prussia, Crown Prince of 430, 436
Prussian army, new (1675 et seq.) 325–
32 pass.
Prusso-Austrian War 413, 427–8
Prusso-Danish War 419
Psychological warfare 56, 57, 234, 554
Public opinion and war 411
Punic Wars: first, 89, 102; second, 89–
96, 102
Pydna ✕ 98, 99
Pyramids, the ✕ 342–3
'Pyrrhic victories' 83, 313
Pyrrhus (king of Epirus) 83, 85

'Quadrilateral', Italian 425
Quatre Bras ✕ 366
Quebec, capture of (1759) 319–20
Quesnoi ✕ 191
Questions, basic military 420
Quinqueremes 102
Quivers (for arrows or javelins) 42, 141
Quoits (as weapons) 398

R.A.F. 482, 502, 503–6, 514, 539
Radar 505, 535
Radetzky, Field-Marshal 425
'Railway of Death' 549
Railways 420, 428, 438, 444
'Raison d'état', doctrine of 212
Ramillies ✕ 301, 304, 311
Ramsay, Admiral Sir Bertram 518
Ramses II (king of Egypt) 41, 42, 45–8
pass., 49
Ramses III 42, 48
Rangoon 532, 540, 543
Rapiers 186
Ratanpur ✕ 405
Rathenau, Walter 477
'Ravelins' 295
Ravenna 131, 133; ✕ 214
Rawlinson, General Sir Henry 493
Raymond, Count of Toulouse 171
Raymond, Count of Tripoli 177, 180
Rebecca (English brig) 315
Recruiting in xvii & xviii centuries (see
also Press-gang) 296, 322, 358
Red Army (Russian communist) 508–
11 pass., 518, 528–9, 553
Red Cross, International 426, 548
Red Indians 30–1, 413
Regino of Prüm 154
Regulations and orders, disregarded
316, 317, 336, 339
Reiter (German mounted pistoleers)
232
Religion and sacrifice in war 269, 566–7
Rennenkampf, General Paul 466–8
pass.
Repulse, H.M.S. 15, 530
Requisitioning (and paying) 301
Retief, Piet 413
Revenge (Grenville's flagship) 241
Revolutionary activities (1815–48) 412

Revolvers 419
Reynald de Chatillon 177
Rheims (1918) 492, 529
Rhine, River 291, 292, 301, 302, 526,
527; as frontier of Roman Empire,
109, 113, 114, 126
Rhineland 274, 498
Rhodes (island) 253, 255, 256
Ribauldequins 191
Richard I (king of England, 'Coeur-de-
Lion') 166, 168, 180, 181
Richborough ✕ 115
Richelieu, Cardinal 265, 269, 274, 276,
279
Richmond (Virginia) 439, 440
Ridanieh ✕ 255
Rifle and bayonet, ancestry of 209
Rifles & riflemen (see also Mauser) 209,
346, 416, 419, 437, 445–7, 452, 453,
471, 472
Rivers (and other waterways), crossing
of 55–6, 63, 77, 82, 250
Roads: Roman, 120–1, 124; European
(in xix century) 420
Robert de Hauteville (Guiscard or the
'Wary') 158–9
Roberts, Field-Marshal Earl 452
Robertson, Field-Marshal Sir William
469
Robins, Benjamin (tactician and bal-
listics expert) 329, 340
Rockets, Hindu and Moghul (see also
V.2) 403
Rocroi ✕ 70, 279, 292
Rodney, Admiral 321
Roger de Hauteville I & II 158, 159
Roger de Lacy 170
Roger de Montgoméry 157
Roman army (see also Legions) 85–124
pass.
Roman camps (fortified) 87, 118, 121
Roman empire 14, 98, 109–33, 135
Roman fleet 14, 91, 92, 97, 102, 110, 127
Roman roads 120–1, 124
Roman soldiers 85–9, 99 (see also
Legions)
Roman towns (military) 118
Romanus Diogenes (Byzantine em-
peror) 146
Rome & Romans 85–133
Rommel, General Erwin 15, 17, 94, 157,
306, 383, 507, 508, 512, 514, 520
Romulus Augustulus (Roman emperor)
125, 131
Roncesvalles Pass 150
Roon, Graf von 426, 427, 430
Roosevelt, President Franklin D. 518,
526, 529, 544, 553
Rose, Sir Hugh 413
Rossbach ✕ 327
Rostov-on-Don 508, 510
Rousseau, Jean Jacques 340
'Rovers' (medieval golf) 197
Roy, Jules 556
Royal Air Force see R.A.F.
Royal Flying Corps 447
Royal Naval Air Service 447
Royal Navy see British navy
Royal Sovereign, H.M.S. 447
Royalists (King Charles I's army) 285–6
Rozhestvenski, Admiral 457
Rubicon, River 105
Rudolf of Erlach 194, 195
Rudolf of Habsburg 185
Ruggiero de Lauria 253
Ruhr, the 515, 526
'Rules of Warfare' (1922) 551
Runstedt, General Gerd von 500, 520,
525

Rupert of the Rhine, Prince 263, 280–5
Russia & Russians (see also Stalin) 313, 329, 335, 351–7, 416, 443, 444, 448, 450, 453–8, 464–8, 482–6, 508–11, 528–9, 558, 559, 561
Russian army (communist) see Red Army
Russian army (Tsarist) 464–8, 482–6
Russian fleet 455–6, 457–8, 480
Russo-Japanese War 455–8

S.O.E. (Special Operations Executive, British) 503
Sabres (including 'Sax') 126, 247, 348, 373, 405
Sabutai 373, 377
Sagittarius, Bishop 147
Saint-Cyr (French military academy (f. 1686) 348, 429
St Gotthard ✕ 261
St Helena (island) 363, 366
Saint-Hubert ✕ 434–5
St Lawrence, River 319
St Lô (in Normandy) 525
St Louis (king of France) 181
Saint-Privat ✕ (see also Gravelotte) 432–5 pass., 441
St Vincent, Cape ✕ 336
St Vincent, Lord (Sir John Jervis, q.v.) 336
Ste Foy de Montgoméry 157
Sakers (small cannon) 227
Saladin (king of Syria and Egypt) 177
Salamanca ✕ 14, 362, 366
Salamis ✕ 14, 60, 64–7
Salonika 488
Saltis (first Hyksos king) 38
Samarkand 376, 402
Samsonov, General Alexander 465, 467, 468
Samurai (Japanese warrior class) 369, 386–90 pass.
San Domingo ✕ 341
San Juan de Ulúa ✕ 236
San Martin, José de 412
Santa Cruz, Marquis of 258, 260
Sapping 169
Saracens (see also Arabs) 152, 159, 178–80 pass.
Sargon (king of Assyria) I, 33; II, 52
Sarissa (Macedonian spear) 73, 398
Satsuma (Japanese clan) 390
Saunders, Admiral Charles 317, 319
'Sax' (see also Sabres) 126
Saxe, Marshal Maurice de 322–3, 325, 332, 364
Saxons 126, 152
Scaling ladders 38, 56, 170
Scanderbeg, George 250
Scapa Flow 480, 481
Schall (cannon founder) 384
Scharnhorst, General Gerhard 414
Scharnhorst (German cruiser) 517
Scheer, Admiral Reinhard 481
Scheer (German pocket-battleship) 517
Schellenberg ✕ 302, 308
Schlieffen, Count von 459, 463
Schlieffen Plan 459, 462–3, 471
Science: in W.W.II, 545; and future warfare, 562–4
Scimitars (see also Swords) 38, 144, 371
Scipio Africanus 92–7; and Hannibal compared, 96–7
Scots under Gustavus Adolphus 273, 274
Scutati 141, 143
Scythes (as weapons) 247
Sea power (see also Nelson) 14, 15, 63–6, 67, 92, 97, 102, 105, 110, 166,

235–41, 250–6, 257–60, 286–9, 300, 335–9, 357, 367, 441, 456, 458, 482, 516–17, 563
Sebastopol ✕ 415, 425
Secret Service 17
Security (of forces) 14
Sedan ✕ 436
Seine, River 526
Sekigahara ✕ 391
Selim I, Sultan ('the Cruel') 247, 254–5, 256
Selim II, Sultan ('the Drunkard') 257
Semerkhet (king of Egypt) 33
Seminole Indians 419
Semitic peoples 33–41 pass., 135
Sempach ✕ 195
Sennacherib (king of Assyria) 51, 54, 55, 57
Senova ✕ 455
Sentinum ✕ 85
'Sepoys' 409
Serbia & Serbs 245, 250, 461, 469, 487
Sergeants (of medieval cavalry) 156
Sertorius, Quintus 100–1
Servile War, first 99
Setnakht (king of Egypt) 48
Seven Years' War 315, 317, 320, 325, 327, 333, 360
Severus, Septimius (Roman emperor) 123, 125
Shells 415–16, 447, 473
Sherman, General William T. 438, 440, 441, 550
Shield-maidens, Viking 155
Shield-walls 57, 154, 155, 163–6 pass., 206
Shields (and 'bucklers') 36, 37, 39, 42, 52, 54, 59, 60, 70, 73, 85, 86, 90, 103, 113, 126, 130, 132, 138, 141, 144, 146, 150, 154, 160, 161, 201, 371, 395–8, 405
Shihabuddin Ghori 402
Shijo Nawate ✕ 382
'Ship-money' fleets 286
Ships (various) 126–7, 198, 201, 211, 232–4, 238, 287
Shock tactics 80, 271, 272, 399, 440, 441, 459
Shoguns, the 386, 389, 390, 391
Shoho (Japanese cruiser) 533
Shorncliffe, Sir John Moore at 359
Sicily (1943) 511, 514
Sidney, Sir Philip 232
Siege towers (beffrois) 68, 73, 77, 155, 170, 171
Siege warfare (see also Fortifications) 38, 41, 45, 56–8, 61, 68, 73, 135, 144, 155, 169–70, 213, 223, 227, 248–50, 284, 295, 298, 373, 379–80, 409
Sikri ✕ 403
Simon de Montfort 186, 196
Sinai Desert 489
Singapore 531
Single combat 39, 59, 75, 387
Sino-Japanese War 455
Sivaji 405
Skippon, Sgt.-Major-General 285
Skobelev, General Mikhail 450, 455
Slim, General (later F.-M.) Sir William 17, 537–43 pass.
Slings & slingmen 52, 54, 57, 70, 85, 94, 247, 253, 398
Sluys ✕ 198, 201
Smigly-Rydz, Marshal Edward 500
Smolensk 508, 511
Smuts, General (later F.-M.) Jan Christian 491
Social implications of warfare 264
Soldiers, British 25 (see also French)

Solferino ✕ 420, 548
Somme ✕ 470–7
Soult, Marshal 348, 349, 351, 354, 361
South African War see Boer War
South-East Europe 487–8, 508
Sovereign of the Seas 287
Spahis (Turkish cavalry élite) 246, 247, 257
Spain & Spaniards 92–3, 99, 135, 138, 211–41, 265, 311–12, 317, 336, 357, 360–1, 365, 443
Spanish Civil War 497, 551
Spanish Succession, War of the 291, 297, 298–300
Sparta & Spartans 25, 59–70 pass.
Spartacus (gladiator) 100
Spears & spearmen (see also Halberds, Lances and Pikes) 34–45 pass., 52–60 pass., 70, 73, 78, 81, 85, 86, 90, 99, 113, 124, 126, 154, 160, 194, 195, 198, 298
Special Operations Executive, British 503
Specialists, military, corps of 247
Spee, Admiral von 480
Spengler, Oswald 416
Sperle, General 504, 505
Spicheren ✕ 432–3
Spinola, Ambrogio 211, 223, 224
Spion Kop ✕ 452
Spiritual values 566–7
Spitfires (aircraft) 505
Spithead, naval mutiny at 336
'Split world, a' 554, 561
Spruance, Admiral 535–6
Spurs 201
Staff & staff work (see also Command and General staffs) 73, 360, 428, 429
Staff colleges 19, 359, 444
Stalin, Joseph 508, 518, 529, 544, 545, 553, 555, 558
Stalingrad ✕ 510
Stamford Bridge (York) ✕ 160, 162, 163
Starvation (in sieges) 170–1
Steinau ✕ 276
Steinmetz, General von 430, 432, 434, 435
Stilicho (Vandal general) 128–9
Stilwell, General Joseph W. 532, 537, 539
Stirlings (bomber aircraft) 515
Stirrups 68, 128, 132, 141, 161
Stopford, General, senior 487
Stopford, General, junior 539, 540
Strategic Air Command, U.S.A.F. 561
Strategy (see also Tactics) 14, 62, 97, 143–4, 236–8, 265, 276, 286, 287, 316, 331, 332, 345–6, 351, 361, 458, 459, 486, 487; Grand, 14, 552; Clausewitz and Jomini on, 413–14
Stumpff, General 504, 505
Sub-machine-guns 497
Submarines (& U-boats) 416, 448–9, 458, 478, 480–1, 512, 517, 537, 550, 561, 563
Sudomer ✕ 194, 208
Suez Canal 489, 511
Suleiman the Magnificent 247, 256–7
Suleiman (Arab admiral) 139
Sulla, Lucius 99–100, 105
Sultan, General 539
Sumter, Fort 437
Sun Tzu 369, 380, 383
Supply to armies (see also Commissariat) 39, 45, 265, 269, 292, 359–60, 512, 532, 538; by air, see Air supply
Suraj-ud-Dowlah 409
Surprise in warfare 22, 285–6, 305–6,

307, 373, 376–7, 497, 530
Surrender: honourable, 295, 548; un-
conditional, 511, 545, 562
Suvla Bay (in Gallipoli) 487
Suvorov, Marshal 349, 352
Sweden (see also Gustavus Adolphus)
265–74, 313
Swinton, Lieut.-Colonel 492
Swiss infantry and mercenaries 194–5,
212–16, 220, 223
Swords & swordsmen (see also Sabres)
35, 38, 42, 43, 54, 59, 60, 70, 78, 85,
86, 89, 90, 103, 124, 126, 130, 141,
146, 154, 161, 178, 197, 201, 216,
247, 259, 266, 271, 280, 282, 284,
298, 379, 386, 390, 398, 403
Syphax (king of Masaesylli) 93
Syracuse, siege of 67
Syrians (ancient) 41, 42, 52

Tabor (Hussite stronghold) 208
Tactics, land (see also Strategy) 14, 21,
22, 37, 60–2, 66, 70, 73, 74, 78–81,
91–8, 132–3, 142–4, 263, 265, 266,
271, 276, 298, 305, 331, 340, 345,
346, 361, 386, 440, 458–9
Tactics, maritime or naval 14, 63, 201,
287–8, 316, 336, 339, 415–16, 458
Taillefer (minstrel) 164
Taiping Rebellion 413
Taira (Japanese clan) 386
Talavera ✕361
Talikota ✕405
Tallard, Marshal 301–10 pass.
Talleyrand-Périgord, Charles Maurice
de 346; quoted, 19
Tamworth Castle 167
Tancred de Hauteville 158
Tanks (armoured fighting vehicles or
A.F.V's; also called 'armour' and
'panzers') 14, 219, 479, 493, 499,
502–3, 512, 513–14, 520, 539
Tannenberg ✕466–8, 482
Tarain ✕ ✕402, 403
Taranto harbour (1940) 507
Tarsus, siege of 143
Tartaglia, Niccolo 227
Tartars (of Crimea) 247
Tashkent, storming of 451
Tattooing 31, 247
Taurus mountains 135, 139, 143, 145
Technology in W.W.II 211, 545
Tedder, A.C.M. Sir Arthur (later Lord
Tedder) 513, 518
Telegraphy, electric 420, 426
Telham Hill (Senlac) 163
Templer, General 555
'Ten Thousand', the 70
Tenchebrai ✕167
Tenochtitlan, siege of 234
Tergoes, relief of 230
Terrible, H.M.S. 316
Testudo (tortoise) formation 113
Teutoburger Forest ✕114
Teutonic Knights (see also Knights) 175
Thames, River 289
Thapsus ✕105
Themistocles 63, 64, 65
Theodoric (Ostrogoth) 131
Theodosius (Roman emperor) 125
Theopompus (king of Sparta) 59
Theory, military 413–15
Thermopylae ✕63, 64
Thirty Years' War 261, 263–79, 297,
323, 550
Thomas (Edward III's flagship) 198, 201
Thot (Egyptian general) 45
Thucydides 67
Thutmose (king of Egypt): I, 39; III,

41, 45; IV, 42, 43
Tiberias, siege of 177
Tiberius (Roman emperor) 110, 113
Ticinus, River ✕91
Tiglathpileser: I, 51; III, 52, 53, 54, 56
Tilly, Johann, Count of 269, 270, 273–4
Timur (Tamerlane) 245, 377, 402, 403
Tirpitz (German battleship) 518
Tito, Marshal 518
Titus (Roman emperor & general) 118
Tobruk 507, 508, 512, 513
Togo, Admiral 456, 458
Tojo, General 529
Tokugawa Shogunate 391
Tomahawks 146, 154
Torgau ✕329
Torpedo boats 448
Torpedoes 416, 448, 456, 458, 481
Torres Vedras 361, 362
Torstensson (Swedish artillery general)
266, 273, 274, 279
Toulon, blockade of 319, 337, 339, 340
Tournaments (& jousts) 187–9
Tours ✕147–8
Tower of London 167
Trafalgar ✕15, 287, 339, 351, 367, 458
Training in arms (medieval) 187
Training, military, importance of 23,
274
Trajan (Roman emperor) 118
Trasimene, Lake ✕91, 97
Trebia (stream) ✕91
Trébuchets 170, 227
Trench warfare 87, 295, 440, 459, 464,
470–5
Tripoli: 1510, 253; 1942, 514
Triremes 60, 63, 64, 65, 102
Trojan horse, legend of 45
Trojan War 59
Tromp, Admiral 263, 287, 289
Trous de loup 204
Troy, siege of 59
'Truce of God', the 172
Truman, President Harry S. 545, 553,
555, 558
Tsushima ✕458
Tullius Servius 85
Tunis & Tunisia 514
Turcopoles 178, 180
Turenne, Henri, Vicomte de 263, 279,
291–3, 295; appreciation of, 292–3
Turkestan 376, 450, 455
Turkey & Turks (see also Ottoman
Empire) 455, 462, 469, 470, 486–7,
489–90
Turkheim campaign 292
Turkish army in W.W.I 486–90
Turko-Islamic (Moghul) invaders of
India 402–6
Turks, Ottoman (see also Ottoman
Empire and Turkey) 243–61
'Turks' (Patzinaks) 135, 143
Turks, Seljouk 146, 173, 244
Turnhout ✕232
Tyre, siege of 74, 77

U-boats see Submarines
Ulm 300, 348, 349, 350
Uluch Ali 258, 260
Ulundi ✕451
'Unconditional surrender' 511, 545, 562
Uniforms 141, 247, 266, 269, 284, 297,
321, 429, 444
United Nations 561
United States of America (see also
American) 443, 495, 545, 556, 558–
9; and W.W.I, 470, 477, 481, 482,
491–3 pass.; in W.W.II, 499, 514,

515, 518–29 pass., 529–32, 533–7,
543
Universal military service 444
Urban (maker of cannon) 248

V.1 (flying-bomb) and V.2 (rocket) 527
VTOL (vertical take-off and landing)
aircraft 563
Vagnoni, Father Alfonso 384
Valdez, Diego de (Spanish admiral) 239
Valmy ✕315, 331–2, 339
Vandals 125, 127, 129, 132–3
Varna ✕245
Varro, Tarentius (Roman consul) 91
Varus, Publius Quintus 114
Vasco da Gama 233
Vauban, Sebastian de 291, 293–5, 313,
319
Vebjorg (Viking shield-maiden) 155
Velites (Roman soldiers) 85
Vendôme, Marshal 311
Venice & Venetians 250, 253, 257–8
Vercingetorix (Gallic guerrilla) 103, 107
Verdun ✕470, 476–8 pass., 495
Vernon, Admiral Edward 317
Versailles, Treaties of: 1783, 321; 1919,
495, 497, 498
Vesontio (Besançon) ✕102
Vespasian 110, 118, 122
Vexillationes 122
Vickers machine-gun 447
Victory ultimately won by the men 24–5
Vienna 274, 300, 302, 351; Congress of,
412, 413; sieges of: 1529, 257; 1683,
252, 261
Vietnam 555–6
Vikings 135, 142, 146, 150, 152–5, 167
Villars, General (later Marshal) 300,
312–13
Villeneuve, Admiral 339
Villeroi, General 300, 301, 302
Villiers de L'Isle Adam 256
Vineiro ✕358
Virginia (U.S.A.) 439
Viriathus (Spanish guerrilla) 99
Visigoths (West Goths) see Goths
Vittoria ✕362
Vladar, Mount ✕208
Vladivostock 456
Von Kluck, General 464
Voronezh 510
Vouglé, ✕146

Wales & Welsh 118, 120, 195–6, 197
Wallace, William 198
Wallenstein, Albrecht von 263, 269,
274, 275, 276
Walls, defensive (see also Maginot Line)
33, 77, 118, 119, 133, 373, 380
Wandewash ✕320
War & warfare (general considerations):
nature of, 13–18; definition of, 14;
causes of, 14, 29–32; types of, 14;
'not concern of soldiers only', 13,
19; study and practice of, 13, 19–21,
24, 25; and civilization, 13, 546;
verdict of, 13; and metal industries,
13; constant factors in, 14, 23;
human side of, 17, 22, 24, 25, 26;
principles of, 23, 34; 'appeal' of, 31;
technique of, 34; religious back-
grounds to, 135, 171, 172, 265;
economic, social and political
aspects of, 263–4; and the State,
265; as a means to wealth, 265;
brutality of (in xvii century), 279;
and politics, 296, 300 (see also
Politics); ethics of, 546–52; 'cannot
abolish itself', 561

War & warfare (kinds of): amphibious, 55; bacterial (bacteriological), 546, 551; Cold, 554–7; desert, 512, 513; dynastic, 315; economic, 234, 315, 554; gas, 472, 473, 546, 547, 548; limited and unlimited, 322, 443, 549, 563 (dangers of escalation, 556, 561); modern, 17–18, 19, 209, 411 et seq.; nationalistic, 315; nuclear, 18, 558–62; political, 554; psychological, 56, 57, 234, 254; total, 13, 17–18, 459, 461, 477, 497, 514, 546, 550, 552; tribal, 30–1, 39; as a game, 31, 187–8
War Academy, Prussian (Kriegsakademie) 428, 444
War crimes see Atrocities
Warnsfeld ✕232
Wars of religion (& Jihads) 14, 138, 177, 211, 223
Wars of the Roses 223
Warsaw (1944) 528
Warships (see also Galleasses, Galleons, Galleys, Penteconters, Quinqueremes, Ships and Triremes) 287, 291, 316, 335, 415–16, 447–9
Washington, City of 438
Washington Conferences 546, 551
Washington, George 318, 321
Water supply (in sieges) 45
Waterloo ✕81, 349, 363, 365, 366, 440, 479
Watson-Watt, R. A. 505
Wavell, General Sir Archibald (later F.-M. Earl Wavell) 24, 25, 320, 383, 506–8, 512, 532, 537
'Way of the Warrior' 387, 547

Weapons (see also under names): ancient, 29, 34; standardization of, 269; modernization of, 411; recent developments in, 499, 558–64
Weirother, General 352
Wellesley, Sir Arthur see Wellington, Duke of
Wellington, Duke of (formerly Sir Arthur Wellesley) 23, 24, 335, 349, 357–63; appreciation of, 365–6
Welsh wars (see also Wales) 196, 197
Western Alliance see NATO
Western Desert Force (see also Eighth Army) 506–8
Western Union Defence Organization 293, 556, 557, 563
Wheel-locks 266, 282
Whips (as weapons) 247
William the Conqueror 13, 157, 159–66
William of Malmesbury 157
William of Poitiers 165
William of Prussia, Prince 426
Wilson, President Woodrow 495
Wingate, Brigadier (later Major-General) Orde C. 537, 539
'Winter Line' (in Italy) 219
Wolfe, Major-General James 315, 319–20, 322, 325
Wolseley, General Sir Garnet (later F.-M. Viscount Wolseley) 444
Women and war 31, 426, 477
Worcester ✕285–6
World War, first (1914/18) 20–1, 22, 23, 219, 414, 415, 419, 446, 447, 461–95, 547, 552
World War, second (1939/45) 15, 20, 23, 24, 25, 219, 419, 497–545, 547, 551

Wörth ✕431, 432, 436, 441
Wounded, treatment of 547, 548

Xenophon 70, 205
Xerxes 63–4
Xyston 73

Yadin, Yigael 34, 39
Yalu River 456
Yamamoto, Admiral 533, 534, 535
Yamashito, Lieut.-General 530
Yarmuk ✕138, 139
Yassa (Mongol legal code) 370
Yi-sun, Admiral 390–1
Yorimoto (Japanese soldier-statesman) 388
York, Duke of 358, 359
York, Harold at 160, 162, 166
Yorktown ✕315, 321
Yorktown, U.S.S. 535
Youth of today 566
Yugoslavia 518, 529
Ypres ✕ ✕ ✕ I (1914), 464, 472; III (1917), 476, 478; IV (1918), 491

Zab river, Greater ✕145
Zama ✕93–6, 98, 396
Zela ✕105
Zenta ✕301
Zeppelins 447, 482
Zhukov, Marshal 510
Zizka, John 208–9
Zorndorf ✕329
Zulus 413, 450–1
Zungarian Gates 376
Zwingli (religious reformer) 221

Belägerung der Vestung Hoch...

A. Vestung Hochen Twiel
B. Vorhofe.
C. Kayserisch Lager.
D. Bayrisch Lager, u lauffg...
E. Kayss. vnd Ostereichische...
F. Battereyen 4 Windmühl m...